The Countries of
North- western Europe

by

F. J. Monkhouse, M.A., D.Sc.
Formerly Professor of Geography in the University of Southampton

LONGMAN

LONGMAN GROUP LIMITED

London

*Associated companies, branches and representatives
throughout the world*

© F. J. MONKHOUSE 1965
Second edition © Longman Group Ltd. 1971

First published 1965
Second edition 1971

ISBN 0 582 31068 7

PRINTED IN GREAT BRITAIN BY
WILLIAM CLOWES AND SONS LIMITED
LONDON, BECCLES AND COLCHESTER

Preface

THIS is a survey of the countries of north-western Europe, defined as extending from the North Cape of Norway to the Bay of Biscay. Finland has been included because of its general associations with the Scandinavian group, East Germany because although *de facto* it is an independent state, this is a provisional status until the final peace treaty between Germany and the Allies is signed. An introductory chapter provides some historical background to the individual countries, and a final chapter deals with the groupings within which for various reasons—economic, strategic and ideological—most states are now aligned.

One major difficulty in regional geography is the maintenance of balance and perspective between an analytical discussion of the various systematic aspects—relief, climate, the economy, communications—and a description of the regional units by means of which the whole geographical picture may be synthesized. In this book a compromise has been sought, whereby the overall systematic aspects of each country are first examined, and then, limiting repetition to a minimum, the regional units are described. Each should be regarded as complementary in the overall survey of the particular country.

The maps and diagrams were drawn with his usual care and patience by Mr A. Carson Clark, Cartographer in the Department of Geography at Southampton, and his team. I am grateful to those who have given permission to base line drawings upon their originals; acknowledgement is made in the caption to each. The heavy labour of the initial typing of the manuscript was carried out by Mrs G. A. Trevett. The photographs have been garnered from a variety of sources listed on p. xv, some my own, and I am happy to pay a special tribute to Mr Eric Kay, B.A., who has contributed a major share, taken during the summer of 1964 for the specific purpose.

Preface to the Second Edition

THE necessity of a new edition has afforded the opportunity of a complete revision of the text, involving the updating of statistical and other information. The original edition surveyed the geographical

v

state of north-western Europe in the early years of the 1960s; this revision presents a review of the closing years of that decade, preparatory to the advance into the momentous 'seventies. Recent years have seen many important, even dramatic, changes: the introduction of large-scale national and regional 'plans'; changes in agricultural policy, notably a move away from the small producing units, a big decline in the labour force, and a marked increase in output, helped by mechanization; the development of large industrial groups and consortia to meet the capital demands of new technologies in industry; the decline of coal as a prime energy resource and its partial replacement by oil, natural gas and nuclear power; the modernization of communications, as indicated by the electrification of railways, the spread of motorways, the growth of a web of pipelines for oil, gas and stockfeed, and the construction of container-ports and bulk-cargo terminals; and the rapid but uneven growth of population, especially in the conurbations, accompanied by decline in many rural areas.

A number of maps and diagrams has necessarily been redrawn and updated, and several photographs have been replaced. In accordance with the official policy towards metrication, quantities are given in S.I. units, though Imperial equivalents (rounded off where necessary) are included. The convenient unit *milliard* is used for the value of a thousand million, and the metric ton (0·9842 long tons) for weights. Statistics are freely included, not to overload the burden on the student's memory, but to give a precise indication of the order of magnitude involved. They refer generally to the years 1967–68, occasionally 1969, except where an earlier Census is the latest available.

F.J.M.

Ennerdale,
1970

Contents

Maps and Diagrams

ix

Plates

xiii

For supplying photographs and permission to reproduce them, I am indebted to the following:

Eric Kay: Plates, I, IV, V, IX, X, XI, XIII, XIX, XXIII, XXIV, XXVI, XXVII, XXXVI, XXXIX, XLVI, XLVIII, XLIX, L, LI, LIII, LIV, LV, LVII, LVIII, LIX, LXI, LXII, LXIII, LXIV; *Aerofilms*: Plate XXXV; *Aero Material A/B (Stockholm)*: Plates II, III; *Aéro-photo*: Plate LVI; *Compagnie Aérienne Française*: Plates LX, LXV; *Deutschen Zentrale für Fremdenverkehr*: Plates XX, XXI, XXII, XXIX; *l'Industrielle de la Photo*: Plate XXVIII; *Institut Belge*: Plate XXXVII; *KLM Aerocarto*: Plates XXXII, XXXIII, XXXIV, XXXVIII; *Krupp*: Plate XXV; *Luftfoto Nowico (Köbenhavn.K)*: Plate XVIII; *N.A.M.*: Plate XLI; *Sabena*: Plate XL; *Swissair*: Plates XLVII, LII; *Widerøe's Flyveselskap og Polarfly A.G.*: Plates VI, VII, VIII, XII. Plates XIV, XV, XVI, XVII, XXX, XLII, XLIII, XLIV are by F. J. Monkhouse.

CHAPTER ONE

The States

EUROPE is divided into a patchwork of independent states. Much of the history of the continent comprises the story of how the states emerged as identities, made war upon each other, grouped into alliances, expanded or declined, and sometimes disappeared, temporarily or permanently; the jigsaw pattern of their boundaries has constantly changed, especially after each period of warfare.

A state consists of a number of people inhabiting a specific territory and organized under a particular system of government. It acquires an outlook which can be best summed up as 'nationality', not easy to define but involving common ties and sentiments, certain traditions and a proud history. Frequently the members of a state speak a common language, though in some countries two or more languages may be recognized as official. Thus French, German, Italian and Romansch are the languages of Switzerland; Walloon (a dialect of French) and Flemish (dialects of Dutch) are spoken in Belgium; and Finnish and Swedish are used in Finland.

Even in a country such as France, where a standard language based on the ancient *Langue d'Oïl* is spoken by most of its inhabitants, nearly 2 million people of French nationality habitually use either another language in its own right or dialects of foreign languages, though almost all have standard French as their second tongue. Over a large part of the South, from Bordeaux across the southern Central Massif and the Midi coastlands to the Italian frontier, is spoken a language sometimes called Provençal, but which is better designated by its ancient name of the *Langue d'Oc*, since it is spoken more widely than in Provence. In the south-western corner of the country about 100,000 speak Basque, a language concerning whose origin there has been much controversy, and which is also used by half a million people of Spanish nationality on the southern flanks of the Pyrenees. In south-eastern France, in Roussillon, a large number speak Catalan, a Romance language transitional between Provençal. French and Spanish. In the north-west about 800,000 speak Breton, a Celtic language closely related to Welsh and to the now extinct Cornish, and indeed of these some 20,000 cannot speak

French. In the departments of Pas-de-Calais and Nord, 60,000 speak one of several Dutch (Flemish) dialects, in Alsace and eastern Lorraine Germanic dialects are spoken, and in the high Alpine valleys some speak Italian. Though few people in Corsica cannot speak the official French, which is taught in the schools, Corsican, an old-fashioned Italian dialect, is used everywhere as the language of familiarity. In addition to these distinctive languages, there are numerous local dialects (*patois*). Yet no one can doubt the unity of France as a nation, despite strong tendencies at times to regionalism, usually manifested harmlessly in cultural movements concerned with the preservation of dialects, literature and traditions. This unity is partly a result of the high degree of administrative centralization associated with the powerful centripetal effect of Paris, partly because of the intensity of national sentiment developed during a thousand years and strengthened especially by the rigours of war. During 1940–45, though France was separated for some time into 'occupied' and 'unoccupied' zones, though Marshal Pétain divided the country into semi-autonomous provinces for administrative purposes, though the Germans incorporated Alsace and Lorraine into the Reich, French national feeling survived strongly, as manifested by the surge of emotion at the time of the liberation.

Some European states emerged early in history and have maintained a long national existence. England within its island boundaries had attained some degree of unity by the tenth century, and after the Norman conquerors had been absorbed a state emerged sufficiently free from continental entanglements to concentrate much of its energies on its projection overseas. France took longer, but soon became the most powerful state in continental Europe. By the end of the Napoleonic Wars, Denmark and Switzerland occupied virtually the same territory as they do today. Belgium and the Netherlands, united in 1815 as a barrier to further French aggression, were finally separated in 1839. The German Empire was created in 1871 largely as a result of the military achievements of Prussia. Norway and Sweden, united during the nineteenth century, were separated in 1905, and Finland was freed from Russian rule in 1918.

The War of 1914–18 and the peace treaties which ended it brought great changes in central and eastern Europe, the results of the collapse of three empires, Austria–Hungary, Turkey and Russia, but the boundaries of western Europe were but little altered. Most of the **changes** involved Germany: Alsace-Lorraine was reunited with

France, part of the Jutland peninsula was returned to Denmark, and some territory in the east was included in a resurrected Poland. The territorial changes in post-1945 Europe were also quite small, mainly involving Germany, though a peace treaty with that country has not yet (1970) been signed. The chief result has been the creation of two German states, with *de facto* (though not *de jure*) independent existence, separated by a boundary as rigid as anywhere in the world because it defines two political ideologies, two distinct ways of life.

France

France, expanding from the 'core' of the Ile de France, emerged from the feudal struggles of medieval times to become an absolute monarchy, striving for administrative centralization amidst the religious wars and seeking to obtain what were considered to be its 'natural frontiers', the Rhine, the Alps and the Pyrenees, involving the country in a long series of dynastic wars, particularly with the Habsburgs. Then for more than a century from 1689, when France had become the premier military power in continental Europe, it was engaged in a struggle with England, whose naval supremacy and deliberate policy of supporting France's continental enemies was to destroy the old French colonial empire in India and Canada. Out of the French Revolution, which swept away the *ancien régime*, emerged Napoleon, who established an empire which sprawled across the continent until his final defeat for which England was largely responsible.

The rise of Prussia became the main threat to France, materializing in the humiliation of 1870–71, in the War of 1914–18 which left France victorious but exhausted, in the collapse of 1940 and the occupation. Yet because it shared in its own liberation, post-1945 France rapidly reasserted its position as a Great Power, as one of the four Allies responsible for zones of occupation in Germany and Austria, and as one of the permanent members of the Security Council of the United Nations Organization. It was faced with grave problems of economic reconstruction and development, with long periods of strife as the overseas territories gradually attained independence, and with internal political instability and unrest until the constitution of the Fifth Republic came into force in 1958.

France has emerged as a vital member of both the Atlantic Alliance and the European Community, able to assert itself to the point of intransigence in world affairs, for long to deny Britain entry to the

Community, to see itself as leader of continental Europe. Its economic development since 1945 has been almost as remarkable as that of West Germany.

Switzerland

Switzerland has had a long and continuous history as a nation-state. Its nucleus was created in 1291, when the Forest Cantons of Schwyz, Uri and Unterwalden, joined by Lucerne in 1332, created a defensive league (the *Bund der Eidgenossen*) around the shores of Lake Lucerne. This group of cantons occupied a strong strategic position in a 'heartland' area controlling the route south to the St Gotthard Pass. Gradually other cantons joined; independence from the Holy Roman Empire was achieved in 1648 at the Treaty of Westphalia; and the Helvetic Confederation of nineteen cantons was created in 1798, though under French influence. By 1815, with the adherence of Valais and Geneva, each piece of the jigsaw had fallen into place.

At the Congress of Vienna the Swiss Confederation was established and its neutrality was guaranteed by most of the Powers of Europe; a brief civil war in 1847 was concluded by the constitution of 1848. Swiss neutrality survived two world wars, partly because it was an armed and determined neutrality. In 1940 the possibility of German invasion seemed imminent; Alpine tunnels and passes were mined ready for demolition, manpower was mobilized at a level greater than that of any belligerent country, and the Swiss were prepared to defend to the last the 'Redoubt', the area around Andermatt in the south. But Swiss neutrality was respected; a potential aggressor weighed the prospects of a bitter struggle among the mountains against the advantages of retaining a neutral state which, wholly surrounded by Axis territory, could supply much desired manufactures to Germany.

This neutrality has been strictly maintained by postwar Switzerland, and it is not even a member of the United Nations Organization, though it belongs to several of the agencies; it contracts no military alliances nor any groupings which might lead to external political or strategic commitments. But its neutrality does not imply isolation; it is the headquarters of many international organizations, including the Red Cross, the Universal Postal Union, the World Health Organization, and the Economic Commission for Europe. Its well-developed roads and railways include several sections of trans-continental routes which negotiate the Alpine tunnels, and such cities as Basle, Zürich and Geneva are centres of international finance and commerce. The country is a member of the Organization for Economic Co-operation and Development (O.E.C.D.), the European Free Trade Association (E.F.T.A., or the 'Outer Seven'), and since 1963 the Council of Europe.

Benelux

The three small states of Belgium, the Netherlands and Luxembourg, known collectively as Benelux, have exercised an importance in western Europe far beyond their size. Their territory has been debatable land throughout history, located as it is within the 'middle kingdom' or 'marchland' formed from the break-up of Charlemagne's empire, a transitional zone between France and Germany. During the sixteenth century the 'Low Countries' (*Nederland*), including numerous individual duchies, counties and lordships, lay within the Habsburg empire. Gradually the differences between the Northern Netherlands and the Southern or Spanish Netherlands became more emphasized. These were the progenitors of the modern states of the Netherlands (which retained the original appellation) and Belgium (in French *Belgique*, in Flemish *België*), a name derived from the '*Belgae*' and the '*Gallia Belgica*' of Roman times, though not used until the time of the French Revolution and officially adopted in 1830.

The distinction between the Northern and Southern Netherlands developed in the sixteenth century on political and religious grounds, though not on the basis of language. Since the early Middle Ages, people in the southern part of the Southern Netherlands had spoken a dialect of standard French, known as Walloon. The remainder spoke '*Duitsch*', or more strictly '*Nederduitsch*', in contrast to '*Hoogduitsch*' or German; this was the origin of the terms 'Dutch' and 'Deutsch'. From the seventeenth century, the name *Nederlandsch* or popularly *Hollandisch* replaced Nederduitsch in the northern provinces, and further south it was known as *Vlaamsch* (Flemish). As a result, the people of the Netherlands speak Dutch, while the Belgians speak both Walloon and Flemish.

In the sixteenth century unrest in the Northern Netherlands steadily increased; this developed into war with Spain, and largely through its maritime supremacy the United Provinces emerged in 1609 as an independent state under the House of Orange. Its national existence was often threatened; war with Spain, naval struggles with

England, and the challenge of Louis XIV's aggressive policies tried and proved the Dutch temper, while their expanding mercantile, colonial and commercial activities increased the national wealth. The Southern Netherlands remained under the rule of the Habsburgs until 1795. Both states were overrun by the French Revolutionary armies, and after various vicissitudes were incorporated into the French Empire. Following the overthrow of Napoleon, Belgium was joined to the United Provinces as the Kingdom of the Netherlands in order to create a stable block against possible French aggression. This union experienced great difficulties, despite considerable economic benefit resulting to Belgium from the opening of the Dutch-controlled Scheldt estuary, which particularly helped Antwerp, and from participation in Dutch overseas trade; industry especially prospered.

But opposition by the Belgians to the union steadily grew, culminating in the revolution of 1830; a year later the Great Powers agreed to the establishment of an independent kingdom of Belgium, though it was not until the Treaty of London in 1839 that the Netherlands finally accepted the terms. Belgium's territory was, however, reduced, for it was obliged to cede the Duchy (now the province) of Limburg to the Netherlands, and the eastern part of the province of Luxembourg was made into an independent Grand Duchy. Since then the two states have pursued separate existences, until the economic *rapprochement* which resulted in the Benelux Union. Both were avowed neutrals in the nineteenth century, Belgium's status guaranteed by the Great Powers at the Treaty of London in 1839. A dispute concerning the navigation of the Scheldt estuary was settled in 1863, when the Dutch right to levy tolls was bought out by a capital payment, to which the maritime powers made contributions in proportion to the use they made of the estuary.

The Netherlands successfully maintained its neutrality during the War of 1914–18, though blockade and unrestricted submarine warfare caused great hardship. But in 1940 its strategic and economic position was too important for Germany to ignore, and the attack on the Netherlands took just five days to complete; on 13 May the centre of Rotterdam was destroyed from the air. The German occupation of the country was bitter, and the combined effects of Allied bombing of essential targets, fighting in 1944 more concentrated than almost anywhere in western Europe, and demolitions by the retreating German forces caused great material destruction.

It is estimated that the Netherlands lost one-third of its capital resources. Moreover, the Japanese attack in the Far East disrupted the valuable colonies in the East Indies, and although the Dutch strove to reassert their position after the Pacific war ended, Indonesian nationalism was so strong that in 1949 they bowed to the inevitable; the Republic of the United States of Indonesia was created, from which almost all Dutch interests have been excluded.

The guarantee of neutrality did not protect Belgium from invasion in 1914, for the German Schlieffen Plan for a mortal blow at Paris involved a major thrust across the country. It was soon wholly occupied, except for the south-western corner behind the river Ijser, which formed the left wing of the Allied line from the North Sea to the Swiss border. At the Treaty of Versailles Belgium was given the former German territories of Eupen, Malmédy and Moresnet, its claim resting on various historical, ethnic and economic grounds; about 60,000 people in the east still speak German. In May 1940 once again German military ruthlessness overrode political morality; in eighteen days King Leopold was forced to admit unconditional surrender, and the country was occupied until September 1944. Since then Belgium has abandoned its unworkable neutral status, and is a member of Western Union, the Atlantic Alliance and the various European Communities. Like the Netherlands, it suffered a loss of overseas territory when in June 1960 the Belgian Congo, with its copper, radium, cobalt, palm oil, cotton, coffee and rubber, attained independence. In 1884 the King of the Belgians had been made sovereign head of the Congo Free State, which in 1907 was formally annexed to Belgium.

The third member of this group is the Grand Duchy of Luxembourg, which likewise has had a long and troubled history. From the fifteenth century its territory was ruled in turn by Burgundy, Spain and the Austrian Habsburgs, and during the Napoleonic era it was incorporated into France. At the Congress of Vienna in 1815 Luxembourg was created a Grand Duchy with independent status, though within both the Kingdom of the Netherlands and the German Confederation of the Rhine. In 1839, when Belgium finally attained independence from the Netherlands, Luxembourg did likewise, but the western, mainly French speaking, portion of the Grand Duchy became the Belgian province of Luxembourg. Within these reduced boundaries the King of the Netherlands remained as Grand Duke on a purely personal basis.

German influence rapidly increased in Luxembourg; at the Congress of Vienna Prussia was granted the right to maintain a garrison in the capital city, and in 1842 the Grand Duchy joined the Zollverein (the German Customs Union), which helped materially in connection with the growth of the iron and steel industry. Ultimately, in 1867 a conference of Great Powers signed a treaty which guaranteed the Grand Duchy as an independent neutral state under the House of Nassau, and the Prussian garrison was withdrawn. Luxembourg remained a member of the Zollverein until its dissolution in 1918.

In 1914 and again in 1940 Luxembourg lay across the path of the German thrust at Paris, and in each case its neutrality was violated and its territory was occupied. After the first liberation in 1918, it seemed difficult for the little state to prosper if it remained economically isolated. A plebiscite indicated that the people wished to enter into some economic union with France, but this France rejected. Finally, in 1922 the Belgo-Luxembourg Customs Union came into being, which gave the Grand Duchy a number of advantages, including participation in Belgium's commercial agreements and use of the port of Antwerp.

In 1940 Luxembourg was incorporated into the Reich and subjected to an intensive 'Germanization', probably greater than in any other occupied country. After the liberation it was abundantly clear to the Luxembourg people that neutrality was no longer a tenable policy, and the revision of the constitution in 1948 abandoned its perpetually neutral status; it has become a member of the various groupings of western Europe.

A convention was signed in 1944 by the three governments in exile, which in 1948 was widened into the customs union known as Benelux, and in 1949 the 'pre-union', or provisional state of economic union, began. The final treaty confirming full economic union was signed in 1958, and came into operation in 1960. The road to economic co-operation has been long and tedious, and few statesmen in 1944 envisaged that the process would take as long as fifteen years. Even the final stages were held up by prolonged arguments about agricultural problems, and several serious differences remain to be settled in detail. All trade agreements with outside countries are concluded by Benelux as an entity, and by 1965 all obstacles to the free flow of goods between the three partners had been eliminated. Gradually economic policies are being harmonized; for example, tenders for constructional work are accessible on equal terms to firms in each of the three countries, labour is allowed to move as it wishes, and there is considerable freedom of transfer of capital, although no monetary union is envisaged. The problems of agricultural policy remain the chief stumbling block, for the efficient, well organized and highly subsidized Dutch farmers can undersell their Belgian counterparts, sometimes by as much as 30 per cent. Belgium reserves the right to close its borders to Dutch farm products if prices fall below a certain level, and a special duty is levied on butter and cheese to equalize the market prices in the two countries. Industrial difficulties have been much less acute, partly because industry is more adaptable than agriculture and the two countries are industrially in many ways more complementary than competitive, partly because their membership in the Coal and Steel Community enforces certain basic agreements. Both countries favour a high degree of free trade and a widening of economic relations; they want an economically unified western Europe but also wish to preserve and extend their contacts with other countries, hence their support for the admission of Britain into the European Economic Community.

Germany

The origins of Germany can be traced back to the kingdom of the East Franks, one of the three states into which Charlemagne's empire was partitioned in 843. But more than a thousand years were to pass before the German Empire was created, during which time the somewhat amorphous Holy Roman Empire occupied a territory substantially larger than Greater Germany ever achieved. Out of it developed the rivalry between Austria and Prussia, decisively settled by war in 1866 in Prussia's favour, and after the crushing defeat of France in 1871 the German Empire was established. By 1914 this great state extended from Lorraine to East Prussia, with a population of just under 70 million; it was a prosperous and rapidly expanding industrial country; it had a mighty army and a large navy; and it possessed colonies in Africa and in the Pacific. The War of 1914–18 cost the lives of 2 million soldiers, the loss of its colonies and its navy, an eighth of its territory and a tenth of its population, the payment of large reparations, and the acceptance of a considerable degree of demilitarization in the Rhineland. But within twenty years, out of the revival of German nationalism furthered by the near collapse of the economy and the rise in unemployment, emerged National Socialism and the Third Reich. Following the absorption of Austria in 1938 and the acquisition of the Sudeten lands from Czechoslovakia in 1939, Gross Deutschland had a population of 81 million, and before the tide of war finally turned Hitler's empire exceeded in extent that of Napoleon.

On 8 May 1945 Germany surrendered unconditionally, and an armistice was agreed. A month later the U.K., U.S.A., U.S.S.R. and France each assumed authority over a zone of German territory, while Berlin, situated far to the east in the Soviet zone, was divided into four occupied sectors. At the Potsdam Conference in July–August 1945, certain rearrangements of German territory were made, insignificant in the west but considerable in the east, though these await ratification by a final peace treaty. Only in respect of Austria, restored to full independence and sovereignty by treaty in 1955, has this ratification occurred, although the western powers terminated the state of war with Germany in 1951, and the U.S.S.R. did so four years later. Some minor boundary modifications were agreed between Germany on the one hand and the Benelux countries on the other, though the Dutch returned their acquisitions in 1963. The only major issue in the west was the future of the Saarland, which the French initially sought to control, first by political then by economic means. But in 1957, as a result of an agreement signed between the two countries, the Saarland returned to West Germany, and by 1959 its economic reintegration was completed.

In the east the position was very different. After the Potsdam Agreement the northern part of East Prussia was occupied by the U.S.S.R. It was agreed that a re-established Poland should administer the southern part of East Prussia, together with all the German lands lying to the east of the line of the Oder and its left-bank tributary the Neisse, from the Baltic Sea to the frontier of Czechoslovakia. In order to give Poland control of the mouth of the Oder, the border was drawn to the west of the river from above Stettin (now Szczecin) to the Baltic coast. Although the destiny of these lands awaits the ultimate treaty, the signing of which seems as far away as ever, in practice they have been very definitely incorporated into Poland and Russia. Within a short time after the end of the War those Germans who had not already fled westward as refugees had been evicted; most reached West Germany, some went on to America, and no minority problem remains.

It was soon apparent that any hopes of a rapid withdrawal of the occupation forces from the four zones and the creation of a reunified Germany were impracticable. The division of the country symbolizes the division of the world into two blocks; the boundary between the three western zones and the eastern zone represents the 'Iron Curtain' at its most rigid. Gradually the three western zones became more closely associated; a central government was agreed for 'Trizonia' in 1948, which a year later became the Federal Republic of Germany (*Bundesrepublik Deutschland*), a state of 250 000 sq. km (96,000 sq. miles) with a population then of about 48 millions, which in this book is referred to as West Germany. In 1955 the three western powers revoked the Occupation Statute, and West Germany became a sovereign independent country. Similarly, the Russian zone became the German Democratic Republic (East Germany). The Federal Republic does not recognize the separate existence of the Democratic Republic and commonly refers to it as *Mitteldeutschland* (central Germany), and to the lost territories under Polish administration as *Ostdeutschland* (eastern Germany) (Plate XXX).

West Germany clearly has an important rôle, strategically and economically, to play in western Europe. One of the major postwar problems was the nature of its contribution to the defence of the free world, on which the U.S.A. was especially insistent. Despite the threat of Communism, there were still justifiable apprehensions, particularly in France and Great Britain, concerning the dangers of a revival of German military strength. Ultimately, after the failure to form a European Defence Community, West Germany joined both N.A.T.O. and Western European Union, and in due course a German general became commander-in-chief of the Allied Land Forces. The U.S.S.R. regards this rearmament of West Germany, even within its controlled limitations, as a breach of the Potsdam Agreement.

Equally if not more vital is the contribution of West Germany to the economic development of western Europe; to play its part a rapid recovery from its war-shattered condition was essential. A radical reform of the currency in 1948 helped to establish confidence and a stable basis for the development of industry and commerce, and American financial aid provided the initial capital. West Germany's membership of the Organization for European Economic Co-operation was of immense benefit both to itself and the other member states, which needed German coal and steel. Though not allowed membership of the United Nations Organization, West Germany has joined a number of its agencies and is a member of the Council of Europe.

The German Democratic Republic enacted its constitution in October 1949, but it has received diplomatic recognition only from twelve Communist states. The country is a member of several organizations dominated by the U.S.S.R., notably the Council for Mutual Economic Aid (*Comecon*) established in 1949, which was concerned at first merely with trading agreements, but has been widened into a joint planning agency. In the military sphere East Germany is a member of the Warsaw Pact, formulated in 1955. In 1950 it concluded an agreement with Poland, by which the Oder–Neisse line was accepted as its permanent eastern border, though this agreement was accepted neither by the Western Allies nor by the Federal Government.

There remains the apparently insoluble problem of Berlin, before 1939 the capital of a great state, with a population of over 4 millions. From 1945 to 1948 the city was administered by a quadripartite Allied government, but then it was divided in the same way as Germany itself. The three western sectors form West Berlin, an enclave of 480 sq. km (185 sq. miles); it is a self-governing city and a *Land* (province) within the Federal Republic (a status not recognized by the U.S.S.R. and East Germany), but separated from it by 160 km (100 miles) of East German territory. East Berlin, the former Russian sector covering an area of 404 sq. km (156 sq. miles), differed from the Allied sectors in that it was contiguous with the Soviet-occupied zone of Germany, so that in 1949 it could become the capital of the Democratic Republic. Berlin remains one of the perennial threats to peace; its future, as that of the two Germanies, remains obscure, for these matters are largely outside German control.

Denmark

The Danes have had a long and proud history, and particularly from the eighth to the twelfth centuries, in common with the other Scandinavian seafarers, their impact on western Europe was considerable. Exploration, trade, piracy and conquest were all part of their activities. At one time the Danes held much of eastern England, and later their colonies were established in Greenland, the Faeroes, Iceland and even the West Indies; the Virgin Islands remained a Danish possession until 1917, when they were sold to the U.S.A. Greenland and the Faeroes are still under Danish sovereignty, sending representatives to the parliament in Copenhagen, but Iceland became independent, though under the personal sovereignty of Denmark, in 1918, and a republic in 1944.

During the long medieval struggles for supremacy in the Baltic region, Denmark for a time made considerable progress in its ambition for leadership; Norway was joined to it in 1380 and remained so until the Napoleonic Wars, when as a result of the ill-judged Danish alliance with the French, Norway was taken away and united with Sweden, which for a time, between 1389 and 1523, had itself been under Danish rule.

After the mid-eighteenth century, in common with its northern neighbours Denmark abandoned external political ambitions and concentrated on internal economic and social progress. But in 1864, after a disastrous defeat by expansionist Prussia, the southern part of Jutland, the provinces of Schleswig and Holstein, was annexed by Prussia and Austria, and later became part of the German empire. Though northern Schleswig was returned to Denmark in 1920 after a plebiscite, the southern part has never been restored. Despite its avowed policy of neutrality, Denmark was invaded by Germany in April 1940, and suffered five years of occupation, a period of stringency, for the country was deprived of its overseas markets and pillaged. After liberation, Denmark was forced to reconstruct its national life. The revival of agriculture, the mainspring of its economy, was inevitably bound up with the economic recovery of western Europe generally; one major factor has been the immense development of West Germany, one of Denmark's main customers. After the disastrous experience of 1940, Denmark realized that neutrality is meaningless in this modern world, and with Norway joined the North Atlantic Treaty Organization. In the desire to further expansion of commerce, Denmark also became a member of the European Free Trade Association.

Norway

Since the days when the Vikings terrorized Europe, established settlements in Orkney, Shetland, the Faeroes, Iceland, around the Irish Sea and in Normandy, and made remarkable voyages to Greenland and to the North American continent, Norway has experienced a varied national history. About the beginning of the fourteenth century the country was drawn into the Scandinavian rivalries and struggles, and its independence soon vanished. For a time it was united with Sweden, then also with Denmark in the Union of Kalmar (1397), then for more than three and a half centuries from 1450 with Denmark alone. From 1814 Norway and Sweden formed a personal union under the King of Sweden; the Act of Union stated that Norway was to remain '. . . a free, independent, indivisible and inalienable kingdom'. Although under a common sovereign, the two states maintained separate systems of government, military forces, tariffs and coinage, but with a joint foreign ministry. Dissension became increasingly acute as the century wore on, at times almost to the point of war, and the arrangement was finally terminated in 1905, when Norway became an independent kingdom.

Norway successfully maintained its declared neutrality until April 1940, when Germany, requiring the ice-free fjord harbours for the battle of the Atlantic, occupied the whole country. This occupation was extremely rigorous, culminating in the devastation in 1944 of Finnmark and Troms in the far north by the retreating Germans as part of their 'scorched earth' policy against the advancing Russian army. Since liberation in 1945, national reconstruction and development have been pushed on apace.

Despite approaches by Sweden in 1949 to associate in some form of strictly neutral Scandinavian block, Norway has realized that its destiny lies with an association of other Atlantic countries, and it joined in 1949 the North Atlantic Treaty Organization. The capital city, Oslo, is the headquarters of one of the N.A.T.O. operational commands.

Sweden

The history of Sweden during the past 1,200 years presents some curious contrasts. Like its neighbours, its people from the ninth century onwards were energetic sailors and colonizers, but Sweden's attentions were primarily directed eastward across the Gulf of Bothnia and overland towards the Black and Caspian Seas. For several centuries Sweden strove to rule the Baltic lands and maintained a state of intermittent conflict with Denmark until the middle of the eighteenth century. At the height of its power, the country had virtually attained its aim of Baltic domination, for it occupied Finland, Latvia, Esthonia and parts of the German Baltic coast. But by the mid-eighteenth century the rise of Russia had forced Sweden to surrender much of its eastern Baltic territory, and Finland was finally lost in 1809.

Sweden was fortunate in being one of the few European countries to remain neutral during both the 1914–18 and 1939–45 Wars. Today the country is still wholly neutral, and while it is a member of the United Nations Organization (the second Secretary-General, Dag Hammarskjöld, was a Swede) and of the economic associations of O.E.C.D. and E.F.T.A., it has remained aloof from such a military grouping as N.A.T.O. and from any proposed 'Scandinavian pact' of a strategic nature.

Finland

As an independent state, Finland has had only a brief existence. From the twelfth century until 1809 it was part of Sweden; many of the people in the west and south still speak Swedish. Then it was a self-governing Grand Duchy within the Russian Empire until the Revolution of 1917, when the freedom-loving Finns with the help of German troops became independent; the republic was recognized in 1920. Its location between Russian and German spheres of influence and ideologies produced an increasingly parlous situation in the late 'thirties, and in 1939 the U.S.S.R. made claims upon certain strategic territories in southern Finland in order to control the approaches to Kronshtadt and Leningrad by way of the Gulf of Finland. On the Finnish refusal the U.S.S.R. launched the 'Winter War' in the Karelian Isthmus; despite a heroic resistance, the Finns ultimately surrendered and in March 1940 a peace treaty was signed. Although Finland later renewed the struggle on the side of Germany in order to regain the territories ceded in 1940, it was obliged in 1944 to sign an armistice. The peace treaty of 1947 imposed a grievous burden; the Finns were forced to cede the Kuusamo-Salla area and part of Karelia (including the town of Viipuri, now Vyborg) in the south-east, a border area in the Karelian Uplands in the east, and the northern outlet to the Arctic Ocean, including the ice-free port of Petsamo (Fig. 14). Nearly 44 000 sq. km (17,000 sq. miles) of territory were lost, including 11 per cent of the farmland, 13 per cent of the forests, and 10 per cent of the industrial capacity of the country. The Russians also compulsorily leased for fifty years the Porkkala pensinsula to the west of Helsinki, though unexpectedly this was returned in 1955. In addition, a huge sum was levied in reparations to be repaid over eight years, of which one-third was to be in the form of timber and timber products, the rest in metal goods; helped by a Russian reduction of about 25 per cent as an example of 'Soviet good-will', the reparation payments were completed in 1952. Finland has signed agreements of friendship, non-aggression and mutual assistance with the U.S.S.R and seeks to remain strictly neutral so as not to afford any pretext for direct or indirect Russian intervention. In 1955 Finland joined the Nordic Council (p. 498), but only on condition that the delegates did not discuss military matters.

In 1961 Finland became an associate member of the European Free Trade Association.

This book deals with the eleven countries of north-western Europe as individuals, for in spite of the undoubted progress which has been made towards some degree of European unity since 1945, which is briefly summarized in Chapter 13, they are still first of all nation-states.

Plate I. Settlement pattern and forest in Jämtland, northern Sweden

Plate II. Sawmill near Fagersauna, Sweden

Plate III. The Göta Canal and the agricultural landscape near Töreboda, between Lakes Vänern and Vättern, Sweden

Plate IV. Stockholm

CHAPTER TWO

Sweden

SWEDEN occupies the eastern part of the Scandinavian peninsula; its boundary with Norway follows for most of its length the main watershed, a broad lofty upland which lies markedly nearer the Atlantic coast than that of the Baltic. The country has an area of 411 000 sq. km (160,000 sq. miles), about one and a half times that of the British Isles; it extends between latitudes 69° and 55° N., a distance of about 1600 km (1000 miles).

Administratively Sweden is divided into twenty-four counties (*län*), replacing the twenty-five provinces which reorganization had deprived of any present administrative significance. Many of the old provincial names are however in current use; thus Skåne denotes that part of southern Sweden in the counties of Malmöhus and Kristianstad, while Småland, the hill country to the north of Skåne, consists of the counties of Kronoberg and Jönköping.

STRUCTURE AND RELIEF

Structure

About three-quarters of Sweden, excepting only the extreme west and south, forms part of the Pre-Cambrian Baltic Shield (Fig. 1), the rocks of which may be divided into those of the older Archaean and the younger Proterozoic eras. The former, occupying by far the greater extent, consist of complex gneisses and granites, probably from 1,800 to 1,300 million years old. Included in the granitic rocks are masses of porphyry, the result of extrusive igneous activity, which frequently contain minerals, notably iron ore. These crystalline rocks were subjected to intense folding and metamorphism in the course of several Pre-Cambrian orogenies. During the Proterozoic era vulcanic activity was common; the resulting rocks include porphyries in the north-western part of central Sweden (the district known as Dalarna) and at scattered places along the Norwegian frontier. In addition, some basic rocks, mainly of dolerite, were intruded.

A long period ensued of denudation of these Archaean mountain ranges, destroying all but the 'roots' of the fold systems, and the

2

materials so derived were laid down in thick beds of the coarse red
Jotnian Sandstone. This was originally deposited over a wide area,
but later denudation has removed it except in north-western Dalarna,
where it was preserved either because it was down-faulted or because
it was covered with protective sheets of extruded diabase, and in
Småland, to the south-east of Lake Vättern. A further group of
Proterozoic rocks, younger than the Jotnian Sandstone, include sand-

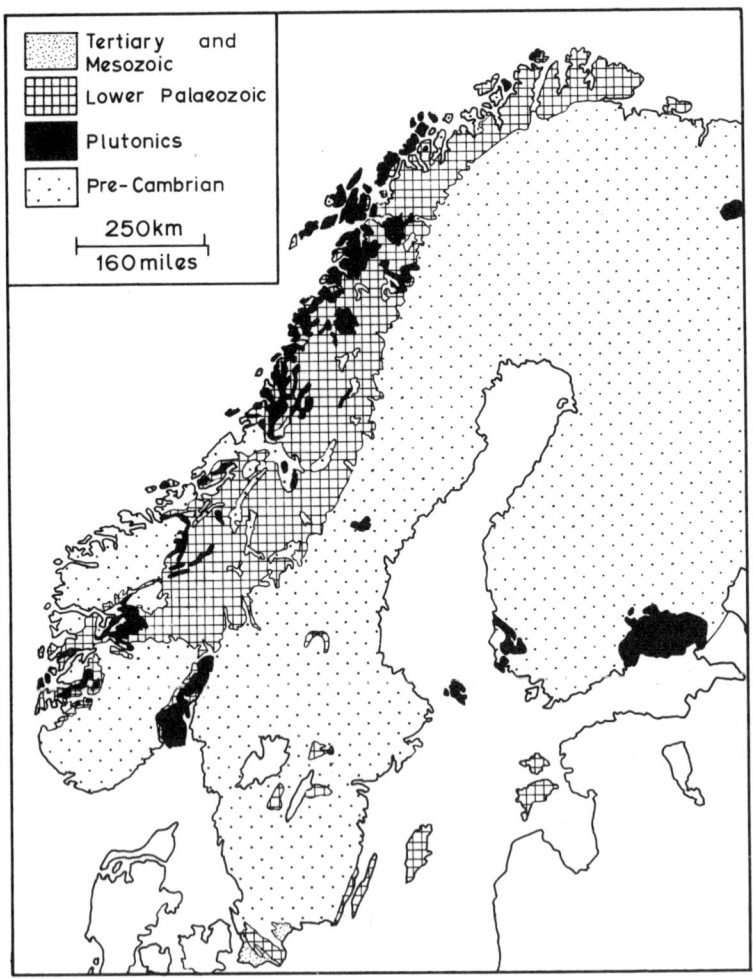

Tertiary   and
Mesozoic

Lower Palaeozoic

Plutonics

Pre-Cambrian

250km

160 miles

Fig. 1. The geology of Sweden, Norway and Finland
(After W. R. Mead)
The shading refers only to the three countries concerned.

stones, limestones, quartzites, slates and schists, found along the Norwegian frontier.

The Baltic Shield has remained relatively stable throughout geological time, subject only to slow movements of uplift or subsidence, possibly the result of isostatic adjustment, and it forms in effect the structural nucleus of Europe. The Pre-Cambrian rocks also appear on the surface in north-western Scotland, the Hebrides and northern Ireland, notably the Lewisian Gneiss and the Torridonian Sandstone which is very similar to the Jotnian Sandstone. It is possible that these rocks are the remnants of an almost completely foundered 'Hebridean massif', perhaps even part of a 'North Atlantic Shield' which included Greenland and Canada.

The Baltic Shield and this Hebridean massif in early Palaeozoic times enclosed a geosynclinal trough elongated from north-east to south-west, in which great thicknesses of sediment were laid down. Probably the Baltic Shield was covered as a result of a subsidence of the Archaean basement with a shallow sea, in which similar sediments were deposited, later compacted and metamorphosed into Lower Palaeozoic quartzite, sandstone, limestone and shale. Since the Silurian, Sweden has experienced no further transgression, except in places along the Baltic coast and in the extreme south of Skåne. As a result, the early Palaeozoic rocks have been largely removed by long-sustained denudation, so revealing the Archaean basement, except for some scattered areas in the centre and south and in the geosyncline where they were very much thicker. These rocks form the islands of Öland and Gotland and parts of the adjacent mainland coast, a band of rock running diagonally across Skåne to the south-east coast, outcrops near Lake Vättern, and others in the Dal valley. In places these rocks can be seen resting directly on the peneplaned Archaean surface.

The Cambrian was a tectonically stable period, but it was succeeded by a series of very active orogenic phases. Their effects can be traced as early as the Ordovician-Silurian transition (the Taconic phase), though the name Caledonian is given to the whole orogeny which attained its maximum at the end of the Silurian, about 400 million years ago. The Caledonian mountains thus created trend from east-north-east to west-south-west across Scandinavia, Scotland and northern Ireland. The north-western front of the orogenic zone can be traced in Scotland, though farther to the north-east it has foundered; possibly the gneissic rocks of the Lofoten Islands represent traces.

In Scandinavia the south-eastern front of the orogenic zone can be readily recognized. The Caledonian stresses were here directed towards the east, resulting in the easterly displacement of some complicated nappe structures along a major thrust-plane, which corresponds to the Moine Thrust on the western margins of the system in Scotland. In Sweden the most easterly zone of the folded area involved only the Lower Palaeozoic sedimentary rocks, but farther west in Norway the Archaean basement rocks were also affected. The nappe structures are extremely complex and are not yet fully understood in detail. Most occur in Norway (p. 61) and are seen in Sweden only in Jämtland, where they consist of schists and slates, with some igneous rocks from associated vulcanicity. Denudation has cut into the main nappes, which probably once extended much further east, as is testified by outliers forming peaks resting on the Archaean basement. The junction between the Lower Palaeozoic rocks and the edge of the Archaean basement is known as the 'Glint Line'. While most of the Archaean peneplain has remained relatively stable, the Caledonian ranges, also reduced to a peneplain, have been subsequently uplifted. Though the nappe structures can still be traced, the mountains consists of a series of high plateaus, dissected into separate blocks and groups of peaks.

Areas of rock younger than Lower Palaeozoic are of small extent in Sweden. Mesozoic rocks are confined to those in Skåne, probably continuous under the Skagerrak and Kattegat with the bed-rocks of Denmark (p. 114). They include Triassic sandstones and clays (which rest on the underlying Silurian rocks), Jurassic sandstones, and the more widespread Cretaceous chalk.

Tertiary rocks are even more scantily represented in Sweden, comprising only a few small patches of clay, marl and sand. Some minor results of the mid-Tertiary tectonic activity which affected much of north-western Europe include the creation of new fault-patterns and the reactivation of some old ones, notably in central Sweden where a shatter-zone of fault-lines, trending markedly north–south and west–east, has left its stamp on the relief features. Other prominent faults trend from north-west to south-east across Skåne, dividing it into three distinct blocks; two in the north are of Archaean and Silurian rocks respectively, that in the extreme south is of chalk, preserved within a down-faulted basin. This tectonic activity also resulted in the formation of several small igneous plugs, necks and bosses in Skåne and elsewhere.

The Quaternary Glaciation

Almost all Scandinavia and the Baltic region formed part of the source-region of the Quaternary ice-sheets. At its maximum, the thickest accumulation of ice probably lay about 160 km (100 miles) to the east of the present watershed, the result of the coalescence of piedmont glaciers on the gentle eastern slope. The ice may have remained over Scandinavia during the whole duration of the Quaternary, though some authorities believe that the glaciation comprised two main periods, an earlier intense one, a later short-lived and less extensive one. Evidence for the double glaciation rests on the discovery of fossiliferous remains, including various pollens, lying between two thick layers of till. During the second phase it is possible that some of the peaks, notably Kebnekaise, the highest in Sweden, projected above the ice like Greenland nunataks, though this also is debatable.

The final retreat stages of the continental glaciation were named after the areas mainly affected (Fig. 2). During the Daniglacial stage (c. 25,000 to 15,000 B.C.), the ice-sheet shrank from western Denmark, though Scandinavia itself was still ice covered. Between 15,000 and 8000 B.C., the Gotiglacial stage saw the gradual withdrawal from southern Sweden, and towards the end of this stage the freshwater 'Baltic Ice Lake' was enlarged into the saltwater 'Yoldia Sea' across south-central Sweden. At this time Skåne probably formed dry land continuous with Denmark and northern Germany.

A pause occurred somewhere about 8000 B.C., when the ice-sheet lay stationary along a line from southern Finland, possibly for a thousand years, resulting in the deposition of the most prominent terminal moraines in Scandinavia. After this episode the ice-sheet shrank with remarkable rapidity during the Finiglacial period, and almost all Sweden was ice-free by about 6500 B.C. The removal of this great weight of ice caused an isostatic uplift of the land, so creating 'Lake Ancylus' which discharged westward across central Sweden by way of what are now the central lakes and the Göta river, and also through the Great Belt. After 6500 B.C. sea-level rose again, the result of water being returned from the melting ice-sheet, forming the 'Littorina Sea' slightly larger than the present Baltic. Probably after 5500 B.C. the ice disappeared entirely, even from the highest plateaus near the Norwegian frontier, during the 'Atlantic' climatic optimum. It has returned in this so-called 'Little Ice Age' as small ice-caps, mainly in Norway, though with about 340 sq. km (130 sq. miles) of ice in Härjedalen and Sulitjelma districts on the

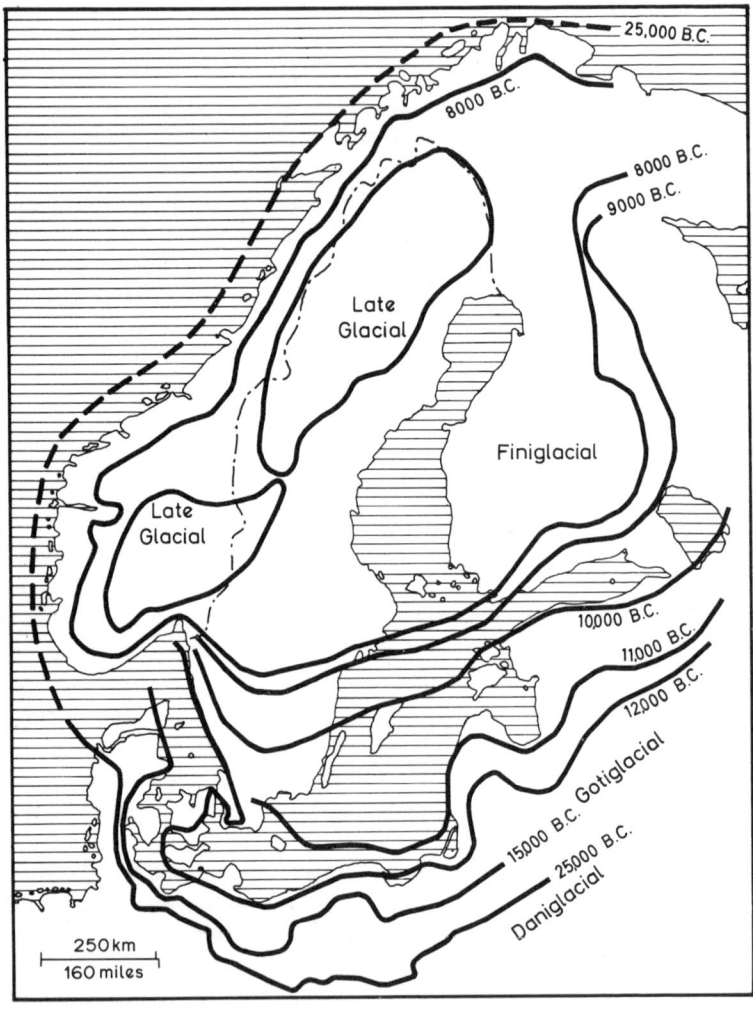

Fig. 2. The retreat stages of the Quaternary ice-sheet in Scandinavia and the
Baltic region
(After *Atlas Över Sverige*)

Swedish side of the border; the present ice-caps are not the final
remnants of the Quaternary glaciation but new ice-bodies.

The ice-sheet produced numerous minor erosive results: well-
marked striae on the Archaean rocks, scoured rock basins, *roches
moutonées* and knobs of all shapes, 'crag and tail', and other features
due to differential abrasion. Many of the erosive results are now

concealed because of the later deposition of drift material, though striated rocks are exposed around Stockholm and along the west coast near Göteborg, where possibly marine erosion during a period of transgression removed the cover of glacial drift. Other results of glacial erosion, U-shaped valleys, cirques, arêtes and peaks, can be seen in the 'alpine' area of Swedish Lapland adjoining Norway. The drift-cover averages 3–5 m (10–16 ft) in thickness in southern Sweden, 8–9 m (25–30 ft) in the north. It is extremely varied in character, for during the various phases sheets of ground-moraine, 'trains' of distinctive boulders, lines of terminal moraine, and drumlin swarms were laid down in chaotic confusion. Ridges of coarse sand and gravel (known in Sweden as *osar*) were deposited by powerful melt-water streams, and fine clays, sometimes in the form of varves, were laid in lakes dammed up along the ice-margins. The largest and most continuous moraines form ramparts across central Sweden, continuations of the Salpausselkä of Finland (p. 94) and the Ra of Norway. The *osar*, deposited as continuously receding deltas of meltwater streams, are found in central Sweden as curving ridges, 25–50 m (80–160 ft) in height, traceable for over 300 km (200 miles). Similar gravel deposits, laid down along the face of the ice-margin as kame-moraines, are also common. Drumlin swarms are found in the uplands south of Lake Vättern and in the central lowlands north of the main morainic ridges. Some of the ice melted under water during periods of marine transgression, thus modifying the character of the deposits; marine erosion of the various materials and their subsequent redeposition elsewhere were common during periods of fluctuating sea-level; and postglacial weathering, mass movement and river erosion of these unconsolidated sediments goes on endlessly.

Drainage

Nearly 10 per cent of the surface of Sweden is covered with lakes and rivers. In the north and centre broadly parallel streams flow south-eastward from the main Scandinavian watershed towards the Gulf of Bothnia, their valleys modified both by glaciation and subsequent uplift of the land. Their upper valleys were deepened by glaciers to form distinct U-shaped rock basins, while morainic deposits created natural dams where they opened out to the east. Thus the valleys now contain narrow lakes or strings of lakes, some as much as 160 km (100 miles) in length, though usually only 5–6 km (3–4 miles) wide. Along the 'Glint Line' (p. 20) the ice to the east dammed the preglacial valleys, ponding up water between this ice-edge and the highlands to the west, and some of the meltwater escaped westward, eroding deep overflow channels. When the ice finally melted, the rivers resumed their preglacial eastward courses, and the over-deepened sections of their channels became lake-filled. Later uplift of the land rejuvenated the rivers, steepening their longitudinal profiles and causing waterfalls and rapids. Since there is much bare rock, runoff is extremely rapid, especially after snow-melt in early summer, and flooding is common, though the lakes form natural reservoirs which to some extent even out the flow.

In the south-centre the uplands of Småland reveal a pattern of almost radial drainage. Still farther south numerous irregularly shaped lakes lie on the uneven morainic surface; these drain south-westward to the Kattegat and south and south-east to the Baltic.

The most extensive area of lakes is in the central lowlands. The two largest, Vänern and Vättern, are respectively about 5400 and 1900 sq. km (2100 and 730 sq. miles) in area, and to the west of Stockholm the irregularly shaped Lake Mälaren (now closed off from the sea by locks) extends inland for 130 km (80 miles). Other lakes are strung out along the valley of the Dal, and hundreds stud the uneven surface of the lowlands; some lie on the undulating morainic cover, others in glacially eroded hollows; many owe their existence to fault-lines in the Archaean floor. The main drainage outlet to the west is via Lake Vänern and the Göta river to the Kattegat. Some of the shallow lake basins have been infilled with sediment and vegetation during post-glacial times, so forming peat bogs, especially in the damper areas of the south-west.

The Coast

The coast of Sweden consists of the irregular edge of the Archaean plateau where it slopes gently under the water of the Baltic Sea. Where faulting has broken up the plateau into a series of fissure-valleys, often crisscrossing in a complex manner, archipelagoes of rocky islands, known as the *skärgård*, are formed, especially well marked in the south-east near Stockholm (Fig. 3), and in the south-west to the north of Göteborg, a district known as Bohuslän. Most of the coast of the Gulf of Bothnia is fringed with archipelagoes of low islands, in the north consisting of partly submerged drumlins.

The southern coasts of Sweden are characterized by broad indentations known as *fjärds*, with parallel, gently sloping shores and fringing islands. These indentations are of glacial origin, eroded both by ice and by subglacial streams, probably taking advantage of the preglacial river valleys. Most of the higher archipelagoes reveal wave-eroded cliffs; striking examples fringe the islands of Öland and Gotland, and also occur at a few points on the coast of Skåne where blocks of Archaean rock project boldly into the sea.

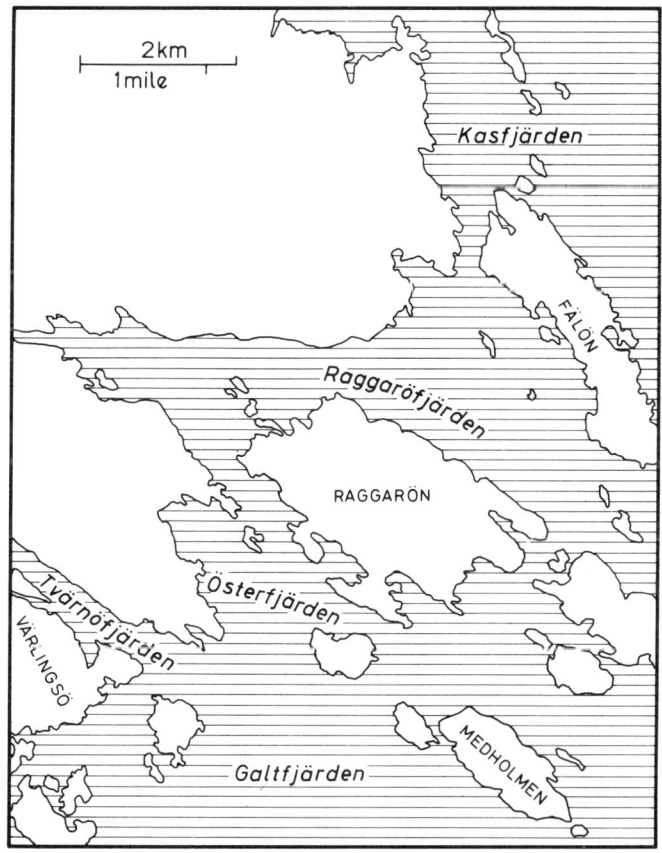

Fig. 3. The 'skerry-guard' (skärgård) near Stockholm

The present form of the coast represents a stage in a long story of changing levels of land and sea. The land is still recovering iso-statically from the depression caused by the overlying weight of the Quaternary ice-sheet, yet at the same time eustatic changes in water level have resulted from the gradual melting of the ice. The land at the northern end of the Gulf of Bothnia is rising at the rate of about

2*

1000 mm (40 in) each century, of only about 400 mm (16 in) near
Stockholm, and none at all in the extreme south.

Relief

Although much of Sweden consists of a somewhat uniform
Archaean peneplain, several distinctive relief units may be distinguished; these are the bases of the main regional divisions (Fig. 9).
In the far north-west, part of the Caledonian fold ranges form high
plateaus (*fjäll*), culminating in the peaks of Kebnekaise (2102 m,
6895 ft) and Sarek (2090 m, 6857 ft), the latter in the Sarek National
Park. To the east of the fjäll the Norrland plateau slopes eastward,
though with a series of steps, to the Baltic coastal plain, crossed by
parallel rivers flowing in deeply cut valleys. Across central Sweden lies
an area of lowland, not a continuous plain but a series of separate
units, in the east around Lakes Mälaren and Hjälmaren, in the centre
between Lakes Vättern and Vänern, and in the west behind the coast
north of Göteborg. These lowlands are interrupted by blocks of
higher land. To the south of Lake Vättern the South Swedish Uplands, sometimes referred to as the Småland Plateau, form an undulating area rising to about 270 m (900 ft) above sea-level, with rivers
flowing outward in a general radial direction. In the south the undulating lowlands of Skåne consist geologically of three blocks
of quite different rock, separated by fault-lines (p. 20), all with a
varied mantle of drift material.

CLIMATE

General Factors

The latitudinal range of the Scandinavian peninsula extends from
about 55° N. to 71° N. In the south during midsummer the days
are 17 hours long, but in winter only about 6·5 hours, while in the
north the continuous daylight of the Arctic summer (for 73 days at
70° N.) alternates with the near darkness of winter. The maximum
altitude of the midday sun in the south in midsummer is about
58°, in the north about 45°; conversely, in winter its maximum
altitude in the south is only about 10°, and to the north of the Arctic
Circle it does not appear above the horizon at midwinter.

Scandinavia lies on the eastern margin of an ocean whose offshore
waters are about 5° C. warmer than the average for the latitude.
The North Atlantic Drift keeps the west and north coasts ice-free
throughout the year right round beyond the North Cape, for its
water rarely falls below 4° C.

A continuous mountain barrier extends from north to south, which reduces maritime influences in the east of the peninsula, produces a marked contrast in temperature between the lands along the coast and the high plateaus, and causes a further contrast between precipitation received on the western slopes and that in the east where a distinct rainshadow effect is experienced. Everywhere local variations are the result of the presence of lakes as temperature regulators, of mosslands and bogs, and of a thick woodland cover.

The situation of Scandinavia between an ocean and a continent causes it to be influenced by various types of air mass: cool, moist Polar Maritime air from the northern Atlantic and Arctic Oceans dominant for much of the time, the less common warm moist Tropical Maritime air from the Atlantic farther south, and in winter the cold dry Polar Continental air from over the Eurasian continent. A succession of low-pressure systems moves across from the Atlantic, resulting in an air flow from a westerly and south-westerly direction, which not only drifts the relatively warm waters northward along the coast, but the air itself, ameliorated by its passage over the sea, 'transports' these higher temperatures, associated with cloudiness and considerable precipitation, to the west coast in winter, though because of the mountains the effects on temperature are not felt far inland.

Polar Continental air may establish itself in winter over Scandinavia, sometimes as a detached area of high pressure over the peninsula, sometimes as an extension of the winter anticyclone of Eurasia, which excludes depressions from the west. During the winter of 1963, the centre of the Eurasiatic high-pressure system lay for long periods over the Baltic, well to the west of its usual position; for a time the Baltic lands were colder than Siberia. The winds during high-pressure dominance are easterly or north-easterly, temperatures are low, precipitation is small and in the form of dry powder snow.

Marked contrasts between the climates of Norway and Sweden are largely the result of their respective locations. The former is much more affected by air streams moving from over the North Atlantic Drift, and its coastal climate is mild and moist. Sweden, lying to the east of the mountains, is partly cut off from these maritime influences and experiences a more extreme and appreciably drier climate of cold temperate type. The differences between the west and east coasts of Scandinavia are illustrated by the fact that while the Norwegian fjords are ice-free throughout the year, the

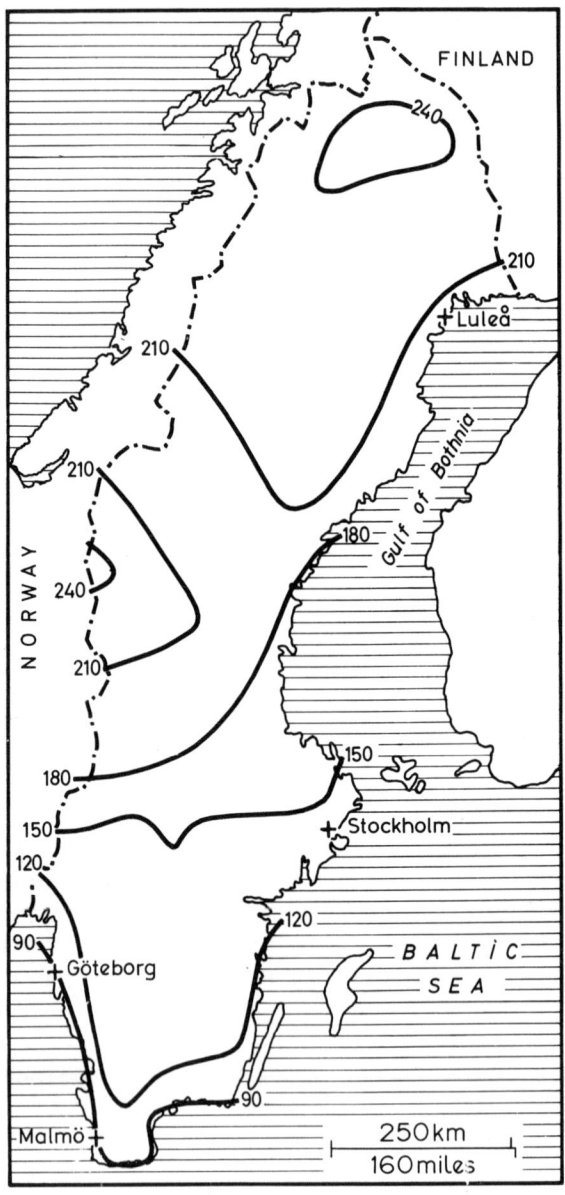

Fig. 4. The mean annual number of days with frost in Sweden
(After *Atlas Över Sverige*)

coasts of the Gulf of Bothnia are frozen for six or seven months (Fig. 15).

Temperature

The climate of Sweden is characterized by appreciable temperature extremes and quite severe winters in the north. While Göteborg on the coast of the Kattegat has a February mean of $-1°$ C., at Stockholm this is $-3°$ C., at Härnösand (at about 63° N.) it has fallen to $-7°$ C., and at Haparanda (on the coast of the Gulf of Bothnia near the Finnish frontier) it is as low as $-12°$ C. The extension of the winter Eurasiatic high pressure, the general absence of cloud cover which allows radiation of heat from the surface, the brief hours of low-angle sunshine even in the south, and the long darkness north of the Arctic Circle, all contribute towards this winter cold and the number of days liable to experience frost (Fig. 4).

The Baltic Sea is an important climatic factor in winter. Its salinity decreases with distance from the North Sea; off the south coast of Sweden it is about 11 per thousand, off Bornholm about 8 per thousand, and at the head of the Gulf of Bothnia it is as low as 2 per thousand. The Baltic receives much fresh water from rivers, including the Oder, the Vistula and the many parallel Swedish streams, and evaporation is low. In an average year ice begins to form around the northern coasts of the Gulf of Bothnia in November, near Stockholm by the beginning of January, and in southern Sweden by early February (Fig. 15). The surface water may remain frozen from a month in the south to six months in the north, and a harbour such as Luleå is closed every year from the end of December until late April. Ports south of Stockholm can usually be kept open with icebreakers, but during the hard winter of 1963 the Baltic was covered with fast ice east of a line between southern Sweden and Denmark; Stockholm was icebound for several months and shipping was diverted to Göteborg.

In summer temperatures are remarkably uniform, for the long hours of the clear northern sunshine to some extent compensate for the decreasing angle of the midday sun. Thus Goteborg and Stockholm each has a mean July temperature of 17° C., and Haparanda a not much lower mean of 15° C. The annual temperature ranges increase steadily northward: 18° C. at Göteborg, 20° C. at Stockholm, and 27° C. at Haparanda. A further point of agricultural significance is the liability of parts of northern and central Sweden to summer frosts, sometimes the result of temperature inversion.

Precipitation

Much of the country lies in a rainshadow relative to the main moisture-bringing air masses from the Atlantic. The greatest precipitation therefore occurs in the south-west (Göteborg, 710 mm, 28 in), brought by depressions crossing the low Danish peninsula from the North Sea, and in the mountains near the Norwegian boundary, where as much as 1900–2030 mm (75–80 in) is received. The driest parts are in the north-east; Östersund has 460 mm (18 in) and Karesuando, on the southern side of the re-entrant of Finnish territory, has a mean of only 320 mm (12·6 in). The south-east is also one of the drier parts; Visby on Gotland receives just 500 mm (20 in). In the island of Öland the combination of a precipitation of about 500 mm (20 in), a potential evaporation rate estimated to be about 400 mm (16 in) and the wide-spread occurrence of permeable limestone are jointly responsible for a remarkable state of virtual semi-aridity.

Precipitation is fairly well distributed throughout the year, though with a distinct maximum during July and August when convectional influences, sometimes in the form of thunderstorms, are most effective. Much falls as snow; in the higher parts of northern Sweden a continuous snow cover is present from the end of September until late May, in southern Norrland from November to April, and in the extreme south from January to early March, though winters vary considerably in respect of the duration, extent and depth of the snow. Spring is the season of least precipitation, but it is also a period of thaw, abundant melt-water and river flooding.

LAND USE AND AGRICULTURE

Soils

Soil types vary considerably in response partly to the bedrock, partly to the uneven cover of glacial drift, marine deposits and alluvium. Many soils are skeletal and immature, since in these cool damp environments the soil-forming processes are slow. The humus content is also varied; the needle leaves of the predominant conifers afford little contribution, while areas of bog peat, though acid in character, are potentially valuable if drained and limed.

Some of the best soils occur in Skåne, derived from the weathering of Cretaceous limestones and Lower Palaeozoic schists, with a contribution of silty morainic material. In the central lowlands the soil is largely derived from marine clays and silts. Farther north where crystalline gneissic and porphyritic rock outcrops are widespread, the soil is thin and acid, sometimes even wholly absent where ice-scarred rocks protrude. The morainic soils vary from coarse sands to clays so boulder-strewn that their utilization is difficult. Much of this drift has been transported by the ice-sheets for only short distances, so that the relationship between bedrock and drift is close, unlike the extensive area of glacial deposition in northern Germany. Among the rocky outcrops and uplands, small areas of potentially useful soil exist: silts on the river terraces, fine clays which fill former lake hollows, strips of marine clay, and patches of sandy moraine. Much of the glacial and fluvioglacial material is of little use: tough stony intractable clays, coarse sands, boulder-fields and tracts of pebbles.

Vegetation

These differences in soil, together with the varied factors of climate and relief, result in a diverse mantle of vegetation. Forest occupies 55 per cent of the total area, arable land about 9 per cent (a figure which has declined recently, with the abandonment of some hill-farms), and meadow and pasture 3 per cent. The remainder, nearly a third, consists of moorlands at high altitude and latitude in the west and north, dominated by mosses, lichens, berried plants, juniper and dwarf birch, bogs on the impermeable crystalline rocks, and extensive bare rock, scree and permanent snowfields in the high mountains.

A large proportion of the trees are coniferous (Plate I); Norwegian spruce occupies 44 per cent, and Scots pine 40 per cent. These cover much of the interior of central Sweden, southern Norrland and the eastern parts of the Småland plateau, where trees occupy almost three-quarters of the area. The deciduous forest, of only small extent, is of two types: birch forest, with some dwarf willows, growing in the far north and on the mountain slopes below the zone of alpine plants, and the oak–beech forests of Skåne and Blekinge, the surviving remnants of an area now largely cleared.

Before the beginning of the nineteenth century, Sweden did not esteem its forest resources highly; some timber, tar and resin were exported to Britain and the Netherlands as naval stores, the oaks of Skåne were used for shipbuilding, and much was consumed locally as fuel, and for building and fencing. The chief enemy of the trees was the charcoal burner, for vast quantities of wood were consumed by the iron industry (p. 42). During the nineteenth century Sweden began to appreciate that its forests were a valuable economic

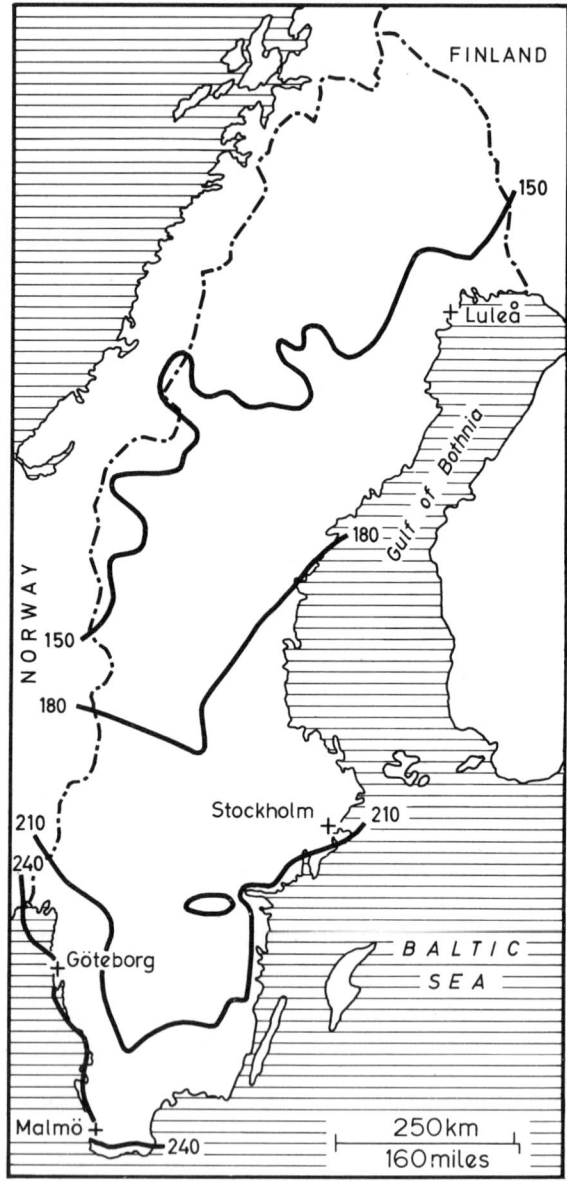

Fig. 5. The length of the farming year in Sweden
(After *Atlas Över Sverige*)
The numerals refer to the period of days between the spring tillage and the
autumn ploughing.

asset, and as the demands of the industrial countries of western Europe rapidly increased the forests were heavily exploited. In Norrland the parallel rivers flowing to the Gulf of Bothnia provided motive power for water-driven sawmills, and many of them have been regularized as 'floating ways', channels from which impediments are cleared and usually bounded by log booms. The logs are cut in winter and dragged on sledges to the frozen rivers, where they await the melting in early summer. About 32 000 km (20,000 miles) of floating way are in use, down which timber rafts are directed to the mills. However, these channels have become less important because of the development of forest roads; tractor haulage can be carried on throughout much of the year, avoiding the short, concentrated effort of the summer-floatings, and it is rather surprisingly less costly.

The timber industry has changed in other ways. Until this century, the emphasis was wholly on sawn timber. This is still important, and 11 million cubic metres were produced in 1968 by about 3,700 sawmills, of which a quarter had five or more workers and a few were giant concerns. But greater diversification has developed during the last few decades; an increasing proportion of the cut goes to make plywood, wallboard, prefabricated houses, furniture, doors and window frames, and matchwood, and since 1945 Swedish furniture has enjoyed growing popularity both in western Europe and America. Before 1850 the sawmills were powered directly by running water, and a large number of small units developed, at least one near the mouth of each river and at each step in the plateau. Since then many of the small mills in the interior have been replaced by large steam-driven plants, notably near Härnösand, Sundsvall and Söderhamn on the coast of southern Norrland. With the twentieth-century introduction of hydroelectricity, some decentralization has again taken place, and the sawmills are widely scattered (Plate II).

The rapid exploitation during the nineteenth century largely cleared the primeval forests, and careful forestry practice has become essential, especially as the more northerly forests take a long time to mature, in northern Norrland as much as three centuries. The State owns about a quarter of the forest land, a number of large companies the same proportion; the rest is in the hands of private landowners and farmers. The position seems satisfactory, since in 1967 the growth was estimated to be about 70 million cubic metres, the cut about 54 millions. The labour force comprises both fulltime forestry workers and sawmill operatives, and also farmers who work in the forests during winter when agriculture is at a standstill.

Arable Farming

The low proportion of arable and pasture land is a result of the limitations imposed by relief, soil and climate. One important factor is the length of the farming year, which is severely restricted by the long harsh winter. While in the south of Skåne the period between spring tillage and autumn ploughing is about 240 days, this diminishes in the north to about 140 days, where work on the land cannot begin until mid-May (Fig. 5). The only compensation in the north is the continuous summer daylight, of which such crops as barley can take advantage. Nevertheless, despite these disadvantages Sweden produces about 90 per cent of its food requirements and has a surplus of dairy products for export.

In the south, with both the best soils and most favourable climate, more than 70 per cent of the surface is classified as arable (Plate III). Along the western coastlands of Skåne where there is little forest or permanent grass the figure is as high as 80 per cent, and in the central lowlands, where the good soils are interrupted by hills and rocks, it is about 40 per cent. Over the northern lands the proportion falls rapidly, so that large areas are uncultivated, the favoured patches comprising less than 1 per cent of the total. Since 1867 an official limit of cultivation, both latitudinal and altitudinal, has been defined, beyond which the land is theoretically reserved for the Lapps and pioneer farming is not permitted.

Sweden has always been a country of small farms worked by their owner-occupiers, though now declining in number (from 230,000 in 1961 to 186,000 in 1966) because of amalgamations. The number of people engaged in agriculture has likewise steadily declined; while 70 per cent of the working population were engaged in agriculture a century ago, this had fallen to only 9 per cent in 1967. Production has, however, increased with the introduction of new techniques, greater mechanization, more liberal use of fertilizers, and improvement in strains of crops.

A broad latitudinal zoning of crops can be distinguished as the length of the growing season decreases northward. Wheat is grown as far as about 61° N., spring and autumn sown varieties each occupying about half of the total; the highest yields are in south-western Skåne. Rye is cultivated in much the same parts of the country as wheat, though more especially on the poorer sandy soils and in the slightly drier climate of the east; its area has steadily declined in favour of wheat as the latter has replaced it in the diet.

Barley is now grown on a much larger area than that of wheat, since its rapid maturing qualities allow it to be grown far north, especially as new varieties have been bred. It is consumed mainly as fodder, though some of the finer varieties in the south are for malting, and in places a type of barley bread is made. Oats is the second most important and widespread cereal both in area and in yield, though it has declined during the last half-century with the decrease in the number of horses. It is grown increasingly on better soils in the centre and south mixed with barley, peas and vetches as a fodder crop, often cut green. In all, 40 per cent of the arable land is under cereals, a proportion rising to 50 per cent in the central lowlands and falling to 30 per cent in some parts of the south as the result of competition on the best soils with sugar beet and industrial crops.

Potatoes are widely grown for domestic consumption, for fodder, and, on sandy soils in the south, for the manufacture of starch and alcohol. The highest yields are in the north, partly because of the freedom from disease in the harder climate, partly because in the south the competition of other more profitable crops tends to relegate potatoes to poorer soils. Though sugar beet was not introduced until the latter part of the nineteenth century, Sweden can now supply its own sugar requirements. This crop is more exacting than the others, and, assisted by state subsidies, is grown only in the south-west of Skåne and on the islands of Öland and Gotland. In recent years, under the stimulus of import restrictions during the War of 1939–45, the acreage of oilseeds, notably rape, has increased to a point of self-sufficiency; in 1968 about 267,000 tons were harvested.

The single most important category of arable land is that under rotation grassland for green fodder and hay, since the long, dark winters, particularly in the north, make essential the indoor housing and feeding of animals for several months. Its increase may be ascribed to the growth in the number of livestock, to the replacement of some meadow, and to the abolition of fallow. A considerable extent of meadow still remains, especially in the north where small boulder-strewn fields are grazed and not cut for hay. Extensive bogs and mosses have been drained to form permanent pasture, in places under the stimulus of the Swedish Moor Culture Association.

Livestock

When in the 1880s the world price of cereals fell sharply, Sweden began to appreciate the importance of animal rearing. By 1968 there were about 2·1 million cattle and 2·0 million pigs. The dairy breeds of cattle have been improved with State encouragement, and increasing use is made of co-operatives on the Danish pattern; 97 per cent of butter and cheese is now produced in factories. The dairy cattle are mainly kept in small herds, while beef stores are reared on the larger farms.

The number of horses has declined substantially from about 600,000 in 1932 to only 69,000 in 1968, mainly the result of the mechanization of agriculture generally, though horses are still used on small farms in forest clearings and in rocky areas where tiny fields make mechanization impracticable. Sheep have dwindled to 286,000 and have almost completely disappeared from the arable lowlands, though some are kept in the mountains, on the islands of Gotland and Öland, and in Norrland.

Reindeer, kept for both hides and meat preserved by smoking or drying, are herded in the north by Swedish Lapps, who roam over the tundra lands, sometimes crossing into Norway and Finland. During the last twenty or thirty years fur farming has become a thriving industry, both as a valuable supplement on small general farms and on large specialized fur farms. The main animals kept are mink (nearly 2 million pelts annually), with a few silver, blue and white fox.

FISHERIES

The Swedish fisheries are substantially less important than those of Norway, in spite of the long coastline, for most of this is along the Baltic Sea, which has never afforded much fish other than the small Baltic herring. Activity is concentrated along the south-western coast, especially north of Göteborg in Bohuslän, where fishing vessels have easy access to the Kattegat, Skagerrak and North Sea. The tendency in recent years has been towards fewer boats and fishermen, less inshore fishing, and the introduction of large motorized fishing vessels operating farther afield. Half the annual catch of about 250,000 tons consists of herring. Many of the harbours in Bohuslän have declined with the growth of Göteborg and more recently of Hönö Klova, 16 km (10 miles) from Göteborg, which is now the largest fishing centre. Fish is sent by rail to many parts of Sweden, and new freezing plants and canneries have been installed.

FUEL AND POWER

Sweden's home supplies of solid fuel are negligible, apart from wood, which is still widely used; it is estimated that 13 per cent of the cut timber is burnt as fuel, equivalent to about 6 per cent of the country's energy needs. At one time great quantities were made into charcoal for smelting, and this fuel is still used for the production of some very high-grade iron. The peat bogs of the centre and north are too isolated to be of much value, especially as most occur in thinly populated areas; farms in some localities burn peat, and about 100,000 tons are briquetted annually. The only coal deposits consist of some brown coal in the Upper Triassic rocks of north-western Skåne, which produce about 200,000 tons a year, temporarily increased to over a million tons during the War of 1939–45. Much of the output is consumed in the kilns of brick-works. With large imports of coal and coke, this type of fuel accounts for 13 per cent of the total energy consumption. Rather surprisingly, water-power has provided in recent years only 15 per cent of the total energy.

Oil

In 1968, oil accounted for about two-thirds of the Swedish consumption of energy. The only home-produced oil is derived from shales of Lower Silurian age, worked near Kvarntorp; though the process is uneconomic, about 100,000 tons are extracted annually. The remaining large requirements of oil are imported, and Sweden is the fourth country in the world in *per capita* consumption of oil in various forms, after the U.S.A., Canada and Iceland, with more than twice that of Great Britain. In all, in 1967 Sweden consumed 20 million tons, of which half entered the country in refined form. Nearly a quarter of Britain's oil exports go to Sweden.

In 1968 five refineries were in operation within Sweden, with a capacity of 9 million tons. Three are quite large, two near Göteborg, the other at Nynäshamn near Stockholm; the two smaller plants are near Malmö and Kvarntorp.

Hydroelectricity

Nature has compensated Sweden for its niggardly supplies of solid fuel by a rich endowment of water-power, although by 1970 all the economically harnessable resources had been developed, mostly in Norrland. For centuries water-wheels were turned by streams flowing from the Scandinavian mountains to the Gulf of Bothnia and radiating from the Småland uplands in the south. Precipitation is well distributed, but because much is held up during the winter freeze a marked winter low water and a summer high water are experienced in the north, though this is less pronounced in the south-west. The abundant lakes serve as natural reservoirs. A disadvantage is the generally limited head of water, the result of the long gradual descent from the mountains as rapids rather than as vertical falls. The 'steps' in this descent provided sites for the earlier stations, but big modern plants require dams and reservoirs to stabilize the flow by storage and to create artificial heads.

The first hydro-station was built in 1882 at Ryfors in the south-west, on the Viskan river. Most of the early stations were installed in the south and centre where power was required for local industrial and domestic use, but as the demand increased and technical problems of long-distance transmission were solved, it became possible to utilize the huge potential of Norrland. The first long 200 KV line was completed in 1936, traversing almost the length of Sweden, and linking the large stations in the north with the industrial and urban consuming centres of the south. By 1960 half a dozen north–south transmission lines were in operation, including one of 380 KV nearly 1000 km (600 miles) in length, linking the Harsprånget station on the Lule river in the far north with the central lowlands. In February 1960 the Swedish and Norwegian transmission systems were linked by a 100 km (60 miles) line to enable the two countries to export power either way as required, though its main purpose is to supply 300 million KWh a year to Stockholm.

The size of the power stations has steadily increased; until recently the largest in Europe (excluding the U.S.S.R.) was Stornorrfors (375,000 KW), near the mouth of the Ume river which has already supplied water to five stations further upstream; this was completed in 1959. The Porjus station was built on the Lule river 32 km (20 miles) from Gällivare, with its generators in underground chambers cut in the solid rock. Two others have been built on the same river, including the second largest Swedish station at Harsprånget. Two rivers in southern Norrland, the Ångerman and the Indals, supply water to the Kilforsen and Krängede stations respectively, and to numerous other plants. The only big unit in the south is Trollhättan on the Göta river, the first large State scheme, which took advantage of the Trollhättan Falls, formerly over 30 m (100 ft) high but now diverted and dry.

In order to cope with an ever-increasing demand for power, particularly during winter low water, the time when domestic demand is at its highest, the State has constructed several large thermal stations, an underground oil-fired plant at Stenungsund to the north of Göteborg, and others at Västerås near Stockholm and at Malmö. A nuclear-powered plant has been built at Björna on the Baltic coast to the east of Norrköping, and others are under construction or projected.

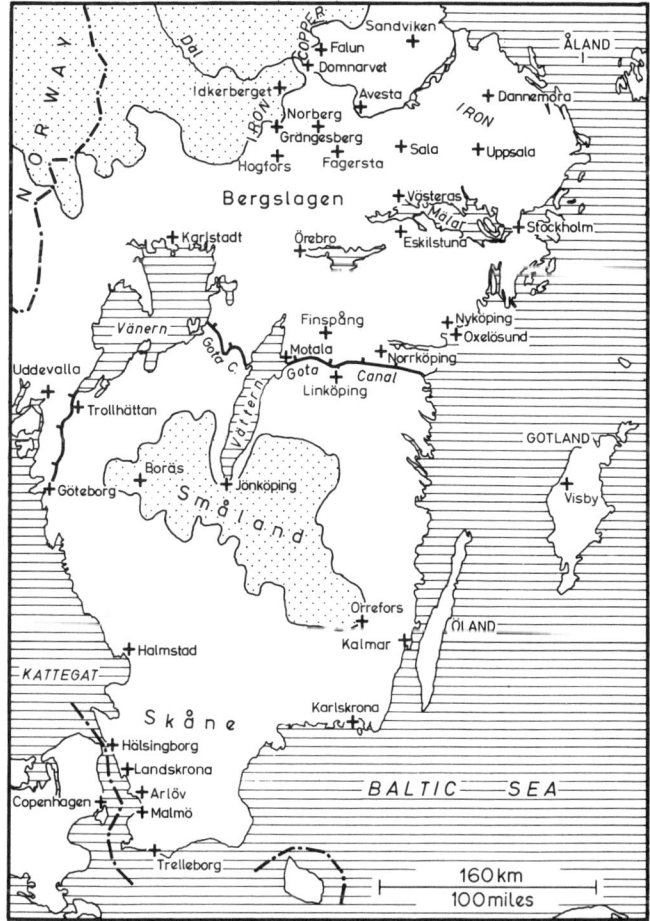

Fig. 6. The industrial area of southern Sweden
The upland areas, above about 180 m (600 ft), are stippled.

Three submarine cables carry power across the Sound from Hälsingborg to Helsingör for consumption in Copenhagen and the island of Zealand; 2 per cent of Sweden's output is usually exported. Sometimes if Swedish supplies are inadequate during a sustained period of frost, the current is reversed and power generated in Copenhagen's thermal stations is transmitted to Sweden.

The total production of electric power has risen from 2·6 milliard KWh in 1920 to 8·6 in 1940 and to 56·2 in 1968. Its value to Sweden's economy can be appreciated by the fact that about three-quarters is consumed by manufacturing industry.

MINING

Iron Ore

One of Sweden's assets is an abundant reserve of iron ore, situated both in the centre of the country and in the north of Norrland. In central Sweden the main mining districts are near Dannemora, Stråssa and Grängesberg (Fig. 6). The ore deposits near Dannemora, 120 km (75 miles) north of Stockholm, are haematites with over 70 per cent metal content; they are free from such impurities as phosphorus and sulphur, and have been used by the Swedish steel industry for many centuries. The Grängesberg deposit, in the district of Bergslagen, is black magnetite containing phosphorus; most of the output is sent by mineral line to the ore-port of Oxelösund to the south of Stockholm. Other smaller deposits in Bergslagen are at Idkerbeget to the north of Grängesberg, at Norberg to the east, and at Persberg, Striberg and Pershytte to the south.

The Norrland ore bodies near Kiruna and Gällivare, by far the largest in the country, were taken over by the State in 1957. Some ore lies near the surface and can be obtained by open-cast working, but the masses are estimated to go down 3 km (2 miles) and some shafts are already 600 m (2000 ft) deep. The probable reserves are about 2,000 million tons at Kiruna and 450 million tons at Gällivare, with a life of at least 150 years at present rates of extraction. Their iron content varies between 60 and 70 per cent, but the phosphorus content is high. The deposits are worked throughout the year, even during the cold and darkness of the Arctic winter, when floodlighting is used. The main disadvantage of the ores is their location in this remote part of the country. A railway was built in 1892 to Luleå on the Gulf of Bothnia, a route which is of use only in summer when the port is ice-free; new large-scale ore-loading equipment which can handle 4,000 tons an hour was installed in 1957. In 1902 a railway was completed across the mountains to the ice-free Norwegian port of Narvik, so that ore can be shipped throughout the year. Since 1961 the third largest mine in Sweden has been developed at Svappavaara,

40 km (25 miles) south-east of Kiruna, producing 3 million tons of ore annually. The new mining town is linked by an electrified railway to the main line.

In 1968 Sweden produced about 32·4 million tons of iron ore, of which just under three-quarters came from the Norrland fields; the average iron content was 61 per cent. Nearly 27 million tons, mostly phosphoric in quality, were exported, a large part to West Germany, some to Britain, the Netherlands and Poland. Though Sweden's output is only about 3 per cent of the world total, its export represents a quarter of the iron ore entering into world trade. It seems probable, however, that as the Basic Oxygen steel-making process (B.O.S. or L.D.) develops, which as yet requires non-phosphoric ore, world demand for these Swedish supplies may decline. Sweden is now importing a considerable amount of non-phosphoric ore from Australia and elsewhere.

Non-ferrous Minerals

The rocks of the Bergslagen district contain a variety of ores, notably copper, silver and zinc, which have been worked since at least the thirteenth century. The silver mines at Sala to the north-west of Stockholm, once known as 'the Treasury of Sweden', were finally abandoned in 1920. For many centuries Falun, north of the river Dal, was the world's chief producer of copper; its operating company claims to be the oldest active mining concern in the world still in operation, for it was inaugurated in 1347. Copper is no longer worked at Falun, for the main lodes are exhausted, but a considerable amount of pyrites is obtained for the chemical industry. A new copper orefield was discovered in 1961 in the Wilhelmina district of western Norrland. Zinc is mined at Garpenberg to the south-east of Falun and at Åmmeberg to the east of Lake Vättern; these mines are owned by a Belgian firm, and the ore is mostly shipped to that country for refining.

In the years following the War of 1914–18, several large ore bodies were discovered in Norrland near Skellefteå, at 65° N., thickly covered with glacial drift and located only by gravimetric and magnetic prospecting methods; other ore bodies have been found in the same neighbourhood during recent years. The main deposit, near Boliden, is said to be one of the largest and most varied in the world, containing copper, gold, silver, bismuth, selenium, arsenic and other metals. Giant smelters, linked to the mines with cableways, have been built on the coast at Rönnskär and Hamnskär; the former possesses the tallest chimney in Europe, designed to avoid damaging the forests with noxious fumes. Automation has been installed; at the Remström mine, one man controls the entire ore transportation system. Most of Sweden's copper ore (85,000 tons in 1968) now comes from Boliden and from the neighbouring Kristineberg and Adak deposits, with lead from Laisvall, and some nickel. Quantities of arsenic, obtained as a byproduct and mostly unsaleable, accumulate in concrete storehouses, creating a steadily growing embarrassment. The main refineries for non-ferrous metals are at Skellefteå, Vasterås to the north of Lake Mälaren, and Finspång near Norrköping. A large aluminium refinery operates at Avesta, using Norwegian alumina.

Granite is quarried in the south-west behind the coast of Bohuslän; for many years it was exported to England and Germany, though this activity had largely ceased before the War of 1939–45. Some granite is still worked for road chippings, but many of the quarries have gone out of production. Limestone is quarried in Skåne, on the islands of Gotland and Öland, and in central Sweden for the cement industry, which is now concentrated in a few large plants. High-quality glass sands are worked in south-eastern Småland.

MANUFACTURING INDUSTRY

Sweden has developed a diverse and highly specialized industrial activity, with a range of products, many of world reputation. Some of these industries owe their antecedents to developments four or five centuries ago, while others are the modern result of the inventive genius of the people. The four main branches are the metallurgical and engineering, textile, chemical and wood-using industries.

Metallurgical and Engineering Industry

From the fourteenth century onwards the accessible lake and bog ores, later the rich non-phosphoric haematite ores of Bergslagen, were smelted with charcoal to produce high-grade steel, for which Sweden had a world reputation; its sword blades rivalled those of Toledo in Spain. Sweden was the leading exporter of bar iron until the end of the eighteenth century, producing about a third of the world total. The Industrial Revolution ended this supremacy, but nevertheless the industry has kept pace with technical developments; the Acid Bessemer process was introduced in 1858, the first Siemens-Martin open-hearth converter in 1868, and the Basic Bessemer process in the last decade of the century. Sweden leads the world in the production of 'sponge iron' used as a raw material for special quality steels; sintered pellets of ore are reduced in a shaft furnace with a circulating mixture of carbon monoxide and hydrogen in a new plant at Grängesberg. Its advantage is that one ton of sponge-iron requires only half a ton of coke, though it consumes 1,000 KWh of electrical energy. The steel industry has probably the greatest diversification of methods of any country in the world. In 1968 5·0 million tons of steel ingots were produced; electric steel accounts for nearly half of this total.

The organization of the steel industry has materially changed, for the scattered small-scale enterprises, originally located where local ore and charcoal could be conveniently utilized, have dwindled in number. Most of the works are in central Sweden, the largest being Domnarvet to the south-west of Falun, where the world's first electrically powered blast furnace was completed during the first decade of this century. Other large plants in this area are at Sandviken, Uddeholm, Högfors and Fagersta. Several modern steel works have been built outside central Sweden. It was logical to construct a state-owned integrated plant at Luleå and a privately owned plant at the ice-free deep-water port of Oxelösund, both coastal terminals of railway lines transporting ore for export. The Oxelösund plant, producing nearly half of Sweden's steel plate, uses in its furnaces coke made from American coal. Two other steel works are at Halmstad on the shores of the Kattegat and at Kallinge on the south coast.

Before 1939 Sweden exported two-fifths of its high-grade steel, but now exports have fallen to one-fifth of the total output. Moreover, imports of lower grades of steel have increased, for in terms of the average *per capita* consumption Sweden is surpassed only by the U.S.A. and Great Britain.

For many centuries small specialist metal-working establishments have operated in the neighbourhood of the Bergslagen smelters and refineries, making agricultural implements, swords, tools, locks and keys. Many of these early enterprises have survived, enlarged and adapted to modern technology but based on a tradition of skilled workmanship and precision. By 1968 about half of the industrial labour force were engaged in engineering, mostly in towns in the central lowlands (Fig. 6). Products include electrical machinery, pulp- and paper-making machinery, mining machinery, cutlery, scissors and tools, surgical instruments, milking machinery and cream separators, telephone equipment, sewing machines, computers, ball-bearings (of which Sweden is the world's largest exporter), lighthouse equipment, refrigerators, and armaments, including the Bofors gun. A large number bear famous trade names, and many owe their success to Swedish inventive genius and adaptability.

Sweden is now the world's third shipbuilding country, with yards at Göteborg, Malmö, Uddevalla, Hälsingborg and Landskrona on the south-western coast, Stockholm and Karlskrona. The *Götaverken* company of Göteborg is the second largest individual shipbuilding company in the world; in 1968 it launched over a million tons, or 6 per cent of the world total. *Eriksberg*, also of Göteborg, is the fourth largest; in 1970 a dry-dock to take vessels of 500,000 tons was completed there. Half of the output, mainly oil tankers, is for foreign orders.

Other engineering industries include the manufacture of electric locomotives at Trollhättan and Motala, rolling-stock at Arlöv, Falun, Linköping and Kalmar, and the *Saab* aircraft at Linköping. An increasing number of cars is exported. The *Volvo* has achieved an international reputation; assembled at a large plant in Göteborg, the components are made at many places in southern Sweden. The *Saab*, with a reputation enhanced by several Monte Carlo Rally and other victories, is made at Trollhättan and Linköping, and the *Scania-Vabis* truck at Södertälje to the south of Stockholm. This list of manufactures could be greatly expanded; apart from supplying a prosperous home consumer market, nearly three-fifths of Swedish exports consist of metals and metal manufactures.

Timber Industries

The growth of the pulp and paper industries has been of immense advantage, particularly as exports of sawn timber have had to meet the competition of North American and Finnish production since the turn of the present century. The first Swedish pulp mill started production as early as 1857, and as the demand for newsprint has grown the pulp industry has replaced the sawmills as the chief consumer of wood. In 1968, 90 pulp mills, many of them large modern plants, produced about 7 million tons, including mechanical pulp for newsprint, sulphite pulp for rayon, and sulphate pulp for wrapping and other papers; about 70 per cent of this is exported, about a third of all pulp entering world commerce.

Associated with the pulp industry is the making of newsprint, fine paper and cardboard. The newsprint mills, which consume great quantities of mechanical pulp, are mainly in the southern parts of the Norrköping area and to the north of Stockholm. Wrapping paper is made in the west around Lake Vänern and near Göteborg, while **fine paper** is produced in Skåne and near Göteborg.

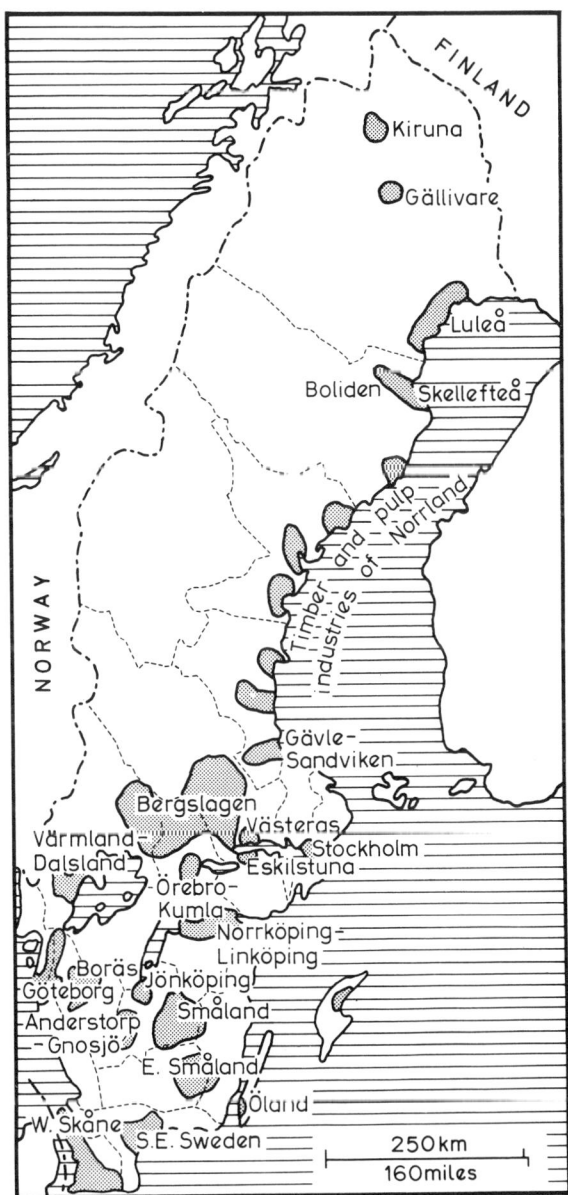

Fig. 7. Industrial regions of Sweden
(After A. Sömme)
The dotted lines are the boundaries of the counties.

Other Industries

Textiles, notably fine cottons, are made at Göteborg, Borås, Malmö and Norrköping. Near Borås a domestic wool and linen industry was active during the Middle Ages, and after cotton manufacture was introduced in the early eighteenth century it went ahead rapidly during the Napoleonic wars and developed on a large scale in the nineteenth century. Norrköping, also with a long tradition, is now the main centre of woollen manufacture; linen and jute are made in the Göteborg–Borås area; rayon in Borås and Norrköping; and clothing in Stockholm and Göteborg. The chemical industry makes explosives, fertilizers, matches and pharmaceutical products. Outstanding expansion has been shown by the petro-chemical industry; for example, a large plant came into operation in 1963 at Stenungsund, north of Göteborg. The manufacture of cement, pottery, high-grade glassware, silverware and many other quality products of high export value may be added to this lengthy list, and widespread industries are associated with food-processing.

The chief industrial areas are in the Stockholm district, in Bergslagen, and to the east of Lake Vättern (Fig. 7). The main districts in the south are near Göteborg and in the valley of the Göta, and along the coast between Malmö and Hälsingborg. The diversity is such that almost every town has some specialized activity, and about 80 per cent of the workers are employed in concerns with fewer than 100 employees. In northern Sweden industry is limited to the working of timber and the processing of mineral ores, except for the integrated iron and steel plant at Luleå.

COMMERCE

Sweden is one of the most prosperous countries in the world, with an average income exceeded only by the U.S.A. and Canada. It can supply much of its own food requirements, it has rich resources of water-power, ores and timber, it has a hardworking, efficient population who can produce specialist commodities in world demand, and it has been neutral since 1814, remaining aloof from war or any outside entanglements. The two World Wars limited imports but stimulated home industry, and during the War of 1939–45 Germany was a large-scale customer; in 1945 the country was prosperous amid a war-shattered Europe.

Until the 'seventies of last century, Sweden was primarily an exporter of grain (mainly oats), timber and naval stores, and a small amount of iron ore which was to increase rapidly as the Gilchrist–Thomas process for using phosphoric ore was more widely used. Gradually the export of grain gave place to that of dairy produce, and much of the sawn timber was replaced by pulp and fabricated wooden articles. In 1968, of a total export value of 25·5 milliard *krona*, minerals (notably iron ore), metals and metal products accounted for half, and timber and timber products for a fifth. Imports were valued at 26·5 milliard *krona*, resulting in only a small adverse visible balance. The protective policy of many countries against foreign manufactured goods has had to be faced; one answer has been Sweden's membership of E.F.T.A., another the creation of Swedish-controlled subsidiaries and associates in the countries concerned, and the issue of manufacturing licences.

Sweden is short of a number of requirements, including coal, mineral oil, cotton, rubber, wheat and other foodstuffs, and tropical and subtropical raw materials. The biggest individual import category is mineral oil, both crude and refined.

COMMUNICATIONS

Systems of communication in Sweden are handicapped for three reasons. In the first place, there are 1600 km (1000 miles) between the north and south of the country. In the second place, the land rises westward to the high Scandinavian plateau, with scattered hills, rock outcrops, and deeply cut valleys where rivers are fast-flowing, steep and rarely navigable. In the third place, the cold of winter, the icebound coasts, the snow-blocked roads, and the floods of the snowmelt are all disadvantages.

Certain compensations are apparent. Though the country is lengthy, it is bordered by a coastline and for nearly seven months connection between north and south for heavy freight can be maintained by coastal shipping. In 1832 the Göta Canal (Plate III), linking Göteborg with the Baltic coast by way of Lakes Vänern and Vättern, was completed; though it has been enlarged, this canal has never attained its anticipated importance as a short cut between the Kattegat and the Baltic. The snows of winter and the frozen lakes and swamps help mobility; in many parts transport can only be carried on at that time of year, partly because the terrain is more solid, and partly because sledges can be used to transport timber.

Roads

Most of the road system is confined to the south and centre. Of a total of about 100 000 km (62,000 miles), only about a quarter are hard-surfaced; a large proportion are 'winter roads' negotiable only when frozen, snow-covered or dry, and at times of snow-melt and in wet weather many are impassable. Some modern roads are of high quality and the radial system around most towns is good. About 65 per cent of all passenger movement is by private car, compared with 20 per cent by rail and only 10 per cent by bus and tram. There is a very heavy urban traffic, for Sweden has nearly 2 million cars (one for each 4 people); the country roads are, however, much more peaceful. Some new roads have been designed to encourage tourist traffic, an example being the Bohuslän route, 290 km (180 miles) long, along the coast northward from Göteborg, crossing into Norway over the Svinesund bridge and so on to Oslo; known as 'the Sunshine Route', it is designed to provide access to the resorts along this attractive coast. Several sections of motorway focus on Stockholm, and about a third of the Malmö–Göteborg motorway is complete.

A distinct feature of recent years has been the increase in lorry transport; half of the total internal freight now moves by this means, compared with only about 7 per cent in 1930. Agricultural products in the centre and south, industrial raw materials and manufactured goods to and from the ports, and timber in increasing quantities move by truck.

Railways

The system originated as horse-powered tramways in the Bergslagen industrial area, linking the mines with furnaces and workshops. The first railway line proper, from Örebro to Arboga, now forming a section of the Stockholm–Göteborg route, was not opened until 1856. There are 12 800 km (8000 miles), about 4000 km less than in 1938, since Sweden has been closing uneconomic lines, though some, particularly in the north, survive because there is no alternative road system in the area served. Nearly two-thirds of the route-length was electrified by 1968, and these lines carry heavy freight; diesels are used increasingly on the rest. Ninety per cent of the lines are state-owned, and this is one of the few countries in the world to run its system profitably.

The important main lines (Fig. 8) are those linking Göteborg with Stockholm; the ferry ports of Hälsingborg (for Helsingör), Malmö

Plate V. Fannaråki (2069 m, 6788 feet) in the western Jotunheim, overlooking the Sygnefjell, Norway

Plate VI. The Lysefjord, which penetrates inland for 70 km. (45 miles) east of Stavanger, Norway

Plate VII. The skärgård *off the coast of northern Norway*

Plate VIII. Glittertind (2481 m, 8140 feet) in the Jotunheim, Norway

(for Copenhagen) and Trelleborg (for Sassnitz in East Germany)
with Stockholm; the ports of Göteborg and Malmö along the south-
western coast; and Stockholm with the Bergslagen towns. Three
lines depend mainly on the transport of iron ore for export: from

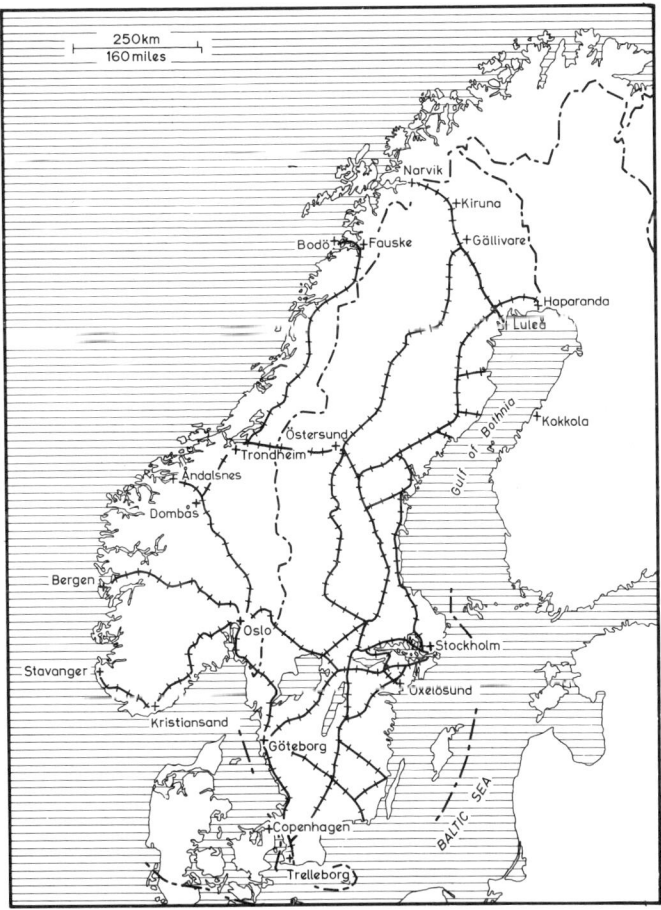

Fig. 8. Railways of Scandinavia
(After the *Continental Bradshaw*)

Kiruna to Luleå on the Gulf of Bothnia; from Kiruna to the winter
port of Narvik (a high capacity line, taking 28 trains daily each with
20,000 tons of ore, controlled by computer); and from Grängesberg
to Oxelösund. A dense network of suburban lines operates around
Stockholm.

3

The opening-up of Norrland by railway was clearly essential to its development, since the sea route can operate only during the summer. Largely because of the difficulty of bridging wide indentations of the sea, the first line was built not along the coast but roughly parallel to it 40–55 km (25–35 miles) inland. A dozen branch lines link this to points on the coast, others run inland up the valleys to mining or timber-working centres. Since 1955 another longitudinal line has been completed, about 190 km (120 miles) inland, linking towns at the southern ends of the lakes and terminating at Gällivare. Only four railway lines continue into Norway. Two in the south form links between Stockholm and Oslo, crossing the border at Kornsjö and Charlottenberg. Another climbs up into the mountains from Östersund, crosses the border at Storlien, and descends to Trondheim, and the fourth is the line to Narvik. In the far north the Swedish coastal line terminates at Haparanda, but as the Finnish railways are on the Russian broad gauge there are no through trains.

Air Transport

Sweden is a partner in Scandinavian Airlines System (*S.A.S.*) operated jointly with Norway and Denmark, and providing international services. Particularly important are the short service between Malmö and Copenhagen and the long-distance Stockholm–Luleå–Kiruna route. Internal routes are operated by Swedish Airlines (*A.B.A.*).

Ports

Sweden possesses a mercantile marine of about 4·8 million gross tons (excluding small craft and fishing vessels), which represents a considerable recent increase; more than half of the vessels are less than ten years old. Nearly half consist of tankers, and most of the remainder are timber boats and ore carriers. Many Swedish owned and registered vessels operate away from their homeland, their earnings affording a valuable contribution to the national income. The *Swedish-Lloyd* passenger services include the thrice weekly Göteborg–Tilbury sailings, and the *Swedish-America* company operates two liners sailing between Sweden and the U.S.A.

In terms of freight handled, Luleå and Oxelösund are the main ports, but their figures are made up almost entirely of iron ore. At Luleå a new shipping-channel has been dredged to take 40,000-ton ore-carriers, and Oxelösund has been equipped with automated loaders to serve ore-carriers bringing non-phosphoric ore from

Australia. In passengers handled the ferry ports, particularly Hälsingborg, are in the lead. The two largest seaports for general activity, installations and value of freight are Göteborg and Stockholm; between them they handle a third of Sweden's foreign trade by value. A large oil-dock able to accommodate tankers of up to 600,000 tons was completed at Malmö in 1967.

The port of Norrköping, near the mouth of the Motala river, has developed appreciably since the completion of the Lindö Canal in 1962. This was designed to provide a direct ship channel 9·6 m (31·5 ft) deep from the port to the open sea, instead of the old circuitous exit via the river. The port is equipped with modern facilities, and adjoining open land is scheduled for industrial development.

POPULATION AND SETTLEMENT

Since Sweden's first census, taken as long ago as 1749, gave a population of about 1·4 million, the figure has increased more than fivefold to its 1969 total of 7·94 millions. The most rapid rise occurred during the first half of the nineteenth century, the result of a high birth rate combined with a rapidly declining death rate. This happened before the development of modern industry, when the traditional agriculture was unable to absorb the additional people despite increased fragmentation of the land into smallholdings; by 1914 over 1·25 million Swedes had emigrated to the U.S.A. With the rapid growth of industrial activity and the increasingly effective use of resources, this emigration has virtually ceased since 1914. A number of emigrants, probably as many as a quarter of a million, have returned to Sweden, and since 1945 about 150,000 migrants from Finland, from the former Baltic republics of Latvia, Esthonia and Lithuania, and from Germany have arrived.

Sweden's population is now growing only slowly. Although there was a temporary rise in the birth rate during the War of 1939–45, it has again declined and in 1968 at 14·5 it was the lowest in the world. The annual excess of births over deaths is only five per 1,000, and the population increase each year is just 50,000. The age structure reveals an increasing top-heaviness and although the twenty to twenty-five age group, representing the rise in the birth rate during 1940–45, has now entered employment, they are being succeeded by smaller groups, the product of the declining post-war birth rate.

The most striking changes are the increase of urban population at the expense of the rural (the former has risen from 11 per cent of the total in 1860 to 78 per cent in 1968), and an increase in the number of industrial workers as compared with those engaged in agriculture. The distribution of population is remarkably uneven. The overall average density is about 19 per sq. km (49 per sq. mile), but because of the hard climate and the poor soils large parts of the high plateau and the north are virtually unpopulated. The rest of Norrland averages only about 1–4 per sq. km (3–10 per sq. mile), rising locally to 100 per sq. km (260 per sq. mile) along the coast where ports and industries are located. Some of the areas in the Småland plateau are also thinly peopled.

By contrast, three areas, the most urbanized and industrialized parts of the country, have outstandingly dense population: the districts around Stockholm, Göteborg and Malmö. The city of Stockholm in 1968 had a population of 757,000, or about 1·4 millions if its suburbs are included; within a distance of 160 km (100 miles) are a dozen flourishing industrial cities, and the aggregate population in this region is about 2·8 millions, more than 36 per cent of the Swedish total. Göteborg, with a population of 445,000 and another 70,000 people living in the nearby valleys, forms a second area of concentration. About half a million people live in Malmö, Hälsingborg and the coastal strip between them, an area of diverse industry and intensive agriculture. Apart from the three large cities, fifty-two towns each have between 20,000 and 90,000 inhabitants; most lie within the spheres of the three cities, but the localized concentration of economic activity in some parts has resulted in a string of rapidly growing though isolated towns along the Bothnian coast, notably Gävle (73,000), Sundsvall (64,000), Umeå (53,000) and Skellefteå (62,000), while the most northerly and most remote is the iron-mining centre of Kiruna (29,000).

REGIONS (Fig. 9)

1. Norrland

This part of Sweden, extending north of about 60° N. to well beyond the Arctic Circle, descends south-eastward from the high plateau along the Norwegian border in a series of steps to the Bothnian coast plain. In detail the structure consists of three roughly parallel longitudinal zones. In the west is the high fjäll, the remnants of one of the crystalline nappes, heavily dissected by former glaciers and bearing some small permanent snowfields; a few peaks exceed 1800 m (6000 ft), the highest being Kebnekaise. Much of the terrain consists of bare rock, patches of lichen, dwarf willows and berried

plants. The central part of Norrland consists of low plateau-blocks
of Archaean rocks, with a thin soil layer and covered with conifers.
Along the coast an undulating lowland, some 180 -270 m (600–900 ft)

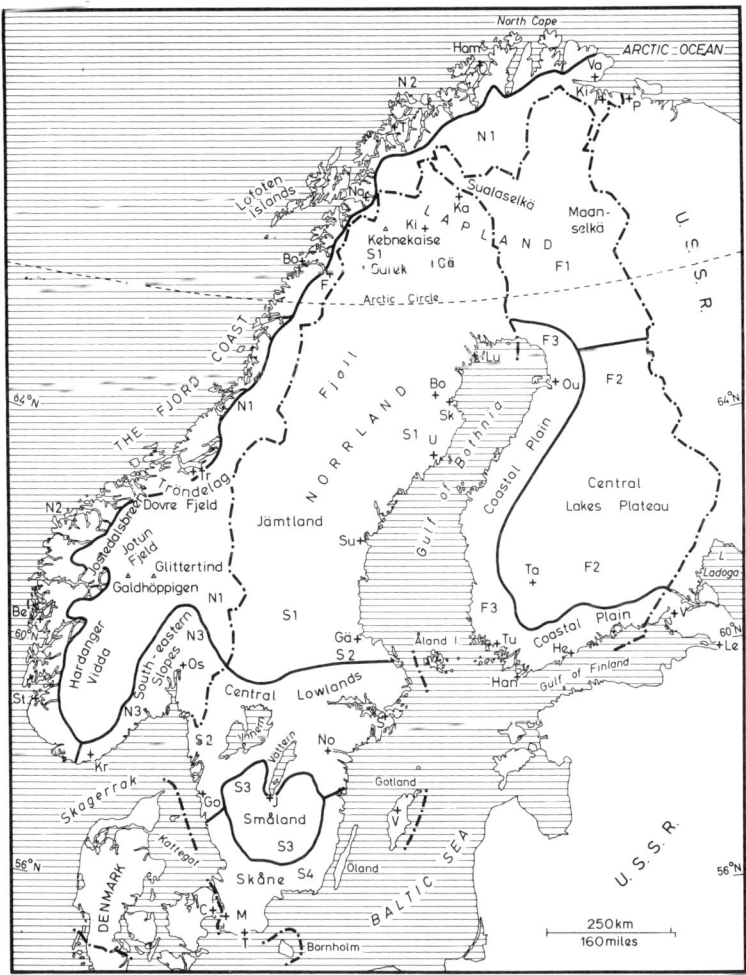

Fig. 9. Regional divisions of Scandinavia

above sea-level, is overlain with recent marine deposits, bounded by
an indented coast with irregular estuaries and in places an offshore
archipelago. These zones are divided into blocks by parallel rivers
flowing from north-west to south-east, their upper valleys containing
strings of long narrow lakes, and their courses interrupted at intervals by falls.

The main resource of Norrland is timber, for nearly three-quarters is forested with pine and spruce. The rivers provide power for the sawmills and afford means of floating logs to the coast, though this is now declining in favour of truck or tractor haulage. In the past most mills were situated well upstream at the fall-lines, where rapids could be used to work the millwheels. While the newer power stations are also sited along these lines, the electricity generated is transmitted to mills and factories on the coast, from which lumber, doors, window frames and pulp can conveniently be exported by sea.

Norrland not only supplies its own industries from the many hydro-stations, but 'exports' power to central Sweden by long-distance transmission line. A second important resource is ore: ferrous and non-ferrous. Agriculture is practised along the coastal plain, despite the long severe winters; the chief crops are barley and potatoes, with roots and fodder crops for the animals.

This part is thinly populated. North of the Arctic Circle many of the people are Lapps, of whom there are now about 7,000 in Sweden; while some still move about with their reindeer, others have settled down as farmers or fishermen, keeping reindeer as an additional source of livelihood. The small towns are located along the coast near the mouths of rivers and in the valleys, where they are usually centres of timber-working. Farther south are more people and the towns are situated in two almost parallel lines, one along the Bothnian coast, the other along a line linking the south-eastern ends of the lakes, where power is available and with some areas of fertile soil.

Norrland is Sweden's problem area, though with only a fifth of its population. It is a region of great distances and of isolation, and with an ice-bound coast in winter. A general recession in the pulp and paper industries has led to the closing of some mills, and there is less part-time forestry to supplement the limited agriculture. Despite Government development grants and loans, few industrial firms have been attracted, and many young people migrate southward.

The province of Jämtland, situated inland from the coast between about 62° and 64° N. latitude, stands out as a more fertile district. Its axis is the Indals river, which flows through a series of lakes, the largest being Storsjön, around which lies a fertile basin floored with morainic and lacustrine deposits and bordered by alluvial terraces. It is an area of prosperous agriculture and a popular tourist district. On the shores of the lake the town of Östersund, although at a height of over 300 m (1000 ft), has a population of 27,000. One advantage is that at Östersund the railway line over the plateau to Trondheim on the Norwegian coast crosses the inland longitudinal railway.

The province of Dalarna forms a transition zone between northern and central Sweden; the river Fal flows across it south-eastward through Lake Siljan. A marked contrast can be seen between eastern Dalarna, which contains part of the mining and industrial district of Bergslagen and is also well cultivated, and the forested west which rises to the fjäll-plateau above 1200 m (4000 ft). This is an important tourist area, especially for winter sports.

2. The Central Lowlands

A discontinuous area of lowland, consisting of down-faulted clay-floored basins interrupted by small rocky uplands and large lakes, extends across central Sweden from the Skagerrak to the Baltic Sea. The main lowlands lie around Lakes Mälaren and Hjälmaren (the province of Södermanland), around Lake Vänern, and to the east of Lake Vänern (the province of Östergötland). The surface is very uneven, with ridges and 'whale-backs' of rock rising above the general level, sheets of till, moraines and long esker ridges of sand and gravel. Patches of good soil have developed on marine clays along the coastal plains, and in former lake hollows filled by sediment or drained by man. The hills and the fluvioglacial deposits are forested with conifers and the higher parts form moorlands. The better soils are under pasture or arable cultivation; oats, barley, rye, a little wheat, sugar beet and potatoes are grown, and dairy cattle are kept.

This has long been an important manufacturing region, and industry is widely dispersed, the result of its traditional activities, supplies of ferrous and other ores from Bergslagen, and ample electric power. The largest industrial centres are Stockholm, Västerås to the north and Eskilstuna (sometimes called 'the Sheffield of Sweden') to the south of Lake Mälaren, Jönköping on the southern tip of Lake Vättern, the steel-making centre of Oxelösund, and Göteborg. Norrköping, with 95,000 people the fifth city of Sweden, is situated in the Östergötland plain; it claims to be the oldest industrial town in Sweden, and manufactures paper, and wool and cotton textiles.

The population is scattered unevenly in villages and small towns, with the two largest centres on either coast: Stockholm in the east and Göteborg in the west. Stockholm (Plate IV), a beautiful city sometimes called 'the Venice of the North', grew up on several islands and along each bank of the narrows linking the fresh water of Lake Mälaren with the Baltic, about 50 km (30 miles) from the sea. The town grew rapidly during the late Middle Ages when Finland belonged to Sweden, for it was then a well placed and central Baltic capital. Gradually it has spread outwards over the rock outcrops to north and south of the lake, many of them now crowned with huge blocks of flats. The approach from the Baltic to the port is not easy through the reefs, islands and channels of the Skärgård (Fig. 3), though the main channels are well buoyed and lighted, and port works line the rocky shores of the numerous creeks and inlets. Though the harbour freezes in winter, channels are kept open by icebreakers, and the port handles a third of Sweden's foreign trade, its outport of Värtahamn dealing with a variety of bulk cargoes. Stockholm, with attractive buildings ranging from medieval churches to modern blocks around central shopping precincts, is served by an excellent, if at times congested, system of roads and railways. Around it have grown satellite residential suburbs such as Vällingby and Farsta, with spaciously laid out blocks of flats. Stockholm and its neighbourhood is the most important industrial centre in the country; its activities include light engineering, clothing manufacture, printing, publishing, food-processing, and the multitude of miscellaneous industries one would expect to find in the capital city of a country with such a high standard of living.

Göteborg, situated on the deep-water estuary of the river Göta, is more important than Stockholm as a port, since it is accessible to larger ships, with several kilometres of quays equipped with container-berths, store-houses, railway sidings and a large floating dry-dock. Apart from its freight traffic, Göteborg has regular sailings to Tilbury, New York, and across the Kattegat to Frederikshavn in Denmark. Into the port opens the Göta Canal, which descends the 44 m (144 ft) between Lake Vänern and the sea by means of locks, but it is not now very important. To the north the Trollhättan station generates power for a range of industries: shipbuilding, car assembly, sugar-refining, flour-milling, brewing and the manufacture of ball-bearings, textiles, calculating machines, glassware and pottery. Inland from Göteborg along the Göta valley, pulp and paper mills obtain their timber from the forested uplands to the north of Lake Vänern.

3. Småland

This low plateau of ancient, mostly granitic rocks forms the central part of the peninsula of southern Sweden, rising to an undulating peneplain at about 270 m (900 ft) above sea-level, with a highest point of 377 m (1237 ft). Småland has a bleaker climate than the surrounding lowlands, with heavy precipitation and three months of snow cover, and the soils are thin and poor; much is covered with moorland, peat bogs in the hollows, and forests. Some of the better soils in the valleys are cultivated, but the region is as a whole thinly populated. Small towns in the valleys and around the upland margins have pulp, paper and glass-making industries; Swedish glass is famous, and factories at Orrefors, as well as small village workshops, produce high-grade glassware for export. Once again water-power is plentiful, provided by the streams descending steeply from the plateau. Jönköping (54,000), the capital of the county of the same name which occupies the northern part of Småland, lies near the southern end of Lake Vättern. With its neighbour Huskvarna to the east, the town is an important industrial area, making pulp, paper and matches (it was once the largest match-making town in the world), and has light engineering. Huskvarna has 80 per cent of its working population engaged in industry.

4. Skåne

The provincial name of Skåne is given to the two counties of Malmöhus and Kristianstad in the south. These undulating lowlands are structurally complex, but much is veneered with glacial and marine clays which have given rise to fertile soils. The climate is appreciably milder than in the more northerly parts of the country.

Two centuries ago much of Skåne was covered either with woodland or pasture, with moorland on the higher outcrops of older rocks, but in the eighteenth and early nineteenth centuries great agricultural developments took place and it rapidly became Sweden's chief arable district, growing wheat, oats, sugar beet and fodder crops; now over 70 per cent of its area is under arable or rotation grass, compared with only 12 per cent over the whole country. The number of animals, notably dairy cattle and pigs, has steadily increased, and the co-operative system has developed.

Skåne is the most densely populated part of Sweden except for the immediate area of Greater Stockholm, and in addition to the well distributed agricultural population several small towns are spread out both along the coast and inland. Malmö is the third town (256,000) and third port of Sweden, handling the heavy ferry traffic with Copenhagen; Hälsingborg (81,000) is also a ferry port, with a busy connection with Helsingor; and Trelleborg at almost the most southerly point of Sweden has ferry services with Travemünde in West Germany and with Sassnitz in East Germany. Other important towns along this coast are Halmstad on the west and Karlskrona on the east.

The coastal region of western Skåne is an important industrial region, dealing with local food products (sugar-refining, flour-milling and brewing), and making cement, pottery, cotton textiles, soap, margarine, leather and rubber articles.

5. *The Islands of Öland and Gotland*

The long narrow island of Öland, parallel to the coast of Kalmar, and the larger, more distant Gotland consist of masses of Lower Palaeozoic rocks, mostly limestone, with some bold cliffs. Though the centre of each (particularly Öland) is rather dry, with an almost karst-like appearance, glacial and marine clays on the coastal margins afford good soils, and intensive farming produces butter, meat, vegetables and flowers; Gotland in particular supplies the Stockholm markets. On each island a large cement works uses the plentiful limestone as raw material. The two islands have a population of about 54,000. Visby, the main town on Gotland, situated strategically in the Baltic, has had a long and at times prosperous history; once a Hansa town, it suffered from the long period of Baltic wars. It is now a pleasant place of about 12,000 people, and a popular centre for visitors.

CHAPTER THREE

Norway

NORWAY extends from the North Cape, the most northerly tip of Europe at latitude 71° N., to the shores of the Skagerrak at 58° N. Its mainland coast, measured in a direct line, is about 3200 km (2000 miles), yet its total length, including the main inlets and larger islands but excluding the thousands of offshore islets, exceeds 20 000 km (12,500 miles). In the north centre the country is narrow, and some of the fjord heads penetrate to only 6–8 km from the Swedish boundary, while in the south its width attains 444 km (276 miles). Norway possesses a boundary with Sweden, unfortified and virtually unguarded, of just over 1600 km (1000 miles), a northern boundary with Finland of 720 km (450 miles), and since 1945 a boundary with the U.S.S.R. of 200 km (125 miles) in the far north-east.

In addition to its homeland area of 324 000 sq. km (125,000 sq. miles), Norway has held sovereignty since 1920 over Spitsbergen (Svalbard), an Arctic archipelago between 74° and 81° N., Bear Island, since 1929 the lonely and desolate island of Jan Mayen lying 480 km (300 miles) north-north-east of Iceland, the small uninhabited dependencies of Bouvet and Peter I Island in the southern Atlantic, and Queen Maud Land and a portion of the Antarctic continent between 20° W. and 45° E., claimed in 1939.

Administratively Norway is divided into twenty counties (*fylker*), though Norwegian geographers distinguish five main regions. North of about 65° N. is Nord-Norge, comprising the three large counties of Finnmark, Troms and Nordland; Tröndelag consists of the area around the Trondheimsfjord; Vestlandet extends inland from the west coast below about 63° N. latitude on to the high plateau; Östlandet comprises the land draining into the Oslofjord lies east of the previous region; and Sörlandet extends along the south coast (Fig. 10).

STRUCTURE AND RELIEF

Structure

The contribution of the Baltic Shield and of the Caledonian orogeny to the physical make-up of Scandinavia has been described (pp. 17–20). While the Shield comprises three-quarters of Sweden, it occupies only about a third of Norway (Fig. 1). The Archaean rocks outcrop in the far north where the boundary makes an easterly

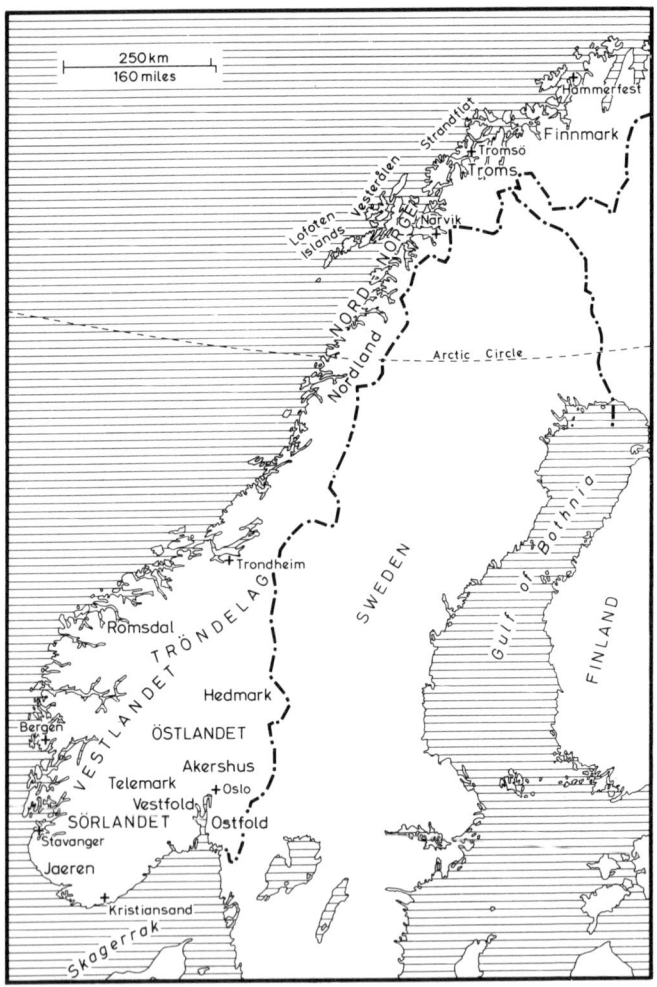

Fig. 10. Regional names of Norway
The more important regional names and towns mentioned in the text are indicated.

embayment, as in a small area behind Narvik, and more extensively south of Bergen. Most of these rocks consist of gneiss, though there are schists and quartzites, and some intrusions of granite.

Almost all the rest of Norway is made up of Lower Palaeozoic rocks in very great variety, laid down in the Caledonian geosyncline (p. 19). In addition to sediments metamorphosed into sandstones, slates and schists, igneous rocks (the product of both intrusive and extrusive activity) occur widely. Within this complex orogenic region of overfolds and nappes, a series of longitudinal zones can be distinguished. In the east the ancient sediments were overfolded on to the edge of the Archaean Shield, though most of this zone lies in Sweden, especially in the north, for the boundary approaches within 30 km (20 miles) of the Atlantic coast. In the next zone to the west the structure is even more complex; the rocks comprise mainly schists metamorphosed from sediments laid down in the deeper parts of the geosyncline, a variety of granites, and some basic igneous rocks, including gabbro, as in the Jotunheim. Farther west again the rocks are mainly granite and gneiss, with some schist. Here the folding was so acute and the subsequent denudation so prolonged that the nappes can no longer be traced and the surface reveals only the 'roots' of the folds. Some of the gneissic rocks may originally have formed part of the basement of the geosyncline; most island groups are composed of gneiss, though the rugged Lofoten Islands also include granite, syenite and gabbro. An outlying area of Lower Palaeozoic rocks occurs in the neighbourhood of Oslo, preserved in a downfaulted trough within the Archaean basement.

With one or two small exceptions, a long gap appears in the geological record between the deposition of the Silurian sediments and of the Quaternary glacial materials. The exceptions include a small outcrop of Devonian sandstones and conglomerates on the west coast to the south of the Nordfjord, and some Permian sediments and igneous rocks near Oslo, lying on the Lower Palaeozoic rocks in the down-faulted trough. The igneous rocks include both intrusive plugs and extrusive lava beds, some of the latter forming caps to the hills around Oslo. A patch of Jurassic sandstones includes a few seams of coal in the island of Andöy in the Vester Ålen, the group to the north of the Lofotens.

A long period of denudation followed the Silurian, reducing the Caledonian ranges to a low peneplain; at least two major erosion surfaces can be distinguished. In mid-Tertiary times the whole area was again uplifted, both the Caledonian mountain 'stumps' and the Archaean shield in the south. This uplift was asymmetrical, especially in the north, so that the watershed lies not far from the Atlantic coast, with a markedly steeper edge on the west. It was associated with widespread faulting, creating a 'grain' which can be distinguished in the present relief, since the shatter-belts formed lines of weakness on which later denudation has acted. Parts of the peneplain have been fragmented into individual blocks, now rising above the general level.

The Quaternary Glaciation

As in Sweden, it is probable that a twofold phase of the Quaternary glaciation can be recognized, succeeded by several distinct stages of withdrawal (pp. 21–2 and Fig. 2). The late glacial stages contributed a striking erosive impress upon the landscape. Numerous glaciers of great thickness, steep gradient and powerful erosive ability flowed westward down the preglacial valleys, carving deeply their U-shaped, steep-sided cross-profiles. The ice accumulated to its greatest depth well to the east of the present Scandinavian watershed, and some westward-moving glaciers eroded through-valleys right across the uplands, several of which can be distinguished south of Trondheim (pp. 23–4). In the higher mountains the characteristic features of alpine glaciation were developed: cirque hollows, hanging valleys, arêtes and prominent pyramid peaks.

The depositive results of the icesheets were small over Norway, since most of their vast burden of material was laid down far to the south; Scandinavian erratics occur plentifully in Britain, Denmark, Poland, northern Germany and even in the Netherlands. Small layers of ground-moraine were deposited on the lowlands around the Oslofjord and on the narrow coastal plains of the south. A prominent line of terminal moraines (known as the Ra) can be distinguished in the neighbourhood of Oslo, formed by the same prolonged ice-pause responsible for the central moraines of Sweden and the Finnish Salpausselkä (p. 94). Some of the glacial drift along the west and south coasts was deposited in the sea, but as the land has since risen this now forms terraces of re-sorted materials.

Only a few scattered icecaps, with an aggregate area of about 5200 sq. km (2000 sq. miles), now exist in Norway. The largest mass of ice in Europe (excluding Iceland) is the Jostedalsbre, to the north of the Sognefjord; this has however shrunk rapidly in recent years and its present area is only 477 sq. km (184 sq. miles), or with the neighbouring smaller ice-masses about 830 sq. km (320 sq. miles). In the north the icecaps are less extensive, though they sustain some glaciers; the Svartisen Glacier and its collecting ground, just on the Arctic Circle, covers about 720 sq. km (280 sq. miles). Farther north at 70° N. the Engabree Glacier reaches the sea at the head of the Jökulfjord.

The mountains of western Norway receive a heavy winter precipitation of snow; the permanent snowline lies at about 900 m (3000 ft) in the north and at 1500 m (5000 ft) in the high southern plateaus (Plate V). In winter most of the country is snow-covered, except on the lower slopes near the fjords (p. 68).

Drainage

Along most of the west coast the drainage pattern is simple; numerous small streams, rising on the high plateau, spill over the edge directly into the fjords or descend from hanging valleys by spectacular falls. Many have cut deeply into the plateau edge to form gorges sometimes 600 m (2000 ft) deep, which are lengthened as the waterfalls erode back at their heads. The international boundary does not always form the watershed, and the headstreams of numerous Swedish rivers flowing to the south-east are in Norway.

Only in the north and south-east are the rivers of any appreciable length. In Finnmark rivers such as the Alta drain the low lake-studded plateaus. Farther south the general direction of the rivers is towards the south-east; some, such as the Trysil flowing into Lake Vänern, continue their courses into Sweden, others find their way into the master-stream of the area, the Glomma, which reaches the sea on the eastern side of the Oslofjord.

Many lakes in this deeply glaciated upland country are long and narrow. They are most numerous in the south-east, strung out along the river valleys; the largest, about 1000 sq. km (400 sq. miles), is Lake Mjösa in the valley of the Lagen. Many irregularly shaped lakes lie on the undulating surface of the high plateaus, and some cirque lakes are found among the high mountains.

Weathering

In an area where slopes are steep, weathering and mass movement play a major part in forming the details of the physical landscape. Rock-falls scar the steep valley sides; scree covers slopes not too steep for its angle of rest; slides and slumps of clay affect the lower slopes; and solifluction processes of a periglacial character are active both on the plateaus and at high latitudes.

The Coast

The coastline comprises the long indentations of the fjords, at least 150,000 offshore islands totalling nearly 23 000 sq. km (9000 sq.

miles), precipitous cliffs, and in the north the Strandflat, a rock platform covered with shallow water and extending far out to sea.

The fjords are partly submerged glacial troughs, long, narrow and rectilinear in plan, with branches joining at right-angles (Plate VI). The Sognefjord is 160 km (100 miles) in length, though rarely exceeding 5 km (3 miles) in width; the Trondheimfjord is 120 km (75 miles); the Hardangerfjord is 110 km (70 miles), with a 37 km (23 miles) branch, the Sörfjord. Their sides are remarkably steep; the north wall of the Sognefjord slopes at from 28° to 34° from the plateau surface at over 1500 m (5000 ft) to 900 m (3000 ft) below sea-level, while one of its branches, the Naeröfjord, has continuous slopes exceeding 50°. While the fjords are for the most part deep (over 1200 m (4000 ft) has been sounded in the Sogne near its head), near the mouth is usually a bar or threshold of solid rock, sometimes with a cover of glacial débris which may be part of a terminal moraine. Deltaic flats at the head are deposited by inflowing rivers from the plateau, but the waters are so deep that these are small. Some of these fjords correspond with faults, possibly even with rift valleys; others follow lines of weak sedimentary rocks, such as the Hardangerfjord which lies along a syncline of schists enclosed between masses of hard gneissic rocks. Along these lines of least resistance the preglacial rivers eroded valleys which the powerful Quaternary glaciers enlarged and deepened. Finally, a rise of sea-level turned the valleys into arms of the sea, although as glaciers can erode below sea-level it is not necessary to postulate much submergence. In the north of the country, in Finnmark, the fjords are broader, shallower and more open, since they lie in valleys eroded in weak schistose rocks by glaciers which were small, thin and slowly flowing, so possessing only weak power of downcutting.

The south coast beyond Stavanger displays merely minor indentations and is quite low-lying, though much is rocky and dangerous for shipping, and markedly exposed to the south-west. Elsewhere in the south hummocky glacial materials are spread over the narrow coastal plain, which in places is lined with sand-dunes.

The Oslofjord is not a fjord in the textbook sense, though it forms a large indentation extending northward from the Skagerrak for over 100 km (60 miles); its shores are low, though in places steep and rocky. The outer part is like a broad funnel, 40 km (25 miles) wide in the south, while the inner fjord branches to form the Sandebukt, the Dramsfjord and the Oslofjord itself. The whole inlet is a down-faulted structural depression within the Archaean Shield.

Much of the west coast of Norway in the centre and north is bordered by the Strandflat, extending offshore in the north for more than 50 km (30 miles). Its landward margin is marked by an abrupt change of slope where cliffs rise steeply from the water. The Strandflat is clearly an abrasion platform, but while some believe it was cut by wave action during preglacial or interglacial times, others claim that potent subaerial erosion under periglacial conditions contributed substantially during periods of lower sea-level, still others that glacial erosion was involved; possibly all these agencies contributed. Subaerial weathering, largely frost action, is certainly so effective that the cliffs are worn rapidly back and powerful waves remove the waste materials from their base; the backwash drags it seawards across the rock platform, so helping to abrade it still further.

From the Strandflat rise numerous islands known as 'skerries', most of bare striated rock, some with a drift cover, behind which lies a stretch of calm water, the 'Led' or 'inner lead'. The outer islands are mostly quite low, rising only to between 8 and 30 m (25 and 100 ft) (Plate VII), though nearer to the mainland some exceed 300 m (1000 ft).

Relief

The main feature of the relief is the high plateau, falling steeply to the indented and island-fringed coast; more than half the country lies at altitudes above 600 m (2000 ft), and a quarter at over 900 m (3000 ft). The surface of these plateaus, gently undulating, with much bare rock and snow-covered in winter, is known as the *fjeld* or *fjell*. In Finnmark the plateau is only about 300–450 m (1000–1500 ft) in elevation, with a few peaks rising to over 900 m (3000 ft). By contrast, farther south the plateau narrows to a ridge, from which rocky peaks rise above the general level to about 1500 m (5000 ft); Snetind, 1599 m (5246 ft), for example, is a nunatak protruding from the ice of the Svartisen Glacier.

Farther south still the upland widens into a series of plateau blocks (*vidder*), deeply dissected on the west by the fjords, on the east by lake-filled valleys draining toward the Oslofjord. The extensive lake-strewn Hardanger Vidda is a compact upland block with a general height of about 1800 m (6000 ft), from which swell ice-rounded hummocky summits.

From the plateaus rise several groups of high mountains, notably the Jotunheim, which include the bold rock peak of Galdhöppigen at 2469 m (8100 ft), the snow-dome of Glittertind at 2481 m (8140 ft) (Plate VIII), and the pyramid of Skagastölstind at 2404 m (7887 ft). The Dovre Fjeld farther north culminates in the Snöhetta at 2243 m (7359 ft) and the Rondeslottel at 2183 m (7162 ft), and the Jostedalsbre to the north of the Sognefjord rises to mountains of almost 2100 m (7000 ft) (Fig. 11).

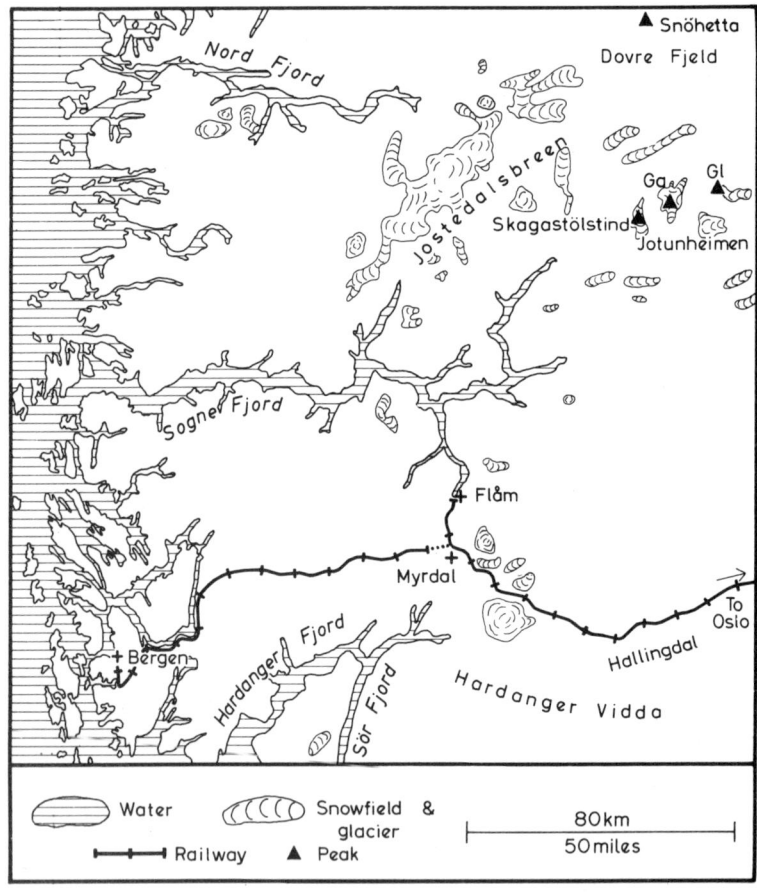

Fig. 11. The coast and mountains of south-western Norway

Only in the neighbourhood of Trondheim, the region known as Tröndelag (where a well marked depression is the result of the greater denudation of the less resistant Silurian schists and limestones), along the south coast, and in the south-east where the land descends to the Oslofjord and the Skagerrak, are slopes comparatively gentle. As a result of isostatic sinking caused by the weight of the icesheets, parts of this area once lay beneath the sea, and subsequent uplift after their melting has revealed marine deposits of sand, clay and gravels. These, with the soft, easily weathered Lower Palaeozoic rocks and the irregular cover of glacial drift, have produced a workable depth of soil, almost the only area of any size in Norway so endowed. The rivers which flow south-eastward into the Oslofjord divide the country, particularly in their upper courses, into distinctive valley units (*dals*). The two most striking are the Gudbrandsdal, the valley of the river Lagen above Lake Mjösa, and the Österdal, the valley of the river Glomma; each forms a re-entrant into the uplands of the Dovre Fjeld.

CLIMATE

Temperature

Norway is markedly affected by its situation on the western margins of the Scandinavian peninsula. During winter the coastal strip and the islands experience remarkably high temperatures for the latitude; the Lofotens have a positive temperature anomaly for their latitude of about 25° C. In spite of the appreciable extent, differences between the north and south are small. Thus Bergen and Svolvaer (in the Lofotens) have a January mean of 1° C., and as far north as Fruholmen, an island beyond the North Cape at 72° N., the January mean is 3° C.

Sea ice never forms around the western and northern coasts because of the relatively warm saline waters of the North Atlantic Drift, and the north-easterly movement of the currents keeps away Arctic drift-ice. In the enclosed fjords, where the water is slightly less saline, some ice may form at the heads or in the branches during severe winters, but even the Varangerfjord, near the U.S.S.R. border, normally stays open.

Away from the coast, both altitude and distance from the sea cause temperatures to fall rapidly, so that Röros at 600 m (2000 ft) has a January mean of −11° C. Altitude seems to have less effect than distance from the sea; Finse, a station on the Bergen–Oslo railway twice as high as Röros but much nearer the coast, has −9° C. as the mean of its coldest month. The coldest part of the country is in the interior of Finnmark, the area farthest north which is also farthest from the sea; for at least three months the temperature never rises above freezing point; and at Karasjok, near the Finnish frontier at 69° N., the January mean is only −16° C., and −50° C. has been recorded. February is nearly always colder than January, mainly because the anticyclonic influences farther east have intensified and the out-moving air is appreciably colder. Local relief has profound effects; very low temperatures are recorded in deep valleys as a result of inversion, and the downward drainage of cold air may be strong enough to form strong, bitter gravity winds. In summer mean July temperatures along the west coast vary from about 10° C. in the north to about 14° C. at Bergen; the proximity of the sea has a moderating effect. The highest summer temperatures are experienced in the lowlands and valleys around Oslo, which has a July mean of 16° C.

Precipitation

Distance from the sea and altitude both affect precipitation, though exposure to or shelter from prevailing air streams exerts a marked local influence. The coastal belt receives considerable precipitation; Bergen, on the edge of the south-west coast, has a mean annual rainfall of 2060 mm (81 in), though Trondheim on a fjord but 50 km (30 miles) from the open sea receives only 910 mm (36 in). The heaviest precipitation is recorded near the coast above 300 m (1000 ft) altitude; Kvitingern on the northern side of the Sognefjord has 3120 mm (123 in). Farther inland the precipitation decreases; Finse, though at 1200 m (4000 ft), has 890 mm (35 in), and Röros only 430 mm (17 in). Since the Oslofjord lies to the east of a broad tract of upland it has a relatively low precipitation; Oslo itself has 580 mm (23 in).

The precipitation is evenly distributed throughout the year, mainly because the frequency of depressions from the west varies little with the seasons. Along the coast the mean annual number of days on which rain falls ranges from about 150 to 180, in some places (as near Bergen) as many as 220. The fewest are in the drier areas of Finnmark (about 110) and around Oslo (130). Spring is usually the driest period almost everywhere, and July and August are the wettest months in the south around Oslo.

Between November and April much of this precipitation falls in the form of snow, and except for the coastal strip most of the country is snow-covered between December and March. On the high plateau near the margins of the permanent snow-caps, the snow may lie for ten months in the year (Plate V).

A high degree of cloud cover is an inevitable result of this coastal location. Even June, usually the sunniest month, has an average cloudiness of about 60 per cent on the coast, though this diminishes to about 40 per cent east of the mountain divide. On the other hand, as a result of the high latitude the summer days are long, so that the total sunshine hours are quite appreciable. The low angle of the winter sun makes aspect an important factor; many villages situated on the shores of a steep-sided fjord may receive no sunshine for several months.

Within these broad generalizations the climate reveals considerable variety, both from time to time and place to place. The country is subject to the passage of non-periodic depressions; their frequency and intensity vary with meteorological conditions both over the North Atlantic and over the Eurasiatic continent to the east. In some years the summer visitor to the fjords may experience days of glorious sunshine, in other years low cloud and constant drizzling rain. In 1959 a long and serious drought lasted throughout late summer and autumn; reservoirs fell so low that hydroelectricity production was markedly affected.

LAND USE AND AGRICULTURE

More than half of Norway is above 600 m (2000 ft) in altitude, with steep slopes, bog, bare rock and scree, poor scanty soils, a long winter snow-cover, and a damp cloudy climate. Very little of the country experiences an average temperature for the summer months exceeding about 10° C., the limit for economic cereal cultivation, though crops such as barley, which can ripen in two months near the Arctic Circle, are helped by the long hours of midsummer sunshine. In consequence 76 per cent of the land area is classified as un-productive, 21 per cent is forested, and only about 3 per cent consists of meadow and arable. Much of the unproductive land consists of fjeld, with lichens and mosses on the higher parts, occasional patches of dwarf birch, willow, alder, juniper and berried plants, and pasture on the lower slopes. Thus agriculture is very limited; despite considerable State subsidies, it occupies only about one-seventh of the working population and contributes a mere 4 per cent to national productivity.

Arable Farming

Small-scale farming is carried on wherever practicable on the lower, less steep parts of hill slopes (Plate IX), on tiny benches along the fjord sides, on deltaic flats at the heads of fjords, and along the lake shores. Many farms are virtually self-contained, isolated units, each worked for the subsistence of its owner and his family. The most valuable farmlands are in the south, where the more extensive areas of lowland and workable soils are found: around the Oslofjord and the valley floors of the rivers draining into it, around the Trondheimsfjord in the district of Tröndelag, and south of Stavanger (the area known as Jaeren) in the south-west. In these limited areas is concentrated two-fifths of the farmland, growing two-thirds of Norway's cereals and root crops; here about one-third of the farms exceed 8 ha (20 acres) in size, although over the whole country the proportion falls to a seventh.

About two-thirds of the farmland is under short-ley grass for hay, about 17 per cent grows barley, and 6 per cent each grows oats and potatoes; oats and barley are mainly regarded as fodder crops. The rotations are usually based on a six-year period: three years of grass, one of potatoes, one of grain, and another of potatoes on the sandier soils, or three years of grass, one of grain, one of potatoes, and one of grain on the better clay loams. Rye, once the chief bread grain, has almost disappeared, and the small area of wheat (only about 3400 ha, 8400 acres) is chiefly found in the Oslo lowlands. Potatoes, cultivated on more sandy soils, form a staple item in the Norwegian diet.

While the arable area has risen but slightly during this century, the yield has been improved by 60 per cent. The main reason is the increase in the application of fertilizers, made available by Norway's thriving chemical industry, and the development of varieties of cereals and roots better suited to these northern conditions. In recent years there has been increasing specialization in the cultivation under glass of early vegetables, tomatoes and cucumbers, especially around Oslo and in Jaeren. Fruit is grown on the sunny lower slopes of some fjords in orchards claimed to be the most northerly in the world, though damp, cloudy summers may make ripening difficult.

Livestock

Some of the physical limitations which restrict arable farming encourage an emphasis on livestock, though most farms are mixed in character. The bases of pastoral activity are the cultivation of fodder (hay, barley, oats, roots), supplemented by imported feeding stuffs, for winter feed when the animals are housed, and the utilization in summer of as much pasture as possible, remote and dispersed though much of it may be.

The location of the farms in the valleys and on the coastal fringes, and the distant summer pastures on the higher slopes and plateaus, have encouraged the development of the age-old *seter* system. A seter is a pasture lying above the treeline, snow-covered in winter, but affording three months' summer grazing in the uplands of the west and as much as six months in the east. Transhumance, the seasonal migration of men and animals, involves several stages; the animals graze progressively higher pastures as the snowline recedes. In the steep fjord country of the west, the seters may lie only a few km from the home farm, though 600–1200 m (2000–4000 ft) higher. In the east the animals may move 30 km (20 miles) or more, occasionally as much as 110 km (70 miles). These high pastures surrounding the chalet-like timber dwellings, sometimes ring-fenced, are allocated to farmers by immemorial usage. The contribution of the seter system to modern Norwegian farming must not be exaggerated, for the number of individual seters has been reduced during this century from about 40,000 to 18,000. The increased production of fodder crops and hay from efficiently farmed rotation grasslands in the lowlands, coupled with increased imports of feeding stuffs, have reduced their essential value, especially of those in the higher, less accessible districts. The practice is, however, still important in some localities. In the south-west, inland from Jaeren, large numbers of sheep move to the high pastures, and in the eastern uplands where slopes are more gentle lorries and even railway trucks are used to convey both the animals and their products.

In 1968 there were about one million cattle. The general emphasis is on dairying to provide milk for the large towns and to meet home needs of butter and cheese. Though much of the production in the west is small-scale and local, co-operative methods have increased, notably in Östlandet; the first co-operative dairy was opened in 1855, appreciably earlier than in Denmark (p. 124). Factories are usually located where valleys converge, down which lorries bring milk for the manufacture of butter, cheese, condensed milk and casein.

Other animals include 1·9 million sheep, 47,000 horses still used on small steep holdings where mechanization would be impracticable, and 98,000 goats which spend the summer near the tree-line, their milk being made on the farms into the famous brown cheese. The number of pigs has increased to over 600,000, and fur farming (silver and blue fox and 2·1 million mink) has become a very profitable sideline.

Farming is not always a full-time activity, but may be carried on in conjunction with fishing, forestry, tourism and more recently with industry; many farmers have become full-time industrial workers in some of the modern factories in western Norway, working their holdings as a part-time occupation.

FORESTRY

The 'productive' forests occupy about 70 000 sq. km (27,000 sq. miles), about a fifth of the area of Norway. Four-fifths consist of Scots pine, most of the rest being spruce which generally grows in areas with heavy precipitation. Deciduous trees are limited to the lower lands of the south, and to a zone of not very useful birch above the conifers. The treeline varies considerably with latitude, aspect and exposure; the pine grows to about 1100 m (3600 ft) in Vestlandet and reaches about 300 m higher in Östlandet, though in Finnmark it is rarely seen above 180 m (600 ft). The pattern of vegetation represents a stage in the natural colonization of the land by plant life since the Quaternary glaciation. A succession of moss, heath, birch, pine, spruce, beech and oak is still in progress, the stage which has so far been reached depending on both altitude and latitude.

Rather more than half of Norway's forests are owned by farmers, many of whom also have rights in the common forests which are still extensive (Plate X). This dual activity sometimes militates against efficient forestry practice because of the rival and varying claims of each, but timber revenues afford an appreciable contribution to incomes, though one which fluctuates according to demand and price. A third of the forests, mainly in the north, are owned by the State, the remainder by large companies. About 31,000 people are employed full-time in forestry, appreciably fewer than the part-time workers. Some progress has been made in forestry practice, especially in Vestlandet and to the north of the Arctic Circle. The disadvantage of the latter area is the exceedingly slow growth; a pine matures in seventy to eighty years in the south, but takes two or three times as long farther north, where in addition the maximum size is much reduced. Other varieties of tree, including Sitka spruce, Douglas fir and hemlock, have been introduced into the wetter parts of Vestlandet from North America.

Apart from the considerable use of the forests to meet home demands for fuel and building, the main value of the commercial cut is for pulp and other forms of processed wood products. Very little sawn timber is exported, but paper, cardboard, wallboard, pulp, sulphite cellulose, wood alcohol and rayon fibre account for about a fifth by value of Norway's exports. Since the first pulp mill was established in the early 1860s, developments in the timber-processing industries have taken place mainly near the mouths of rivers flowing into the Oslofjord. These rivers serve a triple function; they provide routeways down which logs can be floated from the forests of Östlandet, they enable power to be produced, and they supply the 1,000 tons of water required to make each ton of pulp. The Borregaard plant, which produces a range of chemicals derived from wood, is situated at Sarpsborg on the river Glomma; Frederikstad, near the mouth of the same river, has an older steam-powered plant. Many plants stand on the lower reaches of rivers flowing down to Drammen and Skien, which drain the most extensive areas of Norwegian forest. Another large pulp mill is located farther inland at Hönefoss, and a few smaller ones operate in the neighbourhood of Bergen and Trondheim.

Fabricated timber products, notably doors, window frames, buildings and furniture, are made in small factories and workshops, many in the Oslo district and in the valleys of rivers converging upon the Oslofjord, others at points along the west coast, notably in Sunnmöre.

FISHERIES

The sheltered, ice-free waters, rich in plankton, which border the coasts of Norway, have long encouraged its people to turn to the sea, while the limitations of the land have made it essential for them to do so. It is difficult to evaluate the yield of fish, since much is consumed locally by the people who catch it. There are the coastal fisheries (summer herring, brisling), the offshore fisheries (cod, coalfish, winter herring), the banks fisheries on the continental shelf which in places extends over 160 km (100 miles) from the coast (cod, haddock, halibut, catfish, ling), and the distant deep-sea fisheries in Arctic waters (cod, halibut).

In 1968 about 2·6 million tons of fish were caught by commercial enterprise, fifth in order in the world, and greater than any European country except the U.S.S.R. Herring comprised nearly three-quarters by weight, and cod almost a fifth. The most notable cod fisheries are off the Lofoten Islands; between early January and late April several thousand boats and 20,000 men are at work. In recent years the herring catch has declined, as elsewhere in the North Sea; in 1961 it was the smallest for twenty-seven years and totalled less than half that of six or seven years previously. However, there has been some recovery, though the value of cod is almost twice that of herring.

The other contributions, smaller in bulk but quite valuable, include sprat or brisling (the ingredient of Norwegian canned 'sardines') caught in the Oslofjord and in the south-western fjords, coalfish off the Lofotens, mackerel in the Skagerrak, halibut and tuna on the continental banks, dogfish (known in Britain, to which it is mainly exported, as 'rock salmon') off the west coast, and salmon in the western rivers and fjords. The lobster fisheries off the south coast and the trawling of prawns from deep water afford 'luxury' contributions to the total.

Much of the fishing, particularly inshore, is part-time and seasonal; nearly three-quarters of the 40,000 fishing boats are small, open and un-decked. The larger fishing vessels are concentrated at the main west coast ports—Bergen, Stavanger, Trondheim (Plate XI), and farther north at Tromsö and Hammerfest. The diversity of activity is indicated by the fact that of approximately 50,000 men who take part, only about one-third make it their sole occupation.

Another 40,000 people are engaged in activities associated with the immense variety of fish-processing which has developed, partly because of the seasonal and concentrated character of 'glut' catches, especially of herring, partly because of the distance of some fisheries, notably cod, from their markets. The proportion of the total catch processed into meal and oil varies between 40 and 60 per cent. One of the oldest industries, especially in the Lofoten Islands, near Tromsö and in Finnmark, is the drying of cod ('stockfish') by hanging it on racks in the open air. Other activities include the drying and salting of cod laid out on the rocks ('klipfish'), the salting of herring in barrels, the canning of brisling (notably at Stavanger), the preparation of fish oils and edible fats, including some of the new polymerized oils, and the manufacture of fish meal, fertilizers and glue. Recent developments include the packaging of deep-frozen fillets for distant markets, for which a refrigerator plant has been recently opened at Hammerfest. In 1951 two state-owned fish-processing plants began operation at Batsfjord and Honningsvåg to cope with the heavy catches in northern waters during the six-month season. This formed part of the Northern Norway Scheme (p. 86) for the economic development of the three northernmost counties.

Norway is vitally concerned in the international concept of territorial waters, which for long was defined as a distance of 6 km (4 miles) from a line connecting the fjord mouths. This was increased first to 10 km (6 miles), then in September 1961 to 20 km (12 miles) to reduce the amount of competitive fishing in coastal waters where catches are declining. British vessels have been given special privileges in the zone between 10 and 20 km (6 and 12 miles) for ten years, and those from Sweden and Denmark are allowed there indefinitely.

The Norwegian sealing industry has been active for several centuries, so intensively that some species are in danger of extinction, and the hunting season is now restricted to the period from March to May. Each year about sixty vessels sail in early spring for pack-ice areas between Greenland and Newfoundland and in the White Sea. Modern techniques include 'spotting' the concentrations of the animals from aircraft. Many thousands of valuable pelts account for about one-twentieth of the value of the Norwegian fisheries.

Whaling has been carried on for at least a thousand years, but towards the end of the nineteenth century catches in northern waters dwindled rapidly, as most species approached extinction because of such technical improvements as a harpoon with an explosive head. Since 1925 the emphasis has been on pelagic (deep-sea) whaling in the Antarctic Ocean, which reached its climax in the early 1930s, but even in these extensive waters the animals dwindled rapidly, for they were killed faster than they could reproduce. Since 1945 Antarctic whaling has been regulated by international convention; although Norway withdrew from this in 1959, the government rigidly restricts the permitted total catch. Until recently several floating factories and their 'catchers' sailed each autumn from Sandefjord, Tönsberg and Larvik, returning in May with oil from the finwhales, together with by-products such as meat extract, meal and vitamins. Sperm whales were also caught, but their oil is inedible and can be used only for industrial purposes, and the largest species, the blue whale, is now rarely caught since it has become so scarce. But there has been a big decline in activity, and in 1967–68 the value of whale produce formed only 5 per cent of the revenue from fishing, compared with 25–30 per cent a decade ago.

FUEL AND POWER

Except for timber, Norway is deficient in sources of fuel and is obliged to import mineral oil and coal, accounting for nearly 20 per cent of total imports by value. Rather surprisingly, the energy value of these imported fuels is about the same as that of Norway's well known hydroelectricity production. Two oil-refineries are at Slagen and Valloy, both west of Oslo, and in 1968 a third (of 2 million tons annual capacity) was opened at Sola near Stavanger.

Norway has many advantages for the production of hydroelectric power: an ample, well-distributed precipitation, a mild winter so that streams near the coast rarely freeze, waterfalls from the hanging valleys and the plateau edges affording high heads, and lakes on the plateau providing natural storage. The main high-head plants are found in Vestlandet, which also has the greatest precipitation; some have a head of over 900 m (3000 ft), the station of Årdal, near the inner end of the Sognefjord, using a fall of 975 m (3200 ft). By contrast, the plants strung out along the rivers in Östlandet operate with low heads, but their large catchments assure a high volume of water, amplified by reservoirs to store up the rains in summer, when demand for electricity is low, for the winter when demand is high but water supplies are low. A notable example is in Begnadalen, the valley of the river Begna which rises in the Jotunheim and flows south-eastward across the plateau to Hönefoss, so to the Oslofjord. About forty stations are sited along the Begna valley, and a further six in and around Hönefoss. About 80 per cent of the major power developments are south of Trondheim, though a few enterprises in Nordland have been completed, for example to supply the Mo-i-Rana steel works. In Troms and Finnmark the rivers are short, altitudes are less, there are few lake reservoirs, the precipitation is appreciably less than in the south-west, and the winter freeze is more pronounced.

The difficulties and distances involved in the transmission of power have limited the development of a widespread grid; there are fourteen independent systems, and many single stations supply solely an individual town or factory. The icing of transmission lines in winter can cause serious damage to pylons and cables, which limits the lengths of individual spans. Most plants have been built during recent years, by far the largest station, Tokke in Telemark, being completed in 1960. Many small stations have been closed, though not the isolated ones serving a single village or factory. A nuclear station has been opened at Marvik.

The output of electricity has increased very rapidly, from 10,000 million KWh in 1939 to 60,200 million KWh in 1968, though this is estimated to be only 35 per cent of the total potential. This electricity production is the largest per head of population and the cheapest of any country in the world, so that despite the distances involved and the isolation of many settlements 98 per cent of Norwegian houses have electricity. Two-thirds of the total output is consumed by industry. Many new plants have been built underground; it is cheap to make underground shafts and tunnels in solid rock, and they avoid the problems of winter-freeze.

MINING

A variety of metalliferous minerals occurs in the igneous and metamorphic rocks of Norway. For the most part, these are small in scale and suffer the disadvantages of a remote and difficult location, and a low metal content.

The most important is iron ore, of which about 2·8 million tons are mined annually; the largest producer is the Sydvaranger company, which operates 8 km (5 miles) south of Kirkenes near the Russian frontier. About 10,000 people live in this area, directly or indirectly dependent on the mining and shipping of ore. These installations were destroyed during the War, first by Allied bombing then by the German 'scorched earth' policy in 1944, and they did not recommence production until 1952, rebuilt and re-equipped largely by Marshall Aid. The ore is a magnetite of just over 30 per cent metal content, with little phosphorus and sulphur, and is mined in open-cast workings, though these will ultimately be superseded by underground mines. Operations are maintained throughout the year despite the darkness and cold of the winter. The ore is moved by rail to crushing and concentration plants at Kirkenes, from which it is shipped as powder or pellets of about 65 per cent metal content, mostly to the Mo-i-Rana furnaces, West Germany and Britain. The only other iron deposits are some low-grade magnetites near Mo-i-Rana and south-west of Trondheim.

Other large-scale ore deposits are of pyrites, both cupriferous and non-cupriferous, with which are usually associated lead and zinc; in all, about 700,000 tons are produced annually. The chief mines are at Sulitjelma just north of the Arctic Circle near the Swedish border, near Lökken to the south-west of Trondheim, and near Röros, though the last has been worked for centuries and is now almost exhausted. At Sulitjelma and Lökken copper concentrates and metal are produced, and at Lökken sulphur is extracted. Other zinc and lead ores are mined about 80 km (50 miles) south of Sulitjelma. In the south, about 50 km (30 miles) from the sea, is the only mine in western Europe producing molybdenum; another yields ilmenite, the ore of titanium, which is exported as titanium oxide concentrate. The rare metal niobium is mined in the south-east not far from Skien, and others worked in smaller quantities include nickel, cobalt and thorium. Much stone is quarried in various parts of the country, usually near the sea because of transport difficulties. Lower Palaeozoic limestones west of the Oslofjord are used in cement and fertilizer factories, and various ornamental granites, marbles and syenites are worked as facing-blocks for buildings.

Norway proper has no coal except for some thin inferior seams in the Jurassic rocks on Andöy, but there is a coalfield in Spitsbergen at a latitude of nearly 80° N. The mines and settlements, destroyed by the German forces in 1944, were reopened after the War, the Norwegian collieries worked by a State company, while a Russian firm also operates a concession. Coal is mined throughout the year and exported during the summer months when the coasts are ice-free; about 400,000 tons are produced annually.

MANUFACTURING INDUSTRY

Norway's fourfold natural resources, water-power, timber, fish and minerals, form the basis of its industrial activity; the processing activities concerned with timber and fish have been described. The main developments since 1900 have been in connection with the electrochemical and electrometallurgical industries, and many factories and refineries have been built on the shores of the fjords. Here the large quantities of power required to smelt the ores are available, and concentrates can be brought from overseas to the deep-water terminals equipped with modern ore-handling equipment. Some of the plants are owned by the State, but most by large private companies, including *Norsk Hydro*, the biggest industrial unit in the country. Aluminium is produced from imported bauxite; magnesium from sea-water; zinc and nickel ores are refined; and ferrosilicon, ferrochromium and ferromanganese alloys are made. A flourishing chemical industry is based on the fixation of atmospheric nitrogen, also using pyrites and limestone as raw materials, and producing liquid ammonia, calcium nitrate, carbide and cyanamide, silicon-carbide and sodium chlorate (Fig. 12).

The town of Odda was founded in 1926 at the head of the Hardang-

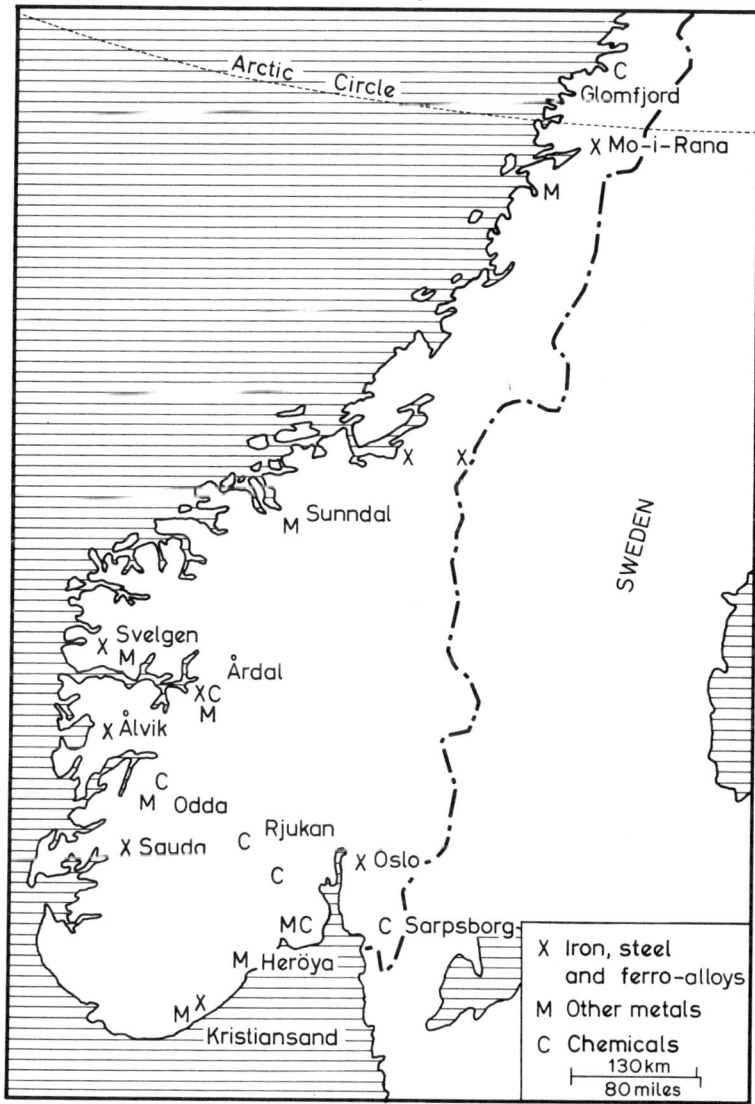

Arctic Circle

C
Glomfjord

X Mo-i-Rana

M

M Sunndal

SWEDEN

X Svelgen
M
Årdal
XC
M
X Ålvik

C
M Odda
X Sauda
C Rjukan
C
X Oslo

MC
M Heröya
M X
Kristiansand

C Sarpsborg

X Iron, steel
and ferro-alloys
M Other metals
C Chemicals
├─── 130km ───┤
80 miles

*Fig. 12. Location of the main electrochemical and electrometallurgical plants in
Norway
(After W. R. Mead)*
The names refer to the towns in or near which the plants are situated.

A new aluminium smelter was opened in 1968 at Karmöy, on an island near
Stavanger.

erfjord, and has chemical works making calcium carbide, and zinc and aluminium smelters. A large aluminium refinery and a factory making carbon paste operate at Årdal near the head of the Sognefjord; another aluminium refinery is at Höyanger on the same fjord. At Heröya, on the Frierfjord in the south-east of the country, a large plant uses local limestone to make calcium carbide, and another produces annually 10,000 tons of magnesium from sea-water and dolomite.

Far to the north on the Glomfjord, *Norsk Hydro* owns a huge plant making liquid ammonia, and on the south coast at Kristiansand a large refinery processes nickel concentrates brought in from Canada. One plant, situated inland at Rjukan, where the nearby falls enable plentiful power to be generated, is the biggest producer of liquid ammonia in Norway, and a nearby plant makes 'heavy water' by electrolysis for use in atomic piles.

In 1955 Norway's largest steel plant was opened at Mo-i-Rana, only a few miles south of the Arctic Circle; extensions have doubled its capacity. It is a State enterprise, sited after careful consideration. Smelting is based on ore and scrap brought by sea, though some low-grade magnetites and haematites are now worked in the Dunderlandsdal to the east of Mo-i-Rana. It is a fully integrated plant, with blast furnaces using coke and electric power in combination, a Bessemer converter, electric furnaces and rolling mills. Other iron smelters are at Stavanger and Bremanger. These and other plants are situated on the coast, mostly on the fjords, often in formerly uninhabited areas so that new small towns have grown up.

The following table summarizes the production of metals and alloys in 1967:

	(*Thousand tons*)
Pig-iron and ferro-alloys	1,232
Semi-finished steel	632
Aluminium	361
Zinc	57
Copper	20

The only other manufacturing activities of any importance are the making of textiles, shipbuilding and engineering. One group of textile mills is situated in the outskirts of Bergen, using partly local, partly imported, wool, and manufacturing both woollens and worsteds. Other mills are in Oslo and Stavanger. Norway has built small ships for many years, but only since 1945 has the industry developed

Plate IX. A seter *near Storlii in the Jotunheim, Norway*

Plate X. A farm and forests near Dombås, western Norway

Plate XI. Trondheim, Norway

Plate XII. Åndalsnes, near the head of the Romsdalsfjord, western Norway. It is reached by a railway which branches from the main line at Dombås

on any scale, mainly because of the country's need to make good its wartime shipping losses and to modernize its fleet. During the last ten years about 700,000 gross tons have been launched, though this represents only a quarter of the amount built abroad for the Norwegian mercantile marine. One group of yards is around the Oslofjord at Oslo, Tönsberg, Horten, Sandefjord and Frederikstad. The others are in the south-west at Bergen, Stavanger (where a dry dock will take vessels of up to 100,000 tons), and at the island of Stord. Ship maintenance and repair work, especially of the whaling fleets, are carried on along the shores of the Oslofjord. Electrical and marine engineering have developed, the former producing turbines and power plant generally, the latter ship's machinery.

Oslo is the centre of miscellaneous consumer-goods industries; these include food-processing (chocolate, tobacco), the making of clothing, printing, a range of light engineering products, and furniture. About a quarter of Norway's industrially employed population lives in and around the capital city.

COMMUNICATIONS

The development of internal communications in Norway is handicapped by its physical features: its latitudinal extent, the mountainous terrain and steep relief, the deep inlets penetrating far into the land, the steep-sided gorge-like valleys, the numerous lakes, the heavy winter snowfall, and the annual damage caused by snow-melt and runoff. The scanty, widely scattered population offers no profitable incentive, and isolated industrial centres prefer to rely on seawise connections. The lengths of railway lines and metalled roads are, in proportion to both the area and the population served, the lowest in Europe (except for Albania), though the growth of tourism has been a stimulating factor.

Roads

In 1968 the official length of roads was about 70 000 km (43,000 miles), but only a seventh had a metalled surface, the rest consisting of rolled gravel or clay. Roads are extremely difficult to construct, especially those which zigzag steeply down from the plateaus to fjord-side settlements, and maintenance is also difficult, for frost and snow-melt severely damage the surface. Many roads are snow-blocked from October or November until June; ploughs are used in increasing numbers to keep open main roads at lower altitudes.

Despite these difficulties, about 13 000 km (8000 miles) of new road have been constructed since 1945, including two short sections of motorway near Oslo, partly to accommodate the increasing numbers of buses, lorries and cars, partly to link settlements formerly only accessible by sea, and partly to cope with and extend the profitable tourist traffic. Some of the high passes are crossed by roads which penetrate superb mountain scenery; the Sognefjell pass, between the northern shore of the Sognefjord and Otta, climbs to 1429 m (4690 ft) through the Jotunheim, and the main road between Oslo and Bergen crosses the Hardanger Vidda at 1241 m (4070 ft). Improvements have been most marked in the north; it is possible to drive from Trondheim to Bodö without using a ferry, and although farther north a few ferries are essential, it is now practicable to take a car to the North Cape. Several road tunnels have been recently opened, five on the route between Oslo and Haugesund. The railways provide conveyance for cars on sections of some routes, such as from Bergen over the Hardanger Vidda, for it is not possible to drive from Bergen to Oslo without using either ferries or rail transport. Several scheduled 'snowmobile' services operate in winter in northern Norway.

Before the War of 1939–45 more than 200 ferries operated in the fjords and between the islands. Some have been closed with the improvement of the road network, but many remain, notably in the deeply indented Vestlandet province.

Railways

The construction of railways is even more difficult than that of roads, and Norway possesses only about 4200 km (2600 miles) of line, almost all owned by the State (Fig. 8). The system is inevitably run at a loss, but it is valuable in that it affords links which can normally be maintained throughout the year even when the high passes are snow-blocked, though screens and avalanche-sheds are required. About half of the lines have been electrified, and diesel traction has replaced steam on the rest.

The first line to be opened was in 1854 between Oslo and Eidsvold in the Glomma valley, and with a few important exceptions the system was completed before the twentieth century. The 480 km (300 miles) of line between Oslo and Bergen, a section not opened until 1909, climbs to a height of nearly 1300 m (4300 ft) across the Hardanger Vidda, and utilizes about 200 tunnels and many km of snow-sheds to provide the only overland connection between Oslo and Bergen for eight months of the year. A branch from Myrdal to Flåm was completed in 1940 (Fig. 11); it is a sensational line dropping over 850 m (2800 ft) in less than 16 km (10 miles) by zigzags and spiral tunnels. Another important link is the 560 km (350 miles) line between Oslo and Trondheim, opened as long ago as 1877, with a branch to

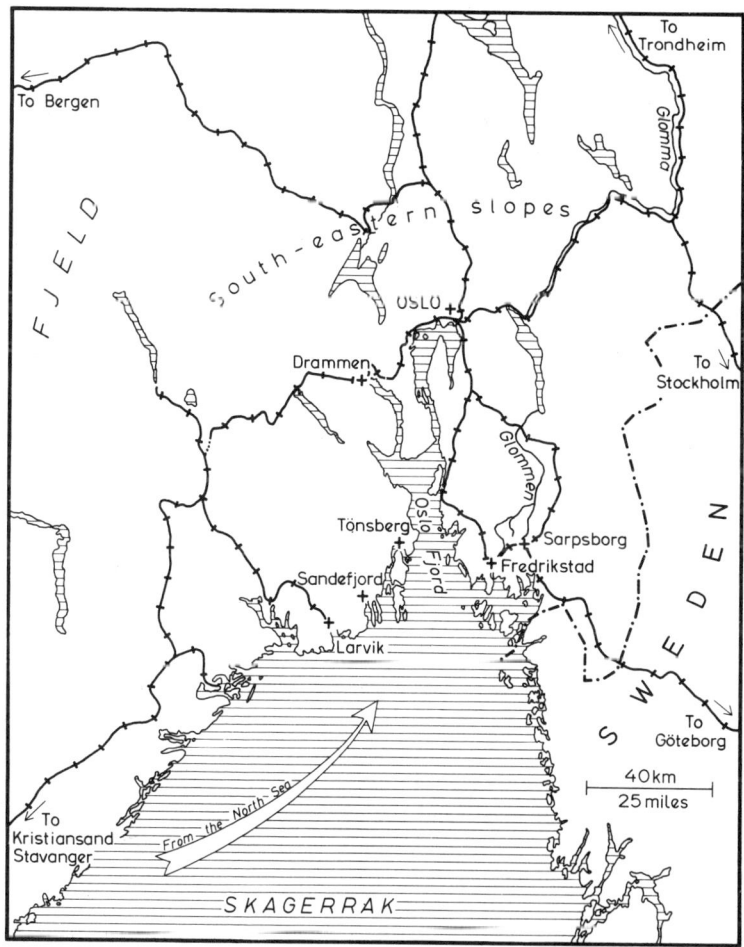

Fig. 13. The location of Oslo

Åndalsnes on the Romsdaljord (Plate XII). A line from Oslo to Stavanger via Kristiansand was completed in 1944 during the German occupation; this is forced to keep about 30 km (20 miles) from the sea, and uses several of the longest tunnels in the country to cross from one deep valley to the next. The Nordland line along the west coast from Trondheim to Bodö has been pushed slowly northward, and was finally completed in 1962. Four lines cross the border from Sweden: between Oslo and Göteborg, Oslo and Stockholm, Trondheim and Östersund, and the ore railway in the north between Narvik and Kiruna (p. 40).

Coastal Traffic

The value of the sheltered 'inner lead' along the west coast has been apparent for over a thousand years, since transport by water affords the only access to many isolated settlements perched on fjord shores or islands. The ease of these water routes must not be overestimated; many thousands of lighthouses, lightbuoys and marker poles are necessary. Large numbers of vessels use these intricate coastal waters, many through the darkness of winter; scheduled sailings operate both for passenger and freight, including regular 'sea buses' serving such towns as Stavanger, and there are innumerable cruising vessels in summer. The most famous service is the Express Coastal Route (the *Hurtigrut*) of over 2000 km (1250 miles), introduced in 1893, which provides a daily sailing throughout the year from Bergen via Trondheim to Kirkenes. Hundreds of small harbours and landings on the coasts of fjords and islands are engaged in local passenger and freight traffic. Fast 'hydrofoil' services operate from Bergen.

Airways

In a country of such considerable distances, airways provide invaluable links between the main towns; the scheduled time between Oslo and Bardufoss, the terminus for Tromsö, the most northerly point served, takes only eight hours. But air services are handicapped by the shortage of level land for airfields, some of which (notably at Bergen) were constructed only with considerable difficulty. Schedules may be disorganized by storm, fog and winter darkness, and the proximity of mountain ranges to most airfields can create hazardous conditions.

Norway is a partner in the Scandinavian Airlines System (*S.A.S*), which operates international routes (p. 50).

Mercantile Marine

The importance of the merchant marine is emphasized by the fact that its earnings pay for about one-third of the country's imports.

The growth of the mercantile fleet dates from the middle of the nineteenth century, and by 1914 it was the fourth largest in the world. Its losses during the War of 1914–18 as a neutral and during that of 1940–45 as an enemy-occupied country were enormous, almost half the total tonnage in each case. After 1945 a big programme of replacement and expansion was launched, mainly in foreign yards (notably in Sweden, later in West Germany), and by 1969 the total gross tonnage had reached 19 millions, one-tenth of the world's total, exceeded only by the fleets of Liberia and Japan. Two-thirds of the tonnage consists of oil tankers, plying between the Caribbean or Middle East oilfields and terminals in western Europe, and other specialized vessels include refrigerated ships, timber boats and ore carriers. About 90 per cent of the tonnage never enters Norwegian waters.

This is a vulnerable if normally profitable position for Norway, since shipping is extremely susceptible to periods of world economic depression. However, most of the fleet is new, efficient and highly competitive, and moreover a large proportion is engaged on time charter by oil companies and other large operators.

Norway's own shipping activity is distributed among a large number of small ports, most of which have their limited hinterlands, in many cases little more than the town itself. For many years since the days of the Hanseatic League, Bergen was the leading Norwegian port, and it maintained this position until the War of 1914–18. Since then, despite its distance from the open ocean, Oslo has been ahead in the value of both imports and exports, because it is the capital and the chief industrial and commercial centre. Bergen is followed by a large group including Tönsberg, Porsgrunn, Haugesund, Farsund and Trondheim. Narvik occupies first place in terms of tonnage of freight handled by virtue of its annual export of some 21 million tons of Swedish iron ore.

COMMERCE

As Norway can produce only a small proportion of the foodstuffs and raw materials required to maintain its standard of living, the volume and variety of imports is considerable. These include ships, automobiles, trucks and tractors, machinery, semi-finished steel, ores, mineral oil, coal, raw textiles, and foodstuffs, expecially cereals. The following table summarises in percentage terms the direction of Norwegian trade in recent years:

	E.E.C. countries	*E.F.T.A. countries*	*North America*	*Others*
Imports from	25·1	42·7	10·4	21·8
Exports to	23·3	44·9	10·2	21·6

Chief trading partners are Sweden, the U.K. and West Germany, in that order. If the U.K. enters the E.E.C., Norway is anxious to follow, for an enlarged market base for her manufactures and fish products would be of advantage.

Exports consist mainly of pulp and paper, fish products, metals and alloys, whale oil, chemicals and light engineering products. The last group has increased markedly in recent years, and now accounts for nearly a third of the total by value, compared with a fifth each for fish and forest products, which were once dominant. Much dried and salted fish is exported to Mediterranean countries, also more recently to Latin America and West Africa.

A wide adverse gap exists between the value of imports and exports; in 1968 these totalled 19·3 and 13·8 milliard *krona* respectively. This is bridged mainly by the earnings of the mercantile marine and by receipts from tourism which, taking advantage of the magnificent coastal scenery, the mountains, and the winter snow cover, attracts about 150,000 visitors a year. These enable the balance of payments to be in surplus in most years, and the gold and currency reserves are almost as high as those of the U.K.

POPULATION AND SETTLEMENT

With a total population in 1969 of 3·83 millions, Norway has the lowest average density (12 per sq. km, 31 per sq. mile) of any country in Europe (excepting Iceland), a reflection of the large proportion of land which is mountainous and virtually barren, or which experiences long winter cold, and is almost uninhabited. About three-quarters of the people live within 16 km (10 miles) of the sea, and over a third are in southern Östlandet around the Oslofjord and in its converging valleys, what may be described as 'the core region', occupying only about 5 per cent of the total area; the densities in 1969 in the counties of Östfold and Akershus, to the south-east and north-east of Oslo, were 56 and 66 per sq. km (145 and 171 per sq. mile) respectively, and in Vestfold it was 80 (207).

By contrast, in the whole of Finnmark, occupying an eighth of the total area, lived only 76,000 people, with an average density of 1·6 per sq. km (4·1 per sq. mile). Since 1945 northern Norway has experienced an appreciable increase in its population, partly as a result of deliberate government encouragement. In 1951 the state-sponsored Northern Norway Scheme and Development Fund were launched, which by taxation concessions and direction of investment have stimulated the introduction and growth of economic activities and therefore of employment. In recent years the same policies have been extended into other underdeveloped areas by the introduction of an official 'Fund for New Industrial Undertakings'.

The total population, which was only 885,000 in 1815, has doubled during the last hundred years, despite considerable emigration, for about 870,000 Norwegians left for America between 1835 and 1940, mainly because of pressure on the limited agricultural land. This movement has now been halted, partly by American restrictions, partly because the increase in industrial activities affords wider scope for employment at home. Whereas in the early nineteenth century 80 per cent of the population were engaged in agriculture and forestry, this proportion has now dropped to 15 per cent, and about 1·2 million (35 per cent) were employed in manufacturing industry at the last Occupational Census of 1960. Commerce and transportation occupy approximately 10 per cent each, administration and services 5 per cent each, and about 4 per cent are engaged in fishing.

A remarkably high proportion of the population, about a third, is classified as 'urban', though the urban units are small by definition. In some of the large northern counties the urban proportions are high because most of their people are concentrated in the few small towns with specialized industrial activities. Oslo had a population of 488,000 in 1969, or about 580,000 including the suburbs beyond the city limits, but only two others, Trondheim and Bergen, had a population exceeding 100,000, and two more, Stavanger and Kristiansand, had over 50,000. The importance of the smaller towns located mainly on the coast, centres of economic activity in their own small districts, is shown by the fact that twenty had more than 10,000 people. Some adjacent towns in the south-east, such as Frederikstad and Sarpsborg, and Skien, Porsgrunn and Brevik, have expanded to form continuous urban areas.

Since 1945 many rural districts have experienced an appreciable decline in population. Most people drift towards the Oslofjord and its neighbourhood, and to the towns on the west and south coasts where industrial employment is offered.

About 20,000 Lapps are in the northern counties of Finnmark, Troms and Nordland. Many of them live along the coast as fishermen, while others move with the reindeer herds from the forest to the mountain pastures, usually disregarding political boundaries.

REGIONS

Norway may be divided into three distinct regions: the long fjord coastline, the interior plateaus, and the south-eastern lowlands with the valleys draining into the Oslofjord.

1. The Fjord Coast

The rugged Atlantic coast is characterized by numerous fjords, and by many thousands of islands ranging from the Lofotens, which rise to over 1265 m (4150 ft), to the low hummocky 'skerries' (Plate VII). Areas of level land are limited to small benches near the mouths of the fjords (Plate XII) and to patches of alluvium at their heads. Farms, isolated or grouped in tiny villages, grow oats, barley and roots (the first two in the north as green fodder), and hay is mown from the lower slopes. Only around Trondheim, where a larger area of lowland occurs, is agriculture practised on a larger scale.

In Finnmark the administrative centre is the town of Vadsö on the northern shore of the broad Varangerfjord, and Kirkenes has a concentration plant and shipment facilities for the iron ore mined at Sydvaranger. The most northerly town is the fishing centre of Hammerfest; destroyed in 1944 by the Germans, it has been completely rebuilt. Farther south in Troms county is Tromsö, founded at the end of the eighteenth century, and now an important fishing port and commercial centre with a population of 37,000. There are sailings from Tromsö to Spitsbergen, as well as regular coastal services. Narvik (15,000) stands at the head of the Ofotfjord; apart from its fishing harbour, it is the terminus of the ore railway from Sweden. Another terminal at Finneid, on the Skjerstadfjord, is used for exporting copper concentrates, refined and processed at Sulitjelma and brought down by narrow-gauge line and lake transport. Bodö (14,000) is now the northern terminus of the west coast railway. Along this section of the coast several small towns have been recently established as industrial centres; these include Mo-i-Rana (iron and steel) and Glomfjord (ammonia), just south and north respectively of the Arctic Circle.

Farther south three larger towns, Trondheim, Bergen and Stavanger, and other smaller industrial centres are strung out along the coast. The rapidly growing Trondheim (124,000) (Plate XI), the centre of Tröndelag, is the focus of three railway lines from northern and south-eastern Norway and across the mountains from Sweden. It is situated on deltaic flats where the river Nea enters the Trondheimfjord, and is surrounded by a prosperous agricultural district; it has pulp mills and industries based on fish products. Trondheim is a fine city, and with its cathedral it forms the seat of an archbishopric and the ecclesiastical centre of the country.

Bergen, the chief town of Vestlandet, is with 116,000 people Norway's third city. Founded in the eleventh century, it became a flourishing Hansa town, and today it has a port used both by the fishing fleets and the mercantile marine; many visitors to Norway arrive through Bergen by the regular sailings from Newcastle. The town has a number of industries, notably fish-processing, flourmilling (a legacy of the days when it was the chief grain port), the manufacture of textiles, and shipbuilding. Bergen's main disadvantage is its difficulty of access inland; although the railway to Oslo was completed in 1909, no road inland is possible without using ferry connections.

Stavanger (81,000), the fourth city of Norway, is a market centre for the fertile farmlands of Jaeren near the southern edge of the fjord country. It is a fishing port, the centre of fish canning, and has several engineering, textile and furniture factories. It is linked by rail around the south coast to Oslo, and by taking advantage of the level land south-west of the city it was possible to construct Sola airport, the terminus of the trans-Atlantic S.A.S air route.

Many flourishing industrial centres are situated at carefully selected points along this southwestern coast (Fig. 12). They include Sunndal and Karmöy (aluminium), Sunnmöre (furniture), Ålesund (herring-meal and -oil), Svelgen (steel and ferrosilicon), Årdal (aluminium and carbon paste), Ålvik (ferrosilicon and ferrochromium), Odda (calcium carbide), Stord (ship-building), Sauda (ferromanganese), Haugesund (shipbuilding, fish processing) and Egersund (fishmeal).

2. *The Interior Plateaus*

The high fjeld is covered with snow in winter, with much bare rock, areas of bog, and shallow irregular lakes (Plate V). Pasture

4*

occurs on the lower slopes, lichens and mosses on the higher parts, with occasional patches of dwarf birch, willow, alder, juniper, ling, and berried plants such as bilberry and cloudberry. These berries, where they grow not too far from settlements, are collected for sale in the towns and for making preserves. Herbaceous arctic plants, including gentians, saxifrages, various heaths and ranunculus, are found particularly on the drier eastern fjeld. The plateaus are used for seasonal grazing, while from some of the more accessible bogs peat is cut for fuel and moss litter. In the north the Lapp herdsmen, their numbers increased during summer by Swedish Lapps who cross the boundary in search of fodder, graze their reindeer. Many of the Norwegian Lapps have now settled down in permanent dwellings as farmers and fishermen, though keeping herds of reindeer as a sideline. Farther south the lower plateaus carry rather better pasture; here are the seters to which animals are brought during the summer.

The mountains form popular holiday districts, both for the Norwegians themselves and for foreign visitors. Many small towns and villages are resorts, serving as ski centres between Christmas and Easter and as summer venues for climbers, walkers and fishermen.

3. *The South-eastern Lowlands*

These lowlands include the coastal districts around the Oslofjord, the valleys draining south-eastward, and the narrow coastal plain of the Skagerrak as far as Kristiansand. Much of the surface is covered with glacial clays and sands, patches of marine clays, and soils weathered from the Lower Palaeozoic shales. This is the most important part of Norway, where over a third of the people live. On the upper slopes is the forest; from the lookout tower at Holmenkollen behind Oslo a sea of conifers can be seen stretching away to the north-west and north. The farms on the lower land grow oats, barley and potatoes, with pasture and fodder crops for the dairy cattle, and intensive market gardening is carried on near Oslo.

Plentiful hydroelectric power from the rivers flowing south-eastward from the plateaus has stimulated the manufacture of pulp, paper, textiles, chemicals, furniture and light engineering products. The most important industrial towns, apart from Oslo, are Frederikstad (30,000) and Sarpsborg, forming an almost contiguous urban area along the valley of the Glomma. Other industrial towns are Drammen (timber, pulp and paper), Skien (newsprint and paperboard), Rjukan (fertilizers, ammonia and 'heavy water'), and Heröya (magnesium and calcium carbide). Many smaller centres manufacture furniture, prefabricated wooden fixtures and textiles. Along the coast to the south-west of Oslo a series of small towns and ports at the river mouths carries on these same types of industry. Horten, Tönsberg, Sandefjord and Frederikstad, each with 10–20,000 inhabitants, are centres of shipbuilding. Kristiansand (54,000), near the mouth of the Ottra river on the south coast, is an important industrial town, refining nickel and copper ores imported from Canada, and making ferrosilicon, carbon paste, pulp and newsprint, and plywood. It has a fishing harbour, many of the boats being engaged in profitable lobster catching.

Oslo, named Kristiania until 1924, is the capital of Norway, with a population of 488,000. Situated 100 km (60 miles) from the sea up the Oslofjord, the original settlement was founded nearly a thousand years ago around Amershus castle on a rocky spur projecting into the bay. But only during the last century has Oslo outstripped Bergen in size and importance, stimulated after 1854 by the growth of railways focusing on it, while Bergen was handicapped by its lack of accessible hinterland. The hills rise steeply behind the shores of the Oslofjord, and the built-up area has spread steadily upward and outward, linked to the city centre with tramways and electric railways, in part underground. The port handles half Norway's imports, and exports pulp, paper, timber, cardboard and cellulose. In the city manufacturing industry includes light engineering, which employs about a third of the workers. Oslo is the administrative and commercial centre of Norway, and has grown rapidly in recent years because of population movement from the rural areas towards this part of the country. An extensive underground railway system is under construction.

CHAPTER FOUR

Finland

FINLAND, with an area almost one and a half times that of Great Britain, extends latitudinally for over 1100 km (700 miles) through more than 10° from the Gulf of Finland to within 30 km (20 miles) of the Arctic Ocean. Yet in this 337 000 sq. km (130,000 sq. miles) live merely 4·69 million people; only Norway and Iceland in Europe are more thinly populated.

STRUCTURE AND RELIEF

Structure

Finland consists of a mass of Pre-Cambrian rocks, part of the Baltic Shield (Fig. 1). The vestiges of at least four Pre-Cambrian orogenies can be traced in the worn-down 'roots' of mountains trending from north-west to south-east, with complex thrusts, faults and folding, but long continued peneplanation has produced a low worn-down plateau. Except for warping along the margins of the Baltic Sea, both upwards and downwards at different times and in different localities, and for patterns of intersecting fault-fractures (especially in the south-west), the rigid Shield has remained largely unaffected by later earth movements. The rocks consist of intensely metamorphosed schists and quartzites into which have been intruded bosses of granite. The ancient structural lines of weakness can be traced in the 'grain' of the country, a sort of 'fault-mosaic', plainly visible where lakes lie in hollows eroded along fault-lines, and again in the pattern of the south-western archipelagoes.

The Quaternary Glaciation

The Finnish plateau was much affected by the Quaternary glaciation, for it formed part of the region of accumulation of the continental ice-sheets, and it was thickly covered with ice until a late stage in the Weichsel glaciation. During the Gotiglacial stage of retreat (Fig. 2), the extreme south of Finland lay under the waters of the 'Baltic Ice-Lake'. Towards the end of this stage, during a

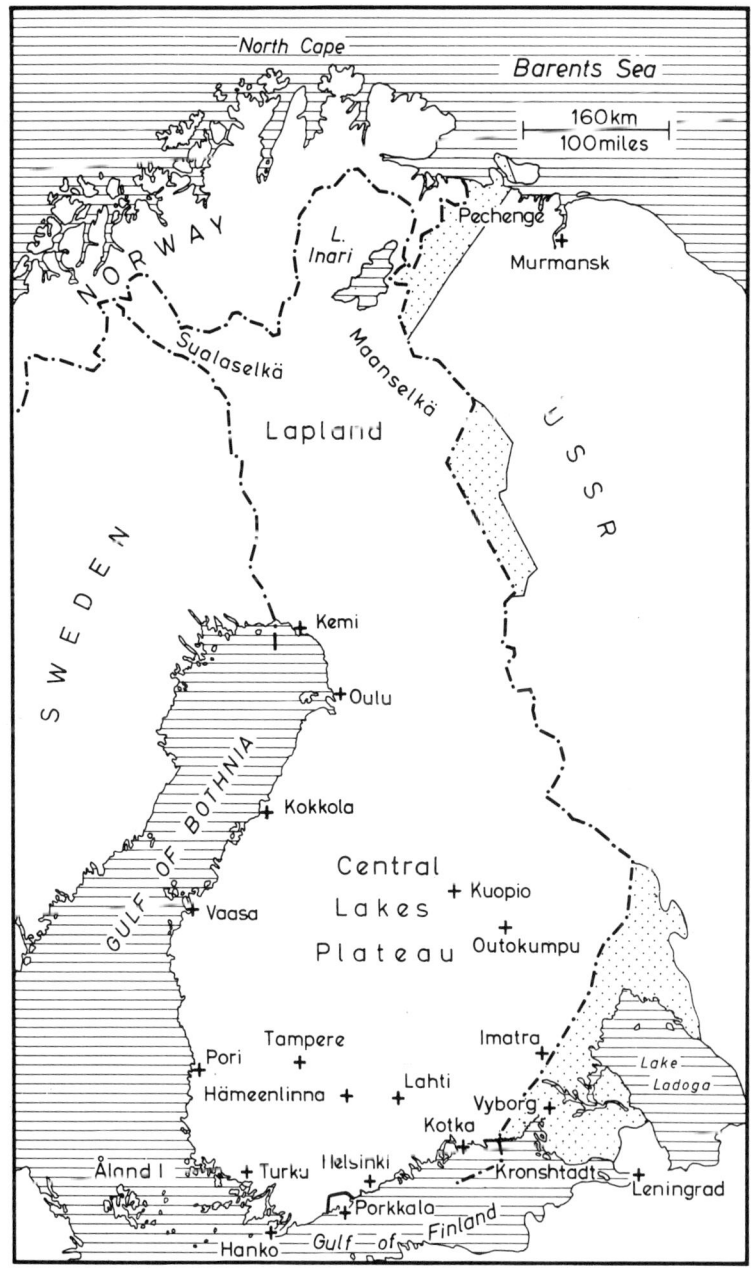

Fig. 14. Finland: general features
Finland's lost territory after the War of 1939–45 is stippled. The area around
Porkkala was returned in 1957.

protracted pause in the ice recession, the double ramparts of the Salpausselkä end-moraines were deposited, 40 km (25 miles) apart, parallel to the coast with the more southerly line 60 km (40 miles) inland. The later Finiglacial stage saw the final withdrawal of the ice-sheets from most of Finland. After 6500 B.C., during the marine transgression responsible for the 'Littorina Sea' (p. 21), marine deposits were laid down along the western and south-western margins for some 30–60 km (20–40 miles) inland. The maximum extension of the 'Littorina Sea' probably occurred about 4000 B.C., since when a gradual though fluctuating withdrawal of sea-level to its present position has taken place as a result of the continued isostatic uplift of the land; at one time this was rapid, of the order of 9 m (30 ft) per century, and it is still rising at about 400 mm (16 in) per century.

The Quaternary glaciation had a profound effect upon the relief of Finland. On the one hand the ice-sheets scoured the plateau, exposing bare rock and gouging irregular hollows, now mostly lake filled. On the other hand the melting ice left, as well as the Salpausselkä moraines, uneven sheets of ground-moraine, consisting of clay in the south but elsewhere mostly of gravels. Swarms of drumlins and trains of erratics can be distinguished trending from south-east to north-west, the direction in which the icesheet finally retreated. Eskers (*osar*), long winding ridges of gravel sometimes rising 60 m (200 ft) above the surrounding country, are common, especially in the south-west.

Relief and Drainage

The uneven surface is now covered with a maze of interconnected lakes, some lying on the clay in kettle-holes, others in rock basins; there are estimated to be about 55,000, mostly quite shallow, varying in depth from 5 to 20 m (15 to 70 ft) and occupying a tenth of the total area of the country. Many have swampy margins, others are now peat-filled or have been artificially drained to provide farmland; about 500 lakes, of an aggregate area of 500 sq. km (200 sq. miles), have been reclaimed during this century. About 12 per cent of the land area is covered with bog and fen of various kinds, the result of gentle gradients and the impermeable nature of the surface.

The physical landscape has been further diversified by the deposition of sediment by rivers in lakes and along the coast as deltas, exposed by subsequent uplift. A veneer of marine clays was laid down south of the Salpausselkä and along the west coast, also to be revealed by uplift. The coastal plains afford the most continuous

area of lowland in the country, 30–100 km (20–60 miles) wide, and the
clay soils are of great value to agriculture.

The relief of Finland is therefore of considerable though subdued
diversity. The highest point, a mountain of 1324 m (4344 ft) in the

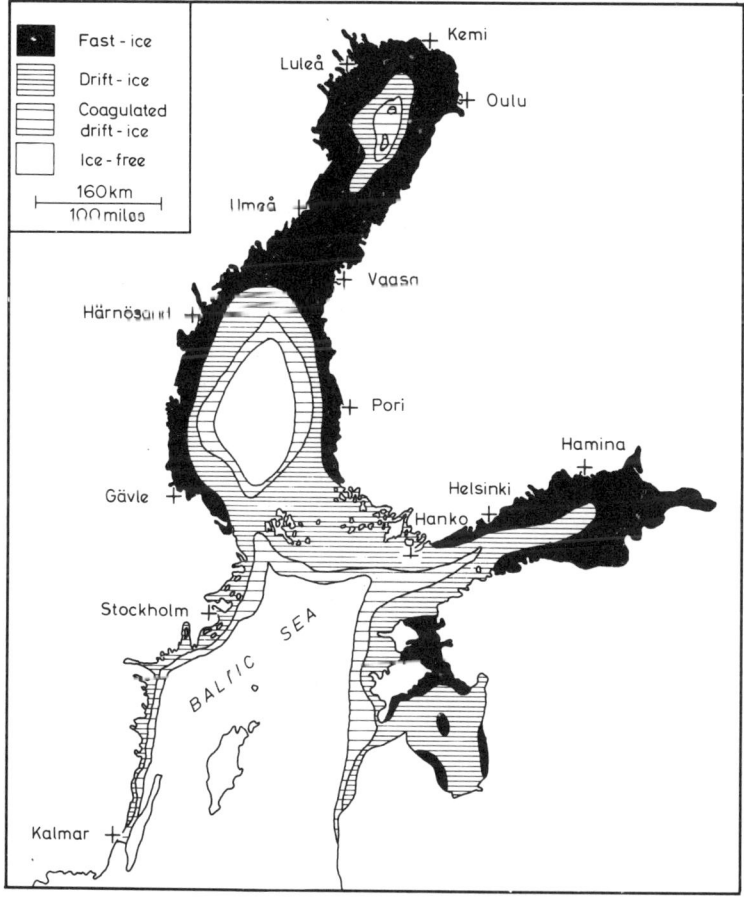

Fig. 15. The closing of the Baltic Sea by ice in winter
(After W. R. Mead)

north-west, stands on the divide between the Arctic Ocean and the
Gulf of Bothnia. Some low ranges of hills rise a little above 300 m
(1000 ft), notably the Sualaselkä and Maanselkä in the north and the
Karelian Uplands in the east, but much of the plateau country lies at

between 60 and 180 m (200 and 600 ft) above sea-level, and two-thirds of the entire area is below 180 m.

While much of the coast has been uplifted and so forms smooth benches, other parts, particularly in the south-west, have been partially submerged as a result of a local southward tilting. The irregular dissected surface of the peneplain has been converted into a rocky archipelago, the highest portions of which form the Åland Islands, and the south coast is diversified by numerous bays and small peninsulas.

CLIMATE

The south coast of Finland lies at 60° N., about the same latitude as the Shetland Isles, while the northern fifth is within the Arctic Circle, extending to 70° N. Yet the far north experiences milder winters than the south, because of air masses moving off that part of the North Atlantic Drift which has rounded the North Cape, and is responsible for the ice-free coasts of the former Finnish Petsamo district (now Russian Pechenge). A gradually diminishing amelioration can be traced as far south as the Arctic Divide.

Central and southern Finland are dominated in winter by the continental features of high pressure and low temperatures, little affected by the Gulfs of Bothnia and Finland. Their brackish waters are frozen for several months, especially in the north of the former where the freeze may last for seven months (Fig. 15). Even Helsinki's harbour is closed, in spite of icebreakers, for a varying period each year between February and April, and only Hanko (Hangö) in the south-west can usually be kept open. The coldest month in Helsinki is February (mean −7° C.), though January is only a degree milder.

The summers, though brief (about 50 days in the north, 110 days in the south), have long hours of sunshine and temperatures of 15° to 18° C., with a mean for Helsinki in June of 17° C. The difference between northern and southern Finland is less emphasized by mean than by accumulated temperatures; the sum of the excess of day temperatures over 5° C. in the north is about 450° C., but along the south coast, which has about 175 days with means above 5° C., it is almost three times that figure.

Precipitation varies from about 635 mm (25 in) on the south coast to only 380 mm (15 in) in the east; its effectiveness is however helped by low evaporation rates. About 60 per cent falls in the six summer and autumn months (the rainiest month on the south coast is August), though no month is dry; February to April average 38 mm (1·5 in) each. The winter precipitation comes in the form of snow; this cover lies for about seven months in the lands north of the Arctic Circle, for three months along the south coast.

LAND USE AND AGRICULTURE

The physical environment which obtains over much of Finland, a harsh climate and a grudging soil, is reflected in the land-use statistics. About 12 per cent of the area is classified as tundra and waste, with much sphagnum and sedge bog or fen, and another 10 per cent is lake covered. The area under cultivation amounts to a mere 9 per cent; this is unevenly spread, ranging from a third of the overall area along the south coast to none at all in parts of Lappland. The crystalline rocks, where not wholly exposed, are covered with stony till, outwash gravels or coarse sand, podzolized by leaching and commonly with a hardpan causing waterlogging. The best soils are derived from lacustrine silts, where lakes have been naturally or artificially drained, and from newer marine clays along the south coast, but these occupy less than 3 per cent of the total area. Agriculture is nevertheless of considerable importance, and about 35 per cent of the working population derives its livelihood thereby. It is not easy to give exact figures, since in the north and east farming is carried on in conjunction with forestry, in places also with fishing and even with hunting. Many a farmer could not exist without ancillary winter employment in forestry or the sale of surplus timber from his holding; these may provide him with a third to a half of his total income.

When Finland attained its independence in 1917, much of the land was in the hands of the large owners, and there were considerable numbers of crofters and landless labourers; the crofts were small and the economic position of the crofters often wretched, for they had little or no security of tenure. During the latter part of the nineteenth century many Finnish families emigrated to America or drifted to the towns.

The policy of the government after independence was attained was the creation of a class of owner-occupiers, later stimulated by the *Lex Kallio* of 1927 which involved expropriation of parts of large estates and the creation of new holdings from the forest and waste. Between 1920 and 1939 the number of tenants diminished from 150,000 to 14,000, and by 1939 over 120,000 smallholdings had been allocated.

After the war with Russia in 1939–40, Finland lost some of its best agricultural land in Karelia and over 425,000 people dispossessed from this ceded territory had to be resettled. This was accomplished partly by a compulsory breaking up of large farms under the Land Expropriation Act of 1945, by which owners of holdings exceeding 30 ha had to give up a proportion, and partly by the creation of other units from neglected farms and from land owned by non-farmers; in addition, about two-fifths came from state-owned land. Most of the Karelian farmers were settled in the south-west, those from the other 'lost lands' on newly reclaimed areas in the centre and north by means of schemes of pioneer clearance and settlement; the last is no new phenomenon, for the Finnish people have always been pioneers. A settler starts with a 'cold farm', a tract of wilderness, and when after long effort he has turned it into a 'warm farm', with fields cleared and farm buildings erected, he receives a payment from the State. About 48,000 farms have been created since the War, and the resettlement programme was completed by 1950.

In all, in 1959 at the last land census there were about 390,000 holdings; only 237 exceeded 100 ha (250 acres) of cultivable ground, situated mostly in the south and south-west, while 90 per cent had less than 16 ha (40 acres), and 30 per cent less than 3 ha (7 acres); the average size is about 7 ha (17 acres), compared with 9 ha (22 acres) before 1939. Many of the farms, particularly in the centre and north, include a large area of unimproved land, beyond the reclaimed infields on which stands a weather-board farmhouse; much of the unimproved holding is a source of fuel and building material. Some farms are quite isolated, situated on lake shores, on eskers and on drumlins.

Arable Farming

In 1968 about 2·7 million ha (6·7 million acres) were classified as land under cultivation; of these 37 per cent were under grass for hay and one-sixth grew oats, the most important crop everywhere except in the Åland Islands, whose best soils form good wheatlands. Barley, cultivated far to the north because of its short growing season, and roots for animal feeding stuffs, bring the proportion of farmland under fodder crops to about 75 per cent. Potatoes, especially in the east and north, turnips, sugar beet (subsidized since the War), and rye occupy the rest of the cropland; in the past rye was the chief cereal, but its place has largely been taken by oats, though it is still the main bread cereal. Rape is grown in the south-west, the oil extracted from its seed at a mill near Turku. Market gardening near Helsinki and other cities has increased appreciably since 1945, especially with the aid of glasshouses.

Between 1920 and 1939 the aim of Finnish agriculture was to make the country as self-sufficient as possible and to develop some surplus of dairy produce for export. By 1939 this had been attained in all but bread grains, and even in this direction the policy had achieved 90 per cent of its objective. But the loss of Karelia was a serious blow, and Finland now imports nearly five times as much grain as in 1939, nearly all from the U.S.S.R. Agriculture in many parts is marginal, and in some years the position is especially serious, particularly when late spring frosts reduce the growing season or early autumn frosts cause damage before harvest. Nevertheless, the farmers seek to make the best use of their land, particularly by the application of subsidized artificial fertilizers and a marked intensification of farming methods; as a result, the yields per ha of most crops are higher than in, say, France. The breeding of new varieties of spring wheat now enables it to be grown as far as the northern end of the Gulf of Bothnia, whereas once it was restricted to the extreme south-west. Frost-resistant and quick-maturing varieties of many other plants have been developed, new crops such as rape have been introduced, and strains of grass in the pastures have been improved. There has been a large increase in the number of tractors, grain harvesters, ditching machines and stump removers, both privately and company owned. Rationalization of farm buildings has been carried out by the creation of unit structures, which facilitate the efficient winter management of stock.

Livestock

The high preponderance of fodder crops and the unreliability of the summer ripening of cereals indicate an emphasis on livestock, and in 1968 there were 2·0 million cows, 679,000 pigs and some 7·0 million head of poultry. The long winter necessitates the housing and feeding of the stock for many months. Co-operation is as lively as in Denmark, and since 1945 some large dairy factories have been built; 101,000 tons of butter and 33,000 tons of cheese were factory-produced in 1968, part for home consumption, the rest for export directly or via Denmark. A Butter Export Association, an Egg Export Society, and a large Central Agricultural Supply Society (founded as long ago as 1905), all help the farmer. Finland, long famous for horses, still has 126,000 (though decreasing), and 155,000 sheep are kept. About 184,000 reindeer are mainly reared by Finns in the north, and other herds are kept by Lapps. Mink are bred on fur farms in the Vaasa archipelago and along the south-western coast; the furs are mostly exported to the U.S.A.

FISHERIES

Fishing is of much less importance than in the other northern countries, for Finland lacks easy access to the open sea. Before 1939 cod fisheries were operated in the Arctic Ocean, and a few Finnish vessels still visit the Icelandic banks. But now the main activity is fishing for the Baltic herring (sild) off the indented coast of the south-west, where 20,000 tons are landed annually. Salmon and other freshwater varieties are caught in the rivers and lakes.

FORESTRY AND TIMBER PRODUCTS

No other country in the world has such a high proportion of its area under forest, about 70 per cent, of which over half, mostly south of 64° N., is classified as productive. A considerable amount of the non-productive forest is waterlogged, forming pine- and spruce-bog, with stunted trees, an undershrub of dwarf birch, and a ground layer of bog moss. About half of the forest consists of Scots pine, a quarter of spruce, 15 per cent of varieties of birch, and some smaller scattered stands of larch, aspen and alder. Spruce is increasing in area, particularly in the south, as the result of afforestation to meet the demands of the pulp industry, though in the centre and north the slow-growing pines are maintaining themselves. Some small groups of oak and lime are found in the south.

Timber has long been cut commercially and there are records of exports as early as the thirteenth century. In the eighteenth and early nineteenth centuries the trade was greatly stimulated by Europe's need of large quantities of naval stores. With the rapidly increasing demands of industrialized western Europe in the mid-nineteenth century, and the replacement of sawmills on the inland rapids by larger steam-powered mills at the coast, exports increased sixfold between 1860 and 1910. Gradually a network of 'floating ways', carefully maintained channels through the system of lakes and rivers to carry the logs to the coast, was developed. Though many small sawmills still operate in the interior, there is now a concentration at the ports, using both hydroelectricity and their own waste wood as fuel for steam raising.

Between the Wars Finland built up a flourishing export, particularly to Britain and Germany, in timber and timber products: sawn timber, boxwood, plywood, spools, matches, pulp and paper, cardboard, cellulose, and such 'forest byproducts' as turpentine, distilled spirit and pine-oil. These items comprised about 90 per cent of the total value of Finnish exports.

The War of 1939–45 had very serious effects on both the Finnish forests and the associated industries. The cession of Karelia lost some stands of high quality, about 12 per cent of the sawmills, 10 per cent of the pulp mills, and 20 per cent of the cellulose factories, and the loss of Viipuri, the main timber port, and of part of the Saimaa Canal (p. 106), the focus of the south-eastern floating way system, meant that considerable forest areas could no longer be easily exploited. The situation was made worse by excessive felling to meet immediate post-war needs, to provide material for rehousing 480,000 people, to clear land for new farms, and to meet the heavy Soviet reparations. However, Europe's increasing demand for timber and the appreciably higher world prices have contributed to the recovery of the industry, and it has largely regained its old emphasis. Much mechanization has been introduced, notably the use of power saws and tractors; the annual winter migration of forestry workers into the centre and north, at one time about 200,000 men, is steadily declining as less manual labour is required. New winter roads are developed to take tractors and trucks, for road haulage direct to the mills is becoming more common, especially in the north and east. The World Bank has made several loans to Finland to help the modernization of its industry; one result is a large sulphate pulp mill at Imatra near the Russian frontier, the most modern in Europe.

In recent years about 60 per cent of the total Finnish exports have consisted of timber and wood manufactures, paper and cardboard (about a million tons in all), and pulp. Various developments have stimulated the production of plywood and wallboard, veneers, prefabricated dwellings, and furniture, whose elegant design, especially when carried out in birchwood, has made it widely popular. Increasing amounts of sulphur and chlorine are imported for the production of sulphite cellulose, and of sodium sulphate for sulphate cellulose.

Timber also provides an essential item in the internal economy; probably 40 per cent of the total cut is consumed domestically. Most houses are of timber: frame houses in the towns, log cabins in the country, and much is consumed for fencing and construction generally. A large amount is burnt by rural households as fuel during the long cold winters, and the high cost of imported coal and oil means that another 10 per cent of the cut is burnt as fuel in industry and nearly as much again as firing for locomotives, though much of the last comprises waste timber.

It is a matter of national importance for Finland to conserve its forests efficiently, especially as the period of regeneration in these northern latitudes is so lengthy. Some concern is felt that the rate of cutting in the south and centre has since the War exceeded the annual increment, which has forced logging further away from the mills, so increasing costs of production. There are, however, virgin stands of unlogged forest in the north-east, and drainage schemes are converting some bog-forest into productive forest. The State owns about a third of the forests, mostly in the north, and exercises considerable legislative control over privately owned forests.

MINERALS AND POWER

The utilization and fabrication of timber is thus the major individual industry, and one-third of the working population is so employed. However, especially since 1945, there has been an increasing diversification of industrial activity, partly to meet domestic needs, partly to cope with Soviet reparation demands, and partly to contribute to the urgent export drive.

Mineral Resources

What is probably the largest copper deposit in Europe was discovered at Outokumpu in 1910, a pyrites body some 3 km (2 miles) in length, estimated to contain about 17·5 million tons of ore with a 4 per cent copper content, as well as some iron, sulphur, zinc, cobalt, gold, silver and other metals. A concentration plant near the mines treats 600,000 tons each year, from which the concentrate is sent to the Harvajalta smelter and Pori refinery in the west; some 30,000 tons of copper, iron, sulphur and smaller quantities of other metals are produced. Intensive geological survey has resulted in several other important finds in recent years. In 1958 a pyrites deposit was located at Pyhäsalmi in the west of the Lake Plateau, and a nickel-copper deposit at Kotalahti in the east; the latter started production in 1959, its output going to the Harjavalta smelter. Another large ore bed was discovered in 1954 to the south of Oulu, containing mainly zinc; about 500,000 tons of ore, yielding 65,000 tons of metal, is processed annually. Nickel and copper are produced at Nivala.

In 1938 a rich deposit of magnetite-ilmenite was found, estimated to contain 50 million tons of ore with an average 37 per cent metal content. Production started in 1953, and output has since steadily increased. More important than the iron, the ore contains about 7 per cent titanium and also a small amount of vanadium. About 100,000 tons of titanium concentrate and 700 tons of vanadium pentoxide are produced annually, as well as a contribution of 215,000 tons of iron concentrate. Another iron ore deposit in the north at Kärväsvaara yields about 100,000 tons a year, shipped through Oulu. A submarine iron ore deposit recently discovered off the south coast may be worked and smelted in a plant which is being built on the Hanko promontory. Other considerable finds of rather low-grade iron ore have been made in the north at Porkonen and at Juvakaisenmaa in Lappland; no development has taken place, nor is this likely, because of transport difficulties and high costs of extraction. Some molybdenum is worked to the north of Outokumpu at Mätäsvaara. The Petsamo nickel mines, formerly owned by the Mond Nickel Company, were taken over by the U.S.S.R. in 1945; this was a serious loss, since the estimated reserves of ore are about 4 million tons. Granite is quarried at Vehma, Uusikaupunki and Keuru, both for home supplies and for export.

Power

Finland is markedly short of fuel, except for wood; the second largest single group of imports by value is oil and coal. A vast amount of wood is consumed for steam-raising in factories, but peat is of little value, since its accumulation in the bogs is usually thin and relatively undecayed; what is cut is for use as animal litter.

In early days most mills were situated on rapids, but when steam-power was introduced, raised by wood or with imported British and later Polish coal, large factories were built along the coast. Then came the development of hydroelectricity, and between 1920 and 1939 the installed capacity of the plants was trebled; the largest plant, the state-owned 120,000 KW Imatra station on the Vuoksi river, distributes power over southern Finland as far away as Helsinki. Many stations are in the south, where streams leave the plateau edge; though flowing from shallow lakes and of low head, mostly only 6–9 m (20–30 ft), they have numerous falls, and except during the winter freeze are well sustained by the lakes on the plateau. But the potential is limited and about 80 per cent has already been developed. The loss of the south-eastern territory to Russia involved nearly a third of the developed power, though fortunately Finland retained the Imatra plant. An ambitious plan to construct a number of big stations has been completed since the War, notably on the Kemi and Oulu rivers, while several new stations have been built in the north and linked into the grid system. But even so, one-third of Finland's power is thermally generated, mainly by Polish coal and Russian oil. An oil-refinery was recently opened at Porvoo, 50 km (31 miles) east of Helsinki.

MANUFACTURING INDUSTRY

Timber-working and food-processing industries have remained dominant in the postwar years. However, Russian reparations demanded considerable quantities of metal manufactures, ships and engineering products, about 60 per cent of the total by value, and this compulsorily stimulated industrial expansion. At first this was geared entirely to the fulfilment of reparations; when these ceased in 1952 Finland found it difficult to break into other markets at competitive prices, and for a time Russia continued to take much of these manufactures. Engineering and metal goods now comprise 23 per cent of Finland's exports by value, and helped by devaluation of the *Finnmark* in 1968, Sweden is now the chief market for these products.

Pig-iron is made at Turku, and several electric furnaces, Martin open-hearth converters (using scrap) and rolling-mills operate on the south coast at Dalsbruk, Fiskars and Vuoksenniska, and in the south-east at Imatra. In 1968 Finland produced 1·1 million tons of pig-iron and 400,000 tons of crude steel; this is inadequate for its internal needs, and much semi-finished steel is imported. Steel-using industries include the manufacture of agricultural implements, turbines, boilers, locomotives (at Tampere), and ships (at Turku and Helsinki). A recent development is the production of paper-making machinery for export, as well as for home use. The Swedish *Saab* company have established a car assembly-plant in Finland.

Other industries include the manufacture of footwear, textiles and clothing, and the production of chemicals. The textile industry is centred in the south-west around Tampere where 40,000 workers are employed, with subsidiary groupings at Helsinki and Turku;

though it was originally based on home-produced wool, most of the raw materials are now imported. One plant in Tampere makes linen from locally grown flax. Pottery and glass of high repute have been produced in Helsinki for a long time. The chemical industry is based partly on byproducts of mining (sulphuric acid and its derivatives from pyrites at Harjavalta), partly on pulp (cellulose), partly on the fixation of atmospheric nitrogen by electrolysis, and partly on the petrochemical industry associated with an oil refinery opened in 1958 to the north-west of Turku. Finnish agriculture makes heavy demands on fertilizers, three-quarters of which must be imported, though large factories now produce nitrates at Oulu and phosphates at Kotka.

Various food-processing industries are carried on, notably sugar refining; four big refineries are owned by the Finnish Sugar Company at Helsinki, Kotka, Turku and Vaasa. About 20 per cent of the beet is home-produced, the rest mostly coming from Denmark and eastern European countries; in addition, about 150 million tons of raw sugar are imported from the U.S.S.R., Poland and East Germany.

Most industrial activity is sited along the south coast in the towns, where there is the highest density of population for labour (40 per cent of which is female), good communications and access to ports; almost half of the industrial workers live in the three main towns of Helsinki, Tampere and Turku. Especially since 1946 considerable developments have taken place farther north in the Lake Plateau, where many sawmills, pulp mills and chemical factories are state-owned. The fastest growing export industry is now the manufacture of furniture. But Finland is worried by industrial unemployment, despite these efforts at diversification, and the position is aggravated during the winter when many forms of employment cannot be pursued.

COMMUNICATIONS

Waterways

The intricate network of interconnected lakes and rivers provides a system of internal routeways, though handicapped by the winter freeze and by rapids which present especial difficulties along the rivers flowing to the coast. Routes for small vessels and timber rafts have been developed through the maze of water and bog; about 40 000 km (25,000 miles) of floating ways are maintained, of which about 6400 km (4000 miles) can also be negotiated by small craft. The Saimaa Canal, 56 km (35 miles), was completed in 1856; it incorporates several lakes in its lower course, and except for crossing the Salpausselkä its construction was not difficult. This afforded a link between Lake Saimaa and the coast, and allowed vessels to move from Viipuri northward as far as Kuopio, 260 km (160 miles) away. In the 'thirties a million tons of freight passed annually along the canal: exports of timber and iron, and imports of foodstuffs. After the War Finland lost Viipuri and most of the canal, so disrupting the waterway system in the south-east.

In 1961 proposals were discussed for a lease to Finland by the U.S.S.R. of the portion of the canal now in Russian territory. Unused for 20 years, this required extensive repairs to the neglected locks, and there have been suggestions of enlargement to accommodate small sea-going ships. There was at first some doubt whether this scheme could be implemented, partly because of the cost, partly because Finland has built new roads and railways from the Saimaa area to the ports of Kotka and Hamina, and new floating ways have been constructed across the watersheds to the west, thus reorientating the Saimaa region away from its former south-easterly outlet via Viipuri. However, the work went ahead; the canal was enlarged and deepened, and new locks built. The southern part was leased from the U.S.S.R., and the whole canal was opened in 1968.

Roads

Road communication is difficult because of the area of lakes and bogs, and because of climatic problems. Most of the trunk roads are now metalled. Since the War a considerable length, including two roads over the boundary into Norway, has been constructed to open up the north for trade and for tourists. The chief maintenance problems involve blockage by snow, though ploughs are now used effectively, and more seriously damage by frost and spring thaw. There are about 40 000 km (25,000 miles) of metalled road and another 32 000 km (20,000 miles) of unsurfaced gravel road, sometimes laid on log foundations. Much of the latter category is used by tractor-hauled sledges and trucks. The length of roads in proportion both to population and area is small, though the increase in the number of automobiles (only 1 for every 32 people in 1961, now 1 for every 9) has stimulated construction during recent years. One problem is that many ferries are still required among the lakes.

Railways

Finland's first railway, between Helsinki and Hämeenlinna 105 km (65 miles) away, was completed in 1862, using a broad gauge (1·524 metres). The network has been steadily extended, and now totals 5717 km (3550 miles), almost all state-owned; this represents a surprisingly high average in terms of length per head of population, higher indeed than any country in Europe with the exception of Sweden. The pattern includes five west–east lines, of which one crosses into Russia, and one from Kemi at the head of the Gulf of Bothnia reaches the Swedish boundary, where there is a break of gauge. The more westerly of the two north–south lines runs south from Kemi via Oulu, Tampere and Hämeenlinna to Helsinki, the other from near Kaajanni via Kuopio and Mikkeli to the port of Kotka. A plan to build a line to the Arctic coast at Liinahamari has never materialized because of the cost and physical difficulties; with the loss of the Arctic seaboard to Russia, it is improbable that this line will ever be constructed.

The railways carried 22 million tons of freight in 1968. A major scheme was completed in 1969 of electrifying 1000 km (600 miles) of track, at first mainly suburban lines in the Helsinki area, then certain main lines.

Ports

The dependence of Finland on the export of bulk products has stimulated the growth of a merchant marine, which before the War totalled 650,000 g.r.t. Destruction and seizure during and after hostilities reduced this tonnage to less than half, though by 1968 it had again increased to 1·1 million tons.

The ports are strung out around the coast, none being dominant, for though Helsinki receives 40 per cent of imports, followed in order by Turku, Hanko and Kotka, it handles only 12 per cent of exports. The leading exporting port is Kotka, which with nearby Hamina has taken Viipuri's place in timber shipments, followed by Helsinki and Turku. The winter freeze presents difficulties, since Hanko and Turku are the only reliable ice-free ports except during mild winters, and even then the approaches are difficult; Helsinki is sometimes ice-bound for three months, despite efforts by icebreakers. The export of timber, nearly three-quarters of the total freight tonnage, is largely restricted to the summer and early autumn.

COMMERCE

After Finland became an independent republic, a large part of its commercial activity was with western Europe, especially with Britain and Germany, good customers for timber and suppliers of coal, metals and manufactures. After 1945 a large part of Finland's exports consisted of reparations to the U.S.S.R. in the form of machinery, ships, prefabricated buildings and other timber products. Finland and the U.S.S.R. have since completed several commercial agreements, and about a sixth of Finnish trade is with its powerful neighbour. During 1960–61 discussions took place concerning Finland's joining the European Free Trade Association. This was approved in 1961, and the E.F.T.A.-Finland Association (E.F.A.) was signed. Gradually, therefore, Finland has widened her trading interests, helped by this associate membership of E.F.T.A. By 1968, the U.K. was responsible for a fifth of the total trade, followed by the U.S.S.R., Sweden and West Germany.

The chief exports in order of value are cardboard and paper, wood pulp, timber and wood products, and machinery. Imports include machinery, mineral oil, chemicals, transport equipment, metals and textiles.

POPULATION

In 1969 the population of Finland totalled 4·69 million, with an average of 15 per sq. km (39 per sq. mile). This represents a very considerable growth since 1749, the date of the first census, when it was only 421,500. When the republic attained independence in 1917, the population totalled about 3 million; the increase during the interwar years was absorbed largely by the towns, in small part by closer agricultural settlement in the south and centre, and by some new colonization in the north. During the War with the U.S.S.R., Finland suffered a grievous drain of manpower, for 78,000 were killed. When territory was ceded in 1945, most of the 425,000 people involved preferred to move rather than become Soviet citizens.

Urbanization has been late, though rapid, in Finland; only five towns date back to medieval times, and Lahti was founded as recently as 1905. Since 1945 the growth of the urban population has gone on rapidly, and between 1950 and 1968 the proportion living in towns increased from 32·3 to 48·0 per cent of the total. Helsinki, the capital, is also the largest town (532,000, or about 708,000 with adjoining suburbs), followed by Tampere (152,000) and Turku

(152,000). Seven other towns have over 50,000 and a further sixteen have over 20,000.

About 52 per cent of the population is classified as rural, a big relative decline from the 88 per cent of 1900. This does not represent an absolute decrease, however, except in parts of the south-west where some actual depopulation has occurred. In the north and north-east the rural population has increased and some parishes in Lappland have doubled their populations during the last twenty years. The most densely populated part of Finland is the south coast plain, with 27–40 per sq. km (70–100 per sq. mile); the department of Uusimaa, containing Helsinki, has a density of 1000 per sq. km (2590 per sq. mile). Over the Lake Plateau the average is about 12–15 per sq. km (30–40 per sq. mile), and in the north less than 4 per sq. km (10 per sq. mile); parts are uninhabited or occupied only temporarily by nomadic Lapps. The two most northerly departments, Lappi (Lappland) and Oulu, have only 2 and 7 per sq. km (5 and 18 per sq. mile) respectively.

The earliest people, probably fishers and hunters, entered the country from the south and east. Unrelated to Slav, Teuton or Mongol, though possibly akin to the Magyars, the Finns speak a Finno-Ugrian language; Esthonian and Lappish are the only other European languages with close affinities. The Finns began to settle in the eighth century, spreading slowly northward; as late as the mid-sixteenth century they were still concentrated along the south and west coasts, though areas farther north and east were used for hunting and fishing. Not until 1800 did the colonists reach the Baltic–Arctic divide as the pioneer fringe was pushed steadily northward. This movement still goes on, especially with the impetus of resettlement after 1945; the county of Lappi, with only 40,000 people in 1880, had 221,000 in 1969.

Two distinct linguistic elements in the population are officially recognized. From the twelfth century Sweden made efforts to conquer the country, and in 1362 Finland became a Swedish province, which it remained for over four centuries until 1809. Swedish settlement in the west and south-west has left a legacy of a Swedish-speaking population of about 330,000, including 95 per cent of those in the Åland islands. The Finnish and Swedish speakers are not distinct racial groups; they are both indigenous to Finland, and the Swedish speaking element has no ties, sentimental or otherwise, with Sweden. Nevertheless, the country is highly conscious of this language division; in the past there have been certain cultural, social and political conflicts, and there is a Swedish People's Party. The number of Swedish-speakers has not increased as rapidly as the rest of the population; moreover, it seems that more Swedish-speaking Finns have emigrated than Finnish speakers. As a result, the percentage of Swedish speakers has fallen from 38 in 1880 to 11 in 1920 and to only 7·4 in 1969. A further element is the Lapp population of the north, in the administrative unit of Lappi; though this comprises nearly one-third of the total area of the country, there are only about 1,300 Lapps.

REGIONS

1. The Northern Lands

The land rises gently northward from the Gulf of Bothnia towards the low rocky ranges which form the somewhat indeterminate Baltic–Arctic divide. These hills, rising but little above 300 m (1000 ft), are known as the Maanselkä in the east and as the Sualaselkä near the Norwegian frontier. In the extreme north-west a narrow promontory of Finnish territory (the 'Enontekio salient') extends on to the high fjeld between Norway and Sweden; here is Finland's highest summit Haltiatunturi, 1324 m (4344 ft). To the north of the divide lies Lake Inari, the outlet of which, the river Pasvik, now forms the Norwegian–Russian boundary for most of its course, reaching the sea at Kirkenes.

The higher part of this region consists of tundra, but farther south towards the Gulf of Bothnia trees become more numerous and less stunted. Reindeer moss, heather and lichen, arctic birch, dwarf willow and alder gradually give place to conifers, though much bare rock and marsh results in a patchy tree cover; most of the forest in these rather remote lands is owned by the State. Until recently these northern areas were inhabited only by Lapps, with their herds of migratory reindeer grazing on the moss pastures. Finnish pioneer settlers have penetrated into the north, living by small-scale agriculture, the keeping of livestock and forestry; some rear reindeer, and are members of a Central Reindeer Breeders' Association. Farther south the amount of settlement increases, though existence is still hard; farms consist of prefabricated buildings, surrounded by a little arable and pasture, and bounded by the edge of the forest.

2. The Central Lake Plateau

Central Finland consists of an undulating peneplain, varying in height from 75 to 150 m (250 to 500 ft) above sea-level, with occasional masses of granite forming rounded hillocks. The uneven surface is studded with a maze of interconnected lakes; the drainage is confused and immature and few river systems of any size have developed. In the south-east the largest river, the Vuoksi, flows from Lake Saimaa into Lake Ladoga, now within Russian territory. In the south-west the Kökemäki drains a considerable area, many short parallel streams flow westward to the Gulf of Bothnia, and the larger Oulu enters the head of the Gulf just east of the Swedish frontier. The plateau is bounded in the south by the Salpausselkä moraines, which end in the west in the sandy spur of the Hanko peninsula. Streams flowing southward to the Gulf of Finland have been harnessed for the production of water-power, as have some of the rapids between lakes at different levels on the plateau.

A large part of the land surface is forested, mostly with pine and spruce; some stands have been planted after earlier logging. Agriculture has penetrated parts of the Lake Plateau, though the extent of level land and good soil is small; low-lying swampy areas have been drained and reclaimed to grow grass for hay, with some barley, oats and potatoes.

Kuopio in the north is on the railway and is also a centre for lake navigation, shipping timber to the south. In the south-west Tampere (152,000), founded in 1782, is now the largest inland industrial town, with saw mills and paper mills, a works making railway locomotives, tanneries and leather factories, timber yards and cotton mills. Tampere is the largest textile-making centre in northern Europe, partly by an historical accident, for a Scottish immigrant installed the first cotton mill in 1820. Power is generated at a large hydro-station on the Tammerkoski river. Lahti (87,000), situated at the southern margin of the Lake Plateau, is a centre of timber industries, the chief furniture-making town, and also has factories making plywood and textiles, and several breweries.

3. *The Coastal Plains*

A lowland extends inland for 80–100 km (50–60 miles) along the coast of the Gulf of Bothnia (a region known as Ostrobothnia) and of the Gulf of Finland. Much of this lowland, once covered by the sea, has been exposed by the gradual uplift in postglacial times which has continued with minor fluctuations to the present; indeed, the original harbour of Vaasa lies 10 km (6 miles) inland from the present port on the Gulf of Bothnia. Parts of these coastal lowlands have been drained and reclaimed to form good agricultural land.

In the south-west the coast is bordered by an archipelago of small, irregularly shaped islands and reefs, Skärgårds-Finland. The largest group, the Åland Islands, is situated only 40 km (25 miles) from the Swedish skerries; its neutral and demilitarized status was confirmed by a decision of the League of Nations. This archipelago is structurally complex, the rocks consisting mainly of granite and other igneous rocks, fractured by an intersecting maze of faultlines. By contrast, the Ångskärsfjörd is a circular bay surrounded by a concentric pattern of irregular islands, outlined by circular faults and ring dykes. In parts the surface of the islands carries a cover of moraine, fluvioglacial gravels and sands, clay and peat in depressions. Farther north in the Gulf of Bothnia is the smaller Vaasa archipelago.

The coastal plain is veneered in places with clay which yields good soils, though here too large patches of sands and gravels are less useful, and the Salpausselkä crosses the plain in the south. The south coast has a more genial climate than the rest of the country; this is the chief farming area, though only about 14 per cent is under cultivation and 70 per cent is still wooded, mostly with conifers but also with some deciduous trees, even a few oaks. Oats, rye, potatoes and a little beet are grown, and permanent grassland provides summer grazing and winter hay. Dairy cattle have increased in numbers, as have the co-operative creameries for butter production.

Over half of the Finnish population live along the coast, over 700,000 in and around Helsinki, founded in the sixteenth century, which became the capital in 1817. Except in mild winters, its port is usually closed in spite of icebreakers for a varying period between February and April, though it has a fine roadstead and extensive quays. Its various industries include timber-working, light engineering, the manufacture of consumer goods, and quality products such as furniture, textiles, glass and pottery. Turku, the first capital of Finland, is now its third town with 150,000 people, and has textile mills, shipyards, marine engineering and diesel works. Farther west is Hanko, Finland's normally ice-free port, which was reached by rail in 1872; its importance as a winter port depends on the severity of the winter and the length of period of closure of other ports. On the Gulf of Bothnia Vaasa (49,000) and Kokkola have sawmills and timber-using industries. Kotka (34,000) in the east near the Russian boundary handles a large export of pulp and paper, and since the loss of Viipuri has become Finland's chief timber port. Its twin, Karhula, on the

Plate XIII. 'Young Moraine' landscape in Jutland, Denmark

Plate XIV. The reclamation of heathland in northern Jutland, east of Holstebro

Plates XV–XVII. Three stages in the reclamation of tidal mud-flats on the island of Römö, western Denmark. Note the wicker fences which are used to accelerate the accretion of mud

opposite (western) bank of the Kymi river, is a new industrial town, specializing in manufactures of steel and glass.

About 70,000 people live in the islands, 22,000 of them in the Åland Islands. From the port of Mariehamn in the south the square-rigged sailing ships left for the Australian 'grain races', last held in 1949. Some inhabitants are fishermen, and the rather better clay soils on some of the islands, with a milder climate than elsewhere, encourage a diversified agriculture, mainly fodder crops for dairy animals, and some cereals.

5

Denmark

THE kingdom of Denmark, a country about half the size of Scotland, comprises the peninsula of Jutland (Jylland), several large islands, and nearly 500 small ones, most of which are uninhabited. Jutland projects towards the angle of southern Scandinavia; its most northerly portion, terminating in the sandspit of the Skaw, is separated from the rest by the winding inlet of the Limfjord. The west coast of Jutland faces the North Sea, beyond the Skaw is the Skagerrak, and to the east lies the Kattegat. The straits between Jutland and Sweden consist of the now bridged Little Belt, the Great Belt between Funen (Fyn) and Zealand (Sjaelland), and the Sound (the Öresund) between Zealand and Sweden (Fig. 16).

STRUCTURE AND RELIEF

Structure

From the point of view of structure, relief and landscape, Denmark is part of the North European Plain, for only Bornholm, a granitic island in the Baltic Sea, is composed of ancient rocks similar to those of the Scandinavian peninsula. The rest of the country consists of Cretaceous and younger rocks, with an almost complete mantle of drift deposits, and more than half is less than 30 m (100 ft) above sea-level.

Far below the surface are ancient Pre-Cambrian granitic and gneissic rocks; deep borings have encountered granite at 900 m (2950 ft) in the island of Funen and at nearly 1280 m (4200 ft) in northern Jutland. These rocks represent the southward continuation of the Baltic Shield, forming the floor or basement of the eastern part of the North Sea basin, in which sediments have accumulated for some 200 million years. On this basement lie Permian rocks, mainly red sandstones and shales with layers of salt; some of the salt deposits in the Limfjord area have been forced upwards as domes to the base of the Quaternary rocks. The oldest rock to appear on the surface, except in Bornholm, is the Chalk of Late Cretaceous age, shaped like a saucer with its rim extending in an arc from northern Jutland through the eastern margins of the islands. The Chalk is revealed here and there along the coast; low cliffs can be seen east of Aalborg in northern Jutland, and in the islands of Zealand and Mön it forms some impressive cliffs, notably the Möns Klint rising to 137 m (450 ft). The Chalk is almost everywhere mantled with a variable thickness of newer rocks, mostly clays, marls and sandstones of Tertiary age. Parts of the southern islands are covered with Eocene clays, which form low but steep cliffs in places along the coast, as at Rögle Klint on the Little Belt where landslips on to the beach are common. Much of Jutland is covered with Miocene sands and clays; these contain occasional seams of brown coal, worked at a number of places during the acute fuel shortage of the War of 1939–45, and now burnt in power stations in Jutland and Funen. Some strata of volcanic ash are believed to be the product of Tertiary volcanic activity in southern Sweden. Like the Chalk, these Tertiary rocks appear only occasionally on the surface, usually along the coast, for they are masked almost everywhere by the products of the Quaternary glaciation, forming a terrain of low, gently undulating plains and rounded hills and ridges. Both the glacial and postglacial periods were complicated by several marine transgressions.

The Quaternary Glaciation

Several distinct advances of icesheets from the Scandinavian and Baltic dispersal centres (p. 21) covered Denmark, as the evidence of distinctive erratics has shown. The effects were partly erosive; the advancing icesheets planed off the rocks in the sedimentary basin, so that the oldest rocks now outcrop concentrically on the northern and eastern margins. But more important, certainly in the later stages, was the widespread deposition of glacial material. The first (Elster) and second (Saale) glacial periods in Denmark directly affected the whole country, and their distinctive tills can be identified. During each interglacial period a marine transgression was experienced; the first covered all Denmark, laying down clays, while the second affected only eastern Jutland and the islands, for western Jutland apparently stood above the level of the sea. This is shown by subaerially eroded valleys in the older till and by the deposition of freshwater sands and clays.

The third (Weichsel) glaciation did not affect the whole country, but clays of the ground-moraine were laid down over eastern Jutland and the islands, forming most of their present undulating surfaces.

The terminal moraines run southward more or less through the centre of Jutland, forming lines of hummocky hills about 150 m (500 ft) in height (Plate XIII); the highest point in Denmark is a gentle eminence which attains 172 m (565 ft). These morainic hills, part of the Baltic Heights, separate two distinctive types of physical landscape (Fig. 17).

Relief

To the west are sheets of outwash sands and gravels, deposited by fluvioglacial streams draining from the icefront during the standstill at the maximum of the final glacial advance. These form gently undulating lowlands crossed by broad shallow outwash channels, the deposits becoming successively finer towards the west. Here and there rounded, broad-backed eminences of till, the product of the second (Saale) glacial period, swell gently as 'hill-islands' above the outwash materials around them; some rise to over 60 m (200 ft). The mature features of these hillocks, the result of weathering, solifluction and erosion by many small streams, show that they are the product of an earlier glaciation than that responsible for the main morainic ridges to the east. Small streams wander indeterminately through boggy depressions towards the dune-lined west coast, which is bordered in places by sandy beaches, offshore bars, small islands and tidal mud-flats (Plates XV–XVII).

To the north and east of the main terminal moraine lies the ground-moraine, gently undulating sheets of clay diversified by drumlins and eskers. Several other lines of terminal moraine can be traced in eastern Jutland, across Funen, and on Zealand parallel to the east coast; these represent successive pauses in the recession of the Weichsel ice-sheets, or possibly minor readvances. Many valleys and hollows diversify the landscape; some are 'tunnel valleys' eroded by subglacial meltwater streams, others are 'kettle-holes' formed by the melting of isolated ice blocks, others are valleys cut by melt-water streams along the ice-front, others are the result of the development of the still immature postglacial drainage system. Small lakes and peat bogs have accumulated in the depressions, though many have been drained by man or infilled naturally, while some valleys form water-less troughs among the moraines. The coastline of eastern Jutland is characterized on the one hand by open bays, probably carved by lobes of the ice-sheet, on the other hand by long winding inlets known as fjords (though quite different from the Norwegian variety), worn by melt-water torrents draining from under the icesheets and later inundated by marine transgression.

Farther east in the islands the lighter morainic deposits afford a smoother landscape than in Jutland. The low clay-covered plains are flat or slightly undulating, though interrupted by occasional

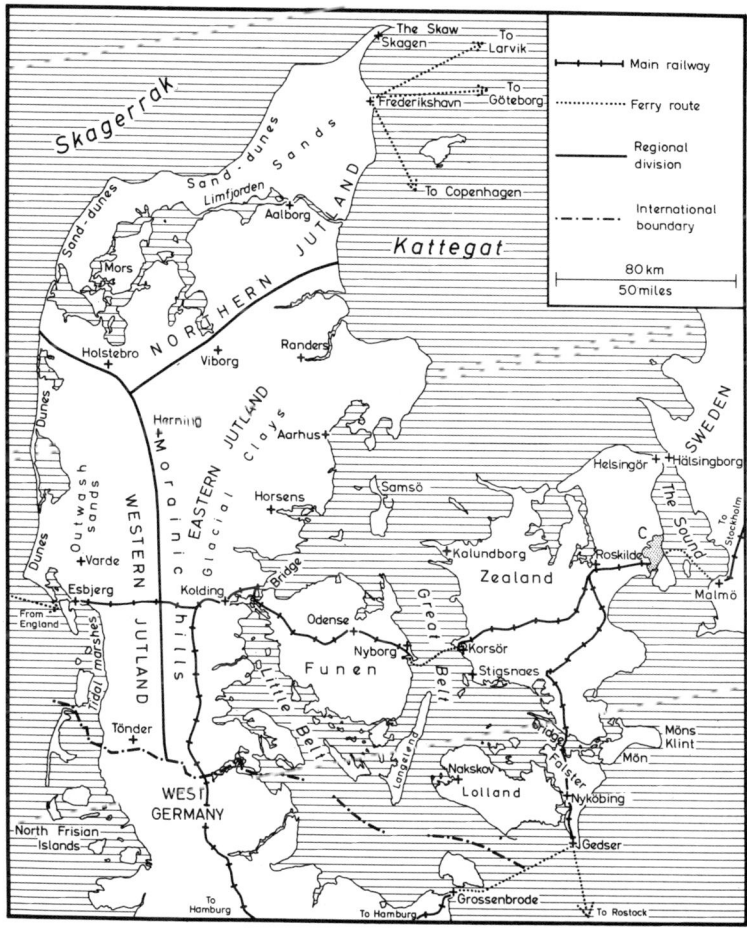

Fig. 16. Regional divisions of Denmark
A new ferry-route has been opened from Rödby on the southern coast of Lolland across the Fehmarn Belt to Puttgarden on Fehmarn island in West Germany.

belts of terminal moraine rising 30–50 m (100–160 ft) above the general level.

Another contribution, accounting for about 10 per cent of the total area, consists of coastal forelands built up by marine sedimentation and now revealed by the late-glacial or postglacial uplift of the sea-floor, as along the shores of the Limfjord. Other coastal flats are the result of the natural accretion of sand, mud and salt-marsh. Along the west and north coasts large areas of dunes have accumulated from blown beach sand.

CLIMATE

The climate of Denmark does not differ appreciably from that of eastern England, though the country is not so open to the ameliorating effects of the Atlantic Ocean. Denmark is more exposed to influences from the east, and very cold spells may be experienced when Polar Continental air masses extend westward from the Eurasian land mass; the country thus lies in a transition region. Because of its small area and low relief, there are no marked differences in climate between one part and another. The 0° C. January isotherm runs from north to south along the length of Jutland; places to the west have means slightly above 0° C., those to the east slightly below. The west coasts experience 70 to 80 days annually with frost, those in the east 110 to 120. Sea ice is rare off western Jutland, though the calm less saline waters along the shores of the Belts, the Sound and the Kattegat may freeze for several weeks during severe winters. During the summer most parts experience mean temperatures between 15° and 20° C.

The country is low-lying and precipitation is nowhere high; western Jutland has an annual average of 635–740 mm (25–29 in), Copenhagen of about 530 mm (21 in). The rainfall on the whole is well distributed, mainly the result of depressions from the west, though August usually reveals a slight maximum because of additional convectional effects.

LAND USE AND AGRICULTURE

About 75 per cent of the surface of Denmark comprises arable land, and permanent pasture a further 9 per cent; the remainder is under woodland (10 per cent) and heath, moor and bog (7 per cent).

Vegetation

The tundra conditions of immediately postglacial times were succeeded in Denmark by birch–pine and then by pine–hazel forests which, as the climate ameliorated during the Atlantic climatic phase, gradually changed to mixed forest in which the oak was dominant. The cool moist conditions which have obtained since about 500 B.C. have caused the beech to become the dominant woodland tree, particularly in the parks and estates of Zealand where they have been carefully preserved. There is much evidence of the former woodland, both from tree trunks found in bogs and from pollen analysis of peat. But since Neolithic times man has lived in this area, and clearance of the forest for cultivation has gone on steadily. The woodland removed from the lighter sandier soils was replaced naturally by heathland, and *Calluna* (ling) and its associates probably covered more than half of Jutland by the eighteenth century.

Land Holding

At the end of the eighteenth century Danish agriculture was still of an almost medieval character; a few hundred lords of the manor owned 80 per cent of the land, and the rest belonged to the Crown or the Church. Some peasants possessed their own plots, but the majority were tenants or serf-like labourers, bound to the land under the manorial system. A holding consisted of a number of strips scattered among the open fields, farmed from a homestead in a central village. For example, in the village of Hejninge in western Zealand a single farm was made up of 115 strips, reallocated annually, and spread throughout the three large fields, one of which was in fallow each year. An Act of 1781 abolished the common-field system, enabling a holder of land to demand that his scattered strips should be exchanged for a single plot, a process of consolidation which attained its major results in the two decades after 1790.

The succeeding century and a half was to see a series of evolutionary, rather than revolutionary, changes in the whole pattern of rural life and the organization of agriculture. A bloodless political revolution in 1784 led to reforms involving on the one hand the emancipation of the tenants, on the other hand changes in land tenure, starting on Crown land and spreading rapidly throughout the country. One feature has been the voluntary break-up of large estates. Government policy has assisted in the creation of a pattern of independent smallholdings by helping the peasants with loans to purchase their rented land. As a result, by 1885 nearly 90 per cent of the workers owned the land they farmed, and the remaining tenants were given security of tenure, long leases and fixed rents. Since 1899 a Government Land Law Board has operated as an agency to buy at full market prices large estates which have come into the open market; compulsory purchase has never been used. This land remains in State ownership, but the estates are divided into lots upon each of which a family is settled, helped by an initial loan. Some 35,000 of these smallholdings have been thus created since 1899; hedges between them are avoided so as not to waste land, and electrified fences are now commonly used.

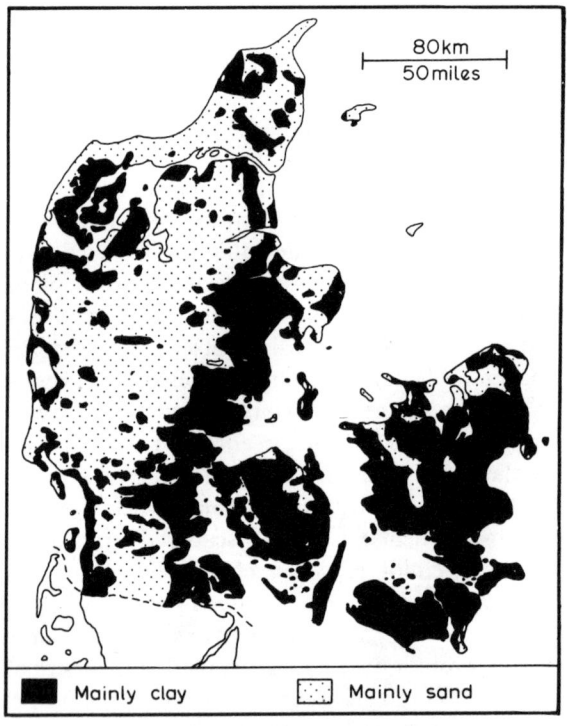

Fig. 17. Main soil groups in Denmark
(After R. Millward)

The net result was that Denmark became a country of small proprietors. There was no industrial revolution to draw men from the land into the towns, or to create an aristocracy of wealth, and an individual was prohibited by law, save in very special circumstances, from owning more than two farms. By the mid-1950's, therefore, Denmark was a country of about 200,000 farms, of which nearly half were smaller than 10 ha (25 acres).

But since then radical changes have occurred, involving a considerable reduction in the number of holdings (of which there are now about 150,000), and an increase in the number of large, heavily capitalised farms, with a greater degree of specialisation and mechanization. The paid labour force has diminished from about 145,000 in 1959 to 44,000 in 1969, though productivity has increased by 15 per cent. Many of the former very small units have either merged to form larger, more viable holdings, or have become market-gardens worked on a part-time basis. About a quarter of all agricultural workers are paid employees, a much higher proportion than in the other Scandinavian countries. This is partly because general inflationary trends and high land prices in recent years have made it increasingly difficult for young people to purchase farms.

Land Reclamation

During the last 150 years, additional land for new smallholdings has been made available, which has involved the reclamation of marshland and bog, both along the coast and inland, and the bringing under cultivation of the heaths which once covered much of western Jutland. In 1780 barely two-fifths of the peninsula was cultivated, and even though the clay soils of the islands presented less difficulty, in all a quarter of Denmark was then agriculturally unproductive.

The reclamation of the heathlands proceeded gradually with the progress of consolidation and with the disappearance of common lands. An impetus was given with the founding of the Danish Heath Society in 1866, stimulated by the loss of Schleswig-Holstein to Prussia in that year, as indicated by the motto of the Society, 'What was outwardly lost shall be inwardly won.' The chief need in the heathlands is the addition of lime to counteract the acid podzolized soil and of marl to make it more coherent. The poorest areas of sand-dunes have been planted with conifers, which grow quite well and also help to prevent the movement of the dunes by the wind; since 1880 about 700 million trees, mainly spruce, Scots pine and silver fir, have been planted in Jutland as wind-breaks and shelter-belts, and marram grass covers much of the dunes. In the inland bogs the peat is stripped off, sometimes for use as domestic fuel, the underlying hardpan is broken by deep ploughing, and drains and ditches are constructed. The success of these measures has resulted in a reduction of the heath in Jutland from about 1·2 million ha (3 million acres) in 1800 to 240 000 ha (600,000 acres), from 40 to 8 per cent of the total area of the peninsula (Plate XIV). So much of the heath vanished that in 1942 the Danish Heath Society acquired an area in the Alheden district of Jutland to preserve as the Kongenshus Memorial Park to show what heath was really like.

Along the coast tidal mud-flats have been dyked and drained; in bays along the Jutland coast the construction of wicker fences has stimulated the accretion of silt and the progressive reclamation from mud-flats to rich pasture (Plates XV–XVII). Numerous small lakes in hollows on the ground-moraine surface have also been drained.

These programmes of reclamation were particularly active during the latter part of the nineteenth century, but they are still important, as more land is taken over for non-agricultural purposes while the population continues to increase.

The Pattern of Agriculture

The pattern of farming practice changed radically during the 'seventies of the last century, before which Denmark was primarily a grain-producing country with an economy based on the export of wheat. Yields were high, the result of the steady improvement in methods brought about by land consolidation and by the Agrarian Revolution, in which Denmark was not much behind Britain. The industrial countries of western Europe, particularly Germany and Britain, were good markets for Danish wheat. But the opening-up of the North American prairies and the reduction of ocean freight rates (which were halved in a decade between 1865 and 1875) flooded Europe with cheap wheat. Denmark, despite its proximity to its customers, could not compete because of higher production costs. Some countries met the competition with tariff barriers to maintain the price of home-grown wheat, but Denmark proceeded to reorientate its economy. It was realized that it was more profitable to turn grain into perishable dairy produce for adjacent markets by using it as fodder, and in addition to take advantage of this cheap American grain to expand the livestock industry.

Even before this agricultural crisis, exports of livestock products had risen as a result of improved farming practices; in 1866 about 58 per cent of the agricultural exports consisted of grain, but by 1878 this had fallen to 28 per cent and a decade later it had virtually disappeared. This change in agricultural practice was due not to direct government action, but to the pioneer work of individuals and societies, though with some government stimulus and financial assistance.

Arable Farming

The farmland has remained largely arable, and in 1968 only about 6 per cent was under permanent grass, comprising water-meadows, salt-marsh and bog-pasture, found mainly in coastal and west-central Jutland. The pattern of arable cultivation reveals a combination of feed-grain, other fodder crops and intensive grass production. Barley occupies 52 per cent of the total arable, mainly in the islands, supplemented with oats, 'mixed grains' of oats, barley, peas and vetches, rye chiefly on the poorer sandy lands in Jutland, and wheat. Practically all this grain, except for some high quality malting barley, is fed to animals, even the wheat, which is too soft for bread-making. The total yield of cereals has trebled between 1914 and 1968, which has helped the economy considerably, since high world prices have enforced a reduction in the importation of feed grains and oil-cake.

About a sixth of the arable land is under such root crops as fodder beet, kohlrabi, sugar beet (especially on the better soils in Lolland and Falster) and mangolds, and a further 4 per cent grows potatoes. Quality strains of potatoes are cultivated as hardy seed for export, but the bulk of the crop is for home consumption, and considerable quantities are used for the manufacture of starch, alcohol and potato flour. A third of the arable land is under green fodder crops (lucerne, clover and trefoil) and rotational short-ley grass grown for silage and for processing into pellets and briquettes. Cereals and sugar beet dominate in the islands, grass in Jutland.

Careful methods of tillage, the heavy use of fertilizers and the development of disease-resistant hybrid seed have increased yields to the highest in Europe. Cultivation is intensive and mechanized, fallow has been almost eliminated since land cannot afford to lie idle, and modern methods of weed control are used. Many fields are underlain by extensive systems of tile drains to remove winter ground-water from the clay soils, so that farmers can work the land in early spring.

Livestock

This intensity of cultivation, together with supplementary imported feeding stuffs, enables large numbers of livestock to be kept. In 1968 there were 3·1 million cattle and 8·0 million pigs, compared with about 3 million and 2·8 million respectively in 1938. Careful breeding has developed pedigree stocks of cattle which give milk of high butterfat content, and Denmark was the first country to eradicate wholly bovine tuberculosis. Friesians and Jerseys have replaced the Jutland and Red Danish breeds of cattle. About 13 per cent of the milk output is sold in liquid form, including large quantities to the U.S. Forces in Europe, the rest is processed into butter, cheese, milk powder and casein. The output of cheese, including such famous types as 'Danish Blue', has increased notably.

There are two other reasons why the standard of Danish agriculture is so high; the first is the widespread use of co-operative methods, the second is the intelligent and progressive nature of the farming population, helped by an outstanding educational system.

Co-operation

Where production is in the hands of a large number of small-holders, some form of co-operation is obviously necessary in order to maintain uniform standards of quality, and to organize collection, processing and marketing so as to obtain the best prices on the world markets. Co-operative dairies, bacon factories, and egg-packing stations have grown up over the country, since the first was established at Hjedding in 1882. Some co-operatives are supply societies, buying fertilizers, feeding-stuffs and implements in bulk for distribution to their members, others are credit societies supplying farmers with long-term low interest loans for the purchase of farms, stock and equipment. Other societies are concerned with animal breeding, butterfat records, insurance, advisory services, and research (Plate XVIII). They are grouped into the Federation of Danish Co-operative Societies which, working with the Federation of Danish Farmers' Unions, have established an Agricultural Council to represent farmers' interests to the government. Such organizations as the Danish Agricultural Marketing Board and its associates ensure quality and uniformity of produce by strict control, enforced by Government inspection; all exports must carry the famous '*Lurmark*' stamp of quality. The development of Danish agriculture is due to the enterprise of the farmers themselves, not of the Government, though the latter may be invited by associations to exercise some control. Farming receives no government subsidies or protective tariffs.

Agricultural Problems and Policies

Denmark has had to face many problems as a result of its high degree of dependence on world markets. The Allied blockade during the War of 1914–18 and the German occupation of 1940–45 cut off both supplies of feeding stuffs and markets; on each occasion a large proportion of the herds was slaughtered. Competition has been increased with the development of refrigeration, enabling more distant producers to compete successfully, and tariffs and quotas (particularly in Britain in favour of Commonwealth countries) have adversely affected Denmark.

For five years after the War of 1940–45 ended, the Ministry of Agriculture was obliged to exercise close control of agricultural exports, by establishing special boards on which the co-operatives and the commercial firms were represented. These were abolished in 1950, but voluntary national export associations have been retained in order to advise on export policy, to ensure the best possible sales in overseas markets, and to negotiate long-term agreements. This was particularly necessary, as between 1946 and 1950 Danish warehouses were filled with produce which other European countries could not afford to buy.

However, the economic recovery of western Europe, the revival of purchasing power and a substantial rise in standards of living have helped Danish exporters. Both output and exports are far higher than before 1939, though achieved by a decrease in the number of workers on the land from 480,000 to only about 200,000. Mechanization and specialisation account for this; for example, between 1939 and 1967, the number of tractors increased from 2,600 to 176,000, and there has been a great increase in the number of pig-, calf- and broiler-houses for intensive production. The net result of this agricultural development is that Denmark supplies more than half of the bacon entering into world commerce, and a quarter of the butter, cheese and eggs. Livestock products now comprise about 42 per cent of exports by value, compared with 55 per cent a decade ago.

By 1968 only about 13 per cent of the working population was exclusively employed in agriculture (compared with 23 per cent in 1960), while 59 per cent were engaged in manufacturing and commerce.

FISHERIES

Situated conveniently between the grounds of the North Sea and those of the Baltic, Denmark has a valuable fishing industry, landing about 750,000 tons annually. A third is taken from the North Sea and the Skagerrak, based on Esbjerg, Hvidesande, Tyborön, Hirtshals and the new port of Hanstholm. There is a little small-boat inshore fishing along the exposed west coast, and mainly large cutters fish for plaice, cod and haddock. In the waters around the Skaw, in the Kattegat and the Belts, fishing takes place from the three large ports, Skagen, the chief Danish fishing port by weight of catch, Frederikshavn and Grenaa, and also from numerous small villages, piers and even open beaches. The main fishing port on Bornholm is Rönne. Herring, whiting, mackerel and plaice are caught, with eels in the bays and sheltered coastal waters, especially in the Limfjord, most of which are exported alive, the rest smoked for home use. A variety of other species, including crustaceans and shellfish, is caught both for home consumption and export.

A large quantity of fish is canned or smoked, or processed for oil, and waste products are turned into fertilizers.

MANUFACTURING INDUSTRY

Denmark possesses few of the basic raw materials, nor any form of power resource except for a little brown coal. Manufacturing followed slowly on the heels of agriculture, yet today it employs one-third of the Danish workers. Obviously the most important branch is food-processing, including the preparation of butter, cheese and bacon, the condensing and canning of milk, the manufacture of dried milk and casein, the refining of sugar beet, the expressing of vegetable oil from imported seeds, the making of cattle cake, the production of beverages such as lager, and the manufacture of margarine, of which the Danes eat more per head than any other European country so that more butter can be exported. Three large breweries in Copenhagen produce 90 per cent of Danish beer, much for export, and several distilleries make noted liqueurs, including 'Cherry Heering'. The total value of processed foodstuffs is greater than that of any other manufactured product, though in numbers of workers employed it ranks only fourth. The large home market for fertilizers has stimulated their large-scale manufacture, using imported phosphates and other raw chemicals, together with waste from the abattoirs and fish canneries. Insulin, hormones, vaccines and other biochemical preparations are further valuable byproducts. Another response to agriculture is the manufacture of such equipment as milking machinery and farm implements; the mechanical cream separator was invented by a Dane.

After food-processing, engineering is the leading manufacturing industry, both in numbers of workers employed and in value of output. Diesel engines, marine engines and motor vessels are made mainly in the Copenhagen district, where more than half the shipyards are located; others are at Odense, Nakskov and Helsingör (Plate XIX). In 1898 the old-established firm of *Burmeister and Wain* bought the patent rights of a new type of power unit invented by Rudolf Diesel; since then they have been one of the world's leading makers of diesel engines and have equipped more than half of the world's motor vessels, directly or under licence. The first diesel-powered motor ship was completed in 1912 in the Copenhagen yards, and tankers and whaling ships are also built.

Another industry of major importance is the production of cement, based on the deposits of pure chalk and Lower Eocene clay easily accessible beneath a thin cover of glacial drift, almost the only home-produced raw material. The large cement-works, grouped around the chalk quarries near the Limfjord and the Mariager-fjord, produce annually more than a million tons, of which 40 per cent is exported to over sixty countries. Almost all the cement works are combined in a single corporation, with a highly efficient sales organization. A Danish firm, the world's largest manufacturer of cement-making machinery, claims to have supplied a thousand cement works throughout the world. Lower Eocene clays containing diatomaceous material are made into refractory bricks. Another development, the result of experience in reinforced and precast concrete construction, is the carrying out of large-scale public works in many countries by Danish construction companies. A refinery in Copenhagen processes cryolite from Greenland, exported to various countries with aluminium smelters.

A prosperous agriculture has naturally created a large consumer market for light industry, though this is wholly dependent on im-ported fuel and raw materials. This activity is concentrated in Copenhagen, and includes light engineering products, leather and leather goods, a wide range of pharmaceutical chemicals, furniture, textiles and apparel, rubber articles, silverware, and pottery such as the famous Royal Danish ware made from kaolin quarried in Bornholm. Some of these handicrafts have attained a high reputa-tion, and the wares are to be seen in the shopping streets of the world's cities. For example, Georg Jensen, whose name is synonym-ous with quality silverware, established his workshop in Copenhagen in 1904, and his hallmark and those of half a dozen other firms are internationally known; more than half the silver is exported to the U.S.A., directly or taken by tourists. During the last decade exports of furniture of elegant design have increased to such an extent that their value now exceeds that of silver and porcelain. These craft industries have been stimulated by international exhibitions and shrewd advertising.

Manufacturing has, in short, developed remarkably; on the basis of an index of industrial production of 100 for 1963, that for 1967 was 127.

Fuel and Power

One of the most serious industrial deficiencies is a source of power, and as a result Denmark's largest category of imports is fuel, mainly oil and coal. Much of the coal, together with some home-produced brown coal, is consumed in large thermal generators, and the output of electricity has increased steadily from 1·69 milliard KWh in 1949 to 11·7 in 1968. A policy of building new large-scale plants has led to a reduction in the number of power stations. Denmark imports power from Sweden by underwater cable, nearly a million KWh annually, though in very severe winters when hard frosts close the Swedish hydro-stations, the direction of current is reversed, and power from Copenhagen's large thermal stations is sold to Sweden.

There are four oil refineries in Denmark: a small one near Copenhagen, another owned by *Esso* at Kalundborg on the north-western coast of Zealand, a *Shell* refinery at Fredericia, and in 1963 the *Gulf Oil Corporation* completed a large refinery near Stigsnaes on the south-western coast of Zealand. The site was chosen partly because of the deep water off-shore, which allows 100,000-ton tankers to berth, partly because of its central position from which coastal tankers can supply *Gulf* depots in Scandinavia.

COMMUNICATIONS

Roads and Railways

Denmark's road and rail systems are not faced with any relief problems, though the morainic surface is undulating and gradient profiles are in places more pronounced than might be expected. The main difficulties are the separate islands and the elongated inlets which penetrate the coasts; long bridges and 240 km (150 miles) of ferries, conveying both cars and trains, are therefore a feature of the communications pattern. Fortunately, the Baltic is virtually tideless. The length of the railway system in 3358 km (2087 miles); about a third is privately owned, the rest, including the main lines serving the principal urban centres and carrying a large proportion of passengers and freight, is state-owned. The efficiently operated train ferries

enable speedy through-journeys to be made; the most notable route
is the main line across the country from Esbjerg, over the Little Belt
bridge to Funen, then via the 26 km (16 miles) Nyborg–Korsör ferry
across the Great Belt to Zealand and Copenhagen, followed by the

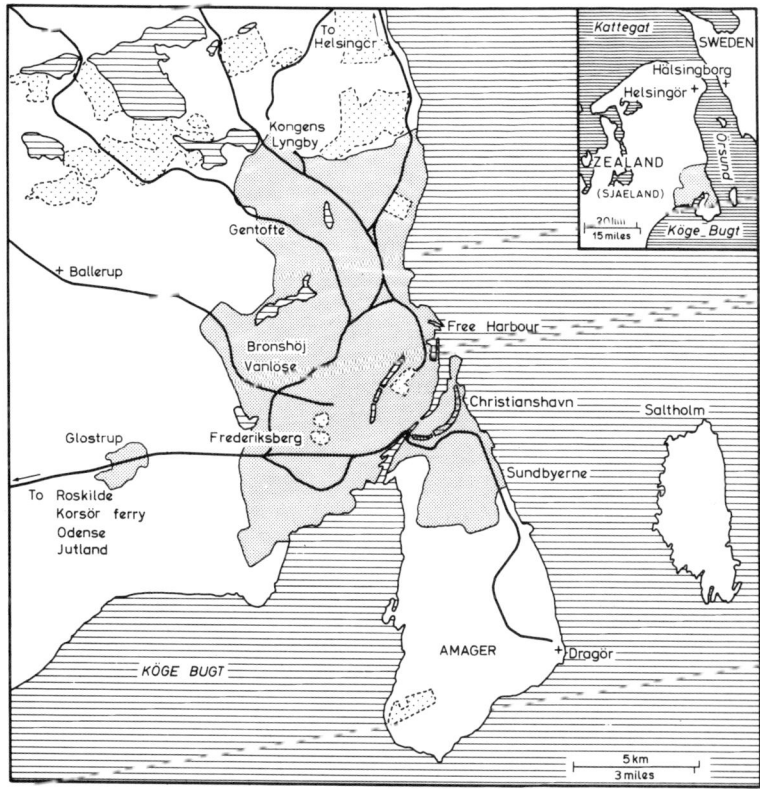

Fig. 18. Copenhagen

Copenhagen–Malmö ferry of similar distance to Sweden, and so to
Stockholm. Another international ferry links Helsingör with Hälsingborg across the northern end of the Sound, and there are several
inter-island ferries.

The main bridges and ferries are shown on Fig. 16. The Little
Belt Bridge between Jutland and Funen, 825 m (2707 ft) in length,
was completed in 1935. The magnificent fifty-span Storströminen
bridge between Zealand and the little island of Masnedö, 3221 m
(10,567 ft) in length (the second longest over-water bridge in Europe)
and carrying both road and railway, was opened in 1937. With the

shorter six-span Masnedsund bridge joining Masnedö with Falster, also completed in 1937, it forms an important link for both road and rail traffic. Another bridge crosses the narrow strait to the island of Lolland, on the southern shore of which Rödby is the ferry-port for the recently inaugurated service across to Puttgarden on Fehmarn, West Germany. The Svendborg Sound bridge between Funen and Taasinge was opened in 1967. A bridge has been proposed to cross the Great Belt, and another across the Sound via the island of Saltholm.

Ports

The position of the archipelago across the passage between the Baltic and North Seas has given Denmark a particular importance, both because in earlier days it could control this passage and for long was an important naval power, and also because its ports could develop as entrepôts for Baltic commerce. The main ports are Copenhagen (Fig. 18) at the south-western end of the Sound between Zealand and Sweden, Aalborg near the eastern end of the Lim-fjord, Aarhus on a large sheltered bay in eastern Jutland, and Frederikshavn on a rather exposed site on the open coast of the Skaw. Odense, the chief town and port of Funen, lies about thirteen miles from the sea, but with access via the Odensefjord and a canal it has a considerable traffic. Numerous smaller ports serve the islands, and much internal freight traffic goes by coasting steamer.

After the Industrial Revolution and the reorientation of agri-culture towards the markets of western Europe, Denmark's economic outlook began to turn westward, though maintaining its Baltic interests. The shallow, marshy and dune-fringed North Sea coast presented no natural port sites of any value, so the harbour of Esb-jerg had to be created artificially in a not very promising position. This has now developed as a major ferry- and container-terminal.

Mercantile Marine

As a result both of its location and its long naval history, it is not surprising to find that Denmark has a considerable mercantile marine, totalling 3·2 million tons and ranking fourteenth in world order. In tonnage per head of population, Denmark is exceeded only by Liberia, Japan and Norway. The Danish fleet is modern, partly because of the heavy wartime losses, but mainly because of a policy of efficient replacement; about a third of the tonnage consists of tankers, another third of special refrigerated cargo ships.

Numerous small vessels carry on a busy coastwise internal trade, transporting about 3 million tons of freight annually, rather less than that carried by the railways.

COMMERCE

About a quarter of Danish exports by value go to Great Britain, a fifteenth each to West Germany and Sweden, and a tenth to the U.S.A. The proportions sent to Britain and Germany are much less than in prewar years, an indication of the diversification of Denmark's interests; the *per capita* value of its foreign trade is now the highest in the world. A striking change has taken place in the nature of trade during the last thirty or forty years. After the War of 1914–18 the pattern was fairly simple, comprising exports of agricultural produce and imports of manufactures. In the decade before the War of 1940–45, imports of raw materials steadily increased in place of manufactures, though exports still consisted largely of agricultural produce. Since 1945 the export of manufactured goods has substantially increased; this category now occupies about 45 per cent of the total by value, while agricultural commodities comprise about a third.

POPULATION

The population of Denmark in 1968 totalled 4,849,000, rather more than four times the figure at the census of 1801. At that time about 100,000 people lived in Copenhagen, and about the same number in other provincial towns; four-fifths lived in nucleated villages and small towns among the open fields or along the coast, and isolated farms were rare.

Two main changes have occurred. As the open fields were abolished and the strips consolidated, farms were rebuilt within their own land, and the rural pattern is now one of fairly evenly distributed farmsteads, each usually built around a rectangular courtyard, with villages at intervals functioning as service centres, generally with one or more co-operatives.

The other change is the growth of the urban population, which now comprises 70 per cent of the total. This has not resulted in rural depopulation, as has happened in so many western European countries; some movement to the towns was inevitable, but it has been less than the natural increase in the rural areas. Copenhagen and the provincial towns accounted in 1801 for about 20 per cent of the total population, but the proportion has now increased to 50 per cent; Copenhagen itself contains 835,000 people, about 18 per cent of the total, a higher proportion for a capital than for any other country but Austria. The disproportion in size between the capital and other towns is exceptional, for with suburbs and adjacent small towns the total is over 1·2 million. The second town, Aarhus, is a provincial centre with 187,000 people, followed by Odense and Aalborg. Only twelve Danish towns have populations exceeding 25,000; most serve as commercial centres for the district around and few have any industrial activity. Some, such as Randers and Kolding, grew up at the heads of fjords where a river could be bridged, others are ferry ports, such as Helsingör, which once collected dues from all shipping passing through the Sound, and Korsör and Nyborg at either side of the Great Belt. Some towns owe their origin or growth to their being religious centres (Odense and Viborg), fishing ports (Esbjerg, Hirtshals, Skagen, Frederikshavn), railway towns (Esbjerg and Herning), fortress towns (Fredericia), and tourist resorts (along the northern coast of Zealand). Only in a few of the larger towns,notably Copenhagen, Odense and Aarhus, has manufacturing industry contributed notably to their growth.

About 1·7 million, or under a third of the total population, live in Jutland, the rest on the islands. Apart from the Greater Copenhagen area, the population is fairly uniformly spread, with no very marked contrasts in density or nature of settlement, since the country has neither industrial conurbations nor barren uplands. It is denser in the islands (Funen 190 per sq. km, 492 per sq. mile), and sparser in the heathlands of central and western Jutland (48–58 per sq. km, 124–150 per sq. mile), but the differences are matters of gentle gradation.

REGIONS (Fig. 16)

1. *Western Jutland*

The coast of south-western Jutland is bordered by wide sandy beaches, shallow lagoons, mud-flats and dunes; the dune-line is almost continuous for nearly 300 km (200 miles) from Skallingen to the Skaw. Several islands, notably Fanö, Mandö and Römö, the last linked to the mainland by a causeway, are a continuation of the German North Frisian Islands, formed by a late Quaternary rise of sea-level which broke through a former outer dune-line. The sea is shallow far offshore, though the exposure to westerly gales and the long fetch often cause widespread flooding through the onshore piling-up of water. To the north of Esbjerg the coast has been naturally straightened by the deposition of an almost continuous sand bar, sweeping northward in a smooth curve from Blaavands Huk. This is backed by shallow lagoons, such as Ringköbingfjord and Nissumfjord, which can be entered by small vessels through locks.

Inland from the coast is an undulating landscape of sand and gravel, from which rise the gently rounded 'hill-islands'. Reclamation of marsh, heath and moorland has gone on steadily during the last century (pp. 121–2), and most of the improved land is under rotation grass, mixed grain, rye on the poorer sandy soils, and potatoes, though parts have been planted with blocks of conifers.

Western Jutland is the least densely populated part of Denmark. Most people live in scattered farms, occasionally in larger clusters around road-junctions and railway stations. A few small towns, usually with a nucleus on a 'hill-island', stand amid the heathlands; originally they were centres from which reclamation was pushed forward, and now form market centres, with agricultural processing and servicing functions. They include Holstebro, Herning and Varde, each of about 10,000 inhabitants. Tönder is a small centre of communications, both for rail and road, near the West German boundary.

A few fishing harbours and boat landings are situated along the coast, but access from the sea is in most places extremely difficult. The chief town in the west, Esbjerg (57,000), was merely a village with thirty inhabitants in 1860. Its port was created partly to replace the loss to Germany of Tönning farther south, partly to foster trade with England by a direct route across the North Sea. The natural advantages of its site were few, though it stands on the only firm ground between the marsh-fringed coast to the south and the dune-fringed coast to the north. An offshore submerged glacial channel has helped to reduce the amount of necessary dredging, and the island of Fanö affords some protection from the west. Port works were started in 1869, with a dock enclosed by moles, and this has been developed so that the port now consists of a series of basins, with one exception all tidal and protected by breakwaters parallel to the coast, and about 20 km (12 miles) of quays. It is only the fourth Danish port in terms of tonnage handled, but it is the main one for English traffic, the terminus of the train ferry route from England to Copenhagen and Stockholm, it has a rapidly expanding container-traffic, and is the chief Danish fishing port. These are several co-operatives and processing plants for dairy produce, fish and meat.

2. *Northern Jutland*

This triangle of land to the north of the Limfjord is bordered by a series of wide, open bays, enclosed by blunt headlands of chalk or limestone and backed by lines of dunes. Much is covered with moraine, other parts with marine clays laid down during a late Quaternary transgression. Areas of sand are extensive, for dunes not only border the coast all the way to the Skaw, but have been blown inland; many villages in the past have been overwhelmed by the sand, and near Skagen a church tower stands among the dunes.

Large areas of northern Jutland are still under heath, moor and bog, bleak and windswept, forming a somewhat dreary landscape; trees are few, stunted and wind-bent. Some reclamation has taken place; oats and rye are grown as fodder, cattle are reared, large flocks of geese are kept, and sometimes tethered sheep can be seen.

The Limfjord is a shallow winding channel, 150 km (90 miles) in length, which links the North and Baltic Seas. It is possible for a shallow-draught vessel to sail right through, but except in the east as far as Aalborg the channels vary both in position and depth, and it is used only by small local vessels and fishing craft. Several little harbours, Lemvig, Struer and Nyköbing, are strung out along its shores.

Aalborg, situated 30 km (18 miles) from the Kattegat on the south side of the Limfjord and linked to its twin Nörre-Sundby on the opposite shore by both road and rail swing-bridges, is the second port of Denmark, though a long way behind Copenhagen. It is an old town, and during the period before 1815 while Denmark and Norway were united it was the main port serving the joint kingdom. Today, with a population of 84,000, its various industries include the crushing of imported oilseeds and the manufacture of cement. The only other port of any size on this coast is Frederikshavn, a fishing harbour protected by breakwaters. It is a centre of fish packing and curing, and is the ferry terminus to Copenhagen, Oslo and Göteborg in Sweden, and to Larvik in Norway.

3. *Eastern Jutland*

The peninsula east of the central morainic line of hills consists of undulating claylands, diversified by drumlins, eskers and ribbon lakes. The soils are on the whole fertile, since the clays are fairly light and contain lime, and much is under arable crops: barley, potatoes, fodder beet and green fodder. Areas of permanent pasture lie in depressions in the uneven glacial cover, the sites of former lakes or bogs.

Many small servicing and processing towns are situated at

intervals within this prosperous farming country, though the only inland town of any importance is the ancient capital of Jutland, Viborg. Most of the towns are located along the coast, either at the heads of the fjords, such as Randers, Horsens, Vejle and Kolding, or on the shores of broad open bays, such as Aarhus on the *bugt* of the same name. Aarhus (113,000), Denmark's second town, is the centre for the farmlands of eastern Jutland, an industrial centre with food packing, the pressing of imported oilseeds for margarine, cattle feed and edible oils, the manufacture of agricultural machinery and implements, and the construction of diesel engines, refrigerating plant and other engineering products. In the north Randers (42,000) is noted for the manufacture of gloves. Farther south Fredericia developed as a rail ferry port where the crossing was made to Funen, though in 1935 the construction of the Little Belt bridge reduced its importance as a transit point. This bridge was a fine engineering feat, since in places the Little Belt is over 40 m (130 ft) in depth. The port still has some foreign trade, notably the import of coal and fuel oil, and several factories make agricultural machinery, fertilizers, footwear and handicraft items.

4. *The Islands*

When the proto-Baltic was a freshwater lake (p. 21), it drained northward by way of a series of channels through the slightly higher hill country then forming a land-bridge between Jutland and Skåne. This hill country was converted by a rise of sea-level into islands, separated by the channels of the Sound, the Great Belt and the Little Belt.

Though of a generally subdued relief, the islands present considerable variety in detail, the result of the diversity of the glacial mantle and occasionally of the outcropping of the underlying solid rocks; in the island of Mön chalk forms impressive cliffs. The elongated Langeland has a gentle backbone of low rounded hills, a terminal moraine resulting from a temporary readvance of the Baltic icesheet. Samsö consists of a series of transverse kame-like hills of sand and gravel, rising to 35 m (115 ft) above the lower ground-morainic material. In northern Funen, Falster and Lolland, the layer of moraine is smooth; the last rises only to 15 m (50 ft) and a few parts are actually below sea-level, protected by dykes. Falster is much the same, though a few gentle hills rise to about 30 m (100ft).

The soils over the islands are fertile, consisting of reddish-brown loamy clays, often with a fair calcareous content, except for the occasional coarser material of the esker ridges. As a result, the land is closely farmed, growing barley, fodder- crops, sugar beet and potatoes, and the dairying industry is highly developed. On Funen particularly there is a close patchwork of farms, the occasional beech copses giving a verdant appearance to the landscape; the population is well distributed and little land remains uncultivated. Market towns, such as Odense on Funen (with 104,000 people the third city of Denmark) and Nyköbing on Falster, serve as centres for the dairying industry. The port of Odense imports coal, oil and feeding stuffs, and exports dairy produce. As the centre of Funen's prosperous agriculture, Odense has a variety of processing industries such as packing, flour-milling, brewing, sugar-refining, saw-milling and the manufacture of margarine. A shipyard north of the port constructs small tankers, and there are several light engineering factories.

The island of Zealand contains the capital, Copenhagen (in Danish Köbenhavn, the 'merchants' haven'), standing on the south-eastern shores of the island and dominating the Sound, the deepest channel of entry into the Baltic Sea. During the centuries when southern Sweden was part of Denmark, Copenhagen was a centrally placed capital, a military and naval base, a 'stepping-stone' between central Europe and Scandinavia. The alliance with France during the age of Napoleon proved disastrous for a time, but in the nineteenth century commerce expanded once more. In 1857 the dues levied on shipping passing through the Sound were abolished, but this actually stimulated the entrepôt trade; the opening of the Kiel Canal in 1895 across the 'root' of the Jutland peninsula was but a temporary setback. The port has grown up along each side of a narrow channel between Zealand and the neighbouring island of Amager to the south-east (Fig. 18), and along the coast of the Sound farther north; there are about 40 km (25 miles) of quay. Goods can be unloaded at a large freeport, stored in bond and transhipped without Customs payment. This entrepôt traffic has declined somewhat since 1945, but it still affords an appreciable contribution to Copenhagen's prosperity, for the port handles about 12 million tons of freight each year, nearly four times as much as at the beginning of this century.

Copenhagen and district now has 1·2 million people, about a quarter of Denmark's population; many live in flats within the city and own 'summer-houses' in the open countryside or along the coast. An almost continuous line of villas, interrupted by a few old fishing villages, lies along the 'Danish Riviera' coast between the city and Helsingör. Copenhagen is an important industrial centre, including shipbuilding, light engineering, the making of agricultural implements, leather manufactures, oilseed-pressing and the manufacture of margarine, and the wide range of light industries to be expected in the capital city of a prosperous country. The home market for fertilizers has resulted in the development of this industry, using imported phosphates and waste products from the abattoirs. At the northern end of Zealand, Helsingör (Plate XIX) (Elsinore) is a tourist centre with Shakespearean associations, a shipbuilding yard and has a ferry service to Hälsingborg in Sweden. The only inland town of any size in Zealand is Roskilde, the medieval capital.

5. Bornholm

This island, about 35 km (22 miles) in length and 27 km (17 miles) in width, lies in the Baltic Sea between Sweden and East Germany, well to the east of the rest of Denmark; it has been Danish since 1522, except for a short Swedish interim in the seventeenth century. It consists of a horst-like mass of mainly Pre-Cambrian granitic rocks, rising inland to ice-smoothed though boulder-strewn hills over 150 m (500 ft) high, diversified by craggy outcrops. In the south and west the granite mass is flanked by Lower Palaeozoic sandstone, shale and limestone, and by some Mesozoic sandstone, clay, conglomerate and limestone. Its margins rise steeply from the sea, in places to well over 60 m (200 ft), with some fine stacks and skerries. The granite in places is strongly jointed and many small streams, taking advantage of these lines of weakness, have eroded narrow clefts (*dals*), usually trending north-east to south-west, which form considerable obstacles to communication by road.

Access from the sea is difficult or impossible in many places, and apart from a few fishing villages the only port and town of any size is Rönne in the south-west, with a population of about 13,000. Though the harbour consists of a shallow bay between reefs, it has been improved by the construction of a series of moles.

About 49,000 people live in Bornholm, engaged in fishing, particularly for cod by line and for herring, and in agriculture. A large part of the surface consists of heathland or moorland used for rough grazing, though parts are well wooded, and in the south the veneer of glacial clays over the sedimentary rocks gives rise to some meadowland and cultivated fields, among which are dispersed numerous farms. Granite is quarried for export as building stone and road metal, and from pits and quarries to the east of Rönne kaolin is worked for shipment to Copenhagen.

CHAPTER SIX

West Germany

THE Federal Republic of Germany (*Bundesrepublik Deutschland*) became an independent state on 5 May 1955 (pp. 10–11). With an area of about 250 000 sq. km (96,000 sq. miles), it had a population in 1969 of 60·46 million. Administratively it consists of eleven provinces (*Länder*) (Fig. 19), including the Saarland added in 1956 and West Berlin, varying in size from the 70 550 sq. km (27,239 sq. miles) of Bavaria to the 404 sq. km (156 sq. miles) of the Free City of Bremen, in population from the 16·9 millions of North Rhine-Westphalia to the 754,000 of Bremen. The state is referred to in this book and in general usage as West Germany.

STRUCTURE AND RELIEF

Bordering the North and Baltic Seas, and extending inland for 240 km (150 miles), is part of the North European Plain. In the south, along the Austrian border, are the northernmost ranges of the Alpine system, known as the Bavarian Alps. Between the lowland and the mountains lies a complex area of uplands, basins and valleys, ranging from about 300 to over 1500 m (1000 to 5000 ft), which may be referred to as the Central Uplands. Along the western margins of the country the Rhine flows from Switzerland to the Netherlands, contributing a unifying element to a region of otherwise varied relief.

Structure

The Pre-Cambrian rocks of the Baltic Shield (pp. 17–19) and the Russian Platform continue southward under the North German Plain and the North Sea. They thus form the basement rocks of much of Germany and the cores of many of the ancient uplands; they appear on the surface in the margins of the Bohemian Plateau.

Towards the end of the Devonian, a geosynclinal trough began to develop across Central Europe from what is now south-western Ireland to the Urals, in which great thicknesses of sediment accumulated. The late Carboniferous and early Permian periods were characterized by a major orogenic phase which created a series of fold-ranges across central Europe. As the present Harz Mountains comprise one fragment, their Latin name (*Hercynia*) has been used to denote both the orogeny and the resultant mountain system, the Hercynian. This involved both Palaeozoic sandstones, quartzites

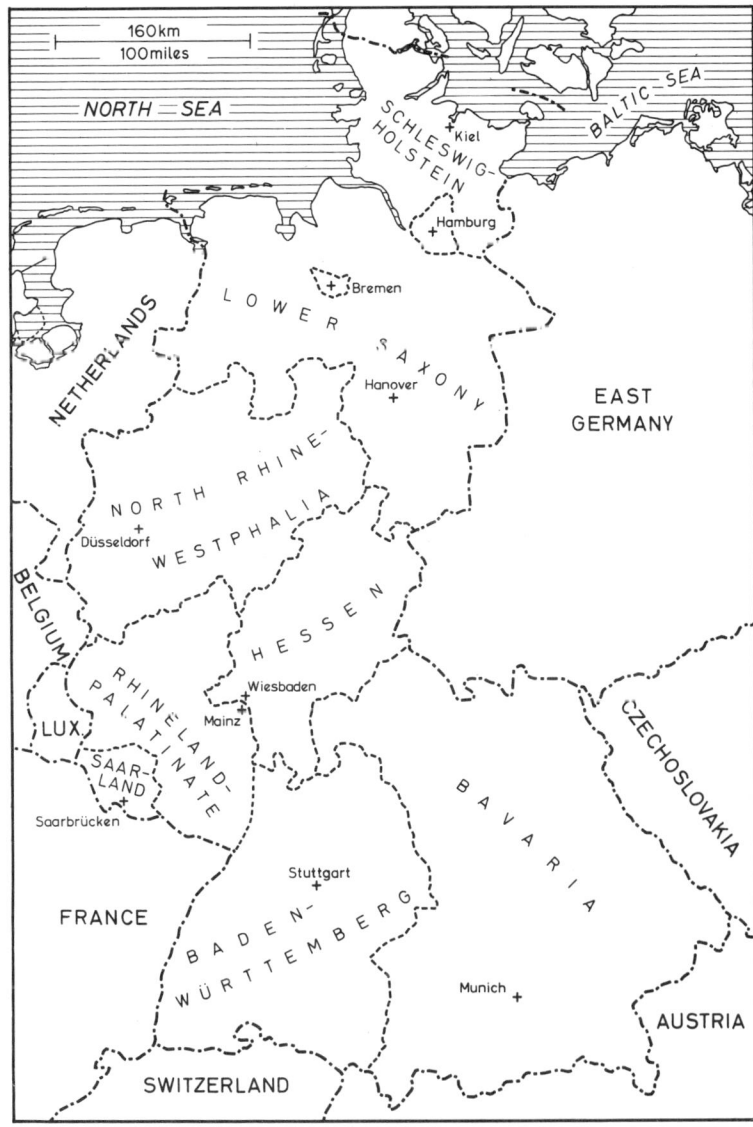

Fig. 19. The provinces (Länder) *of West Germany*
The 'capital' of each province is indicated. West Berlin is now also ranked as a *Land*.

and slates, and also the Coal Measures of Upper Carboniferous times, formed from the remains of swamp forests. During the folding movements masses of granite were intruded into the cores of these ranges, and the ancient sedimentary rocks were extensively metamorphosed.

The Hercynian ranges were then subjected to denudation during Permian and early Triassic times, and were reduced to peneplaned 'stumps'. Some of the Coal Measures were preserved in basins among the uplands, as in the case of the Saar field, and on their northern flanks, as the Ruhr, Aachen and the small Lower Saxony fields. Over much of this worn-down surface spread the Mesozoic seas, in which occurred extensive deposition of limestone, sandstone, marl and clay. These deposits were thin over the Hercynian 'stumps'; possibly the higher ones even protruded like islands from the seas and remained free from deposition. By contrast, in the basins and down-faulted depressions the sedimentary rocks accumulated thickly and are still preserved in the basins of the Main, the Neckar, Weser and the upper Danube. Some of these Mesozoic rocks remain in near horizontal masses, as in the Bunter Sandstone plateaus of Hesse; others were later tilted or folded, and in due course were transformed into scarplands through denudation.

To the south of the Hercynian continent in Tertiary times lay the great Alpine geosyncline, in which sediments accumulated, to be upfolded in mid-Tertiary times to form the Alps, of which only the outer ranges are in Germany. The folding was also felt much farther north in milder form; on the northern margins of the Hercynian uplands were formed some gently folded basins or 'sags', sometimes called 'bays' (after the German *Bucht*).

The Hercynian massifs stood rigidly as a foreland towards which the stresses were directed, and as a result suffered widespread fracturing. The fault-lines follow distinctive trends, for the most part either from south-west to north-east, as in the Middle Rhine Highlands of western Germany, or from south-east to north-west, as in the Harz Mountains. In central Germany these two sets of fault-lines commonly intersect, and contribute a distinctive diamond pattern to many of the relief features. The fracturing of the Hercynian masses also involved their differential movement; some were uplifted and now form upstanding massifs such as the Harz and the Middle Rhine Highlands, from which the younger sediments were denuded. Others, notably the central part of a once continuous block, were depressed, so forming the Rhine Rift Valley, an elongated furrow only 40 km (25 miles) wide but 290 km (180 miles) in length; on the west the Vosges (Plate XX) and the Haardt remained upstanding (p. 474), on the east the Black Forest (Schwarzwald) and the Odenwald. These blocks have steep inward-facing edges and more gentle outward slopes. Associated with these faulting movements occurred vulcanicity in considerable variety. In the Eifel are cinder cones and explosion craters (*Maaren*); in the Siebengebirge, Kaiserstuhl, Hohe Rhön and Vogelsberg are the eroded remnants of basalt flows; and small volcanic 'necks' can be seen in the Siebengebirge.

During late Tertiary times denudation was again widespread, stripping the Mesozoic and Tertiary sediments from the higher blocks, thus exhuming their ancient peneplaned surfaces and creating new ones. In the depressions, both among the faulted uplands and in the 'bays' on the north, the sedimentary rocks were preserved. The most prominent of these in West Germany is the Münster or Westphalian 'Bay', floored with chalk, though largely covered with superficial deposits. In other parts, both to north and south of the Central Uplands, the sedimentary rocks were more pronouncedly folded or tilted. As a result denudation has produced a distinctive scarpland relief, the more resistant limestones and sandstones standing out from the clays. In the north the Weser Hills and the Teutoburg Forest form the outer ridges, with infacing escarpments, of a small unroofed anticline; the former consist of Jurassic limestone, the latter of chalk and greensand of Cretaceous age and of Muschelkalk (Triassic limestone). On the southern margins of the Central Uplands the Mesozoic scarplands again appear. The ridge of the Swabian Jura (or Alb) extends for 200 km (125 miles) from south-west to north-east, and after an interruption by the Ries depression the Franconian Jura curves northward for a further 160 km (100 miles). Both ridges consist of Jurassic limestone, with a distinctive escarpment facing north-west, and rising 300 m (1000 ft) above the general level of the Neckar and Main basins, which are themselves diversified by escarpments and clay vales, somewhat similar in character to those of Lorraine in eastern France (p. 473).

During this late Tertiary period of denudation, further deposition took place in the valleys and basins. The Rhine Rift Valley was filled with sediments, much of Oligocene age, probably while subsidence of its floor was in progress. One valuable contribution is the brown coal of Miocene age, formed from the swamp forests which flourished in the 'bay' around Cologne and on the 'foreland' to the north of the Harz Mountains.

The gently downfolded trough on the northern margins of the Alps, the Bavarian Foreland, was filled with material eroded from the uprising mountains in the same way as the Swiss Foreland (p. 359) farther west. Much of this consisted of sand, compacted as a coarse sandstone known as Molasse; elsewhere masses of pebbles formed a conglomerate called Nagelfluh. The Molasse, the underlying rock of much of the Foreland, appears as low rounded hills to the north-east of Munich, while the more resistant Nagelfluh stands out in places as prominent ridges.

The Quaternary Glaciation

The surface features of the North German Plain and the Bavarian Foreland are largely the result of the Quaternary glaciation: the Scandinavian and Baltic icesheets from the north, the Alpine glaciers from the south. It was in the Bavarian Foreland that W. Penck and E. Brückner worked out in 1905 the concept of a fourfold series of glacial and interglacial stages. They based their conclusions on the distinctive fluvioglacial deposits laid down on the Foreland, an older and a younger gravel complex (*Deckenschotter*)

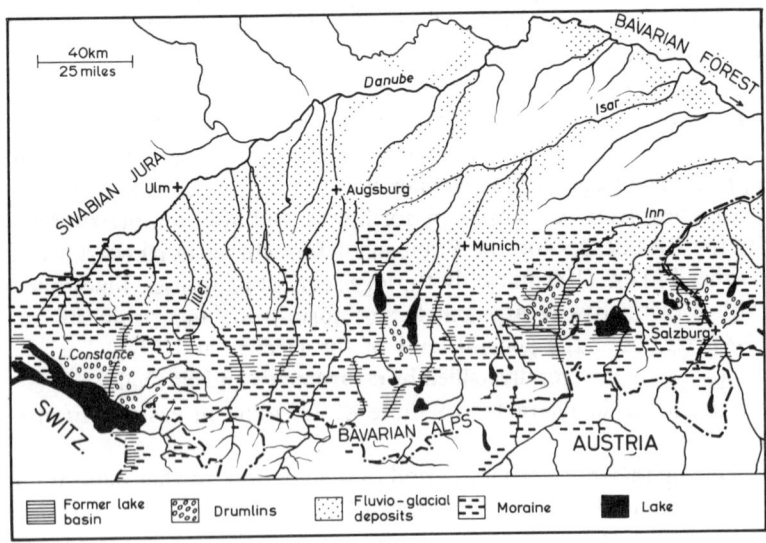

Fig. 20. Glacial and fluvioglacial features of the Bavarian Foreland
(After E. de Martonne)

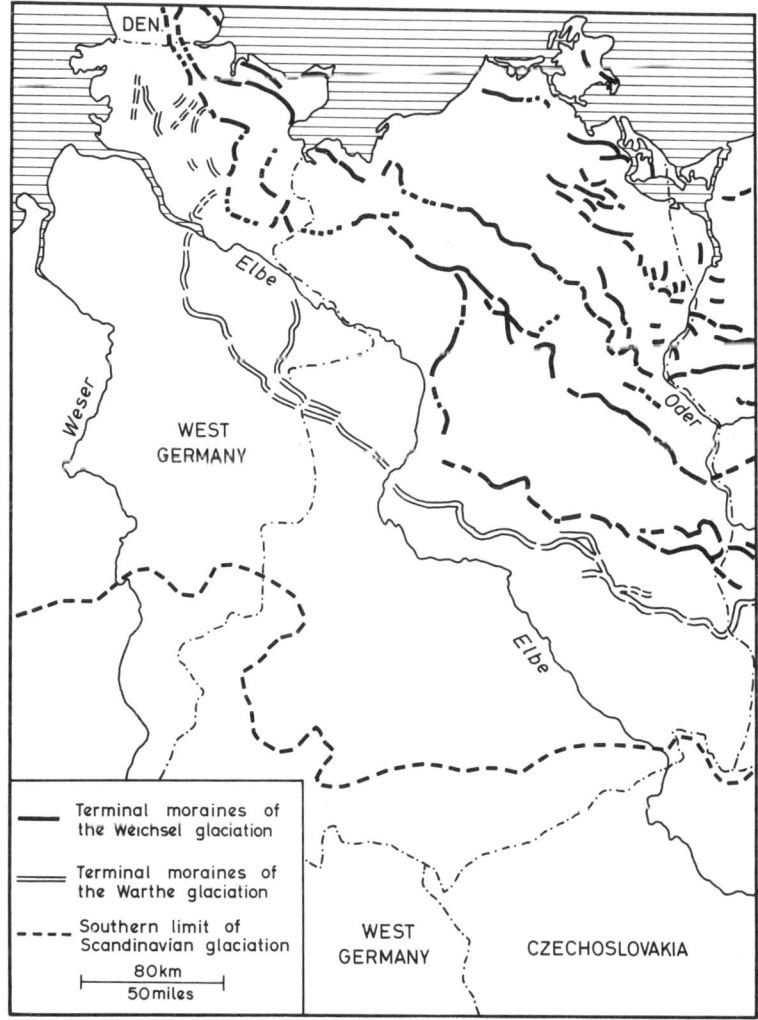

Fig. 21. Terminal moraines of the North German Plain
(After P. Wolstedt)

above the level of the present rivers, and two still younger deposits, known as the High and Low Terrace Gravels. Each of the four gravel complexes was related to an advance of the Alpine glaciers on to the Bavarian Foreland, where they merged to form large piedmont glaciers. To these advances Penck and Brückner gave the names Günz, Mindel, Riss and Würm after tributaries of the river Danube, the last (associated with the Low Terrace) being the most recent and the Riss the most extensive. This classification still basically holds good, though later research workers have postulated additional phases, corresponding to minor fluctuations of the ice margins, and in addition a pre-Günz advance, known as the Donau (Danube), has been suggested. The glacial drift (arranged both in morainic lines and drumlin swarms) and the outwash sands and gravels almost completely mask the Molasse, except to the north-east of Munich. Peat bogs, marshes and lakes are common on the uneven boulder-clay surface (Fig. 20).

The southward advance of the Quaternary ice-sheets from Scandinavia and the Baltic region left profound results on the North German Plain (Fig. 21). Three distinct glacial stages have been distinguished: the Elster, Saale and Weichsel, which correspond to the Mindel, Riss and Würm respectively. The most southerly stage was the Saale, whose ice-sheet extended as far south as the central Netherlands (p. 241). Subsequent evidence suggests that a further phase known as the Warthe intervened between the Saale and Weichsel advances. Its moraines can be traced south of Hamburg and into East Germany and Poland as a discontinuous line of low hills (Fig. 21), trending in a south-easterly direction and rising in places to 200 m (650 ft) above sea-level. The consensus of opinion is that the Warthe stage represents a temporary halt, possibly even a slight readvance, during the retreat of the ice-sheet towards the end of the Saale. Further evidence, though admittedly fragmentary and disputable, indicates that another advance of the ice-sheets, known as the Elbe glaciation and tentatively correlated with the Günz in the Alpine Foreland, may have preceded the Elster.

The Weichsel glaciation involved three distinct pauses in the withdrawal of the ice-sheets, known as the Brandenburg, Frankfurt and Pomeranian stages. Each reproduced the characteristic features of the ice margin zones, with terminal moraines, ground-moraine and drumlin swarms, and outwash sands and gravels beyond the moraines. The most prominent of the terminal moraines is the Baltic Heights or the Baltic End Moraine, which in places rises to over 300 m (1000 ft) above sea-level.

Extensive sheets of till were deposited in the form of ground-moraine during the standstill periods of the ice-sheets. That laid down by the earlier ice-sheets (Elster, Saale, Warthe) is known as the Older Drift, that by the Weichsel as the Younger Drift. The former is much more weathered and leached, re-sorted and redeposited by the

Plate XVIII. The Danish State Research Dairy, near Hilleröd on the island of Zealand, Denmark

Plate XIX. Helsingör, Denmark, with a shipbuilding yard and the castle overlooking the narrowest part of the Sound

Plate XX. The Bärental in the Black Forest, West Germany, with the Feldberg (1495 m, 4905 feet) in the background

Plate XXI. The deeply incised valley of the Danube near Weltenburg, Bavaria, West Germany. Note the monastery on the meander spur

postglacial rivers, the moraines are more eroded, and the clays are more masked by later sheets of outwash material. The Younger Drift is obviously fresher and less weathered, while drainage systems are immature and indeterminate. In West Germany most of the till consists of this Older Drift, in contrast to the Younger Drift found in East Germany and Poland.

During the lengthy standstill period of the Pomeranian stage, the area to the south and west of the icefront was affected in two distinct ways by melt-water streams draining away from the ice-sheets. On the one hand, sheets of bedded sand and gravel, usually 30 m (100 ft), sometimes as much as 90 m (300 ft) in thickness, form low undulating plateaus on which heath and moorland have developed. With their acid sandy soils, these are known as the Geestlands, after an old German word which means infertile.

On the other hand, the melt-waters, prevented from draining northward by the ice-sheets and southward by the Central Uplands, were forced to flow westward towards the proto-North Sea along the ice margins at their halting positions. These melt-water streams eroded broad, shallow troughs, known as *Urstromtäler* (Fig. 22). When the ice-sheets finally disappeared and the postglacial drainage system re-established itself in a more direct northerly direction to the sea, the rivers took advantage of some portions of these east–west troughs. Other sections remained riverless, though usually with marshy floors. Both the Urstromtäler and the postglacial river valleys divide the outwash sands into individual blocks.

Another contribution to the surface features of the North European Plain consists of fine dust transported by the wind, probably during dry interglacial and immediately postglacial periods, exercising its sorting effect on the unconsolidated sands and clays. This *loess* is found only to the west and south of the Baltic Heights, that is, beyond the area covered by the last major ice advance. It occurs at all altitudes, so that the primary agent of transport could only have been the wind, though running water may have been involved in its redistribution. From this fine-textured, lime-rich deposit have developed fertile and easily worked loamy soils as a discontinuous belt along the northern margins of Hercynian Europe, known as the Bördeland or Börde.

Drainage

The rivers beyond the margins of the ice-sheets at times were swollen with melt-water and heavily laden with material. In this

6

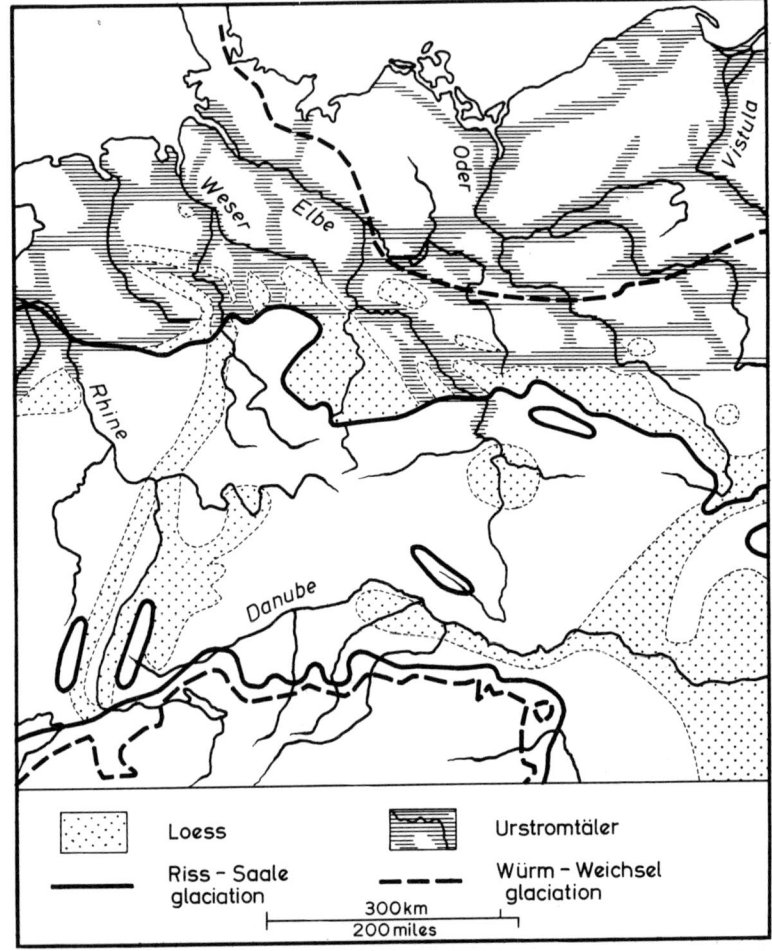

Fig. 22. Urstromtäler *and loess deposits on the North German Plain*
(After W. von Seidlitz)

overladen state they deposited sand and gravel in their valleys, later
to be dissected into terraces when they resumed vertical erosion.
The Rhine was particularly active, creating below its exit from
the Middle Rhine Highlands a huge alluvial fan extending into the
Netherlands, merging with that laid down by its neighbour the
Meuse (p. 293). It also deposited sheets of gravel on the floor of the
Rift Valley to the south.

After the ice-sheets finally went, several major rivers re-established themselves across the North European Plain, and a large part of the drainage is orientated towards the North Sea by way of the Rhine, Ems, Weser and Elbe; the first rises in Alpine Switzerland, the last in the Bohemian 'Diamond' of Czechoslovakia, flowing for the greater part of its course through East Germany, the other two in the Central Uplands. The only exception to this northward orientation is the Danube (Plate XXI), which flows south-eastward, ultimately into the Black Sea.

Relief Regions

The structure of West Germany thus involves four main contributory elements: the Hercynian massifs; the Mesozoic and Tertiary scarplands, basins and low plateaus; the marginal portions of the Alpine folds of mid-Tertiary age, forming the Bavarian Alps (Plate XXII); and the lowlands to the north and the Foreland to the south which owe their features to the impress of glaciation. These elements are so intimately interrelated that the individual relief regions present a veritable mosaic (Fig. 23), summarized as follows:

Hercynian massifs	*Mesozoic and Tertiary scarp-lands and basins*	*Alpine fold-mountains*	*Quaternary lowlands*
Black Forest	Teutoburg Forest	Bavarian Alps	The Geestlands of the North German Plain (Oldenburg, Lüneburg Heath, Schleswig-Holstein)
Odenwald	Weser Hills		
Spessart	Münster Bay		
Haardt	Cologne Bay		
Palatinate Hills	Bördeland of Lower Saxony		The lower river valleys
Hunsrück ⎫	Rhine Rift Valley		Marine coastal plains (the Marschen)
Eifel ⎪			
Taunus ⎪ Middle			
Westerwald ⎬Rhine Main and Neckar		Bavarian Fore-land (with Quaternary veneer)
Siegerland ⎪ High- Scarplands			
Sauerland ⎪ lands Swabian and			
W. Harz ⎭ Franconian Jura			

These, regrouped into five major regions, are the basis of the regional description below (pp. 186–203).

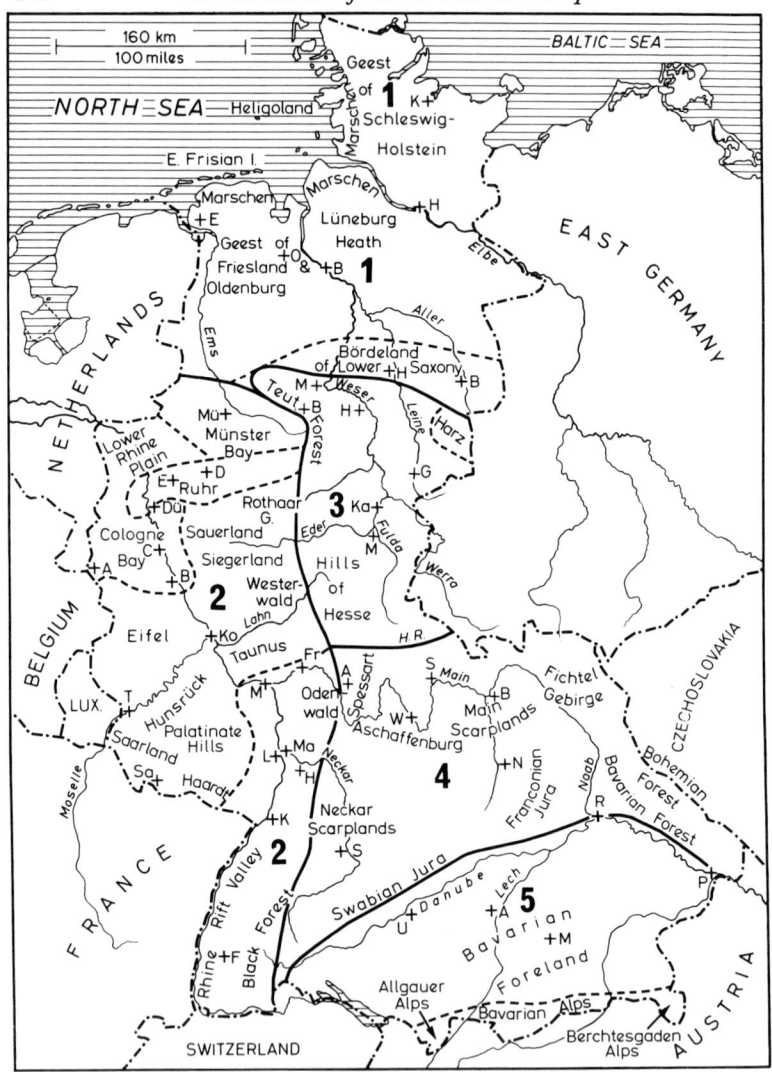

Fig. 23. Relief regions of West Germany
H. R. Hohe Rhön; Teut. Teutoburg Forest.

The Coast

The coastline of West Germany extends from the estuary of the Ems on the Dutch border to the mouth of the Trave just east of Lübeck, where the border between West and East Germany reaches the Baltic Sea. Its continuity is interrupted by Denmark, which occupies the northern part of the Jutland Peninsula.

The present features of the coast are the result of three factors: a slight rise of sea-level over the margins of a plain diversified by an uneven mantle of glacial and fluvioglacial clay, sand and gravel; the accumulation of material from the longshore drift of sand and mud by tidal currents; and the work of man, who has embanked and reclaimed tidal flats, built moles, dykes and groynes, and dredged channels through the estuaries of the large rivers. The coastline is low-lying, interrupted by embayments and estuaries, and fronted by tidal flats and lines of offshore islands.

From about the fourth to the thirteenth century, a continuous belt of sand-dunes stretched eastward from near Calais along the North Sea coastline (p. 243). A slight rise in sea-level, together with a marked increase in storminess, caused the widespread breaching of this dune-belt and the formation of the line of the West (Dutch) and East (German) Frisian Islands, while the submergence of the low-lying margins of the Jutland peninsula produced the North Frisian Islands of more irregular shape. They are separated from the mainland by areas of mud and sand known as *Watten*, exposed at low tide and crossed by a maze of creeks and channels. Since the thirteenth century considerable areas have been reclaimed and converted into rich pasture or 'saltings'. This reclamation has been partly natural, the result of sediment brought down by the rivers and the growth of salt-marsh vegetation, which assists in the accumulation and consolidation of silt (Plates XV-XVII). This has been stimulated by the work of man; wicker fences help the accretion of mud, and dykes have been built to protect the low-lying saltings against exceptional tides.

The submergence of the coastal margins created indentations out of proportion in size to the rivers entering them: the Ems flows into the Dollart, the Jade into Jade Bay, the Weser and Elbe into long tapering estuaries. At low tide the last two rivers are contained in narrow channels, maintained by dredging as fairways for shipping to Bremen and Hamburg respectively.

The island of Heligoland is an exception to the low-lying nature of the North Sea coast of West Germany. It comprises a mass of Triassic sandstone, 1·6 km (1 mile) long, rising in steep cliffs to 66 m (217 ft) above the sea. Marine erosion constantly attacks their base, despite the construction of concrete defensive walls.

Before 1945 some three-quarters of the coastline of Germany lay along the Baltic Sea. The only Baltic section in West Germany is between Flensburger Förde and the mouth of the Trave, characterized by straight-sided inlets which penetrate the low boulder-clay plateau of Schleswig-Holstein. Known as *Förden*, they were formed by the submergence of long narrow valleys, probably eroded by powerful melt-water streams flowing in tunnels under the Quaternary ice-sheet. The three main indentations are Flensburger Förde, Eckernförde Bucht and Kieler Förde. Farther east the coast bends to form a low rounded peninsula, off which lies the nearly flat island of Fehmarn. It then turns south again to form Lübeck Bay, a large rectangular inlet into which flows the Trave, with the port of Lübeck 18 km (11 miles) upstream and its outport of Travemünde near the sea. A few miles to the east is the boundary with East Germany.

CLIMATE

The climate of Germany as a whole is transitional in character, situated between maritime influences from the west and continental influences from the east, though the varied relief introduces distinct contrasts between the exposed plateaus and ridges and the sheltered basins and valleys. The most attractive region climatically is the Rhineland, largely because of its sheltered situation; here the winters are as mild as those along the North Sea coast, spring comes early and the fruit trees are in blossom by the third week in April, compared with mid-May in Schleswig-Holstein. The autumn too is prolonged, and is commonly a delightful golden season.

Temperature

In winter a tendency to high pressure exists over much of continental Europe; cold stable air masses give prolonged anticyclonic conditions, with calm, sunny, but cold weather, sometimes with bleak easterly or north-easterly winds. At times, however, the continental high pressure weakens or even disappears, and West Germany comes under the influences of maritime air masses. Though the associated depressions are commonly occluded, they can bring mild weather and wet, stormy conditions to the North Sea coast, and snow further inland and on the higher ground. The 0° C. mean January isotherm crosses West Germany diagonally from near Lübeck to Basle; west and north of this the temperatures for the coldest month are above 0° C., east and south they are below. Thus Emden and Kiel near the

North Sea coast have figures of 1° C. for January, and Hanover a little further inland a degree less, while Munich (at a height of 520 m, 1700 ft) is appreciably colder with −3° C., and some of the higher stations in Bavaria have January means of about −8° C. The Black Forest and the southern part of the Bavarian Foreland may experience frost on an average of more than 120 days each year, compared with under sixty near the Elbe estuary. The Rhineland also has January means above freezing point (Mannheim, 1° C.), and in the north fewer than sixty days of frost. These figures disguise distinctly cold spells; during the winter of 1962–3, all West Germany lay below freezing point for many weeks, and both the coastal waters and the rivers were frozen, though normally the Kiel Canal is affected by ice for only seven to ten days, the North Sea coast seldom. The Rhine at Mainz experiences ice for about fifteen days in the year, though 'fast' ice occurs only rarely. In the Central Uplands and the Bavarian Alps altitude modifies temperature to such an extent that the observatory on the summit of the Zugspitze at 2963 m (9721 ft) records a mean of only −11° C. for January and February.

In summer heating and convectional overturning results in a tendency to low pressure conditions over central Europe, associated with shallow depressions moving in from the west. The sea-level isotherms trend across the country more or less from west-south-west to east-north-east, with mean temperatures ranging from 15° to 17° C. along the North Sea coast to 18° C. in the south. Temperatures are strikingly uniform over West Germany in summer, except at high altitudes; the summit of the Zugspitze has mean temperatures for July and August of only 2° C. The increasing insolation in southern Germany is compensated by shorter days and higher altitudes than along the northern coast. Mean maxima are higher in the south, however, and in late summer long spells of hot sunny weather are a result of a north-eastward extension of the Azorean high-pressure belt, which sometimes firmly establishes itself across south-central Europe.

Precipitation

This is remarkably evenly distributed over West Germany, the total received being mainly a function of aspect and relief, for the higher land in the south more than compensates for the increasing distance from the sea. On the North German Plain there is a slight decrease eastward as the effects of depressions from the Atlantic diminish; thus Emden has a mean of 740 mm (29 in), Hanover of

640 mm (25 in). The higher areas in the south receive appreciably more; Munich at about 520 m (1700 ft) has 860 mm (34 in), the western Harz about 1520 mm (60 in),- much of the Black Forest 1400 mm (55 in), and the summit of the Zugspitze 1570 mm (62 in). By contrast, there are some striking rain-shadow effects, such as in the southern part of the Rhine Rift Valley, east of the Vosges, which has only about 500 mm (20 in).

Despite the greater incidence of depressions in winter, less rain falls than during the summer. Even along the North Sea coast, where the precipitation is fairly uniformly distributed throughout the year, the wettest months are July and August when 160 mm (6.3 in), or nearly a quarter of the mean total, are received. This tendency is more pronounced farther east and south, where convection influences are marked; thus Munich receives on an average 340 mm (13·4 in) during the months July to September out of its mean annual total of 860 mm (34 in). In the mountains too summer is appreciably wetter than winter; the Zugspitze station records on an average 210 mm (8·2 in) in January to March, but 620 mm (24·4 in) in June to August. The lengthy spells of damp cloudy weather in the mountains during summer, often with violent thunderstorms, contrast with the sunshine and crisp dry air of much of the winter.

Since winter temperatures are near or below freezing for considerable periods, there is an appreciable snow cover; the number of days on which snow falls increases from about thirty on the north-western coast and in the Rhine valley to about fifty-five in Bavaria. The plateaus of the Eifel, Taunus, and Harz experience about sixty days, and the summit of the Zugspitze averages 180. The permanent snowline lies at 2400 m (8000 ft) in the Bavarian Alps, though the winter snowline descends on to the Foreland; the numerous winter resorts include Garmisch-Partenkirchen, where the Olympic Winter Games have been held.

LAND USE AND AGRICULTURE

At a recent land-use survey, about 7·6 million ha (18·8 million acres) or 32 per cent of the area of West Germany was classified as arable land, 23 per cent as pasture, 2 per cent as gardens, vineyards and orchards, 28 per cent was under forest, and 6 per cent under heath and moorland.

Soils

Over much of West Germany, with some notable exceptions, the soil is not naturally very fertile. In the north, along the coast and on the flood-plains of the rivers, are marsh soils, both marine clays and alluvium, considerable areas of which have been drained and support rich pastures. Then comes a broad west–east belt of podzols, developed on the fluvioglacial sands and gravels and on the more sandy clays of the Older Drift. These leached soils, with a thin surface layer of acid humus, are underlain by a hardpan, which prevents the penetration of tree roots and forms an impermeable stratum, causing waterlogging and the formation of acid bog peat from the layers of sphagnum moss.

By contrast, to the south of these podzols occurs a belt of fluctuating width of soils derived from the loess deposits of the Bórdeland. These are loamy in texture, and since this zone once carried deciduous forest, brown earths have developed. In the Cologne 'bay', the loamy soil is similar to a chernozem, but the rather greater leaching it has suffered causes it to be classified as a 'degraded chernozem'. Similar soils are found on the Rhine terraces along the Rift Valley. These soils derived from loess are the best in West Germany, and form the chief areas of wheat and sugar beet cultivation.

The geology and relief of the Central Uplands are so varied that the soils are equally so. The outcrops of the Triassic sandstones are covered with coarse sandy podzols; the limestones of the Swabian and Franconian Jura give rise to rendzina, a black humus-rich soil containing a high proportion of calcareous fragments; brown earths are widely developed, especially in the Main and Neckar basins, where beech forests formerly flourished; and loess soils are scattered in patches throughout the south.

Over much of the Bavarian Foreland, brown earths have developed on the morainic clays, but elsewhere sands and gravels form heavily leached podzols, while badly drained tracts are covered with peat bogs, as in the Dachau Moos, north-west of Munich. The best soils on the Foreland are derived from loess to the north of the terminal moraines and on the terraces along the Danube valley. Finally, on the slopes of the Bavarian Alps are stony 'skeletal' soils.

Forests

The 'natural vegetation' of Germany, as far as it is possible to reconstruct this long vanished cover, consisted almost entirely of forest. Tundra, which gradually moved northward with the withdrawal of the Quaternary ice-sheets, was succeeded by the birch forests of the Pre-Boreal phase, then by the pines of the Boreal, the widespread oak forests of the Atlantic from about 5500 to 3000

B.C., and then a renewal of the pine forests under the cooler, somewhat drier, conditions of the Sub-Boreal. By about 500 B.C. the fairly continuous forest cover of the Sub-Atlantic consisted of oak and birch in the north and over the Bavarian Foreland, and of beech over the Central Uplands. Spruce grew at higher altitudes and firs flourished on the mountains in the south.

From the beginning of the Sub-Boreal period, Germanic peoples of Nordic extraction moved southward into the forests, clearing where the cover was lighter, and later pressing on the northern boundary of the Roman Empire. In the centuries following its fall, when probably three-quarters of the present area of Germany was forested, the first major wave of colonization and clearance began. As population pressure increased in medieval times, more of the woodland was destroyed to make way for the plough, a process accelerated as timber was increasingly required for constructional work and for charcoal. Numerous village names with such suffixes as *-rode* and *-roth* indicate settlements in the forest. By the beginning of this century, the extent under forest had diminished to less than a quarter of the area of Germany; of this nearly three-quarters was coniferous, for both the natural and artificial regeneration of conifers is easier than that of deciduous species.

In the north the clearance of the light mixed forest left the sandy soils exposed to leaching and so furthered the spread of heathland. Planting with conifers sometimes affords the only practicable way of reclaiming this heathland, since conifers are tolerant of inimical soil conditions, and pine plantations have been established on the Lüneburg Heath and on the moors of Oldenburg. The pine is also grown widely on the poor sandy soils of the Bunter Sandstone in the Central Uplands, as in Hesse and the Main basin. Farther south and west flourishes the spruce, more tolerant of winter cold than of summer drought, and now the most widespread species in West Germany, growing in stands on the Hercynian uplands. The silver fir covers the lower slopes of the Black Forest and the Bavarian Alps.

Deciduous trees comprise only about 30 per cent of the total wooded area, though in recent years there has been renewed planting of these types. Beech covers the lower slopes of the Central Uplands, and grows in conjunction with oak on the Middle Rhine Highlands.

During the decade before 1939, afforestation was an important part of the State's land reclamation policy, but during the War overcutting was inevitable, made worse by the shortage of fuel during the cold postwar winters. Since 1950 a highly scientific policy of afforestation has been put into effect; despite the need for timber (24 million cubic metres were cut in 1968), the annual cut must not exceed the increment. This is practicable since West Germany can now afford to import nearly a third of its timber requirements.

Agricultural Policy

In 1938, despite a high proportion of poor soil and upland relief, about three-fifths of the area of Germany was classified as farmland. State policy required a large rural population both for military manpower and the production of a large proportion of the country's food. National Socialism inherited an agricultural system which had been in decline since the end of the War of 1914–18, and programmes of land reclamation and improvement were inaugurated, applications of fertilizer were increased to raise yields, and compulsory labour was drafted on to the land. As a result, by 1938 Germany produced between 75 and 85 per cent of its food requirements and was virtually self-supporting in respect of cereals, sugar and potatoes. There was, however, a marked shortage of fats, and although such countries as Denmark and the Netherlands were anxious to sell, Germany preferred to devote most of its available foreign credits to the purchase of essential industrial raw materials, hence the slogan 'guns before butter'. During the War of 1939–45 production was stepped up still more, so that until a late stage the Germans, using forced labour on the land and with requisitions of food from occupied countries, were probably the best fed people in Europe.

The loss of territory in the east and the division of the country into two parts after 1945 created an agricultural crisis which nearly produced famine. The territory lost to Poland and Russia, especially in Upper Silesia, included large areas of fertile soil which were normally districts of agricultural surplus, contributing between a quarter and a third of the total Reich production. East Germany acquired rather more than half of the prewar arable land, though less than a quarter of the total population. The position became progressively worse for West Germany with the continued arrival of refugees, and because of the diversion of American grain to West Germany to avert famine, bread rationing had to be introduced in Britain, though never required during the War.

At the present time only 10 per cent of the working population is engaged in agriculture, and it contributes less than 9 per cent to the national productivity by value. Nevertheless, large areas of heathland and moorland have been reclaimed since 1948, and immense applications of fertilizers, increased mechanization, and the introduction of new hybrid breeds of crops, have enabled West Germany to produce between 75 and 90 per cent of its food requirements. The yield of wheat, which in the equivalent area of the Federal Republic in 1938 was 2·9 million tons, rose to 6·2 millions in 1968; sugar beet increased even more strikingly from 5·2 to 13·6 million tons. West German agriculture is faced with problems resulting from the policy of the E.E.C.; levies and price maintenance have led to some over-production, notably of butter (as shown by the unsold accumulation by 1969 of 400,000 tons, the 'butter mountain', though now (1970) reduced).

Small farms have always predominated in western Germany, the result of the growth of population in large nucleated settlements within the fields and the hereditary fragmentation of holdings (Plate XXIII). This makes for uneconomic farming because of the impracticability of mechanization on small plots, the waste of time involved in working these scattered parcels, and the general inefficiency of small-scale operations. In 1949, of the 2 million holdings, about 1·2 millions were smaller than 5 ha (12·5 acres). The Government has introduced a series of annual 'Green Plans' to encourage the consolidation of holdings and withdraw agricultural labour through the payment of compensation and grants for retraining. By 1969 about 2·1 million workers had left the land, and the number of holdings had declined to 1·4 millions. At the same time, there has been much State investment in agriculture, including a programme of rural electrification, new farm buildings and roads, etc.

Arable Farming

In terms of yield the most important cereal in West Germany is wheat; a total output of 3·29 million tons in 1952 has been increased to 6·2 millions in 1968, mainly through improvement in yield. It is grown especially on the rich loam soils of the Bördeland, on the drained marine and river clays of the North Sea coastlands and the lower Elbe valley, and on the morainic clays of eastern Schleswig-Holstein. Until 1961 the area under rye was substantially greater than that under wheat, partly because it is so much more hardy that it can thrive on poor soils and at greater altitudes; the amount has however declined to about 3 million tons during the last few years. Some is fed to livestock, though more than half the bread eaten is still of the dark rye variety. Spring barley is grown in the Bavarian Foreland and in the more fertile basins among the Central Uplands; much goes to the breweries at Munich, Augsburg and Nuremberg. Winter barley, consumed mainly as fodder, is grown in much the same areas as wheat, especially in the Bördeland. Both the area under oats and its yield have declined since 1939 by about a third, partly because of the reduction in the number of horses, though it is still grown quite widely as a fodder crop in the moister western parts. A little maize is grown in the Rhineland.

Potatoes are extensively cultivated over most of West Germany, since they are a very adaptable crop and yield well on both sandy and clay soils. About a quarter of the 1968 yield of 19·2 million tons was used as human food, two-fifths for industrial products (alcohol, starch), and the balance as fodder, especially for pigs. The output of sugar beet is now double that of 1938, so that the country is usually self-supporting in sugar. It requires a deep, well-drained, loamy soil and a moderate, well-distributed rainfall, and does well on the loess soils of the Bördeland where it is grown in rotation with wheat, in the basin around Cologne, and in the Rhine Rift Valley. The beet tops and pulp are fed to livestock.

There is a considerable specialization in minor industrial crops grown in small local concentrations, such as rape, from which colza oil is expressed, produced mainly in Schleswig-Holstein under State subsidy. Flax is grown, though in much reduced amounts compared with pre-1939 years, in the north-west along the Dutch frontier; some hemp is cultivated in the Bavarian Foreland; and hops in Franconia and the Rhineland for the huge brewing industry. Tobacco is a specialist crop in favoured localities, particularly along the foot-hills in Baden where cigar tobacco is produced, near Würzburg in the Main valley, and along the valleys of the Moselle and Rhine.

Orchards and Vineyards

Fruit is especially important in the south-west on south-facing slopes in the Rhine Rift Valley and Bavaria. Apples are grown in Württemberg for cider and *Apfelsaft* (apple-juice), along the shores of Lake Constance, and on the slopes of the Taunus hills; cherries in Hesse, to the north of Frankfurt, and especially near Kitzing for the famous liqueur *Kirsch*; plums around Bühl and Kronberg; and even apricots and peaches flourish in the Neckar valley.

Though the area of vineyards is only 60 000 ha (150,000 acres), much wine of high quality is produced and a large proportion is exported. West Germany is in a marginal climatic area for the vine, and its cultivation is confined to the south-facing slopes of the valleys of the Rhine and its tributaries, with tiny terraced vineyards clinging to steep rocky slopes (Plate XXIV). About a third of the wine is produced in the Palatinate along the famous '*Weinstrasse*', which follows the edge of the Haardt uplands. On the southern slopes of the Taunus the Rheingau produces the traditional 'hocks', and on the opposite side of the Rhine, from Worms to Bingen, is Rheinhesse. The vineyards of the Moselle grow on the steep, south-facing slopes of its incised meanders, alternating with rocky cliffs and conifers on north-facing aspects.

Livestock

Though animals are reared widely over West Germany as part of the mixed farming economy, the emphasis is on either grazing in the moister north and west, or on stall-feeding in the Bördeland. The main area of permanent grassland is on the reclaimed coastal marshes and polders and on parts of the western heathlands which have been reclaimed. A second area is on the lower slopes of the Bavarian Alps, where cattle are taken up to the high pastures in summer, and on the neighbouring parts of the Foreland. Pasture and meadows are found on the floodplains of river valleys, on the heavy clays which floor some of the basins, and on the higher parts of the Central Uplands. Livestock kept on dairy farms around the densely populated industrial cities are fed on clover, alfalfa, mangolds, most of the oats and barley crop, and some of the rye. About a quarter of the potato crop is fed to pigs, and sugar beet pulp and tops are also used.

During the last War widespread slaughtering and later requisitioning by the occupying forces reduced the livestock total to a very low figure. In West Germany the prewar figure was not regained until 1953, but by 1968 there were 14·0 million cattle (including 6·0 dairy cattle), 18·7 million pigs, 800,000 sheep and 263,000 horses. Sheep have declined markedly since the beginning of the century and have halved in number since 1949; they are kept on the mountains in the south, and some are folded on roots and stubble in the Bördeland.

A feature of postwar agricultural organization has been the extension of co-operation, especially among dairy farmers. This has helped West Germany to become almost self-sufficient in butter and cheese, though some high-grade dairy produce is imported from Denmark. Yields of milk per animal, as well as its butterfat content, have been substantially improved during the last decade.

FISHERIES

The fishing industry has long made a contribution to the economy of northern Germany. As early as the twelfth century the herring fisheries were important, and salt fish was an appreciable item in the trade of the Hanseatic League. Until the nineteenth century, much of this activity was in the hands of Dutch fishermen.

After the unification of Germany, with the great growth of population, its increase in food requirements, and the development of communications serving inland markets, the fishing industry rapidly developed. Since the beginning of the century Germany has ranked third in Europe, after Norway and Britain, in terms of total catch. The War of 1939–45 caused a big decline in activity, and the widespread destruction of fishing-boats, port facilities and communications, with the lengthy job of mine-sweeping in coastal waters, hampered its revival. The division into two states left almost the whole of the fishing industry in the hands of West Germany, and the need to contribute to the diet of the population, swollen by refugees, stimulated activity. The chief fishing ports are Bremerhaven-Geestemünde, Cuxhaven and Altona-Hamburg, smaller Weser ports such as Nordenham and Brake (the home of the herring drifters), and Emden. The total landings in 1968 were 672,000 tons, appreciably greater than the prewar catch for all Germany; about 40 per cent consisted of herrings. A fleet of 200 large modern trawlers operates farther away, mainly in Icelandic waters.

FUEL, POWER AND MINERALS

A major factor in Germany's industrial development since 1870 has been its large resources of bituminous coal, brown coal and mineral salts (Fig. 24), though the country is poorly supplied with metal ores. For a century the greatest asset was the Ruhr (or Westphalian) coalfield, 'the industrial king-pin' not only of Germany but of western Europe, though now coal is in decline, faced with the competition of oil and natural gas.

Coal

In 1938 Germany was the third largest coal producing country in the world; its output was 186 million tons, compared with 352 million in the U.S.A. and 232 million in Great Britain. At the end of the War, coal-mining was wholly disrupted. The Upper Silesian and

Waldenburg fields lie within the territory now incorporated in Poland. The Saar basin was under French control until 1958, and though it has now returned finally to West Germany, France retained some mining rights until 1970. The small Upper Saxony fields are in East Germany. Apart from these actual losses, the Ruhr had been attacked repeatedly from the air and much of its labour had fled; only 45 million tons of coal were produced in West Germany in 1945.

The recovery of coal production was vital not only to West Germany but to western Europe, and this went rapidly ahead; by 1953 the output had grown to 124 million tons, by 1957 it was 149 millions. But since then there has been a steady decline to about 110 millions in 1968. During the last decade coal's share of the total energy consumed in West Germany has fallen from 69 to 23 per cent, while oil (which is cheaper for many purposes) has risen from 12 to 55 per cent. Moreover, natural gas is replacing coal-gas, and American coal is cheaper than Ruhr coal for West Germany's neighbours. In spite of widespread mine-closures, large stacks of unsold coal have accumulated at the pit-heads. In an effort to rationalise the industry, the Westphalian mines, offloaded by the big steel companies, were merged in 1969 as *Ruhrkohle*. The chief use for coal is coke-making and for fuelling thermal generators.

The Ruhr Basin (Fig. 25), about 150 km (90 miles) from west to east and 100 km (60 miles) from north to south, lies along the northern edge of the Middle Rhine Highlands. Here the Coal Measures dip gently northward, so that while they are exposed on the surface in the south along the valley of the Ruhr, they are concealed to the north by a progressively thicker cover of Mesozoic and Tertiary sediments, where the bulk of postwar mining has taken place; some of the new mines are 900 m (3000 ft) deep. The more northerly part of the field is structurally less disturbed than the exposed field to the south. A total thickness of about 80 m (260 ft) of seams ranges from anthracite and steam coal to high-volatile gas coals. Fortunately, two-thirds is of excellent quality for making metallurgical coke, and the Ruhr is the major contributor to the European Coal and Steel Community. Estimates of the reserves range from 10,000 to 20,000 million tons, of which a third is of coking quality, sufficient for two centuries at the present rate of production.

The Saar Basin is situated well to the south of the main line of fields on the flanks of the Hercynian uplands, orientated from north-east to south-west between the southern edge of the Hunsrück and the plateau of Lorraine. Within the Saarland the Coal Measures are exposed over a considerable area, though south-west of the river Saar they are overlain by Triassic rocks, and workable coal occurs at progressively greater depths over the border into France.

The Saar coalfield (Fig. 26) was worked by France during the Napoleonic period, but it passed to Prussia in 1815 and its exploitation steadily developed during the nineteenth century. This was accelerated after 1871, when much of Lorraine became German, and the field shared the vigorous development of this industrial complex; in 1913 it produced about 17 million tons of coal. Its vicissitudes since 1918 are described on p. 193. The Saar's output of coal in 1967 from 7 collieries (compared with 18 in 1957) was 12·4 million tons. This is not of a good quality for making metallurgical coke, and until recently it was burnt in coke ovens mixed with an equal amount of Ruhr coal. Recent technological advance has reduced the proportion of the Ruhr contribution, and the most modern ovens (notably a large one at Fürstenhausen) can make adequate metallurgical coke from Saar coal alone.

The Aachen Field, separated by faults from the Ruhr coalfield, is geologically continuous with the Dutch Limburg and Belgian Kempen fields to the west. The two main producing basins are near Aachen and Eschweiler, and in recent years the field has been modernized, with several new collieries.

Finally, some small coalfields in Lower Saxony west of Hanover produce about 2 million tons per annum.

Brown Coal

In 1968 the West German production totalled 101 million tons, about two-fifths that of the East (p. 216). The main deposit is in the Cologne 'Bay' 50 km (30 miles) west of the Rhine (Fig. 27), a bed 90 m (300 ft) thick among the Miocene rocks. In the east the Ville ridge was upfaulted, and the brown coal can be worked by open quarries. In the west is the parallel Düren field, separated by the deeply down-faulted Erft basin where the brown coal has been reached by borings but is uneconomic to work. Several large thermal power stations on the Ville field are fuelled by brown coal, including the Knapsack plant south-west of Cologne and the new Frimmersdorf plant. Much is briquetted and shipped from the Rhine port of Wesseling.

Other smaller scattered deposits of brown coal are found near Helmstedt just inside the border east of Brunswick, in Hesse, near Hanover and in Bavaria.

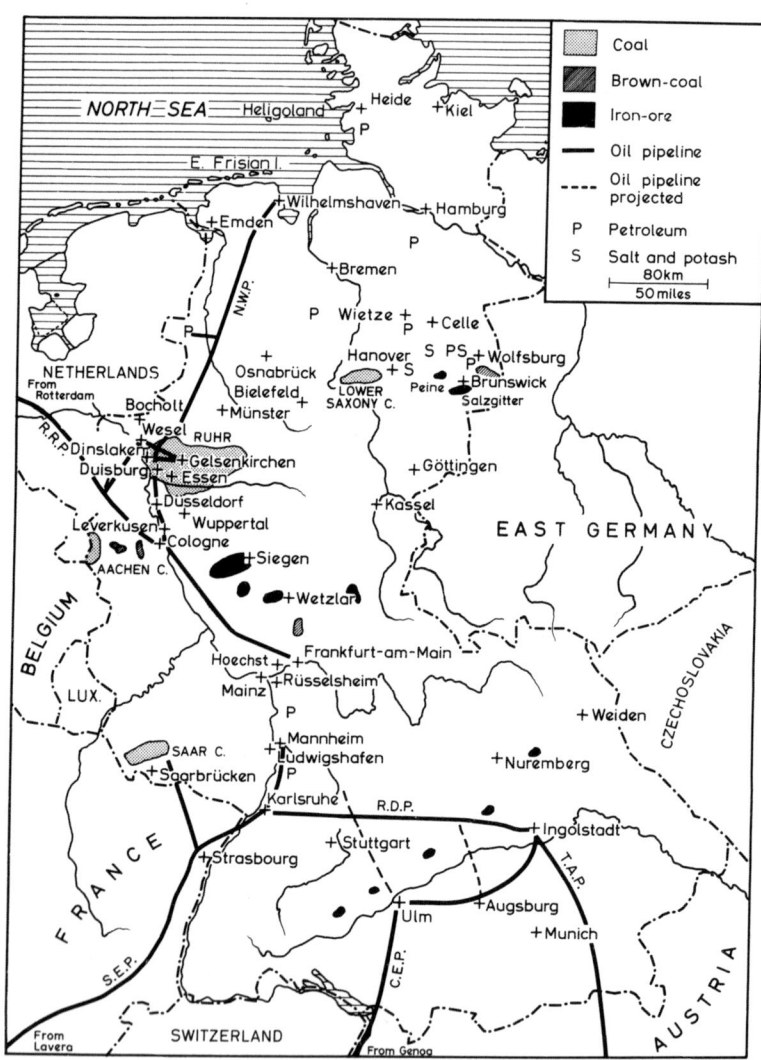

Fig. 24. Mineral resources and industrial towns of West Germany

The pipelines are indicated by abbreviations, as follows: **C.E.P.** Central European Pipeline; **N.W.P.** North-west Pipeline; **R.D.P.** Rhine–Danube Pipeline; **R.R.P.** Rotterdam–Rhine Pipeline; **S.E.P.** South European Pipeline; **T.A.P.** Trans-Alpine Pipeline. There is also a considerable length of products pipelines (carrying hydrocarbon stockfeeds).

Oil

Since the first well was drilled in 1859 at Wietze (north-west of Celle), many efforts have been made to find petroleum along the northern edge of the Hercynian uplands. Until 1930 the annual production of crude oil was only about 100,000 tons, but during the following years the government made desperate efforts to find further reserves, since when war came this would obviously be a vital requirement. The most productive fields were in the Hanover district, notably at Nienhagen and near Reitbrook to the south-east of Hamburg, with smaller producing areas at Wietze, Oberg and Heide in western Schleswig-Holstein (Fig. 24). During the War the Ems field, structurally a continuation of the Dutch field at Schoonebeek (p. 262), and now the chief home producer, was discovered near the Dutch border. These fields have since been vigorously developed, and output has risen from 2.7 million tons of crude oil in 1954 to 8 million tons in 1968. This oil is refined at small plants at Heide and Ostermoor in Schleswig-Holstein, and at Misburg on the Bördeland field.

But home-produced oil supplies only an eighth of West Germany's needs. Crude oil arrives from the Middle East, North Africa and Venezuela through terminals on the North Sea, Mediterranean and Adriatic coasts. From terminals at Wilhemshaven and Rotterdam, pipelines convey it south to refineries at Gelsenkirchen, Oberhausen, Duisburg, Buer and Dinslaken, and on to three refineries on the Rhine at Cologne, Godorf and Wesseling. The Rhineland pipeline was extended in 1963 to the new *Caltex* refinery at Kelsterbach near Frankfurt. The South European Pipeline (p. 437 and Fig. 24) runs to Karlsruhe and Mannheim, where several large refineries have recently gone into production. The most recent development is near Ingolstadt in Bavaria, where the first of five refineries planned was opened in 1963 by *Deutsche Shell*, followed a few weeks later by an *Esso* refinery. These and other plants obtain crude oil through the Rhine–Danube Pipeline from Karlsruhe, from Genoa through the Central European Pipeline which passes in a tunnel under the San Bernardino Pass through Switzerland, and from Trieste by the Trans-Alpine Pipeline. The total annual refinery capacity in 1968 was about 70 million tons.

Natural gas is worked in the Hanover–Brunswick district and in the Rhineland near Darmstadt. These home supplies, together with large amounts imported from the Dutch gasfield at Slochteren (p.262), are distributed through a rapidly extending web of trunk-mains.

Before and during the War, Germany produced a large amount of synthetic oil, mainly at the Leuna plant near Merseburg (now in East Germany) and at Gelsenkirchen in the Ruhr; the former used brown coal, the latter bituminous coal. Though damaged during the War and dismantled immediately after, both are now in production.

Electricity

Before 1938 Germany's power stations had a higher installed capacity and greater output than those of any other European country, with numerous large modern plants and a detailed transmission system. Much of this development took place between 1933 and 1939, but during the latter stages of the War damage to both plants and transmission lines was on an enormous scale, and production fell to less than a quarter in 1945. A major contribution to West Germany's industrial resurgence has been the tremendous increase in electricity production; this has almost trebled between 1955 and 1968 to 209 milliard KWh. The transmission network has been highly integrated, taking power not only from the public and municipal stations but also excess production from industrial units.

Several hydro-stations have been built in the Alpine Foreland on tributaries of the Danube, and others in the Bavarian Alps, notably the Kochel plant which is West Germany's largest. A number of stations, some operated jointly with Switzerland, are located on or near the Rhine above Basle, others jointly with France on the middle Rhine (p. 434), and the Schluchsee plant on the southern flanks of the Black Forest uses the 600 m (1970 ft) fall from the lake to the Rhine near Waldshut. Other stations are in the Central Uplands, where dams have been built to create large heads; the river Ruhr is especially important.

Thermal power production, using coal and brown coal (the use of oil is officially restricted to preserve this outlet for coal), has increased so rapidly that the proportion of hydro is only about 15 per cent of the total. Hydro and brown coal stations provide the base output, the more expensively operated hard coal stations in the Ruhr being utilized for peak loads. The first atomic power station at Kahl on the river Main, 14 km (9 miles) north of Aschaffenburg, began full operation in 1962, since followed by others.

Other Minerals

With the exception of salt, potash and some iron ore, West Germany is not well supplied with minerals, which form a considerable import item.

Germany's early iron ore requirements were obtained from black-band deposits in the Coal Measures, then from the Siegerland and the edge of the Westerwald between the valleys of the Lahn and the Dill near Wetzlar. These ores average about 50 per cent metal content, but reserves are small. About two-thirds of West Germany's requirements are now provided by the Salzgitter and Peine fields in Lower Saxony near Brunswick. This ore, of Cretaceous age, has only about 28 to 30 per cent iron and a high phosphorus content, but it occurs in thick beds with huge reserves, and can be enriched to a 45 per cent metal content by special sintering and washing processes. Other scattered fields are worked in Bavaria, in the Vogelsberg in Hesse, in the Weser Hills, and in Baden.

Output reached a postwar maximum of 13·5 million tons in 1960, but since then has declined to 7·7 million tons in 1968. Most of the balance comes from Sweden and elsewhere (p. 167), for Lorraine ore is not used except in the Saarland.

Some manganese is obtained in connection with the iron ores in the Siegerland near Eiserfeld and Wiedenau, some copper in the western Harz, small amounts of lead and zinc from the Eifel and western Harz, and pyrites from the Sauerland.

Large quantities of common salt, potash and other salts occur in the Mesozoic rocks of the Bördeland, of the same geological age as the Stassfurt field in East Germany (p. 218). The output of potash has steadily increased to about 20 million tons in 1968, and in that year 5·0 million tons of common salt were produced.

MANUFACTURING INDUSTRY

The Industrial Revolution in Germany came later than in Britain and Belgium, but after the unification of the empire industry surged ahead in its contribution to Bismarck's 'blood and iron' policy. Though poor in many raw materials, Germany was centrally situated to obtain them from neighbouring countries, and was able to add to an abundance of coal the skill of its technicians and its scientists, who have gained more Nobel prizes than those of any other country. Most branches of industry were organized into large groups or cartels, placing a concentration of power in the hands of the industrialists; *I.G. Farben* dominated the chemical industry, and *Krupp*, *Thyssen* and the *Vereinigte Stahlwerke* a substantial part of the steel and engineering industries. In the years before 1939 this tremendous industrial strength was controlled by the State and used to further Germany's aggressive policies.

Germany in 1945 was industrially shattered; to prolonged destruction by air raids and military operations was added the policy, enunciated at Potsdam, of reducing the military potential by breaking up the cartels and dismantling heavy industry; the Russians in particular ruthlessly removed factories *en bloc*. At one stage the Allies even discussed turning Germany into a rural agricultural country, and it was impossible to visualize in 1946 that West Germany alone would by 1953 attain an industrial output equivalent to that of prewar Germany, and subsequently increase it enormously. It is now the most powerful member of the European Community, and this industrial development continues; an index of productivity of 100 in 1962 had risen to 131 by 1968.

Without doubt, the hard work, technical skill and commercial acumen of the people was the most important factor accounting for this 'West German miracle'. It was necessary for West Germany to make a major contribution to the economic, political, and strategic strength and stability of western Europe. The refugees from the eastern territories, at first a grave problem, provided an additional 2·75 million workers; many brought their technical and managerial expertise, and about 120,000 new 'refugee industries' and businesses have been established. Capital investment in industry was encouraged by taxation concessions, and overtime pay was for a time exempt from taxation.

The policy of dismantling war factories was soon discontinued, and it was obvious that the cartels were necessary for large-scale industry. In 1945, for example, the Allies began the process of liquidating the shattered remains of the Krupp empire, which the War Crimes Tribunal confiscated, but when it was discovered that this would give the U.S.S.R. a quarter share of the Ruhr properties the decision was speedily rescinded. It has proved to be impossible to break up the company and disperse the holdings; *Rheinhausen A.G.* was created in 1954 to incorporate the Krupp holdings in coal and steel, about a third of the firm's total activities. Soon afterwards the firm was ordered to dispose of *Rheinhausen*, but even now no purchaser has yet been found, so large is the capital involved. Attempts by the Allies to control industry largely ceased when the Federal Republic became a sovereign state. Some of the large organizations have expanded even further through mergers; in 1964 the link-up of *August Thyssen Hütte* with *Phoenix-Rheinohr*

A.G. of Düsseldorf was announced, and the steel industry is now dominated by four large organizations.

West Germany is one of the world's leading industrial powers: the fifth producer of coal, the fourth producer of steel, probably the largest exporter of engineering products, and the second largest shipbuilding country. Though industry is distributed widely, several important concentrations stand out. They may be listed summarily as: (a) the Ruhr-Westphalia; (b) the ports of Hamburg, Bremen and to a less extent Lübeck; (c) the Saarland; (d) the Frankfurt–Mainz region; (e) the Main–Neckar district (Mannheim–Ludwigshafen); (f) West Berlin; and (g) the large cities, notably Munich, Stuttgart, Nuremberg and Augsburg, discussed in the regional section below.

The Iron and Steel Industry

West Germany's steel industry has been based on supplies of coking coal rather than on the small production of iron ore. As a result, the main steel-making area is the Ruhr, which produced about 80 per cent of the total 41·2 million tons in 1968 at large integrated plants at Rheinhausen (Plate XXV), Oberhausen, Dortmund and Duisburg, with Düsseldorf to the south. The industry uses some internally produced ore, but mainly ore brought from Sweden, Liberia, Mauretania, Brazil and Australia, and trans-shipped at Rotterdam, with a large amount of scrap. In the Ruhr a remarkable juxtaposition of coal mines, coke ovens, blast furnaces, open-hearth steel mills, forges and rolling-mills lies within a conurbation about 60 km (40 miles) long and 16 km (10 miles) wide. In 1963 West Germany was the third steel-producing country in the world, after the U.S.A. and the U.S.S.R., but since 1964 it has been displaced into fourth position by Japan.

The Saarland produces just over 10 per cent of West Germany's steel, using Lorraine ore and coke made from local coal with some admixture from the Ruhr. Blast furnaces are located at Dillingen, and integrated plants with basic Bessemer converters at Neunkirchen, Saarbrücken and Völklingen.

Steel plants situated at the source of ore include those in the Siegerland and the Lahn valley, making mainly special quality steels, as at Giessen. Two large plants operate in Lower Saxony at Salzgitter and at Ilsede near Peine. The former is the successor to the prewar *Hermann Goering* concern, completed in 1937, which at its peak during the War produced 2·5 million tons of steel annually, but in 1948 dismantling began and Salzgitter was left almost an empty shell. To find work for thousands of refugees the West German government obtained Allied approval to rebuild the plant. By 1952 its furnaces were producing pig-iron, and two years later steel was made in its open-hearth furnaces; in 1968 it produced about 2 million tons of steel, West Germany's largest single steel plant. It has its own coke ovens, and puts surplus gas and electricity

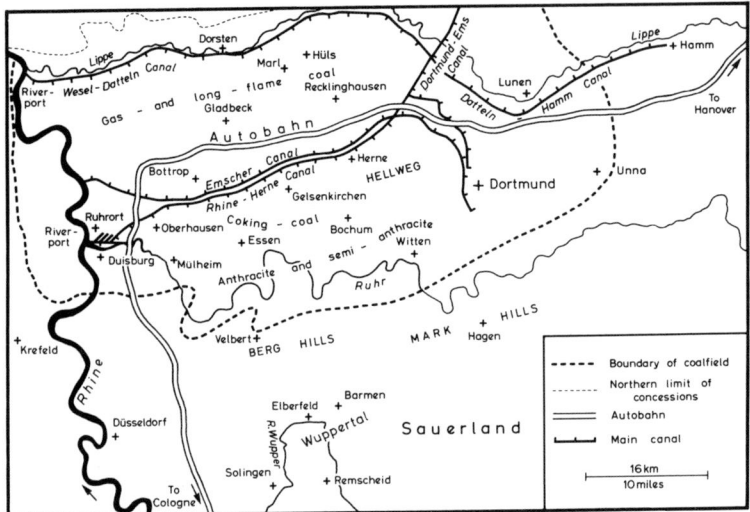

Fig. 25. The Ruhr

into the West German grids. Other outlying steel plants, such as those at Bremen and Lübeck, supply local needs, and another at Krefeld produces high-grade alloys and electric steels.

Engineering

Heavy engineering is closely associated with the iron and steel plants, at the seaports and river ports where steel can be cheaply brought by water, and at cities with plentiful labour supplies. Essen, Dortmund, Oberhausen and Rheinhausen on the Ruhr coalfield, Duisburg, Düsseldorf and Cologne on the Rhine, and Saarbrücken and Zweibrücken in the Saar, make girders, bridges, boilers, plant and heavy machinery. Locomotives are built at Essen, Kassel, Munich and Mannheim; agricultural machinery at

Düsseldorf, Cologne, and large cities in agricultural regions, such as Hanover; and machine tools and cutlery at Solingen, the neighbouring Remscheid, and Wuppertal. Electrical engineering, apart from West Berlin (p. 232), is carried on at Stuttgart, Frankfurt-am-Main, Mannheim and Munich.

Two important aspects of engineering are shipbuilding and the automobile industry. Before 1914 the mercantile marine was second in the world, and a large navy had been built, and though for many years after the 1914-18 War Germany was forbidden to construct warships, by 1939 a fleet of U-boats and some large warships, notably the 'Bismarck' and the 'Tirpitz', had been built, while liners included the 'Bremen' and the 'Europa'. The chief shipyards, situated along the estuaries of the Elbe and the Weser, were heavily damaged by bombing and were dismantled after 1945. Until 1949 West Germany was forbidden to build and launch ocean-going vessels, but once these restrictions were lifted the industry went ahead at remarkable speed. In 1954 *Blohm und Voss* recommenced production at Hamburg, now one of the world's most modern shipyards, as is its neighbour *Deutsche Werft*, and by 1961 the Elbe yards were producing 44 per cent of West Germany's tonnage. Second in importance are the Kiel yards, with 30 per cent of the total, and third is Bremen-Bremerhaven with 17 per cent. Emden, Wilhelmshaven, Flensburg, Rendsburg and Lübeck (which specializes in dredgers) have smaller establishments. By 1960 West Germany had attained third place in the world in tonnage launched, and by 1963 only Japan was ahead. Many factors contributed to this boom: the new yards could give rapid and definite delivery dates; the Korean war was a great stimulus; big orders for tankers were received from Greek shipping magnates; and for a number of years tax-free investment was allowed in shipbuilding. Tankers and bulk-carriers have been the most numerous and profitable launchings. In 1968 West German launchings totalled 1·35 million tons, compared with Japan's 8·6 and Sweden's 1·1 millions.

Gottfried Daimler built the world's first effective motor-car near Stuttgart, and Adam Opel constructed the first small mass-produced German car near Rüsselsheim-am-Main, but it was not until the 1930s that the industry began to expand. At first mainly lorries and military vehicles were produced, and the increasing importance of motor transport was reflected in the construction of the *Autobahn* system. By 1945 most of the plants were shattered, and reconstruction was at first slow. Then both exports and car ownership in West

Germany rocketed, the latter being symbolic of growing prosperity; by 1968 there were 11·7 million cars on the roads, 1 for every 5 people. There are six main firms. *Daimler-Benz A.G.* produce the Mercedes cars, not only at their plants at Untertürkheim and Sindelfingen near Stuttgart, but also at Gaggenau in the Black Forest, at Mannheim and at Wörth in the Rhineland. Then there are the three keenly competitive mass-production firms. At Wolfsburg, north-east of Brunswick, a factory which started in 1937 to provide cars for workers has grown into the enormous *Volkswagen* plant, employing 70,000 people; other

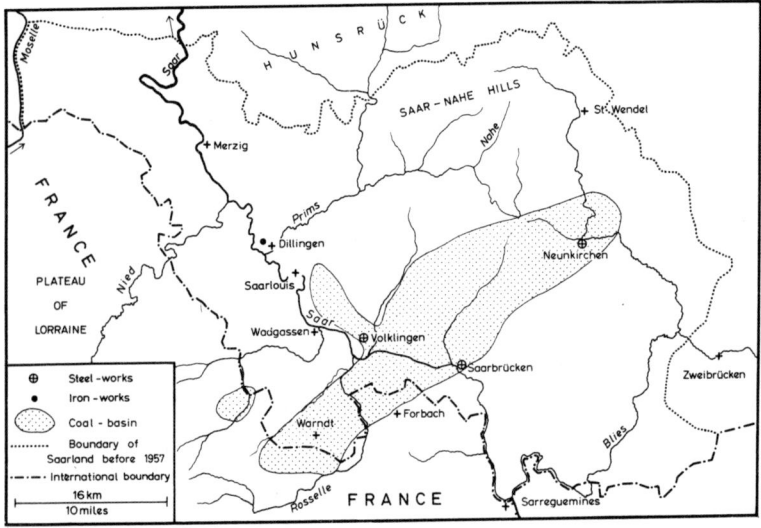

Fig. 26. The Saarland

branches of this firm are at Hanover, Brunswick, Kassel and Ingolstadt. At Rüsselsheim *Opel* is now the biggest unit in the *General Motors* group and the company opened another plant at Bochum in the Ruhr in 1962. The main *Ford* plant is at Cologne, with another at Saarlouis. The *Porsche* firm makes a smaller number of high-quality vehicles at Stuttgart, and *B.M.W.* have a large plant in Munich. *Volkswagen* has now merged with several of the smaller, high-quality firms: *Porsche, Auto-Union, Audi* and *N.S.U.*

The Chemical Industry

Large deposits of salt and potash in the Permian deposits of Lower Saxony represent a major source of raw material for the chemical industry, another being coal, with its range of byproducts. Until

1939 Germany was second only to the U.S.A. in the production of chemicals, largely under the control of *I.G. Farben*, now broken up. The postwar recovery of the industry and its expansion follows the same pattern of success as steel. To salt and coal were added hydrocarbons from the oil refineries and gas wells, leading to the development of petrochemicals. Although rather more than half of the prewar chemical industry was located in eastern Germany, developments in the West have been so rapid that by 1954 output was double that of 1938 for the whole Reich and by 1968 it had quadrupled. Activity is widely distributed, especially in the Ruhr and the Rhineland; the chief centres are at Leverkusen on the Rhine north of Cologne, Hoechst near Frankfurt (Plate XXVI), Duisburg and Ludwigshafen. At the last, *Badische Anilin und Soda-Fabrik A.G.*, employing 45,000 workers, has a factory area along the Rhine of 6·5 sq. km (2·5 sq. miles), the largest chemical complex on one site in Europe. Marl-Hüls, in the north of the Ruhr, is a 'new town', the centre of a new chemical industry based on gas piped from the Ems field to the north; it also makes synthetic rubber. The coke-oven plants in the Ruhr and the Saar produce ammonia, sulphuric acid, tar and benzol.

Textiles

Branches of textile manufacture are widely dispersed, mainly in areas where hand-worked domestic production had long been active. There was a considerable degree of specialization before the War of 1939–45, much less now that each of the two states has sought to make itself self-sufficient, and the development of man-made textiles has also altered the pattern of production. Many branches of the industry in West Germany are operated by refugees from the east, which further contributes to its wide dispersion. Woollens are made at Aachen, Wuppertal, Stuttgart and Augsburg; cottons are manufactured at Wuppertal (Plate XXVII), München-Gladbach and Bocholt; Krefeld, one of the traditional textile towns, produces silk, velvet, nylon and terylene; linen has long been made in the Münster 'Bay', chiefly at Münster and Bielefeld; and Düsseldorf, Cologne and Frankfurt produce man-made fibres. West Berlin, Munich and Düsseldorf are centres of 'high fashion'.

Other Industries

A visitor to the annual Trade Fair at Hanover can appreciate the diversity of West German manufactures. Before 1939 the emphasis

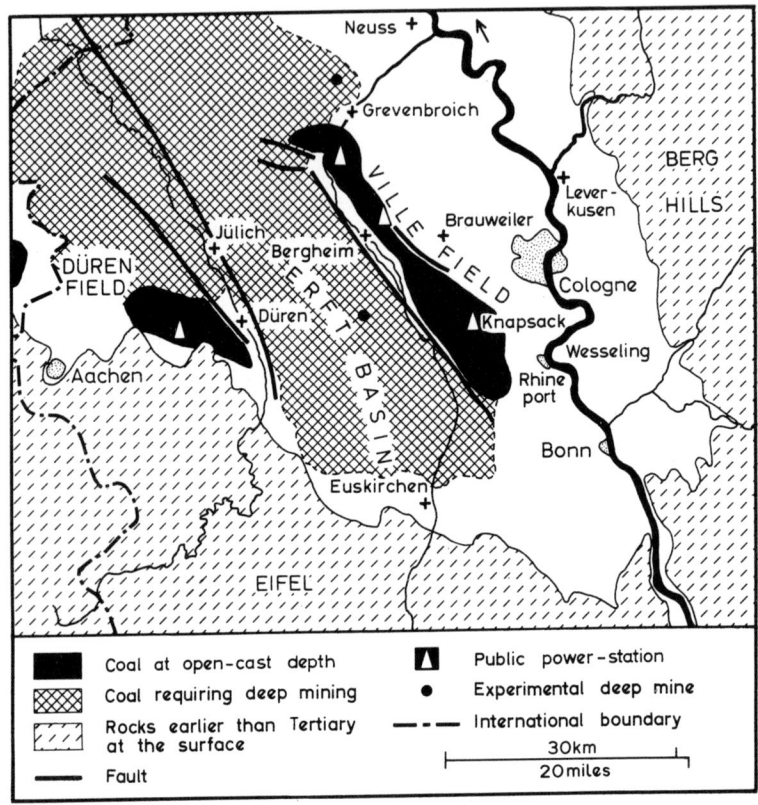

Fig. 27. *The Ville brown coal field*
(After T. H. Elkins)

in western Germany was on heavy industry, but since the War the
virtual severance of trade between the two states has caused a greater
diversification of West German industry, helped by refugees bringing
their specialist skills. Mention may be made of glassware in the Ruhr;
optical instruments and cameras, such as *Leica* at Wetzlar, *Carl-
Zeiss* at Ober Kochen near Heidenheim, *Agfa* at Munich, and others
at Göttingen, Stuttgart and Brunswick; radio and electronics, as
the *Grundig* factory at Fürth near Nuremberg; leather at Weinheim,
north-east of Mannheim, and footwear at Pirmasens in the Palatinate, Stuttgart and Weinheim; pottery at Weiden in Bavaria;
vegetable oil refining at Hamburg, the port of entry of oilseeds;
and brewing at Munich and Dortmund.

COMMUNICATIONS

Before 1938 Germany possessed a well integrated transport system. Much of the country's industrial growth was related to the development of the railways, especially those sections serving the coalfields and major manufacturing regions. The Rhine, Weser, Elbe and Oder provided transportation between south and central Germany and the coasts, while several canals interlinked the natural waterways. A road system, which had hitherto experienced little more than a haphazard local development, achieved both economic and strategic importance with the construction of the *Autobahnen* under the National Socialist régime. *Deutsche Lufthansa* flew 20 million km (12 million miles) a year, providing both internal and European schedules and a regular mail and freight service to South America.

This transportation system was disrupted by the War of 1939–45, when strategic bombing of lines of communications was an inevitable part of military operations. Then came the division of the country into two, so that routeways were arbitrarily severed, with only a few limited links and crossings, while the previous focusing of routes on certain nodes, particularly Berlin, created enormous problems. Apart from the extensive reconstruction of destroyed or damaged facilities, numerous new links and alignments were required.

Roads

By 1968 the *Autobahn* network, still under development, totalled 3617 km (2248 miles). Fig. 28 indicates how efficiently this network and its future extension links the main cities and industrial areas. These express highways are used very heavily; it is possible at certain times of day to see even a six-lane motorway choked with traffic, especially in the section through the Ruhr and south to Cologne and Stuttgart. The amount of motor traffic on West German roads has increased phenomenally; in 1968 over a million heavy trucks were operating (it is estimated that the tonnage carried is twelve times that of 1938), and 11·7 million private cars.

The road system apart from the *Autobahnen* is not however particularly good, despite an overall length of classified roads of about 160 000 km (100,000 miles) in 1968. Many are narrow, with poor surfaces, and the average density of road-length per unit of area is little more than half that of Great Britain.

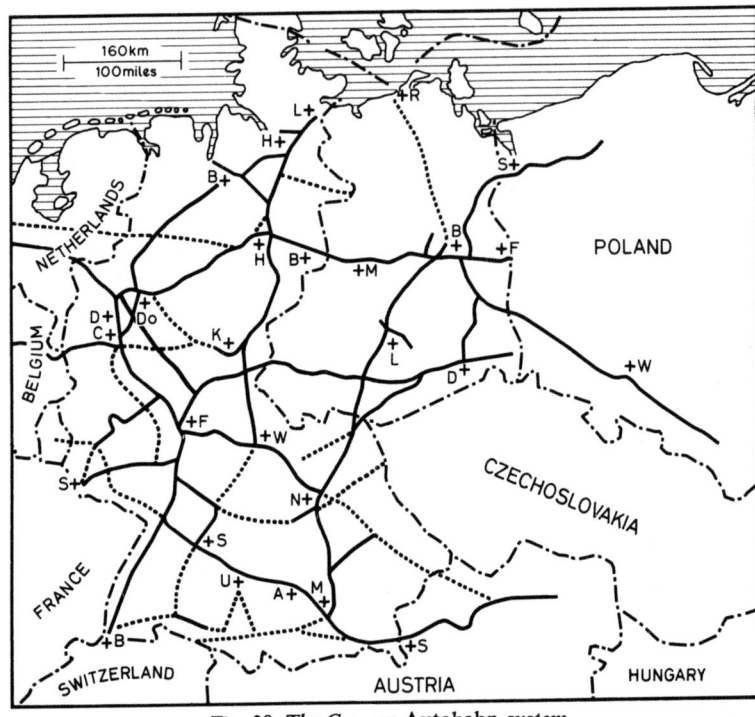

Fig. 28. The German Autobahn *system*
The dotted lines indicate sections under construction (1970).

Waterways

The inland waterways of West Germany totalled 4424 km (2749 miles) in 1968. The main physical advantages of the system are the great rivers, the existence of the Urstromtäler (p. 145) which have facilitated the construction of west–east links, and the low-lying nature of much of the North German Plain. These waterways serve areas of heavy industry and many large cities are situated on their banks, which accounts for the 233 million tons of freight transported in 1968, about 25 per cent of the West German total.

Though the rivers have been used since Roman times and a few canals were built in the Middle Ages, traffic was unimportant until the industrial age of the nineteenth century. The rivers had considerable navigational difficulties, and vexatious tolls were levied by the numerous riparian states. No great period of canal building occurred, as in Britain's pre-railway age, and in the nineteenth century the improvement of roads and the creation of the railway network received much more attention. The formulation of the status of international river at the Congress of Vienna in 1815 helped to reduce tolls on the Rhine, Elbe, Weser and Ems. But before 1871 it was difficult to obtain any concerted action of improvement on

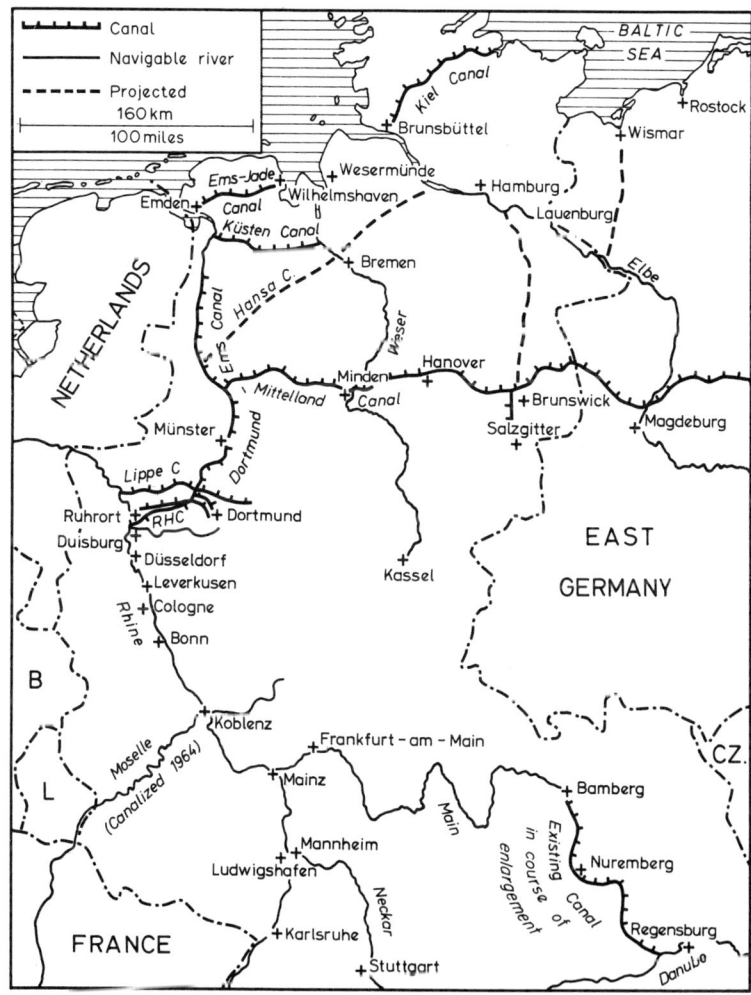

Fig. 29. The West German waterway system

waterways passing through more than one state, and even after that date their administration was left in the hands of individual states.

Before the end of the century several rivers had been regularized, and some canals were built. The most important, though it never fulfilled original expectations, was the 269 km (167-mile) long Dortmund-Ems Canal built in 1892–99, which was intended to be a wholly German alternative to the Rhine as an outlet to the North Sea from the Ruhr industrial district, and as an entry for Swedish iron ore. In 1895 the Kiel Canal was completed across the root of the Schleswig-Holstein peninsula from Brunsbüttel to Kiel, 85 km (53 miles) long and taking sea-going vessels of up to 9·5 m (31 ft) draught; though originally designed to allow the German navy to move between the Baltic and North Seas, it has proved of assistance to Germany's trade with the Scandinavian countries.

In 1905 the Prussian government sanctioned the construction of several new waterways, including the Rhine-Herne Canal through the Ruhr coal-basin (1914), and the western part of the Mittelland Canal between the Ems and the Weser (completed in 1915). The eastern section of the Mittelland Canal to Magdeburg was completed in 1938, so providing a west–east waterway of 360 km (224 miles).

Since 1945 a number of new projects has been planned and some started, partly as a result of the position of the new boundary (Fig. 29). A large canal (the Hansa) will run south-west from the Elbe, make a locked connection with the Weser, and continue to the Dortmund-Ems Canal, and another (started in 1968) from the Elbe above Hamburg will go directly south to join the Mittelland Canal near Brunswick. The perennial project of a first-class link between the Main near Bamberg and the Danube above Regensburg is in progress; two sections were opened in 1968. Several direct links between the Rhine and the Meuse, one from Duisburg to Venlo, and another across the hill-country from Grimlinghausen via Maastricht to the Meuse below Liège, have been seriously considered.

A major contribution, the regularization of the Moselle (Plate XXVIII), was completed in May 1964. In 1956 West Germany agreed to carry out the work on the 187 km (116 miles) of this river within its territory, France was to be responsible for the work on 30 km (19 miles) and Luxembourg for the remaining 39 km (24 miles); about half of the total expenditure fell on France, and under 1 per cent on Luxembourg. France has much larger interests in the navigation of this river, though West Germany gains from the electricity generated at power stations sited at the barrages. From Thionville to Koblenz, a total distance of 260 km (160 miles), the channel has a minimum width of 37 m (120 ft) and a depth of 3 m (10 ft), is navigable by the standard 1,500-ton European barge, and

Plate XXII. Garmisch-Partenkirchen in Bavaria, West Germany, with the Bavarian Alps in the background culminating in the Zugspitze (2963 m, 9720 feet) on the right

Plate XXIII. Fragmented farm holdings in the Spessart, east of Frankfurt-am-Main, West Germany

Plate XXIV. Terraced vineyards on the slopes of the Rhine Gorge near St Goar, West Germany

Plate XXV. The Krupp blast-furnace plant at Rheinhausen, the largest and most modern in West Germany

descends by means of thirteen locks from 140 to 55 m (460 to 180 ft) at the Rhine junction.

The Rhine handles two-thirds of West German waterway freight, for it is navigable for 713 km (443 miles) within German territory. Its regularization has been a long and expensive task, and there are still times of year when the river above Strasbourg may be temporarily unnavigable because of low water, floods or occasional freezing. Small sea-going vessels can normally reach Cologne; barges of 6,000 tons capacity go as far as Duisburg and Düsseldorf, of 5,000 tons to Mannheim (Plate XXIX), and of 2,000 tons to Basle. The construction by the French of the left-bank canal loops in the south, known as the Canal d'Alsace (p. 460), has helped in the southern section of the Rift Valley, and joint Franco-German action is improving the remainder.

Several Rhine river ports have been developed, the largest being Duisburg-Ruhrort, the former on the south bank, the latter on the north bank, of the Ruhr confluence; it handles coal, coke, iron ore, crude steel and petroleum, totalling 35 million tons annually. Düsseldorf, Leverkusen, Cologne and Mainz are also important, while further upstream are the twin ports of Ludwigshafen-Mannheim, second to Duisburg in terms of freight.

Upstream Rhine freight from the Dutch border comprises iron ore, grain, petroleum, timber and oilseeds, while downstream traffic

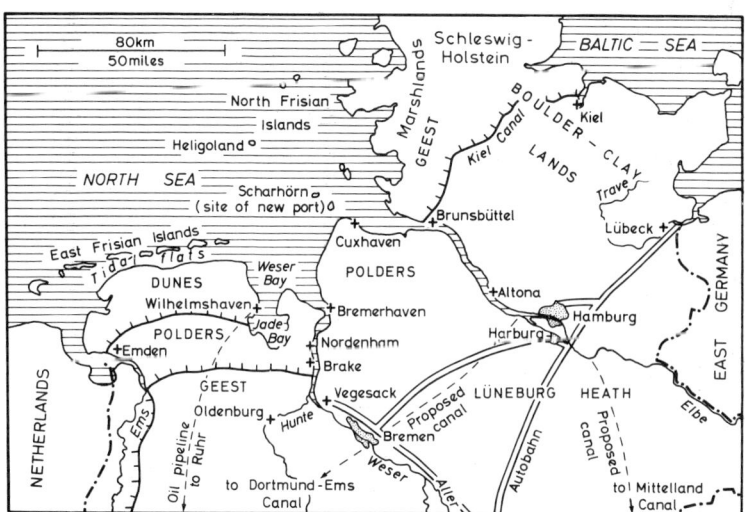

Fig. 30. The North German lowlands
The two proposed canals are now under construction.

includes coal and coke, brown coal briquettes, steel, fertilizers and chemicals. About 75 million tons of freight passes the German-Dutch customs-post at Lobith annually, of which two-thirds goes upstream, carried in Dutch, German, Belgian, French and Swiss barges, in that order of importance. The Ruhr canals are chiefly concerned with coal and coke, especially the Rhine-Herne Canal, which continues the Dortmund-Ems canal into the Ruhrort docks, and the Lippe Canal. The Dortmund-Ems Canal was built to accommodate only 750-ton barges, but its enlargement has recently been completed, so that 1,500-ton barges can go through from Emden to the Ruhr.

The Mittelland Canal, which can take barges of 1,000 tons capacity, suffered a considerable reduction in importance after 1945 through its severance by the West–East German border. However, the West German section carries a considerable traffic in coal and coke from the Ruhr, steel, petroleum, chemicals and fertilizers, bricks, cement, and local agricultural produce such as sugar beet, potatoes and grain, from the Bördeland. A locked connection with the Weser near Minden enables barges to pass between the canal and the river.

Railways

Germany's first railway was opened between Nuremberg and Fürth in Bavaria; the original two locomotives on this line were built by Robert Stephenson and operated by British crews. Within fifteen years there were 5000 km (3000 miles) of railway, and by 1937 Germany had a total length of nearly 55 000 km (34,000 miles), exceeded in length only by the U.S.A. and U.S.S.R., and in density only by Great Britain and Belgium. A pattern developed with no single focal point, for much of the rail net originated as individual systems serving a particular state and focusing on its capital city. However, as early as the mid-nineteenth century four main groupings began to develop: a northern group based on Berlin, a lower Rhineland group based on Cologne, a south-western group based on Frankfurt-am-Main, and a Bavarian group based on Augsburg. Gradually the main lines were interlinked, but up to the War of 1914–18 there were seven individual State railways; in 1924 they were reconstituted as the *Deutsche Reichsbahn*.

The division of Germany in 1945 left 35 000 km (22,000 miles) of route in the West, though with only seven crossings into the East, and a tremendous task of rebuilding the war-damaged system was necessary. It was reorganized in 1951 as the *Deutsche Bundesbahn*, quite independent of the *Deutsche Reichsbahn* in East Germany; the only through trains are between West Germany and Berlin (with connections for Warsaw and Moscow), and these do not convey passengers for internal journeys in East Germany. The main pattern of flow of both passengers (about a million annually, a decline of a third in the last decade) and freight (319 million tons) is now north–south, rather than west–east, with the exception of the heavily used line from Essen via Hamm and Hanover to Brunswick. Considerable modernization has been effected, including the electrification of lines in the Rhineland from Basle to Cologne, in the Ruhr and in Bavaria, and the extension of high-speed diesel haulage, of which Germany was a pioneer in the 'thirties.

West Germany makes a considerable contribution to international routes, and several famous express trains still run, including 'Helvetia' (Hamburg–Frankfurt–Basle–Zürich), 'Saphir' (Ostend–Cologne–Frankfurt), 'Rheingold' and 'Loreley' (the Netherlands to Switzerland along the Rhine valley), 'Tauern' (Belgium–Aachen–Munich–Austria), 'Ostend–Vienna', and 'Nord' (the Netherlands, Belgium and France across northern Germany to Copenhagen, Malmö and Stockholm). The position of West Germany, lying athwart west-central Europe between the North Sea and the Alps, accounts for the importance of these international routes.

A new ferry route has been introduced from Puttgarden on Fehmarn island (linked by a bridge to the mainland) with Rödby on the Danish island of Lolland (p. 130), and so to Copenhagen. This replaces the Warnemünde-Gedser and Sassnitz-Trelleborg ferries now operated by East Germany.

Air Transport

After 1945 Germany had no airlines, but numerous military aerodromes and civil airports were brought into use by the Allies as soon as the crippled facilities could be repaired. Berlin Tempelhof, fortunately from the point of view of the Allies, lay in West Berlin. Under the Potsdam Agreement, all Allied aircraft flying to Berlin are strictly confined to three 'corridors' from Hamburg, Hanover and Frankfurt, and it was by these routes that West Berlin was supplied during the blockade of 1948–49 (p. 231). Gradually foreign airlines began to serve West German airports, and in 1953 a national airline was created, most of its capital owned by the Federal Republic; in 1955 this began commercial operations, first internally, then to other parts of Europe, North and South

America, and the Middle and Far East, and today *Deutsche Lufthansa* is an airline of world status.

Mercantile Marine and Ports

In 1938 Germany had twenty seaports which each handled annually 100,000 tons or more of shipping. Hamburg was of 'world' class, fifth in order after New York, Rotterdam, London and Antwerp, in terms of tonnage of shipping entered and cleared. Despite the set-backs of the War of 1914–18 and its aftermath, Germany's merchant fleet in 1938 ranked fifth in the world, with about 4·5 million g.r.t. But in 1945 the ports lay idle, their installations devastated by aerial bombardment, and their channels blocked by sunken shipping; the mercantile marine had been mostly destroyed or captured.

The first port to be revived was Bremen, since it was the main entry for the American forces, and facilities were speedily made usable. Situated 56 km (35 miles) up the estuary, Bremen now forms (with Bremerhaven-Geestemünde) West Germany's chief passenger port, the terminus of liner services with New York. It also imports raw cotton and jute, supplying a large part of central Europe.

Hamburg is the largest cargo port of West Germany, situated 120 km (75 miles) up the Elbe and reach by a channel dredged to 12 m (39 ft). Its outport is Cuxhaven, but with the decline of passenger traffic in favour of Bremen-Bremerhaven this has become mainly a fishing port. The destruction of 80 per cent of Hamburg's port facilities was made good by 1953, when installations along the river front and in the basins were completed, and a year later the freight handled, about 24 million tons, surpassed pre-1939 figures. By 1968 this had increased to 38 million tons, its imports including grain, mineral ores and raw materials, its exports comprising manufactured goods, much less than imports in both bulk and value. A large container-traffic is developing. Hamburg still handles some trade to and from East Germany, Czechoslovakia and Hungary, but a large part of their imports and exports which formerly passed along the Elbe now goes via Polish ports and increasingly via Rostock (p. 225). Hamburg is again the third port of continental Europe, though some way behind Rotterdam and Antwerp (Fig. 44). The citizens of Hamburg envisage the creation before the end of the 'seventies of a large port off the mouth of the Elbe among the sandbanks and mud-flats between the small islands of Scharhörn and Neuwerk, for which hydrographic surveys began in 1963. The new harbour will handle bulk cargoes of grain, ore and coal. The projected new canals from the Elbe (p. 176 and Fig. 29) will also be a great asset. One striking feature which has contributed to the port's success is the excellent labour situation. Other West German ports include Emden, Wilhelmshaven and Kiel (Plate XXX). Emden, on the estuary of the Ems, is the entry for Swedish iron ore and Norwegian timber, much of which proceeds by barge along the Dortmund-Ems Canal to the Ruhr. Wilhelmshaven has been developed as an oil terminal, with a pipeline to the Ruhr (p. 163) and in 1968 its naval base was re-opened. Kiel is a fishing port, with rapidly expanding ship-building.

In 1968 sea-going vessels unloaded 87 million tons of imported foreign freight at West German ports, and loaded 24 million tons for export. The total is more than three times the pre-1939 figure, an indication of West German economic recovery and development. The mercantile marine, including numerous tankers, totalled 7·0 million g.r.t., compared with 4·5 million in 1939 for Germany as a whole.

COMMERCE

Germany's economy was entirely controlled by the occupying powers during the years following 1945. Extensive aid, mainly from the U.S.A., was needed to avert starvation in the three western occupation zones. The formation of the Federal Republic in 1949, helped by credits from the Western Allies and the rapid growth of industry, produced a remarkable resurgence of economic activity, for West Germany has contributed to, stimulated and benefited from the revival of western Europe. As a result of its geographical position, its possession of the Ruhr coalfield and much of the Rhine as the 'economic artery' of the West, the technical ability of its industrialists, the skill of its statesmen, the hard work of its people, and the aid of its former enemies, it was well able to take advantage of its membership of various international organizations. Until recently West Germany had to bear no crippling burden of armaments. As early as 1952 the country not only had a favourable trade balance, but the value of its commerce considerably exceeded that of prewar Germany, and the *Deutsche Mark* (*DM*) rapidly became one of the strongest of currencies.

West Germany's main imports are foodstuffs, forming about a third of the total by value, and raw materials, mainly iron ore, textile fibres and petroleum. Its exports consist of raw steel, especially to its partners in the Coal and Steel Community, and manufactured goods; for example, the *Volkswagen* car, with its cheapness, reputation of reliability, and after-sales service, has permeated the world's markets, selling even in great auto-producing countries such as the U.S.A.

In 1968 about 41 per cent of West Germany's imports came from the E.E.C. countries, 16 per cent from the E.F.T.A. group (of which the U.K. supplied a third) and 12 per cent from North America. About 38 per cent of exports go to the E.E.C., 22 per cent to the E.F.T.A., and 12 per cent to North America. West Germany has made successful efforts to increase its trade with the 'new' and former underdeveloped lands; such capital goods as agricultural machinery, factory plant, power station equipment, mining machinery and railway rolling-stock are exported. In recent years trade with the Communist bloc has also increased. Though there was little commercial intercourse between West and East Germany for some years, there has recently been an appreciable increase (p. 227); West Germany imports from the East brown coal briquettes, chemical raw materials and textiles, and exports coal and steel.

POPULATION AND SETTLEMENT

In 1946 the population of all Germany was about 65 million, of whom 44 million lived in the West. This was a decrease of over 4 million compared with 1939, largely the result of war deaths, both military and civilian. Since 1945, while the population of East Germany has declined (p. 227), that of West Germany has increased; by 1954 it had reached 52 million, with a further 2 million in West Berlin, and by December 1968 it was 60·5 million. This rise was at first due to refugees, consisting partly of *Reichsdeutsche*, Germans from the territories lost to Poland and the U.S.S.R. (about 7 million), partly of *Volksdeutsche* expelled from Czechoslovakia, and partly of escaped citizens of East Germany. The number of arrivals in West Germany until the Wall (p. 231) was built in 1961 was about 12·5 million, very nearly a quarter of the present population; since 1961 27,500 have arrived, in spite of the great risk involved. The average density has increased from about 160 per sq. km (420 per sq. mile) in 1945 to 243 per sq. km (630 per sq. mile) in 1968. There are over a million foreign workers, mainly Italians, Spaniards and Greeks.

Distribution of Population

The area of greatest density of population stands out as an inverted 'L', with the right-angle in the north-western corner of the country. The west–east bar of the 'L', 60–100 km (40–60 miles) wide, extends from the boundary near Aachen through the industrialized Ruhr and along the prosperous Bördeland, with its resources of salt, petroleum and iron ore, its cities, notably Hanover and Brunswick, and its rich agriculture. The north–south bar of the 'L' follows the Rhineland, also an area of prosperous agriculture, and with the concentrated urban industrialization of Düsseldorf, Cologne, Koblenz, Mainz-Frankfurt, Karlsruhe and Stuttgart, strung out along the lines of communication.

The Saarland is an outlying area of density above average, dependent on the coalfield and heavy industry, and separated by Hercynian plateaus from the Rhineland. Other centres of dense population form 'islands' around widely separated cities: the North Sea ports, Kassel, Nuremberg, Augsburg and Munich.

By contrast, considerable areas have average densities of less than 40 per sq. km (100 per sq. mile). These include the coastal polders, the heaths and moorlands of northern Germany (Hanover, Oldenburg, the Lüneburg Heath and western Schleswig-Holstein); the Middle Rhine Highlands and the sandstone and limestone Central Uplands; parts of the Bavarian Foreland, with its gravels and sands covered with moorland; and the foothills and mountains of the Bavarian Alps. The density of rural population is higher than it was in pre-1939 days; between 1939 and 1950 the population of villages of less than 5,000 people increased by about a third, mainly because the cities and towns were so damaged that they were unable to accommodate many refugees. Since 1960, however, urban growth has been rapidly resumed.

Towns and Cities

In 1938 just under a third of the population of Germany lived in cities with more than 100,000 inhabitants. For the first decade after the War, this proportion was appreciably lower, but by 1958 reconstruction and expansion had enabled the cities to recover and in the main improve upon their former position. By that year only Cologne and Wilhelmshaven had not attained their 1939 figures, and a few other towns, mostly industrial centres in North Rhine-Westphalia, had expanded into the category of those with 100,000 people, including Herne, Bottrop and Wanne-Eickel. Salzgitter, the steel-making town in Lower Saxony founded only a few years before the War, also exceeded 100,000. By 1968 fifty-seven towns had populations of 100,000 or more, apart from West Berlin.

Most of the cities and towns are old established; some were Roman garrison centres and route foci, which developed with the growth of ecclesiastical power into cities ruled by powerful bishops: Trier, Cologne, Mainz, Worms, Regensburg and many more. In early medieval times, as commerce began to flourish, merchants settled for protection around the castles and cathedrals of the temporal and spiritual lords, and the towns well sited for trade, especially on the rivers, in gaps through the uplands, in fertile basins, and on estuaries, developed a prosperous civic life, many of them as members of the Hanseatic League. Some of the architectural glories of the cities are cultural legacies of the wealthy merchant families; an example is Augsburg, which the Fugger family dominated for so long. Other towns, especially in central and southern Germany, developed because they were the capitals of small states and principalities, with their courts; after the unification of the empire much of their political significance vanished, though their fine civic buildings remained, at least until 1940–45. Many a city possessed a medieval 'Altstadt', containing a chaos of picturesque buildings; around it the line of the former walls could sometimes be traced as a modern ring road or a green belt of gardens, with the later residential areas and nineteenth century industrialization lying beyond.

The War of 1939–45 took a tremendous toll of the cities; few, notably Heidelberg and Wiesbaden, escaped entirely. Rebuilding has presented a tremendous challenge to West Germany; most cities have been planned for the mid-twentieth century, with broad thoroughfares, apartment blocks of ferroconcrete and glass, and spacious industrial quarters, though a few, of which Lübeck is an example, have reconstructed part at least of the former 'Altstadt'.

Rural Settlement

The distinctive types and patterns of German village structure owe their origin and form mainly to historical rather than geographical causes. They reflect the eastward expansion of settlement, the 'colonization' of land through both peaceful penetration and military conquest; some are the result of the reclamation of forest, swamp and heath, and the creation of new farms out of the wasteland. This colonization and settlement, however, affected chiefly the lands beyond the Elbe (p. 228).

One type of settlement in West Germany is the individual, sometimes quite isolated farm (*Einzelhof*), found mainly in upland areas such as the Middle Rhine Highlands and the higher parts of the Bavarian Foreland. These farms were concerned mainly with pastoral activities, and on the well-watered hills they had no problem of water supply. Later other isolated farms were created in the heathlands of north-western Germany, almost of a 'squatter' type of settlement, by enterprising families.

Over most of the fertile arable lands the dominant form of rural settlement was a nucleated compact cluster of dwellings, revealing no very distinctive arrangement; this is termed a *Haufendorf*, meaning 'a thrown together village'. Agriculture was based on the cultivation of three large fields, following a common rotation, within which was a centrally placed village. The original large fields have become divided into small unenclosed plots, the result of fragmentation through inheritance, despite some progress in consolidation. Where the original individual strips of cultivation were clearly defined, the settlement is known as a *Gewanndorf*, after the word for furlong.

Gradually settlements of a more planned character were established during the process of land reclamation. In the marshlands bordering the North Sea coast, along the lower valleys of the rivers, and in the bogs among the Geestlands of Hanover, Oldenburg and Schleswig-Holstein where settlement depended on drainage, houses were arranged on each side of a canal, or along the inner margin of a dyke; such a village is known as a *Marschhufendorf*. Each homestead has its land extending back at right-angles to the central line; a striking example is Papenburg, not far from the Dutch frontier.

Another characteristic village type is the *Waldhufendorf*, created in early medieval times in the Black Forest, the Odenwald, the Spessart and the Hohe Rhön. Such a settlement is usually located in a valley, strung out in a line; each farmer gradually cleared the land behind his house in a long strip which was pushed back up the wooded slopes. Many of these settlements have characteristic suffixes which indicate a clearing in the forest, such as *-rode*, *-holz*, *-feld* and *-brand*.

By the end of the medieval period, the pattern of settlement in western Germany was virtually complete, and many of these basic village forms have come down through the ages with strikingly little change, except where they have been overtaken and absorbed by the modern development of a large city.

7*

REGIONS

1. The North German Plain

The main ingredients in the physical landscape are the offshore islands, the low-lying coastal lands, the sandy heath and moor country, and the narrow belt of loess-covered Bördeland. These are not continuous latitudinal zones, for they are interrupted by the valleys of the Ems, Weser and Elbe. Farther east, in Schleswig-Holstein, lies a small area of country covered with till.

The Offshore Islands. The North Sea coast of Germany, west of the Elbe estuary, is fronted by a wide extent of sand- and mud-flats, exposed at low tide. About 6 km (4 miles) from the dykes which border the mainland is the line of the East Frisian Islands, seven in number, the largest being Norderney, about 14 km (9 miles) in length, 3 km (2 miles) across. The islands are little more than sand-dunes, rising in places to 18–21 m (60–70 ft), strengthened on their seaward faces against the open North Sea by breakwaters and groynes, and with patches of empoldered pasture on the south. These islands are popular resorts, and several villages cater for visitors, while fishing is active.

To the north of the Elbe estuary are the more irregularly shaped North Frisian Islands, the remnants of the former undulating coastal plain inundated by the sea. They too consist mainly of sand-dunes, with marshland on the landward side, though in places solid rock is visible; on Sylt, the largest, cliffs of red sandstone rise to 41 m (135 ft). Some, known as *Halligen*, covered with bright green grass, are used for grazing, sometimes with a farmhouse perched on an artificial refuge mound. The small fishing villages are crowded with holiday-makers in summer; Westerland on Sylt, Wyk on Föhr, and Amrun are the main resorts, reached by coasting-steamer, except for Sylt, which is linked with the mainland by rail over the 11 km (7 miles) long Hindenburg Dam.

Heligoland is a mass of sandstone 1·6 km in length, situated about 30 km (20 miles) from both the Friesland and Schleswig-Holstein coasts, its steep cliffs rising to a grassy plateau. Captured by Nelson, Heligoland remained British until 1890 when it was exchanged for Zanzibar with Germany, who made it into a powerful naval base, especially for U-boats. Though it was ordered to be demilitarized by the Versailles treaty, this was never wholly carried out, and in the War of 1939–45 it remained a strong point until a thousand-bomber raid by the R.A.F. caused the surviving inhabitants to be evacuated, and in 1947 all the casemates and submarine pens were blown up. Until 1952 it served as an R.A.F. bombing range, but then it was handed back to West Germany and most of its former inhabitants returned. It has become a popular resort, with the attraction of duty-free status, and has resumed its function as a fishing base, especially for lobsters.

The Coastal Lowlands (Fig. 30). The low-lying *Marschen* along the North Sea coast are usually only 8–16 km (5–10 miles) in width, though extending farther inland along each side of the estuaries. The story of their reclamation is similar to that of the Dutch polders, involving the construction of coastal dykes and networks of drainage channels, but only in a few areas are they below sea-level, and the last really bad flood along this section of the German coast was in 1570. The coastlands behind the Baltic Sea in eastern Schleswig-Holstein are covered with undulating sheets of clay of the Younger Drift ground-moraine, which affords a heavy soil of a brown earth category.

Both the marine clays and the tills are fertile and well farmed. The former favour the growth of pasture, which forms the basis of a flourishing dairying and stock fattening activity, especially in Friesland and in western Schleswig-Holstein, where the fields are dotted with the familiar black and white cattle. The till, however, is almost all under arable, growing mainly fodder crops for dairy cattle and pigs. Some of the marine clays are also under the plough, particularly between the Elbe and the Weser, where wheat and oats are grown, while the presence of several large towns has stimulated market gardening, especially along the valley of the lower Elbe. In these coastal lands agriculture is prosperous; a familiar feature is the large farmhouse, with its gable-roof covering house, barns and byres in one sweep.

The functions of the main ports along the coast of West Germany, Hamburg, Bremen, Emden and Kiel, have been described (pp. 180–181). With a population of 1·8 million, Hamburg is both the largest port and city and, excluding West Berlin, the largest industrial centre in West Germany. The Elbe flows in braided channels across its wide, alluvium-floored floodplain, bounded by the low but distinct edges of the Geestlands on either side, and joined from the north by the Alster. The original settlement was sited on a spur of slightly higher Geestland projecting between the Elbe and the Alster, and commanding a ford across the main river. On this spur a castle, the Hammaburg (hence the city's name), was built in the early part of the ninth century, and a small port later developed at the mouth of the Alster. Farther downstream grew the town of Altona; on the south side of the floodplain Harburg was established; and Wilhelmsburg developed to the east. In 1937 these four towns were amalgamated into the *Freie und Hansestadt Hamburg*, a federal state of the Reich; in 1952 it was reconstituted as a *Land*, though retaining its city status. Hamburg has had a long and eventful history, first as a member of the Hanseatic League, then as a North Sea port; during the nineteenth century it grew rapidly with Germany's industrial development. The alluvium of the Elbe valley facilitated the construction of basins; the tidal range in the estuary is so small that ships can arrive or depart at any state of the tide, and enclosed docks are not necessary. Hamburg suffered great destruction during the War of 1939–45, but by 1953 the city had been magnificently rebuilt. Its industrial activities include oil-refining, especially at Harburg, the manufacture of chemicals, soap and margarine, engineering and metallurgical industries, grain-milling and sugar-refining, and the processing of rubber. Most striking has been the development of shipbuilding and marine engineering. The ambition of its civic leaders is to make Hamburg the centre of a large North German industrial region with a population of 10 million, based on the ease of transportation of raw materials and manufactured products by sea. A large steel works is a major feature of the plan, which it is hoped will be completed during the 'seventies.

Bremen (605,000), now West Germany's chief passenger port, is situated 56 km (35 miles) up the Weser at a crossing point of the river, where the higher Geestlands approach the former marshy floor of the valley. The original city is on the right bank of the river; the '*Neustadt*' on the left bank was established in the seventeenth century as a defensive bridgehead. The silting of the Weser and the increasing size of shipping forced the city to develop outports: Vegesack, Brake and Bremerhaven-Geestemünde. After the War of 1939–45, Bremen was reconstituted as a *Land*; it was made an outlying portion of the American zone of occupation to serve for the entry of personnel and materials. Its industries include shipbuilding, grain-milling, tobacco-processing and jute-spinning; it has general and electrical engineering industries.

Emden, the third North Sea port, is on the Ems estuary at the entry of the Dortmund-Ems Canal; much of its imports consist of iron ore and timber. It is also the home port of a large fleet of drifters. Kiel (270,000), once a great naval base, is a fishing port and a rapidly expanding centre of shipbuilding. Wilhelmshaven, which has recently returned to its rôle as a naval base, is now an oil terminal, handling over 20 million tons annually, which flow along a pipeline to the Ruhr. Lübeck, a Baltic port with steel works and engineering activities, has been rebuilt after its extensive wartime damage.

The Heathlands. Behind the coastlands and at a higher elevation, in places up to 90 m (300 ft), lies the heath and moor country: in the west the Geest of Friesland, Oldenburg and western Hanover, in the centre the Lüneburg Heath, in the north the Geest of Schleswig-Holstein. Despite the disadvantages of the acid sandy soils, efforts have been made to improve these areas. Large areas of bog have been drained, the peat stripped off and the sand below mixed with marl and silt; deep ploughing was used to break up the underlying hardpan; and heavy applications of chemical fertilizers were used to enrich the soil. Though some parts, including a nature reserve in the Lüneburg Heath, still support the typical heath vegetation and large areas have been planted with conifers, there is much improved grassland, and some rye, oats and potatoes are grown. The former large flocks of sheep have almost entirely been replaced by cattle and pigs; store cattle are raised and shipped away for fattening to the Bördeland and the estuarine pastures.

The Geestlands are thinly populated; the only towns are small market centres, usually on the edges of the sand country. Oldenburg, on the river Hunte, has food-processing industries; Delmenhorst, 16 km (10 miles) west of Bremen, has the manufacture of woollen textiles and jute, and the production of linoleum; Lüneburg has chemical works based originally on its brine springs, and is a centre for visitors.

The Bördeland. To the south of the Geestlands is the narrow strip of the Bördeland of Lower Saxony, of which the eastern part between Hanover and Brunswick is sometimes referred to as the Harz Foreland. This is a favoured region; much of the loess soil grows wheat and sugar beet, and cattle are fattened on pulp from the sugar refineries and fodder crops grown in the rotation. Deposits of oil, salt, potash, iron ore, a little coal and brown coal have resulted in the development of manufacturing industries. Some activities are associated with the processing of agricultural products: sugar-refining, grain-milling, leather-tanning, the making of starch, glucose and industrial alcohol. Others are of relatively recent introduction, notably the steel works at Salzgitter and the *Volkswagen* plant at Wolfsburg.

The two most important Bördeland towns are Hanover (Hannover) and Brunswick (Braunschweig). Hanover grew up as a bridge town at the head of navigation of the Leine (a Weser tributary); it was first a medieval market town, then capital of the kingdom of Hanover, next capital of a Prussian province, now the chief town (522,000) of the *Land* of Lower Saxony, and a centre of communications by rail, *Autobahn* and the Mittelland Canal. These efficient transport links are a major reason why Hanover is a great industrial centre where an annual Fair, West Germany's show piece to the world, is held. Its activities, some of which were introduced by refugees from East Germany, include the production of tyres at the largest individual tyre plant in Europe, chemicals, machinery, tractors and heavy vehicles, radios and gramophones, a wide range of light consumer goods, milling and sugar-refining.

Brunswick (226,000), also in Lower Saxony, is situated in a fertile part of the Bördeland at a crossing-point of the Oker, a tributary of the Aller. It was the capital of a Duchy, then of a federal state, then of a *Land*, though in 1945 this was merged with that of Lower Saxony. In the Middle Ages Brunswick was a centre of transit traffic, goods were sold at its fairs and markets, and it was important for domestic craft industry. In the nineteenth century the nearby brown coal at Helmstedt was worked. Its activities include milling, sugar-refining and vegetable-canning, and in recent years it has developed optical industries (especially the production of cameras), engineering, and the making of pharmaceutical chemicals; it too has numerous 'refugee' industries.

2. The Rhineland

The Rhineland has been one of the transitional zones of Europe for nearly two millennia, the scene of long struggles between Frank and Teuton and since 1870 between the modern nation-states of France and Germany. Since the creation of the European Communities, however, the Rhine has become more than ever the axis of western Europe.

The Rhine Rift Valley. For about 300 km (190 miles) from Basle, the Rhine flows northward through a flat-floored valley, 30–50 km (20–30 miles) in width. The Black Forest and the Odenwald along its margins are mainly of granite, forming rounded summits covered with coniferous forest, the highest being the Feldberg (1495 m, 4905 ft). During the Quaternary glaciation, the Black Forest nurtured some small snowfields and glaciers; several lakes, notably the Feldsee and Titisee, lie in glacially eroded hollows. The northern part of the Black Forest is covered with Bunter Sandstone, most of which carries spruce and fir forest, with patches of pasture.

The sides of the Rift Valley descend in steps to the Jurassic limestone foothills, interrupted by the deeply cut valleys of streams joining the Rhine, and by small basins and depressions, including the Breisgau of which Freiburg is the centre. Farther west, near Breisach, the Kaiserstuhl rises prominently to 557 m (1827 ft) from the valley floor; it is a mass of basalt, the product of some mid-Tertiary volcanic activity.

A series of well-defined terraces borders the floodplain, which is in places 8 km (5 miles) wide; over it the Rhine formerly wandered in braided branches, with backwaters separated by marshland and gravel islets, an area known as the *Ried*. Much has been reclaimed and drained, and the river is confined in a straightened channel between embankments both to check flooding and to assist navigation. Areas near the river form damp pasture, sometimes bearing patches of alder wood, while the higher terraces, especially where there is a veneer of loess soils, are well cultivated. The summers are warmer than in most parts of West Germany, and maize, sugar beet, fruit (including apricots and peaches in the south), hops and tobacco are grown. Though not as famous for quality wines as the Rheingau and the Moselle valley, nearly three-quarters of the German output comes from the Rift Valley.

The Rhine as far north as Lauterbourg forms the international boundary and few towns stand near its banks. Kehl is opposite Strasbourg (p. 476), linked to it by rail and road bridges. Away from the river, in the Breisgau, is Freiburg (168,000), a pleasant tourist town with minor industries such as wood-carving and the manufacture of toys, clocks, pottery and jewellery. Farther north on the right bank stands Karlsruhe, with a river port, metallurgical and electrical engineering industries, and an oil refinery. At the confluence of the Neckar (Plate XXIX) the old town of Mannheim (326,000) stands on the right bank, and the mid-nineteenth century creation of Ludwigshafen (173,000) on the left. The joint river port has 50 km (30 miles) of wharves, and the towns are important for electrical and general engineering. Ludwigshafen has a big chemical plant, using natural gas piped from near Darmstadt, petrochemical feedstocks from Karlsruhe, and coke oven gas piped from the Saarland. Farther east, on the banks of the Neckar where it breaks through the sandstone hills, is Heidelberg (121,000), with its narrow winding streets and famous university (founded in 1386), an attractive centre for visitors.

The Rhine-Main Basin. At the northern end of the rift valley, the Main comes in from the east, while the Rhine turns at right-angles to the west for 30 km (20 miles). The joint basin forms a densely populated industrial district. Mainz (172,000), on the left bank of the river, was an ancient city with Roman antecedents, then a prosperous medieval town, the seat of an archbishopric, before the War of 1939–45 the capital of Rhine-Hesse, now the capital of *Land* Rhineland-Palatinate. Recovered from its war damage, it is an important centre of communications, with large-scale industries (engineering, optical, chemical and cement-making). Wiesbaden (259,000), across the river from Mainz, is a residential and tourist town with mineral springs famous since Roman times, and is one of the centres of the wine industry. By contrast, part of its suburbs along the Rhine now has engineering, chemical and cement-making industries. It has also become the administrative capital of Hesse.

Frankfurt-am-Main (660,000) has been a centre of communications since early times, as its name ('the ford of the Franks') indicates. It too was a medieval commercial centre and for long an Imperial City. It gradually became active industrially, obtaining bulky requirements of fuel and raw material by river; its activities include engineering, the manufacture of chemicals, plastics and furniture; and since the creation of West Germany it has taken over much of Leipzig's pre-eminence in the fur trade. Other industrial towns include Rüsselsheim, the home of the *Opel* car, and Darmstadt (140,000) with a chemical industry which has grown rapidly in recent years, partly due to local supplies of natural gas.

The Middle Rhine Highlands and Gorge. From Bingen to Bonn, a distance of about 110 km (70 miles), the Rhine flows in a gorge across the Middle Rhine Highlands, which have been divided into individual blocks by the river and its tributaries. These plateaus, their surfaces mostly above 450 m (1500 ft), are covered with thin soils and bear poor pasture and forests, though parts, especially in the Taunus, are cultivated. The gorges, with castles perched on crags and small towns at crossing-points, some of them spas (-*baden*) with mineral springs, are visited by many tourists. Despite the narrowness of the valleys, they are followed by railways and roads, and the Rhine is used by steamers and strings of barges.

Though many parts of the gorge are rocky and precipitous, the south-facing slopes are terraced for vineyards (Plate XXIV). The most renowned wine-producing areas are the Rheingau along the southern edge of the Taunus, and the Moselle valley with such attractive centres as Bernkastel. The canalization of the Moselle was completed in May 1964 (p. 176).

The largest town in the Rhine gorge is Koblenz, near the confluences of the Moselle and the Lahn with the Rhine, where the valley widens to form a distinct basin. Apart from being the centre of the wine trade, Koblenz has developed industries, making tinplate, cement, paper and pottery. Other small towns situated in neighbouring valleys include Wetzlar in the Lahn valley, the home of the renowned *Leitz* optical firm. The chief town in the Moselle valley is Trier, an ancient fortress with Roman remains, a former ecclesiastical city, and the centre of the Moselle wine trade.

The Saarland. This territory, now a constituent *Land*, occupies part of the basin of the river Saar, which joins the Moselle above Trier. Much consists of sandstone hills and plateaus, dissected by steep-sided valleys; about a third is forested, but the wider valleys and basins contain pasture and arable land. Its most valuable asset is a productive coal basin (Fig. 26 and p. 161).

Between 1920 and 1935 the Saar Territory was administered by a council appointed by the League of Nations and the coalfield was operated by the *Mines Domaniales de la Sarre*, a company controlled by the French government. This was intended to afford some compensation to France for the destruction wrought in Nord and Pas-de-Calais in 1914–18. The French exploited the coalfield vigorously, but in 1935 the Saarland returned to Germany after a plebiscite. In 1945 it was assigned to the French occupation zone, and France clearly hoped to incorporate it permanently, but gradually the political climate changed, and under an agreement in 1957 it returned to West Germany, although France retains until 1981 certain mining rights in the coalfield near the border. An oil-refinery, with associated petrochemical industries, has been opened at Klarenthal.

Apart from its collieries, the Saarland has several coke-oven plants, and gas is piped both westward to Lorraine and eastward to Ludwigshafen. Integrated steel works, consuming Lorraine ore, are at Völklingen, Saarbrücken (132,000) and Neunkirchen, with blast-furnace plant at Dillingen (Fig. 26).

The Cologne 'Bay'. Where the Rhine leaves its gorge, the hills fall back to form a 'bay' of lowland. Much is covered with alluvium, while the gravel terraces on each side of the river are capped in places with fertile loess soils. This is a well-cultivated area, with fields of wheat, potatoes and sugar beet, orchards and pasture.

Numerous towns line the banks, the three largest being Bonn, Cologne and Düsseldorf. Bonn, in pre-1939 days a pleasant residential and university town, has expanded rapidly since 1949 as the capital of West Germany, and now has 138,000 inhabitants. Cologne

(Köln) (856,000) was founded by the Romans as *Colonia Agrippina*, and grew up as a river-crossing place, a religious centre with an archbishop who was a powerful prince and an elector of the Holy Roman Empire, and a prosperous commercial and industrial city. It stands at the head of navigation for sea-going vessels, and here the first railway bridge over the Rhine was constructed. West–east routes skirting the edge of the Hercynian uplands cross north–south routes along the Rhine valley. The city suffered great damage during the War of 1939–45, and it was not until 1958 that it reached its prewar population total. Its factories make engineering goods, *Ford* cars, chemicals, rayon and nylon, perfume and chocolate. A group of large oil refineries is situated near Cologne, and on the right bank below the city is the Leverkusen chemical plant. The Ville brown coal field to the west (Fig. 27) supplies large quantities of power (p. 161), in the form of thermal electricity and briquettes.

Düsseldorf (683,000), though within the 'Bay', is sufficiently near the Ruhr to have been greatly affected by it. On the one hand, it is a great industrial centre, with steel-making, heavy engineering and the manufacture of steel tubes, chemicals and synthetic textiles, helped by river transport for its bulky needs. On the other hand, it is one of the chief financial centres in West Germany, the capital of *Land* North Rhine-Westphalia, a renowned shopping district, and a focus of fashion and art.

The only town of any size to the west of the Cologne 'Bay' is Aachen (177,000), the centre of a small industrial region utilizing coal from the nearby field which produces about 6 million tons yearly. It is the largest manufacturing town for woollen textiles in West Germany, and a new large factory makes electric light bulbs.

Siegerland and Sauerland. To the east of the 'Bay', the most northerly parts of the Middle Rhine Highlands are the Siegerland and Sauerland. Much consists of uplands with forests and pastures, and many reservoirs have been created by damming the valleys. There is a considerable amount of industry, much of it long established. In the Siegerland occurs some of West Germany's limited home supplies of iron ore, which nurtured an early smelting industry, both here and in the valleys draining the flanks of the Sauerland, using running water for power and charcoal from the forests for fuel. The rapidly diminishing output of ore now largely goes to the Ruhr, from which the local industries obtain their raw steel. Industry has survived in specialized forms, especially west of the Sauerland in the district of Berg. Solingen (174,000), sometimes known as 'the Sheffield of Germany', is noted for cutlery, the neighbouring Remscheid (135,000) for tools. The small town of Velbert, the old-established home of locksmiths, is still the largest centre for locks in West Germany. The other important activity in this area is the manufacture of textiles, notably at Wuppertal (412,000), a town extending for 16 km (10 miles) along the valley of the Wupper, created in 1930 by the union of Elberfeld and Barmen (Plate XXVII). Its textile products are highly specialized.

The Ruhr-Westphalian Industrial Region. Below Düsseldorf the Rhine valley opens into a lowland, and between the right-bank Ruhr and Lippe tributaries lies the Ruhr coalfield, the greatest industrial region in Europe. The result of nearly a century of intense development is an area of 11 700 sq. km (4500 sq. miles) of towns, collieries, steel works and factories, with a population of 8 millions (p. 167).

The Ruhr's activities are not limited to steel. Coking plants along the Emscher valley provide raw materials for the heavy chemical industry, and a new large plant in the north at Marl-Hüls makes synthetic rubber and plastics, using coal gas from the Ruhr and natural gas from the Ems and Dutch fields to the north. There are several oil refineries, and the Ruhr is responsible for almost half the total electricity generated in West Germany. Duisburg is a centre of non-ferrous metal refining and of heavy chemicals as a byproduct. Textiles are made at Krefeld and München Gladbach to the west of the Rhine. In all, fourteen Ruhr municipalities have populations exceeding 100,000, the largest being Essen (700,000).

The Ruhr region is served by the Rhine, and Duisburg-Ruhrort, at the confluence of the river Ruhr, is one of the biggest inland ports in the world. Its quays and basins extend for 20 km (12 miles) along the Rhine, the Ruhr and the Rhine-Herne Canal.

In spite of this accumulation of urban and industrial activity, much farmland survives among the built-up areas. This is particularly true of the narrow zone to the north of the Ruhr valley known as the Hellweg, which is part of the loess-covered Bördeland. It grows wheat and sugar beet, and extensive dairying and market gardening supply the huge urban populations.

The Münster 'Bay'. This area of lowland, sometimes known as the Westphalian Bay, consists mainly of Upper Cretaceous rocks, with an outer rim of chalk surrounding outcrops of clay. Much is covered with superficial deposits of loess in the south, sands and gravels in the centre and north. In the south on the loess soils cereals, especially barley, are grown; the clay-lands mainly carry hedged-in pastures; on the sands are clumps of pines and patches of heath. It is a prosperous farming area, producing milk, butter and meat for the population of the Ruhr to the south and barley for the Dortmund breweries. The centre of the region is Münster (203,000), founded as a see at the time of Charlemagne. It is the market centre of the lowland, handling grain and cattle, and it has food-processing industries and a variety of light engineering.

The Lower Rhine Plain. Below the industrial region of Ruhr-Westphalia, the Rhine flows north-west across an almost featureless floodplain to the Dutch frontier. The river is enclosed between massive embankments, beyond which lie water-meadows and polders.

3. *The North Central Uplands*

Extending from the Weser Hills along the Bördeland margins in the north to the volcanic hills of the Vogelsberg and the Hohe Rhön in the south, this region is one of considerable physical variety and complexity. It can be regarded as a unit only because it comprises the basin of the Weser and its headstreams, the Fulda (with its tributary the Eder) and the Leine. The Vogelsberg and Hohe Rhön represent a watershed between the Weser drainage and that of the Main in the south.

The Northwestern Scarplands. To the north-east of the Münster Bay projects an area of scarpland country, the dissected remains of an anticline of Mesozoic rocks trending from north-west to south-east. The crest of the anticline has been removed by erosion, leaving a clay-floored valley, the western part of which drains by the small river Hase to the Ems, the eastern part in the opposite direction by the Else to the Weser. On either side are cuestas: the Teutoburg Forest on the south-west, and the line of the Wiehen and Weser Gebirge on the north-east, each with prominent infacing escarpments.

The Teutoburg Forest consists mainly of chalk and greensand, with a narrow strip of Muschelkalk, rising to about 300 m (1000 ft) and culminating in the Völmerstod (468 m, 1535 ft). The ridges carry forest, mainly beech on the chalk and conifers on the sandstone, while the limestone bears excellent pasture.

The Weser gap, the '*Porta Westfalica*', cut by the river (though probably deepened by glaciation), divides the Jurassic limestone ridge into two, with the Wiehen Gebirge on the west, the Weser Gebirge on the east, rising to about 335 m (1100 ft). Some of the higher parts are covered with moorland or beech forest, the valleys (floored with marls and glacial drift) with pasture. The several towns in this area include Minden, commanding the northern exit of the Weser Gap, Osnabrück (140,000) in the north-east, and Bielefeld (169,000), situated in a minor gap through the Teutoburg Forest followed by a main railway from the Ruhr to Hanover. These towns have long-established textile industries and light engineering activities.

The Hill-country of Hesse. This structurally complex region lies between the Middle Rhine Highlands on the west and the Harz-Thuringian Forest on the east. It consists of low plateaus and ridges of Bunter Sandstone, mainly forested, crossed by the valleys of Weser headstreams, which widen out into marl- and clay-floored basins linked by narrow gaps. These areas of lowland are well cultivated with wheat, oats, rye, potatoes, hops, tobacco and sugar beet, and orchards and vineyards flourish on south-facing slopes. In parts, however, the farming is of a rather poor mixed character, with many small farms and little mechanization.

The main town is Kassel (213,000), standing on the banks of the Fulda at about 150 m (500 ft) above sea-level, while wooded basaltic ridges rise to over 600 m (2000 ft) to west and east. It is a remarkable centre of communications, the head of river navigation, and with railways running north–south along the Fulda valley, westward to the Ruhr and eastward to Thuringia, though now much less important since the division of the two states. When the present road-building programme is complete, it will be one of the foci of the *Autobahn* system near the junction of highways to Dortmund, Hanover, Frankfurt and Nuremberg. Because of its communications, it is also an important industrial centre, making locomotives, rolling stock, electrical machinery, optical instruments, textiles (partly the result of the enterprise of seventeenth-century Huguenot refugees), and chemicals. Other small towns include the bridge town of Hamelin in the north, Münden at the Fulda–Werra confluence, and the university towns of Marburg and Göttingen, the last with a specialized production of optical and scientific instruments, on the river Leine.

The Harz Mountains. Only the western part of this isolated Hercynian horst (p. 210) lies in West Germany, the border crossing the highest summit, the Brocken. In the valleys which dissect its western margins are several small towns with a long association with mining and smelting, notably Clausthal and Goslar. One valuable feature of these valleys is that they have been dammed to form reservoirs supplying the Bördeland towns.

The Volcanic Uplands. Large parts of southern Hesse were covered in Tertiary times with lava-flows, now eroded to leave two large masses in the south, the Vogelsberg (950 m, 3117 ft) and the Hohe Rhön (774 m, 2539 ft), and smaller isolated areas as far north as Kassel. These lava masses interrupt the line of what is structurally a continuation of the Rhine Rift Valley. The Fulda depression between the two, and the Wetterau depression between the Vogelsberg and the Middle Rhine Highlands, therefore form important north–south routeways.

Parts are thickly forested with spruce, other areas carry pasture, and the heavy winter snowfall has made them popular winter-sports resorts. The lower areas are agriculturally prosperous, with their fertile loess-covered vales and basins.

4. The South Central Uplands

The greater part consists of scarp-and-vale country developed in Mesozoic rocks, with the Main scarplands in the north, the Neckar scarplands in the south-west, and the long line of the Swabian and Franconian Jura (or Alb) in the south-east. The Hercynian uplands form the western borders of Bohemia: the Bavarian Forest, the Bohemian Forest and the Fichtel Gebirge.

The Main Scarplands. The Main, whose headstreams rise in the Fichtel Gebirge, flows westward across a region of escarpments and valleys in the pattern of a 'W', prominently incised below the general level, before its junction with the Rhine. It drains a considerable area, receiving the Saale from the north, the Regnitz from the south. In the west, the Spessart is an outlying continuation of the Odenwald, a crystalline massif covered in the east with Bunter Sandstone.

Considerable areas are thickly wooded, especially where sandstone outcrops as ridges in the east and in the Spessart (Plate XXIII). The extensive areas of Muschelkalk bear rather poor pasture, while the better soils derived from Keuper marls, loess and glacial drift are under arable, with large fields of wheat, sugar beet and potatoes. Water-meadows extend along the floors of the valleys, and vines, fruit and hops are grown on south-facing slopes.

Several towns are strung out along the Main valley. In the east is Bayreuth, home of the Wagner festival; Bamberg, with small textile mills, is at the limit of navigation and is being linked to the Danube by a new canal; Schweinfurt makes ball-bearings; Würzburg (120,000) has light engineering works; and Aschaffenburg has industries utilizing timber from the Spessart uplands, and textile and clothing factories.

The most important town is Nuremberg (Nürnberg) (471,000) on the Main's tributary, the Regnitz. Founded over a thousand years ago, it was an Imperial City for five centuries, and has long been a centre of learning, the arts, handicrafts and inventive skills. Its advantages included supplies of timber, small quantities of ore in the hills, wool and hides, and plentiful water for power, for floating down timber, and for the textile industries. The city was severely damaged by bombing, which destroyed many of its medieval buildings, but it has been rebuilt. Its industries comprise the production of electrical apparatus, engineering (the making of diesel engines, tractors, boilers and cranes), musical instruments, the traditional toys, pencils, radios, motor-cycles, glassware and a wide range of similar consumer articles.

The Neckar Scarplands. The Neckar drains a triangular area between the Swabian Jura and the Black Forest, flowing successively over the Muschelkalk limestone, Keuper marls and sandstone, and Lias clay. These rocks have been eroded to form low but steep sandstone escarpments such as the Löwenstein Berge overlooking the Neckar near Heilbronn, undulating limestone plateaus, and clay-floored depressions. Equally varied is the land use; the sandstone ridges are thickly wooded with pines, the thin stony soils on the limestones carry poor pasture, the clay soils and alluvial valleys have permanent pasture, and the marls and loess soils grow cereals, hops, sugar beet and tobacco.

The chief town is Stuttgart (617,000), now the capital of *Land* Baden-Württemberg, situated near the banks of the Neckar in a basin surrounded by wooded hills. Before the nineteenth century it was a state capital, with some small textile manufactures, but the development of communications led to a great increase in its industrial importance. Here Gottfried Daimler made his first automobile, and now the *Mercedes* factory is located in the industrial suburb of Untertürkheim. *Porsche* cars are also made, and precision instruments, watches, ball-bearings, accordions and other musical instruments, textiles, shoes, gloves, chemicals and photographic materials. Farther downstream is the port of Heilbronn, with engineering and food-processing industries.

The Swabian and Franconian Jura. This crescentic belt of Jurassic limestone curves for over 300 km (200 miles) from the margins of the Black Forest almost to the Fichtel Gebirge, from which it is separated by the clay-floored Naab valley. Its escarpment overlooks the basins of the Neckar and the Regnitz; even the well graded *Autobahn* from Stuttgart to Munich has to ascend quite steeply to surmount it. The highest point is the Lemberg (1015 m, 3330 ft) in the Swabian Jura. The south-eastern slope to the Danube is much more gentle, forming a sloping plateau dissected by narrow valleys, with many examples of subterranean drainage. The surface of these hills is somewhat bleak, covered with pasture and on the higher eminences with coniferous woodland, though the eastern slopes, particularly where marls are overlain by loess, afford good arable land.

The Swabian Jura is separated from the Franconian Jura by the Ries basin, drained by the Wörnitz, which ultimately joins the Danube at Donauwörth. The basin, floored with fertile soils, is agriculturally productive, and the small town of Nördlingen is a route centre.

The Hercynian Uplands. In the extreme south-east of West Germany lie the western margins of the Bohemian 'Diamond', one of the major Hercynian masses, consisting mainly of gneiss, granite and crystalline schists. The crestline of the Bohemian Forest, rising to rounded summits over 1200 m (4000 ft) high, is followed by the Czechoslovakian boundary. Farther west, separated by the narrow valley of the Regen, a Danube tributary, is the lower but rugged Bavarian Forest. At the north-western corner of the Bohemian 'Diamond', the complex upland mass of the Fichtel Gebirge culminates in the Schneeberg (1053 m, 3455 ft); this is one of the drainage dispersal centres of Europe, for streams rising on its flanks flow to join the Rhine, the Elbe and the Danube. About half of the uplands are thickly forested, mainly with spruce and fir; meadows and pastures occupy the cleared areas, and most of the arable land is used for fodder crops as the result of an emphasis on cattle rearing. The exploitation of timber, timber-using industries, and small-scale but long-established specialized watch-making, pottery and glass industries in the little towns, together with a growing tourist activity, contribute to the economy of a rather thinly populated, though scenically very attractive area.

5. *The Bavarian Foreland and Alps*

The Danube, rising on the slopes of the Black Forest, flows in a sweeping curve across southern Germany (Plate XXI) to its junction with the Inn, where it enters Austria. The bottom lands of the valley are marshy, though the loess-covered terraces are well cultivated. The riparian towns, which have long been bridge-points, include

Tuttlingen, specializing in the manufacture of musical instruments; Ulm, the head of navigation for small vessels and a focus of routes across the Swabian Jura, with light engineering industries and particularly the manufacture of radio valves; Ingolstadt, where five oil refineries were in operation by 1970, served by a branch from the South European Pipeline; Regensburg (126,000), the limit of navigation for larger vessels and an old commercial city on the trading route to northern Europe from the Brenner Pass; and Passau at the junction of the Danube and the Inn.

The Foreland. Between the Danube valley and the Bavarian Alps lies an easterly continuation of the Swiss Plateau, sloping gently northward from about 900 m (3000 ft) in the Alpine foothills to 300 m (1000 ft) in the Danube valley. The underlying rocks consist of Tertiary Molasse sandstone and Nagelfluh conglomerate, which occasionally appear on the surface as low whale-backed hills or irregular ridges between the valleys of the Danube tributaries. Most of the area is covered with glacial and fluvioglacial deposits laid down during the Quaternary glaciation (pp. 354–5): festoons of moraine, drumlins, uneven sheets of till, low gravel plateaus, terraces along the rivers, and expanses of coarse sand. Farther north are considerable deposits of loess, especially on the margins of the Danube valley. There are numerous lakes, some of the larger ones being moraine-dammed, such as the Ammer See and the Würm See to the south-west of Munich, and the Chiem See farther east; peat bogs indicate the existence of former lakes filled in with sediment and peat, known as *Moosen*.

The Foreland, with its rather poor soils, its northerly aspect, its elevation and cool moist climate, is not a prosperous agricultural area. In the south the country is under permanent grassland, and the ridges and dry gravels are forested with conifers. Farther north, especially where loess soils are present, the amount of arable land increases; oats, rye, potatoes, hops (especially in the Hallertau district north of Munich) and animal fodder are grown, though the extent of poor pasture, heath and forest is still considerable.

One of the most favourable districts is in the west around Lake Constance, partly because this water-body slightly ameliorates the climate, partly because of the sheltered, south-facing slopes descending to the lake. These slopes carry vineyards, orchards, hop fields and market gardens. Early man also found it favourable, as evidenced by substantial remains of Neolithic and Bronze Age settlements, including lakeside pile villages.

The population is scattered, with market towns commonly situated on the higher terraces above river crossings, but two cities, Munich and Augsburg, afford a striking contrast to the generally thinly populated Foreland. Munich (München) is the administrative capital of *Land* Bavaria. Situated where the road from Augsburg to Salzburg crossed the river Isar, it did not become really important until the nineteenth century, when it grew rapidly, first as a railway centre, then as an industrial city. Now with a population of 1·28 million, it is the second city of West Germany (excluding West Berlin). It has electrical and other engineering works (now the headquarters of *Siemens*), the famous *B.M.W.* motor-works, factories making aero-engines, the clothing industry, the manufacture of optical instruments and cameras (such as *Agfa*), and large breweries. It has West Germany's largest university, several technical colleges, art galleries and museums, and is the centre of the country's film industry.

Augsburg (212,000) was a Roman town (*Augusta Vindelicorum*), and later played an important part in medieval commerce because of its situation on a trade route crossing the Alps to northern Europe. It has a long-established textile industry (cotton, silk, now nylon), and engineering industries; the first diesel engine was made here.

The Bavarian Alps. The Foreland rises on the south to irregular foothills of Cretaceous rocks and of Molasse and Nagelfluh, then steeply to the northern wall of the Alps. The western section between Lake Constance and the valley of the river Lech, which cuts right across the ranges from Austria, is known as the Allgäuer Alps, consisting mainly of sandstones and shales. Farther east are the Triassic and Jurassic ridges of the Bavarian Alps proper, the crest-line of which is followed by the German–Austrian border. The limestone precipices, playgrounds of Bavarian rock-climbers, rise from the meadows, pine forests and scree slopes to jagged ridges and pinnacled summits. The Zugspitze has a small permanent snowfield and a glacier under its peak; one can travel by rack railway and cable-car to the summit. Numerous lakes are set in cirques and deep valleys, notably the Alpsee and Schwansee near Füssen. Farther east the border makes an abrupt salient to the south, enclosing a group of limestone peaks around the Königsee, known as the Berchtesgaden Alps, and culminating in the Watzmann (2714 m, 8904 ft).

The mountains, lakes, valleys and pine-woods are attractive to visitors at all seasons. The Winter Olympic Games of 1936 were at

Garmisch-Partenkirchen, and other resorts are Füssen, Oberammergau, where the famous Passion Play is held every ten years, and Mittenwald where violins have been made for centuries. Apart from tourism, forestry and the rearing of cattle, grazed in summer on the high pastures, are the main occupations.

CHAPTER SEVEN

East Germany

SOON after the three western zones of Germany became a Federal Republic (p. 11), the Russian-occupied eastern zone became the German Democratic Republic (*Deutsche Demokratische Republik*). Its constitution was officially enacted on 7 October 1949, but it has been recognized only by thirteen Communist countries. The state comprises an area of 108 174 sq. km (41,722 sq. miles), and in 1949 had a population of about 18 million, which twenty years later was almost a million less (despite a small rise in recent years), the result of the steady flight of refugees to the West.

East Germany at first consisted of five *Länder* (provinces), but in 1952 these were replaced by fourteen *Bezirke* (districts) (Fig. 31), their administration highly centralized under the Communist government. The capital is East Berlin, the former Russian sector of the city, separated from West Berlin by the rigorously guarded Wall.

STRUCTURE AND RELIEF

The northern areas of East Germany form part of the North European Lowland, which merges eastward across the river Oder into the plains of Poland and the U.S.S.R. In the south of the country lies a series of crystalline massifs of Hercynian age. Between the two is a confused area of basins, valleys and low plateaus, mainly composed of Mesozoic rocks.

The Northern Plain

This undulating lowland, occupying three-fifths of East Germany, extends southward for about 300 km (200 miles) from the Baltic coast. Its surface is covered with superficial deposits which almost completely mask the underlying 'basement' rocks. The evidence of borings and of occasional outcrops, such as chalk in the island of Rügen, indicate that Cretaceous and Tertiary rocks form the foundation of the lowland. These in turn are underlain by Palaeozoic rocks, which appear on the surface in the southern Hercynian uplands. As a result of the spread of the Quaternary icesheets over this lowland (p. 144), two

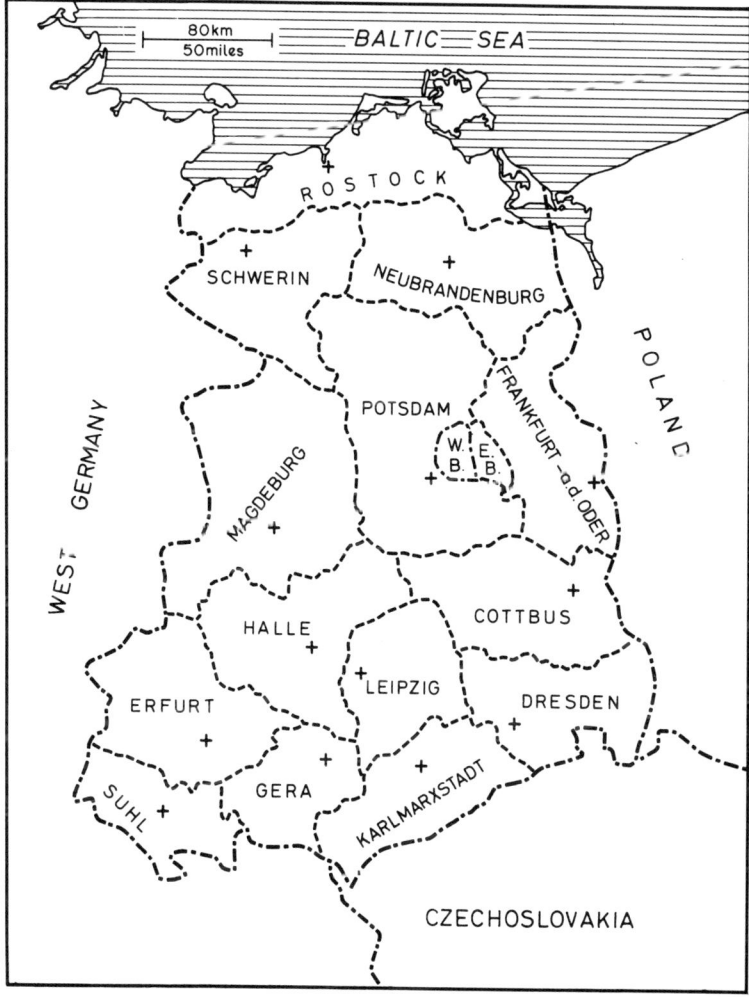

Fig. 31. The districts (Bezirke) *of East Germany*
The 'capital' of each district, after which it is named, is indicated by a cross.

main types of physical landscape may be distinguished: the ground-moraine and the fluvioglacial outwash zone.

Behind the dune-fringed Baltic coast lies an area of almost level ground-moraine, its surface at about 45 m (150 ft) above sea-level and extending inland for 80 km (50 miles). This low plateau is flanked on the south by the line of the Baltic End Moraine, deposited during

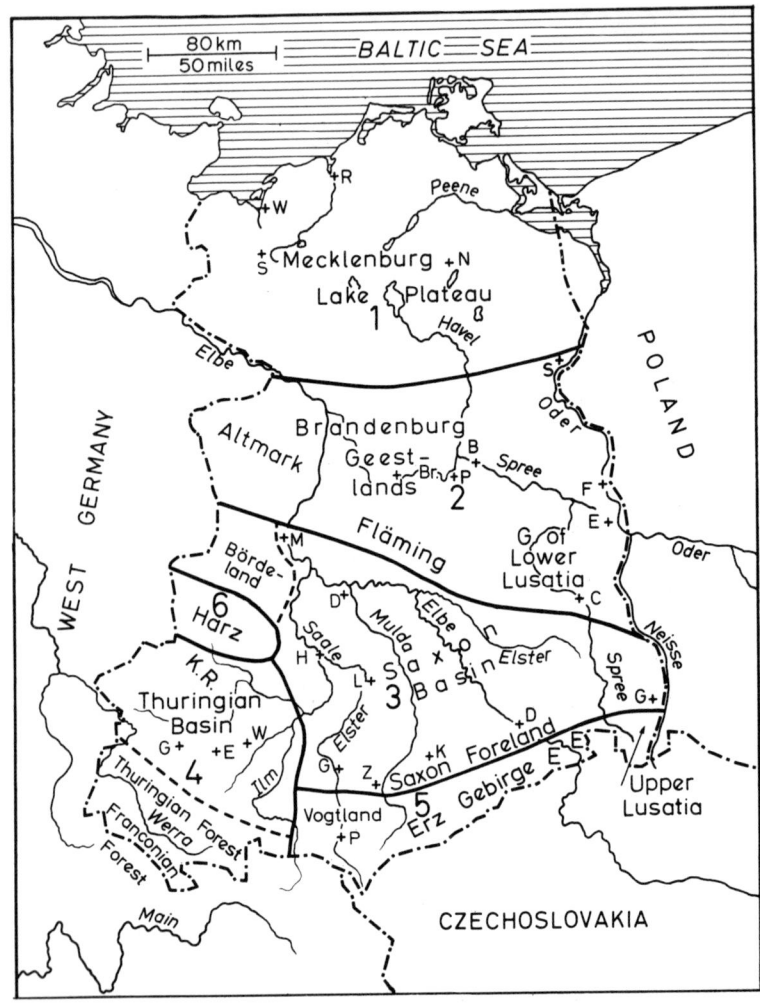

Fig. 32. Relief regions of East Germany
K.R. Kyffhäuser Ridge. **E.** Elbesandsteingebirge.

the Pomeranian stage of glacial retreat, rising in places to 250 m (800 ft) and in Poland to over 300 m (1000 ft). Some 50 km (30 miles) further south still is another terminal moraine, the product of the earlier Frankfurt glacial stage. Between the two lines a zone of irregular ground-moraine forms a confused landscape of hillocks, ridges and hollows, the Mecklenburg Lake Plateau. It extends diagonally across the country, with many hundreds of irregular sheets of water, some small, others quite large, such as the Plauer See, the Schweriner See and the Ratzeburger See in the west, and the Müritzer See in the centre.

The drainage pattern is extremely indeterminate, with low vague watersheds; some streams wander northward directly to the Baltic Sea, others westward to the Elbe. The Peene flows eastward to enter the Stettiner Haff at the mouth of the Oder, while the Havel meanders southward, receiving the Spree to the west of Berlin, and continuing north-westward to join the Elbe near Werben.

An area of fluvioglacial sands and gravels, part of the Geestland, extends across the north-centre of East Germany, diversified by occasional morainic hills of an early glacial stage. The deposits are divided into individual blocks, both by the present river valleys and by sections of the Urstromtäler (p. 145 and Fig. 22). In the west, beyond the bend of the Elbe below Magdeburg, a continuation of the Lüneburg Heath (p. 189) is known as the Altmark. To the east and north of the Elbe and its tributary the Schwarze Elster is the extensive heathland of the Fläming, bordered on the south by the terminal moraines of the Warthe glacial stage. Farther east the heathland of Lower Lusatia (Nieder Lausitz) is bordered by the valley of the Schwarze Elster on the west and that of the Neisse on the east, and is cut across by the valley of the Spree.

The floors of the Urstromtäler lie 30 m (100 ft) or so below the general level, and they commonly form elongated marshy depressions. Sometimes these contain braided misfit rivers, with a maze of cut-off lakes and backwaters (as in the case of the Spree), and with areas of marsh. Others have no surface drainage, but are shallow sandy troughs, sometimes with clusters of dunes. Some Urstromtäler have facilitated the construction of canals, linking the Oder with the Spree, the Spree with the Havel, and the Havel with the Oder.

The Elbe crosses the western Geestlands in a broad trough 8 km (5 miles) in width, between Magdeburg and its junction with the Havel. Its floodplain is a kilometre or two across, floored with alluvium, with braided channels and abandoned meanders, though the main channel has been regularized and dyked for most of its length.

The South-Central Basins and Lowlands

A complicated area of river basins and valleys across south-central East Germany drains to the Elbe by way of its sheaf of tributaries (Saale, Elster, Mulde and Schwarze Elster), each separated by low plateau-like interfluves. The central and eastern part is sometimes called the Upper Saxony Basin (or 'Bay'), the western part the Thuringian Basin.

The underlying rocks of the Upper Saxony Basin are of Mesozoic age, laid down in widespread shallow seas and including shelly limestones (Muschelkalk), sandstone (Bunter), marls and clays. Within the sandstones occur beds of salt and potash of great value, while in parts a thin cover of Tertiary rocks contains very large deposits of brown coal (Fig. 33) of Miocene age. Farther south a

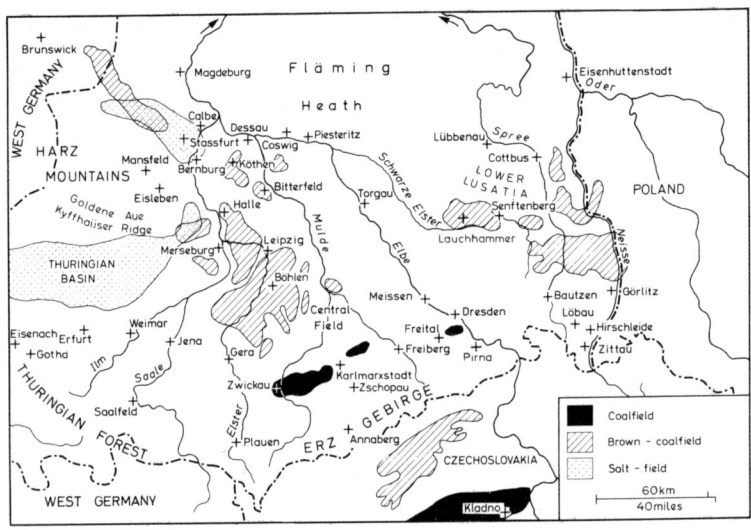

Fig. 33. The industrial region of southern East Germany

few small hard coal basins lie near the margins of the uplands. Rarely are the Mesozoic rocks revealed, for the valleys are floored with alluvium, low morainic ridges diversify the landscape in the north, and there is a cover of loess in the west and south forming part of the Bördeland (p. 145).

The Thuringian Basin lies between the Harz Mountains on the north and the Thuringian Forest on the south, and is drained by two left-bank tributaries of the Saale: the Ilm and the Unstrut. This basin is floored with Triassic rocks outcropping in a concentric pattern, with Keuper marls in the centre, surrounded by an interrupted exposure of Muschelkalk, and on the other rim the Bunter Sandstone. The rivers have developed well defined valleys; the easily eroded marls in the centre lie at 150–180 m (500–600 ft) above sea-

Plate XXVI. A large chemical plant at Hoechst, West Germany

Plate XXVII. Wuppertal, West Germany

Plate XXVIII. A barrage and locks on the canalized Moselle

Plate XXIX. The confluence of the Rhine and the Neckar at Mannheim,
West Germany, with a 'tank farm' on the peninsula between the two

level, while the more resistant sandstones and limestones stand out as prominent outward facing escarpments.

The Hercynian Uplands

The Hercynian orogeny of Carbo-Permian times and its later vicissitudes (pp. 138–40) are responsible for several crystalline massifs in the centre and south of East Germany. The Bohemian 'Diamond' is sharply defined on its north-western margins by fault-lines, forming the Vogtland, the Erz Gebirge (Ore Mountains), the Elbe Sandstone Mountains, and the hills of Upper Lusatia. The Thuringian Forest projects north-westward from the corner of the Bohemian 'Diamond', and the Harz Mountains, only the eastern part of which are in East Germany, rise isolated to the north.

The Vogtland comprises a group of uplands between the Thuringian Forest and the Erz Gebirge, lower than their neighbours, and deeply dissected by the headstreams of the Elster. The block of the Erz Gebirge was tilted, so that its steeper south-eastern edge lies in Czechoslovakia, while it slopes more gently north-westward into the Upper Saxony Basin. In the west the rocks consist of slates, schists and sandstones, though farther east great masses of gneiss and granite form rounded summits, the Fichtelberg (1214 m, 3982 ft) being the highest point within East Germany, though the Keilberg (1244 m, 4080 ft) in Czechoslovakia is the highest in the range. The Erz Gebirge are also characterized by masses of basalt, the product of mid-Tertiary volcanic activity; most appear in Czechoslovakia, though the Hässberg (990 m, 3248 ft) is a fragment of a dissected basalt flow in East Germany. Many valleys, containing the head-streams of the Elster and the Mulde, descend from the border ridge. The presence of mineral ores in the Erz Gebirge is indicated by the name, though centuries of mining have removed most of the more accessible deposits.

The Elbe breaks through the rim of the Bohemian 'Diamond' in a district called the Elbe Sandstone Mountains (the Elbesandstein-gebirge) sometimes fancifully referred to as 'Saxon Switzerland'. The rocks are mainly yellowish Cretaceous sandstones, which have weathered into fantastic pinnacles and buttresses, rising to 450 m (1500 ft). The river flows in a gorge 180 m (600 ft) in depth and in places the valley floor is only about 90 m (300 ft) above sea-level.

East of the Elbe gorge the border with Czechoslovakia makes a kink to the south, leaving the uplands of Upper Lusatia (the Lausitz Gebirge) in the angle with the river Neisse. These consist mainly of sandstone, though in places masses of crystalline rocks are exposed; the highest point is the Lausche (793 m, 2600 ft).

The Thuringian Forest projects north-westward from the corner of the Bohemian 'Diamond' as a ridge 16–25 km (10–15 miles) in width, with a general altitude of 900 m (3000 ft); its highest summits are the Grosser Beerberg (982 m, 3222 ft) and the Schneekopf (978 m, 3209 ft). It consists mainly of Permian sandstones and conglomerates, with some older Palaeozoic slates, while denudation has revealed masses of granite and other crystalline rocks. This ridge originated as a Hercynian fold which was denuded and then again uplifted during the Alpine orogeny. It has been cut into by numerous rivers flowing to the Saale on the north and north-east, to the Werra (hence the Weser) on the north-west, and to the Main on the south and south-west. The part of the Thuringian massif lying beyond the Werra valley is known as the Franconian Forest.

The Harz Mountains form an isolated upland to the north of the Thuringian Basin; the border between West and East Germany crosses the highest point, the Brocken (1142 m, 3746 ft). The Harz is an elliptical horst some 90 by 30 km (55 by 20 miles), sharply defined by marginal faults, especially on the north. It consists of folded Devonian slates and quartzites flanked by Carboniferous and Permian sandstones, with several granite intrusions, notably those which culminate in the Brocken and in the Raumberg farther east. Denudation has resulted in the formation of a series of distinctive erosion surfaces. The eastern part of the massif is deeply dissected by rivers draining either north-eastward directly to the Elbe or south-eastward to the Unstrut, hence via the Saale also to the Elbe. As in the Erz Gebirge, the deposits of ores occurring around the margins of the intrusive masses have made the Harz a famous mining area; some mines are still productive, especially of copper near Mansfeld.

The Kyffhäuser Ridge, a small outlying massif rising to 474 m (1554 ft), is separated from the Harz by a little rift valley known as the Goldene Aue. This ridge consists of a crystalline core of granite and gneiss, with Carboniferous and Permian limestones and sandstones on each flank, and falls steeply to the Goldene Aue in the north, more gently to the south.

The Coast

The Baltic coastline of East Germany extends from Lübeck Bay near the mouth of the Trave to that of the Oder. Its features are mainly the result of a rise of sea-level along an uneven land margin, so that low hills of glacial material form numerous irregular islands. Waves and longshore currents drift sand and shingle in an easterly direction, creating spits and bars which link the islands to each other and to the mainland, so straightening off the coast and forming inlets known as *Bodden*; for example, the sandspit of Fischland, the cuspate foreland of the Darss and the elongated island of Zingst together enclose the extensive Saaler Bodden.

The oddly shaped island of Rügen, separated from the mainland near Stralsund by a narrow channel, consists of several formerly separate islands, some of chalk, others of glacial material, which have been connected by spits to enclose several Bodden. In eastern Rügen the chalk outcrops boldly in the cliffs (*Klinten*) of the Stubbenkammer rising to 128 m (420 ft) above sea level, forming an exception to the usual low earthy or sandy shoreline of the Baltic. Shallow open bays front the coast, notably the Wismar Bucht and the estuary of the Warnow; both have sandbanks and rocky shoals, and the creation of a deep-water harbour at Rostock on the Warnow estuary has been a major task (p. 228 and Fig. 35).

The coast has been straightened out farther east by the formation of the dune-fronted islands of Usedom and Wollin across the mouth of the Stettiner Haff, the bay into which flows the Oder. The East German–Polish border lies to the west of its mouth, so that only part of the more westerly island of Usedom lies in East Germany.

CLIMATE

East Germany lies in a transitional area between the temperate oceanic climate of western Europe and the continental climate of the Russian steppelands. It is a zone of contact between maritime and continental influences, with a slight tendency in favour of the latter, as compared with West Germany where the tendency is in favour of the former. The winter climate depends on whether moist Atlantic air masses or cold Polar Continental air masses are dominant. Occasional periods of damp mild conditions may spread across the country from the west, alternating with longer periods of cold, calm and often bright weather. The farther east, the more likely are these continental conditions to prevail, and for longer periods.

Much of East Germany in winter is an area of uniform cold. Berlin and Magdeburg have January means of $-0.5°$ C., Leipzig of

−1° C. On the higher land, these figures are lower; the mean January temperature for the summit of the Brocken in the Harz Mountains at 1142 m (3746 ft) is about −4° C. The Elbe at Magdeburg is frozen over for an average of thirty days each year and the Oder at Frankfurt for forty-three days.

The climate in summer depends on the outcome of another struggle between the occasional depressions which penetrate from the Atlantic, the shallow low-pressure conditions which may cover eastern Europe as a result of heating and convectional overturning, and the occasional extension over central Europe of stable subtropical high-pressure conditions, most common in late summer when long periods of hot sunny weather may be experienced. Temperature means increase slightly toward the east with progressive continentality; Magdeburg, for example, has a mean July temperature of 18° C., Berlin of 19° C. Day temperatures are high; Berlin has an average daily maximum in July of 24° C. Again altitude modifies these figures; the July mean for the summit of the Brocken is only 10° C. The mean seasonal range between the warmest and coldest month is 18° or 19° C., rather higher than in West Germany (Aachen, 15° C.) but rather lower than in Poland (Warsaw, 22° C.), affording an indication of its transitional location.

Apart from the uplands, there is little variation in the annual amount of precipitation over the country, averaging from about 580 mm (23 in) in the west to about 480 mm (19 in) in the east. In the central and southern uplands the total may exceed 1000 mm (40 in), though intervening basins and valleys in rainshadow locations receive less than 510 mm (20 in). The winter precipitation results from depressions moving eastward from the Atlantic coast; in summer, the season of maximum precipitation, it is caused by short-lived thunderstorms produced by convectional heating. Berlin receives 230 mm (8·9 in) during the period May to August out of a mean annual total of 550 mm (21·7 in), Leipzig 340 mm (13·3 in) from May to September out of a total of 630 mm (24·9 in). Precipitation during the winter months is usually in the form of snow; the surface bears a thin cover for a month or more, affording a sparkling landscape in the winter sunshine.

LAND USE AND AGRICULTURE
Soils

The soils are largely derived from superficial deposits of glacial, fluvioglacial, alluvial and loessic origin. Much of this cover is not particularly fertile, despite recent efforts at improvement.

Brown forest soils have formed on the recent tills which formerly carried beech forest to the south of the Baltic. The sands and gravels farther south have been to some extent leached, so that podzols have developed, though the leaching has not progressed as far as in the heathlands of West Germany, partly because the sands are the product of a more recent glaciation, partly because the precipitation is rather less. These sands require heavy fertilizing, and drainage measures have been necessitated by the indeterminate streams and extensive areas of marsh.

In the central and southern parts of East Germany the soils are diverse, the result of strikingly different superficial deposits and rock outcrops, and of varied relief and altitude. They include podzols on outcrops of Bunter Sandstone and on the crystalline rocks of the Harz Mountains, and brown forest soils which have formed under the former oak-beech cover. To the south of Magdeburg the brown earths have developed on loess, forming loamy soils of high quality. In the Thuringian Basin and the Goldene Aue the loess deposits have developed a type of 'black earth' soil, though as they have suffered some leaching they are known as degraded chernozems. A thin layer of rendzina occurs on some of the limestone hills. On the broad floors of the valleys of the Elbe and its tributaries alluvial soils, once covered with marsh and alder-scrub, are now mainly drained and reclaimed.

The soils can therefore be divided into three groups: the leached sandy soils, mainly growing rye and potatoes; the brown earths and chernozems, especially on loess, used for wheat and sugar beet; and the heavier clay and alluvial soils, mostly under pasture.

Forests

Nearly a third of the surface of East Germany is wooded, an area which has steadily increased since 1945–48, when wartime over-cutting and felling for fuel during the postwar winters had taken a heavy toll. About 100 000 ha (250,000 acres) of woodland have been planted annually during recent years.

Some 80 per cent consists of coniferous species; the most widely grown is the Scots pine, especially on the poorer sands in the east where areas of former heathland have been afforested in solid plantations, notably the Spreewald near Berlin. Other conifers are spruce, growing particularly in the Harz Mountains, and fir in the Thuringian Forest and the Erz Gebirge. Deciduous trees include beech behind the Baltic coast, oak and birch in favoured areas on the sands, open oak woodland around the flanks of the Harz Mountains, and beech on the southern uplands.

Agriculture

In 1939 a large proportion of the agricultural land in the northern half of what is now East Germany was still held in huge estates, divided into square fields. By contrast, in Upper Saxony and Thuringia farms were mainly small, usually less than 10 ha (25 acres), each worked by an individual family. After 1945 a series of ruthless agrarian reforms were put into effect. First the lands of leading Nazis, the Prussian Junker class, and war criminals were sequestrated, then any estate over about 100 ha (250 acres) was compulsorily confiscated; about 45 per cent of the area of East Germany was affected. On to these lands were settled over half a million landless peasants and refugees from beyond the Oder. Farmland became fragmented to an uneconomic extent, and output diminished considerably, adding to both the economic and social difficulties of the country.

Since 1952 a policy of compulsory consolidation and integration has been pursued. Almost all the farmland is now in either collective farms (officially known as 'Agricultural Producer Co-operatives'), of which there are about 13,000, averaging 400 ha (1000 acres) in size, or in 650 state farms. Much capital has been put into agriculture, and programmes of mechanization, involving the creation of huge machine and tractor stations, have been carried out; the number of tractors increased from about 11,000 in 1950 to 100,000 at the present time. Agriculture is working towards highly ambitious targets of food production, involving appreciable increases in yield. These have been achieved in spite of a reduction in the labour force from 1·7 million in 1950 to about 1 million.

About 60 per cent of East Germany is classified as farmland, of which a third consists of meadow and pasture, compared with about two-fifths in West Germany. This lower proportion is mainly the result of cold winters and warm summers, together with extensive areas of sandy soil which do not support good grassland.

In 1968 about 13 million tons of potatoes were grown on the till soils behind the Baltic coast, on the sands in the centre, and on the loess lands in the south. They form a staple item in the diet; large quantities are used for feeding pigs, and for making starch and alcohol. The other important root crop is sugar beet (7·0 million tons), mainly cultivated on the fertile loess soils near Magdeburg and in Upper Saxony, and on the black soils of Thuringia, in rotation with wheat or barley.

The yield of wheat in 1968 was 2·4 million tons (double that of a decade ago), of rye 1·93, of barley 2·12 (also greatly increased), and of oats 0·9. Rye still occupies the largest area of any crop because of its hardiness and tolerance of soil and climate, growing both on the poor sandy soils and on the heavier claylands; it is used both as a bread grain and to feed stock. Wheat is grown on the loess and black-earth soils, and its yield per hectare has been greatly increased. Spring-sown barley, mainly for malting, is grown on the same terrain, taking advantage of the sunny summers, and some oats are produced on the northern claylands. The main vegetable oil crop is rape, cultivated in Mecklenburg.

Shortages of milk and meat have been so serious in recent years that strenuous efforts have been made by the government, and despite the small amount of pasture the number of cattle has increased from about 3·8 millions in 1955 to 5·1 millions in 1968. The chief area of dairy farming is in Mecklenburg, where the animals are kept in conjunction with rotation grass and the cultivation of potatoes and other fodder crops. Some cattle are grazed on the upland pastures of the Thuringian Forest, the Vogtland and the Erz Gebirge, others on the drained marshes along the floodplains of the Elbe and its tributaries, and on the floors of some of the Urstromtäler. Elsewhere the animals are stall-fed on sugar beet tops and pulp and on other fodder crops, including an increasing amount of alfalfa. The most important animal for meat is the pig (9·5 millions), kept widely throughout the country. The number of sheep almost doubled between 1955 and 1968 to 1·8 million, kept both in the uplands and folded on stubble and roots on the arable farms of Upper Saxony and Thuringia. But despite these various efforts, the production of meat, milk, butter and cheese is still inadequate to meet internal requirements.

FISHERIES

The fishing industry is of relatively little importance, since the Baltic Sea has few fish of value. Small fleets operate from Rostock and Sassnitz, and recently there has been some deep-sea fishing farther afield.

MINERALS AND POWER

Coal and Brown Coal

The only deposits of bituminous coal in East Germany comprise some small basins (Fig. 33) on the flanks of the Erz Gebirge: one between Zwickau and Karlmarxstadt, another farther east, and the Döhlen basin between Freital and Dresden. The seams are little disturbed and mining is easy, but the coal is mainly of gas and long-flame varieties with a high ash content, unsuitable for making metallurgical coke. Before 1939 the annual output of coal was about 5·5 million tons, but after the War this averaged only 3 million tons and in recent years has steadily declined (1967, 1·8 million tons). Coal is imported from Polish Upper Silesia, Czechoslovakia and the U.S.S.R.

The chief industrial asset of East Germany is the enormous deposits of brown coal (Fig. 33). Until recently the main producing area was the Central (Halle-Leipzig) field between the valleys of the Saale and the Mulde, but the much larger Lower Lusatian field, centred on Senftenberg to the north-east of Dresden, is rapidly increasing in importance. A third smaller field lies to the north of the Harz Mountains, west of Magdeburg and Stassfurt, and extending into West Germany. The brown coal, of Tertiary (Miocene) age, occurs in beds 9–18 m (30–60 ft), sometimes as much as 100 m (330 ft), in thickness, covered by only a thin overburden, and easily mined by large-scale excavators in opencast workings. The ease of extraction compensates in part for its low calorific value, only about one-ninth that of the same bulk of bituminous coal, and for its high water content.

Before 1939 the Upper Saxon brown coal fields were relatively unimportant, since Germany had not only large reserves of hard coal, but the Ville brown coal deposits in the Rhineland (p. 161) were extensively worked. Some 60 million tons annually were produced in the Central Field and another 40 to 50 million tons from the Lower Lusatian deposits east of the Elbe. Since 1945 the brown coal has been exploited with great vigour, especially in Lower Lusatia, which is now responsible for 60 per cent of the output. By 1954 the annual total had reached 180 million tons, by 1968 about 247 million tons.

About a third of the brown coal is compressed into briquettes, of which 50 to 60 million tons are produced, used widely as domestic fuel. Much is burnt *in situ* in large thermal generators, which supply 90 per cent of East Germany's power requirements; the pre-1939 annual output of about 14 million KWh in this equivalent area had been increased to 63·2 million by 1968. The main plants are at Trattendorf, Vockerode, Berzdorf, Hirschfelde, and the giant '*Schwarze Pumpe*' near Spremberg, all in Lower Lusatia. During the last few years plants have gone into service at Lübbenau and Vetschau to the south-east of Berlin, and at Boxberg, which is claimed to be the largest brown coal fired station in the world. A power station at Eisenhüttenstadt is operated by blast-furnace gas, and an atomic power station at Rheinsberg now puts power into the grid; brown coal is, however, the dominant source of energy.

Some of the brown coal is consumed directly for steam-raising in factories, and increasing amounts are used as raw material in the chemical industry; oil, benzene and phenol are produced synthetically at the Leuna plant at Merseburg and at another near Zeitz to the south-east of Leipzig, and gas is piped through a grid from Lower Lusatia. At Lauchhammer, to the south-west of Cottbus, a large plant made metallurgical coke from compressed brown coal briquettes; mixed with Polish coke, this was used in the low-shaft blast furnaces at Calbe (p. 220), but the process has now been abandoned as uneconomic.

The largest multi-purpose concern for utilizing brown coal is the *'Kombinat Schwarze Pumpe'*, completed in 1963; it produces annually 5 million tons of briquettes, gas, thermal electricity and chemical raw materials. Another similar *Kombinat* was completed at Weiswasser, to the south-east of Spremberg.

The deposits of brown coal are of paramount importance to the East German industrial economy, and their utilization has been a feature of the various Plans (p. 219). But this cannot entirely supersede bituminous coal, and each year about 2 million tons of coal and the same amount of coke are imported from Poland, the U.S.S.R. and Czechoslovakia.

Oil

Extensive geological research so far indicates that little or no oil is present in East Germany. The Leuna plant was opened near Merseburg as long ago as 1927 for making oil from brown coal, and for a time was the largest in the world; though it was repeatedly bombed, production was rarely interrupted during the War. After 1945 the plant was dismantled by the Russians, but in the mid-fifties it was rebuilt; it is now the largest industrial plant in East Germany. It now also refines crude-oil brought from Schwedt by pipeline.

Synthetic oil production is, however, inadequate for internal needs, and the U.S.S.R. has been obliged to make available meagre supplies of petroleum. The position was improved when in 1963 a large refinery was completed at Schwedt-an-der-Oder, north-east of Berlin, fed by the 'Friendship' pipeline bringing crude oil from Brody in the

Ukraine via Ughgorod, Kosice and across Poland and also by a new pipeline from Rostock.

Other Minerals

Supplies of iron ore, scanty and of poor grade, include scattered deposits in the Thuringian Forest and near Ilsenburg in the Harz Mountains; about 1·4 million tons, with an average 30 per cent metal content, are produced annually. The Harz and the Erz Gebirge have been famous since the early Middle Ages for ores of silver, lead, copper and zinc, but most of the more accessible ore bodies had been worked out by the seventeenth century, and by 1900 there was only sporadic mining activity. Since 1949 non-ferrous mining has been substantially revived, largely with infusions of Russian direction and technology. Near Gera, in the Elster valley, and also at various places in the Erz Gebirge, uranium is mined under conditions of great secrecy. The mining of copper has been revived in the eastern Harz (1·3 million tons in 1967) and of other metals in the Erz Gebirge, including cobalt, bismuth, arsenic and antimony. Magnesium is derived from the salt deposits of Stassfurt, obtained in the form of magnesium chloride; before 1939 this area produced more than half the world's magnesium, and this has been substantially increased.

Huge beds of salt, including chlorides and sulphides of potassium, sodium and magnesium, in places 300 m (1000 ft) or more thick, were laid down when the waters of the Permo-Triassic sea spread over the land, possibly in enclosed basins under arid conditions. They form a crescent curving around the eastern margins of the Harz towards Halle (the name of which means salt) and Stassfurt. In terms of pure potassium oxide, these East German fields produce about 2·2 million tons, or nearly a third of the world output.

MANUFACTURING INDUSTRY

The rapid development of Germany's resources after 1870 made it the most powerful industrial country in Europe (p. 165). Though what is now East Germany was less developed than the West, Upper Saxony had a thriving industrial life, based on the production of textiles, precision instruments, pharmaceutical products, leather and footwear, pottery and glass, toys, musical instruments, paper and printing. The limited heavy industry included the manufacture of fertilizers and acids, synthetic petroleum and synthetic rubber. There was only one steel works, the *Maximilianhütte* at Unterwellenhorn near Saalfeld in Thuringia, except for a few small foundries and rolling mills using steel scrap.

The division of the country after 1945 left East Germany in a disadvantageous position. Most of the industrial plants which had survived the War in Upper Saxony were dismantled and removed to Russia, and many skilled personnel from the specialized industries fled to the West. In addition, 200 plants were placed under Russian control, though these were returned in 1953, except for the highly secret uranium mines in the Erz Gebirge.

Organization

Under the rigid control of the U.S.S.R. and within the overall pattern of economic expansion in eastern Europe, it was soon evident that despite the lack of natural advantages heavy industry in East Germany was to be stimulated at the expense of lighter categories. This caused grave difficulties which have manifested themselves in shortages of consumer goods, and have contributed to the low standard of living and considerable discontent. Some 94 per cent of industry has been nationalized, and of the remainder most firms have State capital participation.

A first Five Year Plan, almost wholly concerned with heavy industry, was launched in 1950 by the State Planning Commission under the National Economic Council. To this Plan belongs the Stalinstadt (now Eisenhüttenstadt) steel works concept, which has never attained or even approached the enthusiastic forecasts. The Second Plan ran from 1955 to 1958, a Third Plan began in 1958, and the Seven Year Plan ran from 1964 to 1970; rarely have the targets so far been attained, mainly because of shortages of capital, fuel and raw materials, which the U.S.S.R. was willing or able to alleviate only in small part. Since 1955 the Plans have operated in conjunction with those of the other eastern European countries within *Comecon*, the Council for Mutual Economic Aid. After 1960 less emphasis was placed on East German steel development in favour of Poland and Czechoslovakia, and East Germany has concentrated on its chemical and engineering industries.

Despite obvious shortcomings, industrial expansion in East Germany has been on a considerable scale. The introduction of modern technology has made some progress, and improvements have been made in the light 'consumer' industries, for long neglected. The output of crude steel has grown from 2·2 million tons in 1953 to 4·7 million tons in 1968, and that of electric power from 19·5 thousand million KWh in 1950 to 63·2 in 1968. There has been a considerable increase in the production of such consumer goods as refrigerators, TV sets and washing machines, welcome to many East Germans who have been starved of such goods. Manpower remains a problem, for as a result of the low and declining birth rate (only 14·3 in 1968), more old people are leaving industry than young people are entering it; as a result, 70 per cent of all women are in employment.

Steel Production and Engineering

During the years following the end of hostilities, much of the small amount of heavy industrial equipment in East Germany was systematically dismantled and removed by the Russians. Since 1950 the output of steel has been slowly increased to 4·7 million tons in 1968, small compared with the West German 41 million tons, despite the propaganda associated with it. There are three large plants: the rebuilt *Maximilianhütte*, the 'Eastern Combine' at Eisenhüttenstadt on the Oder just north of the Neisse junction, and the 'Western Combine' at Calbe on the Saale; the first two are integrated plants, that at Calbe is a blast furnace plant smelting low-grade ore from the Harz Mountains. The Eisenhüttenstadt combine was developed on an ambitious scale, using Polish coke and Russian ore from Krivoi Rog, and with a large new workers' city built in what was open heathland. Other steel foundries and rolling mills have been reconstructed at Riesa on the Elbe and at Gröditz, Brandenburg, Mirchmöser, Hennigsdorf (near Berlin) and Thale. Plants at Döhlen near Leipzig and at Freital near Dresden produce special alloy steels in electric furnaces. Several non-ferrous refineries include copper smelters at Eisleben and Ilsenburg on the flanks of the Harz, and at Oranienburg to the north of Berlin, a zinc foundry at Freiberg, a nickel foundry at St Egidien, and lead and zinc smelters at Annaberg in the Erz Gebirge.

The Five Year Plans laid considerable emphasis on engineering, which is responsible for about a third of the total industrial production and for two-thirds of the exports. Its output includes machine tools at Karlmarxstadt, Dresden, Gera, Magdeburg and Leipzig, electrical machinery especially in East Berlin, mining machinery at Magdeburg and Leipzig, agricultural machinery at Leipzig, electric locomotives in East Berlin and at Hennigsdorf, textile machinery at Karlmarxstadt, cranes at Eberswalde, Köthen and Schmalkalden, and small cargo ships of up to 15,000 tons in the shipyards at Rostock,

Warnemünde, Stralsund and Wismar. Motor-cars are produced in increasing numbers, though still only about 250,000 a year, including the '*Trabant*' 'baby car' at Zwickau and the '*Wartburg*' in Eisenach and Karlmarxstadt. Lorries are made in Zwickau and Werdau, motor-cycles at Zschopau and Suhl, and tractors at Schönebeck.

Chemicals

The production of chemicals is the second largest branch of industry in East Germany, accounting for 25 per cent of the output by value, based on the deposits of potash and other salts and of brown coal. Before 1939 about two-fifths of the German chemical industry was located in the East, largely controlled by the giant *I.G. Farben*. After 1945 the chemical industry was nationalized, and growth has been especially rapid since 1955. East Germany is now the producer of such heavy chemicals as potash, nitrogenous fertilizers, sulphuric acid, caustic soda and ammonia for the countries of eastern Europe. Most are manufactured in large combines in the Stassfurt-Halle area, notably at Bitterfeld, Calbe and Magdeburg. Another important branch is the production, with typical German inventive genius, of a range of synthetic substances dependent on brown coal. These include *Buna* rubber at Zschopau near Leipzig, and plastics and fibres based on the large-scale production of polyethylene at new factories at Premnitz, Wolfen and Schwarza. Several large plants fix nitrogen from the atmosphere, as at Piesteritz near Wittenberg; these are usually located near thermal generators. The manufacture of petrochemicals is based at Leuna. A very large output of light chemicals includes drugs and photographic materials.

Textiles

Upper Saxony has long been famous for the manufacture of textiles on the northern flanks of the Erz Gebirge at Chemnitz (now Karlmarxstadt) and Plauen, in Thuringia at Erfurt, in the Elster and Mulda valleys at Zwickau, Gera and Leipzig, and in many smaller towns. Zittau and Löbau in the south-east of the country make linen, as they have for centuries. To the woollens, linens and cottons, a wide range of man-made fibres has been added. Textiles are now third in importance after engineering and chemicals in value.

Other Manufactures

After the collapse of Germany, most of the varied industrial activity of Upper Saxony ceased. Skilled technicians and managers from firms with world-famous names fled to West Germany, where they restarted their activities, taking their expertise and goodwill. Nationalization of industry, shortages of steel and raw materials, the emphasis on heavy industry in the plans, and the low priority given to consumer goods, were all grave handicaps. Only in recent years, with a desire both to improve standards of living and to export to other eastern European countries, has the position improved; refrigerators, washing machines and television sets are being produced in increasing numbers; a factory making television tubes, for example, has been opened in rural surroundings in Lower Lusatia at Friedrichshaim. Many world-famous products are now made in East Germany, sometimes using the same name as those in the West, but with a wholly independent organization. The *Carl-Zeiss* company left Jena, its original home, in 1945 and established itself at Ober Kochen near Heidenheim in West Germany, but the Jena works have restarted activity and now export cameras to many other countries.

This urgent need to export has encouraged the revival of some of the old craft industries, an example being the making of Meissen porcelain; the 'Dresden shepherdesses' were among its products famous since 1710. Not until 1951 did the Meissen factory, operated by a State corporation under Russian control, recommence work; now it is claimed that standards are as rigid and quality as high as ever, and about 70 per cent of the output is hand-made. The factory was the first enterprise to be allowed to transact foreign business without passing through the normal channels of the State trading organization, an indication of the importance attached to its earnings of foreign credits.

It is fair to say that East German industry has made some progress in its postwar struggles, not as spectacular nor as publicized as that of the more fortunately placed West Germany, but it is still impressive even when shorn of propaganda. By 1955 output had achieved a level about 50 per cent above that of pre-1939, and by 1960 it had been doubled; by the end of the Seven Year Plan in 1970 it had trebled.

COMMUNICATIONS

The division of Germany into two states cut across the unified systems of communication which had been developed before 1939 as part of the economic and strategic pattern. The position was made more difficult by the damage suffered during the War and in the east by Russian dismantling; equipment from the electrified lines was removed, and rolling-stock and locomotives vanished. The position of Berlin, on which many of the main routeways focused, greatly complicated the problem.

Roads

East Germany inherited several sections of *Autobahn* (Fig. 34), including the Brunswick–Magdeburg–Berlin–Frankfurt route, along which Allied convoys and West German transport have transit rights to West Berlin, and another west–east one from Erfurt to Karlmarxstadt, Dresden and Cottbus. The former Berlin–Breslau *Autobahn* affords a direct link between Berlin and Polish Upper Silesia, and another runs from Szczecin (Stettin) in Poland via Berlin to Leipzig. Most of these highways were in a bad state of repair after the War, with shattered bridges and viaducts, but they were rapidly made good. The main postwar addition to the network is an *Autobahn* from East Berlin to Rostock, intended to improve the links between the centre and south of the country with its main port. There are only about 800,000 cars, 1 for each 20 of the population, compared with 1 for each 5 in West Germany.

Railways

The railway system inherited by East Germany in 1945 was in a chaotic state and has been almost completely rebuilt, with an increase of track length of about 2000 km (1250 miles). This includes new lines eastward into Poland via Frankfurt-an-der-Oder, direct main lines north from East Berlin to Rostock and Stralsund, and a ring-line around East Berlin, linking the only prewar main line station located in the eastern sector of the city, the Ostbahnhof, directly with lines from north and south without passing through West Berlin. Programmes of modernization include the introduction of diesel railcars and the electrification of some main lines. Railways are more important for freight transport than in most countries, handling over 80 per cent of the total.

Waterways

Before 1939 the German rivers, flowing from south-east to north-west, were connected latitudinally by the Mittelland Canal, completed only a year before the War to take 1,000-ton barges. Its most

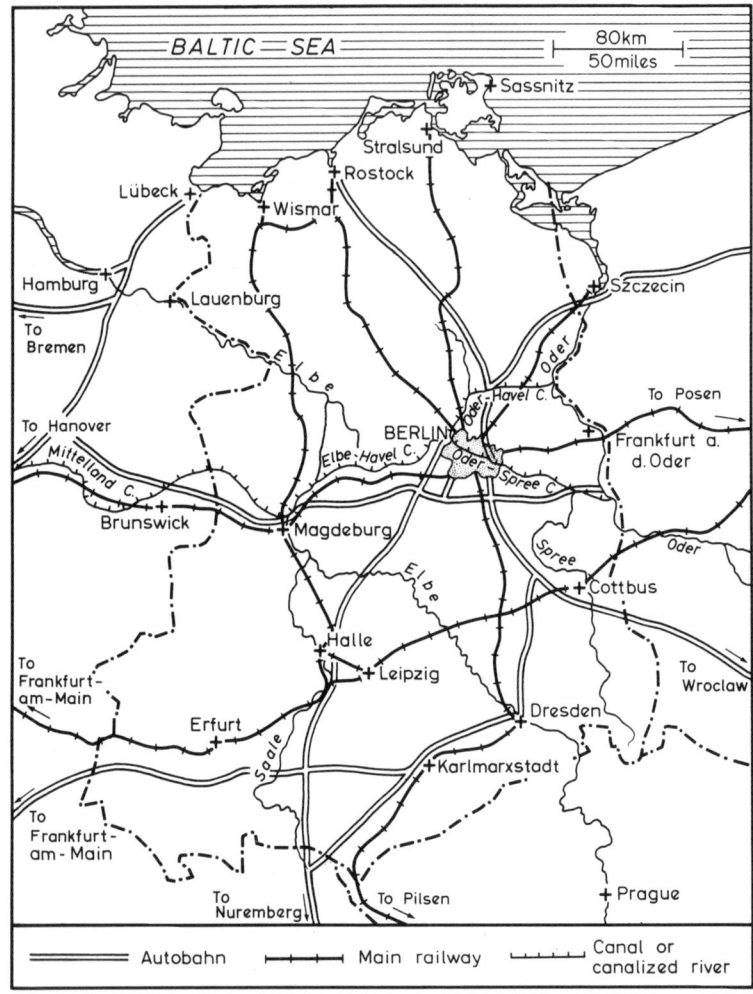

Fig. 34. The pattern of communications in East Germany

easterly section, the Elbe-Havel Canal, linked the Oder-Havel and Oder-Spree Canals within Berlin. The division of the country disrupted the waterways, leaving those in East Germany of relatively little importance. The Elbe flows into West Germany just above Lauenburg, the Mittelland Canal is cut between Brunswick and Magdeburg near Helmstedt, and the Oder is a wholly Polish river. Much of the freight traffic that once passed down the Elbe from Upper Saxony to Hamburg has ceased; some now goes down the

Oder for shipment via the Polish port of Szczecin, but much more moves by road and rail to Rostock. The East German canals converging on East Berlin pass through West Berlin, where the controlling locks are situated; these can cause delays, sometimes as deliberate reprisals for the holding up of Western traffic on the Mittelland Canal through East Germany to West Berlin.

Civil Aviation

During the first decade after 1945, civil aviation was controlled by the U.S.S.R., but in 1955 *Deutsche Lufthansa* (since 1963 known as *Interflug*), began operation. The main Berlin airport, Tempelhof, lies in West Berlin, and as a result the new Schönefeld airport has been constructed in the East. *Interflug* operates direct international services to Moscow, Warsaw, Prague, Budapest, Bucharest and Cairo.

A heavy air traffic crosses East Germany to West Berlin by means of three 'corridors' from Hamburg, Hanover and Frankfurt-am-Main, carrying both passengers and freight. West Berlin was entirely supplied for a year from June 1948 by the famous 'air lift', when ground communications were severed by a Russian blockade. These air corridors are a source of friction and potential danger to peace.

Ports and Mercantile Marine

In its early years East Germany had no mercantile marine, and no figures are yet available of the present merchant fleet. Its only ports are the small Baltic harbours of Wismar, Rostock and Stralsund, with Sassnitz the ferry port for Sweden. Rostock (Fig. 35), with its outport of Warnemünde, was selected for development as the main outlet, and its deep-water harbour was completed in 1960, with an annual capacity of 20 million tons of shipping; an oil-terminal and container-berths have recently been opened.

COMMERCE

Foreign trade, at a standstill in 1945, recovered only very slowly under the State monopoly. In recent years about 75 per cent of the total by value was with the Communist countries, including 45 per cent with the U.S.S.R. About a third of the imports by value consist of food, the rest of mineral ores, pig-iron and crude steel, raw textiles, coal and oil. Exports comprise machinery (about a quarter of the total), chemicals and manufactured goods; East Germany is now fourth in the world as an exporter of machinery, after the U.S.A., the United Kingdom and West Germany.

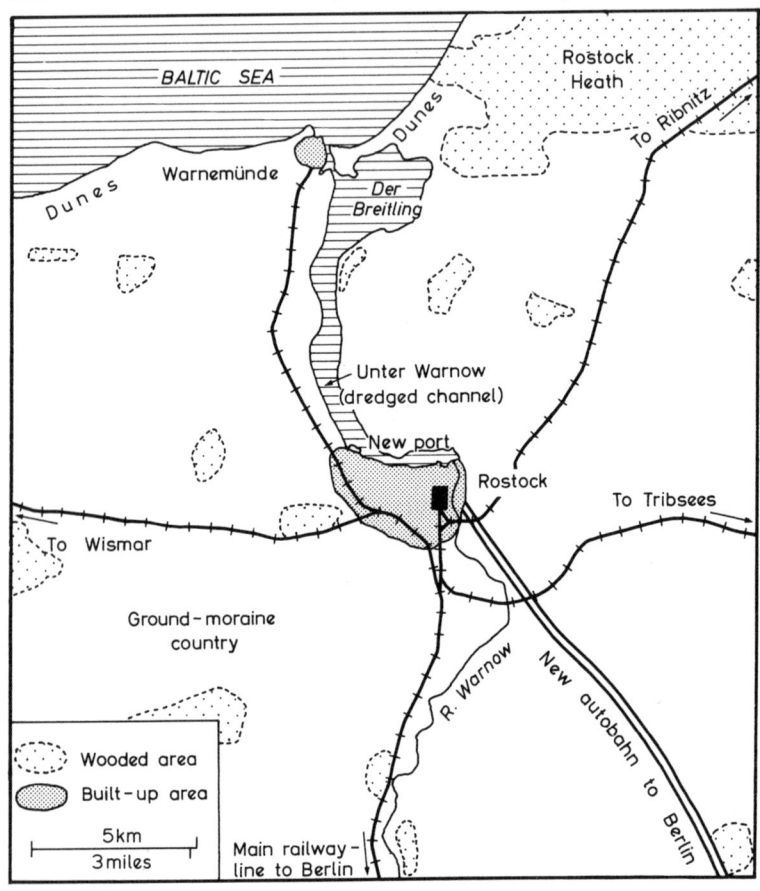

Fig. 35. The port of Rostock

Since 1955 East Germany, despite its lack of political recognition
by many countries, has sought to widen its trading connections and
has concluded agreements with thirty-five non-Communist states, as
well as with the usual Communist bloc. Profitable fields of enterprise have been opened up in the Arab countries (its single largest
extra-European trading partner is the United Arab Republic), in
south-east Asia, among the new states of Africa, and in Latin
America. There has been a substantial increase in trade with West
Germany, and in 1968 about £29 millions worth with the United
Kingdom. The East German government now uses the Leipzig Fair
(pp. 233–4) as its 'shop window'.

POPULATION AND SETTLEMENT

The great upheavals which affected Germany following the end of the War complicate the demographic picture. The population of the Soviet-occupied zone in 1945 was about 18 million, and although there was a constant movement of refugees across the country, the figure was much the same when the Democratic Republic was created. In 1950 the total was 18·4 million, but as the flow of refugees continued, seeking a more attractive life in West Germany, it dropped to 17·6 million in 1956 and to 17 million by 1964, though since then there has been a slight increase. The birth rate has declined, largely because many who fled from the East were of the younger generation, and in 1968 the birth- and death-rates were identical at 14·3 per thousand. Since 1961 the East German government has rigidly closed the border between the two states in order to cut off the flow of refugees, culminating in the construction of the Wall across Berlin.

In 1968 East Germany had an average population of 158 per sq. km (409 per sq. mile), a figure appreciably below that for West Germany, 243 per sq. km (630 per sq. mile). There is a marked contrast between the northern half of the country, with its forests, heaths and thinly populated arable land, and a belt of much denser population across the Bördeland, with its rich loess soils, and with many towns which have had a prosperous commercial and industrial life since the Middle Ages.

Urban Settlement

With the exception of East Berlin, which with a population of 1·2 million stands as an 'island' within the thinly peopled sand country, the large towns of East Germany are in the south, including ten with over 100,000 people, the largest being Leipzig (608,000) and Dresden (468,000). Most of these cities have been largely rebuilt since the War; new factories and blocks of flats have risen in their suburbs. The urban population has increased markedly at the expense of the rural element; the drift to the towns goes on steadily, partly because mechanized agriculture requires fewer workers, partly because of the demand for labour in industry.

Rural Settlement

Much of East Germany was colonized during medieval times by a steady eastward movement, in part the result of military conquest, in part peaceful agricultural settlement involving the draining of marshes, the clearing of woodland, and the improvement of the sandy soils. Villages of distinctive and recognizable pattern were created, including the 'long-street village' (*Strassendorf*), where the farmhouses are in two rows, facing each other across the street; and the 'long-green village' (*Angerdorf*), where the farmhouses are similarly arranged but with a long narrow village green between them. Behind the villages lay the large open fields, with narrow strips worked by individual farmers. Farther north, in Mecklenburg, the settlement pattern was long dominated by the large estate farm (*Gut*), with its associated village inhabited by the estate workers. This pattern of settlement changed little through the centuries until the end of the 1939–45 War. Since then the estates have been expropriated, the manor houses pulled down, and collective and state farms established.

REGIONS (Fig. 32)

1. *The Mecklenburg Lake Plateau*

This region extends across East Germany between the valleys of the Elbe and the Oder; most of its physical features are the result of the Quaternary glaciation (p. 144). The mainly heavy clay soils were once covered with thick forest, mostly beech, into which German colonization has pushed since medieval times. The region now forms one of the chief agricultural districts, growing potatoes, wheat and sugar beet.

In medieval times several ports along the indented Mecklenburg coast were important. Rostock, with a population of over 10,000 by the end of the fourteenth century, Wismar and Stralsund were Hanse towns, with a valuable trade in herrings, timber and grain, but they subsequently suffered from the general decline in Baltic trade; the agricultural hinterland had little need for outlets, and Hamburg and Lübeck to the west, Stettin to the east, served the needs of the industrial regions in southern Germany.

The post-1945 boundary gave a new importance to this stretch of coast, since its small ports are East Germany's only direct outlets by sea. Development has been concentrated at Rostock (Fig. 35), and in 1960 a new deep-water harbour was completed 11 km (7 miles) from the sea along the left bank of the river Warnow, together with improvements at its outport of Warnemünde. The city, badly damaged from the air during the War, for its shipyards, aircraft factories (*Heinkel*) and engineering works were important targets, has been rebuilt, and its 1938 population of 113,000 had grown in 1968 to 188,000. The *Neptun* and *Warnow* shipyards build vessels for the Communist countries. The fishing port has been reconstructed, and a fish-processing industry established. Rostock has been linked directly to Berlin by railway, and a new *Autobahn* is under construction.

Away from the coast the density of population in this primarily agricultural area is low, and the only inland towns of any size are Schwerin and Neubrandenburg. The former was the capital of Mecklenburg-Schwerin, and is now, with nearly 100,000 people, the administrative centre of a *Bezirk*. Considerable industrial developments have taken place since 1950, including engineering, chemical manufactures and food-processing. Neubrandenburg is a planned 'colonial' town, its core revealing a rectangular pattern of streets, surrounded by gardens occupying the site of the former fortifications, outside which are the modern suburbs.

2. *The Heathlands of Brandenburg*

The heathlands extending across the north-centre of the country have developed on sands and gravels over a series of low plateaus between 45 and 200 m (150 and 650 ft) above sea-level, separated by the river valleys and by sections of Urstromtal. Although there has been considerable reclamation, parts are still heath (*Heide* or *Sandgeest*), with vegetation such as ling and heather which can grow on the poor leached sands. Other higher areas form moorland (*Moorgeest*), where an impermeable hardpan has developed, resulting in water-logging and the accumulation of sphagnum moss to form peat. About a third is under woodland, mostly pines in plantations on the less tractable sands. The better sandy soils grow potatoes and rye, patches of clay soil produce wheat and sugar beet, and the drained floors of the Urstromtäler are mainly under permanent grass, of which there is otherwise little. Around Berlin the urban market has encouraged intensive market gardening, especially in the Western sector, where as much food as possible must be produced.

Apart from the dominance of Berlin, this region is not character-ized by much urban development. In the west Brandenburg (70,000) is an important engineering centre, with a steel plant using scrap, a rolling mill and a large tractor factory. Frankfurt-an-der-Oder, a natural crossing-point of the river where its valley narrows, is less important than in pre-1939 days; its population is only about 60,000, compared with 76,000 in 1938. The new boundary not only severs it from half its former hinterland but also from its original suburbs, now a Polish town on the eastern bank of the river. Potsdam (111,000) originated as the royal residence, then formed a suburb of Berlin, with many fine houses, then it became a dormitory town, and is now a manufacturing centre, with the largest locomotive-building plant in East Germany, and other engineering works. Two industrial towns have grown up in the east: Eisenhüttenstadt, with its integrated steel plant and workers' city, and Schwedt-an-der-Oder, with its oil refinery.

During the last twenty years a new industrial region has developed in the heathlands of Lower Lusatia to the south-east of Cottbus, which is the administrative centre of a *Bezirk*. This development is based on the brown coal field (p. 216) coking and chemical plants at Lauchhammer, an integrated plant using brown coal at '*Schwarze Pumpe*', and thermal power stations at Trattendorf and Laura.

3. *Berlin* (Fig. 36)

The origins of the city comprised two small twelfth-century settlements, Alt Kölln on an island in the Spree, and Alt Berlin on its right bank. The site was not naturally good, although a west–east Urstromtal, in which flows the Spree, is here crossed by north–south routes across the heathlands. Its growth into a large city only occurred because it became the capital first of Brandenburg in 1470, then of Prussia in 1800, and finally of the German Empire in 1871. In that year its population was about 900,000, and by 1939 this had reached 4·3 million, the fourth largest in the world. Berlin is surprisingly compact, covering about half the area of Greater London. Both to west and east are extensive interlinked lakes, and beyond them open drift-covered plateaus, with immense areas of pine forest. As the capital of a great state it became a centre of administration and of commercial and financial activity, a focal point of communications by road and water (Fig. 34), from which in 1939 no less than fourteen main railway lines radiated. Industrial quarters developed at Spandau and Charlottenburg in the west, Treptow and Schöneweide in the south-east, Tegel and Reinickendorf in the north-west, Mariendorf and Tempelhof in the south, Lichtenberg in the east. The main activities were electrical engineering (*Siemens* and *A.E.G.*), the construction of diesel engines, aircraft components, precision instruments, machine tools, cars and lorries and pharmaceutical chemicals.

Sustained bombardment from the air, together with the devastation caused during the final siege, shattered much of Berlin; it has

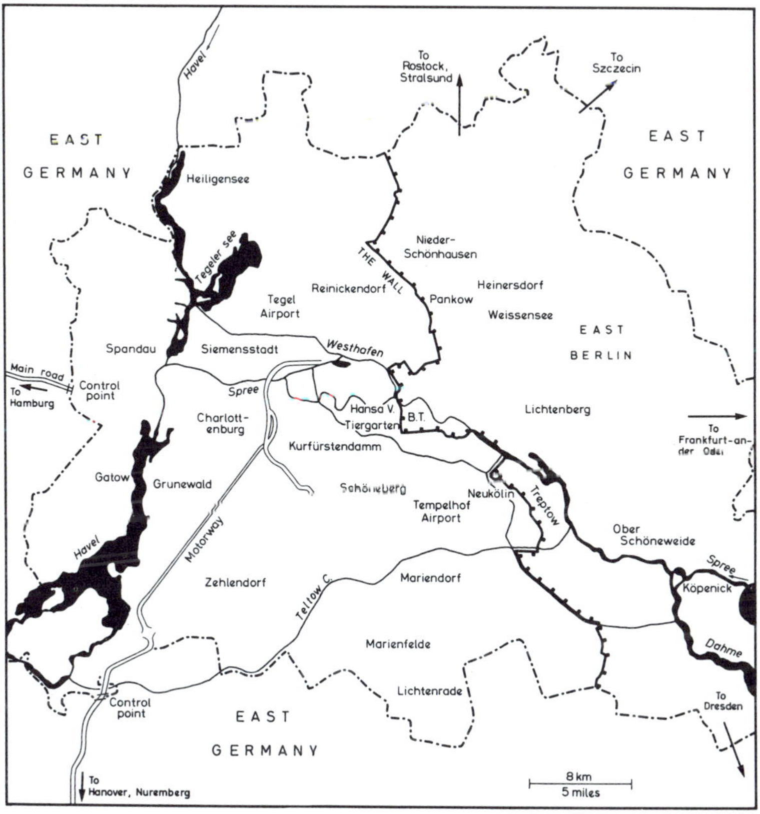

EAST
GERMANY

Heiligensee

To
Rostock,
Stralsund

To
Szczecin

EAST
GERMANY

Havel

Tegeler see

THE WALL

Nieder-
Schönhausen

Tegel
Airport

Reinickendorf

Pankow

Heinersdorf

Weissensee

EAST
BERLIN

Spandau

Siemensstadt

Westhofen

Spree

Main road
To
Hamburg

Control
point

Charlott-
enburg

Hansa V.
Tiergarten

B.T.

Lichtenberg

To
Frankfurt-an-
der Oder

Kurfürstendamm

Gatow

Grunewald

Schöneberg

Neukölin

Treptow

Tempelhof
Airport

Ober
Schöneweide

Spree

Havel

Motorway

Teltow C.

Zehlendorf

Mariendorf

Köpenick

Dahme

Marienfelde

Lichtenrade

To
Dresden

Control
point

EAST

GERMANY

8 km
5 miles

To
Hanover, Nuremberg

Fig. 36. Berlin
B.T. Brandenburger Tor
Canals and canalized rivers are shown by black lines and named. (Based on
various large-scale city plans).

been estimated that 25 sq. km (10 sq. miles) of built-up area, including
the 'heart' of the administrative district, were utterly destroyed.
Though from 1945 to 1948 Berlin was administered by the quadripartite Allied government, the three western sectors now form West
Berlin, 480 sq. km (185 sq. miles) in area and with a population of
2·16 millions, separated from the Federal Republic by 160 km (100
miles) of East German territory. For every three laden trucks entering
West Berlin, two must return empty, and East Germany charges an
excessively high toll. Despite the blockade of 1948–49, overcome by
the air lift, despite tension, threats and pressures, despite the building
of the Wall across the city, West Berlin, with the support of the Federal

Government and of the Western Allies, has maintained its independence, forming a political and economic 'island' within the Communist world. Most of the city has been magnificently rebuilt, serving as a showpiece of the West, much in strikingly modern architecture, especially the Hansa Viertel and the luxury shops of the Kurfürstendamm. Helped by direct West German grants and investments, tax remissions and special credit terms, West Berlin's industry has flourished to such an extent that output is estimated to be twice that of pre-1939. Many industrial groups in West Germany, including *Telefunken, Osram* and *A.E.G.*, have expanded their branches in the city, or have developed new ones, and the *Siemens-Halske* electrical firm now has 40,000 workers. Many foreign concerns, such as *I.B.M., Gillette* and *Philips*, as a sign of confidence now have branches in West Berlin.

East Berlin, the former Russian sector, covering an area of 404 sq. km (156 sq. miles), differed from the western sectors in that it was contiguous with the Soviet-occupied zone of eastern Germany, and in 1949 it could become the centrally situated capital of the Democratic Republic. But for long it remained largely a ruined city, except for the façade of the Karl Marx Allee, built by the Russians as a showpiece, and the slow rebuilding appeared drab in the extreme, although the last few years have seen a substantial improvement. Its population of 1·08 million in 1968 was appreciably less than the 1950 figure of 1·2 million, the result of the westward drift of refugees. New administrative buildings serve the East German government. Factories, mainly concerned with electrical and other engineering, chemicals and clothing, have been built in the northern suburbs at Heinersdorf, and on the east at Köpenick and Treptow. A new airport has been developed at Schönefeld.

The division between West and East Berlin is highly artificial and remains one of the main threats to world peace. At present the problem seems insoluble; no West Berliner wishes to be incorporated into the Democratic Republic, and the creation of Free City status, even under guarantees, seems impracticable and unworkable. For most of the time West Berlin carries on in a quietly normal way, with a status which has been described as 'permanently provisional', but at any time a crisis could be developed at the Communist whim.

4. *The Upper Saxony Basin*

In the 'embayment' between the Harz on the west and the Erz Gebirge on the south lies an undulating lowland, rising gently southward from about 90 m (300 ft) near the edge of the Fläming heathland to about 300 m (1000 ft) along the foothills of the Erz Gebirge. With the exception of a small area in the east, which drains north via the Neisse and the Spree, the drainage of the whole basin focuses to the north-west by way of the Elbe, each of its numerous tributaries in turn being picked up by the line of the Urstromtal occupied by the Schwarze Elster and the middle Elbe as far as Magdeburg. Much of the surface is covered with soils derived from loess, underlain by Tertiary and Mesozoic rocks within which are found the two chief economic assets of the region: brown coal and potash.

The Upper Saxony Basin has long been a prosperous region, with flourishing agriculture (wheat, barley and sugar beet), some woodland and pasture, craft industries resulting originally from the presence of water-power, timber on the hill slopes, local wool, ores from the mountains, and highly skilled labour. The cities enjoyed a European reputation as commercial and cultural centres. The specialized industries have experienced a renewed activity under modern conditions; most of the factories have been rebuilt and enlarged after wartime destruction or postwar dismantling. New large-scale industry is based on brown coal; a dozen large thermal power stations are within a 50 km (30 mile) radius of Leipzig.

Except for the Greater Berlin district, this is the most densely populated part of East Germany, including six cities with populations of over 100,000. The largest is Leipzig (608,000), situated on the eastern side of the Elster valley. The twelfth-century town was built on a promontory of alluvium rising above the junction of the Elster with the Pleisse, and with extensive marshes around, not a particularly favourable site. But at an early date it became a commercial centre and a focus of routes, and established its fairs as international events as early as 1268. Other activities included paper-making, printing and publishing, the fur trade, the textile industry, mechanical and electrical engineering, and the making of pianofortes and other musical instruments, as befits its associations with J. S. Bach and Richard Wagner. The War disrupted its importance; much of its nodal position disappeared, for the railway lines south-westward to Frankfurt-am-Main, Würzburg and Nuremberg were crossed by the boundary between East and West Germany. Though the city has recovered and even extended its industrial activity, its population is still below that of 1939, when it was over 700,000. Its spring fair has been revived, not only as a showpiece of East German manufactures but as a meeting point for mutual trade between East and West. While two-thirds of the exhibitors are from the Communist countries, more than 200 British firms are usually represented, and the fair in some ways rivals that at Hanover.

Halle (266,000), 40 km (25 miles) to the west of Leipzig on the right bank of the Saale, is the centre of the chemical industry, located on the brown coal field and near the salt deposits, and has engineering works, especially the construction of mining machinery, and sugar refineries. The city has a reputation as a centre of culture and learning. Before the creation of the Second *Reich* in 1871, Leipzig was in Saxony, Halle in Prussia, and for this political reason the latter became a focus of communications. Other towns in this part of East Germany are Dessau (heavy engineering), Merseburg (the Leuna synthetic oil refinery) and Köthen. Farther south, on the foreland flanking the margins of the Erz Gebirge, Karlmarxstadt (formerly Chemnitz until 1953), Zwickau and Gera, each with over 100,000 people, are situated in the valleys of the north-flowing rivers. This has long been a flourishing textile area; Chemnitz was known for its linens in the Middle Ages, during the nineteenth century it became pre-eminent for cottons, and since 1950 much of this activity has been revived. Karlmarxstadt is also a centre of both heavy and light engineering, including textile machinery and machine tools.

Dresden is farther east on the Elbe near the edge of the foothills of the Erz Gebirge, where the river flows through an open clay-floored basin. A fortress and bridge town since the thirteenth century, it became the capital of Saxony in the fifteenth, and also a commercial, industrial and cultural centre, though somewhat overshadowed by Leipzig. By 1938 its population was 625,000, but it was heavily damaged during the War, though by 1968 the total had partly recovered to 500,000. Its industries are mainly of a precision character, such as the making of optical instruments, laboratory apparatus, glassware and machine tools; food-processing and cigarette-making are also important. The river port has been developed since the War, helped by the improvement of the Elbe as a waterway from Czechoslovakia. Other small industrial towns in the Dresden basin include Meissen, the home of fine porcelain, Pirna with pulp, paper and glass, and Freital with alloy steels. Farther east, near the Polish border on the left bank of the Neisse, is Görlitz (92,000), with engineering and textile industries.

At the most westerly point of the bend of the Middle Elbe stands Magdeburg, a military fortress against the Slavs in the Middle Ages, and subsequently a focal point for the neighbouring Bördeland. In the nineteenth century the Elbe became increasingly important for navigation, partly because of improvements in its channel, partly because of the progressive reduction of tolls charged by the riparian states. The Mittelland Canal was built between 1905 and 1938, linking Magdeburg with the Dortmund-Ems Canal and hence the Rhine, while the Elbe-Havel Canal continues the water route to Berlin. An east–west *Autobahn* passes to the north of Magdeburg, and the city has also become a railway focus. It suffered heavily during the War, and is now very much a peripheral rather than a focal town, since it is only 50 km (30 miles) from the border, which cuts across road, rail and canal communications. However, there has been a considerable recovery; its population by 1968 had reached 268,000, though still well below the 1939 figure of 330,000. Located within a rich farming district, its industries include food-processing, sugar-refining, oilseed-pressing, the making of agricultural machinery, milling and the manufacture of fertilizers. It is also an important producer of heavy machinery and of chemicals.

5. *Thuringia*

The south-western corner of East Germany is commonly given the historic name of Thuringia after one of the early tribes, though for many centuries there was no political unit, merely a collection of small states. In 1945 Thuringia became a province, but when the new *Bezirke* were created in 1952, its territory was divided between Erfurt, Suhl and Gera.

Thuringia consists of two quite different physical regions. The northern part is the Thuringian Basin, the drainage area of the rivers Unstrut and Ilm, with their valleys eroded across concentric outcrops of Triassic clays, limestones and sandstones. Much is covered with Keuper clay, though its surface is diversified by superficial deposits of alluvium in the valleys, till in the northern and central parts, and loess generally. A small outlying part of the Thuringian Basin is the Goldene Aue ('the Golden Meadows'), a narrow rift valley between the Harz and the Kyffhäuser Ridge. It is floored with clays and marls, with a sporadic loess cover, and its soils are fertile.

By contrast, the southern part of Thuringia consists of the ridge of the Thuringian Forest, parallel to which on the south-west are the valley and the headwaters of the Werra, flowing north-westward to join the Weser.

Thuringia presents very marked contrasts in landscape and land use. Extensive woodland still grows on the Thuringian Forest and less continuously on the sandstone escarpments. Most of the Basin, together with the Goldene Aue, is an area of prosperous agriculture, with fertile soils growing wheat, barley and sugar beet in large fields, and near Erfurt is a market gardening and fruit-growing area, including the cultivation of flowers and vegetables for seed. The heavier clays carry pasture and support livestock farming.

Population is distributed evenly over the centre of the Basin, more thinly on its wooded upland margins. Some towns were capitals of their respective little states in past centuries. The largest is Erfurt, one of the oldest towns in central Germany, a market town since the ninth century and a member of the Hanseatic League, though its growth was checked by a stormy political history, and it was constantly involved in interstate struggles. It is the centre of a *Bezirk*, one of the few towns in East Germany to have a greater population (193,000) than in 1938, and with activities including light engineering, clothing and shoe-making, and seed-packing. Toy-making has long been famous in the nearby Sonneberg district. Other towns include Jena (85,000), with its optical industry; Gotha, with printing and publishing; Eisenach, with engineering and chemical industries; and Weimar, with the traditions of the enlightened educational life of its court, its associations with Goethe and Schiller, and the meeting place of the first National Assembly of the post-1918 German Republic.

6. *The Southern Uplands*

Upper Saxony is bordered on the south by the uplands which form the rim of the Bohemian 'Diamond' of Hercynian age. The fact that these slope gently to the north into Upper Saxony, together with their ores, plentiful water, wool from local sheep, and timber on the hills, encouraged settlement and industry, and many mining villages and small towns were established. Annaberg and Freiberg have been important in this connection for centuries; the latter still has smelt-mills for non-ferrous metals. Modern methods of prospecting and of working ores previously regarded as uneconomic have caused renewed activity since 1950.

Industry began on a domestic or rural craft basis, and has remained specialized and small-scale, including the making of musical instruments in the Vogtland, and of toys, clocks, textiles, gloves and cut glass in the Erz Gebirge. This activity is associated with the larger towns (Dresden, Karlmarxstadt, Zwickau) along the margins of the foothills. The chief town in the Vogtland is Plauen (82,000), with industries such as pulp and paper making, textiles and machine tools.

7. *The Eastern Harz*

The massif of the Harz is a clearly defined block between the Bördeland in the north and the Thuringian Basin in the south. Its century-old mining activity and traditions have been stressed (p. 197), though in recent decades its only significance has been in the mining of copper and its smelting at Mansfeld.

Though the original forests which swathed the Harz were cleared during centuries of mining and settlement, recently there has been extensive planting and the surrounding slopes are swathed in fir forests. The highest granite summits are covered with poor pasture and moorland, and experience a heavy winter snow cover. Many small towns and villages are situated in valleys on the flanks of the massif, those with the suffix *-rode*, such as Harzgerode, indicating their origin in clearings.

CHAPTER EIGHT

The Netherlands

THE kingdom of the Netherlands consists of the delta lands of the Rhine, Maas (Meuse) and Scheldt, and adjacent parts of the North Sea Lowland; these rivers reach the sea through an interlaced series of distributaries (Fig. 38). The country is sometimes referred to as 'Holland', though this name properly applies only to the provinces of Noord- and Zuid-Holland, which extend from the mouths of the Rhine to the island of Ameland. This is the 'hollow land', much of which is below sea-level; but for the dykes, 40 per cent of the Netherlands would be either permanently inundated or temporarily flooded during high tides and river floods (Fig. 37). Much of Dutch history has been concerned with the reclamation and defence of this land; in the words of the old saying, 'God made the world, but the Dutch made Holland'. Problems concerning the indeterminate margin of land and sea are emphasized by the considerable area between the mean high- and low-water marks. The official land area of the Netherlands in 33 808 sq. km (13,053 sq. miles), but the total to the mean low-tide mark is 40 893 sq. km (15,789 sq. miles).

STRUCTURE AND RELIEF

Structure

The whole of the Netherlands, two-thirds of Belgium and much of northern France are part of the North Sea Lowland, which for long periods of geological time has been an area of depression and sedimentation; its floor is the peneplain of Hercynian Europe. These Palaeozoic rocks, buried beneath newer sediments, contain great thicknesses of Coal Measures, located by the deep borings put down by the Dutch and Belgian geological surveys and by oil-prospecting companies. In South Limburg, where the dip of the concealed Coal Measures is to the north-west, workable coal is found at a depth of about 60 m (200 ft) in the east, but at over 600 m (2000 ft) in the west. This field, structurally a continuation of the Kempen in Belgium (p. 301), is bounded by major faults. Farther north, separated from the South Limburg field by a downfaulted trough in which the Upper Carboniferous strata occur at 2400 m (8000 ft) below the surface, is the

Fig. 37. The polders and heathlands of the Netherlands
The areas liable to indundation by the sea are shown in black, those by the rivers
with a stipple. Heathlands in the east and south are named.

Peel coalfield. Coal was reached in 1906 near Helenaveen at a depth
of 978 m (3208 ft), but the immense development costs which would
be entailed have precluded any exploitation. Further north still
other deep fields have been proved in Overijssel (near Winterswijk)
and Gelderland, both likewise unexploited.

The Mesozoic era was a period of extensive deposition over the
North Sea Lowland. Triassic and Jurassic rocks have been found
beneath the surface of north-eastern Belgium and the southern part
of the Netherlands. In Upper Cretaceous times a rise of sea-level

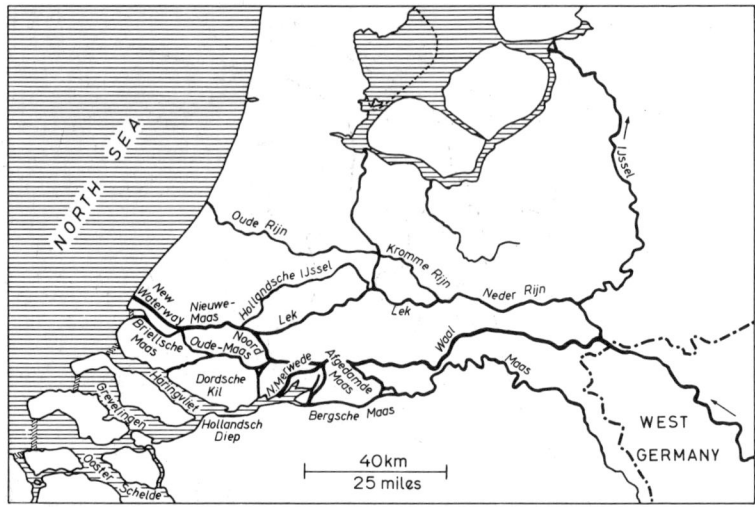

Fig. 38. The Rhine–Maas distributaries
The outer dykes of the Delta Plan are indicated, but they will not all be completed until 1978.

caused the 'Chalk Sea' to spread over much of western and central Europe, when an extensive cover of chalk was laid down. This now appears on the surface in the Paris Basin (p. 470), in parts of south-central Belgium (p. 288) and in South Limburg, but elsewhere it has either been removed by subsequent denudation before the Tertiary rocks were laid down, or is deeply masked by newer deposits.

In early Tertiary times a further marine transgression covered the lowlands of western Europe; though the resultant deposits are to be found over much of central Belgium (p. 289), in the Netherlands they are buried beneath younger deposits. In later Tertiary times (Miocene and Pliocene) occurred the last of the major transgressions, and great thicknesses of coarse sand were laid down in the North Sea basin. Towards the end of the Pliocene began the steady shift northward of the coastline, as the seas gradually receded, mainly the result of a widespread tilting movement. Areas to the south of a line indicated approximately by the Belgo-Dutch boundary were slowly uplifted, so that surviving patches of Lower Pliocene rocks now lie at approximately 150 m (500 ft) above sea-level in southern Belgium and northern France. Conversely, to the north of this line the tilting movement was downwards; the Lower Pliocene strata have been located at 360 m (1200 ft) below sea-level by borings near Utrecht.

Plate XXX. *The harbour at Kiel, West Germany, with a striking piece of propaganda against a divided and diminished Germany*

Plate XXXI. *Berlin. A view of the boundary between East and West Berlin, with the Wall in the foreground, at 'Check Point Charlie', one of the few official crossing-places*

Plate XXXII. Sand-dunes along the Dutch coast, with groynes to check beach-scouring

Plate XXXIII. Emmeloord in the North-east Polder, Netherlands

The Quaternary Glaciation

The North Sea Lowland lay at the very edge of the maximum advance of the Scandinavian ice-sheet during the third (Riss or Saale) glacial period, about 150,000 years ago, when it extended just to the south of the Zuider Zee. Dutch geologists have given the name *Drenthian* to this glacial phase, the only one during which an ice-sheet actually reached the Netherlands. Its limit is indicated by a series of low sandhills to the south of the Zuider Zee, interrupted by the Rhine valley, and continued to the south-east of Nijmegen into West Germany. These ridges were probably caused by ice pressure from the north, 'rucking-up' the drifts; in several quarries layers of sand and gravel can be seen, folded and even overthrust in a remarkable way, if on a miniature scale. If this supposition is correct, the name of 'push-moraine' (in Dutch, '*stuwwall*') is justified.

Farther north an extensive area in the eastern Netherlands, extending into West Germany, was covered by ground-moraine. Here sand, with irregular gravel patches, is dominant, though there are also considerable tracts of till. Farther west the till occurs at greater depths, buried under newer fluvial and marine deposits, though isolated upstanding masses form the nuclei of some of the West Frisian Islands; it also underlies part of the Wadden Zee and the IJssel Meer. Occasional erratics of Scandinavian origin have been found. In the province of Groningen and in the neighbouring parts of Drenthe, these erratics have been assembled by man to form dolmens, the '*Hunnebedden*' or burial places, the oldest traces of human occupation in the Netherlands.

The Quaternary glaciation was but a temporary interruption to the development of the drainage system. By the beginning of the Pleistocene these northern lowlands were dominated by a great proto-Rhine, to which the Scheldt, Meuse and Thames were confluents, and sedimentation proceeded in the areas to the south of the icesheet. As the ice fluctuated, so did the base-level of the rivers, corresponding to the changing sea-levels which resulted from a withdrawal of water when the ice advanced or a return of water when it withdrew. Extensive deposition of gravel and sand took place at times when the rivers were heavily charged with detritus, while renewed erosion occurred during stages of low sea-level, when the rivers entrenched their beds deeply into their own deposits to form terraces; these occupy a large part of the southern and eastern Netherlands.

9

Postglacial Developments

The greater part of the western half of the Netherlands and the valley floors of the Maas and Rhine are covered, in places to considerable depths, with recent marine and alluvial deposits, laid down since about 20,000 B.C. At the end of the Pleistocene, sea-level was about 60 m (200 ft) below its present position, because of the amount of water still contained in the icesheets over northern Europe, and the floor of what is now the North Sea formed continuous land between Britain and the Continent. The melting icesheets caused a gradual marine advance, the 'Flandrian Transgression', which ultimately formed the English Channel, the Straits of Dover and the North Sea. From archaeological evidence, the final breaching of the Straits of Dover is dated at approximately 5000 B.C., the accepted end of the Lower Holocene, when the sea-level was 5–6 m (16–20 ft) below the present, and the coastline lay broadly parallel to, but a few kilometres seaward of, its present position.

During the last few millennia, there has been on the one hand the accumulation of sand-dunes and marine clays, the deposition of river silt, and the growth of fen peat. On the other hand, there has been a slight but continuous relative rise of sea-level, still in progress at the rate of 100–150 mm (4–6 in) per century, the result of the continued sinking of the floor of the North Sea basin. On to the results of these processes has been superimposed man's contribution of reclamation and coastal defence, though repeatedly interrupted by temporary setbacks due to storm and flood; the latest of these disasters flooded 160 000 ha (400,000 acres) in 1953.

The Rivers

The broad, alluvium-floored valleys of the lower Rhine and its distributaries form a distinctive physical region across the south-central part of the Netherlands from the West German frontier to the North Sea (Fig. 38). The Rhine in preglacial times entered the sea farther to the north than at present, by way of what became the Zuider Zee, but since then its outlets have been gradually displaced to the south. In Roman times the main stream flowed westward along the line of the Kromme Rijn and the Oude Rijn, so reaching the sea to the west of Leiden; this was for long the defensible northern boundary of the Roman Empire. The major discharge of water is now by the Waal, which carries three times the volume of the Neder Rijn (Lek) and six times that of the IJssel, the other distributaries.

The bulk of Waal water passes through the artificial Nieuwe Merwede, cut in the latter part of the nineteenth century, then via the Hollandsch Diep and the Haringvliet to the sea.

The Maas flows northward from Liège for about 160 km (100 miles), forming the boundary between Belgium and the Netherlands as far as Maasbracht (except in the Maastricht district), and then becomes a wholly Dutch river. Past changes in its course and base-level have caused the formation of a valley, 3 km (2 miles) broad and with distinct terraces on each side, between Liège and Maasbracht. Farther north in the Netherlands, the plateau edge becomes less marked and falls back from the Maas, although the floodplain is still bordered by low bluffs, until the river begins to swing westward and approach the Rhine. It finally reaches the Hollandsch Diep through the Bergsche Maas, cut in the latter part of the nineteenth century to form a direct outlet then distinct from that of the Waal.

The gradients of these rivers are gentle, and they bring down large quantities of alluvium and sand, much of which is deposited in their beds, so gradually raising the level above the surrounding country. The resultant danger of flooding is aggravated by the sinking of the adjacent land through drainage and compaction. The Rhine distributaries are massively embanked along almost their whole length from the Dutch frontier, and the Maas is dyked below Grave. This dyking, with the construction of stabilizing barrages, the cutting across of meander-loops, and constant dredging are part of the process of regularization, not solely for flood control, but also to improve navigation. Between the main dykes, set well back from the summer channel, lies a considerable area of land; these lateral strips, usually inundated in winter, afford valuable summer pasture. Outside the dykes are the river polders, enclosed units wherein pumping may be necessary to remove excess water; they are covered with clay and occasional patches of gravel and coarse sand.

The Coast

By the end of the Lower Holocene, the coastline of the Netherlands lay a few miles offshore from its present position. A great sand-bar developed, sweeping in a curve from the coast of western Flanders near Calais to the Scheldt-Maas-Rhine delta, and continuing again along the coast of Zuid- and Noord-Holland. Its nucleus consisted of sand mixed with shelly fragments, forming a basal layer on which windblown sand accumulated to form dunes.

As this so-called 'old dune-line' developed into a continuous barrier, the sea was excluded and mud steadily accumulated in the shallow freshwater lagoons behind; and the surface level gradually rose. Vegetation contributed layers of fen peat (*laagveen*), which now occurs extensively in Zuid- and Noord-Holland, Friesland and Groningen, in places as much as 5 m (16 ft) thick.

During the first millennium A.D., the position of the offshore bar gradually changed as a result of erosion in the south and of accumulation in the north. The southern part of the old bar and dune-line south-west of The Hague was destroyed, and the present coastline lies 5–8 km (3–5 miles) farther inland. In the north the bar moved seaward until it reached a mass of boulder-clay which now forms the 'core' of the island of Texel, and then curved eastward along the line of the Frisian Islands. On this bar a second series of dunes accumulated, which probably originated about the beginning of the fourth century A.D. The two dune-lines can still be traced along the coast of Zuid- and Noord-Holland, the older one 6 or 8 km (4 or 5 miles) inland of the newer dunes bordering the beach. The older dunes form gently undulating terrain of considerable agricultural value, known as the *Geestgronden*.

Beyond the inner dune-line in Roman times lay a broad plain covered with peat fen and shallow meres, above mean sea-level but liable to inundation by spring tides. An extensive shallow lake, the *Lacus Flevo*, formed the ancestor of the Zuider Zee. Until the beginning of the fourteenth century the sea generally gained on the land. There are, it is true, records as early as the seventh century of reclamation around the shores of the *Lacus Flevo* and some dykes were constructed in Friesland and Groningen, but by 1300 the sea had advanced considerably; the new dune-line north of Den Helder had been breached in several places, each fragment forming one of the Frisian Islands. The mud-flats behind were inundated to form the Wadden Zee, which extended southward into the *Lacus Flevo*, flooding the low-lying lands around its margins and creating the Zuider Zee, under whose waters vanished many villages. Farther to the south, the province of Zeeland and much of southern Zuid-Holland became an archipelago separated by tidal channels, into which the Rhine-Maas-Scheldt distributaries poured their waters.

Other temporary changes occurred in the coastline as a result of flooding and inundation; many floods have been recorded, caused by storm surges when exceptionally high tides coincided with onshore gales to which the fourteenth and fifteenth centuries seem to have been particularly prone. As the technique of coastal defence improved, really disastrous floods became rarer, but they still occasionally happen, as in February 1953.

DYKES AND POLDERS

Sea Dykes

The sea dykes extend without a break from the West German border along the coast of Groningen and Friesland to the IJssel Meer, and the Frisian Islands are also faced with dykes to amplify the dunes. The main IJssel Meer dyke runs from the coast of Friesland for 29 km (18 miles) across what was open sea to the shores of Noord-Holland. From Den Helder to the Hook of Holland the sweeping curve of coast is bordered by a dune-belt, with a width near Zandvoort of about 5 km (3 miles). Dykes are rarely necessary, though groynes cross the beaches below the low-water mark (Plate XXXII), fortified by sunken mattresses of interwoven boughs and recently of polypropylene to afford protection against tidal scour and to stimulate the accretion of sand and mud. On the sand-flats fronting the dunes osier fences form 'drift dykes' which, supplemented by the planting of marram grass, help to stabilize the moving sand. The seaward faces of some of the narrower dune-lines are faced with stone, and sea walls and promenades front the resorts. This section of the coast, therefore, while needing constant maintenance, does not normally cause any major concern.

The Delta Plan

The 'delta region', with its islands and deep-water channels, affords the most critical problems, for approximately 1100 km (700 miles) of dykes are required, some merely earthen banks, others massive structures. Difficulties arise because the land behind the dykes, as a result of drainage and compaction, is frequently lower than the beach; tidal scour removes material from the foreshore and so undercuts the dykes, causing them to slump forward. For many years there has been discussion over the two possible methods of coping with the ever-present threat of flooding in the delta region. One was to strengthen and raise every dyke by about 2 m (6·5 ft), the other was to build new massive dykes across the entrances to the estuaries, so excluding tidal water.

The floods of February 1953 made it emphatically clear that an overall 'Delta Plan' was a matter of urgent priority. The cause of the disaster was a storm surge in the North Sea, associated with gale-force winds and waves of exceptional power. Many dykes were over-topped and the inrushing water eroded and breached their inner slopes, while the wave attacks undermined others which slumped forwards. The area flooded totalled 150 000 ha (375,000 acres), about 47,000 houses were destroyed or damaged, and 1,800 people lost their lives. The cost of this disaster was half the estimate of the Delta Plan.

When completed, this master scheme will exclude the sea from the delta region by means of a series of major dykes interlinking the islands and shortening the coast by about 680 km (420 miles) (Fig. 37). The mouths of the Wester Schelde and the New Waterway will not be sealed, since these are the shipping approaches to Antwerp and Rotterdam respectively, and traffic is too heavy to pass through locks without considerable delay. The former estuaries will be con-verted into a large freshwater reservoir; when the rivers bring down flood water, the excess will be discharged through the sluices into the sea at low tide. The whole scheme will, it is anticipated, be completed by 1978. In 1956 preliminary work began in the Haring-vliet, between the islands of Voorne and Overflakkee, with the sinking of mattresses of fascine work weighted with ballast. Above these were laid threshold dykes of shale and basalt, and on to this a line of concrete caissons was floated and sunk in position. The first major step was completed in May 1961, when the Veersche Gat dyke, between Walcheren and Noord-Beveland, was closed. The Haring-vliet was closed in 1968, the Brouwershavensche Gat in 1970.

Some Dutch engineers look farther ahead and envisage a series of dykes which will interlink the West Frisian Islands and so reclaim the Wadden Zee. This would provide the Netherlands with a smooth coastline, unbroken but for the shipping channels.

The Polders

The unit of organized reclamation behind the dykes is the polder, which varies in size from a tiny patch of land reclaimed from a tidal inlet or a piece of fen to a major unit such as the 54 000-ha (133,000-acre) East Polder of the Zuider Zee scheme. Some polders lie below sea-level, occupying former areas of open sea or deep lakes, and con-stant pumping removes water from rainfall and seepage, so maintain-ing the water-table at a predetermined level. Other polders lie just above mean sea-level, surrounded by lower dykes; water can normally be removed from these by gravity flow through the sluices at low tide. Still others are well above sea-level, but may be subject to temporary winter waterlogging; a system of ditches and channels usually provides adequate drainage.

Lowlying polders reclaimed from the sea or a lake are enclosed by a ring dyke, with a perimeter canal into which water is pumped from the drainage channels intersecting the polder floor. Formerly these were drained by pumps worked by a ring of windmills standing on the dykes; in the nineteenth century they were largely superseded by steam pumps, then by diesel pumps, and most windmills are now inoperative, though many remain as a picturesque feature of the landscape.

Although each polder is reclaimed as a unit, its maintenance must obviously be integrated with that of its neighbours, as well as with the navigable waterways, which requires detailed and vigilant organization. The local administrative body, the *Waterschap*, consists of representatives elected by landowners within the polder or group of polders concerned. Formerly powerful autonomous bodies, their powers have been reduced as the growing complexity of drainage schemes and the sometimes conflicting needs of navigation have necessitated centralized administration, with financial assistance from the State and provincial authorities.

The net result of a millennium of effort is that there are about 2,500 polders, of which 400 000 ha (1 million acres) are drained by gravity flow and two and a half times as much by pumping. Reclamation is still going on; there are two large polders to complete in the Zuider Zee, and while the Delta Plan is not primarily intended as a scheme of reclamation it will add between 10 000 and 16 000 ha (25,000 and 40,000 acres) of new land. Some lakes in Noord- and Zuid-Holland remain as storage reservoirs, and others in Friesland, lying in uneven hollows on fluvioglacial sand and gravels, have hardly been touched, for the poor soils would not be worth the cost. But with these exceptions the polders cover almost all the Netherlands below the one-metre contour, and form as a result of man's unending efforts the country's main agricultural lands.

The Reclamation of the Zuider Zee (Fig. 39)

The Zuider Zee, 3704 sq. km (1430 sq. miles) in area, penetrated far south into the heart of the country, and 320 km (200 miles) of dykes were required to safeguard the surrounding lands. It has long offered a challenge to the enterprising Dutch, for even a partial reclamation could add ten per cent to the cultivated area of the Netherlands. The plan finally adopted involved first the construction in 1927–32 of a

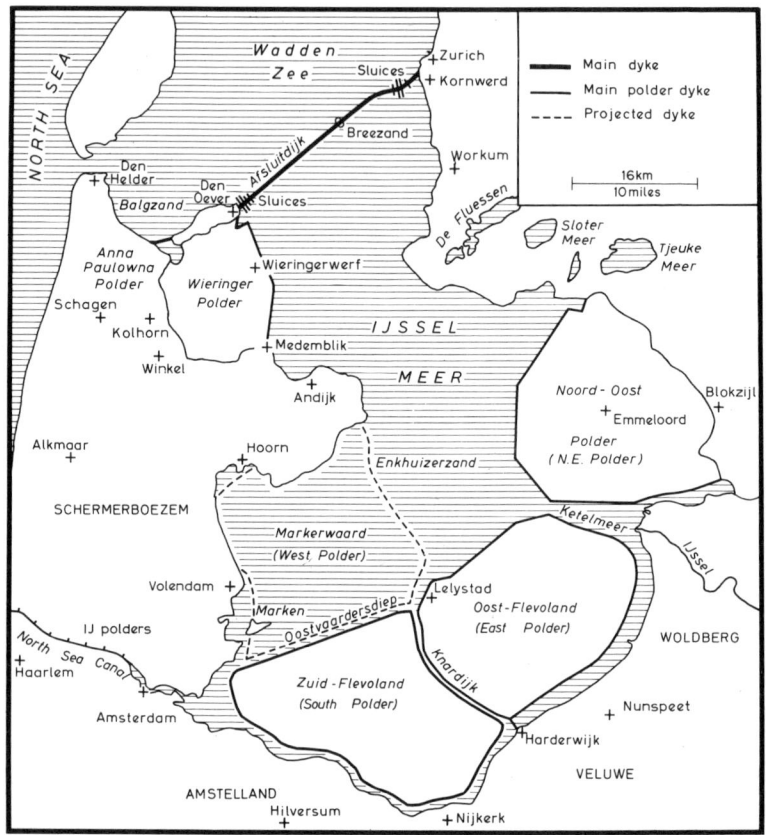

Fig. 39. The reclamation of the Zuider Zee
The reclamation of Zuid-Flevoland was completed in 1967, that of the Markerwaard will be completed by 1975.

29-km (18-mile) dyke across the narrow exit into the Wadden Zee, so converting the tidal gulf of the Zuider Zee into a freshwater lake. Within this enclosed area five individual polders are being reclaimed, leaving a much reduced body of water, the IJssel Meer, the level of which is automatically controlled by sluices in the main dyke. In times of obstructed discharge, when exceptionally high tides are experienced in the Wadden Zee, the sluices remain closed, and the level of the IJssel Meer then rises, so acting as a temporary storage reservoir. By 1937 the IJssel Meer was fresh, and it incidentally provides a useful source of water, particularly for agricultural purposes; its summer level is maintained above that of winter, so that water can be extracted.

Work started in 1927 on the first unit, the North-west or Wieringer Polder, and before the War the whole area was under cultivation. The North-east Polder was drained by 1942, but was not in full cultivation until 1958. In the original plan the large South-east and South-west Polders remained. It was later decided that the former was too big to handle as a unit and it was divided into two, the East Polder (Oost-Flevoland) and the South Polder (Zuid-Flevoland), (Fig. 39). The dyke around the East Polder was completed in 1956, and two years later nearly 2000 ha (5000 acres) were under cultivation; by the beginning of 1963 about 2,400 people were living there. Work on the South Polder was completed in 1967. The final stage, the reclamation of the West Polder (known as the Markerwaard), will total 60 000 ha (148,000 acres) and should be completed by 1975.

The reclamation of each polder represents a tremendous effort, first by state-employed contractors, then by carefully selected tenant farmers. The initial work involves the construction of the perimeter dykes, pumping stations, major canals both for drainage and transport, and a close network of minor canals and ditches. A problem is the desalinization of the soil by leaching; rainwater is periodically pumped away, gradually removing salt in solution, a process accelerated by spreading gypsum over the land to form a highly soluble compound with the sodium chloride. The land is deep-ploughed several times to mix the light sands with the underlying clay, and to expose as much material as possible to the beneficial effects of weathering. The whole process takes several years, but gradually early crops of rye and kale are replaced by wheat, potatoes and sugar beet, as the soil is improved. Individual farms are built, each in its 20-ha (50-acre) holding, and complete villages and towns, such as Emmeloord (Plate XXXIII) in the North-east Polder and Lelystad in the East Polder, are created.

The whole scheme will be completed, it is hoped, by 1975, thus realizing an enterprise spread over more than half a century, which will have cost the equivalent of £200 millions.

Relief Regions (Fig. 40)

Despite the generally lowlying character of the Netherlands, several relief regions can be distinguished. The first comprises the delta-lands of the Rhine, Maas and Scheldt, together with the coast-

9*

Fig. 40. Relief regions of the Netherlands

lands to the north; this includes most of the provinces of Zeeland and Noord- and Zuid-Holland, the seaward portions of Friesland and Groningen, and the West Frisian Islands. Behind the sea-dykes and the dune-lines lie the polders covered with marine clays and peat, for the most part below sea-level.

The second region, across the south-centre of the Netherlands, consists of the joint floodplain of the Maas, the Rhine and its distributary the IJssel, floored with clay and protected from flooding by dykes.

In the east and south of the country several areas are covered with sheets of sand and gravel, on which has developed a distinctive heathland vegetation. South of the curve of the lower Maas, continuous across the boundary of Belgium with the Kempen, are the heathlands of Noord-Brabant (Plate XXXIV) and northern Limburg. Between the southern shores of the IJssel Meer and the valley of the river IJssel is the Veluwe, and to the east along the West German frontier are the heathlands of Overijssel, Drenthe, eastern Friesland and Groningen. Though broadly similar in aspect, the sands and gravels are of two different origins. Those in Noord-Brabant are fluvial, laid down by the late glacial and immediately postglacial Maas when swollen in volume and bearing an immense load, while those to the north and east of the Rhine-Maas valley are of glacial and fluvioglacial derivation.

The fourth region, the southern part of the province of Limburg, is very different from the rest of the country, consisting of an 'appendix' projecting southward for 40 km (25 miles) on the eastern side of the Maas, except for the Maastrict district which stands on the left bank where the boundary makes a small loop to the west. South Limburg is a plateau from 90 to 180 m (300 to 600 ft) above sea-level, consisting mainly of chalk, with patches of Younger Tertiary sands and marls. Rarely do these rocks appear on the surface, for they are largely covered with loam-like deposits, similar to the limon found in Belgium and northern France. The plateau is cut into several individual blocks by the valleys of the Geul and the Geleen, two right-bank tributaries of the Maas. The rounded summit of the Vaalserberg, almost at the junction of the Dutch, Belgian and West German boundaries, is the highest point (322m, 1056 ft) in the Netherlands.

CLIMATE

No marked contrasts in climate are appreciable over the Netherlands, for it is low-lying and is nowhere much more than 160 km (100 miles) from the sea. The country is open to air masses moving eastward from the North Sea and to others, though less frequent, from eastern Europe and beyond; the weather is characterized by the usual variability of these latitudes. Mean temperatures are of much the same order as in East Anglia, though the winters are slightly colder because of the more marked continental influences. On the North Sea coast at Flushing the January mean is about 3° C., at Groningen about 1° C. Prolonged periods of frost are more common and sustained than in Britain, particularly when a continental high-pressure system extends its influence westward. The lowest temperature recorded at the Eelde (Groningen) observatory between 1921 and 1960 was −23° C., and at De Bilt (Utrecht) the record is −25° C. Mean summer temperatures scarcely differ over the country, the July mean varying little from 16° C.

Equally uniform is the distribution of precipitation. The mean annual rainfall for Flushing is 680 mm (26·8 in), spread throughout the year, for even the driest months (April and May) average about 36 mm (1·4 in) each. The wettest part is in the south-east, where the land rises to just over 300 m (1000 ft); here the mean is about 800 mm (31·5 in), though over South Limburg as a whole it is a little lower (about 620 mm (24·5 in)) than over the rest of the country, because of the slight rain-shadow effect of the Kempen plateau in Belgium. Some precipitation falls as snow, the average annual number of days with snowfall varying from about ten to forty-four.

LAND USE AND AGRICULTURE

The Netherlands is one of the most intensively farmed countries in Europe, partly because of its high density of population providing both labour and markets, and partly because of the inherent Dutch characteristics of resourcefulness, thoroughness and ability to work hard. Natural advantages were limited, but centuries of diligent effort have reclaimed farmland from the sea, the marshes, the lakes and the heathlands, and after reclaiming it the Dutch have defended it and continued to improve it. Production has continued to rise steadily; an index number for the early 1950's of 100 has risen to 129 for 1967.

Soils

The soils depend mainly on the nature of the superficial deposits from which they have developed. The Soil Survey Institute at Wageningen has published figures of the different soil types, as follows:

	Per cent	
Old sea-clay	3·1 ⎫	
Young sea-clay	28·8 ⎬ Polders	
Peat	7·8 ⎭	
Dune-sand	2·1	Coastal margins
River-clay	9·8	River valleys
Fluvial and fluvioglacial sand	46·4	Heathlands
Loess-loam	1·9	South Limburg

Behind the coast, areas of sand derived from the old dune-line are known as the *Geestgronden*; these contain shelly fragments which afford a source of lime, and being light and warm the resulting soils are valuable for horticulture. Much of the polderland is covered with marine clays; the older ones, exposed by the drainage of lakes or the stripping away of overlying layers of peat, are largely under pasture, while the younger clays, when desalinized after reclamation, form the main arable soils. The peat soils, derived from beds of fen peat, are mainly under permanent pasture. In these polderlands the water-table can be regulated according to requirements; it is usually maintained at a higher level if the land is under permanent grassland than if under crops.

The floodplains of the rivers are covered with clays and occasional patches of gravel and coarse sand. The soils derived from these materials are not as good as the marine clays, since the alluvium tends to be damp and often rather sour, the result of the constant infiltration of water. Farther east, where the land is slightly higher and a lower water-table can be maintained, the soils are better drained and are used for mixed farming.

The soils over the heathlands are for the most part poor. The podzols developed on the sands are dry because of their low water-holding capacity, and they are subject to rapid leaching by percolating rain water which removes the soluble bases, particularly calcium, leaving the soils deficient in nutrients. Only a small amount of humus forms, derived from the fibrous remains of mosses, lichens and woody heath plants, and highly acid in character. Waterlogging may be caused by the formation of a hardpan, an impermeable stratum sometimes consisting of sand grains or gravel cemented by ferric salts, sometimes of humus compounds.

In the north-east the depressions among the undulating areas of boulder-clay developed tracts of waterlogged peat, formed from sphagnum and other bog plants. This is the *Hoogveen*, much of which has now been stripped off as part of reclamation.

The loams of South Limburg are probably derived from deposits of loess, though some geologists regard them as the result of the modification and redeposition of chalky rocks by weathering and stream action. The resultant soils, known as 'loess-loam', cover about a quarter of Limburg, and are among the most fertile in the Netherlands.

The soils are constantly being modified as a result of intensive cultivation. Drainage, the heavy application of lime and fertilizers, and the reclamation or improvement of land formerly of little value have enabled the Dutch to make the best use of their somewhat limited environment.

Land Reclamation

The reclamation of the polderlands has already been described. Less widely recognized, but of considerable importance, is the problem of making available for agriculture the heaths and moors of the south and east. In 1888 the Dutch Heath Society was founded, with its headquarters at Arnhem; helped by the State, it distributes financial assistance, carries out reclamation schemes, leases the resultant land to approved tenants, fosters research, facilitates mechanization and disseminates information. The Society itself carries out about half the reclamation orders it receives, putting the rest out to contractors, though maintaining supervision.

Sometimes the stimulus has come from cities such as Groningen and from individual communes. Groningen began reclamation in the sixteenth century, when its citizens began to remove peat for fuel from the surrounding moorlands; as each section was cleared, agricultural settlements were established. Manure from the flocks and herds and garbage from the city were dug in, and in the nineteenth century cheap chemical fertilizers from Germany were used.

The low-lying areas of damp river-clay between the Rhine distributaries and the Maas are known as the *Komgrondengebieden* ('basin soil districts'). Because of their sour soils and also because of isolation due to the absence of roads and railways and the stretches of unbridged rivers, they have long constituted areas of agricultural underdevelopment. Since 1945 the State has carried out schemes of drainage, provided financial help and advice for colonists, and fostered programmes of research. The work was furthered in 1953 by the creation of the 'Foundation for Basin Soil Districts' as a co-ordinating and stimulating organization.

Reclamation is still in progress generally; between 1950 and 1968 a total of 120 000 ha (300,000 acres) was reclaimed, almost exactly half each by way of drainage of new polders and improvement of the sandy wastes. But during the same period as an inevitable result of the growth of population, towns, industry and communications, nearly 60 000 ha (150,000 acres) of agricultural land were lost.

Land Use

The Netherlands has about 2600 sq. km (1000 sq. miles) of woodland, about 9 per cent of the total area; most of it is found on the sandcountry in the form of plantations, as in the Veluwe and in the eastern heathlands. Much planting is the work of the State Forestry Service, created in 1899. Many valleys of South Limburg are wooded, and clumps of beech trees add to the verdant character of the countryside.

In 1968 the agricultural area of the Netherlands amounted to about 2·22 million ha (about 5·5 million acres), or approximately 70 per cent of the total land surface. About 33 per cent of the farmland is under arable, 36 per cent under pasture, the rest under the category of horticulture, including market gardens, bulb-growing, flower-cultivation, glasshouses and nurseries. This horticultural land totalled only 120 000 ha (300,000 acres), but it is the most intensively farmed category and yields the highest cash returns per unit of area.

Land-holding

A major problem is the fragmentation of land, the result of the Law of Succession; in 1950 there were no less than 410,000 individual farms, of which nearly 60 per cent were of less than 3 ha (7·5 acres). Even though these proportions were exaggerated by the inclusion of 38,000 market gardens, this fragmentation was economically unjustifiable, and the government has taken measures to consolidate holdings. Increasing opportunities in industry, especially in new development areas, the transfer of farmers to holdings in the IJssel Meer polders, and payments under the Land Administration Fund simply 'to give up and get out' has reduced the number of separate holdings by a third in twenty years. The increase in larger holdings has also resulted in greater mechanization.

Other government assistance includes land-grants for improvements, allocations for research, the increased availability of advisory services and further education, price support for such staple commodities as milk, and the protection of cereals by import levies.

Co-operation

Most farmers belong to co-operative societies, which lay down regulations for the grading and marketing of produce, especially in horticulture. The first co-operative was founded in 1886; now there are over 4,000. Most are dairy co-operatives, handling about three-quarters of the milk produced, others are concerned with the bulk purchase and distribution of feeding stuffs and fertilizers. Co-operative auctions are held at centres to which farmers bring their produce; for example, the famous cheese auction at Alkmaar takes place every Friday.

Livestock

The importance of livestock is shown by the fact that they contribute two-thirds of the value of all agricultural produce. In 1968 there were about 4·1 million cattle in the Netherlands, compared with 3·7 million before the War, distributed widely except in the mainly arable province of Zeeland. The traditional dairy-farming areas are on the grass polders, where a high water-table can be maintained within the clay soils, the fen peats, and the riverine alluvial soils. Areas of former heathland support large numbers of animals on imported concentrates and fodder crops grown with the aid of fertilizers. The province of Noord-Brabant, much of which is sand country, has over half a million cattle.

Along the coastal lowlands of Friesland and Noord- and Zuid-Holland, the relatively mild winters and well-distributed rainfall enable dairying to be based on permanent pastures, which occupy 61 per cent of the farmland, and cattle are kept out of doors most of the year. Little short-ley pasture and few fodder crops are grown, although hay is cut and stored for winter feed. In Zuid-Holland a large urban market exists for milk; in Noord-Holland and Friesland, by contrast, much milk is sent to processing factories. In 1968 about 118,000 tons of butter and 245,000 tons of cheese were produced under strict State control. Notable varieties are Gouda, made in western Utrecht and eastern Zuid-Holland, and the red-crusted Edam, made on the polder farms near the IJssel Meer. Rather less than half of the butter and rather more than half of the cheese were exported. Developments have taken place in the output of condensed milk and of dried milk. In various ways the equivalent of a third of all milk produced is exported.

The production of beef and veal in association with dairy farming is now sufficient to meet the Netherlands' requirements. Bullocks are fattened in a number of areas; in the neighbourhood of Schiedam, for example, they feed on residues from the distilleries. The number of pigs too has increased remarkably; in 1950 the total was about 1·9 million, but this had risen to 4·7 millions in 1968. The two provinces of Utrecht and Noord-Brabant contain between them about half the pigs. After a period of decline, the numbers of sheep have risen to about 550,000 in 1968, compared with 330,000 in 1938.

Arable Farming

The cultivation of crops is to a large extent associated with the rearing of livestock; the produce, including rye, barley, oats, fodder beet, clover and alfalfa, from about three-fifths of the arable land is fed to animals. Rye is grown on the sandy soils of the south and north-east, oats on the clay polders and the former heathlands, especially in Groningen, and barley in Zeeland and Groningen. The most striking change has been the increase in both the area and production of wheat, which was behind both rye and oats in 1950, when its yield was only 295,000 tons, but this increased to 739,000 tons by 1967; the chief cereal-growing province is Zeeland. Potatoes, both for human consumption and for industrial purposes, are produced chiefly in Friesland. Sugar beet is grown, especially in Zeeland and on the loam soils of South Limburg, and fodder beet appears generally within the rotations.

Industrial crops include flax, mainly in Zeeland, and small amounts of rape, chicory, mustard, colza, hemp and caraway. The cultivation of flax has fluctuated appreciably. Until the end of the nineteenth century it was grown very widely, then it dwindled to as little as 7000 ha (17,000 acres) in 1931. Since the War there was first a steady increase, and then a subsequent decline to about 10 000 ha (25,000 acres); much is now imported from Poland.

Horticulture

Horticulture and fruit cultivation supply both home and export markets, especially in Great Britain. Market gardens are important to the east of The Hague on the sandy soils of the Geestgronden, which being light and warm are extremely productive when fertilized. The district to the south of The Hague, known as the Westland, and the neighbouring Delfland and Schieland, have an immense area of glasshouses; the chief province for glasshouse cultivation is Zuid-Holland.

One of the most renowned and profitable aspects of Dutch horticulture is bulb-growing, and a string of centres extends along the sandy strip between Leiden and Haarlem, concentrated at Sassenheim, Lisse and Hillegom. In 1968 some 12 000 ha (30,000 acres) of the heavily fertilized sandy soils were devoted to bulbs, almost entirely for export. An elaborate cut-flower trade, both for home and export, is centred near Leiden, around Utrecht, and at Aalsmeer near Schiphol. Nursery gardens are widespread, the most famous, with azaleas, rhododendrons, clematis and roses, being at Boskoop, 16 km (10 miles) north of Gouda.

Fruit is chiefly grown in the inter-riverine district between Arnhem and Nijmegen, usually known as the 'Betuwe' ('the good land'), where the trees are commonly in grass orchards. In South Limburg large orchards of apples and pears have been established, also in grass. Considerable areas of bush fruit support canning, preserving and jam-making industries at such small towns as Elst and Tiel. Other areas of bush fruit include the island of Zuid-Beveland (especially red currants) and parts of Noord-Brabant, where raspberries are grown in the light sandy soils.

This diverse agricultural activity, carried on with an intensity and an enthusiasm rivalled perhaps only in Denmark, makes a valuable contribution to the Dutch economy and 45 per cent of the agricultural output is exported. The horticultural districts are claimed to have the densest rural population in the world. In 1968 about 8 per cent of the working population were engaged in agriculture and though this is the lowest proportion in Europe, they were responsible for 10 per cent by value of the total productivity of the country.

FISHERIES

In response to their location near the fishing banks of the North Sea and to the numerous estuaries and islands with sheltered waters, the Dutch have been engaged in fishing for many centuries. In the Middle Ages they had a virtual monopoly of the European herring fisheries, one factor leading to the growth of the mercantile activity. Although this pre-eminence gradually disappeared during the eighteenth and nineteenth centuries, fishing still makes a contribution to the economy; in 1968 about 144,000 tons of fish were landed.

The fishing activities may be divided into three: sea, coastal and inland, though in contrast to those of neighbouring countries, the Dutch fisheries are confined almost entirely to the North Sea, and few trawlers visit the ocean fishing grounds. Herrings, for long the most important fish, are caught by vessels operating from IJmuiden, Scheveningen, and Vlaardingen on the Nieuwe Maas between Rotterdam and The Hook. But the general decline of the herring fisheries in the North Sea is shown by the fact that in recent years they contributed only a fifth of the total catch by weight and a seventh by value.

The coastal fisheries are important in the estuaries and in the Wadden Zee. They are concerned mainly with oysters, mussels, shrimps and prawns, contributing one-fifth to the total value of the fisheries. The Delta Plan is having serious effects on these inshore fisheries, which flourished particularly in the Rhine-Maas delta; in

May 1961, just before the final closure of the Veersche Gat, a fleet of nearly a hundred fishing boats sailed sadly from the harbour at Veere, never to return, for no longer would they have access to the open sea.

The inland fisheries are chiefly concentrated in the IJssel Meer, where since 1937 salt water fish have been replaced by pike, perch and eels; the last come from the Sargasso Sea and pass through the sluices in their millions. Between 7,000 and 9,000 tons of freshwater fish are caught each year by IJssel Meer fishermen, apart from another 8,000 tons of inedible varieties used for fishmeal.

FUEL, POWER AND MINERALS

In 1968 about two-fifths of the working population were employed in mining, manufacturing industry and constructional work. This may seem high since industrial advantages are few, home-produced raw materials are limited, and the only worked coalfield is the small South Limburg basin. Manufactures include some with a long tradition, others are highly specialized, based on modern scientific and technical developments and on a high degree of capitalization. Since 1950 the development of these 'new' industries has proceeded apace, helped by a remarkable amount of investment, much from abroad and especially from the U.S.A. One of the most notable developments has been the recent discovery of huge deposits of natural gas.

Coal-mining

The South Limburg field has for long been important to the Netherlands because it is the only productive one (Fig. 41); the Peel coalfield, though proved, is not worked. Though possibly the earliest to be exploited in Europe, it was not until 1895 that the first large-scale concession was granted; during the succeeding five years further leases were obtained by companies with French, German and Belgian interests. Towards the end of the nineteenth century it was considered desirable for the State to assume some interest in the coalfield, and most of the non-conceded proven area was reserved. A State company, the *Staatmijnen in Limburg*, was established with its headquarters at Heerlen, and the first coal was produced in 1906 by the Wilhelmina colliery in the south-east; three other State collieries were built, including the great Maurits undertaking in 1923, at one time the largest in Europe in terms of production. Since 1926 these State collieries have been responsible for about two-thirds of the annual

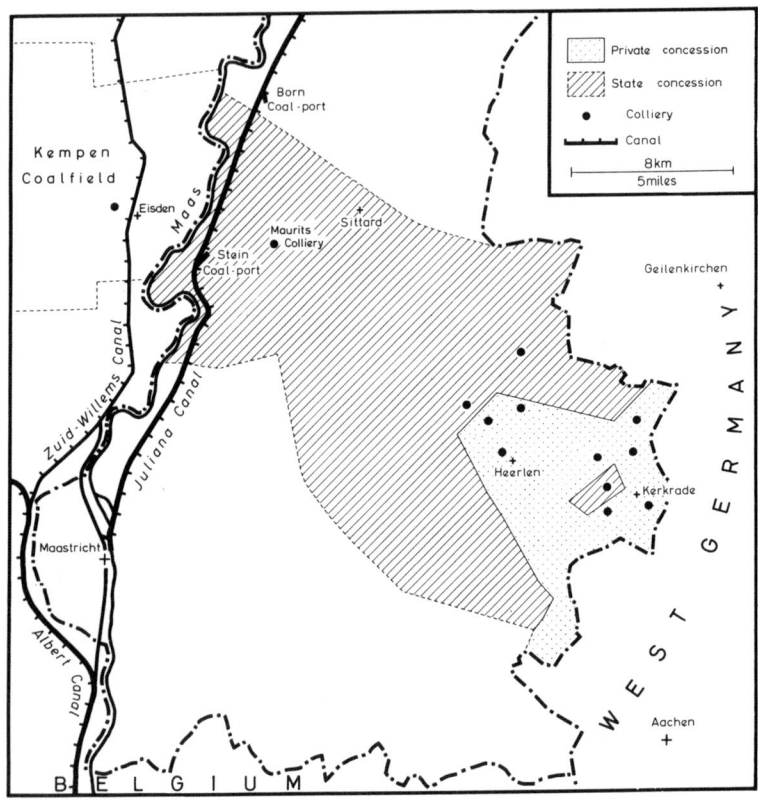

Fig. 41. The South Limburg coalfield

Several of these collieries have been closed during the last few years.

production (Fig. 42), while the balance was supplied by eight privately owned collieries.

The South Limburg field reached its peak of production in 1937 (about 14 million tons), and even during the German occupation output was maintained until the end of the war. Great efforts were made to increase production from the 1945 figure of 5 million tons, and a post-war peak of 12·6 millions was attained in 1961, providing about 60 per cent of the country's needs. Since then, however, the Limburg field has experienced increasing competition from American and Polish coal (which can be supplied to the steelworks of IJmuiden more cheaply than Dutch coal), and from oil and natural gas. Production has fallen steadily, reaching 6·7 million tons in 1968; several

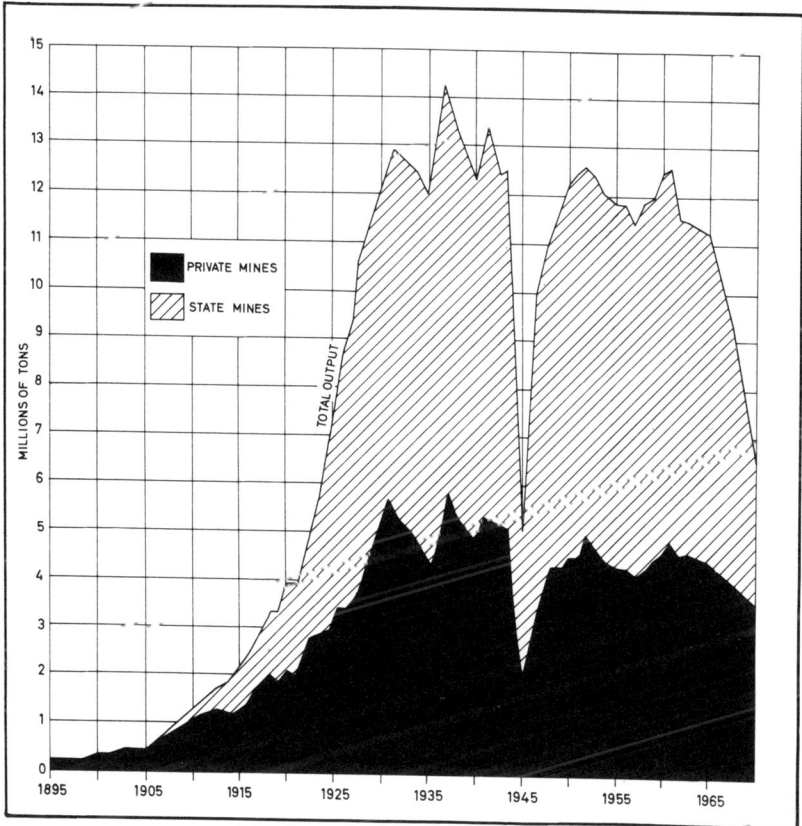

Fig. 42. Output of coal by private and State mines in South Limburg, 1895–1968
(Based on statistics from *Jaarcijfers voor Nederland*)

collieries have been closed, including *Maurits* and *Hendrik* (the latter is now the headquarters of the Alfcent command of N.A.T.O.). By 1968 there were only two State-owned and seven privately owned mines. Under the policy of the E.C.S.C. (see page 497), the Limburg field will be completely phased-out by 1972.

Oil

Oil was first located in 1944 near Schoonebeek in south-eastern Drenthe, and in 1953 some other scattered deposits were found in the west between Rotterdam and The Hague. Output slowly climbed from 0·7 million tons in 1950 to 3·1 million tons in 1962, but although this is a valuable contribution the estimated reserves are a mere 15 million tons, and while exploration continues it is believed that the present wells have passed their peak; the output in 1968 declined to 2·1 million tons.

By comparison, imports of crude oil through Rotterdam (Europoort) have risen to over 100 million tons in 1969, though nearly half of this is re-exported by pipeline to West Germany (p. 163); the rest is refined in Rotterdam (Plate XXXVI) at five large refineries, with a total annual capacity of about 55 million tons. Another refinery has been completed on the banks of the North Sea Canal at Zaandam, near Amsterdam, supplied by pipeline from Europoort. This refining of oil and the associated petrochemical processes represent a very important sector of Dutch industry.

Natural Gas

The Dutch position concerning resources of power was abruptly transformed when in 1959 an enormous gas field, said to be the largest in Europe, was discovered near Slochteren (Plate XXXVII) in the province of Groningen, at a depth of 2700 m (9000 ft), by the *Nederlandse Aardolie Maatschappij (N.A.M.)*, owned jointly by *Royal Dutch-Shell* and *Esso*. Reserves are estimated to be at least 1,100,000 million cubic metres. Recently this company and others have found further deposits near Delfzijl, Noordbroek and Annerveen, in the West Frisian Islands, and in offshore waters, and research continues. It is officially estimated that when the Slochteren field is in full operation it will cover a quarter of Dutch energy requirements. A web of gas pipelines has been constructed from Groningen to other parts of the Netherlands, which has been linked to the pipeline system of the *Internationale Gas Transport Mij.N.V.*, another joint enterprise of *Shell* and *Esso*, to supply other countries; half of the gas produced is sold abroad. One pipeline runs from Slochteren across the Netherlands and Belgium, and on through northern France to Paris, another runs to Mannheim in West Germany.

Electricity

The production of electricity, all of which is thermal, has grown rapidly in recent years; the output of 34 milliard KWh in 1968 was nine times the pre-1939 figure. The big power stations are mainly located in the cities, though about a sixth of the energy is produced by stations attached to the South Limburg collieries, and by large industrial enterprises which put excess power into the grid. Several trans-border links enable power to be both exported and imported between the Netherlands, West Germany and Belgium.

Other Mining and Quarrying

The only other mineral products are sand, gravel and clay, common salt and chalk. Salt was discovered in 1919 at Boekelo in Overijssel near the German border, contained in Triassic beds at a depth of about 400 m (1300 ft). Other borings have located salt near Winterswijk in Gelderland and near Hengelo; its output has grown enormously from only 76,000 tons in 1936 to 585,000 tons in 1955 and to 2·4 million tons in 1968. Chalk is quarried in the Maastricht district to supply several large cement works.

MANUFACTURING INDUSTRY

While the northern Netherlands were not as important industrially as Flanders during the Middle. Ages, cloth was manufactured at Haarlem, Leiden, Dordrecht and Utrecht, the last well known for its velvet, and Delft was famous for its pottery. As Dutch mercantile and colonial interests developed, so did shipbuilding to provide the vessels and new industries to process materials brought from overseas. But until the nineteenth century manufacturing was subordinate to commerce, and while the Industrial Revolution made rapid progress in Belgium, development was much slower in the Netherlands until the last quarter of the century, when in a desire to widen the economy industrial activity was stimulated. Shipbuilding and textile manufactures were revived, and the processing of home-grown and colonial agricultural products developed: oilseed-crushing, the making of chocolate, starch, strawboard and margarine (invented in 1871). Gradually the scope widened, and the specialized production of highly fabricated articles dependent on imported raw materials developed at the ports, notably Rotterdam and Amsterdam. The discovery of coal in South Limburg encouraged chemical industries in that area. Other activities were started in more remote sites, where labour and spacious land for development were available; examples are a tin smelter at Arnhem, and the *Philips* factory at Eindhoven now producing a fifth of the world's electric light bulbs, radio and television sets, and electrical equipment generally. Despite the diversity of industry, 35 per cent of all Dutch production comes from three giant firms: *Philips*, already mentioned, *Royal Dutch-Shell* and *Unilever*.

Since 1950 the government has given both direct and indirect encouragement to development in the southern and eastern parts of the country, partly to ease industrial overcrowding in Zuid-Holland, partly to assist the rural economy where agricultural unemployment and overpopulation were increasing. Foreign firms have been encouraged by non-discriminatory or even specially favoured treatment, stable labour conditions, and favourable wage structures to establish their own plants and those of subsidiaries. A large number of American firms have created plants, operated under licence by associates and subsidiaries or by Dutch firms, to manufacture their products and use their patents.

The Twente district in south-eastern Overijssel, which for long had only a rather meagre textile industry, has grown into the main cotton manufacturing area, and recently rayon and nylon have also become established. Emmen, in the extreme east of Drenthe, is one of the 'new towns'; in the past it was little more than a centre of peat-digging, but the peat has now almost gone, and new industries are being deliberately introduced into the south-east of the municipality, where chemical plants, strawboard mills and a nylon-spinning factory have already been built. Most of the larger provincial towns have manufacturing of various kinds; thus Groningen, the 'capital' of the north-east, has industries connected with agricultural commodities: flour-milling, brewing and distilling, and the making of industrial alcohol, starch and strawboard.

Industrial production has risen especially rapidly during the last decade; between 1963 and 1968 the index of production has risen from 100 to 143, while output per worker has increased by 25 per cent. These figures are the highest of any West European country.

The Rotterdam conurbation forms the largest single industrial region in the Netherlands. From Vlaardingen up-river to Dordrecht fifty yards build tankers, cargo ships, warships, motor coasting steamers, tugs, dredgers, hoppers and floating cranes, both for Dutch and foreign needs. The 'Rotterdam' (38,650 g.r.t.) was completed in 1959 as flagship of the *Holland-America Line*. During recent years several 200,000-ton tankers and 100,000-ton bulk-carriers have been built. Marine engineering is well developed, while the manufacture of lock gates, pontoons, pumps and bridges is a reflection of the country's own requirements. Dutch firms carry out contracts for port works, drainage and regularization schemes in many parts of the world. There is a wide range of port industries, including oil-refining, petrochemicals, distilling (especially at Schiedam), vegetable oil-pressing, the manufacture of paper and timber products. *Unilever* has two factories, one making soap at Vlaardingen, the other margarine at Feijenoord. Some 16 km (10 miles) south-east of Rotterdam is Dordrecht; its industrial activities are of much the same character as those of Rotterdam, though on a smaller scale.

The Amsterdam industrial district, second in the Netherlands to Rotterdam, extends along the North Sea Canal to IJmuiden and along the north bank of the IJ. Varied branches of metallurgical and engineering industry are carried on, many of a precise nature and requiring a high degree of fabrication. Dutch firms have a reputation for specialized machinery, including plants designed to process colonial products (machinery for sugar refineries, margarine factories, oilfields and tin mines), refrigeration machinery and electrical equipment. Although not as important as at Rotterdam, there is considerable ship-building activity; the 'Oranje' (20,166 tons) was built for the *Netherlands Royal Mail Line*. Marine engineering is highly developed; one firm, *Nederlandsche Werkspoor*, accounts for a fifth of the Dutch output of marine engines, and several foreign firms build their engines under licence. Plants which assemble cars and lorries include the *Ford* works at Hembrug, a few miles west of the city on the shores of the North Sea Canal; the *Fokker* works on the northern side of the port builds aircraft. Consumer goods include clothing, pharmaceutical chemicals, footwear, paper, printing and bookbinding; food-processing industries comprise chocolate- and cocoa-making, sugar-refining, tobacco-processing, flour-milling, brewing and distilling; other activities are associated with the 'colonial trade': oilseed-crushing, rubber and timber manufactures. The long-established diamond-cutting and setting still exists but on a much reduced scale, partly because of the growth of Antwerp as a rival centre, partly because of developments in the Republic of South Africa. In all, about 110,000 people are employed in factories within the Amsterdam district.

The town and port of IJmuiden came into existence with the construction of the North Sea Canal between Amsterdam and the North Sea. Adjacent to the northern side of its basins are the coke ovens, blast furnaces and steel works of the *Koninklijke Nederlandsche Hoogovens en Staalfabrieken* (*N.V.*), the only fully integrated steel plant in the country. The original plant was constructed, as a result of the shortage of steel during the War of 1914–18, on a coastal site because the industry could be advantageously supplied with high-grade ore imported by sea. After 1945 the Netherlands was faced with a greatly increased consumption of steel for the reconstruction of its cities, communications and factories, for its new manufactures, and for its contribution to West European defence; by 1955 this had risen to 2·4 million tons, a figure only half a million tons less than the Belgian consumption. The government, in conjunction with the industrialists, expanded the IJmuiden plant; the open-hearth furnaces were increased to five, and several rolling mills and a tinplate plant were built. By 1968 the IJmuiden steel works were producing about half per cent of the steel used in the Netherlands, and this integrated concern is now the third largest steel firm in the E.C.S.C.; its output of raw steel in 1968 totalled 3·7 million tons. The need for still greater supplies of steel has led *Hoogovens*, in conjunction with the West German firm of *Hoesch*, to construct a large integrated steel-plant on a 'green field' site at Maasvlakte, near Rotterdam.

Several byproduct plants have been erected near IJmuiden. Coke-oven gas is utilized in a nitrogen fixation plant to produce ammonium sulphate, benzol, toluol and tar, while the excess is piped to Amsterdam, Zaandam and Haarlem. Portland cement is made from furnace slag, with an annual output of 200,000 tons, and another slag-processing plant produces road-surfacing materials. A large power station was built, utilizing blast-furnace gas for thermal electricity production, and now supplying much of the province of Noord-Holland.

Despite this concentration of industrial activity in the west of the country, the provinces with the highest proportion of their working population engaged in industry are Overijssel and Limburg. This is partly because agricultural development is limited in these largely heathland provinces, but in addition Overijssel has the textile manufactures of Twente and varied activities in some of the 'new towns'. In Limburg much of the industrial activity is associated with the coalfield; for example, a nitrogen fixation plant, built in 1930 near the Maurits colliery, was enlarged in 1949, and liquid ammonia, carbon dioxide, ethylene and a range of other derivatives are produced. As the coalfield closes down, this activity will be based on hydrocarbon stock-feeds piped from the Rotterdam refineries.

COMMUNICATIONS

The Netherlands is not only well supplied with dense networks of internal communications, but is situated at 'the gateway to Western Europe'. A vast amount of transit freight passes across the country to other countries by road, rail, water and pipeline.

Roads

Since the end of the war of 1939–45, the Netherlands has embarked on a considerable road-building programme to make good wartime destruction, especially of bridges, and to develop a system capable of handling the increasing traffic. Land is precious and expensive, but even so the Dutch have created a number of multi-lane motorways, including sections of several European highways. Rotterdam, Amsterdam, The Hague and Utrecht are linked by motorways, and European Road 8 runs east to Arnhem and on to join the Rhineland *Autobahn*. The Netherlands is well served with straight, well-surfaced main roads, with flyover junctions and new bridges over the rivers. The road on the IJssel Meer dyke forms a direct link between Noord-Holland and Friesland, continuing through Leeuwarden and Groningen into West Germany. When the Delta Plan is completed, an important through-road along the dykes will serve the province of Zeeland, and with the help of a new ferry service across the Wester Schelde will afford a direct link between Rotterdam and western Belgium. One important link is the fine Oosterschelde bridge, between the islands of Duiveland and Noord-Beveland; 5022 m (5492 yd) long, it is the longest road-bridge in the world outside North America.

Railways

The first railway in the Netherlands was opened in 1839 between Amsterdam and Haarlem, and the network was virtually completed by 1890, though the density of track is only half that of Belgium. The route length totals 3227 km (about 2000 miles), of which half, including all the lines in the south, is electrified, the rest worked by diesel locomotives. Most of the lines are operated by *Nederlandsche Spoorwegen*, a company formed in 1938 by the amalgamation of existing companies with the State as sole shareholder.

A single track, standard-gauge line is operated in South Limburg. Each colliery has its own sidings, with a main marshalling yard at Susteren, and the system is linked to the State Railway at several points.

Some of the lines in the Netherlands form sections of international routes. Famous international express trains operating from the chief ferry port, Hook of Holland, include the 'Rheingold' (to Milan), the 'Loreley' (to Basle), and the 'Holland-Scandinavia' (to Stockholm); others from Amsterdam include the 'Edelweiss' (to Zürich), the 'Etoile du Nord' and the 'Ile de France' (to Paris), the 'Holland–Italy' (to Rome), the 'Rhein–Main' (to Frankfurt), and the 'Riviera' (to Ventimiglia). The 'Delta' express container-service, operating between Rotterdam, Frankfurt and Mannheim, was inaugurated in 1968.

Waterways

The importance of waterways to the Netherlands results from its position at the mouths of the major arteries of the Rhine, Maas

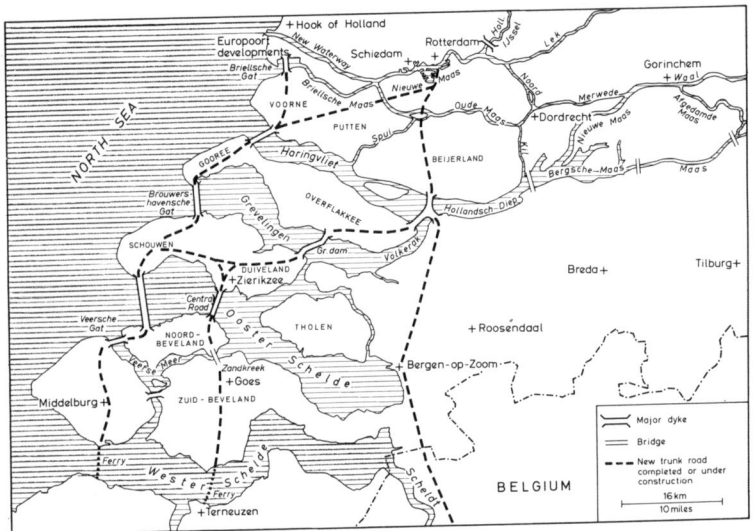

Fig. 43. The waterways of the Rhine-Maas estuaries

and Scheldt, while the level and lowlying nature of much of the country has facilitated the construction of link canals. In 1968 there were about 6400 km (about 4000 miles) of navigable waterway, just over a quarter negotiable by vessels exceeding a thousand tons capacity (Fig. 43). In 1968 the Dutch waterways transported about 242 million tons of freight, of which 147 millions were classified as international. This represents an increase of over a third in ten years, indicating the importance of Rotterdam and the Rhine as a major entry to Western Europe.

The main artery of navigation through the maze of waterways is the line of the Waal–Merwede–Noord–Nieuwe Maas, focusing on Rotterdam and its outlet to the sea through the New Waterway,

29 km (18 miles) in length. No locks are required on this route, other than where branch canals enter, and barges drawing 3 m (10 ft) or more and with a capacity of up to 4,000 tons can navigate with ease, while small sea-going steamers can pass up the waterway into West Germany. The Waal is linked at several points with the Maas, as at St Andries, where the locks take 2,000-ton barges, and by the short Maas–Waal Canal. The Neder Rijn–Lek waterway is far less important than the Waal, although 2,000-ton barges can use it under normal conditions.

While minor canals have for long provided links between Rotterdam and Amsterdam, for many years the latter wanted a direct connection with the Rhine; in 1952 the Amsterdam–Rhine Canal was completed, passing Utrecht to the west, crossing the Lek at Wijk, and joining the Waal near Tiel through the huge Prince Bernhard locks.

The importance of the Rhine navigation is shown by the fact that 110 million tons of freight in 1968 passed Lobith, the West German–Dutch customs post, of which about 62 million moved upstream. A large proportion of this upstream traffic consisted of grain, oil, timber and bulk raw materials transhipped at Rotterdam for despatch to West Germany, France and Switzerland. Most of the remaining upstream freight originated in Belgian ports and moved direct to the same three countries. Downstream traffic was mainly from West Germany, particularly steel and manufactured goods for export, and potash from Alsace for the Dutch and Belgian chemical industries.

While the Rhine is the premier waterway of the Netherlands, the Maas is of importance for the south of the country. The improvement of navigation downstream from Maastricht has assisted the economic development of South Limburg, and is particularly valuable for the exploitation of the coalfield. The Maas is contained between massive embankments, several meanders have been cut across, and locked barrages have been built to stabilize depths. These schemes, completed just before the War of 1939–45, made the Maas navigable for vessels of 1,500 tons capacity, and as a result of further postwar improvements the river can now be negotiated by 2,000-ton barges. These measures were concerned with the Maas below Maasbracht, where it becomes a wholly Dutch river. With the exception of the short stretch through the city of Maastricht, the Dutch–Belgian boundary runs from Lanaye to Maasbracht along the centre of the river, whose course is impeded by gravel- and sandbanks, islets and backwaters. With Belgian unwillingness to undertake any joint scheme of regularization, unilateral action by the Netherlands to improve the river was impossible. The Dutch solution was the construction of the Juliana Canal, 34 km (21 miles) in length, along the right bank wholly in Dutch territory, between Maastricht and Maasbracht. This carries about 10 million tons of freight annually, two-thirds (mainly coal, cement and fertilizers) moving north from the coalfield; coal freight is, however, decreasing rapidly with the shut-down of the coalfield. The portion of the river between Maastricht and Maasbracht has remained unnavigable.

Air Transport

In a country as small as the Netherlands, internal air transport is of little importance; by contrast its international services are among the most extensive in the world. *Royal Dutch Air Lines (K.L.M.)* was founded in 1919; though a private company, the State holds a controlling interest. It operates six internal airports, the largest of which is Schiphol (near Amsterdam), completed in 1967 on a reclaimed area of 1600 ha (4000 acres), with others at Eelde (Groningen), Rotterdam, Hilversum, Beek and Texel, and heliports at Eindhoven, Maastricht and Rotterdam. In 1968 its aircraft carried 2·1 million passengers, on a route mileage of 27 000 km (17,000 miles), of which a quarter was inter-European.

Mercantile Marine

The Netherlands has a mercantile fleet totalling 5 million g.r.t., the twelfth largest in the world, of which nearly 3 million tons have been built since 1955. Almost half of this consists of freighters, another 1·6 million tons of tankers, and ten passenger liners have a total tonnage of 180,000. The last include the fleet of the *Holland-America line*, the second largest company in the trans-Atlantic service, with its flagship the *Rotterdam*.

One activity in which the Netherlands has long specialized is long-distance ocean salvage and towage; it possesses some of the most powerful ocean-going tugs in the world.

Ports

In terms of goods handled by Dutch ports, Rotterdam is over-whelmingly pre-eminent (Fig. 44); of a total of 160 million tons in 1968, Rotterdam accounted for 140 millions, and it is now ahead of

New York as the world's leading port. Six other ports are associated with Rotterdam (Schiedam, Vlaardingen, Maasluis, Hook of Holland, Dordrecht and Zwijndrecht), and two with Amsterdam and the North Sea Canal (IJmuiden and Zaandam). The only other ports are Harlingen, Delfzijl and Groningen (where a new harbour was opened in 1967) in the north, and Terneuzen and Flushing (Vlissingen) in Zeeland.

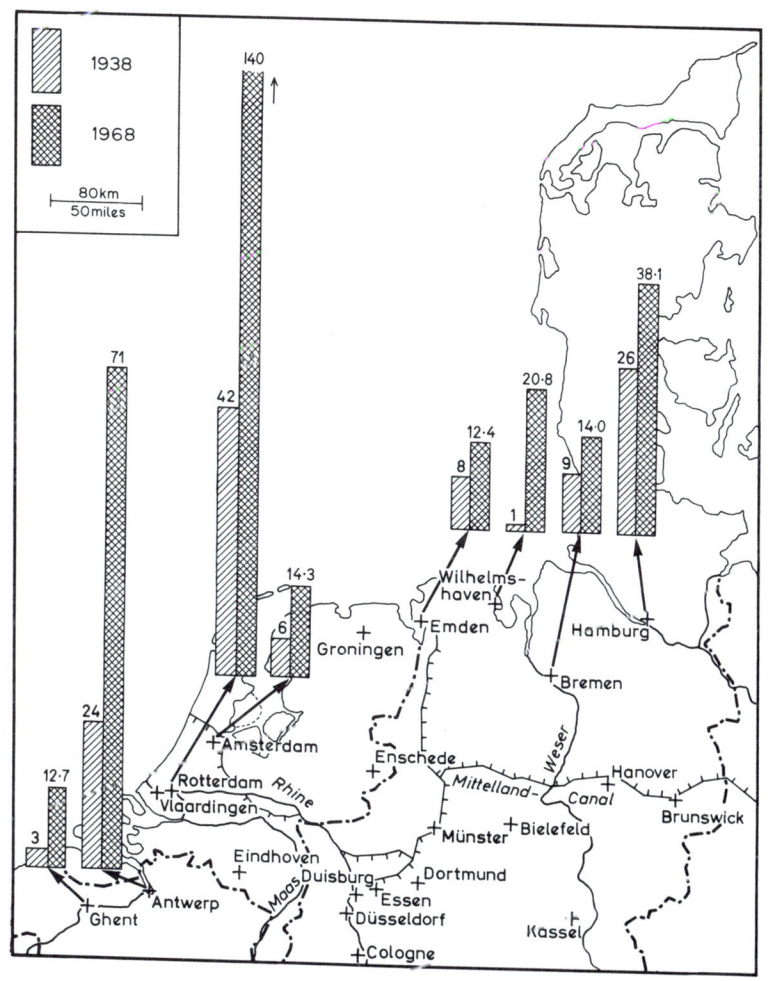

Fig. 44. The major ports of western Europe
(After an official publication of the Rotterdam Port Authority)
The figures refer to total tonnage of freight handled.

Rotterdam stands about 30 km (18 miles) from the sea on the northern bank of the Nieuwe Maas, which is formed by the junction of the Lek and the Noord, near the confluence of the small river Rotte. At first its trade was subordinate to that of Dordrecht, for long the leading Dutch port, but in the seventeenth century it began to forge ahead. The problem of its approach channels became increasingly acute as the size of vessels increased. The ultimate solution in 1872 was the construction of the New Waterway (Nieuwe Waterweg), a direct cut to the North Sea through the sandspit of the Hoek van Holland. This channel was originally only 3 m (10 ft) deep, but it has been enlarged several times, and can be negotiated by vessels of up to 40,000 tons drawing 10 m (33 ft). Ships enter between moles nearly 800 m (2600 ft) apart at Hook of Holland (Hoek van Holland), which also handles the ferry traffic with England.

The port of Rotterdam consists of quays along both banks of the Nieuwe Maas and a series of basins with unlocked connection with the river. Approximately 40,000 ships use the port and its subsidiaries each year. Much freight consists of bulk imports of petroleum, ores, cereals, timber, and such 'colonial' materials as groundnuts, soya beans, sugar and bananas. Over 63,000 containers were unloaded in 1968, of which 32,000 came from North America.

Since 1950 major developments have taken place at Rotterdam (Fig. 45). Freight-liner and container berths and roll on/roll off truck terminals have been completed. At the eastern end of the island of Rozenburg the port of Botlek has been developed to handle bulk imports of mineral and vegetable oil, and of chemicals. New industrial undertakings nearby include an *Esso* refinery, a shipyard for supertankers, and a chemical complex. The Botlek port works were completed in 1959.

On a still bigger scale is Europoort ('the gateway to Europe'), the construction of which started in June 1958 and was about half completed by the end of 1969. Situated at the North Sea end of the island of Rozenburg, opposite Hook of Holland (Fig. 45), it is mainly intended to cope with the import of bulk cargoes, such as oil from the Middle East and iron ore from Labrador, South America and Africa. The construction of Europoort involves extensive excavation of basins and channels, using the derived spoil to build up the level of the land. The new direct entrance from the North Sea can accommodate 250,000 ton tankers, with channel depths of 19 m (62 ft). On the Europoort site *Shell*, *Caltex*, *Esso* and *Gulf* have built terminals, refineries and tank-farms. The Rotterdam–Rhine Pipeline has been

Plate XXXIV. Heathland to the south-east of Eindhoven, Netherlands

Plate XXXV. City of Rotterdam

Plate XXXVI. The Oude Maas and the Botlek refinery, west of Rotterdam

Plate XXXVII. The Slochteren gas-field. A well-head, near the village of Kolham, is enclosed in a steel cage in the back-ground

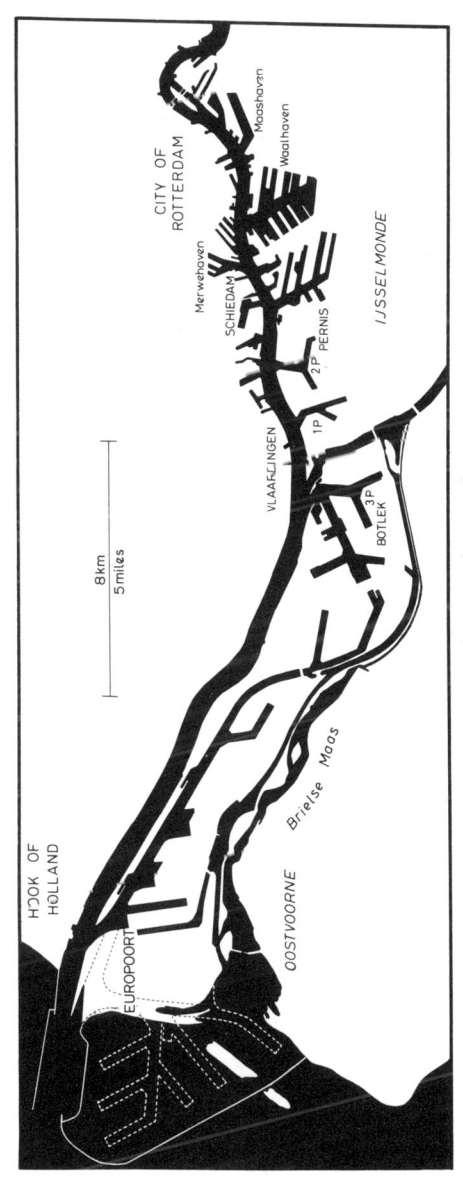

Fig. 45. The port of Rotterdam

(After an official publication of the Rotterdam Port Authority)

Pecked lines indicate the extension of Europoort, much of which has now been completed. 1P, 2P and 3P indicate the petroleum basins where crude oil is discharged. Newer and larger terminals are being opened at Europoort.

laid from Europoort to Godorf, Wesseling and on to Kelsterbach near Frankfurt, with a branch line from Venlo to Wesel; 290 km (180 miles) in length (of which 150 km (95 miles) are in the Netherlands) and 600 mm (24 in) in diameter, it has an annual capacity of 8 million tons. Europoort will handle cargoes of ore and coal for a new steel works to be built on the site and for western Europe generally; a ship canal has been cut parallel to the New Waterway; and new industrial sites have been made available. To cope with the workers employed in Europoort, the town of Spijkenisse to the south will be enlarged from a population of 3,500 to 80,000.

The port of Amsterdam lies along a stretch of water known as the Afgesloten IJ, separated by locks from the IJssel Meer, with some new basins for special purposes lying to the west. It comes considerably behind Rotterdam, handling in 1968 14·3 million tons of seaborne freight, though this represents a three-fold increase since 1950. It is well connected with inland waterways, notably to the Rhine via the Amsterdam–Rhine Canal. In 1876 the North Sea Canal, 24 km (15 miles) in length, was completed, by which the city turned its back on the Zuider Zee and reorientated itself towards the North Sea. This waterway, several times enlarged, can take vessels up to 100,000 tons; its entrance locks at IJmuiden are the largest in the world. New moles have been built out into the North Sea at IJmuiden, so enclosing a spacious outer harbour, opened in 1967. It is claimed that the most modern bulk trans-shipment facilities in Europe have been installed.

COMMERCE

Trade and commerce have become the lifeblood of the Dutch nation, born of its maritime traditions, nurtured by colonial expansion, consolidated first by agricultural specialization and then by modern highly capitalized industrialization, and carried out with brilliant acumen. Some 40 per cent of the national income is derived through commercial activities, including receipts from a large volume of transit trade to and from other European countries. Normally the value of visible imports exceeds that of exports (in 1968 about 34 and 30 milliard *Fl.* respectively). The chief trading partners, in order, are West Germany (a fifth of the total), Belgo-Luxembourg, the U.S.A., France and the U.K.

The keynote of both imports and exports is their diversity. Before 1939 agricultural products comprised half of the total exports by value; now this proportion has fallen to about a fifth, though still the largest single group of items. Next in order come machinery (20 per cent), other manufactured items, chemicals, coal and coke, refined oils and lubricants. Imports consist mainly of such raw materials as crude oil, iron ore, pig-iron and raw steel, fertilizers, non-ferrous ores, coal, oilseeds and wheat.

POPULATION AND SETTLEMENT

The total population of the Netherlands at the beginning of 1969 was 12·80 millions, with an average density of 379 per sq. km (982 per sq. mile), the highest of any European country. This would be higher still but for the inclusion of the southern IJssel Meer polders, where as yet the density is only 5 per sq. km (12 per sq. mile). The population has grown steadily since 1945; in 1923 the total was only 7·1 millions, and in 1938 about 8·7 millions. The birth rate, about 20 per thousand, is high for a western European country, while the death rate, about 8·5, is the lowest in the world, resulting in a rate of natural increase which is exceeded in Europe only by Albania and Poland. These trends are likely to continue, since the age-group composition reveals a high proportion in the younger categories. Since 1945 an average of about 50,000 people have emigrated annually, mainly to the U.S.A., Canada and Australia, but about half as many, including a considerable number of repatriates from Indonesia, have immigrated each year.

This high population density is a reflection of the standard of prosperity achieved mainly through the enterprise and skill of its people. About 8 per cent of the active population is engaged in agriculture, utilizing more than 70 per cent of the area through centuries of effort. More than half are employed in industry, and the value of international commerce is the highest per head in the world.

This average density conceals considerable regional variations. Three provinces, Zuid-Holland, Noord-Holland and Utrecht, comprise only a fifth of the total area of the country, but they contained two-fifths of the total population. Zuid-Holland, with an average density of 1037 per sq. km (2686 per sq. mile), must be one of the most densely populated parts of the world, and that of Noord-Holland is 832 per sq. km (2156 per sq. mile). This density is the result on the one hand of a remarkable urban development, with flourishing industrial and commercial activities, on the other of a rarely equalled intensity of agriculture. The density in western Utrecht is also very high, but as this province includes the sandhills of Gooiland, with their parks and recreation areas, the average is reduced to 590 per sq. km

1528 per sq. mile), though nevertheless third in order. Despite the heath and bog in the northern part of Limburg, its average is 456 per sq. km (1181 per sq. mile), a reflection of both the activity based on the coalfield and the prosperous agricultural life.

Seven of the eleven provinces have densities below the national average, the lowest being Drenthe with 136 per sq. km (352 per sq. mile). These thinly populated areas correspond to the sandy heathlands in the east and south. Even so, the densities in these provinces have increased quite appreciably since the War, for the 1938 density for Drenthe was only 92 per sq. km (238 per sq. mile). This is mainly the result of the creation of patches of high local density through the development of new industry. The government is seeking to move a million people from the overpopulated western areas to the eastern provinces by the attraction of new industries and the provision of housing, communications and general facilities. A memorandum presented to parliament in 1961 stressed the fact that 35 per cent of the population lived on only 6 per cent of the land.

Towns

A major reason for the high average density is the degree of urbanization. It is not easy to state exact figures, since population statistics are returned only for municipalities; thus Emmen, in the east of Drenthe, had a population of 77,000, yet only about 16,000 lived in the town of Emmen, for the municipality covers about 310 sq. km (120 sq. miles), including several hamlets, 'fen colonies' and a 'new town'.

No less than 89 municipalities each had more than 25,000 inhabitants, and fifteen had over 100,000. Three are regarded officially as conurbations: Amsterdam (1,046,000), Utrecht (448,000), and Rotterdam (1,059,000) with The Hague ('s-Gravenhage) (738,000); the outskirts of the last two are only 13 km (8 miles) apart, yet they contain more than 14 per cent of the total population.

The southern part of Zuid-Holland is known as the '*Randstad Holland*' (an urban agglomeration), and affords great problems of 'overspill', housing and communications. There are in effect two 'wings' of this conurbation, the northern (Haarlem, Amsterdam, Hilversum, Amersfoort, Utrecht), and the southern (Leiden, The Hague, Vlaardingen, Rotterdam, Dordrecht). A commission of 1958 emphasized that the farming area between these two 'wings' must be preserved from further encroachment. It is feared that an unbroken chain of towns may develop eastward to Arnhem, also including Eindhoven, Tilburg and Breda on the south, to form a '*Randstad Midden-Nederland*', with a population of 7·5 millions. Further, urban planners forecast that soon after 1970 a great 'West-European ring-town' will encircle the Rhine mouths and enclose the southern and central part of the Netherlands. This is sometimes referred to as the 'A-B-C Ring-town', after the three 'corner stones' of Amsterdam and the other parts of the Randstad, Brussels with Antwerp, Ghent and Liège, and Cologne with Aachen and the Ruhr towns. Such is the expected growth of population in western Europe.

Other large regional and industrial centres include Eindhoven (187,000) in Noord-Brabant and Groningen (168,000), the commercial, industrial and servicing centre of the north-east.

Rural Settlement. In Friesland and Groningen some villages are associated with earthen refuge mounds built for protection against floods. In many parts linear villages have been constructed along the line of a canal, with the farm land running back in strips at right-angles from the houses. In the compact heathland villages the householders have their arable fields nearby, and rough grazing, sometimes held in common, at some distance. Small towns and large villages are situated in the reclaimed polderlands, often surrounded and sometimes intersected by canals. In the most recently reclaimed polders in the IJssel Meer, the settlements are dispersed, with each individual farm standing within its 20 ha holding. Much of Zuid-Holland consists of a dense 'suburbanized landscape', a confusion of houses and glasshouses among market gardens and orchards, a dense but formless pattern. Finally, there are carefully planned 'new towns' in the heathlands and the IJssel Meer polders.

THE REGIONS (Fig. 40)

1. The Northern Coastlands

The coastal lands of the provinces of Groningen and Friesland extend from the Dollard to the shores of the IJssel Meer, a smooth coastline indented only by the rectangular Lauwers Zee. The reclaimed marine-claylands extend inland for 16–30 km (10–20 miles), mostly empoldered, though the surface is 1 to 2 metres above sea-level and normally drains by gravity flow. To the south lies the sand country, the higher parts once covered with peat which has now been stripped off; little outward sign can be seen in the agricultural landscape of the transition from the clays to the sands. These coastal lands form rich farming country, and nearly four-fifths is under rotation grass, clover, potatoes (for which Friesland is the chief growing area in the country), cereals, chicory and mustard. Although the emphasis is on arable crops, Friesian cattle are grazed on the reclaimed coastal pastures and on temporary leys; their milk goes to the factory production of butter and cheese, frequently on a co-operative basis. Some cattle are bred for beef, others for export.

The spacious landscape of these provinces is interrupted only by straight tree-lined roads, quiet villages and large prosperous farm-houses, with their glazed-tile, sometimes part-thatched, roofs. There is little urban development except for the provincial capitals, Groningen and Leeuwarden, partly because the two provinces have depended almost wholly on an agricultural economy for many centuries, partly because this was always a somewhat remote corner of the Netherlands.

The city of Groningen is situated where the clays, sands and peat-bogs meet. It is a market centre for the country around, and has industries connected with the processing of agricultural commodities: flour-milling, brewing and distilling, and the making of strawboard. Groningen is linked by the Eems Canal (enlarged in 1967) to the Dollard at Delfzijl, which has developed as its outport and generally serves the prosperous north-east. Delfzijl imports coal, fertilizers, timber and animal feeding stuffs, and exports strawboard, paper, potato flour and dextrine from the factories of Groningen; it handles annually about a million tons of freight.

In Friesland, Leeuwarden (88,000) was once a port on the Friesche Middelzee, a long arm of the sea reclaimed as early as the end of the thirteenth century. The old town is still surrounded by a moat, and several minor canals, used by small barges carrying agricultural produce, fertilizers, coal, bricks and timber, focus on it from Harlingen, Groningen, Zwolle and Meppel. Leeuwarden is the administrative centre for a rich agricultural district and has markets for cattle, butter and cereals; only Rotterdam handles more cattle annually. Once the city was renowned for gold and silver work, but this has been replaced by industries carried on in small efficient factories: the manufacture of shoes, vinegar, paint, soap, electro-plate, butter, cheese and margarine.

Harlingen is a small artificial port, built during the years 1870–77 to serve Friesland. It handles mostly exports of dairy products and strawboard, and imports of oil, timber and raw materials for Leeuwarden's industries. Other small activities include the building of coasting vessels and barges, the canning and salting of fish, and leather tanning.

2. The West Frisian Islands

Between the dyked coast of Groningen and Friesland and the line of the West Frisian Islands lies the Wadden Zee, a considerable extent of tidal waters, with sheets of mud and sand uncovered at low tide and crossed by a maze of creeks. The shoals have long been notorious for the wrecking of ships.

The West Frisian Islands are strung out in a smooth curve, each consisting of sand-flats with a line of dunes fronting the open sea. All except Vlieland, which is wholly sandy, have small areas of marine clay on their inner sides. On the larger islands cattle, sheep and goats are kept; the famous Texel 'green cheese' is made of ewes' milk. Most of the villages are popular summer resorts, and some inshore fishing is practised.

3. The Polderlands of Noord- and Zuid-Holland

These provinces are characterized by an intense agriculture and by the presence of large towns with flourishing manufactures and commerce. Most towns grew up in the Middle Ages as commercial centres on the banks of navigable waterways. In Noord-Holland several bordering the Zuider Zee, once important as centres of commerce, have suffered because of their position on a shallow near-inland sea; Enkhuizen, Edam, Hoorn and Medemblik are now little bigger than they were in the seventeenth century, some indeed are smaller, and function as quiet market centres.

The only Zuider Zee town to flourish in modern times is Amsterdam, by reason of its development of administrative functions, commercial life and industrial activities, and the construction of the North Sea Canal. The city grew up in what was in many ways an unpromising position among tidal flats and sand-banks. Early in the thirteenth century, near where the little river Amstel entered the IJ on the south, a dam was built to provide a sheltered harbour where sea-going craft could transfer their cargoes to smaller vessels using the inland waterways. The urban area was gradually extended southward in a semicircle, with houses on piles driven into the marsh; its outward growth can be traced from the concentric semi-circular canals crossed by radial channels, and in effect the city stands on three hundred islands (Fig. 46 and Plate XXXVIII). Occasionally

drastic flooding forced the citizens to undertake large-scale reclamation schemes, and the city then spread a stage farther on to the
newly available land. Since the War of 1914–18 Amsterdam has
developed rapidly; in 1921 the area of the municipality was quadrupled, and great building programmes were put into operation.

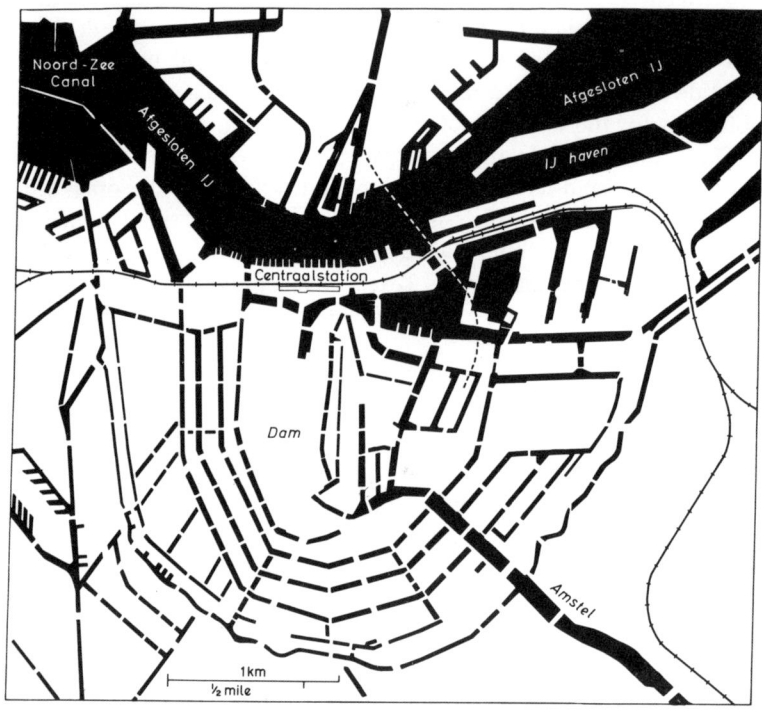

Fig. 46. Amsterdam
(After *Falk-Plan Amsterdam*)

To the north of the IJ garden cities were built, including Oostzaan
in 1920–21 and Nieuwendam in 1925–6. A 'Master Plan' for
Amsterdam was published in 1936, involving several more garden
cities to the west, industrial development in the port area, and carefully integrated systems of communications, including a 'belt
railway' raised on an embankment and a series of radial highways.
Though delayed by the War, a revised plan is now making progress;
several garden cities are being developed, including Slotermeer
around an artificial lake. Although the country's political seat of
government is at The Hague, Amsterdam is the capital, and is

an important industrial (p. 265), commercial, financial and cultural centre.

There are few other large towns in Noord-Holland, partly because of its predominantly agricultural character, partly because it lies between the IJssel Meer and the sand-dune coast with its almost complete lack of harbours. In Zuid-Holland and western Utrecht, by contrast, there are several large conurbations. The city of Rotterdam is second to Amsterdam in size. Much of its centre was rebuilt following extensive war damage (Plates XXXV, XXXIX); one of the most striking new features is the Lijnbaan, completed in 1953, a shopping centre from which vehicular traffic is excluded. The port and industrial activities of Rotterdam have been described on pp. 264, 270–4.

The Hague (known in Dutch both as 's-Gravenhage and Den Haag) is an attractively laid out town, with tree-lined avenues and imposing squares, substantial houses and government buildings, new residential suburbs, gardens and parks. Originally situated 3–5 km (2–3 miles) from the coast, it has expanded into the dunelands, and Scheveningen, one of the most popular Dutch seaside resorts, and Loosduinen are now officially within the commune. Its functions are primarily political and administrative, and it has been the seat of the Permanent Court of International Justice since 1922. Formerly the city had little commercial or industrial importance, but in the last few decades new industries include printing (notably at the government Stationery Office), paper-making, clothing, minor metal manufactures, furniture and food-processing. Scheveningen is the second Dutch fishing port; about 40 per cent of the catch is landed there.

Some 8 km (5 miles) to the south-east of The Hague is Delft (81,000), standing on the Schie, with the old quiet town enclosed by a rectangular moat. It was long famous for its pottery, and although the industry nearly died out a revival has taken place since the end of the nineteenth century. In addition, Delft has a variety of light industries: the making of cigars, dyes, alcohol, gelatine, margarine and electric cables; and it is a pleasant residential town with attractions for tourists.

Leiden (103,000) lies north-east of The Hague, 8 km (5 miles) from the coast of the North Sea, among the branches of the Oude Rijn which flow sluggishly through the town. A former flourishing cloth trade now survives only in the manufacture of blankets and liveries, and its other few industries include printing and publishing, distilling and cigar-making. At the height of its prosperity in the early seven-

10*

teenth century it had a population considerably greater than at the present.

Dordrecht (88,000) stands mainly on the south bank of the Oude Maas, and until the seventeenth century it was the leading Dutch port, but silting and the increasing size of ships caused Rotterdam, 24 km (15 miles) nearer the sea, to outpace it. Its industrial activities are of much the same character as those of Rotterdam, although on a smaller scale: marine engineering, metallurgical industries, a *Unilever* oilseed-crushing plant, and the manufacture of chemicals and quality glassware.

Utrecht (448,000), the fourth city of the Netherlands, is situated on the Kromme Rijn where it splits into the Vecht and the Oude Rijn; these rivers are markedly entrenched, and the city grew up on the high firm banks. It has long been a centre of communications, for it stands in the 'isthmus' between the IJssel Meer and the Lek, at the junction of the polderlands to the west and north-west, the river claylands to the south, and the morainic hill country to the east. The completion of the Amsterdam–Rhine Canal and the new state highways have further improved its situation. As the result of this central position, Utrecht has some metropolitan functions; it is the seat of the Roman Catholic archbishopric, the headquarters of the State Railways, and has an international commercial and industrial fair. It is an important industrial town, with engineering, the manufacture of railway rolling-stock and chemicals, tobacco-processing, and a large output of factory-made dairy produce. To the north-west have developed the new industrial suburbs of Zuilen and Maarssen.

4. *The Delta Region*

This region includes the province of Zeeland and the extreme south of Zuid-Holland; this is the delta-land, including the four major estuaries: the Wester Schelde, the Ooster Schelde, the Grevelingen Maas and Volkerak, and the Haringvliet, the area which will be transformed by the 'Delta Plan' (p. 245).

It is one of the main arable districts of the Netherlands; two-thirds of the area of Zeeland is classified as arable land, and only a sixth is under permanent pasture. About a quarter grows wheat, barley is also important, approximately a quarter of the Dutch sugar beet and flax is produced, together with potatoes, onions and leguminous crops; cultivation is intensive and yields are high. In Zuid-Beveland there is a large acreage of orchards and bush fruit, especially red currants.

Only about a fifth of the cattle are dairy animals; this proportion is by far the lowest of any Dutch province.

Because of the absence of large towns, only Friesland and Drenthe have a density of population lower than that of Zeeland; its figure of 173 per sq. km (448 per sq. mile) is less than half that of the country and about a sixth that of Zuid-Holland. The only town of any size is Flushing (Vlissingen, Flessingue) (39,000) on the southern tip of Walcheren, and the third port of the Netherlands, though its former packet services with Harwich have not been resumed since the War of 1939–45. It has oil-bunkering facilities, and a large shipbuilding yard. The capital of the province is Middelburg, once a port, now linked by canal to Flushing; it is a quiet administrative and market centre, with the old town still surrounded by a moat. Terneuzen, at the point where the ship-canal to Ghent enters the Wester Schelde, is the centre of a large chemical complex, mainly controlled by American interests.

5. The Heathlands

The heathlands of the Netherlands fall into three distinct blocks, separated by broad river valleys: Noord-Brabant, the Veluwe, and the heathlands of Overijssel, Drenthe and Groningen. These form undulating tracts between 45 and 90 m (150 and 300 ft) above sea-level, sometimes known as *Geest*, as in Germany. Depressions in the higher parts contain bogs, the largest tracts of which are the Peel near the Belgian border and the Bourtanger Moor along the German border. Expanses of ling and heather, birch scrub and poor pasture are common, and there is much bare sand, some in the form of dunes. The sands are remarkably continuous in the Veluwe, and as a result it forms the largest area of sparse population in the Netherlands, with some solid tracts of coniferous plantations. Wide expanses of ling still exist, some in nature reserves, and the several large estates include the royal summer residence.

Much reclamation has taken place even on the high moors, which now have fields of potatoes, rye, oats and sugar beet. Root crops are grown and cattle reared, both grazed on permanent pastures and stall-fed, so providing manure for the sandy soils. Pigs are fed on skimmed milk, poultry and bees are kept, and in places market gardens produce early vegetables and bush fruit.

Coal has been located in the Peel, though not mined, oil has been found in south-eastern Drenthe near Schoonebeek, and gas near Slochteren in Groningen, now a centre of radiating pipelines. In central Overijssel such towns as Enschede and Hengelo in the district of Twente make cotton textiles. At Eindhoven in the south is the *Philips* electrical equipment factory, employing 25,000 workers, and also a works producing lorries, road-tankers and the *D.A.F.* car, the only Dutch make of automobile.

6. *The Rhine-Maas Valley*

On each side of the rivers the polders, protected by dykes from inundation, are covered with clay, patches of gravel and coarse sand. The soils are rather damp and much is under pasture, supporting dairying. The most prosperous part of these riverlands, known as the 'Betuwe' (the 'good land'), is in the east. Because of the liability to flooding until recent years, there are few towns and the riverine lands are sparsely populated. The two main towns are Arnhem (134,000) on the northern bank of the Neder-Rijn, and Nijmegen (147,000), 16 km (10 miles) away on the southern bank of the Maas, at crossing places where low hills rise from the floodplain and afford flood-free sites. Their positions have always been of strategic importance, and in the closing stages of the War of 1939–45 desperate attempts were made by Allied airborne troops to secure the crossings. Arnhem has rayon, rubber, chemical, clothing and metallurgical manufactures, and a smelter which refines a fifth of the world's tin output. Nijmegen, with a port on the Waal, also has a varied industrial activity, including the manufacture of electrical apparatus, barges and river steamers, chemicals, rayon and food products. Large brickyards are situated along the banks of the Waal.

7. *South Limburg*

The southern part of Limburg consists of an 'appendix' projecting southward between West Germany and Belgium for more than 40 km (25 miles), and widening from a corridor merely 5 km (3 miles) across to more than 30 km (20 miles) further south. All South Limburg lies on the east side of the Maas, except for the district of Maastricht where the town stands on the left bank, with the border making a loop 5 km (3 miles) to the west on to the plateau of Hesbaye. At the end of the War of 1939–45, the Netherlands made strong claims for a number of frontier revisions at the expense of Germany, one of which concerned the 'Selfkant', to the east of the narrow corridor. Although not all the original Dutch demands were met, part of the Selfkant was transferred to the Netherlands in 1949 and placed under a special commissioner, and in 1952 was incorporated into the province of Limburg. In 1963 this territory was returned to West Germany.

South Limburg, with its fertile loamy soils, is a prosperous agricultural area, it contains the only Dutch worked coalfield, and has a variety of associated activities. The industrial centre is Heerlen (77,000), where the mining companies have their headquarters. Other towns are Kerkrade (50,000) near the West German border, Brunssum and Hoensbroek. Near Lutterade several chemical by-product plants are situated. The coalfield is gradually diminishing in importance, as coal is phased-out of the industrial economy and mines are closed, and other industries (light engineering), a *D.A.F.* plant (at Born) and petrochemicals are being introduced as replacements. Market towns include Sittard (34,000) and Geleen serving the northern area, Valkenburg in the Geul valley, Margraten on the plateau to the south, and Vaals on the West German frontier.

The regional centre of South Limburg is Maastricht (95,000), mostly situated on the left bank of the Maas, and which has owed much to being a crossing point of the river since Roman times. During the latter part of the nineteenth century the town expanded rapidly as the result of new waterways (the Liège-Maastricht and Zuid-Willems Canals), the arrival of the railway, and the development of the coalfield, while in the 1930s its position was further improved by the construction of the Juliana Canal. The city has various steel-using industries, brick, tile and cement works, a tannery, a soap works, several rubber factories, a woollen mill, a tobacco factory, a glass factory, and one of the largest paper mills in the country. It is an important marketing and servicing centre for South Limburg, spaciously and attractively laid out, and still retains much of its old interest and charm.

CHAPTER NINE

Belgium

BELGIUM occupies an area of 30 513 sq. km (11,778 sq. miles), rather less than a fifth of the size of England and Wales. Yet it is situated in a vital part of western Europe, it displays considerable diversity of geology, relief and land use, and with its highly developed agriculture, industry and commerce, and an average density of population of 314 per sq. km (814 per sq. mile), it has an importance quite out of proportion to its size.

Belgium consists of nine provinces, which correspond approximately to medieval territorial divisions. The western provinces of Oost- and West-Vlaanderen (East and West Flanders) are the Belgian portion of the old county of Flanders; Hainaut and Namur were counties within the Holy Roman Empire; Brabant, Luxembourg and Limburg were duchies; and Liège was an episcopal principality. Though a walled city and a port since the early Middle Ages, Antwerp appeared as a territorial unit only during the period of French domination (1795–1814), when it formed part of the French department of Deux-Nèthes. In 1818 this was divided into two; the northern section now comprises part of the Dutch province of Noord-Brabant, the southern forms a Belgian province, Antwerpen. Other names have survived with no administrative significance though with a distinctive identity, such as Hesbaye, the Kempen or Kempenland (Campine), the Pays de Herve, the Condroz, and in the extreme south-east Belgian Lorraine.

STRUCTURE AND RELIEF

The rocks on the surface of Belgium vary from slates and quartzites of Lower Palaeozoic age to recent alluvium, peat and dune sands (Fig. 47). Its relief ranges from the 'high plateau' of the Ardennes in the south-east to the 'low plateaus' and plains in the centre, west and north; these two main divisions, 'Upland Belgium' and 'Lowland Belgium', are demarcated by the line of the rivers Sambre and Meuse.

Structure

The 'basement rocks' consist of Cambrian and Silurian slates and quartzites, which outcrop in the higher parts of the Ardennes

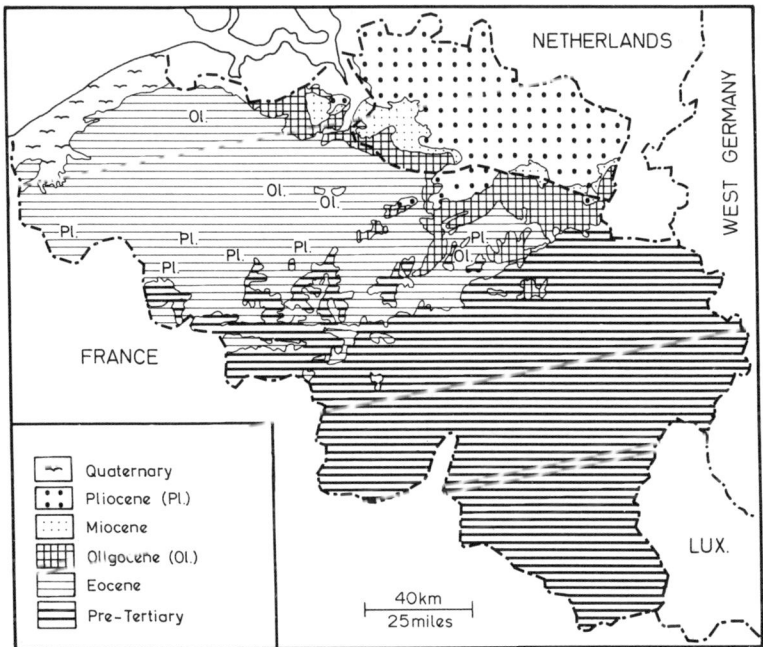

Fig. 47. The generalized geology of Belgium
(After J. Halkin)
The letters refer to very small, but significant, surviving deposits of Oligocene
and Pliocene rocks.

and are also exposed farther north in the deeply cut valleys of the
Senne and Dyle. On top of the Silurian were deposited Devonian
rocks; the lower series are mainly sandstones and quartzites, the
upper ones limestones and shales. These in turn were succeeded by
limestones and Coal Measures of Carboniferous age, which have
been denuded from the higher parts and survive on the surface only
in the northern Ardennes near Dinant and in a major structural
syncline extending from Mons to Liège. These two areas of Carboniferous rocks are separated by a narrow outcrop of Silurian and
Devonian rocks which form the Condroz hill country, sometimes
called the Crête du Condroz because of its long ridge-like character.
Coal Measures are also present in the north-east of Belgium, though
hidden beneath a thick layer of newer rocks.

The Ardennes owe their structural character to the Hercynian
orogeny of late Carbo-Permian times (p. 139). Though this folding
was extremely complex, certain major trend-lines of the alternate

anticlinoria and synclinoria, approximately south-west to north-east in direction, can be traced (Fig. 48). The northern edge of the Ardennes is defined by the Namur synclinorium, in which the Coal Measures are preserved; this is the exposed portion of the southern coalfield, though farther west the Coal Measures are concealed beneath a cover of chalk and newer rocks. The complexity and intensity of the folding and associated faulting have made mining conditions difficult; in some cases Devonian, Carboniferous Limestone and Lower Coal Measure strata have been thrust over the younger Upper Coal Measures, and deep shafts have to be sunk through the older rocks to reach the underlying coal.

The Palaeozoic rocks to the north of the 'coal-furrow' were also involved in the Hercynian folding, which created the 'Brabant anticline' across central Belgium, though of a much less intensely folded nature than those in the Ardennes. Its northern limb dips gently under a thick cover of newer rocks as the Kempen syncline, which also contains Coal Measures, forming the northern coalfield of Belgium.

During the long span of Mesozoic time, the Hercynian ranges were worn down to a peneplaned surface. During the Cretaceous the widespread 'Chalk Sea' (p. 240) covered much of western and central Europe, when an extensive cover of chalk was laid down, now appearing on the surface in the neighbourhood of Mons and farther east the Hesbaye and Herve regions. In the Kempenland the colliery shafts pass through chalk and other Cretaceous rocks at considerable depths. In some places on the Ardennes plateau, patches of Triassic and Cretaceous rocks still survive, resting on the Devonian rocks, testifying to the extent of the now vanished Mesozoic cover.

Another widespread marine transgression in early Tertiary times was responsible for the deposition of the Flanders Clay of Eocene age on the Flanders Plain and of sandstones in Brabant and northern Hesbaye. A narrow interrupted belt of Oligocene clays outcrops along the southern border of the Kempenland, and patches of sandy clay of similar early Tertiary age can be seen at several localities in the Ardennes at heights exceeding 550 m (1800 ft), lying both on the Cretaceous and Palaeozoic rocks.

During the mid-Tertiary (Miocene) period of orogenic activity which created the Alps (p. 351), the worn-down remnants of the Ardennes were once more uplifted, so that they stood above the Miocene and Pliocene sea which extended over much of south-eastern England, the Netherlands and Belgium. In this sea a considerable thickness of sand was deposited, surviving in the Kempenland as a continuous cover and in western Belgium as scattered patches on the hill summits.

Towards the end of the Pliocene a widespread tilting movement (p. 240) affected much of western Europe. As a result, the Lower Pliocene cappings on the hills of western Belgium are now at a height of about 150 m (500 ft) above sea-level. The Ardennes were further uplifted, so standing prominently above the surrounding lowlands; in

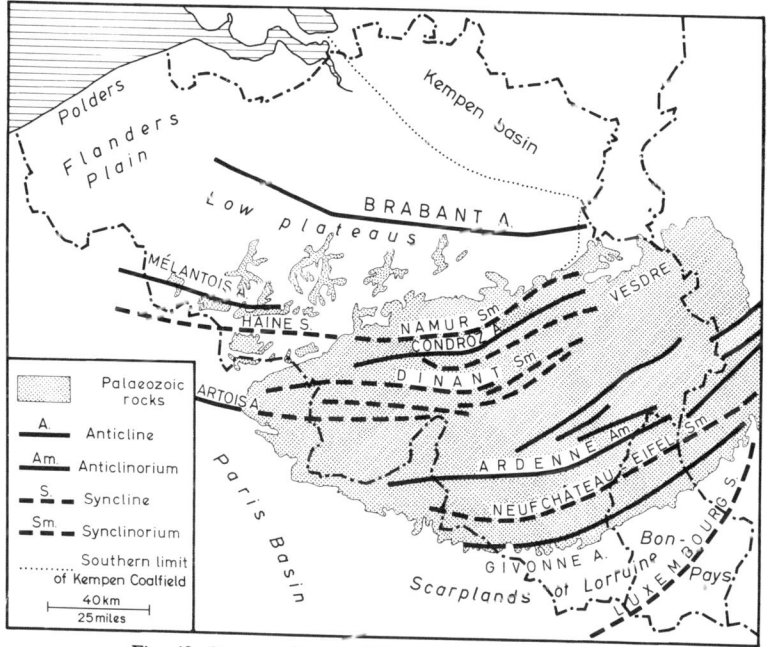

Fig. 48. *Structural map of the Ardennes and its margins*
(After J. Halkin)

effect, the ancient structures have been resurrected and their 'grain' revealed. Along the axis of the Ardennes anticlinorium (Fig. 48), where the elevation and resultant denudation was most pronounced, the Cambrian–Silurian rocks are exposed as gently rounded summits just exceeding 600 m (2000 ft) in altitude; these High Ardennes are the 'roots' of the former Hercynian fold ranges. The effects of the various periods of denudation and uplift are shown by several distinct erosion surfaces.

By the end of the Pliocene, therefore, uplift and denudation had combined to produce a broad surface sloping northward from the

High Ardennes away to the North Sea basin. On this surface developed a pattern of consequent rivers, flowing northward to the retreating Plio-Pleistocene sea. The evolution of the present landscape is largely the result of the development of the Meuse and Scheldt drainage systems, with modifications in the coastal lowlands as the result of fluctuations of sea-level, the deposition of mud and sand, and the accumulation of peat.

Belgium lay to the south of the maximum advance of the Quaternary icesheets, though it was affected indirectly by accelerated periglacial weathering processes, especially in the Ardennes, and the heavily laden Meuse deposited vast amounts of material. A further contribution in interglacial and postglacial times was the deposition of a widespread cover of fine-textured *limon*, similar to the loess of Germany (p. 145), from which have developed brownish loam soils. This limon occurs at all heights in central Belgium, both on the high interfluves and plateaus and, though redeposited by subsequent river action, also on the terraces. As a result, the underlying solid rocks, whether chalk in Hesbaye or Tertiary sands and clays in Brabant and Hainaut, are wholly masked over large areas.

The Rivers

The natural drainage of Belgium is concentrated into two main systems. In the south-east is the sweeping curve of the Meuse, flowing northward along the Belgo–Dutch border into the Netherlands, while the numerous rivers which comprise the Scheldt system converge across the Plain of Flanders and central Belgium towards its estuary. The only exception is the little river Ijzer (Yser), which breaks through directly to the North Sea in the south-west.

After crossing the scarplands of French Lorraine (p. 473) into Belgium, the Meuse flows northward across the Ardennes to its junction with the Sambre at Namur. This course lies transverse to the general trend of the structure, superimposed on a former cover of Cretaceous and Tertiary rocks now almost wholly removed. The valley is in places spectacular, particularly where the river erodes across bands of compact limestone, forming gorges which alternate with more open basins.

At Namur the Meuse undergoes a marked change of direction, as it enters the line of the 'coalfield furrow' flanking the northern edge of the Ardennes, following the trend of its main tributary, the Sambre, from the west. This direction, at right-angles to the original consequent drainage lines, was obviously initiated after the younger rocks had been removed, revealing the structural line of the Namur synclinorium. Below Liège the river bends northward, forming the international boundary for 160 km (100 miles) before it becomes a wholly Dutch river, called in that country the Maas (p. 243).

The various rivers which comprise the Scheldt system (the Lys, Scheldt, Dender, Senne, Dyle and Demer), form a gridiron pattern focusing on the Scheldt estuary above Antwerp. Their upper courses trend from south-west to north-east, that is, approximately parallel to the North Sea coast, a pattern which originally developed during the gradual emergence of the Pliocene sea floor (p. 240) as a series of independent consequents. Many of the physical features of the Plain of Flanders and the low plateaus of central Belgium are the result of erosion by these rivers in Quaternary times; the valleys are too wide to have been formed by rivers of their present size. This erosion removed almost completely the newer Tertiary deposits, except for the isolated interfluve cappings on the hills in Flanders and Brabant, and so exposed the older Tertiary rocks such as the Flanders Clay and the sandstones of Brabant and Hesbaye. In central Belgium erosion went even further and cut completely through the Tertiary deposits to reveal Cambrian and Silurian rocks in some valleys.

In immediately postglacial times the heavily laden rivers covered the floors of their valleys with alluvium, in places to thicknesses of over 30 m. The rivers meander through floodplains 6–8 km (4–5 miles) in width, though their courses have now been artificially stabilized.

The western members of the Scheldt system (the Lys, upper Scheldt and Dender) join the middle Scheldt, which flows in an easterly direction. The lower Demer has eroded a distinct east–west 'furrow' between the southern edge of the Kempen plateau and the northward slope of central Belgium. This furrow 'taps' the consequents flowing northward (the Senne, Dyle and Demer) from the plateaus of Brabant and Hesbaye, and so leads their waters to the Rupel, hence to the Scheldt estuary. The only other major Scheldt tributary is the Nethe in the north-east, which drains the gentle south-western slope of the Kempen plateau.

The Coast

The Belgian coastline, only 68 km (42 miles) in length, is remarkably straight, with a broad sandy beach uncovered at low tide in places for a width of nearly 400 m (440 yd.). It is backed by a rampart of dunes, cut through only at the mouth of the Ijzer, at Ostend, near

Zeebrugge where a ship canal from Bruges reaches the sea between twin moles, and at the shallow inlet which marks the former mouth of the Zwin estuary. In many places the dune-belt is over 2 km wide and is chaotic in appearance, with clusters of crests, the highest rising to 51 m (167 ft), separating broad depressions, and with a steep slope to the beach. Behind this dune-line a flat plain, seamed with drainage channels, extends landward for some 10–16 km (6–10 miles).

The coastlands of Flanders experienced several phases of marine transgression during historic times; the maximum probably occurred during the fifth century A.D., when the sea extended 16–24 km (10–15 miles) inland of its present position. But from the eighth century onwards it slowly receded, and the gradual drying-out of the shallow lagoons was assisted both by sedimentation and by some small-scale reclamation by man; documents as early as the tenth century relate to the building of dykes. Another less extensive transgression in the tenth century caused several breaks through the dune-line, when the estuary of the Ijzer became a broad sheet of water, and the enlargement of a breach near Knokke was responsible for the estuary of the Zwin. Towards the end of the eleventh century a renewed transgression widened and deepened this, resulting in the growth in importance of Bruges; its later silting-up was responsible for the decline of the port.

Reclamation went steadily on, though many set-backs were experienced; sometimes too extensive an area was reclaimed with inadequate defences, so that storms did grievous damage. A disastrous flood occurred in 1404, as a result of which a dyke which can still be traced was built by the Count of Flanders. However, since the seventeenth century little serious flooding has taken place along the Belgian coast. The strengthened dune-line is straight and continuous, and no part of the land lies below mean sea-level. The only area flooded since the seventeenth century is the Ijzer estuary, for defensive purposes in 1783 and in 1914–18, and again in 1928 by the collapse of a dyke during a storm. A very small area to the east of De Zoute was inundated by the floods of 1953.

Relief Regions

This complicated geological evolution has resulted in a variety of relief divisions (Fig. 49). Behind the North Sea coast lies a lowland known by its historic name of Flanders, though this applies also to the adjoining parts of the Netherlands and France. Maritime Flanders, the area behind the dune-fringed coastline, is an almost

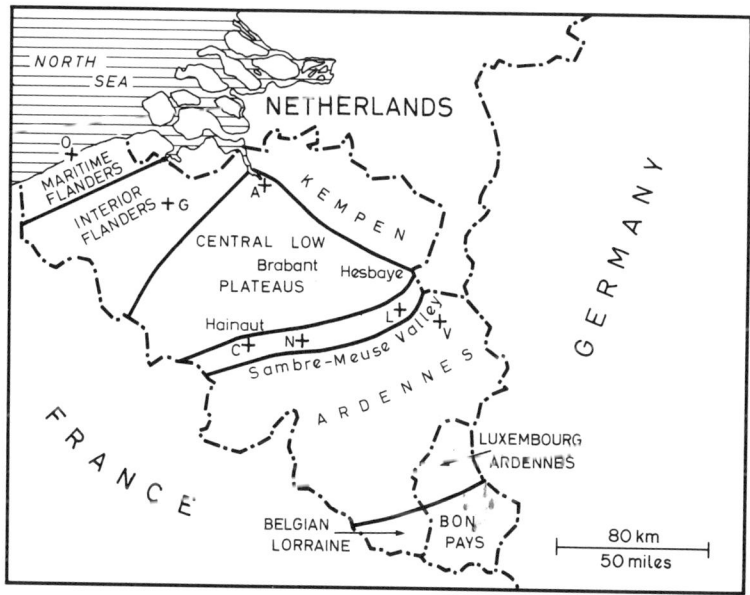

Fig. 49. Relief regions of Belgium and Luxembourg

level plain seamed with drainage channels, interrupted only by shallow depressions, usually the result of peat-cutting, and by low sandy hillocks. This is succeeded inland by Interior Flanders, a gently undulating lowland covered mainly with Flanders Clay, across which the Lys, Scheldt and Dender flow north-eastward in broad alluvium-floored valleys.

From the eastern margins of Interior Flanders the land rises gently inland to about 200 m (660 ft) above sea-level, until terminated by a marked descent to the Sambre–Meuse valley. This area is known as the central low plateaus: in the west in Hainaut, in the centre Brabant, and in the east Hesbaye. The underlying Palaeozoic basement is covered with Flanders Clay in the west, Tertiary sands in the centre and north, and chalk in the east, with a superficial limon mantle in many parts.

In the north-east the low Kempen plateau is bounded by the valleys of the Meuse and Demer. A sheet of coarse sand and gravel, laid down by the Meuse as a 'fan' during a late stage in the Quaternary, thickly covers the underlying Pliocene sands. Its surface rises to about 100 m (330 ft) in the east, dipping gently westward and north-ward towards the Scheldt estuary and the Dutch boundary. Below the surface of the Kempen plateau, buried by Mesozoic and Tertiary rocks, is a concealed coalfield.

To the south of the 'furrow' of the Sambre and the Meuse lies a dissected peneplain at about 300 m (1000 ft), known in the west as Entre Sambre-et-Meuse and in the east as the Condroz. South of this the broad Famenne depression trends from south-west to north-east, drained by two Meuse tributaries, the Lesse and the Ourthe. Widespread limestone here accounts for complex underground drainage systems; the Grottoes of Han consist of interconnected caverns through which the Lesse flows for about a mile.

The upland of the High Ardennes is defined by the 300 m (1000 ft) contour, but rises in places to rounded summits, the highest being the Botrange (694 m, 2277 ft) and the Baraque de Fraiture (652 m, 2140 ft). These gentle elevations are separated by shallow depressions, usually containing bogs. As they flow to join the Meuse, the rivers have cut deep winding valleys through the Palaeozoic rocks, the result of repeated rejuvenation.

A small part of Lorraine extends into the south-eastern corner of Belgium. Several lines of sandstone and limestone hills, as north-facing cuestas, trend across the country. Between them are vales, floored with clay and marl, upon whose less resistant outcrops streams flowing to the Meuse have developed their courses.

CLIMATE

Though Belgium is small in extent, its climate presents some marked contrasts, the result of the two main physical divisions, 'Low Belgium' and 'High Belgium', and of increasing distance from the sea. On the coast the mean temperatures for January and July vary little from 3° C. and 17° C. respectively. The mean daily minimum is slightly above freezing for the winter months, though within a 20 km or so of the coast frost may be expected on about thirty days each year. Farther inland the extremes of temperature increase by a few degrees; the mean figures for Brussels in January and July are 2° C. and 17° C. respectively, and for Stavelot 0° C and 15·5° C. In the Ardennes uplands frost may be expected on 120 days in the year. Farther south still, in Belgian Lorraine, although the land is generally lower than the Ardennes and has a southerly aspect, winters are quite severe, as is indicated by an annual average of 103 days with frost at Arlon. The seasonal range is shown by mean monthly temperatures for Arlon of 1° C. in January and 18° C. in

July. However, Belgian Lorraine, sometimes referred to as '*la petite Provence belge*', is the only part of Belgium where the vine can be grown in the open.

Along the coast the mean annual precipitation is about 710 mm (28 in), with a distinct maximum in autumn and early winter and an early spring minimum; February is the driest month. Over much of central Belgium the mean annual total is of the order of 760–840 mm (30–33 in) (Uccle, near Brussels, 760 mm (30 in)), with a late spring minimum, and maxima in July–August and again in October. Over the Ardennes precipitation is heavy, with low cloud and frequent hill fogs; Baraque Michel has a mean annual total of 1220 mm (48 in), and Chiny, in the Semois valley to the south-west, has 1270 mm (50 in), officially the wettest place in Belgium. Some of this precipitation falls in the form of snow, which lies above 600 m (2000 ft) during an average year for as long as eighty days, and at an altitude of 300 m (1000 ft) for about thirty days; the German offensive in the Ardennes in January 1945 drove westward over deeply snow-covered country. The mean annual precipitation for Belgian Lorraine is about 740 mm (29 in), with a distinct maximum between November and February, not markedly less than that of the Ardennes to the north, though summers are appreciably drier.

LAND USE AND AGRICULTURE

Soils

The Belgian Ministry of Agriculture defines thirteen agricultural regions, largely on the basis of their predominant soil types. Along the coast the narrow strip of dunes is backed for 10–16 km (6–10 miles) by sandy soils, naturally poor but light and warm, and when adequately fertilized suitable for market gardening. Behind this lies polderland, far less extensive than in the Netherlands, with soils mainly derived from heavy marine clays, though locally there is considerable variety; patches of yellow sand, black silt and grey or blue clay can be seen within a few metres. This is succeeded by Interior Flanders, covered with Eocene clays in the south-west, Eocene sands in the north-east, and alluvium over the floodplains of the Lys and Scheldt; the soils vary accordingly. The Kempenland in the north-east has poor leached soils developed on superficial sheets of sand and gravel deposited by the Meuse, similar to those of the Dutch heathlands (p. 250).

The region of the low plateaus across central Belgium is the country's most important agricultural area. The widespread cover of limon has developed brownish loams of excellent quality, with heavier clay loams in the west and sand loams in the east. In the north a transition can be seen from these loams to the coarse sands and gravels of the Kempenland.

Over the Ardennes the soils on the slates, quartzites and sandstones are thin and acid; waterlogging is common in the depressions on the high plateaus. Only in some of the alluvium-floored valleys and on the Carboniferous Limestone of the Famenne are soils of reasonable quality. Some of the soils of Belgian Lorraine are light and sandy, developed from Triassic sediments, others are calcareous, and still others are of heavy clay.

Forests

Forest covers approximately a fifth of the total area of the country, a surprisingly high figure. The main wooded regions are in the Ardennes. More than two-thirds of the total grows in the three provinces of Luxembourg, Namur and Liège, both on the sides of the deeply cut valleys and on the exposed plateau surface. The southern portion along the French border is thickly wooded; from the Meuse valley the dark forest wall can be seen in the distance. In the valleys grow some attractive oak–birch, oak–hornbeam and beech forests, while the plateau surface bears plantations of spruce and Scots pine. Some of the best maintained forests are in the Eupen and Malmédy districts, acquired from Germany in 1919. About half of Belgian Lorraine carries a tree cover, mainly of oak, beech, hornbeam and hazel, often grown as 'standards with coppice' on the escarpments.

The establishment of plantations of softwoods has been carried out in the eastern Kempenland by the State, communes, public bodies and private individuals. In the province of Limburg the proportion of communally owned woodland forms one-third of the total, for this is the most profitable way for the communes to make the heathlands contribute to their revenues, especially as the State assists in the cost of clearing and planting. Scots pine and occasionally Corsican pine, which have the advantage of attaining maturity within thirty or forty years, are planted in large rectangular blocks. Only occasionally do the trees occur less formally; a few scattered pines have naturally colonized adjacent heathland, and clumps of trees have been established to help fix the sand-dunes, or for shelter and decorative purposes near collieries, factories and housing estates. In all, about one-seventh of the heathland has been planted with conifers.

Elsewhere in Belgium the woodland is sporadic, occurring in

small isolated patches; West Flanders has less than 2 per cent of its area wooded. On the coastal dune belt, conifers have been planted to assist the fixation of the sand, and in the polders are lines of pollarded willows or poplars, with occasionally a clump of trees around an isolated farm. Over the central low plateaus the land is too valuable to carry much woodland, except for avenues along the roads, groups of trees around some of the big farmhouses, and in the parks of private estates. The most continuous woodland is the carefully preserved Forêt de Soignes, to the east of Brussels, with its magnificent beeches and oaks.

Arable Farming

About 54 per cent of Belgium is defined as farmland, with rather more than half under arable, the rest under meadow and permanent pasture. Though only about 6 per cent of the active population is engaged in agriculture, the second lowest proportion in Europe, and though only about a third of the soil can be described as fertile, agriculture is highly developed. The farming is intensive and affords high yields; it is specialized and extremely varied; it produces many industrial crops; and supplies four-fifths of all home consumption of foodstuffs. Despite efforts at consolidation, there is a very large number of small units. Many of these are part-time holdings, owned and cultivated by industrial workers, and others are market gardens worked as family units. This is particularly true in Flanders, where farming is little more than patient laborious spade cultivation. The biggest farms are on the loam soils of Brabant and Hesbaye, where wheat and sugar beet are grown (Plate XL).

During the last hundred years the area under cereals has decreased from about 850 000 ha (2·1 million acres) in 1866 to 469 000 ha (1·2 million acres) in 1968, because of the change to the more profitable dairying and stock rearing. Except for rotation grass, wheat is still the most important crop; about half is grown in Hainaut and Brabant. Oats are produced for fodder in West Flanders and in the Ardennes, barley is cultivated on the loam soils in the centre of the country, and rye is still grown (27 000 ha, 67,000 acres in 1968) on the sandy soils of the Kempen and in parts of Flanders, though in declining amounts. Potatoes are grown mainly in Flanders, though the area is only a third of what it was eighty years ago. By comparison, both fodder beet and sugar beet have doubled in area during the same period, the former in Flanders and Hainaut, the latter in Brabant; the country is normally self-supporting in sugar.

For some centuries flax was a most important crop, mainly in Flanders, but scarcity of labour and the competition of cheap foreign flax caused a general decline, and now only about 30 000 ha (74,000 acres) are grown, by no means adequate for the linen industry. Hops are cultivated in western Flanders, tobacco in Hainaut and in the Semois valley in the south, and chicory in Brabant.

Horticulture

Horticulture, including market gardening and fruit growing, is extremely well developed, especially around such cities as Ghent, Mechelen and Antwerp, with their large markets. The neighbourhood of Brussels has a tremendous concentration of market gardening, dairying, pig and poultry farming, and the cultivation of flowers. To the north-west of the city, particularly between Berchem and Assche, immense areas of glasshouses produce early vegetables and flowers, while to the south-east other glasshouses are devoted to grapes. Much of the polderland near Antwerp is intensively cultivated, especially nearby in the reclaimed Waasland where market gardens specialize in cauliflowers and tomatoes and where there are orchards of bush fruit, dairy farms and poultry farms. On either side of the Demer valley in the north-east, the light warm sandy soils, heavily fertilized, are used for the intensive cultivation of vegetables, particularly of early varieties; peas, sown at the end of January and picked in early June, asparagus, early potatoes, carrots and chicory are grown along a 'golden belt' of horticulture between Mechelen and Diest.

Livestock

Nearly half the farmland is under permanent pasture, notably in the polderlands, the Ardennes and Belgian Lorraine. Much of the Kempen heathland has been reclaimed as pasture; only one-tenth of the total area of the two provinces of Antwerpen and Limburg were under grass in 1866, but this has now risen to one-fifth, of markedly better quality.

The number of cattle increased from about 1·2 million in 1870 to 1·7 in 1938, and, after a fall due to wartime slaughtering, to 2·7 in 1968, of which nearly half were dairy cattle; a large proportion of the milk is consumed in nearby industrial towns. The country is self-supporting in veal and almost so in beef. About 2·5 million pigs are kept, mainly on smallholdings or in association with dairy farms. The 83,000 sheep indicate a big decline from the 700,000 of a century ago, partly because mutton is unpopular, partly because of the relative cheapness of imported wool.

Although the coast of Belgium lies near the North Sea banks, fishing is not an important occupation; only 31,000 tons were landed in 1968, though this is somewhat greater than in pre-1939 years. About four-fifths of the catch is handled at Ostend, whose fishing harbour is equipped with packing sheds, ice factories and canneries. Other fishing ports are Zeebrugge, Nieuwpoort and Blankenberge. The chief catch by weight consists of cod, though the most important by value is sole. The inshore fisheries are profitable; shrimps are consumed in great quantities at the coastal resorts.

The two Belgian coalfields are the Sambre-Meuse or southern field (Fig. 50) and the Kempen or northern field (Fig. 51). Belgium developed into one of the world's most highly industrialized countries during the nineteenth century, when the production of coal increased from 2·6 million tons in 1835 to 16·8 million tons in 1880, and then to 23·5 million tons in 1900, at which total it more or less remained until 1914. But the consumption of coal increased more rapidly still, and it became increasingly obvious that this field was unable to supply Belgium's needs. Imports of coal and coke, which in 1835 amounted to less than 10,000 tons, had attained 3 million tons by 1900.

The southern coalfield forms part of an elongated series of Coal Measures which extend from the departments of Pas-de-Calais and Nord in France (Fig. 85) across the border. This field is extremely difficult to work, for faulting and overthrusting interrupt the continuity of the seams, some dip at a high angle, and minor anticlines divide the field into individual basins. In the Liège district mining is concentrated in three distinct areas, separated by less productive or wholly barren ground. Sometimes the coal is so shattered that it has to be briquetted, used in thermal generators, or burnt *in situ* for underground gasification. The fractured seams hinder mechanization, and firedamp is prevalent, contributing to a high accident rate. Further disadvantages are that the exploited seams are thin, though numerous, and many of the mines are deep, particularly in the west near Mons where they exceed 1000 m (3300 ft). The nine-teenth century saw the removal of the most accessible coal and many parts of the field have been worked out or abandoned as uneconomic.

Increasing attention therefore was paid to the possibility that the Dutch Limburg field (p. 238) might extend below the Meuse valley westward into Belgium. Because of the thick cover of younger rocks, only trial borings could verify this, and the first was put down in 1877

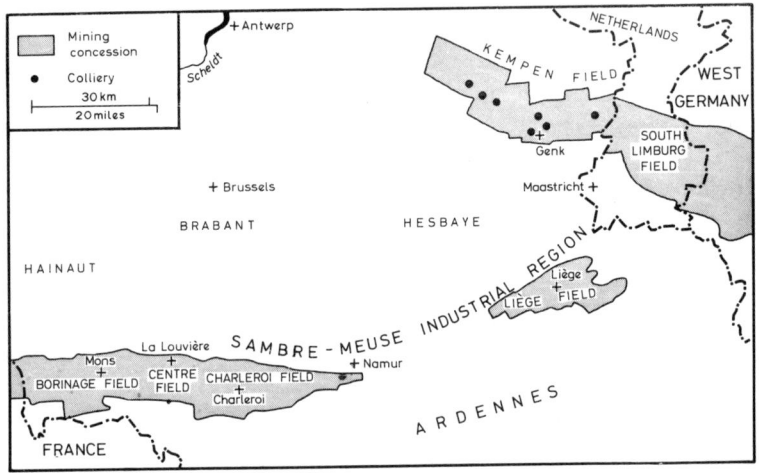

Fig. 50. The Belgian coalfields
The individual collieries are shown only for the Kempen field; one of these was closed in 1966.

to the north of Liège; success was finally attained when in 1901 a boring reached a coal seam at a depth of 541 m (1775 ft). As a result of the immense initial difficulties of exploitation, this northern basin pro-duced no marketable coal until 1917, but since then progress has been continuous, and until recently seven collieries produced annually from 9 to 10 million tons (Fig. 51). The proportion of the Belgian total contributed by the Kempen field steadily increased to about two-thirds. The Kempenland was not a promising area for industrial development, for it consisted of heathland, with few settlements. The shortage of labour was met by importation from other countries, and from 1922 onwards trainloads of workers arrived in Belgium. Foreign labour, mostly Italian and Polish, now comprises a third of the total mining force of about 50,000, and a higher proportion, three-sevenths, of the underground workers. The result of this popu-lation increase was that housing estates where the workers could live had to be built near the collieries in the heathlands (Plate XLII); over parts of the Kempen the heathland is replaced by new towns.

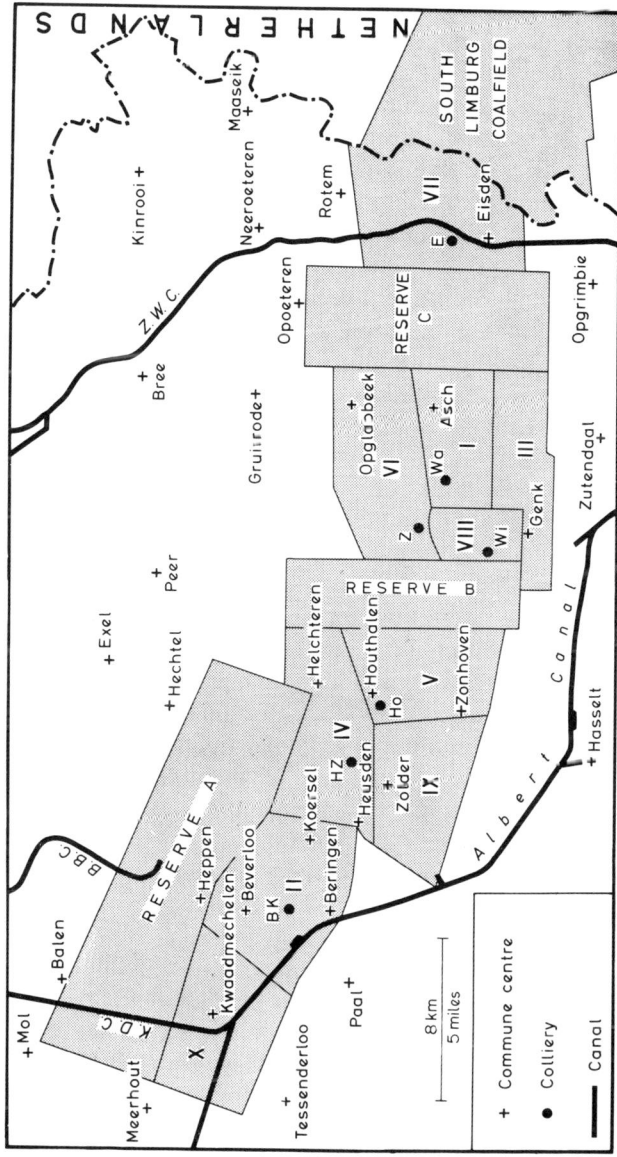

Fig. 51. The Kempen coalfield

The three areas A, B, C were retained as State reserves when concessions were granted, and have not yet been exploited. Z.W.C., Zuid-Willems Canal; K.D.C., Kwaadmechelen-Desschel Canal; B.B.C., Beverloo Branch Canal. The Roman numerals refer to individual concessions. The Zwartberg colliery (Z) was closed in 1966.

Problems and Policies

Although damage to the collieries during the German occupation of 1940–44 was relatively slight, the postwar mining industry has had to face many problems. Belgium is a high-cost producer of coal, partly because of wage rates above average for western Europe, partly because of the heavy contributions which the industry must bear towards social security and miners' housing, and partly because of the increasing operational difficulties of the southern field. To increase and maintain production called for a vigorous system of rationalization in the southern field, a ruthless policy of closing unproductive mines, and heavy State investment to modernize the installations. Although industrial unemployment has caused great unrest in southern Belgium, there was a constant shortage of mining labour, particularly in the north. In the immediate postwar years prisoners of war, political *détenues* and 'stateless' people were employed, and the Belgo–Italian agreement of 1946 brought many Italian workers.

Belgium's membership of the European Coal and Steel Community has posed some special problems. The policy of the High Authority imposed a levy on below average cost producers in West Germany and the Netherlands, which with contributions by the Belgian government enabled temporary compensation to be paid to the collieries in the southern field to cover the difference between the Community's common-market price and the economic selling price. The modernization policy has involved gradually closing or amalgamating many of the southern collieries, and the Community has tried to help the government to mitigate the social effects of the dismissals; many foreign miners have returned to their home countries, new industries have been introduced into the worst hit districts, and retraining of former miners has been undertaken. There is, however, considerable unemployment, with consequent social and political unrest (see p. 321).

Output has fallen steadily, and in 1968 it was only 14·8 million tons, less than half its peak; only 22 mines are active in the southern field, compared with 193 in 1938, and 6 in the Kempen field (producing 8·5 million tons). This output is less than half Belgium's requirements, the balance being met by imports of cheap American and Polish coal, especially for making into coke. Yet home overproduction of some types of coal has led to stock-piling at the pitheads, partly because the consumption of oil and gas fuel has trebled in the last ten years.

Other Mining and Quarrying

Belgium is poorly supplied with ores, although in the past small deposits have helped to establish the metallurgical industry. Zinc and lead ores were mined along the Meuse valley and towards the German border near Moresnet and Montzen, but these ceased production in 1939. A small section of the Oolitic Limestone escarpment of Lorraine lies within Belgium, but only one mine is now active, which produced 82,000 tons of ore in 1968, a very small proportion of the ore required to make 10·4 million tons of pig-iron.

The varied geological outcrops result in a range of quarry products. These include slate and sandstone in the Ardennes; limestone and marble in the Sambre-Meuse valley and the upper valleys of the Dender, Senne and Dyle; and porphyritic rocks for road setts in the Dyle and Senne valleys. Clay is excavated in great quantities for making bricks and tiles near the Rupel estuary and in the northern Kempen near Turnhout.

POWER

Gas

Apart from some small hydroelectric stations in the Ardennes, Belgium's only home-produced source of power is derived from its coalfields. Much coal is burnt to produce gas, and Belgium was a pioneer in the integration of its distribution by means of a grid. Instead of a multiplicity of small local concerns, a few major companies operate high-pressure grids through which they distribute gas derived from gas works (such as the huge plant at Pont-Brûlé to the north of Brussels), from the metallurgical coke ovens (as at Tertre and Monceau on the southern coalfield, and at Hoboken near Antwerp), and from chemical works and other industrial plant, taking their excess output. The main grid runs from Antwerp through Brussels to the southern coalfield. Gradually, however, natural gas piped from the Netherlands (p. 262) and that derived from the Belgian oil-refineries is replacing coal-gas.

Electricity

Belgian policy concerning electricity differs markedly from that of most industrial countries, in that numerous small stations are in operation, sited as near as possible to each area of consumption, so minimizing the transmission distance. The industry is not nationalized, and the programme is co-ordinated by several regional organizations such as the *Union des Centrales Electriques* and the *Union des Exploitations Electriques en Belgique*. An interconnection network has been developed, which in recent years has been linked to neighbouring countries, and an increasing amount of power is both imported and exported via this international grid.

The output of electricity has grown enormously since 1945. Whereas in 1938 a mere 5·1 milliard KWh of energy were produced, by 1968 this had been increased to 25 milliard. Production is mainly in the hands of private companies and of industrial concerns which sell excess power, though there are also ten publicly owned stations. A few small hydro-stations are situated on tributaries of the Meuse in the Ardennes. The big thermal generators are located in the industrial areas of Hainaut and Liège, and in the outskirts of Brussels, Antwerp and Ghent.

Oil

Belgium produces no oil or natural gas, and the whole of its considerable requirement of oil is imported, a large though declining proportion in refined form. While in 1938 only half a million tons of crude oil were imported, this has risen steadily since 1945, as refining facilities have been increased, to over 24 million tons. Most of this is processed in the Antwerp district, where *S.I.B.P.*, *Esso–Standard* and smaller concerns operate refineries (Plate XLI). A large refinery has been constructed near Ghent, supplied by pipeline from a terminal at Zeebrugge.

MANUFACTURING INDUSTRY

A notable feature of Belgian industry is that its control is concentrated in the hands of a few large trusts. The dominant concern is the *Société Générale*, which owns 40 per cent of Belgium's coal, 50 per cent of steel, 65 per cent of non-ferrous metal manufacture, and 35 per cent of electricity production. The *Groupe Solvay* dominates chemicals, the *Banque Lambert* has a major interest in oil.

The Iron and Steel Industry

In 1968 Belgium produced 10·4 million tons of pig-iron and ferro-alloys and 11·6 million tons of crude steel; more than 80 per cent came from the Sambre–Meuse valley. A large proportion is mild

Plate XXXVIII. Amsterdam. Note the semicircular pattern of the canals,
with the IJ in the background

Plate XXXIX. The flyover at the entrance to the Maas Tunnel at Rotterdam

Plate XL. The arable lands of the Dyle valley between Leuven and Mechelen

Plate XLI. The petroleum-port at Antwerp, showing the oil-docks, storage tanks, refineries and petrochemical plants

'Thomas steel', made in Basic Bessemer converters at large integrated plants, though these are being replaced by Basic Oxygen Steel
converters, which in 1968 made 4·5 million tons. About 190,000 tons
of 'Martin steel' was produced in open-hearths, using imported pig
and both local and imported scrap, and another 311,000 tons of
'electric steel', mostly alloys and tool steels, was made in electric
furnaces, especially in the Liège area.

The iron and steel industry can be traced back at least to medieval
times, perhaps in the Liège district to Roman times. The main areas
throughout the centuries have been the Sambre-Meuse depression
and the Lorraine scarplands. Iron ore occurred widely, although in
small-scale deposits which have been gradually exhausted; alluvial
iron ores were worked in the valleys of the south, and hematites,
with as much as 52 per cent iron and little or no phosphorus, were
mined in the Devonian rocks outcropping along the Sambre-Meuse
valley. Limonite, with an iron content of about 45 per cent, occurred
widely in fissure veins, often in conjunction with rich zinc and lead
ores for which it was primarily exploited. A peak year's output of
778,000 tons of iron ore was attained in the mid-nineteenth century.

The early iron industry used charcoal obtained from the forests
of the Condroz and the Ardennes, and the furnaces were located on
exposed hilltops to obtain an adequate draught. When water-driven
bellows were introduced, smelting migrated to the valleys of the
Sambre, Meuse, Ourthe and Lesse; the pig-iron was taken to Liège,
which since the thirteenth century had been the home of metal-
working guilds. Open-cast mining of coal along the Meuse valley
can be traced back at least to the twelfth century, providing fuel for
the forges of the skilled iron workers. Liège became an industrial
centre of European pre-eminence long before the Industrial Revolution. In 1823 John Cockerill, son of an English mechanic who
migrated to Belgium at the end of the eighteenth century, built the
first coke-fired blast furnace at Seraing on the banks of the Meuse;
the name of Cockerill has since then been pre-eminent in Belgian
industry, and the Seraing works still stand on the original though
greatly enlarged site. The western part of the Sambre-Meuse coalfield developed rapidly during the first half of the nineteenth century,
and although Charleroi did not possess the industrial antecedents
of Liège, the metallurgical industry expanded rapidly. Later still
furnaces were installed at La Louvière, using the good coking
coals of the Mons-Centre basin.

Most steel is now produced by a few integrated concerns in the southern industrial region (Fig. 52). For many years two of the largest, both in the Liège district, have been the *S.A. John Cockerill* and the *S.A. d'Ougrée-Marihaye*, also on the banks of the Meuse; in 1955 these merged to form one of the largest metallurgical combines in Europe, producing a third of Belgian steel, and later were joined by the *Providence* company. The Charleroi district contains several other large-scale combines, situated along the banks of the Sambre; the *Hainaut-Sambre* company was the result of an amalgamation in 1955, and is now the second largest.

Outlying plants include a group of blast furnaces in the south-east at Halanzy and Musson, originally based on local ore from the small extension of the Lorraine field into Belgium, but now using French ore; a large plant on the Brussels–Charleroi Canal at Clabecq,

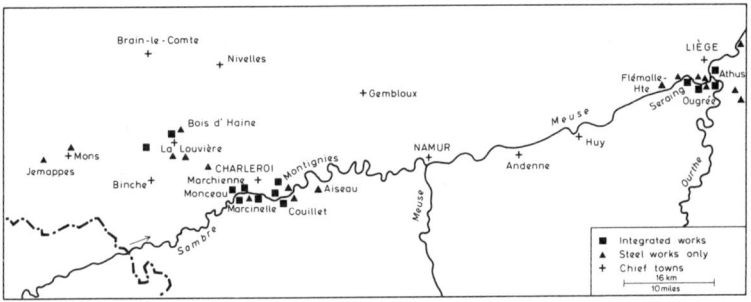

Fig. 52. The major iron and steel works in southern Belgium

24 km (15 miles) south of Brussels; a few small though specialized steel works at Turnhout, Court-St Etienne and St Michiels (near Bruges); and rolling-mills at Schoten near Antwerp. In 1962 the High Authority of the E.C.S.C. authorized the construction of a new sheet-steel plant, known as *Sidmar*, at Selzaete near Ghent, which began production in 1965; it includes blast furnaces, converters and rolling-mills, where steel production is highly computerized, the most modern plant in the world, with an annual output of 1·5 million tons of sheet steel. The works are linked to the Wester Schelde by a ship-canal; the recently enlarged locks at Terneuzen can take 60,000-ton ore-carriers.

Heavy Engineering

The heavy engineering industries are located mainly on the southern coalfield and particularly near the sources of steel, many closely integrated with steel works on the same or an adjacent site. The products include boilers, girders, bridges, diesel engines, electrical apparatus, locomotives and rolling-stock. The first Belgian locomotive was built at Seraing in 1835 and used on the Brussels–Mechelen railway, the first Continental line operated with steam locomotives, which were for long constructed at Seraing, Couillet, Tubize and Haine-St Pierre.

Most of the big towns along the Sambre-Meuse valley have heavy engineering works. Namur lies on a now exhausted coal basin, but its heavy industry has continued: the manufacture of boilers, cranes, rolling-stock and agricultural machinery. Not all industry is concentrated on the southern coalfield. Several large concerns to the south of Brussels make diesel engines, steam engines, turbines and marine engines. Antwerp is the centre of Belgium's small ship-building industry; the largest yard is at Hoboken on the right bank of the Scheldt above the city, building motor vessels, trawlers, barges and tugs for the European inland waterways, marine engines, ships' boilers and propellers, and much steel is used for ship repairing. Ghent is another non-coalfield centre of heavy industry: diesel engines, diesel-electric locomotives, turbines and other electric motors, pumps and textile machinery are all made.

Light Engineering

Light engineering is widely distributed, many branches with age-old traditions. Liège and its satellite towns are of major importance; in the Herstal region, to the north of the conurbation, many small firms are engaged in the production of hardware, motor-cycle, bicycle and aircraft parts, jet engines, electrical goods and small arms. Liège has had an international prestige for weapons since the fourteenth century, and a number of firms still make sporting weapons of high reputation; the *S.A. Fabrique nationale d'Armes de Guerre* produce the *F.N.* rifle adopted by the armies of the N.A.T.O. countries. Wire, nails and screws are produced in the Charleroi area, notably at Fontaine l'Evêque and Anderlues.

While the conurbations of the Sambre-Meuse valley still dominate the industrial scene, there has been a rapid development of light engineering in other parts of the country. The small size of Belgium, its dense population, its towns with a long tradition of commercial life and skilled labour supplies, its possession of the port of Antwerp and a well-knit system of communications have all assisted this development. Bruges has engineering works near the terminal basin of the Bruges–Zeebrugge Canal; Ghent and Tournai manufacture textile and other machinery; Leuven makes agricultural machinery;

Turnhout has a small steel works which, using steel billets brought by waterway from Liège, produces agricultural implements; Verviers makes textile machinery, not only for its own woollen industry but also for Flanders and for export; and Vilvoorde specializes in machine tools. Brussels as the capital is the most important organizing and distributing centre for an immense range of products. This lengthy catalogue reflects the variety and importance of Belgium's metal-using industries. More than two-thirds of the products are exported, accounting for between a quarter and a third by value of Belgian exports.

Textiles

The Plain of Flanders has been one of the world's leading textile manufacturing areas since the Middle Ages. In early times there was a concentration on woollens, first using wool from sheep on the neighbouring hills and then importing it from the Cotswolds. Though some specializations in woollens survive at Ghent, Kortrijk and Eeklo, the main centre moved as early as the fifteenth century from Flanders into the Verviers district, east of Liège. The reasons are partly geographical (plentiful soft water and wool from the Ardennes and the Eifel) and partly historical (freedom from the restricting guild regulations of Flanders, the introduction of the first carding and spinning machines in Europe by William Cockerill in 1798, and the enterprise of the local merchants).

The linen industry, with the advantages of locally grown flax, the pure water of the Lys for retting, and a dense hard-working population, has flourished for centuries along the Lys valley at Wevelgem, Kortrijk, Ghent and many smaller places. As late as the nineteenth century most of the flax was cultivated on smallholdings and harvested by large firms who retted the flax and sold the fibre to the mills. Now home-produced flax supplies only a fifth of the requirements and the rest is imported from the Netherlands, Poland and France; high quality yarn for fine linens (which still constitute a valuable export item) comes from Northern Ireland.

Cotton is now the pre-eminent textile in Flanders, despite increasing competition from Japan and India. Though more than half of the spindles are located in and around Ghent, the industry has also spread along the valley of the Scheldt at Oudenaarde and Ronse and of the Dender at Aalst, Ninove, Geeraardsbergen and Ath. Many small firms specialize in branches of the industry, though a few large combines have been created, and even the independent companies have grouped themselves into marketing organizations. The textile industry has extended into Brabant, particularly at Brussels itself (clothing, carpets, blankets), Braine-l'Alleud, Anderlecht and Court-St Etienne. In all, about 170,000 people are employed, with another 30,000 who produce ready-made clothing. There is still a considerable number of small enterprises; more than 800 weaving firms employ fewer than fifty people each, and the 700 cotton mills have an output equal to only a hundred in the Netherlands.

Other Industries

Such is the importance and variety of industry in Belgium that only a few special examples can be mentioned. The heavy chemical industry is highly developed in the Sambre-Meuse coalfield, based on the products of coal distillation and coke making, in the Kempen where several large factories make explosives, fertilizers and copper sulphate for vine-spray, and at Brussels, Antwerp (based on petro-chemicals), Ghent and other large towns. Light chemicals, such as pharmaceutical products and photographic materials, are manufactured very widely. Glass has been made since the fourteenth century, and Belgium is now responsible for nearly a fourth of the world's output. A works at Seraing has had an international reputation for crystal glass for over a century, and other glass works are at Zeebrugge, Brussels, Boom on the Rupel estuary, and Charleroi. Belgium is the chief producer of plate-glass, made near Liège and at Mol-Gompel in the Kempen. Both local Kempen sands and fine quality sands from near Fontainebleau in France are used. Brick-making is concentrated near Boom, where plentiful supplies of clay are available, and at Turnhout, Liège and Bruges. Cement is made in the Sambre-Meuse valley, using the outcrops of chalk and limestone. Articles of rubber are made at Anderlecht and Aalst, and the famous *Englebert* tyres at Liège.

Belgium's traditional heavy industries, mainly established in the Sambre-Meuse region, are now lagging behind the new industries of the Antwerp district, the Kempen and Flanders, and this has undoubtedly resulted in some critical economic and social problems. For many years unemployment has been higher in Belgium than in other western European countries, and in 1959 a special law was passed facilitating government aid to depressed areas, including the Borinage, the province of Luxembourg, the Verviers district, and around Ypres (Ieper) in Flanders. These have been designated 'development areas', where firms opening factories are given subsidies, tax concessions, and other benefits and inducements, in order to inject new life into near-moribund districts. Special schemes are in operation to help the rehabilitation and retraining of former miners, the worst-hit section of labour. Many towns have sponsored their own incentive schemes; Mechelen, for example, has offered land at low prices, erected factories, and given reliefs from local taxes. Foreign firms have established new industries during recent years, many of them American concerns seeking a foothold in the European Economic Community.

COMMUNICATIONS

Roads

Belgium possesses a detailed pattern of communications, the result of its small size, dense population, and situation on the coast of the North Sea. About 10 500 km (6500 miles) of State roads provide the country with a remarkably even network, the result of the regular distribution of the towns which they interlink. Between them a much greater length of local roads varies from earth tracks to paved or macadamized surfaces. The density of these local roads varies in response to the agricultural and industrial possibilities of each district, whereas the uniform network of State roads has been superimposed overall. The areas of high local road density are in the neighbourhood of large towns, in the industrial areas of Hainaut and Liège, and in the intensive agricultural districts of Flanders, Brabant and Hesbaye. Conversely, the areas of low density are in the Kempen heathlands, the Ardennes, and the more marshy parts of Maritime Flanders.

The road system is seriously inadequate for the present volume of traffic; the number of vehicles on the roads has increased from 210,000 in 1930 to 2·2 millions, and Ostend is the entry port for large numbers of British motorists visiting the Continent. A considerable programme of reconstruction has been in progress since 1920, much accelerated during the last decade; it has involved the improvement of surfaces, the realignment of existing roads, the elimination of narrow bridges and the construction of new ones, the creation of bypasses to towns whose narrow though picturesque streets were major obstacles, and of underpasses at major junctions. In Brussels three ring roads have been constructed since 1945, with underpasses to avoid obstruction of flow at intersections with the radial arteries.

The difficulty of superimposing a motorway network upon such a crowded country is acute, but a national *autoroute* plan was formulated in the early 'thirties, now integrated with those of neighbouring countries. This includes the Ostend–Brussels motorway, which runs straight across country, bypassing Bruges, Ghent and Aalst. A motorway carries very heavy traffic between Brussels and Antwerp, and another has been completed across the Kempen from Antwerp via Liège to Aachen in West Germany, where it links up with the *Autobahn* system. Others under construction will link Antwerp and Brussels with the Lille Paris motorway in France, Antwerp with Rotterdam and Eindhoven, and Liège with Charleroi and Mons.

Railways

Belgium has a route mileage of 4320 km (2684 miles), with an average density which is the highest of any country in the world, though it varies appreciably in different parts of the country. In Flanders, Hainaut and Brabant ease of construction and the presence of many towns encouraged a close net. In the wooded Ardennes uplands the difficult terrain and the sparse settlement precluded much construction, except for the international Brussels–Namur–Arlon–Luxembourg line, completed in 1859, which provides a through-route between the North Sea coast and Switzerland.

The state-owned *Société Nationale des Chemins de Fer belges* operates at a profit in most years, though helped by a government subvention. Freight remains fairly constant at about 60 million tons annually, about two-thirds of that carried by the inland waterways.

Though a postwar programme of reconstruction (mainly to make good war damage) and of modernization is still in progress, only about a quarter of the route-length has been electrified; the number of diesel locomotives has been doubled during the last few years. Several stations have been modernized, notably in Brussels, on which converge seven lines carrying international traffic; the country's largest marshalling yard is at Schaerbeek in the north-eastern suburbs. Its two main stations are *Nord* and *Midi*, formerly linked only by circuitous belt-lines, although only 3·2 km apart in a straight line. Their junction by an underground link was begun as long ago as 1902, but the interruptions of two wars and more urgent reconstruction delayed until 1955 its completion, together with a new underground *Gare Centrale*.

The importance of the Belgian railway system lies not merely in its internal services, but in its international and transit contributions. Of the total 63 million tons of freight carried in 1968, about 32 millions were classified as international, and a further 9 millions as transit, i.e. from one country to another across Belgium. The International Sleeping Car Company was founded at Liège in 1873, and established its headquarters at Brussels in 1876, where it remained until its transfer to Paris after 1945. Some of the famous 'named' trains still running through Belgium include 'Etoile du Nord' and 'Ile de France' (Amsterdam–Antwerp–Brussels–Paris), 'Edelweiss' (Amsterdam–Antwerp–Brussels–Namur–Luxembourg–Zürich), 'Parsifal' (Paris–Namur–Liège–Aachen–Cologne–Hamburg), 'Oiseau Bleu' (Brussels–Paris), 'Saphir' (Ostend–Brussels–Liège–Aachen–Cologne–Frankfurt-am-Main), 'Tauern' (Ostend–Brussels–Liège–Munich–Austria), 'Ostend–Vienna', 'Nord' (Ostend–Brussels–Cologne), and many more express trains from Ostend, one of the main passenger entries for western Europe, to Basle and other cities, coping with a large part of Europe's steadily increasing tourist traffic.

The Belgian 'light' or 'local' railways, the *chemins de fer vicinaux*, were originally operated by a number of separate organizations, privately, communally or provincially owned, though supervised by a state-controlled company created in 1884. By 1938 the services totalled 4800 km (3000 miles) of track and 800 km (500 miles) of bus routes. These light railways served a very useful purpose in catering for the rural populations in areas which did not merit standard-gauge lines and in transporting industrial workers to the factories. Since the War of 1939–45, the policy has changed. The route length operated has been doubled, but only a tenth consists of tracks with electric or diesel locos; the rest are bus routes, which are cheaper to run, more flexible, and less inconvenient than tramways along the roads. They contribute to Belgian mobility, for about 1·7 million people (excluding the urban systems) travel by them.

Waterways

Belgium is situated in close proximity to the triple delta of the Scheldt, Meuse and Rhine, though it controls the outlet of none of these. The system of natural waterways consists of two groups: the rivers focusing on the lower Scheldt, and the long curve of the Sambre–Meuse in the south-east. The steep northern edge of the Sambre–Meuse trough is the major physical obstacle to a unified waterway system, and is crossed by only two canals, the Albert in the east and the Brussels–Charleroi in the south.

The total length of navigable waterway is 1535 km (954 miles), of which a fifth are rivers, regularized and improved for navigation. The waterways in 1968 carried about 93 tons of freight, appreciably more than the railways; this is a considerable increase in recent years, for in 1949, when most of the war damage had been made good, the total freight handled was only 30·5 million tons. Since then government policy has stimulated the use of the waterways by a modernization programme, which when completed will allow 1,350-ton capacity barges to use all but the most minor waterways.

In 1955 the Government introduced a bill for a long-term plan to widen and deepen the Charleroi–Brussels and the Centre Canals, the Sambre between Monceau and Namur, the Meuse and the upper Scheldt. It is also intended to enlarge the Bruges–Zeebrugge (now renamed the Baudouin), the Bruges–Ostend and the Bruges–Ghent Canals.

The outstanding feature is the eastern circuit of the Albert Canal, the Sambre-Meuse, the Brussels canals and the Rupel-Scheldt estuary, linking the two coalfields, the industrial area of the south, the capital and the chief port. The Albert Canal (Fig. 53), 130 km (80 miles) in length, forms a direct link between Antwerp and Liège, an immense undertaking which took ten years to complete and was officially opened in 1940. The chief obstacle was the plateau to the west of the Meuse valley, which had to be pierced by a series of cuttings (Plate XLIII), one of which is 10 km (6 miles) long and in places 60 m (200 ft) below the plateau. The fall of 56 m (184 ft) between Liège and Antwerp is negotiated by six groups of locks. Its importance is shown by the fact that in 1968 over 60 million tons of freight were transported. Several ports have been constructed along it, notably the Genk coal port (Plate XLIV), which ships coal from two big Kempen collieries.

Useful, though less important, is the western circuit of the Scheldt, the Brussels canals and the southern link canals: the Antoing–Pommerœul, the Mons–Condé and the Centre Canals. The line of the Ghent–Bruges and Bruges–Ostend Canals is the only link with the North Sea, apart from ship canals from Bruges to Zeebrugge and from Ghent to Terneuzen on the Wester Schelde.

Such bulky commodities as coal, coke, stone, bricks, cement, oil and timber account for almost half the total freight.

Belgium's situation in western Europe is emphasized by the fact

11*

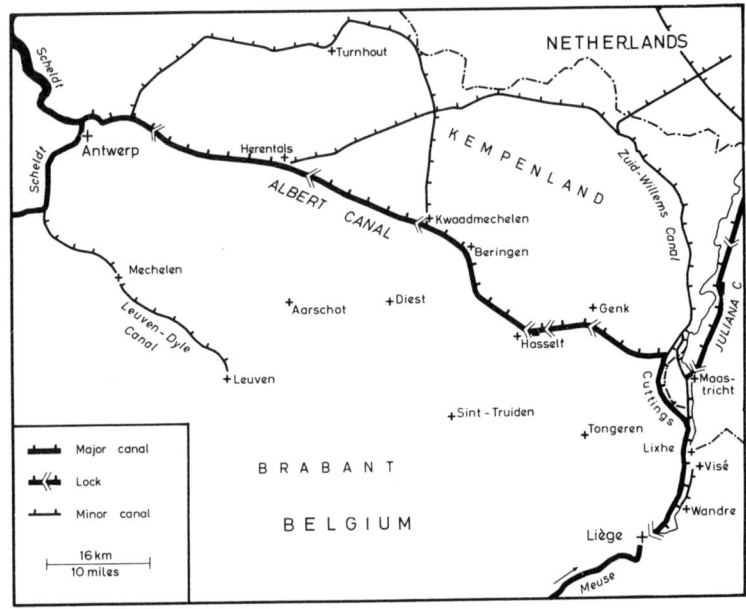

Fig. 53. The Albert Canal
(After A. Delmer)

that international and transit freight appreciably exceed inland freight. Its three neighbours, France, West Germany and the Netherlands, have well-developed systems of inland waterways; there are seven water links across the Franco–Belgian boundary and two across the Belgo–Dutch, apart from the delta route via the lower Scheldt and the Wester Schelde. A considerable amount of German traffic moves between Antwerp and the Rhine, working its way through the delta region and via the Zuid-Beveland Canal to the Wester Schelde (Fig. 43). Even 1,700 Swiss barge journeys were made in 1968 on Belgian waterways. One of the most important links is the Lanaye lock, completed in 1960, which enables large barges to pass from the Albert Canal into the port of Maastricht and so to the Juliana Canal.

Civil Aviation

Belgium follows France and the Netherlands in relative importance among European countries in the development of civil aviation. A monopoly is held by the *S.A. belge d'Exploitation de la Navigation aérienne*, founded in 1923, and known by its initial letters as *Sabena*. In the last decade the number of flights handled by the airports at Brussels, Antwerp, Ghent and Ostend has trebled, Brussels being an airport of international importance.

Ports and Mercantile Marine

Despite its North Sea coastline, Belgium does not share the well-developed maritime traditions of neighbouring countries. Its mercantile marine consisted in 1968 of only 92 vessels, of a total 885,000 g.r.t., which however represents a doubling of its prewar size and includes several motor vessels, oil-tankers and cross-Channel ferries. While Belgium's external trade is considerable, fourth in total value in Europe, a large proportion is carried in foreign vessels; only a ninth of the vessels which docked in Belgian ports in 1968 were registered in that country.

Mercantile trade is dominated by Antwerp, partly because it has long been one of the main commercial cities of Europe, partly because it stands on the Scheldt estuary; in the words of the proverb, 'Antwerp owes the Scheldt to God, and everything else to the Scheldt'. But because 55 of the 93 km (34 of the 58 miles) between Antwerp and the mouth of the estuary lie in Dutch territory, there has been the long-debated 'Scheldt question'. The Dutch sought to cripple Antwerp's trade by denying maritime access, and so closed the Scheldt from 1648 to 1792. It was not until 1863 that the Dutch right to levy tolls on Scheldt navigation was bought out by Belgium and other maritime countries. The Wester Schelde has a dredged and buoyed fairway. Until the mid-19th century most traffic used the river quays, but gradually a series of docks was opened below the city, entered through locks. Successively larger docks have been constructed downstream, east of and parallel to the Scheldt. In 1956 work began on a major scheme to extend the port; several new docks have been constructed still further downstream, almost to the Dutch border, including one with the large Zandvliet lock (opened in 1967) to accommodate super-tankers. Through the Antwerp docks passes about four-fifths of the foreign trade of Belgium and Luxembourg. In 1968 unloadings totalled 53·2 million tons and loadings 17·7 million tons. A wide range of commodities is included: imports of mineral oil, ores, coal, timber, foodstuffs, 'colonial goods' and other raw materials; exports of manufactured goods, especially steel, chemicals, glass and textiles. But although Antwerp's trade has steadily increased, that of Rotterdam has grown more rapidly (p. 270 and Fig. 44), although about 85 per cent of the latter's huge total consists of bulk cargo, compared with Antwerp's 70 per cent; this is because of Rotterdam's position at the mouth of the Rhine as the 'gateway of Europe'. Antwerp has also developed a highly efficient series of container-terminals.

The North Sea coast of Belgium has few ports, for it is straight, unbroken except for some sand-choked estuaries, and bordered by extensive banks and shoals. Ostend, Nieuwpoort and Zeebrugge require considerable port works, piers and moles, and constant dredging. Zeebrugge is wholly artificial, protected by a mole nearly 8 km (5 miles) in length; it handles imports of oil, raw chemicals and glass-sand, and exports coke, manufactured chemicals and cement. It has developed a busy container-terminal and a roll on/roll off car terminal. Apart from its fishing harbour, the main importance of Ostend is as a ferry port for England at the terminus of international railway routes and of a motorway; thousands of visitors use Ostend each year. Ghent is Belgium's second port, vessels entering by way of a recently enlarged ship canal from the Wester Schelde at Terneuzen; about 2,400 ships docked at Ghent in 1968, and 12·7 million tons of freight were handled.

COMMERCE

Belgian economy is highly dependent upon a thriving commercial activity; a third of its revenue is derived from foreign trade. As a densely populated, industrialized country, with a high standard of living, the trading pattern involves imports of raw materials and foodstuffs, and exports of manufactured goods, particularly those made of metal. The value of imports usually exceeds that of exports, but the adverse balance is normally not excessive; in 1968 the value of imports was 417 milliard fr., of exports 408 milliard fr. These statistics refer to the Belgo–Luxembourg Customs Union, as no individual returns are available for the two countries.

The main import items include ores (iron and a wide range of non-ferrous metals), raw cotton and wool, wheat and other foodstuffs, tobacco, coal and coke, timber and pulp, and a host of materials required by a diverse manufacturing industry. Some manufactured goods are imported, notably automobiles and their components; foreign-made cars are assembled, as at the *General Motors* and *Ford* plants in Antwerp and the *Ford* plant near Genk. Manufactured metal goods comprise more than two-fifths of the exports by value, followed by textiles, electrical apparatus and electric light bulbs, chemicals, cement, and glass (of which Belgium is the world's leading exporter). Though Belgium has fostered a policy of worldwide trade development, her chief trading partners for both imports and exports were the Netherlands, West Germany and France in that order, a reflection of the increasing collaboration of the Benelux countries and of the members of the E.E.C. Then follow the U.S.A., the U.K. and Italy.

Belgium was forced to accept the independence of the Congo in 1961. The material loss was considerable, for Belgium had maintained a favourable trade balance with the Congo which largely offset an overall adverse balance with other countries. In 1961 and subsequently several missions were sent to Latin America and Asia to stimulate Belgium's extra-European trade.

POPULATION AND SETTLEMENT

The population of Belgium at the end of 1968 was officially estimated to be 9·63 million, with an average density of 314 per sq. km (814 per sq. mile), a figure exceeded in Europe only by the Netherlands. During the nineteenth century the growth of population was rapid, associated with industrialization; between 1850 and 1914 the annual rate of natural increase varied between 8 and 11 per thousand. The War of 1914–18 marked a turning-point; between 1920 and 1939 the birth rate revealed a decline almost every successive year, while the death rate remained virtually stable. By 1935 the rate of natural increase per thousand had fallen to 2·6, compared with 11·0 in the Netherlands, whose population in that year exceeded the Belgian total for the first time; by 1967 the excess had reached 3 millions. Since 1945 the Belgian birth rate has remained fairly stable at between 16 and 17 per 1,000, and the rate of natural increase, about 5 per 1,000, is still one of the lowest in Europe.

Foreign Population

Since 1920 an appreciable increase has taken place in the number of foreigners resident in Belgium, for the marked shortage of labour, especially in the less attractive branches of industry, was met by importations of workers. From 1922 onwards trainloads of foreigners, mainly Poles and Italians, arrived, particularly in such new industrial areas as the Kempen. Since 1945 the same tendency has been evident, particularly after the Italo–Belgian Coal Agreement of 1948. In 1968 about 678,000 foreigners were domiciled in Belgium.

Distribution of Population

The average density figure of 314 per sq. km (814 per sq. mile) screens considerable differences between various parts of Belgium. The most densely populated province is Brabant (640 per sq. km, 1658 per sq. mile) but without the Brussels conurbation the average would be below the national figure, partly because agriculture, though productive, is on an extensive basis with large mechanized holdings. The second province in density in Antwerpen, the result of the presence of the Antwerp conurbation, for much of the eastern part of the province consists of thinly populated heathlands. The two Flanders provinces are also above the national average, though the figure for the East is greater than the West, the combined result of the intensity of agriculture, the numerous farms and houses, the large number of towns, including Ghent, and the highly developed industrial life. Hainaut includes the western part of the industrialized Sambre–Meuse region.

The remaining four provinces have densities markedly below the national average. In the north-east is the largely heathland province of Limburg, though the development of the coalfield and of other industry has caused a more rapid proportional growth of population in this province since 1900 than in any other, 133 per cent, compared with 34 per cent for Belgium as a whole. The provinces of Liège, Namur and Luxembourg contain the wooded Ardennes uplands, though the first includes part of the Sambre-Meuse industrial region, as well as the city of Liège and its neighbourhood, so that its average density is still comparatively high. The density of Namur was 104 per sq. km (269 per sq. mile), and Luxembourg, which includes the High Ardennes and the rather remote Belgian Lorraine, had a density of only 50 per sq. km (130 per sq. mile).

Towns and Cities

Urban life flourished early in Belgium, and medieval towns grew with the industrial and commercial prosperity of the country. Although many were adversely affected by long periods of warfare. they expanded rapidly in the nineteenth century with modern industrialization. Belgium is not as highly urbanized as the Netherlands, for it has only ten towns with more than 50,000 people, compared with forty in the latter, though the Brussels conurbation exceeds a million inhabitants.

It is, however, difficult to evaluate the urban population, since figures are available only on a commune basis. On the one hand, several contiguous communes may fuse to form a single town or city; thus Brussels consists of eighteen, Antwerp and Liège of six, and Ghent of four. Charleroi, with a commune population of only 24,000, is surrounded by the satellite towns of Jumet, Gilly, Montignies, Marcinelle and Marchienne-au-Pont, giving a total population of 283,000. Conversely, a single commune figure may be the aggregate of a number of villages; Genk has a population of 56,000, comprising the old town, some hamlets, and several large housing estates where live the workers at the collieries and factories, separated by farmland, heathland and coniferous plantations.

It is probably more difficult in Belgium than in any other country to differentiate between the urban and rural, industrial and agricultural population, for many people live at considerable distances from their places of employment and some industrial workers own and work smallholdings. The population of the suburbs of some towns has steadily grown, while the number living in the centre has declined, so that town and country are often intermingled. The Sambre-Meuse industrial region, for example, consists of an almost continuous line of 'urban villages'. This tendency has been encouraged by the excellent systems of suburban railways, light railways and bus services, which facilitate the journey to work.

Rural Settlement

In Belgium three basic types of rural settlement can be distinguished: nucleated, dispersed and agglomerated, though with the growth of population much of the distinctiveness of the three types has disappeared as settlement has spread into and filled much of the intervening spaces.

Nucleated settlements imply the grouping of houses into compact units, separated by open agricultural land, woodland, or heathland. They occur in the plateau of Hesbaye, in part because the chalk terrain localizes water supply, so that houses are grouped around a single deep well. They occur too, for different reasons, in the Ardennes, many of them originally sited in isolated forest clearings.

Dispersed settlements consist of individual houses, each standing in its own fields or smallholding, sometimes with only a church to indicate the commune centre. Occasionally an inn with a few shops may be grouped at a cross-roads, or where a road crosses a canal. Flanders is the type area for dispersed settlement, with the houses scattered over the countryside. Another area of dispersion lies in the east of the country in the Pays de Herve, between the Meuse valley and the West German border, where the landscape is very similar to that of Hesbaye to the west of the Meuse, with the same combination of limon soils developed on chalk. The fact that settlement is dispersed in Herve but nucleated in Hesbaye shows that water supply is not always the determining factor.

In the agglomerated settlement buildings are loosely grouped, though separated by open country with dispersed houses. Agglomeration is found mainly in northern and central Belgium, with an extension from south of Liège to the West German frontier. Subtypes include hamlets located where local roads cross State highways, hamlets with a double line of houses down a single street, formless hamlets with outlying farms (the well-named '*villages-nébuleuses*'), and industrial villages and housing estates located near a large factory or colliery.

The Flemish–Walloon Problem

During recent years such statements as 'Belgium is harried by chronic disunity', and 'Racial antagonism divides Belgium' have appeared in the press of western Europe. The basis of this disunity is linguistic, the two languages involved being Walloon, a French dialect, and Flemish, a form of Dutch, of which there are several dialects, though 'standard Dutch' is the language of instruction and of educated Flemings, and is used in newspapers and books. The dividing line between the two languages runs from Menin (Meenen) in the west to Tongeren in the east; Brussels lies just north of this line, and is officially a bilingual city. Approximately 56 per cent of the population speak Flemish alone, 11 per cent are bilingual, and about 32 per cent speak Walloon alone, except for about 61,000 German speakers in the east. The bilingual group are mostly Flemings, for they have more incentive to learn a second language of worldwide use than have the Walloons to learn Flemish.

Since the early Middle Ages, French has been the language of the educated classes and of the administration, especially in the nineteenth century after the attainment of Belgian independence; the Walloon element was then clearly dominant and Flemish became merely 'the language of the home and the inn'. During the nineteenth century a Flemish movement made headway, partly through the influence of the Roman Catholic Church, partly through a literary and cultural revival. Towards the end of the century this movement acquired an increasingly political flavour and purpose, in its more extreme aspects with nationalist tendencies, and as the numbers of Flemings increased, so did their influence in national elections.

After the War of 1914–18 some reforms were effected, culminating in the law of 1932 which established the 'language line'; to the north of it Flemish place names were made the official form, to the south place names are in French, though alternative forms of most exist. Local administration is carried out in the official language for the area, but for State purposes there is a complete basis of equality; simultaneous translation is used in Belgian parliamentary proceedings. Since the War of 1939–45 the problem has become more acute; the language line separates Flemish-speaking Roman Catholic conservatives from French-speaking anti-clerical socialists, though these divisions are far from clear-cut. Economically the disparity has increased; the flourishing new industries of the north contrast with the declining southern coalfield, its obsolete factories and its increasing unemployment. The average Walloon family has one child, the average Flemish family has four or five, and the Flemings now outnumber the Walloons by 2·4 millions.

Several attempts have been made to modify the position of the language line, as recently as 1967, but the whole problem has been exacerbated between 1968 and 1970. Certain militant groups have even suggested the creation of two separate states within a federation. The Flemings protest that they are still treated as second-class citizens, and that all the senior posts in the civil service, in business, and in the army are held by Walloons. The latter are worried at the growing economic ascendency of the Flemings, and complain that most new factories are established in the Flemish districts.

REGIONS

1. *Maritime Flanders*

This coastline is an almost continuous holiday resort, for as well as the major centres, Ostend and Blankenberge, many -*baden* and -*plages* are fronted by promenades and sea walls, and among the dunes are hotels, holiday camps and caravan parks. Ostend (Oostende in Flemish, Ostende in French) (57,000) is an important ferry port at the terminus of an international railway route. It is also the chief Belgian fishing port, with associated fish-curing and canning plants, refrigeration plants and fertilizer factories. A large shipyard builds trawlers and such specialized craft as dredgers. Nieuwpoort (Nieuport), situated about 3 km (2 miles) up the Ijzer estuary, has a harbour for tramp steamers and fishing boats, and its industries include a chemical works. Zeebrugge handles a varied commercial traffic, mostly imports of oil and exports of coke, chemicals and glass-sand; it is the terminus of container-traffic with the U.K.; its activities include the *Solvay* chemical works, a coke-oven plant and the largest glass furnace in the world.

Behind the coastal dune-belt an area of polderland extends inland for from 8 to 16 km (5 to 10 miles) to approximately the 5-m contour. The polders are covered with a maze of drainage ditches, many in orderly geometrical patterns, others in irregular chaos; some of the latter were formerly tidal creeks. They lead into larger channels and then into a few major outfalls. About 50 per cent of the polders are under permanent grassland, while much of the remainder grows rotation grass, with oats and green crops as fodder for the large dairy herds which produce milk for the towns of central Belgium. Pig-rearing is usually associated with dairy farming. Sheep, the basis of the medieval Flemish woollen industry, once grazed in large numbers on the salt-marshes and grass-covered mud-flats; some are still to be seen, mostly in the east, but are few in number in comparison with the past. Farther south on the slightly higher lands sugar beet, flax and malting barley are grown. The demands of neighbouring urban markets have resulted in market gardening, producing early vegetables on the sandy soils where the dune belt meets the polders.

Farms stand on sandy ridges or hillocks away from the damp pastures, and with an occasional line of pollarded willows or poplars they form the only interruptions to the open countryside. A few small market towns include Veurne (Furnes), the focus of four waterways, six roads and a railway, the market centre of the frontier district; it has a few small processing industries, but its population is only about 7,300.

Bruges (Brugge) (51,000) is situated on the edge of the polderland 13 km (8 miles) from the sea, to which it is linked directly at Zeebrugge by a ship canal and also by a much longer waterway, the Ghent–Ostend Canal, which wanders across the plain. The old town, encircled and intersected by canals, exists mainly on its dual function as a tourist centre and as a market for the northern parts of West-Vlaanderen. Considerable industrial developments have taken place outside the old town along the canal basins, including small ship-building yards, engineering works which construct bridges and rolling-stock, breweries, flour mills, a yeast factory and several timber yards. Craft industries (lace-making, embroidery, wood-carving, fine printing and glass painting) cater both for tourists and for export.

2. *Interior Flanders*

Inland of the coastal lowlands lies the plain of Interior Flanders, between the 5- and 50-m contours, across which the Lys, Scheldt and Dender flow slowly north-eastward in their alluvium-floored valleys towards the Scheldt estuary.

Interior Flanders has for centuries been one of the most closely settled and densely populated areas in Europe, with a flourishing agricultural, industrial and commercial economy, and its many towns have been prosperous centres of urban life, as their architectural glories testify. Agriculture is carried on intensively, much of it on a horticultural scale, for holdings are small. Long before the Agrarian Revolution in England the hard-working Flemings had discovered the value of heavily manuring the sandy soils, thus obviating the necessity of a wasteful period of fallow. Hops, potatoes, sugar beet, chicory, flax and wheat are grown in small patches, often by spade cultivation. On many holdings more than one main crop is produced each season; turnips, for example, sometimes follow a cereal, and high yields are general, the result of heavy manuring both with artificials and dung. Clover and fodder crops are included in the rotations to feed dairy cattle; each holding has a small herd of two or three animals to produce milk, butter, cheese and veal, contributory items in a mixed farming economy.

Towards the south, in West-Vlaanderen and Hainaut, the size of farms increases, mechanization replaces the spade cultivation of northern Flanders, and large fields of wheat and sugar beet become evident. Some specialization has developed in industrial crops: flax in the valley of the Lys near Kortrijk and Tielt, tobacco in the Ieperle valley, and chicory between Kortrijk and Roeselare, while potatoes are widely grown in the sandy soils.

To this intensive agriculture Interior Flanders adds a considerable industrial development, mainly concerned with textile and metallurgical manufacturing, at Ghent, Tournai, Kortrijk and Ronse. Two large towns are situated in this lowland, Ghent and Antwerp. Ghent is a focus of waterways, for the Lys and the upper Scheldt meet in its south-eastern suburbs, the lower Scheldt flows eastward towards the estuary, a recently enlarged ship canal from Terneuzen enters the docks in the north-east, and a smaller canal leads eastward across the plain from Bruges and Ostend; there are said to be over 200 bridges within the city, and the built-up area lies on twenty-three islands. Ghent has had a long and prosperous history; as early as 1500 it had a population of over 100,000, as a result of its industrial

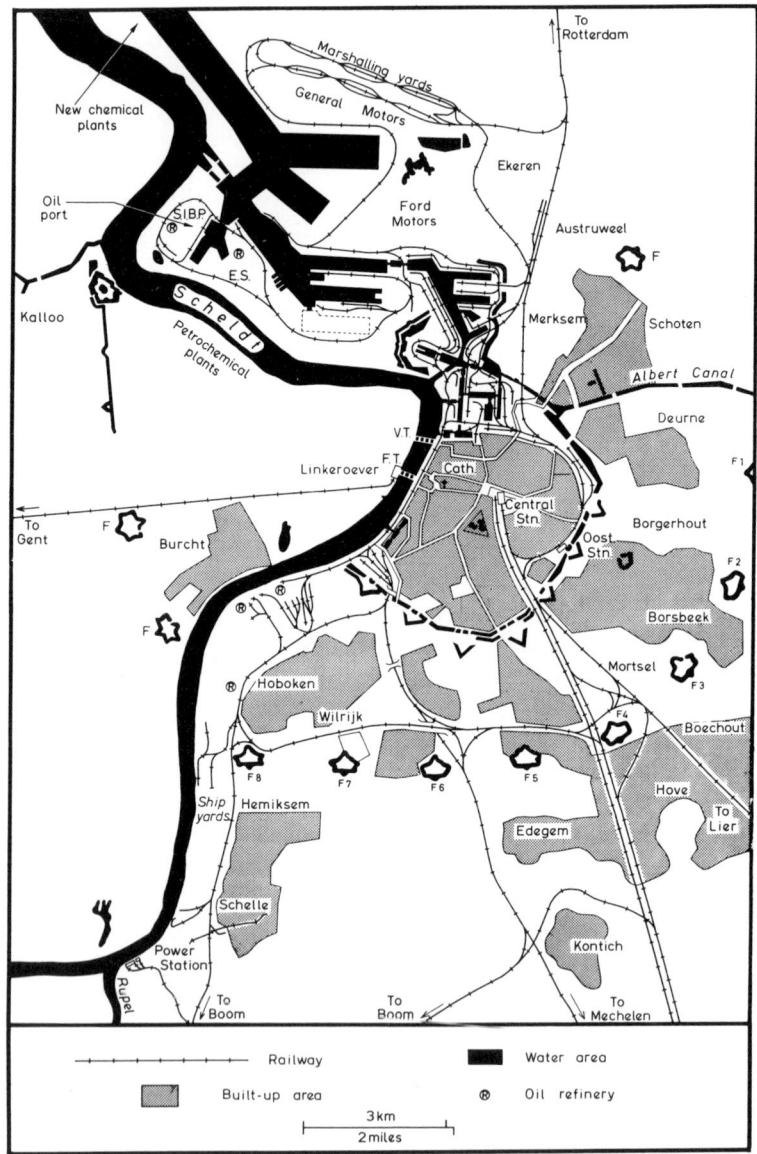

Fig. 54. Antwerp
(After *Falkplan von Antwerpen*)
A new vehicular tunnel under the Scheldt, part of the E3 motorway (Stockholm–Paris–London) was opened in 1968.

and commercial activity. In 1968 the population of the commune was 153,000, though several adjacent suburbs brought the total for the agglomeration to over 230,000. Ghent is the dominating centre of the Belgian textile industry (except for woollens), and it has an immense variety of related manufactures, such as carpets and clothing. Chemicals (especially dyestuffs), fertilizers, metallurgical products and glassware are made, and around the docks and in the eastern and northern suburbs are flour mills, sawmills, tanneries, paper mills (one of these produces half of Belgium's requirements of newsprint), a low temperature carbonization plant, an electro-chemical works, a new large steel-plant, and an oil-refinery. These modern industrial developments and the new suburban housing estates contrast with the old inner town, where stand some of the architectural glories of Belgium: the Hotel de Ville, the Halle aux Draps (Cloth Hall) and the cathedral.

Antwerp (Fig. 54) is not strictly in the Plain of Flanders, but is really the focus of the whole lowland. On its barge docks converges inland waterway traffic, and its port functions (p. 315) and commercial and industrial traditions have caused it to grow into a city of 234,000; with its half-circle of contiguous communes to east and south, the total population of the conurbation exceeds 650,000. A variety of industry has developed in the suburbs: vegetable oil and sugar refineries, flour mills and tobacco factories, and chemicals, soap, margarine, chocolate and rubber articles are manufactured. There are several oil-refineries and petrochemical plants, for a quarter of Antwerp's imports now consist of crude oil. The metallurgical and engineering industries include shipbuilding, marine engineering, car assembly, the construction of cranes, bridges and heavy machinery, and non-ferrous metallurgical products; and along the estuary are large glass, pottery, brick and cement works. The diamond industry, established for a little over a century, is now considerably more important than that of Amsterdam.

Much of the neighbouring polderland is intensively cultivated, largely to supply the demands of Antwerp's population. Numerous prosperous villages are the homes of Antwerp commuters, who travel daily into the city.

3. *The Central Low Plateaus*

Most of central Belgium forms an area of prosperous agriculture, varying in character according to the quality of the soils. The clay soils in the south-west are mostly under permanent pasture, while the sandy and loamy soils farther east are under the plough and large hedgeless fields grow wheat and sugar beet. Intensive market gardening and horticulture are practised in the neighbourhood of the towns, particularly near Brussels.

Farther east the plateau of Hesbaye consists mainly of chalk covered with limon, with a countryside of open fields; arable farming is predominant, and in southern Hesbaye the emphasis is almost exclusively on the cultivation of wheat and sugar beet on large holdings. Farther north agriculture becomes more mixed in character, and includes market gardening and fruit growing on the sandy loams, as in the neighbourhood of Tongeren.

Central Belgium has an average population density of 150–190 per sq. km (400–500 per sq. mile), figures swollen by the considerable urban population, for some of the towns have had a flourishing existence for a thousand years or more. The Flemish textile industry extends eastward into Brabant, particularly at Brussels, Braine-l'Alleud, Anderlecht and Court-St Etienne. In the Senne valley the towns of Halle, Braine-le-Comte and Soignies have metallurgical, textile and food-processing industries. At Clabecq in the Sennette valley a large integrated iron and steel works is situated on the banks of the Brussels–Charleroi Canal.

Farther east Leuven, Nivelles and a host of smaller towns, many within the orbit of Brussels, share the well-developed industrial life of Belgium. Leuven (Louvain) (33,000) stands in a gap through the northern edge of the Brabant plateau. It is a market centre for the surrounding agricultural countryside, and has extensive food-processing industries, particularly brewing, flour-milling, the manufacture of potato starch and vegetable-canning, while metallurgical industries include the manufacture of agricultural machinery, and there are chemical works, tanneries and sawmills. The Leuven–Dyle Canal, linking the town with the Rupel and the lower Scheldt, carries a considerable tonnage of such commodities as fertilizers, flour, bricks and timber.

Vilvoorde (34,000) is situated where the Senne cuts through the northern edge of the plateau of Brabant in a well-defined gap, also followed by the Willebroek Canal. Following a long period of decline, the town shared in the nineteenth-century expansion of industry, and particularly in the prosperous period of 1896–1914. The manufacture of fertilizers, vegetable oils, glue, starch and leather is established in the suburbs, and many specialized factories, such as those making textiles and gloves, still operate within the town itself.

Brussels (in French Bruxelles, in Flemish Brussel) has for long been one of the great cities of Europe (Plate XLV). The agglomeration, including fifteen contiguous communes, has a total of 1·1 million people. The city originated in the sixth century on one of the islands among the marshland of the braided Senne, which flows through the western part of the city, now mostly vaulted over and incorporated within the city's drainage system, although it emerges in the north-western suburbs. The town developed rapidly from the eleventh century as its industrial and commercial activities increased. The built-up area grew on the drier terraces along the east bank, and it has now spread on to the sandstone plateau beyond; there is a clear distinction between the lower town, with the commercial quarter, the spacious Grand' Place flanked by the fifteenth-century Hotel de Ville, the docks and the canal port, and the residential upper town with its parks, boulevards and squares. Considerable developments have taken place since the War of 1939–45, including a great extension of suburban housing estates and the building of blocks of flats and offices within the central area. Brussels has numerous administrative functions, is a great commercial centre and the main industrial district of Belgium. Its industries include metallurgical products, textiles (carpets, blankets, clothing), chemicals, paper, furniture and consumer goods generally. It is a port in its own right, with a series of basins in the north-west of the city; the Brussels–Rupel Canal enables barges and small sea-going vessels of up to about 3,000 g.r.t. to reach the capital from the Scheldt estuary via the Rupel. From the southern end of the port the Brussels–Charleroi Canal crosses the plateau of Brabant to the Sambre industrial region. The city is an important railway focus, for seven lines carrying international traffic converge upon it and the country's largest marshalling yard is at Schaerbeek in the north-eastern suburbs.

Southern Hesbaye has many small towns and villages, most with fewer than 5,000 inhabitants; they have agricultural industries and occasional specializations, such as cutlery manufacture at Gembloux. Farther north a line of larger towns is strung out along the medieval trade-route from Antwerp and Bruges via Leuven to the Rhineland; these include Tienen in the valley of the Grande-Gette, Sint-Truiden and Tongeren. Tienen (Tirlemont) (23,000 inhabitants) lies on the northern margins of the sugar beet area, and possesses the largest sugar refinery in Belgium, as well as other agricultural processing industries: flour mills, tanneries, starch factories, and a factory making citric acid.

The northern margins of the low plateaus are defined by the broad Demer valley; its light warm sandy soils when heavily fertilized are suitable for the intensive cultivation of vegetables, particularly of early varieties. Numerous villages and towns form market centres, both for the southern Kempen and the Demer valley, and have flourishing industries. Diest (9,695) is a centre of flour-milling and other forms of food-processing, brewing and distilling; Aarschot (12,140) also carries on food-processing; Lier (29,000) manufactures textiles and chemicals, and Duffel (13,000) has textile and metallurgical works. The most important industrial town is Mechelen (Malines) (66,000), situated at only 8 m (25 ft) above sea-level on the banks of the Dyle, which flows through the town in several branches. It is an agricultural and market-gardening centre and its industries include food-processing, furniture, textile and clothing factories, paper mills, printing works and tanneries. The town of Boom (17,000), on the northern bank of the Rupel, is one of the main centres of brick-making; yards line the river banks between Boom and Rumst.

4. *The Kempen*

The Kempen plateau, lying mostly between 45 and 75 m (150 and 250 ft), but rising in the south-east to about 100 m (330 ft) above sea-level, forms a watershed between the Scheldt and the Meuse systems. This south-western section of the European heathlands is characterized by poor leached soils developed on superficial sheets of sand and gravel; a considerable extent of bare sand, often blown into dunes; a vegetation cover of heath associations, notably ling; and in the higher bleaker parts tracts of moorland. Reclamation of these heathlands has gone on for centuries. Around each village the sandy soils have gradually been improved by adding humus, marl and fertilizers; and potatoes, wheat, rye, sugar beet and vegetables are grown. It is, however, usually more profitable to put the land under permanent pasture with carefully selected types of grass suitable for dry sandy soils. At one time the Kempen supported large flocks of sheep, but they have been replaced by cattle to supply milk and veal to Brussels, Antwerp, and other large towns. Plantations of Scots and Corsican pine have been established, and about a seventh of the region is forested.

In the higher eastern Kempen the sparse population lives mostly in small villages near the plateau edge, with another line on the terraces along the western banks of the Meuse. Very few settlements are to be found on the plateau itself; one is Asch, at a height of 80 m (260 ft), a focus of roads across the plateau, a minor railway junction, and a small servicing centre. Of recent construction are the housing estates (Plate XLII), built for the labour in the collieries and at the chemico-metallurgical works sited near the industrial units they serve. The regional centre of the eastern Kempen is Hasselt (39,000) in the Demer valley; it is the administrative centre of the province of Limburg, a market and shopping centre, with a busy port on the Albert Canal, and industrial activities including food-processing (flour mills, distilleries, tobacco factories, breweries and a gelatine works), brick and tile works, timber yards, several tanneries, a glue works, a soap works and some fertilizer factories.

The character and aspect of the Kempen change gradually westward towards Antwerp, with progressively less heathland, more deciduous trees, more fenced fields, more market gardening and dairy farming, and more villages and small towns. The regional centre of the western Kempen is Turnhout (38,000), a prosperous market, industrial and administrative town on the railway line between Antwerp and Tilburg, and on the Desschel–Turnhout–Schoten Canal. One group of factories carries on the manufacture of drawing-paper, stationery and fine papers, situated within the city in blocks among the houses and shops; it has important printing and bookbinding trades, and is the world's largest centre for the manufacture of playing cards. Other old established industries include the manufacture of coarse linen, twill, sacking and canvas, and lace is still made as a piecework domestic industry. A second newer group of factories operates to the north-west of the town near a basin on the canal: timber yards and sawmills, a cement works, a flour mill, and a steel works making agricultural implements. Turnhout is the centre of a brick-making district and the yards, producing a quarter of the Belgian output, are along the banks of the canal. Cement is made near Turnhout and Beerse, using lime brought by barge from the kilns near Visé in the Meuse valley. Mol is another small industrial and market town on the railway between Antwerp and Neerpelt; within the town several factories make cigars, leather goods, pottery, small articles of metal and wood, textiles and clothing. Herentals has similar industries, including also articles of copper and bronze, and glassware.

The Kempen contains a number of major industrial units, deliberately sited in the heathlands, and these, with the six collieries, make it one of Belgium's industrial regions. Its advantages include cheap land for spacious factory sites and for the housing estates required to accommodate their workers, unpopulated areas available for the segregation of noxious or dangerous industries, the presence of the coalfield, and the proximity of the port of Antwerp, while the building of the Albert Canal in the 'thirties was a major contribution. Most of the industrial establishments are on the waterways, usually at a rail–water intersection. They include zinc, copper and other non-ferrous refineries, chemical plants making sulphuric acid, copper sulphate, fertilizers and explosives, glass works (notably at Mol-Gompel), a *Ford* car assembly plant opened in 1963 in the commune of Genk on the banks of the Albert Canal, and a Belgo–American plant making stainless steel, also opened in 1963.

Much of the landscape has been strikingly modified by these collieries (one now closed), factories and housing estates. The commune of Genk in the heart of the heathlands, for example, contains two collieries which produce one-seventh of Belgian coal (Fig. 55). Its population was 1,776 in 1846, and still only 3,422 in 1910, but by 1968 it had risen to 56,000, of whom about a quarter were foreigners. But a third of the Kempen is still heath-covered, and the ceaseless activity at the collieries and factories only emphasizes the emptiness and loneliness of the sombre heathlands within which they stand.

5. *The Sambre–Meuse Valley*

In this 'industrial crescent', more than 160 km (100 miles) in length but only 5–16 km (3–10 miles) wide, live approximately a quarter of the people of Belgium. There are several large towns, Liège, Namur and Charleroi on the Sambre, which enters the industrial area a few miles above Charleroi, with Mons situated in the western part of the coalfield. These towns, surrounded by large sprawling villages, contain the greater part of Belgium's heavy industry: iron and steel, chemicals, glass and non-ferrous metallurgy, for which the coalfield provided the initial momentum and which it still helps to sustain. It is obvious from its appearance that this southern coalfield is an 'old' industrial area. Derelict collieries, overgrown spoil-banks, a chaos of pit shafts, blast furnaces and steel works, chemical factories, and long rows of small, drab dwellings in irregular rows, are typical of the crowded industrial development of the nineteenth century.

Not all the southern coalfield is like this. New housing estates and, particularly in the western part of the field, industrial villages, smallholdings and farmland intermingle in a manner characteristic of many parts of Belgium; and to the north of Mons, away from the cramping bounds of the Meuse valley, are the limon-covered arable

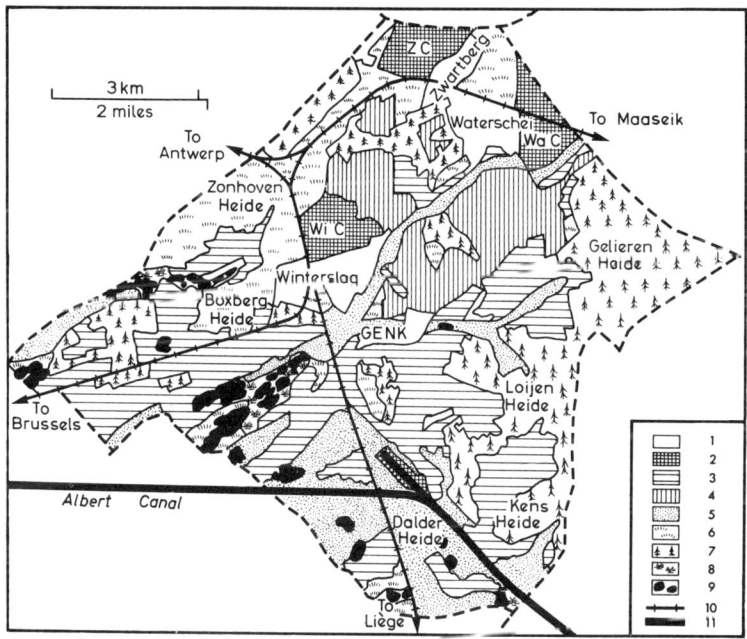

Fig. 55. Genk
(After a manuscript map made available by the commune of Genk, with additional field survey)
The numbers are as follows: **1.** built-up areas; **2.** industrial sites; **3.** smallholdings; **4.** field cultivation; **5.** pasture; **6.** heathland; **7.** woodland; **8.** marsh; **9.** meres; **10.** main-line railway; **11.** canal. The key refers only to the area of Genk commune. The three collieries are indicated by abbreviations, as follows: **Wa. C.** Waterschei; **Wi. C.** Winterslag; **Z.C.** Zwartberg (now closed).

lands of the Hainaut plateau. But elsewhere the concentration of industrial activity along the narrow valley leaves little space for planned development.

Liège is the fourth city of Belgium (Fig. 56), with a commune population of 150,000 and an official agglomeration exceeding 450,000. It stands in the trench of the Meuse near the junction of the Ourthe, with its tributaries the Vesdre and the Amblève, which have cut transversely across the Ardennes; the Ourthe valley provides one of the few routeways from the Meuse valley into the Famenne and the southern Ardennes, and Liège has long been a centre of communications. The Sambre and the Meuse upstream of the city are useful waterways, although they have required much regularization, while a few miles below the city the Albert Canal leads off the Meuse (p. 313) to form a link with Antwerp. The modern road system shares this focal character, which will be emphasized when the Belgian contributions to the European network are completed,

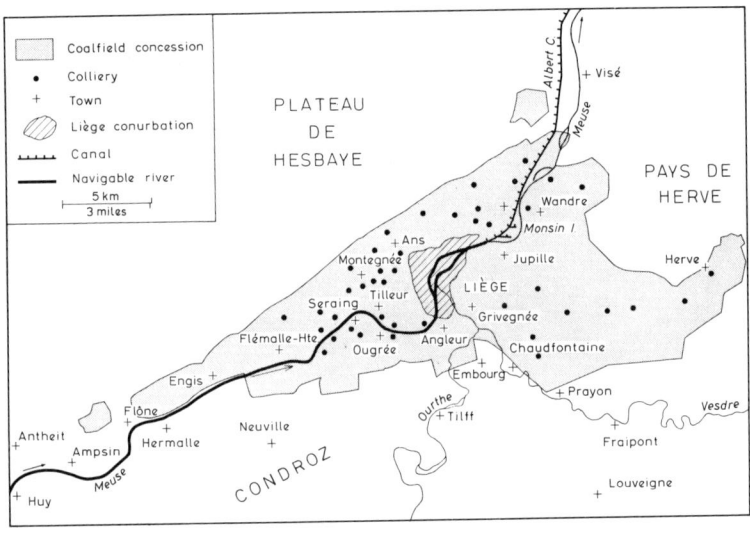

Fig. 56. The Liège industrial district
(After *Atlas de Belgique*, T. H. Elkins and J. A. Sporck)

for six arterial roads will converge upon the city. As a railway centre it has its problems; the main line from Brussels has to negotiate the northern edge of the Meuse valley, and routes southward through the Ardennes are difficult. Nevertheless, Liège is crossed by several international routes (Paris–Charleroi–Cologne following the Meuse valley, Amsterdam–Luxembourg–Basle, and Ostend–Brussels–Leuven–Cologne), and it is the focus of five other lines. It is not surprising that the city should have nurtured a flourishing commercial life. Its industrial activities, based originally on local iron ore, charcoal from the Ardennes forests, and water power from the many streams, have long been of major importance, and the coalfield has been worked from at least the twelfth century. Since the Industrial Revolution, the development of the Liège mining and metallurgical industries has been on a very considerable scale. It is a large producer of refined zinc, and has other non-ferrous refining and consuming industries. Many factories produce heavy chemicals, glassware, tyres, leather, fire-arms, pottery and light consumer goods.

Namur is a much smaller town (32,000), but it has an important position at the junction of the Meuse and the Sambre as 'the gateway to the Ardennes'. As a result, it has been a fortress town for centuries, and suffered many sieges, down to 1914 when the Germans captured it. Although the Namur basin's exploitable deposits of coal are exhausted, its heavy industries are well established, using coal brought by the waterways. In addition to steel-using industries ranging from cranes and boilers to cutlery, it has many miscellaneous manufactures: cement, glass, paper, leather, glue, soap, tobacco and even pianos. It is also an important market town and the centre of market gardening on the limon-covered area within the south-eastern angle of the Meuse.

Charleroi forms the heart of a considerable urban agglomeration on a basin of the southern coalfield, with metallurgical industries and two of Belgium's largest glass factories. Mons (28,000) is the centre of the most westerly part of the coalfield, known as the Borinage; villages and collieries spread beyond the town to the south-west. Unlike the other large towns, the Mons district has few heavy industries, except for some coke ovens, briquetting plant and chemical byproducts. On the other hand, various lighter industries include pottery and refractory ware, soap, textiles, tobacco, ropes and cement. Several large sugar refineries process beet grown in northern Hainaut.

6. *The Belgian Ardennes*

The Ardennes form the western part of the uplands lying across the Middle Rhine basin (p. 192). Their margins rise boldly from the surrounding lowlands, though the surface consists of an undulating plateau mostly above 300 m (1000 ft), from which swell rounded summits. Rivers flow westward or northward to the Meuse in deep winding valleys across the plateau. Shallow depressions contain bogs, while the drier eminences are heath-covered; woodland, mostly plantations of spruce and Scots pine, occupies about half of the area. Except in the lower, more sheltered parts of the Famenne, the thin infertile soils and the poor drainage of the bleak plateau are not favourable for agriculture. Precipitation is heavy, between 1000 and 1250 mm (40 and 50 in), partly in the form of snow which may lie for two months. Only a small part, mostly under permanent grass, consists of farmland. Beef cattle are bred to be sent to lowland districts for fattening, some dairying is practised in the Famenne, and oats, rye, clover and potatoes are cultivated in the valleys. The sheltered Semois valley in the south has a specialized production of tobacco, the chief cash crop of the farmers; it is grown intensively year after year on the same land with heavy fertilization, and smallholdings devoted to it are found on alluvial flats below the steep sides of the valley. The only other occupations of the scanty population are forestry for the production of pit-props and constructional timber, and quarrying.

The density of population is well below 40 per sq. km (100 per sq. mile) and much is quite unpopulated. A few small towns stand on the plateau, mainly along the railways which cross it: Butgenbach and Bullange in the north-east, St Vith, Bovigny, Bastogne and Libramont. St Vith was almost completely destroyed during the Ardennes offensive of 1945 and has been attractively rebuilt. Several railways negotiate this barrier between central Belgium and the Rhineland; the Brussels–Namur–Arlon–Luxembourg international line crosses the watershed near Libramont at a height of 490 m (1608 ft). Bastogne is particularly important as a route centre, for seven roads converge on it; it was therefore the focal point of the German offensive in 1944–45. These small towns are minor market centres for the high plateau areas, and some are tourist centres among attractive wooded valleys and pleasant walking country. The most famous is Spa, once called 'the café of Europe'; situated on the northern edge of the Hautes Fagnes, at a height of 240 m (800 ft) in a wooded valley, its mineral springs have made it a health resort since the sixteenth century, and in the eighteenth it was at the height of European fashion.

7. Belgian Lorraine

A small part of Lorraine, with an area of about 1000 sq. km (400 sq. miles), lies in the south-east of Belgium, with a succession of Jurassic calcareous sandstones, limestones, shales and marls trending in roughly parallel outcrops from west to east. These rocks offer a varied resistance to denudation, and form a series of north-facing escarpments (*côtes*). The most northerly escarpment consists of yellowish Lower Lias Sandstone, crossing the country to the north of Arlon; it is much dissected, rising to a number of wooded summits, the highest being the Hirtzenberg (465 m, 1526 ft) consisting of Mid-Lias calcareous sandstones. A few km farther south a second escarpment trends eastward from near Virton into the Grand Duchy, and rises in the east to form several hills. The third escarpment in the south comprises a short section of Oolitic Limestone, rising to 403 m (1322 ft), which can be traced for about 140 km (90 miles) from the Chiers valley almost to the Moselle, though only a small part is in Belgium; this gave the country a tiny portion of the iron ore field. Between these sandstone and limestone ridges appear Lias clays, marls and shales, within whose less resistant outcrops the river systems have developed their east–west vales. The Semois rises near Arlon, and flows westward until it crosses on to the Palaeozoic rocks of the Ardennes. Most of the remainder of Belgian Lorraine drains to the Chiers and so to the Meuse.

Belgian Lorraine was once completely under forest and almost half is still wooded, mainly with birch and pine on the sandy soils of the escarpments, although patches of beech and oak survive on the heavier clays. About two-thirds of the farmland is under pasture, while most of the remainder grows oats and other fodder crops, indicating the importance of animal rearing; of the 55,000 cattle, nearly a third are dairy stock, and in addition there are 11,000 pigs. Some fruit is cultivated, usually in 'grass orchards'.

The small portion of the Lorraine iron-ore field extending into Belgium stimulated developments in this southern district, and blast furnaces near Musson and Halanzy and an integrated steel works are still active, now mainly using ore imported from French Lorraine. The total population of Belgian Lorraine is 90,000, with a density of about 80 per sq. km (210 per sq. mile), mostly grouped in small nucleated villages in the vales. Arlon (13,000), situated at a height of 410 m (1350 ft), is the administrative centre of an *arrondissement*, a market town and a route focus; on it converge eleven main roads and it is the frontier station for the Brussels–Namur–Luxembourg international railway. The only other place of any size is Athus (7,000), chiefly important for its steel works.

CHAPTER TEN

The Grand Duchy of Luxembourg

LUXEMBOURG is a sovereign state with an area of 2586 sq. km (just under 1000 sq. miles), and with maximum north–south and west–east dimensions of only 82 km (51 miles) and 56 km (35 miles) respectively. It is situated in a critical strategic angle between France, Belgium, and West Germany. The population in 1968 totalled only 336,000, yet this small state plays a full part in world affairs: it is a member of the United Nations Organization, the North Atlantic Treaty Organization, the Organization for Economic Co-operation and Development, and the three European Communities. The city of Luxembourg is the seat of the 'High Authority' of the Coal and Steel Community.

STRUCTURE AND RELIEF

Luxembourg can be divided into two distinct physical regions (Fig. 57). The northern third (sometimes called the Oesling) forms part of the Ardennes; the southern portion, a section of the scarplands of Lorraine, is lower, with a milder climate, better soils and more productive agriculture than the Ardennes, and is given the name of the Bon Pays, or in German Gutland.

The Ardennes

The part of the Ardennes which extends into Luxembourg is structurally similar in character to that in Belgium (p. 287); the succession of Hercynian anticlines and synclines can be traced on Fig. 48. Devonian quartzites and slates predominate, appearing in parallel bands from south-west to north-east.

The Luxembourg Ardennes, situated on the eastern margins of the whole massif, are appreciably lower in elevation than in Belgium. The highest points, although inconspicuous as summits, reach 563 m (1847 ft) in the Burgplats in the north, and 555 m (1821 ft) in the Napoléonsgard in the west. The plateau varies in height from about 400 to 500 m (1300 to 1650 ft), but is deeply dissected by rivers

Plate XLII. Housing estate in the heathland near Genk, in the Kempen, Belgium

Plate XLIII. The Albert Canal west of the Lanaye lock, where it cuts through the edge of the plateau overlooking the Meuse valley in the Caster cutting

Plate XLIV. The coal port at Genk, opening from the Albert Canal, Belgium

Plate XLV. Brussels

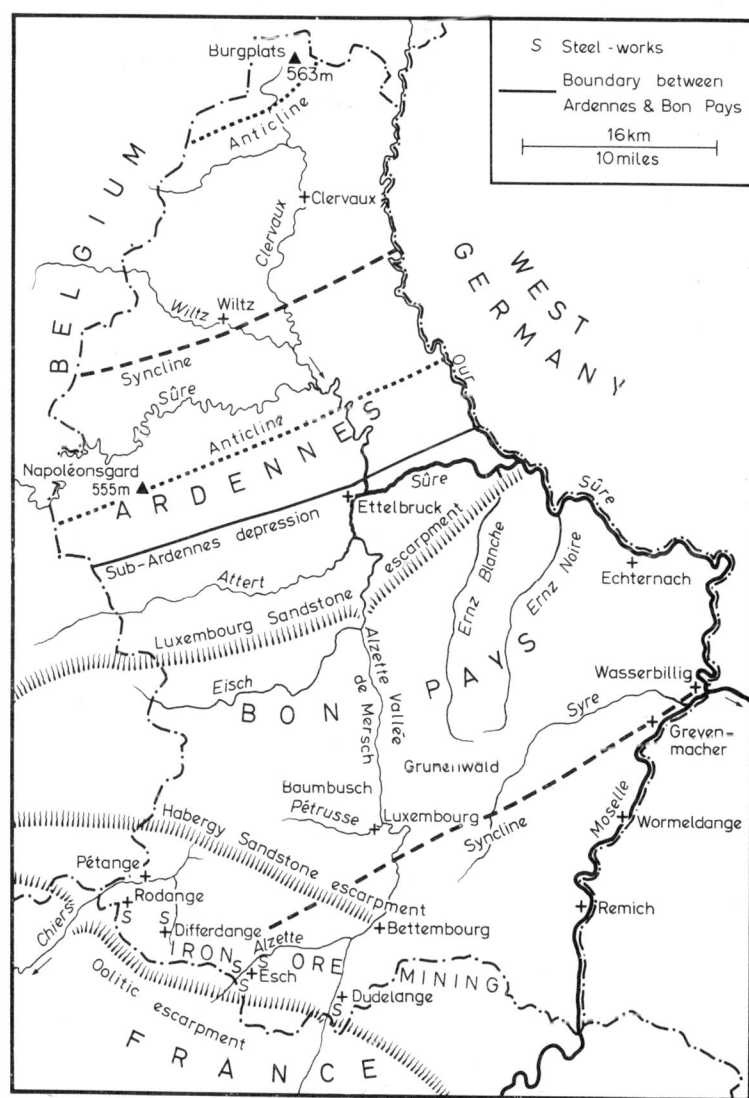

Fig. 57. Relief features of Luxembourg
The north-facing escarpments are indicated by hachures.
Heights are given in metres.

which, flowing south-eastward to the Sûre and so to the Moselle, have cut deep winding valleys, leaving rocky spurs within the meander-curves.

The Bon Pays

The southern edge of the Lower Palaeozoic rocks of the Ardennes recedes to the north-east, forming a triangular 'embayment' extending into West Germany beyond Trier. This re-entrant indicates the line of the broad Luxembourg Syncline, a Hercynian downfold parallel to the folding of the Ardennes, now infilled with Mesozoic rocks which have been subjected to a long period of differential denudation. As a result, the several outcrops of Triassic and Lower Jurassic rocks present the pattern of an acute angle pointing north-east, with successively younger rocks appearing to the south-west.

A pattern of drainage has developed in the Bon Pays which, except for the headstreams of the Chiers in the south-west, focuses entirely on the Moselle in the eastern angle of the country. This has produced a diverse landscape of low plateaus, steep-sided valleys, prominent escarpments, and open clay-floored vales. The oldest outcrop, that of the Bunter Sandstone, follows the edge of the Devonian rocks of the Ardennes; in it the Attert, Wark and Sûre have eroded a broad trough, the Sub-Ardennes Depression. The next formation, the Muschelkalk, is represented both in the north, where it succeeds the Bunter parallel to the edge of the Ardennes, and in the east along the Moselle valley. The Muschelkalk here differs from its usual shelly limestone character, for it consists rather of sandstones and marls in the lower beds, and of dolomitic limestones and sandstones in the upper. It forms a distinctive escarpment, though cut completely through by the Alzette, and in the east rises to some prominent little peaks 360–400 m (1200–1300 ft) in height. Within the angle of the Muschelkalk outcrop the Keuper rocks, mainly clays and marls, but including also layers of sandstones, limestones and some gypsum.

The central part of the Bon Pays consists of a low undulating plateau of Luxembourg (Lias) Sandstone, ending in the north in a distinctive escarpment. Most of this plateau lies between about 300 and 400 m (1000 and 1300 ft), the highest point occurring in the Grunenwald (437 m, 1434 ft) to the north-east of Luxembourg city. In several places this sandstone forms very impressive scenery. As the Alzette approaches the capital, its valley becomes a gorge with sinuous loops; the surface of the plateau lies almost 60 m (200 ft) above river level, and the tenth-century fortress which formed the nucleus of the city was built on the rocky peninsula between the Alzette and its tributary the Pétrusse. The winding valley of the Sûre between Reisdorf and Echternach, where the sandstone continues into West Germany, is also spectacular, though the most striking scenery is in the valley of the Ernz Noire, where not only has erosion cut deep gorges, but rain water has percolated into the fissures of the calcareous sandstone, enlarging them by solution, and forming chasms, grottoes and caverns. The rocks vary in resistance, and in places strata of siliceous sandstone, much less easily attacked than the calcareous sandstones, stand out boldly as buttresses and pinnacles, and rapids and falls occur where the harder strata outcrop across the valleys. These sandstones are densely wooded with beech, and the district, known as the Petite Suisse, is much visited by tourists.

To the south-west of the Luxembourg Sandstone plateau, outcrops of Middle and Upper Lias clay, shale and marl form undulating country between 240 and 300 m (800 and 1000 ft) above sea-level, while an outcrop of calcareous sandstone produces another distinct escarpment. In the extreme south-west a small part of the edge of the Oolitic Limestone escarpment is in Luxembourg; limited as it is, it provides the Grand Duchy with valuable deposits of iron ore. The edge of the escarpment forms hills overlooking the valleys of the Chiers and the Alzette; near Dudelange the Gintzenberg, on which stands Radio Luxembourg's transmitter, attains a height of 425 m (1394 ft).

The Moselle valley forms a depression along the south-eastern boundary; the lowest point in the Grand Duchy is 129 m (423 ft) near the Sûre confluence. The floodplain is covered with alluvium and gravel, and the valley slopes cut in the Keuper rise gently to the west. Where the Muschelkalk approaches the river the slopes are steeper, and step-faults have resulted in a series of terraces facing south-east, each backed by a prominent steep slope.

Extensive Quaternary deposits include Pleistocene gravels, coarse sands, and narrow strips of recent alluvium along the valleys. The Pleistocene deposits are found on the higher land along the Ardennes margins, in the west of the Bon Pays, and along the foot of the limestone scarp in the south-west. These gravels formerly contained alluvial iron ore in nodules or grains, redeposited from the ore beds to the south; the early iron industry developed because of the ready availability of these non-phosphoric ores, which could be smelted with charcoal.

CLIMATE

The climate of the Luxembourg Ardennes is neither so bleak nor so wet as that of the Belgian Ardennes, since it is appreciably lower and also lies in the rain-shadow of the higher plateau to the west; Clervaux in the north has a mean rainfall of about 810 mm (32 in). Few meteorological stations are situated on the plateau, but mean figures probably nowhere attain 1000 mm (40 in). Nevertheless, the elevation and exposure of the uplands result in bleakness, cloudiness and a mean snow cover of from twenty to thirty says, sometimes much longer, and frost occurs on an average on about a hundred days in the year.

Considerable climatic variations are experienced over the Bon Pays, in spite of its limited size. The Moselle valley lies to some extent in a rain-shadow and has a south-easterly aspect; as a result, it experiences a pleasant climate, with a mean annual rainfall of 660–710 mm (26–28 in), monthly temperatures varying from about 18° C. in June to 2° C. in January, only about forty-five days with frost, and long hours of sunshine. The rest of the Bon Pays has a higher rainfall, from about 810 to 960 mm (32 to 38 in), and is generally cooler and cloudier than the Moselle valley. Indeed, the highest rainfall figures for Luxembourg are found not in the Ardennes, but in the south on the exposed Oolitic escarpment, where the mean total exceeds 1000 mm (40 in). Considerable local variations occur; sheltered south-facing valleys experience more pleasant conditions than do the exposed plateau surfaces.

LAND USE AND AGRICULTURE

This marked contrast in physical features and climate between the Ardennes and the Bon Pays is reflected in the land use and agriculture. About a tenth of the country is forested, though rather surprisingly the proportion under woodland in the Ardennes is not much greater than in the Bon Pays, for large parts of the former consist of high moorland, poor grassland and bogs. Elsewhere solid blocks of conifers, mainly spruce, and more scattered beechwoods grow on the plateau surface, while the steep valley sides are thickly tree-covered.

In the Bon Pays extensive felling by charcoal burners in the eighteenth and nineteenth centuries provided fuel for the iron furnaces. The main surviving woodlands are on the Luxembourg Sandstone, notably in the neighbourhood of the capital, with the

Grunenwald to the north-east and the Baumbusch to the north-west, while the Marscherwald lies to the east of the Ernz Noire valley. Beech is the most common tree in the Bon Pays, though oak woods and mixed beech–oak woods are found. Conifers have been planted extensively, especially on the sandstone ridges, by the State Forestry Service.

The Ardennes

The Luxembourg Ardennes is not a favourable agricultural area, though potatoes and oats are grown on the plateau as subsistence crops and rye is still cultivated. One result of the more severe climate is that potatoes are grown for export as seed to the milder south. The rearing of livestock, particularly cattle and pigs, has recently become more important, and in an effort to improve the standard of animal husbandry, developments in co-operative livestock breeding and dairying have been effected. Syndicates have been created by voluntary associations of farmers, and co-operative dairies in northern Luxembourg send cream to a butter factory at Hosingen, or to another at Ettelbruck on the southern edge of the Ardennes. The agency operates a fleet of lorries to collect cream and despatch butter to retailers.

In the last few decades the pastures on the plateau have been improved as a result of ploughing and seeding with better grasses and the use of lime and fertilizers on the sour soils. The valleys, with their steep sides and winding narrow floors, are of little value for arable farming, although some of the alluvial flats produce hay, especially where they are intersected with irrigation channels, forming water-meadows which yield two crops annually.

The Bon Pays

The Bon Pays is a region of mixed farming, although local variations in relief, soils and climate are reflected in differences in emphasis. The damp alluvial valley floors and the heavier marls and clays in the west and the south-west tend to be under permanent pasture, while gentle slopes with well-drained soils on the calcareous sandstones are devoted to arable, in favoured areas to orchards and vineyards. Over the Bon Pays the land is divided more or less equally between cereals, roots, green fodder and permanent pasture. Oats make up almost half the grain crops, with some winter wheat for human consumption. Potatoes, fodder beet, turnips and swedes comprise the root crops, the first occupying two-thirds of the total arable area, and red clover and lucerne are grown to supplement the hay crop. Since the War of 1939–45 there has been a marked decrease in arable land and an increase in pasture and meadow. While the area under cereals has declined but little, in 1968 root crops occupied only half the area in 1938 and fodder crops only three-quarters.

Both dairy and beef cattle, mostly Friesians, are kept in the Bon Pays, and every holding has a few animals, large herds being rare. Milk is produced for the capital city and for the industrial towns in the south, as well as for sale to dairy co-operatives which supply the butter factories at Saeul and Ettelbruck. The skimmed milk returned to the farms is fed to pigs. There is not only a considerable demand within Luxembourg, for pork is one of the main items of diet, but some export to neighbouring countries.

Many fruit trees, including apples, cider apples, plums and damsons, are scattered through the Bon Pays in every village for local needs, and some large orchards, mainly on the south-eastern valley slopes, are owned by commercial growers. Rose bushes are cultivated on the heavy marls and clays of the Vallée de Mersch, though the area devoted to them has considerably declined; before 1914 about six million bushes a year were produced, but in the years before 1939 output fell to below a million, and since the War less than half a million have been grown annually, though they are still exported.

The Moselle valley is famed for its vines, and Luxembourg produces a range of both dry white and sparkling wines from the vineyards situated on the south-eastern slopes on terraces above the river. The valley is marginal for wine production, for the altitude is considerable, bitter winds from the uplands to the north may be experienced despite the sheltered slopes, and both late frosts and wet summers with sunshine below average are common, so that yield and quality fluctuate considerably.

MINING AND INDUSTRY

The basis of the iron and steel industry of Luxembourg is the extension of the Lorraine ore field for a few km across the French border into the Grand Duchy. As a result, the country is the thirteenth steel producer in the world, and until 1939 was fifth in order. Its economy is predominantly dependent on steel, which accounts for 65 to 75 per cent of the total productivity by value, and for 80 to 90 per cent of its exports. In 1968 about 23,000 people, one in every six of the working population, were employed in the steel industry; compare the relative figure of one in eighty for Great Britain.

Iron-ore Mining

The area of iron ore extends over little more than 36 sq. km (14 sq. miles), but the deposits are estimated to comprise 300 million tons of exploitable ore, with a metal content of 63 million tons. The field is divided into three basins by the river valleys. In the western basin, within the triangle of Rodange, Pétange and Differdange, and bounded on the south-west by the French border, the ore is mainly siliceous, with an iron content of about 28 per cent. Between the rivers Alzette and Kayl lies the Esch field, and east of the Kayl valley is the eastern field; these two deposits are calcareous, with an iron content of only about 24 per cent. Before 1939 the overall average content of ore mined varied between 30 and 31 per cent; this reduction over only twenty years indicates partly the working-out of the richer beds, partly the technological improvements which have enabled poorer ores to be economically utilized.

In 1968 some 6·4 million tons of ore were produced, of which about half was calcareous; the highest ever was in 1926 with 7·8 million tons. The number of mines in operation has been steadily reduced, though their individual output has increased. Two-thirds are open-cast, where the ore is worked in shallow quarries; the other mines are exploited by galleries driven horizontally into the escarpment and the sides of the valleys. The dip of the strata is for the most part gentle, with little structural disturbance, so that costs are low. Eleven mines, producing three-quarters of the total, are owned by three Luxembourg steel companies, six others by Belgian companies, and the remainder are small independent concerns.

The calcareous ores are almost wholly self-fluxing, and can be blended in the furnaces with siliceous ore. But the more accessible calcareous beds are being rapidly exhausted, and Luxembourg is unable to produce sufficient to supply its furnaces; consumption totals 12 to 13 million tons. Moreover, as a result both of geographical proximity and of industrial collaboration and financial relationships, the Grand Duchy exported a million tons, mostly to Belgium. About 7 million tons are imported annually from France.

Steel Production

The pattern of the steel industry has been dominated by the gradual integration of individual enterprises (Fig. 58), the largest of which is *Arbed*, created in 1911 by the merging of three companies. The *Terres-Rouges* company, incorporated in 1919 to take over installations and properties owned and operated by German interests, entered into association with *Arbed* in 1926, and they have now merged to form one of Europe's largest combines, employing 22,000

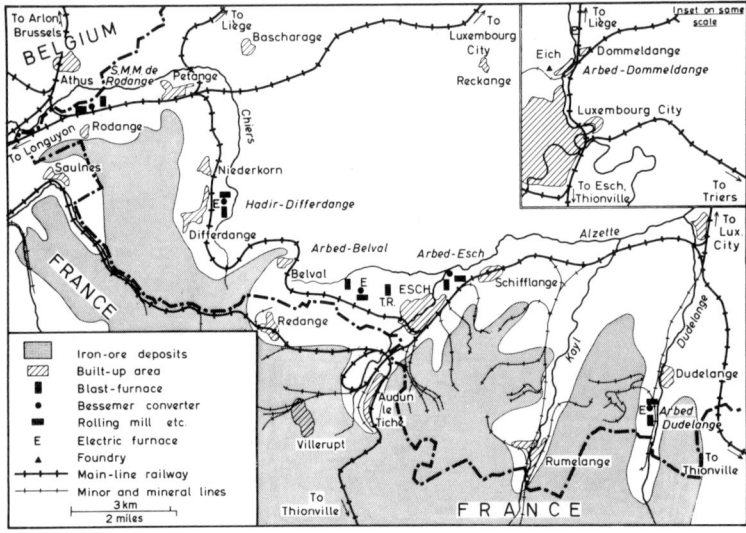

Fig. 58. The iron and steel industry in southern Luxembourg

people. *Arbed* has five plants in operation: blast furnaces and Bessemer converters at Belval, Esch and Dudelange, blast furnaces at Terres-Rouges to the north-west of Esch, from which molten iron is conveyed through conduits to the Belval and Esch converters, and electric furnaces at Dommeldange which produce alloy steels. The *Arbed* group has a capacity of 3 million tons of pig-iron, the same amount of crude steel, and 2 million tons of rolled steel products. In addition to its ore mines in Luxembourg, *Arbed* owns others in France, connected with its blast furnaces by mineral lines and in places by overhead cables. It operates another integrated steel plant in the Saar, it owns collieries and coking plants in the Eschweiler field, it has financial interests in the Kempen and South Limburg coalfields, and it controls a number of metal-using industries in Belgium, French Lorraine, the Saar and the Rhineland. At present

Arbed's steel plants are being modernized; efforts are being made to remove the phosphoric content from the ore, so producing basic pig-iron, and thus enabling the B.O.S. (Basic Oxygen Steel-making process) to be introduced.

A second corporation in Luxembourg is *Hadir*, formed in 1920, with its plant at Differdange, where its furnaces have a capacity of a million tons of pig, its Bessemer converters produce 800,000 tons of crude steel, and its rolling mills process 700,000 tons of semi-finished steel. While not of the industrial stature of the *Arbed* group, *Hadir*'s interests are wide, and include iron ore mines in Luxembourg and French Lorraine, and a large rolling mill at St Ingbert in the Saarland.

The third company, a subsidiary of the Belgian *Cockerill–Ougrée–Marihaye* group, has its plant near the Belgian border adjacent to the Luxembourg–Pétange–Paris railway, with blast furnaces, Bessemer converters, rolling mills specializing in rails, steel foundries and a brick-making plant. The company owns ore mines both in the Grand Duchy and in French Lorraine.

In 1968 these three steel companies, operating eight individual groups of plant, produced 4·3 and 4·5 million tons of pig-iron and of crude steel respectively. Though the industry consumed over 4 million tons of coke, there are no ovens in Luxembourg; it has always been considered more economical to import fuel in the form of coke, and no outlet is afforded in the Bessemer converters for the use of coke-oven gas. About 3·5 million tons of coke come from West Germany, most of the rest from Belgium.

Engineering Industries

The largest steel-using firm is at Hollerich in the southern suburbs of the capital, with a wide range of activities developed over the years from a small foundry and boiler works; it builds and erects bridges all over the world, it specializes in installations and equipment for steel works, and it manufactures cranes, factory machinery and railway rolling-stock. Another long-established firm near Wasserbillig manufactures agricultural implements and machinery serving the Bon Pays and the Moselle valley. Situated in the vine country, it has for long made wine-presses for local use; this has developed so much that presses are exported to the wine-making centres of Europe and even to vine-growing areas in the southern hemisphere. The firm also manufactures extractive machinery for cider and for vegetable oils. Lesser centres of engineering and metal manufacturing include Lintgen and Keispelt to the north of Luxembourg city, where tools and kitchen implements are made, and Hunsdorf which manufactures mining equipment.

Other Industries

Other industries, most of them concentrated in the capital, include textile factories (survivors of a widespread domestic industry) making woollen cloth, hosiery and knitted goods, leather tanning for shoes and gloves, brewing and distilling, and the manufacture of cigarettes. Small brick works, cement works and sawmills are found in most towns and villages. Luxembourg city has many small-scale industries, particularly in the suburb of Hollerich to the south.

COMMUNICATIONS

Though Luxembourg possesses only about 340 km (210 miles) of standard-gauge railways, they are of great importance, since the lines form sections of international routes passing through the city of Luxembourg. One line from Ostend links Brussels–Namur–Arlon–Luxembourg–Metz–Strasbourg-Basle, while a cross-line through Paris–Longuyon–Luxembourg–Trier–Koblenz affords a direct route between Paris and the Rhineland. Both lines carry a heavy international passenger traffic, and the second also conveys coal, coke and iron ore. A less important north–south line links Liège through Luxembourg city to Metz, Nancy and Dijon, and a branch from Liège runs eastward to Aachen and Eschweiler, which is important since *Arbed* owns collieries in the Eschweiler coalfield. The Grand Duchy derives considerable financial benefit in the form of transit dues from this international transport.

Until recently the rivers had no commercial importance, and were used only by small pleasure craft, ferries and canoes in summer, with some barges carrying limestone and gravel dredged from the river beds. The canalization of the Moselle (p. 176), which forms the south-eastern boundary with West Germany for about 40 km (25 miles), now affords an efficient link between the French Lorraine iron and steel district and the Rhine, and will undoubtedly be of value to Luxembourg as a riparian state. A new river-port has been constructed at Grevenmacher, with an annual capacity of 4·5 million tons of freight.

The road system, totalling about 2800 km (1740 miles) of State roads and 2100 km (1300 miles) of local roads, has been considerably improved in recent years. It carries a heavy and increasing traffic both of private cars and bus services, to which tourist traffic makes a substantial contribution. The tourist industry is fostered by State encouragement and propaganda, and the attractive little country, situated in the heart of western Europe, is visited by large numbers every year. The chief centre is the capital, partly because it is a charming and historic city, partly because it is an excellent centre. Many small towns and villages cater for visitors: Echternach for the Sûre valley and the 'Petite Suisse' district, Remich and Wormeldange for the Moselle valley, Vianden, Diekirch, Ettelbruck and Clervaux for the Ardennes, and Mondorf-les-Bains, with its mineral springs, for the south. The system of youth hostels attracts large numbers of younger visitors.

POPULATION AND SETTLEMENT

The total population in Luxembourg in 1968 was 336,000, giving an average density of 130 per sq. km (336 per sq. mile). This figure conceals considerable regional variations, especially as between the Ardennes and the Bon Pays.

In the Ardennes the average density of population is low as a result of large areas of moorland, woodland and pasture, and people live in isolated villages and hamlets. The Ardennes support only 15 per cent of the total of the Grand Duchy, although occupying 32 per cent of the area. The population of some rural cantons is steadily declining, for the attractions of better paid employment in the southern industrial area have caused many to leave the more rigorous uplands. The only town of any size is Wiltz (3,900), situated on the railway line running westward to Bastogne in Belgium, and the focus of a number of roads, so acting as a market centre for the eastern Ardennes; it is also a pleasant resort. Vianden is a tourist centre in the Our valley near the West German border, and Clervaux grew up around a castle in the wooded valley of the river Clervaux, a tributary of the Wiltz. Other villages are situated along these valleys, and a few, such as Beiderscheid and Putscheid, are on the plateau itself.

The density of population over the Bon Pays was about 143 per sq. km (370 per sq. mile) in 1968; occupying two-thirds of the total area, it contains 85 per cent of the population, the result of a diverse agriculture and a highly developed steel industry. The region also includes both the capital city and the industrial area, notably Esch-sur-Alzette (27,000), the centre of the steel industry. Differdange (18,000), Dudelange (15,000) and Pétange (12,000) were other towns almost exclusively preoccupied with steel manufacture.

The city of Luxembourg (Fig. 59), with a population of 77,000, is

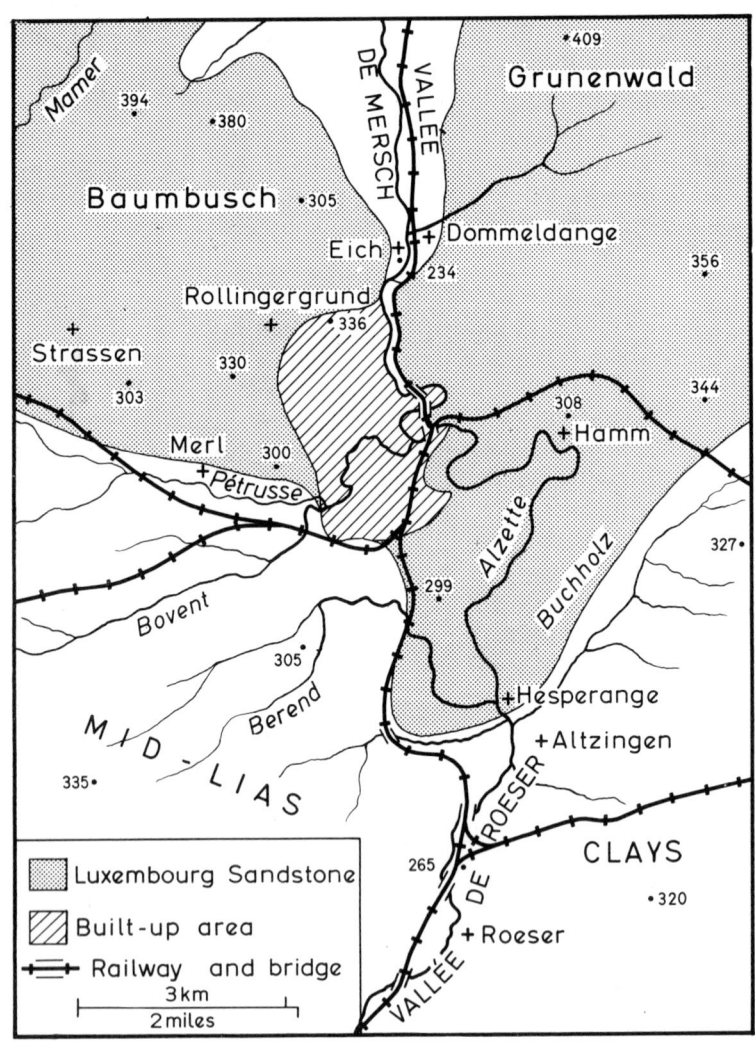

Fig. 59. The city of Luxembourg

Heights are given in metres.

situated in the south-centre of the country at the confluence of the Alzette and the Pétrusse. It is a focus of railway communications, and an administrative and commercial centre. In the southern suburbs engineering and other industries (brewing, distilling, the making of textiles and electrical apparatus) are carried on.

Both French and a Germanic dialect known as *Luxembourgeois* (or *Letzeburgesch*) rank as official languages. During the occupation of 1940–44, the authorities decreed that German was to be the sole official language, and the use of French in speech, place names or personal names was prohibited. This effort to exterminate French failed, and the bilingual ability of most people survives.

CHAPTER ELEVEN

Switzerland

SWITZERLAND occupies an area of about 41 000 sq. km (16,000 sq. miles), a little more than a quarter that of England and Wales; it had a population of about 6·1 millions in 1968. Its limitations are obvious: a quarter of the area consists of rock, snow and water, there 'are virtually no minerals, a large part is snow-covered in winter, and its small extent of arable land, though assiduously tilled, can provide only about three-fifths of the nation's food requirements. Its prosperity and high standard of living depend on imported raw materials fabricated with power partly derived from running water; on its highly organized tourist industry; on its commerce and finance; on its position in the 'heart' of central Europe; and on its long-standing and rarely interrupted neutrality.

Switzerland consists of twenty-two cantons (Fig. 60), of which three, Unterwalden, Basle and Appenzell, are each divided into two. The cantons maintain a considerable degree of independence and traditional decentralization and there is strong local feeling, emphasized by the isolation of many districts and by differences in language, creed, culture and way of life. Nevertheless, to the outside world the Swiss Confederation presents a firm united front; the working compromise between federal and cantonal authority and the constant use of nation-wide referenda in deciding important issues is conspicuously successful.

STRUCTURE AND RELIEF

Structure

Towards the end of the Palaeozoic era, the old Hercynian continent of Europe formed a stable 'foreland', with a geosyncline to the south. Into this materials eroded from the continental blocks were deposited, varying in character according to whether they were laid down in the shallow bordering seas or in the deeper parts of the geosyncline. Towards the end of the Mesozoic era the southern (African) block began to move northward, thus squeezing and in part metamorphosing the geosynclinal sediments, and causing

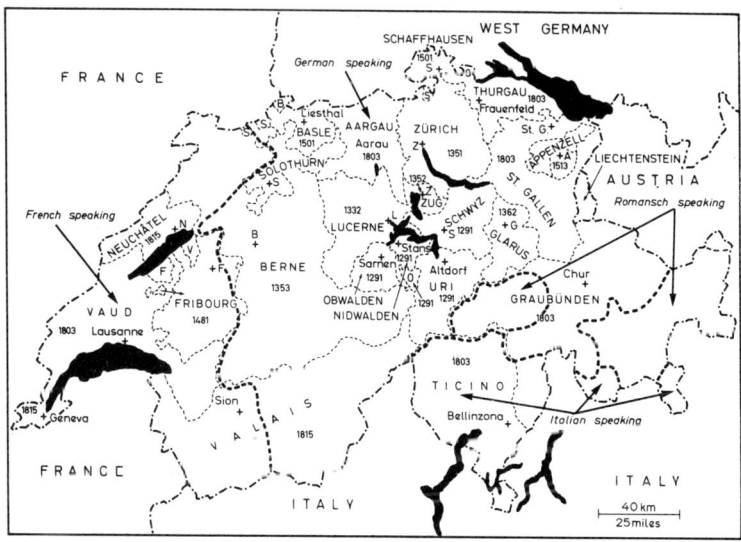

Fig. 60. The cantons of Switzerland
The heavy pecked lines indicate the approximate boundaries between the four official languages.

them to fold and splay forwards on to the edge of the foreland. This involved the formation of huge recumbent folds and thrusts. Ultimately several masses of rock were thrust bodily northward, in the form of nappes separated from their 'roots'. The nappes were not carried forward at a uniform level; when traced from west to east, at right-angles to the direction of movement, their surfaces seem to rise and fall in a series of 'culminations' and 'depressions'. The 'culminations' have been exposed to greater denudation, and so the upper nappes have been removed and the lower ones exposed, or in extreme cases completely removed to reveal the crystalline basement. By contrast, in the 'depressions' the upper nappes have been preserved.

Several series of individual nappes can be distinguished (Fig. 61). The most northerly group are isolated '*Klippen*' known as the Pre-Alps, situated to the north-east of Lake Geneva and also to its south in France. They consist of an isolated pile of sandstones, shales, conglomerates and limestones, very different in character from those of any nearby mountains.

To the south and east of the Pre-Alps, the line of the High Calcareous Alps forms the northern wall of the whole Alpine system.

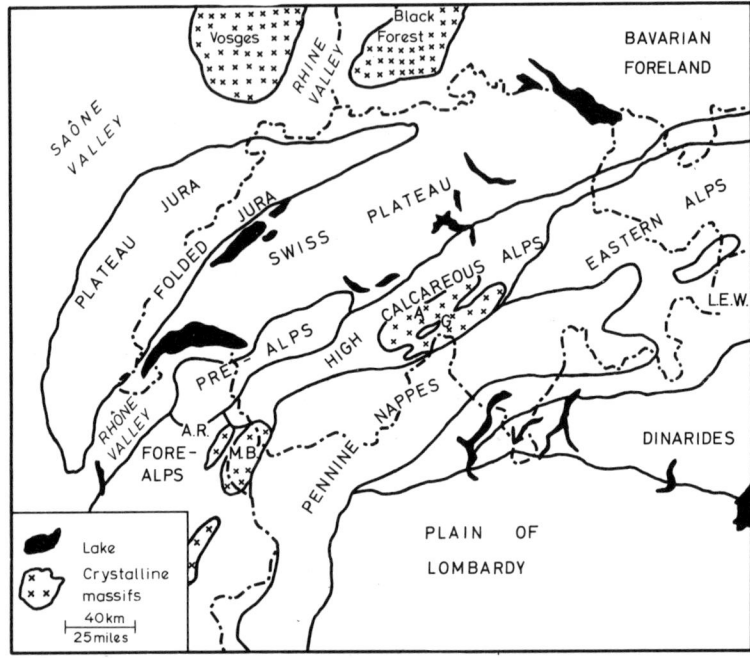

Fig. 61. The major structural divisions of Switzerland
(After L. Collet)
A.R. Aiguilles Rouges; **M.B.** Mont Blanc; **A.** Aar massif; **G.** St Gotthard massif;
L.E.W. Lower Engadine 'window'.

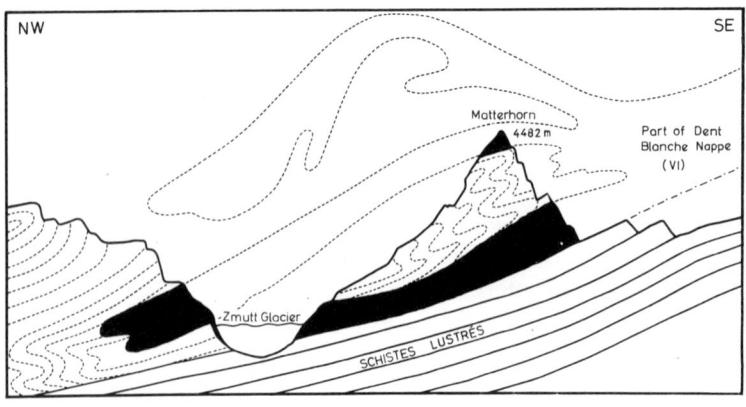

Fig. 62. Simplified section of the Matterhorn
(After L. Collet)

Six separate nappes, sometimes called the Helvetides, have been preserved.

The group of the Pennine nappes, lying to the south of the Rhône valley, extends more or less parallel to the Swiss-Italian border; although generally referred to as nappes, in the strict sense these structures are not nappes but a pile of recumbent folds. Six have been distinguished; numbers I to III are the Simplon nappes, lying mostly in France, number IV is the Great St Bernard nappe in the neighbourhood of the pass of that name, number V is the Monte Rosa nappe, and number VI the highest overriding Dent Blanche nappe. The last two consist of ancient crystalline gneisses, wrapped round by highly metamorphosed sediments (*schistes lustrés*), out of which have been carved such peaks as Monte Rosa, the Dent Blanche and the Matterhorn (Fig. 62). Farther east the Pennine nappes are lower, forming the Lepontine Alps, and farther east still in eastern Switzerland they are hidden by the overlying nappes of the Eastern Alps, sometimes called the Grisonides, which have been denuded from the Western Alps. But denudation has stripped off the cover in two places, forming 'windows', one of which, the Lower Engadine, lies in eastern Switzerland; here the rocks of the Pennine nappes are exposed. The most southerly tectonic region, represented in Switzerland only in the Ticino, is the 'zone of roots', where the Pennine nappes appear to turn vertically downwards.

The Alpine orogeny was so intense that several blocks of granitic rock, probably parts of the 'splintered edge' of the foreland, were overwhelmed by and caught up in the folding. These blocks, exposed by denudation where they occurred in the 'core' of a 'culmination', form a discontinuous chain of massifs, notably the Aiguilles Rouges–Mont Blanc mass, mostly in France (p. 402), and the Aar–Gotthard mass, wholly in Switzerland.

The orogenic movements died out in late Tertiary times, except for local uplift and depression between fault-lines. Some authorities believe, however, that the deep-seated folding in the geosyncline was so intense that its base was ultimately warped or buckled downwards, so forming deep mountain 'roots'. This could well have resulted in the bodily uplift of the superficial folds through isostatic compensation, perhaps doing more to account for the present altitude of the Alps than the fold movements themselves. During and since the main orogenic period, denudation has progressed steadily; the Alps are a complicated tectonic pile out of which the present mountains have been carved by the processes of earth sculpture.

The northern flanks of the folded region formed an elongated depression, now occupied by the Swiss and Bavarian Forelands, extending from the Jura Mountains into West Germany. At times this contained lakes or shallow seas into which much of the débris worn from the uprising mountains was deposited. In early Tertiary times this consisted mainly of a coarse sandstone (Flysch), which appears on the surface in Bavaria and in the uplands of east-central Switzerland. Over much of the Swiss Foreland an appreciable thickness of Molasse was laid down, occasionally interrupted by beds of Nagelfluh (p. 142).

To the north-west of Lake Geneva lie the Jura, whose structural features are also the result of the Tertiary folding, though here it is a more superficial phenomenon, for only rocks younger than the Permo-Triassic beds were affected. Many individual anticlines were formed; some estimates put the total at about 160, but this is difficult to calculate since many pitch out and are succeeded by others emerging from a neighbouring syncline.

Glaciation

During the Quaternary (Pleistocene) era, the Alpine snowfields and glaciers were far more extensive than at present. On the Bavarian Foreland farther east the classic sequence of the four main glacial episodes was first worked out by Penck and Brückner (p. 142). Over the Swiss Foreland, too, the glaciers pushed outward, at their maximum reaching to or beyond the Rhine valley between Constance and Basle; much of the Foreland at one stage may have been covered by a single piedmont glacier. The four glacial episodes (Günz, Mindel, Riss and Würm) distinguished by Penck and Brückner farther east are certainly represented, but two additional major glaciations have been postulated, the Kander and Glütsch, which occurred between the Mindel and Riss. The Riss, as elsewhere, was the most extensive.

At the present time about 1800 sq. km (700 sq. miles) of snowfield and glacier exist in Alpine Switzerland (Fig. 63). During the postglacial climatic optimum of the 'Atlantic Stage', between about 5500 and 3000 B.C., these were appreciably less extensive than at present. Since then the glaciers have fluctuated considerably; during the early Middle Ages the climate was distinctly mild and the glaciers shrank accordingly, but by the end of the sixteenth century they advanced again to a minor maximum, overwhelming pastures, forests, mines and villages. Other shortlived advances have occurred at intervals,

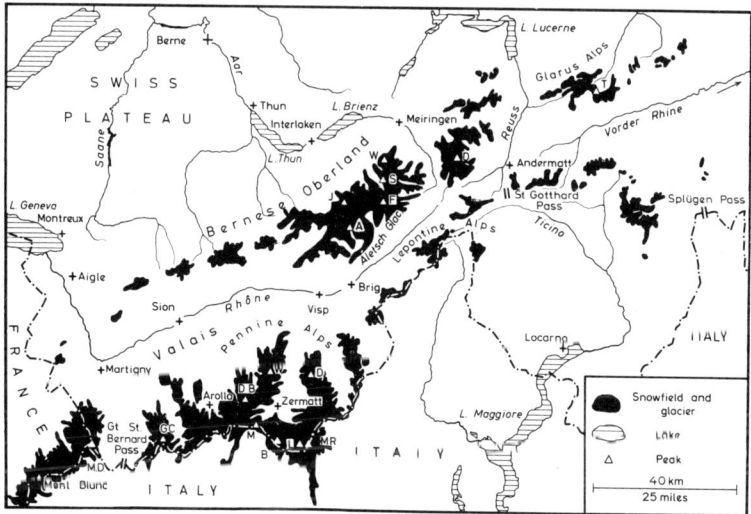

Fig. 63. Snowfields and glaciers in the Swiss Alps
The peaks should be identified by their abbreviations from an atlas.

the last notable one in 1850. During the last fifty years there has been a general shrinkage in length, the result of a slight rise in atmospheric temperature. For example, the average shrinkage of all glaciers observed by a Swiss Commission between 1957 and 1961 was 12 m (39 ft). The recession is very sporadic; the Zmutt Glacier near the Matterhorn decreased by 69 m (225 ft) between 1960 and 1962. During the last few years, however, it has been reported that one-third of the 110 under observation are once again increasing in length.

The glaciers and snowfields not only afford an attractive ingredient in the Alpine landscape (Fig. 64 and Plate XLVI), but they continue their work of denudation, as the lines of moraine and the milky glacier streams, laden with their burden of 'rock-flour', testify. Below the level of present glaciation, overdeepened trough-like valleys, hanging valleys, valley steps and alp benches are eloquent testimony to glacial erosion. In the valleys lines of moraine, uneven dumps of till, and outwash sands and gravels are obvious results of deposition.

The Jura Mountains were also affected by glaciation, though there is now no permanent snow. Some of the high cols were probably cut down by tongues of ice pushing north-westward. Till lies in undulating mounds in the valleys and on the plateaus, and erratics of Alpine origin have been traced as high as 1800 m (6000 ft) on the southern ridges. Many small lakes have been dammed-up by crescentic terminal moraines, or lie in uneven depressions on the clay cover.

Drainage

The neighbourhood of the St Gotthard Pass is the very heart of the drainage pattern of central Europe. The two master streams, the Rhône and the Rhine, take advantage of a longitudinal structural line, though flowing in opposite directions along it. The Rhône emerges as a turgid glacier stream from the 'snout' of the Rhône glacier (Fig. 69), and flows for 130 km (80 miles) in a west-south-westerly direction. It then makes an abrupt right-angled bend near Martigny, and continues through the gorge of St Maurice into the south-eastern wing of Lake Geneva. The lake lies at about 375 m (1230 ft) above sea-level; into its still waters the river is building out a lacustrine delta, and from the air the underwater banks stand out from the clear waters of the rest of the lake. The Rhône leaves the western end of Lake Geneva and 24 km (15 miles) below passes into France.

The Rhine, rising on the eastern slopes of the Oberalp Pass, flows in an east-north-easterly direction along the structural furrow for about 100 km (60 miles), until it too breaks northward and continues into Lake Constance. It leaves the western end of the lake and flows westward to Basle, where it enters its rift valley section (p. 190). The Rhine drains nearly three-quarters of Switzerland, for it is joined by two major tributaries which have pursued circuitous routes across central Switzerland. In the west the Aar, formed from the melt-waters of the northern Oberland glaciers, passes through the twin Lakes Thun and Brienz, and later receives the outflow from Lakes Neuchâtel and Bienne in the north-west. Not long before the Aar joins the Rhine it receives the Reuss, which rises only a few km from the Rhine but flows north through the Aar massif into Lake Lucerne and across east-central Switzerland.

Except for the extreme south and south-east, the whole of Switzerland is drained by either the Rhône or the Rhine. The canton of Ticino lies south of the main Alpine watershed, and its drainage proceeds via the river Ticino and Lake Maggiore to the Po, hence to the Adriatic Sea. In the south-east most water finds its way into the trench of the Engadine, through which the Inn flows from its source on the Maloja Pass to its junction with the Danube at Passau.

These rivers are formed from a multiplicity of head-streams and tributaries, many beginning as the melt-water streams of glaciers.

The glacial over-deepening of the main valleys has resulted in a profusion of hanging valleys, from which streams spill in cascades. The rapid downcutting of torrential streams in the mountains, possibly accelerated by the slow isostatic uplift of the range, has created spectacular gorges, including those of the Trient, which joins the Rhône below Martigny, the Lütschine below Grindelwald, the Hinter Rhine near Thusis (the Via Mala) and the Schöllenen Gorge of the Reuss near Andermatt crossed by the well-known 'Devil's Bridge'.

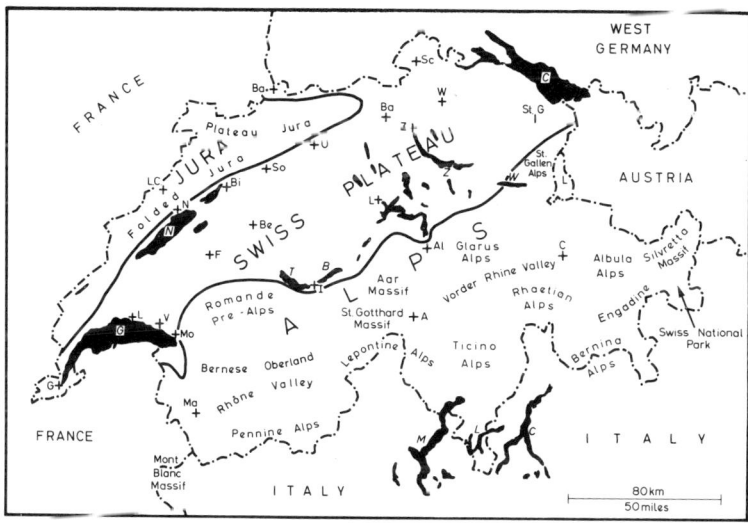

Fig. 64. Relief regions

A characteristic feature of the Swiss landscape is the number of lakes, the largest of which are Geneva (Léman) and Constance (Boden); parts of these lie in France and West Germany respectively. Other large lakes are Neuchâtel and Bienne (or Biel) in the northwest near the margins of the Jura, the irregularly shaped Lucerne, Zürich and Zug in the centre of the country, Thun and Brienz on the Alpine margins, and in the south, beyond the main watershed, most of Lugano and the northern end of Maggiore, which are two of the Italian Lakes. Some, especially the southern lakes, lie in deep glacial valleys; others, notably Geneva and Constance, are contained in 'sags' or depressions of tectonic origin.

Relief Regions (Fig. 64)

Switzerland can be divided into three main regions on the basis of relief: the Jura in the northwest, occupying about a tenth of the total area; the mountain complex of the Alps, comprising rather more than half; and the Swiss Plateau in the centre and north.

The Jura. The border between Switzerland and France crosses the Jura obliquely from Basle to Geneva, leaving most of the 'folded Jura' in Switzerland, though the highest point, the Crêt de la Neige (1723 m, 5653 ft), is in France, as is most of the 'plateau Jura'. In the latter the Jurassic limestones have been faulted, probably at the same time (during the Oligocene period) as the Rhine Rift Valley (p. 140) was created, forming low tabular plateaus and undulating hills. Much of the limestone is buried beneath a covering of the Molasse and of later glacial drift.

In the Folded Jura the upfolds for the most part still correspond to the upstanding ridges and the synclines form the valleys, floored with sandstones and clays and occupied by longitudinal sections of rivers. Often torrents flowing down the sides of the upfolds furrow deeply into the limestone and erode headwards into the less resistant underlying clays and marls, sometimes cutting back into an anticline and so forming a high-lying depression or combe along its crest. These combes are walled with infacing scarps, commonly culminating in a limestone cliff, below which a gradual slope, covered with scree, descends to the floor.

Another prominent feature of the Folded Jura is the transverse valley (*cluse*) which cuts across an anticline, often as a steep-sided gorge; the river existed before the anticline, and maintained its course by erosion as uplift progressed. There are between sixty and seventy *cluses* in the Folded Jura, of which three-quarters are in Switzerland. The drainage as a result reveals an alternation between longitudinal and transverse sections, with sudden changes of direction, elbow bends and frequent river captures. For example, the river Doubs at its most easterly point makes a complete reversal of direction; probably it once flowed to the Rhine but its beheaded 'trunk' is now a misfit, the small river Birse, which joins the Rhine just above Basle.

Most of the other drainage of the Swiss Jura finds its way into Lake Neuchâtel, via the Lac de Joux and the rivers Orbe or Areuse, hence by way of Lake Bienne and the river Aar to the Rhine.

The Swiss Plateau (Plate XLVII) has an overall slope from 1200 m

(4000 ft) near the margins of the Alps to about 400 m (1300 ft) in the Rhine valley along the West German border and near the foot of the Jura. Though the term plateau is commonly used, the name *Mittelland* is perhaps better, for its surface is far from uniform; wooded ridges rise above the general level, lakes lie in hollows, and the rivers Aar and Reuss, with their tributaries, flow northward to the Rhine in steep-sided valleys which dissect the surface. It consists structurally of a synclinal foreland, filled with the soft, gray Molasse sandstone of Upper Oligocene and Miocene age and with patches of Nagelfluh conglomerate. These rocks outcrop only locally, since the plateau is covered with uneven sheets of ground-moraine, curving festoons of terminal moraines, swarms of drumlins, and sheets of terrace-gravel.

Some authorities believe that the Molasse and Nagelfluh were upfolded to form a gentle anticline extending between Lakes Constance and Geneva, whose eroded remnants, particularly where it consists of the more resistant Nagelfluh, form prominent hills, sometimes with impressive cliffs. These include the Napf (1408 m, 4620 ft) and the Rigi, which rises to 1800 m (5905 ft) above Lake Lucerne. Farther east the hills between Lakes Wallen and Constance are also formed mainly of Molasse and Nagelfluh.

The Swiss Alps. In the north-west the Pre-Alps, known in Switzerland as the Romande Pre-Alps, overlie both the Molasse rocks of the plateau and the frontal folds of the High Calcareous Alps. The group is carved into a chaos of ridges by streams draining north by way of the Saane and the Simmen. The district is sometimes called the 'Zone des Cols', because numerous passes leading west to Lake Geneva cross the ridges. The most prominent peaks include the Niesen (2362 m, 7749 ft), Trüttlisberg, Krinnen and Pillon.

The Swiss Alps proper may be divided into a northerly and a southerly zone, separated by the structural line of the Rhône–Rhine valleys. The more important mountain groups and ranges have separate names, marked on Fig. 64.

The northern group consists of the High Calcareous nappes, known as the Bernese Alps (or Bernese Oberland) in the west and the Glarus (or Glarner) Alps in the east. Much of the rock is limestone, but there are also outcrops of dolomite, shale, sandstone, and in places highly metamorphosed gneissic rocks. The northern wall of the Oberland rises abruptly in such peaks as the Eiger, the Mönch and the Jungfrau (4166 m, 13,668 ft) (Fig. 65). The North Wall of the Eiger overlooking Grindelwald is an 1800 m (6000 ft) bastion of limestone, remarkably steep, hard and smooth-in its lower sections, equally steep but of a more crumbling limestone above; the latter section, interspersed with several icefields, sends down a constant barrage of avalanches which render the North Wall one of the most notorious climbs in the Alps. Behind this wall lies a series of snow-fields, such as the Ewig-Schneefeld and the Jungfraufirn, from which glaciers move outwards, including the Rosenlaui, Unter-Grindel-wald and Ober-Grindelwald Glaciers on the north (Fig. 65), and the Grosser-Aletsch on the south (Plate XLVI). The Glarus Alps form a much dissected mass between the valleys of the Reuss and the Rhine, culminating in the Tödi group, the highest of which is the Tödi itself (3623 m, 11,887 ft).

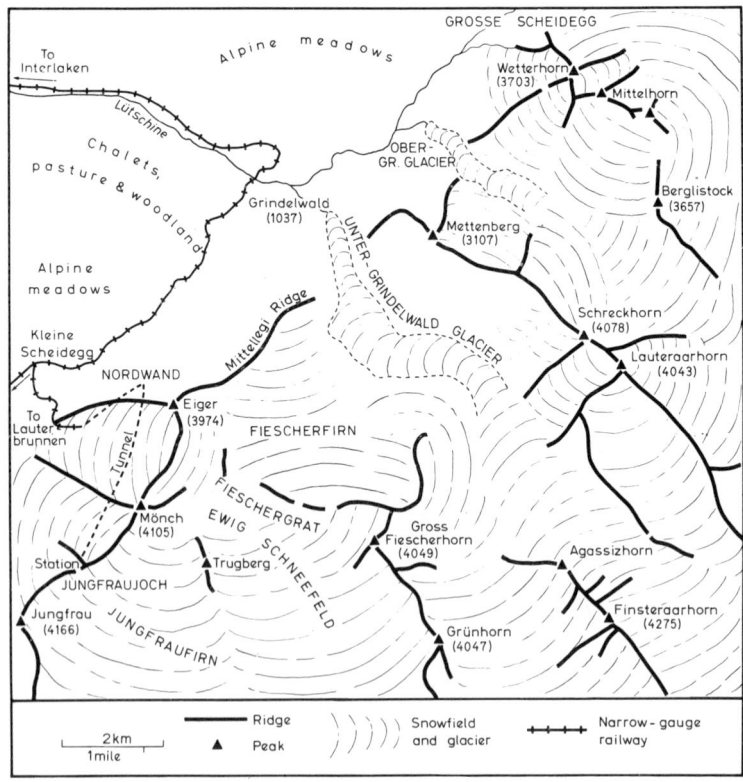

Fig. 65. Snowfields and glaciers in the Bernese Oberland in the neighbourhood of Grindelwald
(After *Landeskarte der Schweiz*)

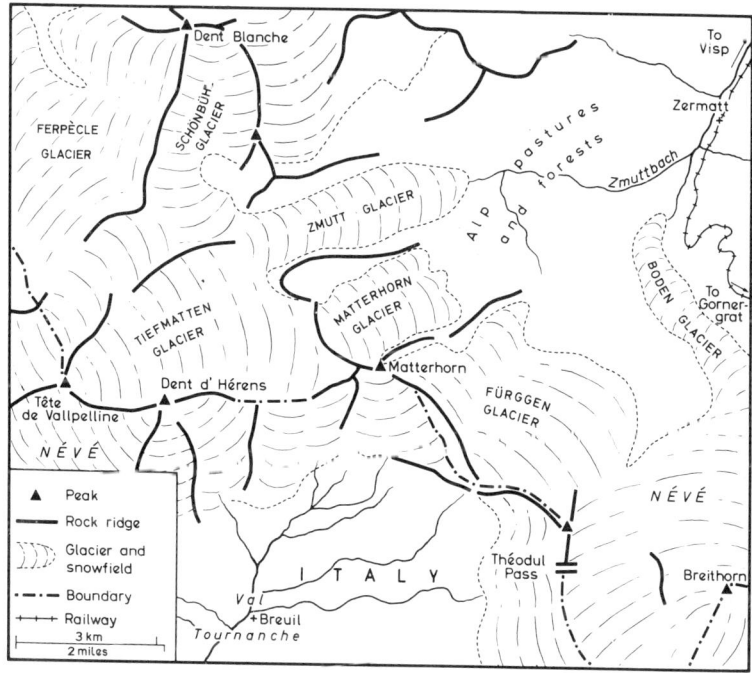

Fig. 66. The Pennine Alps near Zermatt, Switzerland
(After *Landeskarte der Schweiz*)

These two sections of the High Calcareous Alps are interrupted by a granitic massif, one of the isolated fragments of the Hercynian foreland. There are two blocks, the larger Aar massif to the north, the St Gotthard to the south, with a slice of sedimentary rocks between them. Out of this granite is carved the Finsteraarhorn (with an altitude of 4275 m (14,026 ft) the highest peak in the Oberland), the Aletschhorn and the Bietschhorn. Their clean-cut ridges contrast with the crumbling limestones and shales of some of the other Oberland mountains.

To the south of the Rhône valley are the Pennine Alps (Plate XLVIII), the highest mountains in the Alps but for Mont Blanc itself; four summits exceed 4500 m (15,000 ft) and seventeen rise to over 4200 m (14,000 ft). One line of peaks and ridges, which forms the Rhône–Po watershed (Fig. 66), includes the snow-covered bulk of Monte Rosa (4634 m, 15,204 ft) and the rock obelisk of the Matterhorn (4482 m, 14,705 ft). From this border ridge other mountain groups separate such deep north-trending valleys as the Val d'Anniviers and the Val d'Hérens. Many of these peaks are famous in the annals of mountaineering: the Dent Blanche, the Weisshorn with its three gleaming faces, the Obergabelhorn with its dangerous double-corniced ridges, and the Dom which is the highest peak (4554 m, 14,941 ft) situated wholly in Swiss territory.

Farther east are the lower ranges of the Lepontine Alps, the Ticino Alps occupying a southerly salient of Swiss territory beyond the main Alpine watershed, and the Rhaetian Alps drained by the Hinter Rhine. The finest mountains in eastern Switzerland are the culminating points of the Bernina group, called after its highest peak, the Piz Bernina (4052 m, 13,294 ft), and of the Silvretta massif, culminating in Piz Linard (3410 m, 11,188 ft).

CLIMATE

The country is situated in the heart of the continent, transitional between western or 'maritime' Europe and the Mediterranean lands on the one hand, and between western and east-central Europe on the other. There are marked contrasts between the climate in the north of the Plateau and that of the valleys to the south of the Alpine watershed, which experience much of the warmth and sunshine associated with the Mediterranean lands.

A narrow 'tongue' of high pressure extends westward in winter over central Europe, a prolongation of the Asiatic anticyclone, forming a 'barometric backbone' separating the low pressure systems crossing north-western Europe from those passing through the Mediterranean basin. But this high-pressure area is by no means a permanent feature, though for considerable periods it may bring calm, cold and sunny conditions, except in deep valleys where inversion fog may linger. But at any time the high pressure may weaken, and depressions penetrating from the Atlantic may bring precipitation in the form of rain on the lower ground and snow at higher altitudes. In summer the long periods of high-pressure conditions usually cause bright sunny weather, interrupted by occasional convectional storms, especially among the mountains. It is possible to experience summers with weeks of fine weather, what the mountaineer calls 'a good season', and others when the weather is rainy and stormy and only occasionally does a brief break in the clouds reveal the high peaks in their new snow mantle.

Temperature

The Swiss Plateau conforms on the whole to a 'central European' climatic type. The mean temperatures in January are at or just below freezing (Basle, 0° C., Berne, −2° C., Lucerne, −1° C.); in July they are generally about 18° C. (Basle, 19° C., Berne, 17° C.). In the Jura winters are quite severe, with mean January temperatures of −4° C. to −2° C., and frost is experienced on the higher ridges on about a hundred days annually. Summer days are sunny, with mean July temperatures of 19° C. in the more southerly valleys, 16° C. to 17° C. farther north.

The difficulty of generalization applies with particular force to the Alps. The first factor is altitude; the station on the Säntis (2500 m, 8202 ft) in the St Gallen Alps has a January mean of only 10° C., the resort of Davos (1561 m, 5121 ft) has −7° C., and Bevers (1710 m, 5610 ft) has −10° C.; the summer temperatures are correspondingly reduced, being 5° C., 12° C., and 12° C. respectively. The mean temperatures at the station on the Jungfraujoch (3380 m, 11,090 ft) never rise above freezing point, even in high summer.

The normal lapse rate is frequently upset by prolonged inversion, the result of the downward drainage of cold, heavy air, especially in the deep valley trenches. One can, for example, stand in the brilliant sunshine at Mürren, and look down into the fog-filled Lauterbrunnen trench. Much of the attraction of the higher resorts in winter lies in their long hours of sunshine, with clear skies; air temperatures may be low, but sun temperatures are high, and skiers have to be careful not to over-expose the skin to the sun's burning rays. Aspect is extremely important; the south-facing slope (*Sonnenseite* or *adret*) of a valley aligned from west to east will record much longer sunshine hours than the north-facing slope (*Schattenseite* or *ubac*). A further example of situation and aspect is in Ticino, sheltered by the main ranges from the north, yet open to Mediterranean influences from the south. Such resorts as Locarno on Lake Maggiore and Lugano on the lake of that name have remarkably mild winters, with January means above freezing, and early springs, as indicated in favoured locations by the subtropical gardens.

Another important factor is the influence of local winds. The *föhn* is experienced when a depression lies to the north of the Alps and moist air is drawn northward from the western Mediterranean basin. Warmed by adiabatic compression, it descends the northern slopes, following the valleys of the Rhine, the Aar, the Reuss, and the Rhône from Martigny to Lake Geneva. It can raise the air temperature between 10° and 20° C. in a few hours, yet the wind is so dry that fire danger becomes serious, and in many villages smoking out of doors is prohibited during föhn weather. It melts the snow rapidly, often causing avalanches of partially thawed snow and widespread flooding.

Precipitation

In the Jura precipitation averages 1000 mm (40 in) annually in the valleys and 1650–1800 mm (65–70 in) on the ridges, much falling as snow. At Monthe, near the French border, the total annual snowfall averages about 3 m; it may lie for about 55 days in the valleys at around 600 m (2000 ft) and for as many as 125 days at 1200 m (4000 ft). No passes are, however, sufficiently high to cause regular snow-blocking, although the Col de la Faucille between St Claude and Geneva may be intermittently closed. During the summer, continental influences reveal themselves in appreciable convection rain, some 75–100 mm (3–4 in) a month.

In the Swiss Plateau precipitation varies with location from means of 830 mm (32·7 in) at Basle and of 860 mm (33·9 in) at Geneva to about 1270 mm (50 in) near the margins of the Alps, where the influence of altitude is apparent. A distinct summer maximum shows the effect of convectional influences; Basle receives about 360 mm (14 in) during the months June to September. Even in the lower parts of the plateau, snow may lie for two to four weeks in winter, sometimes, as in 1962–63, for very much longer.

In the Alps precipitation is varied in amount and distribution, and the effects of altitude and exposure are profound. Generally the total increases with altitude up to about 2700–3000 m (9–10,000 ft), though short term records near the summits of some of the peaks indicate that the total decreases again at higher elevations still. The Säntis (2500 m, 8202 ft) has a mean precipitation of 2440 mm (96 in), and the St. Gotthard Pass receives about 2540 mm (100 in). By contrast, the effects of rain-shadow reduce markedly the totals in the valleys and on the eastern slopes. The floor of the deep Rhône valley averages only 560–610 mm (22–24 in), though the peaks around may get three to four times as much. Davos and Bevers in the eastern Alps, lying in sheltered valleys, though at over 1500 m (5000 ft), have mean totals of only 910 mm (36 in) and 840 mm (33 in).

Much of this precipitation is in the form of snow; above about 1500 m (5000 ft) rain is rarely received, except perhaps in July, though the valley resorts may have depressing periods of rain in summer, while snow falls on the peaks. Precipitation in winter is mainly cyclonic, in summer convectional; the southern peaks and valleys are particularly subject in summer to sudden and violent thunderstorms, which seem to build up from the heated lowlands of northern Italy. The snowline varies with season and locality, and the extent of the snow cover is a serious matter for ski-ing resorts. Sometimes the entire Alpine region may be snow-covered down to the floors of the lowest valleys, but on an average it lies for about 125 days at 1200 m (4000 ft), 180 days at 1800 m (6000 ft), and 240 days at 2400 m (8000 ft). The permanent snowline is at about 2700 m (9000 ft) in the western Alps, and about 300 m higher in the east. North-facing hollows retain snow for weeks after the south-facing slopes have been stripped bare, and drifts persist throughout the year well below the general snowline. Most of the passes above about 1800 m (6000 ft) are closed by snow between October and June (pp. 379–80).

LAND USE AND AGRICULTURE

Analysis of the main categories of land use reveals that 24 per cent of the total area is wooded, 46 per cent is under pasture, 6 per cent is arable, and the remaining 24 per cent consists of bare rocks and scree, permanent snowfields and glaciers. The Alpine cantons of Valais and Graubünden have, naturally, a very much lower proportion of cultivable land. Much of the country has a short growing season because of the long winter snow-cover and the lateness of spring, though a south-facing aspect may mitigate the severity of the conditions, and cereals and fruit are grown at surprisingly high elevations.

Soils

The soils are in many parts poor, thin or absent, especially in the mountains, where the 'skeletal' soils can support only an Alpine flora. On some of the alp benches, however, the accumulation of 'flushed' soils from the downwash of weathered material is rich in bases, and on the valley floors the lighter tills and alluvium give rise to patches of fertile soil. On the Plateau the soils are derived from glacial and fluvioglacial materials, with some patches of loess, and some of the most fertile soils occur on the sites of now drained lakes or marshes; the largest of these reclaimed areas lies between Lakes Neuchâtel and Bienne. The Jura valleys are floored with soils derived from till and alluvium, though in higher depressions thin reddish soils of the terra rossa type, derived from the disintegration of limestone, are widespread.

Forests

The visitor gains the impression that Switzerland is much more extensively wooded than the proportion of 24 per cent of the total area would imply. Much of the Swiss Plateau has been cleared by centuries of cultivation, so that 70 per cent of the forest grows in the Alpine region, and another 20 per cent is in the Jura. The rest is found in smaller patches on the Plateau: on the morainic ridges and outwash sands, on the Molasse hills, and around the lakes.

Though small areas of mixed deciduous trees (oak, beech, chestnut) occur in favoured places, about 70 per cent of the forest is coniferous, mainly spruce, by far the most common tree, and silver fir, with some larch and various species of pine, notably the Arolla pine and the stone pine near the treeline. The conifers can grow on remarkably steep slopes, and most north-facing valley sides are thickly covered. As the treeline is reached, the close stands are replaced by progressively more stunted individual pines (the name *Krummholz*, or 'crooked wood', is applied to the curiously twisted and scrubby trees), then by dwarf birch, juniper, Alpine rose, rhododendron and other bushes, and passing into an Alpine flora which extends up to the permanent snowline.

The treeline is commonly higher on north-facing than on south-facing slopes, because those trees on the latter are usually cleared to provide pasture. On the northern slopes of the Oberland, it lies at about 1700 m (5500 ft), in Valais at 2100 m (7000 ft), in the southern Ticino Alps as high as 2700 m (9000 ft).

There is virtually no federally owned forest, and about two-thirds belongs to individual communes and public bodies, about 30 per cent is privately owned, mainly by farmers, and the remainder is the property of the cantons. Until the middle of last century, there was little forest legislation or conservation practice, but a series of flood disasters drew attention to the dangers of deforestation in the high valleys. Accordingly, a Federal Forest Law decreed that the overall area of woodland must not be reduced, and that clear-felling should be prohibited in the protective or 'shelter forests'. The Swiss forests are carefully managed, and programmes of felling and planting, and the encouragement of regeneration, are methodically worked out.

The forests are useful in several ways: they have a protective value as breaks against avalanches and as checks to the torrential runoff on steep, bare slopes which causes flooding in the valleys; they afford shelter-belts for settlements; they have a distinct amenity value in the landscape; and they produce annually about 3·5 million cu. m. of commercial timber, pulpwood and firewood, out of the country's average requirements of about 4·5 millions. Forestry work affords employment for the rural population, especially in remote valleys where there is little possibility of earning additional to subsistence agriculture.

Organization of Agriculture

Only 9 per cent of the working population is now employed on the land, compared with 20 per cent in 1940, which is indicative on the one hand of some rural depopulation, on the other of the rationalization of agricultural methods which require a smaller labour force. Between 1940 and 1968, while the number of agricultural workers decreased from about 415,000 to 260,000, the real value of agricultural produce increased by a quarter. The majority of farmers own their land, which in many cases has remained in the same family for several generations.

Considerable importance is attached to the rôle of agriculture in the national economy, but it was not until 1947, as a culmination to the difficulties of the war years, that a new clause was embodied in the constitution, authorizing the Federal Government to take steps . . . 'to maintain a large rural population, ensure agricultural productivity and consolidate rural properties'. In 1951 a law was passed for the maintenance of rural landed property, and another which has been described as 'the keystone of Swiss agricultural policy'; it enabled import quotas for various commodities to be fixed, and guaranteed the maintenance of prices so as to give an economic return to farmers. The co-operative system has been widely developed, both for marketing produce and for the provision of fertilizers and machinery, and numerous organizations are concerned with technical progress in agriculture.

In recent years efforts have been made to reduce the number of small farms through policies of voluntary amalgamation known as '*remaniement parcellaire*'. Though sponsored by the State, for a scheme to be operated the majority of landholders in a commune have to agree to it, and those who give up their land are financially compensated.

Livestock

The damp climate in many parts, the steep slopes, the high alp benches which are clear of snow for only a few months but produce rich grass in the Alpine sunshine, nurtured by the melting snow, are clearly more favourable for pasture and livestock than for arable. For centuries the slopes were grazed only by sheep and goats; it was not until the eighteenth century that the emphasis shifted to cattle, then primarily reared for beef. Young stores, born in spring, were fattened on the summer grazings, then driven south into Italy.· Much of the former arable was converted into meadow to provide winter hay for the breeding animals. Dairying until the nineteenth century was secondary, producing only sour-milk cheese, such as the still popular 'Glarner green' variety, for transport problems and the absence of refrigeration precluded any other development. In 1815, however, a cheese-making factory was established at Kiesen near Berne; since then the commercial development of dairying has proceeded, not only in the Alps and the Jura, but also on the Swiss Plateau.

In 1968 there were 1·8 million cattle, of which 900,000 were dairy animals. Cattle-rearing is based on winter stall-feeding and outdoor summer grazing, both on the Plateau and in the mountains. Transhumance, the age-old transference of animals from their winter quarters in the valleys to the high pastures, is still widely practised, since it is the most efficient way of utilizing the available pasture at different times of the year. Most villages possess their own alps (Fig. 67), with rough summer dwellings for the people who accompany the cattle (Plate XLVIII), thus freeing the valley meadows of animals for the summer months so that several crops of hay may be taken; the winter feed is stored in lofts over the byres or in barns dotted among the meadows, and much of the arable is devoted to fodder crops such as alfalfa, colza and clover.

Large-scale dairy factories manufacturing cheese and butter on a commercial scale are situated both in the Alpine valleys and on the Plateau; some are in such towns as Vevey and Lausanne, others in the open countryside. These factories, supplied by tanker lorries, cable transporters, and in recent years by polythene pipelines (*pipelaits*) down the steep valley sides, consume two-thirds of the milk yield. Large quantities of cheese and butter are produced. Many cheeses have a high reputation; over a hundred named brands are produced, such as Gruyère, Emmenthaler and Greyerzer on the Plateau, Piora in Ticino, and the Vacherin du Mont d'Or of the Jura.

Plate XLVI. The Aletsch Glacier, Switzerland

Plate XLVII. The Swiss Foreland near Büren, with the northern peaks of the Bernese Oberland in the distance

Plate XLVIII. The village of Bettmeralp, looking across the upper Rhône valley towards Monte Leone (left) and the Fletschhorn, Switzerland

Plate XLIX. A barrage control on the upper Rhône near Leukerbad, Switzerland

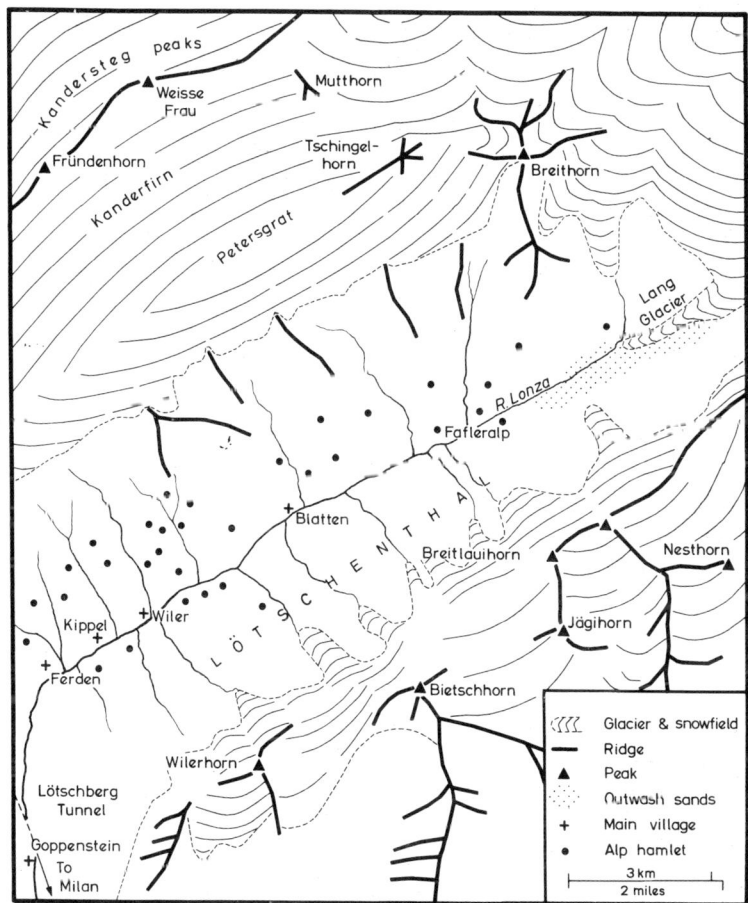

Fig. 67. The Lötschenthal
(After *Landeskarte der Schweiz*)
This is the valley of the Lonza, a right-bank tributary of the Rhône; until recently
it had no access for motor traffic.

A well-known national dish, *fondue*, is made by melting Emmenthaler
or Gruyère cheese with wine. Boxed and processed cheeses are produced by such firms as *Nestlé*; condensed and dried milk, and milk
chocolate (such as *Nestlé* and *Tobler*) account for the rest of the milk
yield not consumed in liquid form.

About 1·8 million pigs were kept in 1968; pork products, including
highly flavoured sausages, are an important part of the diet. Sheep

13

and goats, formerly so important, have become much less so, partly because cattle-rearing is much more profitable, partly because little grazing is available in winter and they cannot be practicably housed.

Arable Farming

Apart from fodder, the main arable crops are wheat, barley, rye, sugar beet, rape, potatoes, sun-flowers and a small amount of tobacco. Though the Plateau is the chief arable area, some crops are grown in the mountains on steep slopes and at surprising altitudes. Winter wheat can be grown up to about 730 m (2400 ft) above sea-level, spring wheat to about 1300 m (4200 ft), and on some of the south-facing slopes in Ticino up to 1500 m (4800 ft). Rye appears even higher; fields can be seen at Findelen, near Zermatt, at about 1900 m (6300 ft).

During the War of 1939–45, Switzerland as a result of its isolation was obliged to grow more food, and land which had been under meadow since time immemorial was ploughed up and the area of cereals doubled. Since 1945 the area under cereals has declined once more, though not to the prewar level. Much progress has been made in plant selection and in scientific methods of cultivation; the average yield of winter wheat has been almost doubled between 1940 and 1968. The potato crop is normally adequate for home requirements.

Fruit

Fruit trees are grown in orchards on the Swiss Plateau, in Valais and in the valleys of Ticino, and very commonly in rows of trees between fields and along the roads. Apples, pears, cherries and plums are widely grown; apricots are a feature of the Valais, peaches of Ticino.

Switzerland is not much regarded outside its borders as a wine-producing country, yet vineyards cover 12 000 ha (30,000 acres), and about 1 million hectolitres (21 million gallons) of wine are produced annually. The Romans introduced the vine on to the sunny slopes above Lake Geneva, and in the Middle Ages it spread into the Rhône and Rhine valleys, mainly cultivated by the religious foundations. Today the slopes to the north of Lake Geneva are still the most important; many villages and towns have their annual wine festivals, Lausanne is the headquarters of the Swiss Wine Growing Association, and Vevey is the home of the long-established *Confrérie des Vignerons*. The Chasselas grape, grown in other countries for dessert, yields the most popular Swiss wine, Fendant. Other esteemed wines are Dézaley and Aigle in canton Vaud, the 'flinty' red Dôle of the Rhône valley, the delicate red wines of Ticino, and the sparkling wines of Neuchâtel from grapes grown in the calcareous soils of the Jura slopes.

POWER AND INDUSTRY

In spite of the poverty of its mineral resources and raw materials, and its distance from the seaports through which these needs may be imported, Switzerland ranks as an important industrial country. Between 1900 and 1968 the number of manufacturing undertakings increased from 5,000 to 13,100, and the number of workers from 200,000 to 880,000. The only advantages are the quality of this labour force and the availability of water power, hence a high degree of skilled fabrication is involved, and as André Siegfried wrote, 'Switzerland has been saved from the temptations of mass production and condemned to superiority'. In 1880 an average hundredweight of raw material of value 100 francs was fabricated to an export value of 500 francs; in 1957 the comparable export value per hundred-weight was 1,170 francs, about 1·5 times the corresponding value in Great Britain, twice that in West Germany, and three times that in France. The smooth transformation from a skilled but domestic peasant industry, producing toys, wood-carvings, embroidery, ribbons, watches and clocks, has been accomplished through the application of power, heavy capital investment in plant, high standards of craftsmanship, inventive genius, creative energy and trained skill. That the Swiss universities and technological institutes have an international reputation is a reflection of these qualities.

Minerals

Some coal deposits of poor quality are worked in Valais and near St Gallen, and brown coal and peat occur in the Swiss Plateau, though in insignificant quantities. Iron ore was formerly mined at Gozen near St Gallen, at Herznach in the Aargau, and at Choindez in the Jura, but the mines were closed during 1965–7. Rock-salt is worked near Bex in the Rhône valley, and at Schweizerhalle, Rheinfelden and Ryburg in the Rhine valley. Limestone is quarried in the Jura and the northern Alps as the basis of cement making. About 200,000 tons of salt are mined annually at Bex and Schweizerhalle. Granite and gneiss for road-metal are quarried in the mountains.

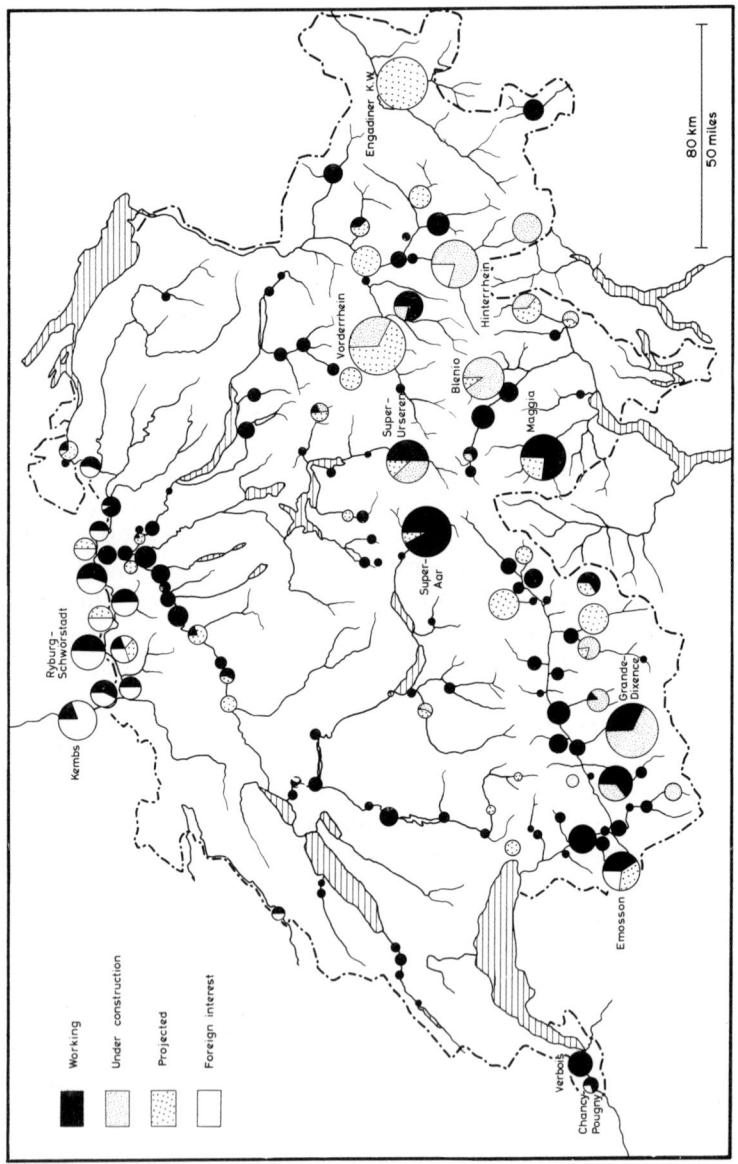

Fig. 68. The production of electricity in Switzerland
(After a map in a brochure published by the *Union des Centrales Suisses d'Electricité*, Lausanne, 1966, with revisions).

Coal, crude and refined oil, pig-iron, raw steel, non-ferrous metals, chemicals, alumina, cotton and timber must be imported, mostly up the Rhine valley, though also some from Italy.

Hydroelectric Power (Fig. 68)

Water-power has been utilized in Switzerland since the Middle Ages, when small wheels were installed along the rivers to provide motive power for flour mills, sawmills and forges. In modern times the country has played a pioneer rôle in the development of hydro-electricity; the first power station was built in 1879, a small plant installed by a hotel proprietor in St Moritz, while the first station for a town system began operation in Lausanne in 1882. Gradually larger installations were built: at Chèvres on the Rhône in 1896 and Rheinfelden on the Rhine in 1898, while in 1908 the first high-head storage reservoir impounded by a dam was completed. Since then development has continued steadily; the output of power, which totalled 600 million KWh in 1900, has grown to about 31 milliard KWh, of which about 94 per cent was hydro. The balance came from thermal plant in Basle and Zürich, mainly functioning as reserve stations in a state of suspended animation, but used in the event of a reduction in hydro supplies. The consumption of current per capita in 1968 was fourth in the world, after Sweden, Norway and U.S.A.; about 40 per cent is used domestically, the same proportion industrially, and the remainder by the railway system. In past years Switzerland has been able to export as much as 20 per cent of its production of power to neighbouring countries, but internal requirements have grown so much that the country is now a net importer. The transmission network is linked to those of West Germany, France, Italy and Austria.

The early stations were small units built to supply local factories or sections of the railway, especially in the Alpine tunnels, among the earliest lines to be electrified; the Amsteg plant furnishes power for the line through the St Gotthard tunnel and a plant near Visp supplies the Simplon section.

The rivers Rhine and Rhône supply energy for several low-head stations, notably at Schaffhausen and Ryburg-Schwörstadt on the Rhine, and at Chancy-Pougny below Lake Geneva on the Rhône. A string of smaller stations is situated along the Aar, another along the Reuss. The main difficulties are the 'locking-up' of water by the winter freeze, the wasteful and concentrated runoff of flood-water in early summer, and the periods of late summer low water. Barrages have been constructed in an effort to equalize the seasonal flow (Plate XLIX). The fluctuating nature of the river régimes is indicated by the ratio of high to low water flow on the Rhône, which is 11:1 at Sierre and 14:1 at Brig, while at Zermeiggern in the Visp valley it is about 45:1. Many of the early schemes were 'run-of-the-river' projects, leading water from a river through an aqueduct, which may result in appreciable variation in output; thus Lavey in Valais has a mean production of 130 million KWh during the winter half-year and of 270 million KWh during the summer half-year.

Most of the big projects recently completed or under construction are in the Alps, utilizing the heavy precipitation, the storage capacity of the snowfields and glaciers, the deep valleys and the steep gradients. They usually involve the construction of a high gravity or arch dam to create a large storage capacity deep enough to allow water to be taken off from beneath the ice when the surface is frozen. Examples include Super-Grimsel on the upper Aar, Super-Urseren on the upper Reuss near Andermatt, and the recently (1965) completed Grande-Dixence (Plate L) in the Val d'Héremence in the Pennine Alps, behind whose dam, 284 m (932 ft) high, water is collected from neighbouring valleys through a complex system of tunnels. The new reservoir supplies three power stations at Chandoline, Fionnay and Nendaz; the last two are underground. About 400 stations, with a total installed capacity of 9 million KW, are in operation; some of these are being enlarged, and a number of others are under construction. Much capital has also been put into developments in Austria, Italy and West Germany.

In Switzerland electricity production and transmission are not nationalized, and large numbers of individual concerns are in operation; some are private, others are owned by a commune, a municipality or a canton. The *Union des Centrales Suisses d'Electricité* has a membership of over 400, including industrial firms and the Federal Railway; some are producers, others distributors, still others perform both functions. There is nevertheless a high degree of integration, supervised by the Federal Electricity Office.

Switzerland is unlike Norway, where the undeveloped hydro-potential is still enormous (p. 76), for it is estimated that 90 per cent of the water resources are being used, and that by 1974 the last economic hydro-station will have been completed. To meet increasing demands a nuclear power station at Lucens in the canton of Vaud began to put electricity into the transmission network in 1965, and three others have been opened at Mühleberg near Thun and at

Beznau near Zürich. The first big oil-fired thermal station, near Aigle, was opened in 1966. Six per cent of Swiss power is now thermally produced.

Other Sources of Power

It is surprising to find that only about a third of the overall energy requirements is derived from hydroelectricity; even that is a substantial increase over 1938, when it was only 17 per cent. An enormous amount of wood is consumed for domestic heating, especially in the mountains, where a mound of logs is stored beside each chalet as winter approaches. About 2 million tons of coal are imported annually; nearly half a million tons of coke are made, gas is distributed in the larger towns, and schemes are in progress to pipe natural gas from the Dutch field at Slochteren (p. 262).

Consumption of oil is increasing rapidly, partly because of the rise in the number both of Swiss cars and lorries (now totalling 1·2 millions) and of tourists' cars, partly because of the greater use of oil as an industrial and domestic fuel. A consumption of 3·2 million tons in 1958, which could be economically supplied by refineries elsewhere in western Europe, has grown to over 12 million in 1968. Both crude and refined oil products come to Basle by tanker-barge and rail-tanker. But port facilities at Basle are strained, despite improvements (p. 382), and in the event of a prolonged period of frost or of summer low water navigation may be hampered or even closed. A trunk pipeline with an annual capacity of 3 million tons has been constructed from Genoa via the Great St Bernard road-tunnel (p. 380) to a refinery at Collombey, near Aigle, to the south-east of Lake Geneva. Other refineries near Cornauz, Cressier and Olten, in the northwest of the country, are supplied with crude oil through spurs from the South European Pipeline (p. 437 and Fig. 89). Another spur brings oil via the Trans-Alpine Pipeline (p. 162), leaving it at Splügen and running to a refinery at St Margrethen. A small refinery has been completed at Bellinzona in Ticino for the use of a local chemical industry.

Manufacturing Industry

At a recent Basle Commercial Fair, about 30,000 different Swiss-made items were on show. About 460,000 people are engaged in metalwork, engineering and watch-making, 166,000 in textiles and clothing manufacture, and 130,000 in food-processing. Other manufactures include chemicals (57,000), a rapidly expanding industry, footwear, soap, detergents and plastics.

While the main centres of manufacturing are at Zürich, Basle, Geneva, Berne and St Gallen, activity is decentralized to a remarkable extent; almost every village has a factory of some sort, often small but modern and highly efficient, producing a type of precision instrument, a piece of specialized machinery, or some other item of quality (Plate LI). An exacting and highly critical home market is the result of one of the highest standards of living in the world.

The manufacture of machines, machine tools, turbines, generators and other electrical equipment, diesel-electric locomotives, textile machinery, printing machinery, pumps and refrigerating machinery is concentrated in the larger cities on the Swiss Plateau. These engineering industries developed initially to meet home requirements, and the degree of skilled specialization involved led to the development of precision instruments, optical products, typewriters, computers, radios, gramophones, acoustic equipment and tape-recorders. The home demand for presses, grinders, milling-machines, automatic lathes and machine tools produced first an excess for export, then an actual concentration on the export market. Much machinery is sent to other parts of Europe; in 1968 the European Economic Community took two-fifths of the Swiss output, and the European Free Trade Association another fifth. Much of the metal required is imported from West Germany and France in the form of either pig-iron or raw steel; most is made into alloy steel, especially at large plants at Bienne, Wintherthur and Schaffhausen. About 400,000 tons of finished steel are made annually in electric furnaces, mostly from scrap.

A wide range of non-ferrous metals is consumed, and several plants produce copper wire, brass, zinc and lead. Until 1906 Switzerland was the world's largest producer of aluminium, the result of its pioneer development of electricity. The output from the smelters at Neuhausen and Rheinfelden on the Rhine and another near Orsières in Valais now totals about 50,000 tons.

At one time Switzerland produced about four-fifths of the world total of watches and clocks, but today the share has fallen to 45 per cent, mainly as a result of the growing competition of Japan, the U.S.S.R. and the U.S.A. Until recently the industry was in the hands of more than 2000 separate undertakings, but production methods are being rationalised within a smaller number of highly automated factories. Several of the great watch firms are internationally renowned; most have their headquarters in Le Locle, Neuchâtel, Geneva, La Chaux-de-Fonds, Solothurn, St Imier and Schaffhausen, though drawing on dispersed factories and workshops. The Swiss Horological Research Laboratory and the Horological Electronic Centre, both in Neuchâtel, carry out research on behalf of the industry. The craftsmanship and creative energy that produced the carved wooden clocks of four centuries ago now build atomic clocks and a new type of watch of incredible accuracy, powered by a vibrating quartz crystal strip.

The textile industry had its origins in the fine lace and embroidery made in the homes during the long winters, and in the linens and woollens woven in small workshops at St Gallen, Burgdorf and Berne. For centuries these textiles dominated Swiss exports and at the beginning of this century they still accounted for 52 per cent of the total by value; now they occupy only fourth place after machinery, chemicals and watches. The industry found it impossible to compete with cheap mass-produced textiles and concentrated on quality products, exported not to the mass markets of Africa, Latin America or the Far East, but to West Germany, Britain and the U.S.A. The establishment of freer trading relationships in western Europe since 1945, together with the rise in the standard of living, has benefited the textile industry very markedly. Since 1950 exports of synthetic fibres and yarns have quadrupled in value, of ready-made clothing have trebled, and of embroidery have doubled. Factory production is now dominant, though the units are still for the most part small and widely dispersed, and there is much piece-work on a semi-domestic basis. Cottons are made at St Gallen, Zürich and Basle; linen at Berne and St Gallen; woollens at Schaffhausen and Solothurn; silk at Zürich and Basle; and branches of the various textile industries are found in small towns throughout the Swiss Plateau.

The chemical industry, initiated mainly to provide aniline dyes for textiles, has developed in Basle where it originated. The great names in Swiss chemicals (*Ciba, Roche, Geigy* and *Sandoz,* among others) produce a range of industrial and pharmaceutical chemicals, dye-stuffs, photographic materials, cosmetics and perfumes, plastics and agrochemicals, and are affiliated with concerns in many parts of the world.

Food-processing developed because certain types of farm produce, notably milk, were among the few raw materials available, and once again inventive initiative led the way in creating new methods of food preparation and preservation. In 1867 Henri Nestlé developed an easily digestible milk food, the first commercial infant food; today the firm he founded owns 200 factories in thirty-four different countries stemming from the parent organization, and numerous other concerns have international reputations. The production of processed milk, chocolate, instant drinks, soups, processed cheese, meat extracts, concentrates, baby and invalid foods, as well as biscuits and pasta, cigarettes and tobacco, provides not only for a large home market but for a considerable export.

This catalogue of manufacturing activity has listed only the more important items. Wooden objects, soap, musical instruments, jewellery, silver plate, footwear and many more appear on the world's markets. They consume little raw material but are of high value and require much fabrication in proportion to their bulk.

TOURISM

The skilful and attractive organization of hotels and catering, together with efficient transport systems, enable the advantages of Swiss scenic beauty to be profitably and accessibly capitalized, both in summer and winter, offering holidays from the most leisurely to the most strenuous. About 150,000 Swiss are employed in hotels and many more indirectly benefit from tourism. About 6 million foreign visitors come each year.

COMMUNICATIONS

Situated in the heart of the continent, with Alpine ranges bordering its southern margins, the barrier of the Jura in the north-west, and a snow cover for much of the winter, the Swiss transport systems have to cope with considerable physical difficulties. Most of the main routes cross the country from north to south, while the mountain barriers run from west to east. Yet these problems had to be faced for Switzerland to take advantage of its central position and to change isolation into accessibility, in order to import essential raw materials, export the goods by which it lives, and afford access to tourists. Internally it was necessary to provide links with relatively isolated districts as a contribution to federal unity.

Roads

Since earliest times Switzerland has lain at the crossroads of Europe; some of the Alpine passes were crossed by Roman legions, followed throughout history by pilgrims, merchants and soldiers. The passes separated the trading cities of medieval Italy from the Hansa towns of northern Europe, and though the routes were then little more than mule tracks they were well used. Napoleon required effective routeways to help keep his empire together, and at his direction a road was constructed over the Simplon Pass.

During the modern period some remarkably good routes have been constructed, both trunk roads and secondary roads penetrating the remote valleys. Not only has this system to cope with the influx of foreign vehicles, but there is one Swiss car for every five inhabitants, and the network is heavily overburdened. A programme of about 1900 km (1200 miles) of motorway is under development; some sections, including Geneva–Lausanne, Zürich–Berne and Zürich-Liechtenstein, are complete.

Constant engineering is necessary on the Alpine roads to improve their alignment, width and surface, to carry out programmes of protection against avalanche and flood, and to effect repairs after each winter. The Susten Pass, for example, which climbs to 2262 m (7421 ft) between Meiringen and Wassen, was transformed from a track into a good motor road, though it is closed by snow between

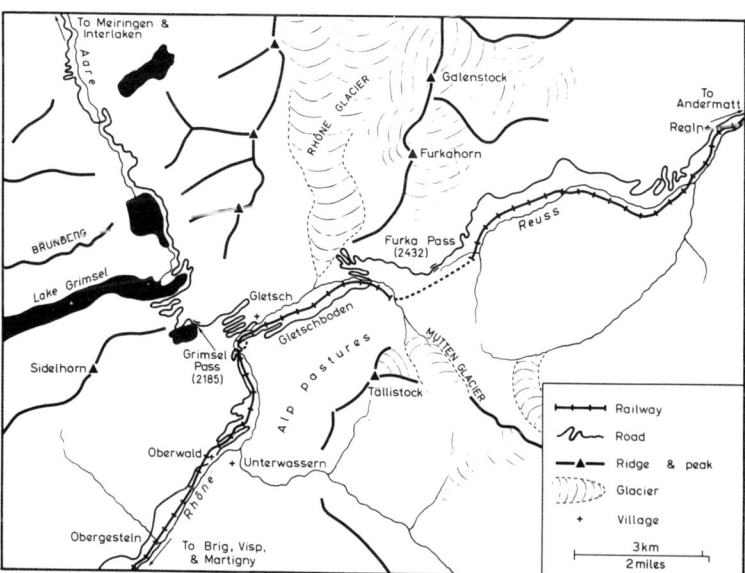

Fig. 69. Alpine roads and railways in the neighbourhood of the Furka and Grimsel passes
(After *Landeskarte der Schweiz*)

October and June, as are most of the Alpine passes. The highest are the Umbrail Pass (2505 m, 8218 ft) in the east between Sta Maria and Bormio in Italy (Fig. 77); the Great St Bernard between Aosta and Martigny; and the Furka, one of the west–east links between the upper Rhône and Rhine valleys (Fig. 69). Though snow-blocking of passes is a serious disadvantage, it is partly remedied by the speedy convey-ance of cars on rail trucks through the St Gotthard and Lötschberg–Simplon tunnels and by some new road-tunnels.

A major project was completed in 1964, when the road tunnel, 5·6 km (3·5 miles) long, between Bourg St Pierre and St Oyen under the Great St Bernard Pass was opened. It is a high altitude tunnel, entering at 1915 m (6282 ft) above sea-level, but is approached by roads with wide curves and gradual inclines, protected by snow-sheds, and will be kept open throughout the year. The boring of the San Bernardino Tunnel, 6·4 km (4 miles) long, in eastern Switzerland was completed in May 1965, and it was opened to traffic in 1967.

Apart from private motorists, the Swiss roads carry a heavy tonnage of freight, and local systems operate 1300 km (800 miles) of route by bus, trolleybus and tram. The *Autoreiseposter*, or coach routes operated by the Swiss Post Office, penetrate into the most isolated valleys, providing economic transport for passengers, mails and light freight.

Railways

Since the first railway was opened in 1847, the system has grown steadily; there are now 2914 km (1811 miles) of Federal standard-gauge line (Fig. 70), 2140 km (1330 miles) of privately owned line, both standard- and narrow-gauge, and a further 400 km (250 miles) of rack, cable and funicular services. The Federal system is concerned only with main line internal and international traffic, and has few branch lines. It is financially one of the soundest in the world, because it has been efficiently electrified for over thirty years, it carries a heavy and remunerative international transit traffic, it charges high fares, it does not have to subsidize uneconomic branch lines, and competition from road haulage is less serious than in many countries.

The private railways consist of numerous separate concerns, ranging from a few large units, such as the Rhaetian Railway, to a multiplicity of narrow-gauge lines, existing to supply a local service which a viable main line Federal system could not provide. They are private in that they are run by limited companies but no private capital is involved, for they are financed by federal, cantonal and municipal funds. The

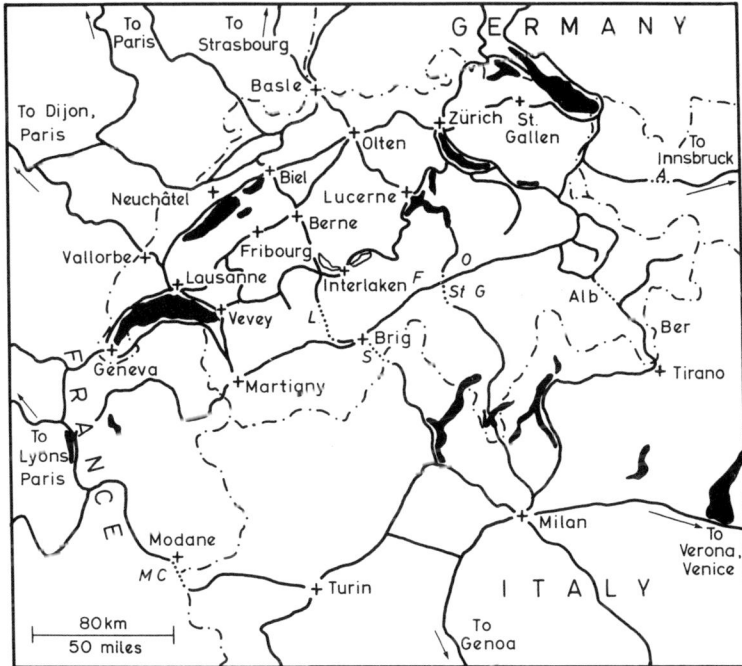

Fig. 70. The mainline railway system in Switzerland
Passes and tunnels are shown by abbreviations, identifiable in an atlas.

mountain railways and funiculars carry a heavy traffic of visitors in summer and of winter sports enthusiasts in winter; the *Jungfraubahn* takes passengers through the heart of the Eiger peak to the Jungfraujoch at 3380 m (11,090 ft), Europe's highest railway station (Fig. 65).

Several main lines serve the Plateau in a west to east direction, notably the Geneva–Neuchâtel–Bienne–Olten–Zürich–St Gallen line, and the Lausanne–Fribourg–Berne–Olten line. Farther south it is not so easy to travel from west to east. One line pursues a most scenic route from Vevey via Interlaken to Lucerne and Zürich. Another takes advantage of the troughs of the Rhône and the Rhine; from Montreux one travels by the main line to Brig, there takes the Furka-Oberalp Railway (Fig. 69), and then proceeds down the Rhine valley to Chur by the Rhaetian Railway. From Brig much of this line is single-track, operating only in the summer.

Several transcontinental lines cross Switzerland from north to south, focusing on the two main tunnels. The 15·3 km (9·5 miles) St

Gotthard tunnel, completed in 1882, links Zürich with Milan via Como. Two other routes converge on Brig in the Rhône valley; one crosses the French frontier at Vallorbe and passes through Lausanne, Montreux and Martigny, the other comes from Basle or Belfort via Berne, and penetrates the Oberland ranges by means of the Lötschberg tunnel. Both lines enter the Simplon tunnel and continue via Domodossola and Stresa to Milan. The only other railway to cross into Italy runs south from St Moritz via the Bernina pass to Tirano in Italy, hence to Lake Como and Milan; this attains a height of 2068 m (6786 ft), and with the protection of snow-sheds and galleries operates throughout the year.

Switzerland is well serviced by through services from France, West Germany and the Netherlands. Among the famous trains are 'Helvetia' (Hamburg–Zürich), 'L'Arbalète' (Paris–Zürich), 'Edelweiss' (Amsterdam–Zürich) and 'Loreley' (Hook of Holland and Amsterdam–Basle). Highly efficient freight-liner and container terminals have been constructed at Basle and Geneva.

Air Transport

For a country in the heart of a continent air transport can solve many problems, and two civil air companies were formed as early as 1919; they merged in 1931 as *Swissair*, the privately owned and unsubsidized national airline. The airports are, however, federally owned and operated, though *Swissair* enjoys no more privileges or status than foreign operators. The three international airports are at Basle-Mulhouse (on French territory and operated jointly with France), Geneva-Cointrin (where a new airport was opened in 1968) and Zürich-Kloten.

The Port of Basle

One of the compensatory features of Switzerland's inland position is that the Rhine becomes navigable at Basle, which, located 800 km (500 miles) from the sea, has developed into an active port (Fig. 71). But the rift-valley Rhine is not a good natural waterway (p. 460), with its fluctuating volume and liability to freezing, and few vessels could go above Strasbourg until the beginning of this century. Basle has been helped considerably by the French construction of several sections of the Grand Canal d'Alsace (p. 434), and by joint French-German improvements on the Rhine itself, enabling adequate navigational depths to be maintained. Occasionally winter freezing or summer low water may halt navigation, but normally barges of

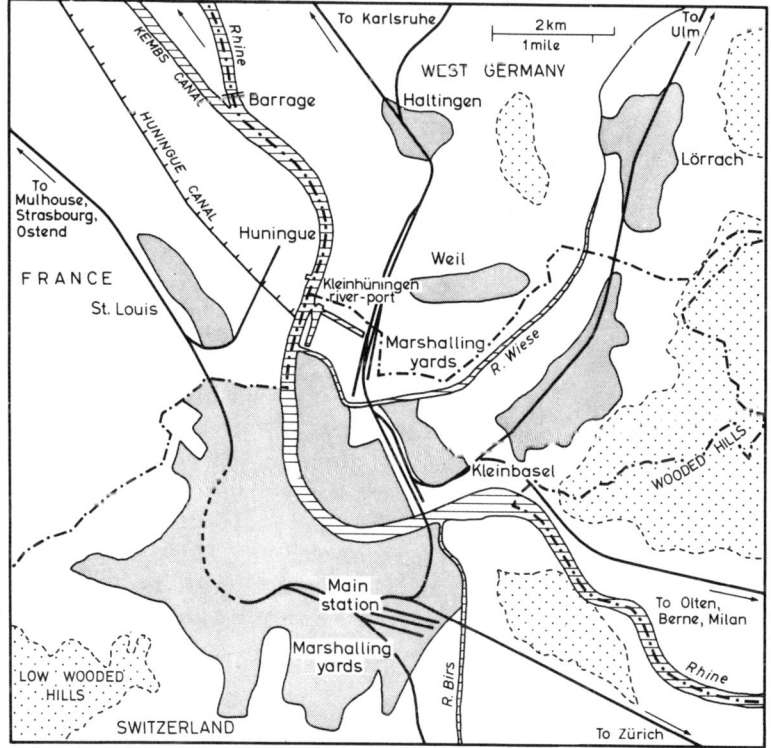

Fig. 71. Basle
(After *Landeskarte der Schweiz*)
For key, see Fig. 72.

up to 2,000 tons can use the port. There are two main harbours (Plate LII), with modern quays and facilities which in 1968 handled 7·8 million tons of freight; over 95 per cent by volume consisted of imports (oil, coal, coke, wheat, pig-iron and raw steel, timber). Thus Basle can regard Rotterdam, Amsterdam and Antwerp as functioning as its 'outports'. About half this freight is carried in Swiss vessels, the rest in mainly Dutch and some Belgian, French and West German barges.

COMMERCE

Switzerland is obliged to import the large quantity of food which it is unable to produce, and even larger quantities of raw materials and fuel. To pay for these it is necessary to export manufactured products: 95 per cent of its dyestuffs, 90 per cent of its textile machinery, and 80 per cent of its machine tools. Of these and other manufactures, about two-thirds are sold in Europe. The country normally has an adverse visible balance of trade, for in recent years exports have paid for only about 80 per cent of the imports. Most of this deficit is met by invisible exports: receipts from tourism (equivalent to about 10 per cent of the value of visible exports), foreign investment and insurance, transit dues, and the earnings of its banking system. Switzerland's rôle in international finance has come about through the stability and unrestricted convertibility of the Swiss franc, the large deposits from overseas in Swiss banks, and a bank rate (now $3\frac{3}{4}$ per cent) that has fluctuated only slightly in recent years.

Switzerland is very concerned with problems of European integration, especially in the economic sphere, since its existence depends on the maintenance and extension of markets for its exports. The creation of the European Economic Community caused some anxiety, since nearly a third of Switzerland's exports normally go to the Six. It is a full member of the European Free Trade Association, and sought in 1962 (without success) to establish some form of association with E.E.C. One difficulty is that Switzerland cannot join any grouping which involves political implications or affects in any way its independence and neutrality.

POPULATION AND SETTLEMENT

The population of Switzerland in 1968 was about 6·1 millions, having risen steadily from 2·4 millions at the census of 1850. This rise has been almost entirely in the urban population, especially in the larger towns. Though the average density over the country was 148 per sq. km (382 per sq. mile), if this average were calculated on the basis of only the permanently inhabited area, it would come to the more representative figure of about 700 (1800). Rather more than two-thirds of the population live on the Swiss Plateau, which is little more than a third of the area. The shortage of industrial labour is indicated by the presence of over 500,000 foreign workers on labour permits.

The most densely populated parts are in the 'greater Zürich', 'greater Basle' and 'greater Geneva' urban districts; along the northern shores of Lake Geneva, with an almost continuous string of flourishing small towns; around Lake Lucerne; to the south of Lake Constance in the triangle between Winterthur, St Gallen and

Constance; and in the piedmont lake zone between Neuchâtel, Bienne and Berne. Even the low figures for the mountainous cantons of Valais and Graubünden conceal some concentrations of population along the floors and south-facing slopes of the Rhône and Rhine valleys. Strings of small towns (Martigny, Sion, Sierre, Leuk, Visp and Brig in the Rhône valley; Disentis, Flims, Ilanz, Tamins and Chur in the Rhine valley) are linked by agricultural settlement, with occasional factories.

The urban population, defined as those living in towns of 10,000 or over, amounts to just over 2 millions, or about 40 per cent of the total. Five towns have populations exceeding 100,000: Zürich with 435,000 by far the largest, followed by Basle (215,000), Geneva (172,000), Berne (169,000) and Lausanne (139,000). The cities are attractive, for they have been spared both destruction by war and desecration by the Industrial Revolution; the guild houses of the Altstadt in Zürich, the patrician dwellings and arcades of Berne, the baroque cathedral of Solothurn, the eleventh century cathedral of Schaffhausen, the arcades of Lugano, all remain unspoilt. Yet fine modern buildings have risen in Zürich and Geneva, and the many factories and workshops are clean and smokeless.

Religion and Language

Switzerland's national unity is the more remarkable because its people are of diverse religion and language. At the last census Protestants numbered 2·7 millions (about 52 per cent of the total), Roman Catholics about 46 per cent. These proportions have changed little during the centuries; there have been bitter religious controversies, but today there is complete liberty of creed and conscience.

Four officially recognized languages are spoken, and again the pattern has changed little with time. Dialects of German (*Schweizerdeutsch*) are used by about 69 per cent of the national population, who are in a majority in nineteen of the twenty-five cantons, those in the centre, east and north (Fig. 60). Just under a million (19 per cent) are French-speaking, almost wholly in the western cantons, and about 280,000 speak Italian, most of these living in Ticino, the others in the more southerly valleys of Graubünden. The majority of the people in the last-named canton (about 50,000) speak *Romansch*, which became an official language in 1937; it is derived from the Latin once spoken in the Roman province of Rhaetia, but isolated from the neighbouring Romance languages and largely surrounded by a German-speaking population, it has survived in the valleys of the Vorder Rhine and its tributaries, and in the Engadine.

REGIONS (Fig. 64)

1. *The Jura*

The arc of the Jura Mountains extends from the Rhine valley between Basle and Schaffhausen south-westward across the French frontier. It is bounded on the south-east by a depression in which lie Lakes Neuchâtel and Bienne and the river Aar. The northern portion comprises part of the 'Plateau Jura', the remainder the 'Folded Jura'.

The Plateau Jura is an undulating area of Molasse in the east, of Jurassic limestone in the west, on which good soils have developed, especially where a covering of loess is present. The countryside is well cultivated with wheat and sugar beet, vines and orchards on south-facing slopes, and there is a flourishing dairying activity. Most of the small towns are centres of specialized industry: silk, chemicals, cement and engineering, especially along the valley of the Birse. These towns include Brugg, a main crossing point of the Aar, with a large cable works, Liestal, Delémont and Porrentruy; the last two are on the main railway line from France to Berne via Belfort.

The centre of this region, indeed of all north-western Switzerland, is Basle (Fig. 71), a river port and a focus for rail and road routes from France, Germany and the North Sea through the Rhineland. It owes much to its situation on the right-angle bend of the Rhine at the head of the rift valley, with the Belfort Gap on the west leading into France and the upper Rhine valley affording a route to eastern Switzerland and Austria. Its site is so congested and hilly that its airport is on the Rhine plain in France, operated jointly by the two countries. Basle is an important bridge town, with five road bridges and a rail bridge, the main part of the city being on the west bank, Kleinbasel on the east. The settlement was first mentioned in A.D. 374, when it was named *Basilia*, and it flourished as a Free City in the Holy Roman Empire. Since then the city has spread outwards from its well preserved twelfth century Altstadt, and many small towns and villages have been incorporated within the conurbation. Its port is on the right bank below the city at Kleinhüningen, with modern dock basins and installations (Plate LII). Basle is an important industrial city, especially for pharmaceutical chemicals, engineering products, and silk and cotton textiles, and it is a centre of commerce and finance, holding an annual Swiss commercial and industrial fair.

Though the greater part of the 'Folded Jura' lie in France, the more easterly ridges and valleys are in Switzerland. Numerous parallel ranges culminate in limestone cliffs with pinnacled crests, separated by long steep-sided valleys. Some of the higher valleys contain such rivers as the Doubs, which marks the Franco-Swiss frontier for some distance, and in the south the Orbe follows a trench from its source in France through the Lac de Joux and so into Lake Neuchâtel.

About a third of the Jura is forested, mainly with spruce and pine; steep slopes rising from the green meadows of the valley floors are swathed with conifers, interrupted by limestone cliffs too steep to support vegetation. Though there is a varied agricultural activity, the emphasis is on pastoral farming based on the meadows; here dairy cattle graze in summer, supplying milk to the factories in Geneva and Neuchâtel which make condensed milk, chocolate and cheese. Transhumance is still practised, families taking the animals to the high pastures from May to September, though many cattle are now kept permanently in the valleys. On the lower slopes a patchwork of small fields grows wheat and oats, potatoes, turnips, and in the south some tobacco; orchards of apples, plums, medlars and cherries flourish on sunny, south-facing aspects.

Prosperous cottage industries, such as wood-carving and the making of watches and clocks, have long been an important feature of the Jura. Small rural workshops still make watch parts for assembly in towns such as Geneva and Neuchâtel on the margins of the hills, but this activity is now concentrated in La Chaux-de-Fonds (43,000) situated at a height of 900 m (3000 ft), Le Locle, Tavannes and St Imier. At Ste Croix tape-recorders, gramophones and cine-projectors are made.

2. *The Swiss Plateau*

The surface of the Swiss Plateau is far from flat (Plate XLVII); wooded ridges rise above the general level, lakes lie in hollows, and the Aar and Reuss with their tributaries flow northward to the Rhine in deeply entrenched valleys. This is the most important part of Switzerland; here live two-thirds of the population, here are all the large towns except Basle, and here flourish both intensive agriculture and diverse industrial activities. More than half the farm-land is under pasture and fodder crops; sugar beet, potatoes and cereals are also grown. A considerable area of orchards produces apples, pears, and black cherries which are used for making pre-serves; vineyards cover the south-facing slopes, especially along the shores of Lake Geneva. The most prosperous farming areas are in the Thurgau to the south of Lake Constance and extending beyond Zürich to the Reuss valley, the Emmenthal in canton Berne, the Saane (Sarine) valley, the pleasant country to the north of Lake Geneva, and the reclaimed lands around Lakes Neuchâtel and Bienne.

Apart from Zürich, Berne and Geneva, the Plateau contains many small busy towns, linked by an efficient network of roads and railways and set in a well-populated countryside. In the north-east Winterthur (93,000) was originally a textile town, but is now more famous for its diesel engines and electric locomotives, and St Gallen (78,000) is the centre of cotton textiles, lace and embroidery. In the Rhine valley Schaffhausen, a bridge town for both road and railway, is situated two miles from the Rhine Falls at Rheinau, where a power station produces electricity used by engineering works and by an aluminium refinery at nearby Neuhausen. Other towns on the Swiss Plateau include the railway junction of Olten, the industrial centre of Baden (with machine tools and electrical engin-eering) and Fribourg, a centre of factory-made cheese, standing on a prominent spur almost surrounded by an incised meander of the Saane. Many towns, with their specialized industries tucked dis-creetly away, are visited by tourists. Lucerne (74,000) is situated around the foot of the lake near the exit of the Reuss; steep wooded hills rise from the shore, along which are numerous resorts and hotels. The 13·7 km (8·5 miles) Axenstrasse, a roadway cut from the solid rock, closely follows the shore between Brunnen and Flüelen. Along the northern shores of Lake Geneva is an almost continuous line of pleasant towns: Nyon, Rolle, Morges, Lausanne, Vevey and Mon-treux. The largest is Lausanne, its steep streets ascending the terraced slopes of Mont Jorat, crowned by a cathedral and castle; a funicular links Ouchy, its port on the lake, with the railway station in the city.

Zürich is the most important city of Switzerland, with flourishing industrial, commercial and financial activities, and a general air of wealth and efficiency. It is situated at the northern end of Lake Zürich, where the river Limmat leaves the lake on its way to join the Reuss (Fig. 72). The settlement developed in Roman times as

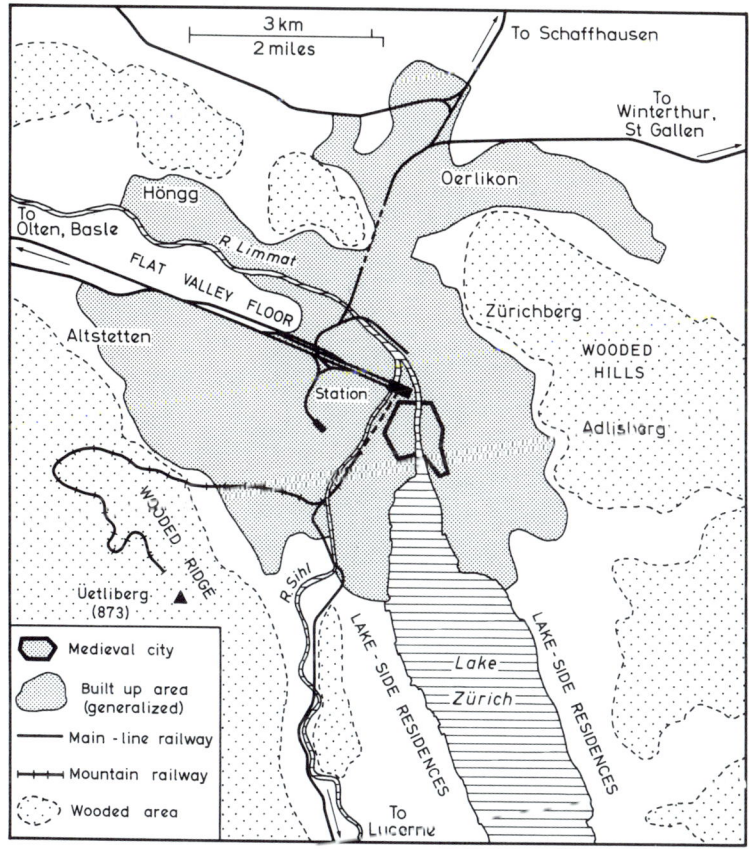

Fig. 72. Zürich
(After *Landeskarte der Schweiz*)

Turicum, it later became a bridge and market town, and then began
its industrial life as a centre of silk manufacture. Zürich has grown
rapidly in recent decades to the west beyond the river Sihl on to the
slopes of the Uetliberg, with a mountain railway to its summit, and
to the east on to the Zürichberg and Adlisberg. It has also extended
to the north to include Oerlikon, the home of world-renowned
engineering and armament industries. The guild houses of the Altstadt on either side of the Limmat, the elegant shopping centre of the
Bahnhofstrasse, the flourishing commercial and financial quarters,
the blocks of modern flats, and industrial districts which must be
the cleanest in the world, combine with the setting of Zürich to make
it a most attractive city.

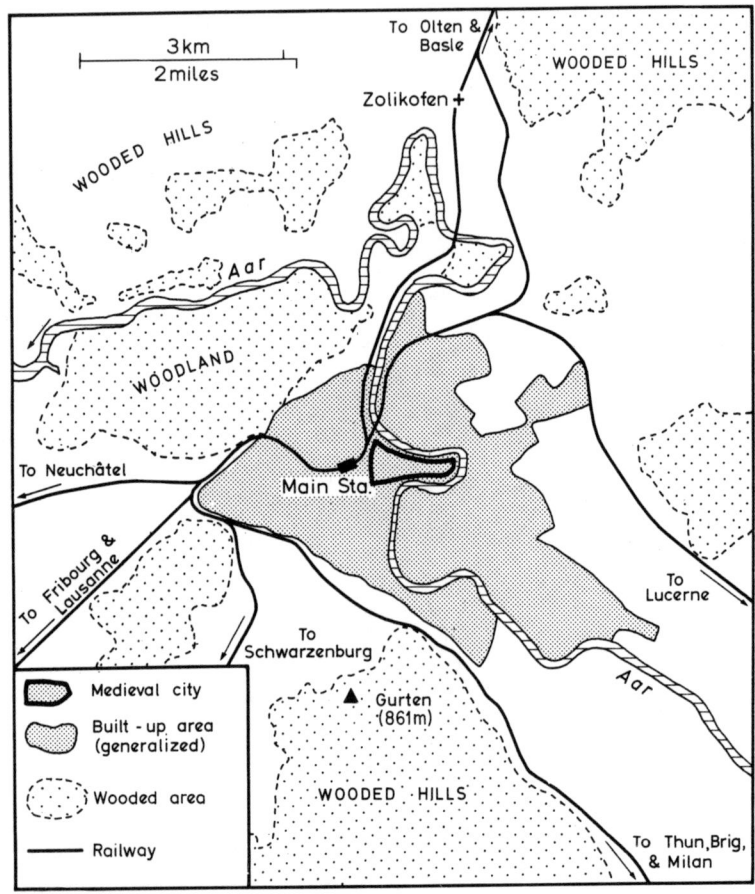

Fig. 73. Berne
(After *Landeskarte der Schweiz*)

Berne (Plate LIII) has been the Federal capital only since 1848, though it was founded at the end of the twelfth century. Its site, chosen for its defensive value, is a sandstone peninsula, surrounded by the Aar flowing swiftly 30 m (100 ft) below in an incised meander-gorge (Fig. 73). Much of the medieval city, with its arcades and fountains, still survives, surrounded by the modern town. Apart from its administrative importance, Berne is a route centre of remarkable nodality, for here the Geneva–Lausanne–Fribourg–Zürich–St Gallen–Austria line over the Swiss Plateau crosses the transcontinental Basle–Olten–Lötschberg–Simplon–Milan line. Its

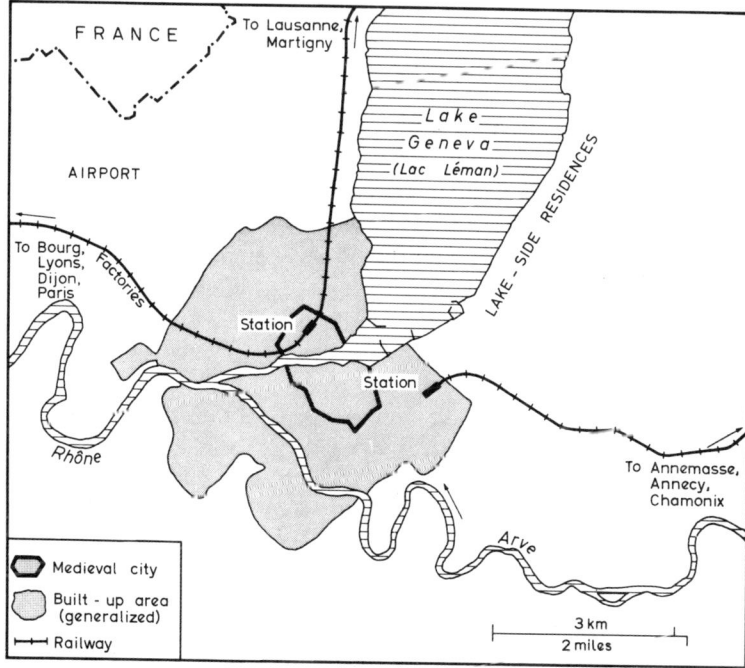

Fig. 74. Geneva
(After *Landeskarte der Schweiz*)

industries include the manufacture of textiles, chocolate, light engineering products and furniture.

Geneva lies at the western end of Lake Geneva, where the Rhône leaves as a clear fast-flowing stream, to be joined 1·5 km below by the Arve (Fig. 74). In the first century B.C. Geneva was the capital of a Celtic tribe, later of a Roman province. During the troubled times of the Reformation, the city espoused Protestantism, and in 1536 John Calvin established himself there, for it has always offered a haven for refugees of all kinds. It is the home of international organizations, including the former League of Nations, the International Labour Office, the World Health Organization, the World Meteorological Organization, and the World Council of Churches. Geneva is also a centre of banking houses, commercial firms, and the watch and jewellery industry. It is spaciously laid out, with its hotels, shops and gardens making the most of its extensive lake frontage. Several railway lines from France focus on it, and it is at the western end of the railway system across the Swiss Plateau to Lake Constance. It has an international airport, and from the city a motor-way follows the northern shores of the lake to Lausanne.

3. *The Alps*

This diverse region of high ranges and deep valleys can be divided into several distinctive units.

The Rhône Valley. The Rhône flows through its glaciated trench for about 130 km (80 miles), regularized and embanked between Sierre and Martigny against the floods of early summer. Particularly in its upper parts, the valley reveals well the striking contrast between south- and north-facing slopes. Most settlements are sited along the northern side, on alluvial fans formed by tributaries descending from the Oberland snowfields, and away from the flood-threatened floor of the trough. The valley lies in a distinct rain-shadow area and usually has a warm sunny summer; it has been described as 'an Alpine land with a Mediterranean climate' and as 'the Côte d'Azur with glaciers'. Vines for the Fendant white wine and the Dôle red wine, apricots, plums, peaches, cherries, almonds and figs, and market-garden crops are cultivated. Irrigation is widely practised, using water led by gravity from the Rhône tributaries over the fertile fans. By contrast, the north-facing slopes are thickly forested. In the tributary valleys age-old patterns of life can still be observed, though affected in some by the construction of new power stations and factories. On the north the Lötschenthal, the valley of the Lonza (Fig. 67), was until recently accessible only to walkers or mule trains, and was wholly cut off for long periods in winter. Now there is a motor road and a postal bus service, but the villagers of Ferden, Kippel, Ried and Blatten still take their herds in summer on to the south-facing alps below the Petersgrat.

At points along the Rhône valley small towns serve as collecting centres for agricultural produce and as markets for the side valleys. Most have in addition some industries based on hydroelectric power (Fig. 75); thus Brig has a furniture factory, Visp an electro-chemical plant, Chippis an aluminium refinery, Sierre a small engineering works, Sion a textile mill and a factory making pharma-ceutical chemicals and cosmetics, Ardon a small steel foundry, and Martigny a chemical and an engineering works.

The lower part of the valley is served by the railway line from Lausanne to Milan, which follows the Rhône until it turns south at Brig to penetrate the mountains by way of the Simplon tunnel. Both a road and a railway follow the Rhône valley to its head (Fig.

69). The road climbs by remarkable zigzags to the Furka Pass near the snout of the Rhône Glacier and continues eastward to Andermatt; the motorist can escape north by an equally sensational road over the Grimsel Pass, though both roads are blocked by snow from October until June. A railway crosses the Furka with the aid of several spiral tunnels, operating through-services in summer.

Both the Oberland and the Pennine Alps are renowned tourist districts. The valleys opening out on to the Swiss Plateau on the

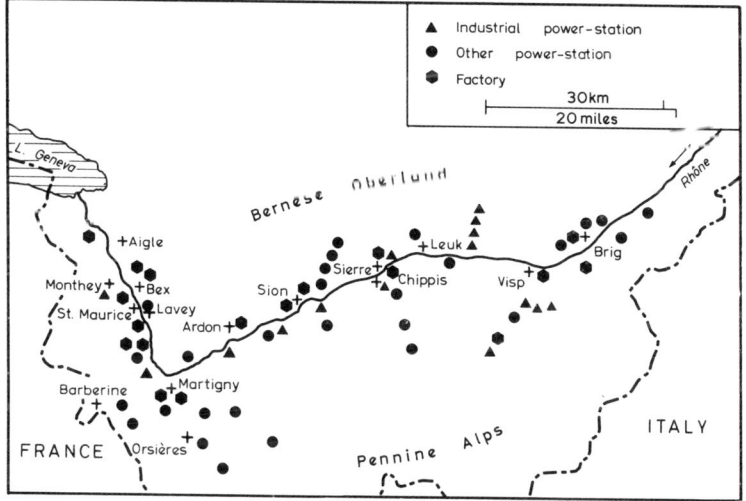

Fig. 75. Power and industry in Valais
(Plotted in the field by a student-group)

northern margins contain many resorts; Gsteig, Lenk, Adelboden, Kandersteg, Lauterbrunnen, Interlaken, Grindelwald and Meiringen are all popular in both winter and summer. The southern slopes of the Oberland are less interrupted by side valleys and fall steeply to the Rhône, but a few small resorts, such as Leukerbad, perch in the hanging valleys or, such as Belalp, on the alp shoulders overlooking the Aletsch Glacier.

The southern valleys, from their heads among the peaks on the Italian border to their junction with the Rhône trough, have their own characteristics, though dairy farming, forestry and tourism are familiar repeating patterns. Here are sited many of the new power stations, dams and reservoirs. Each has its resorts, famous climbing- and ski-ing centres with hotels, mountain railways and ski lifts, superimposed upon the traditional pastoral and forestry economy. Saas Fee in the Saas valley, St Niklaus and Zermatt in the upper Visp valley, Zinal in the Val d'Anniviers, Evolène, Les Haudères (Plate LIV) and Arolla in the Val d'Hérens, all have their Alpine traditions, their corps of guides and their ski schools. Farther west, near the bend of the Rhône at Martigny, the Dixence (Drance) and Trient valleys join the main trench. The Dixence valley leads via Orsières and Bourg St Pierre to the Great St Bernard Pass, thence to the Val d'Aosta in Italy. On the summit of the pass is the Hospice, founded by St Bernard de Menthon in 962 A.D., since when travellers have been given shelter and succour; the pass is open to motor traffic from June to October, but since April 1964, when the new road tunnel (p. 380) was opened, it has been but little used. At Orsières the Val Ferret joins the Dixence, retaining much of its peaceful character since no road crosses the Col de Balme at its head into Italy, but there is a succession of small villages, their inhabitants keeping cattle and goats, with a few small hotels.

Below Martigny the Rhône flows north-west in a narrow gorge flanked by the Dent du Midi on the west and the Dent du Morcles on the east. The valley opens out below Bex, with a marshy floor which has in parts been drained and reclaimed. Several large factories are in this section: cement works supplied with local limestone at St Maurice and Vouvrey, engineering and chemical works at Monthey, and an oil refinery at Collombey.

The Rhine Valley. Crossing eastward over the Furka Pass, one descends into the Urserenthal, a short section of valley separated by the Furka Pass from the headstreams of the Rhône and by the Oberalp Pass from those of the Rhine. Down the Urserenthal flow the turbulent headwaters of the Reuss, which continues northward through Altdorf into Lake Lucerne; this valley is most spectacular,

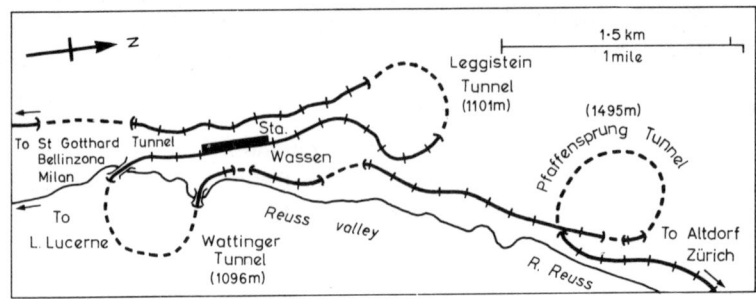

Fig. 76. *The mainline railway north of the St Gotthard Tunnel*
(After an official railway map)

since the river cuts through the granite in the Schöllenen Gorge. The line from Zürich to Milan avoids these problems, for after negotiating some remarkable loops and spiral tunnels (Fig. 76) it enters the St Gotthard tunnel at Göschenen. The road pass over the St Gotthard rises to 2112 m (6929 ft), but many motorists bound for Italy put their cars on railway trucks for conveyance through the tunnel. At Göschenen an underground power station has been recently completed, part of the 'Super-Urseren' scheme.

The Vorder-Rhine flows in the glacier-deepened 'furrow' between the Glarus Alps to the north and the Lepontine, Adula and Rhaetian Alps on the south as far as Chur, the capital of Graubünden. These mountains are extremely dissected; there are said to be 150 side-valleys, each containing a river and one or more lakes. Though broadly similar to Valais in appearance, the Rhine trough has fewer villages and farms, and life seems simpler and more traditional. Each village consists of a group of wooden chalets and a church, with small patches of potatoes, cereals, vegetables and fruit on the valley floor and the lower slopes. Above are the steep forested valley walls, and higher still the summer pastures with their rough seasonal settlements. The railway from the Furka and Oberalp Passes continues to Chur, but operates only from Andermatt during the winter; it passes through such small places as Sedrun, Disentis and Ilanz.

Numerous tributaries enter the main valley from either side, notably that of the Hinter-Rhine, whose headstreams rise in the snowfields of the Adula Alps. This branch of the river flows transversely across the 'grain' of the country, in one section through a magnificent limestone gorge. Despite its difficulties, the Hinter-Rhine valley was negotiated by a Roman road from Chur (Cura Rhaetorum) to Thusis and Splügen, and so over the Splügen Pass to Chiavenna and Lake Como in Italy (Fig. 77). The spectacular Via Mala was built through the Hinter-Rhine gorge above Thusis in 1822, crossing the river several times and penetrating the ravine by tunnels and a roadway cut in the solid rock, with the river 50 m (160 ft) below; a new road at a higher level has been constructed during the last few years. Another road from Splügen crosses the San Bernardino Pass within Swiss territory to Bellinzona in canton Ticino and to Lake Maggiore.

Other right-bank tributaries, including the Landwasser, which joins the Rhine at Chur, and the Landquart, drain the mountains and valleys to the south-east of the Rhine. These sheltered and sunny valleys have an attractive appearance; fruit trees and vines grow on the terraced slopes and irrigated meadows are on their floors. Several pleasant if sophisticated resorts have developed, especially for winter sports, and some with sanatoria, notably Davos, now with a population of 11,000, Klosters and Arosa.

Below Chur the Rhine flows northward for about 150 km (90 miles) to Lake Constance, forming the Swiss-Austrian border for most of its length, with the St Gallen Alps on the west. Much of its formerly marshy floor has been drained and the river has been regularized.

The Engadine Valley, through which flows the Inn, is another structural trough following the main 'grain' of the Alps, more or less parallel to the Vorder-Rhine to the north. It is a clearly defined regional unit, though it is usually divided into the Ober (Upper) and Unter (Lower) sections, the division being at Susch. Away in the south-east, this might seem to be a remote part of Switzerland, and until this century this was largely the case. The high Upper Engadine has a mainly pastoral economy with traditional ways of life, and the limited opportunities have resulted in considerable emigration into the Italian valleys to the south. The Lower Engadine is more favoured, with irrigated water-meadows on its floor, small fields growing barley, oats, potatoes and other vegetables on terraced slopes, and thickly forested north-facing hillsides. The Inn leaves Switzerland through the Finstermünz gorge; the river has cut its valley through the resistant rocks revealed in this structural 'window' (p. 353).

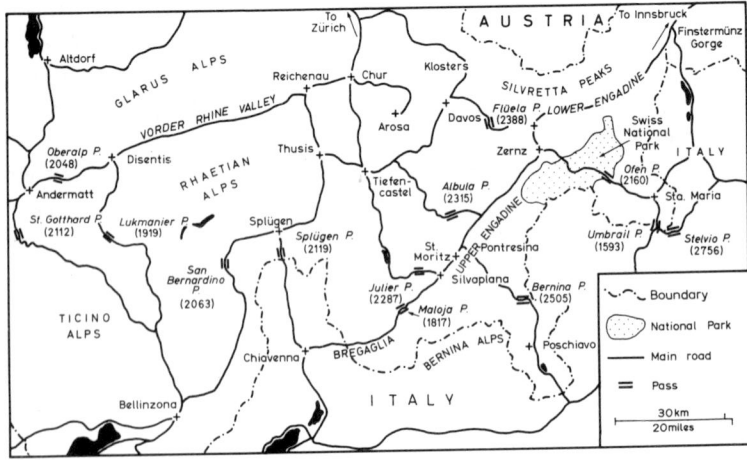

Fig. 77. Road passes in eastern Switzerland

During this century the Upper Engadine has become a very popular district for tourists, with highly developed winter sports and mountaineering, notably among the peaks and snowfields of the Bernina group, such as Piz Bernina, Piz Palu and Piz Morteratsch. The Rhaetian Railway from Chur via Tiefencastel and the Albula Tunnel penetrates to the fashionable resorts of St Moritz and Pontresina, and several well-engineered roads interlink the valleys. The Maloja Pass (1817 m, 5961 ft) crosses the col at the head of the Engadine, continuing into the Val Bregaglia and Italy; the Albula and Julier Passes lead northward to Chur; the Flüela Pass goes to Davos; and the Ofen Pass to Sta Maria, thence via the Umbrail Pass to Bormio in Italy. The last road traverses the Swiss National Park, some 180 sq. km (70 sq miles) in area, the boundary of which is shown in Fig. 77.

Ticino. The mountains and valleys of Ticino canton lie to the south of the main Alpine watershed, and partake in many ways of the character of the Italian Alps. Access from the rest of Switzerland is not easy, though the St Gotthard tunnel carries the main line south to Bellinzona and to the cosmopolitan lakeside resorts of Locarno and Lugano. There are also three road passes, the St Gotthard, Lukmanier and Splügen, though they are usually snow-blocked from October to June.

The Ticino Alps, though not high, have some impressive ridges and peaks cut in the granite of the St Gotthard massif. The bare slopes, the scanty pastures and the impression of poverty in the upper valleys contrast markedly with the luxuriance, even opulence, of the lakeside settlements further south. The sheltered nature and southern aspects of these valleys combine to favour the cultivation of fruit such as vines, peaches, apricots and in places even citrus. The olive is grown in favoured spots, its most northerly habitat in Europe; there are groves of sweet chestnut; and around the lake shores flourish magnolia, mimosa, cypress, acacia, palm and bamboo, and flowering shrubs.

CHAPTER TWELVE

France

FRANCE has an area of about 552 000 sq. km (213,000 sq. miles), more than three times the area of England and Wales. Its population on 1 January 1969 totalled 50·1 millions, an appreciable increase on the 1962 Census figure of 46·5 millions. It is a country of considerable variety of relief, soils, climate and resources, and its early national existence and long-established traditions have enabled good use to be made of these resources. Yet many problems have beset France, especially during the last sixty years: two crippling European wars, long periods of strife in overseas territories, and political unrest at home. The creation of the Fifth Republic in 1958 (p. 3) has given some degree of political stability, despite the uncertainties of the future. Membership of the European Economic Community has contributed to material development and particularly to improved relationships with West Germany, though the French ban on Britain's entry to the Community caused dissension among the members. In an attempt to solve the problems of the dwindling overseas empire, which during the last decade has involved France in a series of colonial wars, the French Community (*La Communauté*) was established in 1958. But seventeen of its members are now independent states, though seven remain within the Community, and all are in '*la Zone franc*'. France Overseas now consists merely of four departments (Martinique, Guadeloupe, Réunion and Guyane) and a few 'overseas territories' (St Pierre and Miquelon, French Polynesia, Comoro, New Caledonia and French Somaliland). New Hebrides is administered under an Anglo-French Condominium, established in 1914.

For administrative purposes, metropolitan France is divided into 95 departments, most of which were created in 1790, when the old provinces were abolished. They cover the country in a mosaic and though they rarely correspond with units of any geographical identity, statistics are available in great detail on this departmental basis. In 1964 the French government carried out a regrouping of the departments in the Paris region. The department of Seine was divided into the *Ville de Paris* and three new departments: Seine-St. Denis, Haute-de-

Seine and Val-de-Marne. The department of Seine-et-Oise was divided into Val-d'Oise, Yvelines and Essonne. There are, therefore, 95 departments, together with the *Territoire de Belfort* and the Ville de Paris.

STRUCTURE AND RELIEF

Three distinct structural elements may be distinguished: the ancient upland masses, the young fold mountain ranges, and the surrounding and intervening lowlands floored with Mesozoic, Tertiary and Quaternary rocks (Fig. 78).

The Uplands

The upland blocks are the product of alternations of folding, peneplanation, uplift and renewed denudation through long periods of geological time. The Hercynian orogeny of Carbo–Permian times (p. 139) was responsible for the basic structures, when the Archaean and Palaeozoic rocks were folded to form ranges across central Europe. The trends of folding in the west are referred to as Armorican, after the Breton name '*Ar-Mor*', 'the country of the sea'; here the structural lines run from west to east, gradually changing in central France until their direction is almost north-west to south-east. Farther east the trend is from south-west to north-east (Variscan), as in the Ardennes and the Vosges.

These ranges were slowly reduced to peneplains by a lengthy period of denudation during the Permian and Triassic, and then were covered during the prolonged Mesozoic and Tertiary marine transgressions by limestones, sandstones and clays. Renewed denudation, followed by *en masse* movements of uplift, produced a number of blocks projecting from the surrounding plains. During the Alpine orogeny of mid-Tertiary times, these uplands acted as stable bastions against the fold movements from the south, and helped to determine the alignment of the ranges. In addition, the blocks again suffered renewed *en masse* movement with tilting and faulting, associated in some areas, particularly Auvergne, with volcanic activity. Since then denudation has modified the uplands still further. They thus comprise massifs of Pre-Cambrian and Palaeozoic rocks: slate, schist, sandstone, quartzite and limestone, together with intrusive granites and with some superficial products of volcanic activity. Small areas of newer rocks are preserved in basins and depressions within the uplands or on their margins.

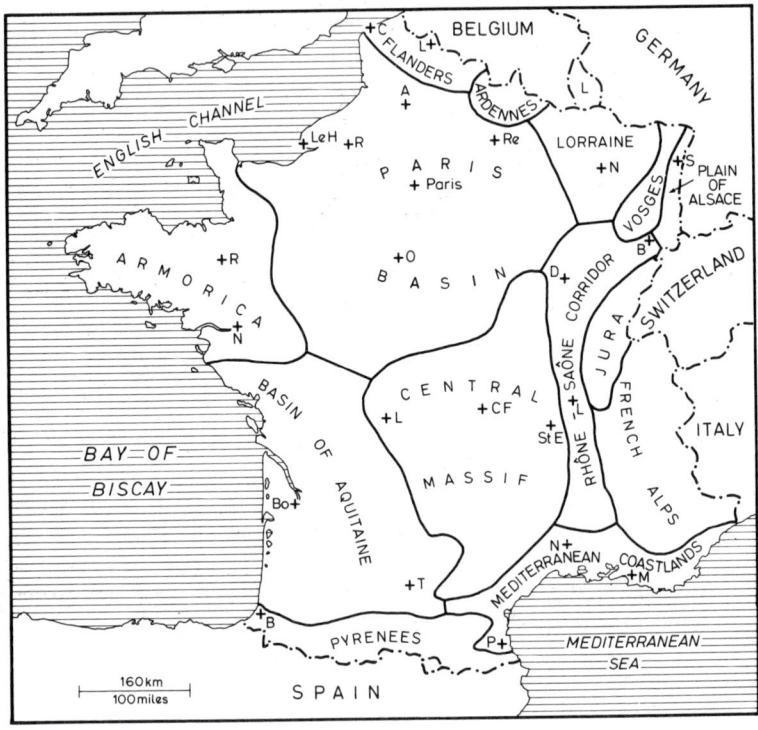

Fig. 78. Relief regions of France

In the north-west is Armorica, a triangular peninsula projecting into the Atlantic Ocean. Although the original Carbo–Permian folds have been largely destroyed by denudation, the ridges to the north and south represent the 'reincarnation' of the ancient anticlines, while a central synclinorial furrow (Châteaulin), eroded in weak shales between them, can be traced eastward from the bays which furrow the west coast. In its broadest structural sense, Armorica includes Brittany (the old province of Bretagne), the western parts of Normandy, Maine and Anjou, and Vendée to the south of the lower Loire.

The Central Massif, enclosed by the 300 m (1000 ft) contour, stands prominently above the surrounding lowlands, with a steep drop along its uptilted eastern and south-eastern margins to the Saône–Rhône valley and the Mediterranean coastlands. Although its average height is about 900 m (3000 ft), its maximum altitude attains only 1886 m (6188 ft). Four distinct structural elements can be

Plate L. The Barrage de la Grande Dixence in the Val des Dix, Switzerland

Plate LI. An aluminium plant in the Swiss Jura near Leisberg

Plate LII. The Rhine port at Basle

Plate LIII. Berne, the Federal capital of Switzerland, viewed across the river Aar

distinguished. The first and most extensive is the Hercynian basement block itself of granite, gneiss and schist, forming extensive plateaus. The second element is the remnants of the former continuous cover of Mesozoic rocks, mainly limestone, which has been removed from the Massif itself except in the Grands Causses in the south, but makes an essential contribution to the marginal plateaus. The third element is a series of down-faulted basins, trending broadly from south to north, formed in Tertiary times and now occupied by the upper courses of the Loire and its tributary the Allier. The fourth element is the result of late Tertiary vulcanicity, including basalt plateaus, the large cones of Cantal and Mont Dore, and the many small cones of the Puy district. Several distinct erosion surfaces can be distinguished on the surface of the massif.

The Vosges (Plate LV) is an upland mass rising in a series of steps along the western side of the Rhine Rift Valley (p. 190), falling away more gradually westward towards the scarplands of Lorraine. The core of these uplands consists of ancient crystalline rocks, especially granite, forming the High Vosges, with an average altitude of about 900 m (3000 ft) and rising in places to individual rounded summits, known as *ballons*. Farther north, the Low Vosges are covered with Triassic sandstone. A small part of the Ardennes (p. 333) extends into France.

Finally, the western part of the island of Corsica comprises a mass of crystalline rocks, a remnant of the foundered margins of the Hercynian continent. The north-eastern part, by contrast, consists of folded metamorphosed rocks, similar in character to some of those found in the French Alps (Fig. 103).

The Fold Mountains

The mountainous region of south-eastern France, between Lake Geneva and the Mediterranean Sea, forms part of the fold system of the Alps (Fig. 79). From the Mont Blanc massif, the Franco-Italian border runs southward along the watershed between the tributaries of the Rhône and of the Po, leaving within France many mountain groups, including the main summit of Mont Blanc.

The Alps are primarily the result of the mid-Tertiary earth-movements which upfolded the Mesozoic and Tertiary sediments accumulated in the geosyncline between the Hercynian foreland of Europe and the continent of Africa (pp. 350–3). Of the six major nappes which are developed in the Pennine ranges of the Swiss-Italian Alps, the Great St Bernard nappe, of highly metamorphosed

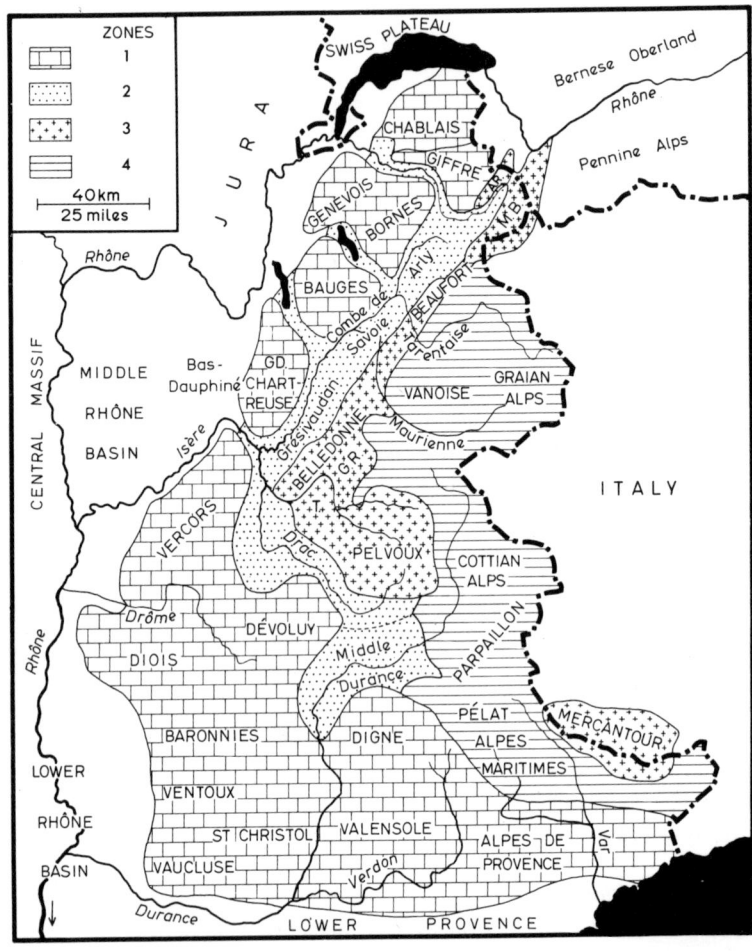

Fig. 79. The French Alps
The four main structural divisions are as follows: **1**. The Fore-Alps; **2**. the Sub-Alpine Furrow; **3**. the Hercynian massifs; **4**. the High Alps.

sedimentary rocks, is extensively represented in the French Alps, forming the high mountain ranges along the Italian boundary. Involved in the folds are several blocks of crystalline rock, the so-called 'inner horsts', which represent portions of the edge of the Hercynian continent overwhelmed by and caught up in the folding, the deep-seated 'cores' of the folds, and some batholithic intrusions within the folds or overrun by them. The most striking of these are the Mont Blanc massif (Plate LVI), Pelvoux and Mercantour.

The outer margins of the folded zone are separated from the High Alps by a discontinuous 'Sub-Alpine Furrow', occupied by sections of several rivers in turn. These margins are represented by the curve of the limestone Fore-Alps, and by the ranges of the Jura extending in an arc from the southern end of the Vosges to the Rhône valley east of Lyons. The border between France and Switzerland crosses these uplands obliquely from Basle to Geneva, leaving the south-western Jura in France.

The Pyrenees comprise a third system of fold mountains, the crestline of which for the most part demarcates the Franco–Spanish border. Rising abruptly above the Basin of Aquitaine, these ranges are not as lofty as the highest Alpine peaks, but are continuous and afford few passes. They owe their origin mainly to the Tertiary orogeny, but the fold movements occurred rather earlier than those of mid-Tertiary times mainly responsible for the Alps. The orogeny was one of great complexity, involving masses of Pre-Cambrian granite and gneiss strung out along the main axial line, highly metamorphosed Palaeozoic slates, and Mesozoic and Tertiary limestones forming the flanking plateaus and foothills.

The Lowlands

The main continental water-parting runs north-eastward from the eastern Pyrenees, along the south-eastern edge of the Central Massif to the Plateau de Langres, so to the 'Belfort Gate' and the Rhine at Basle. To the south and east of this line most drainage finds its way via the Saône–Rhône system to the Mediterranean. To the west and north are the basins of the Garonne, Loire, Seine and Scheldt, the last known in French as the Escaut. Seven separate lowland areas may be defined; though differing in scale, each has an undoubted individuality.

In the north the Plain of Flanders is crossed by the headwaters of the Lys and Scheldt. The extensive lowlands of northern France comprise a structural synclinal depression enclosed by the Ardennes, the Central Massif and Armorica, filled with Mesozoic and Tertiary sedimentary rocks (Plate LVII), and occupied by the Seine, its family of tributaries, and the middle Loire. The heart, the focus of these lowlands, as of France itself, is Paris, and the term Paris Basin is commonly applied. In the east these lowlands merge into the scarplands and vales of Lorraine, where outward facing cuestas of Jurassic limestone alternate with clay-floored valleys (Fig. 80). The Meuse and Moselle flow northward across Lorraine.

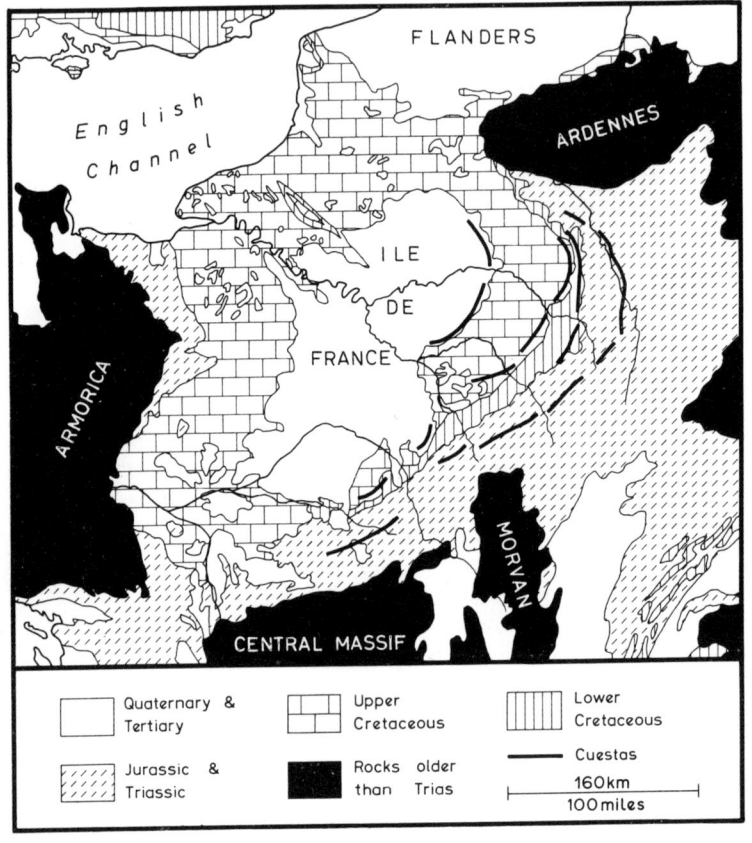

Fig. 80. The Paris Basin and its environs
(After the *Carte géologique de la France*, 1:1,000,000)

Through the broad gap of Poitou between Armorica and the Central Massif, the lowlands of northern France are continuous with those of Aquitaine. This undulating triangular lowland is crossed by a fan of rivers flowing from both the Central Massif and the Pyrenees, and focusing on the Gironde estuary.

The coastal plain of southern France, between the uplands and the Mediterranean Sea, is known as the Midi. From the point of view of structure and relief it exhibits great diversity, with outcrops of limestone, gravel-covered terraces, sheets of alluvium, sand-dunes and lagoons, but on to this the climate has imposed a unifying stamp reflected in both the landscape and the way of life. To the north the

Midi is continued by the Saône–Rhône valley, forming a lowland re-entrant far into central France. Another 'gateway', the Gap of Belfort, leads from the upper Saône valley into the Rhineland. The valley of the Rhine from Basle to Strasbourg consists of a rift valley bordered by the Vosges and the Black Forest. The plain of Alsace, varying in width from 16 to 40 km (10 to 25 miles), lies on the western side of the Rhine, which for about 140 km (90 miles) forms the international boundary.

Fifteen distinctive structural and relief regions have thus been defined: five Hercynian uplands, three series of fold mountain ranges, and seven basins, valleys and coastal lowlands.

CLIMATE

From a climatic point of view, France has a notably transitional location. It experiences in the north-west and west a typically maritime régime, characterized by Polar Maritime air masses associated with the passage of a succession of low-pressure systems from the Atlantic Ocean. In the centre and east it displays distinct features of continentality; winter is usually dominated by a westerly extension of the Eurasiatic high-pressure ridge, summer by a tendency to convectional low pressure. In the south the Mediterranean régime is characterized by summers dominated by mid-latitude high-pressure conditions, its autumn and winter by low-pressure systems, some originating in the western Mediterranean basin, others penetrating eastward from the Bay of Biscay.

Temperature

The latitude of France varies from 51° N. to nearly 42° N., its altitude ranges almost to 4900 m (16,000 ft), and parts in the east are 500 km (300 miles) from the sea. The combined effects of these factors result in striking seasonal and annual differences in temperature. The highest temperature ever recorded was 42° C at Perpignan, the lowest −40° C. at the observatory which once stood on the summit of Mont Blanc.

In January the controlling factor is distance from the sea, and the isotherms (reduced to sea-level) trend almost parallel to the west and south coasts. A narrow coastal fringe experiences mean temperatures of about 6° C., and the mildest areas, virtually frostless, are the coasts of Brittany, Provence and Roussillon; the mean January temperatures for Brest and Nice are almost identical, about 7° C. With increasing distance east the January mean temperature decreases; Paris has about 3° C., Strasbourg just below 0° C. Severe winters are quite common in the Rhineland, and the Rhine occasionally freezes over.

In summer the effects of latitude are more pronounced, and mean temperatures reach about 17° C. on the Channel coast, 19° C. in the Rhineland, and 22° C. on the Mediterranean coast where diurnal maxima of 35° C. are frequent. The hottest part of France is Roussillon, where Perpignan has a July mean of 24° C., and the sunbaked plains shimmer in the heat.

The seasonal range of temperature thus varies with distance from the sea. The smallest range is only 7° C., experienced at Roscoff in Brittany, the result of the ameliorating effects of its peninsular location. The highest is in the Rhineland, the most continental part of the country; Strasbourg has a range of 19° C.

If actual temperature figures are considered, the effect of altitude becomes significant in the upland and mountain areas, most of which experience mean sub-zero temperatures for several months, with a lengthy period of snow cover. Above 1200 m (4000 ft) frost is experienced daily for about four months. The high valleys among the mountains record markedly low winter temperatures as a result of inversion, with spells of frost and cold fog; it is noticeable that in many valleys the vines are grown 30 m or so above the floors to avoid frost damage.

'Local' temperatures are largely the result of aspect and exposure. The Vosges, for example, cause considerable differences between Lorraine on the west and the Rhineland on the east; spring comes appreciably earlier in Alsace in spite of the cold winter, and the south-easterly aspect is of great importance to such crops as the vine. Grapes and tobacco flourish, and peaches, apricots and almonds grow in favoured localities, evidence of the pleasant climate. In the Alps the distinction between the south-facing slope (the *adret* or *endroit*) and the shady side (the *ubac* or the *envers*) is so profound that it dominates patterns of settlement and land use in the narrow west–east valleys.

Associated with aspect is the degree of exposure to winds from particular directions; some are so regularly experienced that they possess specific names, such as the 'mistral' and the 'bise' from the north-west, and the 'marin' from the Mediterranean Sea. The mistral is notorious; cold dry air, originating as an air stream behind a depression passing eastward through the Mediterranean, moves from the Central Massif down the Rhône 'funnel', and the air flow may become established as a strong, bitterly cold, and extremely dry wind. It can do much harm in spring to fruit trees, vines and gardens, both by physical damage and by its desiccating effects. The landscape of the lower Rhône valley is diversified by wind-breaks of poplars, cypress hedges and hurdle fences, erected to mitigate the effects of the mistral.

Precipitation

The amount and seasonal distribution of precipitation are related to moist air masses moving in from the Atlantic and to a less extent from the Mediterranean, to convectional influences in the more continental environment in the east, and to the distribution of the uplands, which produce profound contrasts on their windward and rain-shadow slopes. The combined effects of these factors result in several distinctive rainfall régimes.

The areas behind the north and west coasts receive mean annual totals of 710–760 mm (28–30 in), though rather higher on the exposed Breton moorlands where it is between 1000 and 1270 mm (40 and 50 in). The precipitation is well distributed, since depressions come at all seasons, though the Channel coast has a spring minimum when rather fewer disturbances are experienced. Along the Biscay coast the summer minimum and autumn maximum become more marked as summer high pressure over the Mediterranean is approached. Bordeaux has a mean annual total of 760 mm (30 in) and Brest about 810 mm (32 in), the latter with more cloud and periods of fine drizzling rain.

In central and eastern France the distinct winter minimum and summer maximum of precipitation are indicative of a modified continental régime. Because of its low-lying nature and a slight rain-shadow effect, the centre of the Paris Basin is one of the driest parts of the country (Paris, 580 mm, 23 in). An appreciable summer maximum is the result of convectional tendencies; the months May to October each have mean rainfall totals of over 50 mm (2 in), while the other months have less, the driest being February with 30 mm (1·2 in). The summer maximum is still more pronounced in the Rhineland; the wettest months at Strasbourg are June and July, the driest January and February when the continental high-pressure conditions are well established.

In southern France the Mediterranean régime, with its pronounced summer minimum of precipitation, is the result of high pressure and light winds, but the maxima in spring and autumn are caused by moist southerly and south-westerly air-streams from the sea, associated with depressions in the Gulf of Lions. In Provence, backed by the Maritime Alps, the precipitation totals about 710–810 mm (28–32 in), while to the west of the Rhône in lower Languedoc it ranges from about 500 mm (20 in) at Narbonne to 760 mm (30 in) at Montpellier. The rainiest month is October, most falling in a few intense showers, but July averages less than 25 mm and in many years is wholly rainless. Farther south Perpignan has a mean rainfall of 560 mm (22 in), occurring on only sixty-four days in the year, and the nearby Salses, with 430 mm (17 in), is probably the driest place in France, having on an average only thirty-four days with rain; here the summer drought is virtually complete.

Southern Aquitaine reveals broadly the same pattern of distribution as the Mediterranean coast, but there are indications of an Atlantic régime, with cloudier skies and an annual precipitation of from 760 mm (30 in) in the plain to 1520 mm (60 in) in the Pyrenean foothills. The autumn–winter maximum results from depressions moving from the Bay of Biscay to the Mediterranean along the northern flanks of the Pyrenees and through the Carcassonne gap. Hendaye, for example, has a mean annual precipitation of 940 mm (37 in); the driest month is July with 60 mm (2·4 in), the wettest is October with 140 mm (5·5 in).

This general pattern of the distribution of precipitation is modified in detail by the relief. Even the low hills in the east and south of the Paris Basin have 740–810 mm (29–32 in), appreciably more than Paris, though farther from the sea. The windward slopes of the Central Massif in places receive over 2000 mm (80 in), though Clermont-Ferrand, on the rain-shadow side of the Limagne basin, has only 640 mm (25 in). Similarly, Epinal on the western flanks of the Vosges, with a mean annual rainfall of 940 mm (37 in), contrasts with Colmar in the eastern rain-shadow with only 480 mm (19 in); Modane, in the deeply cut valley of the Arc in the French Alps, has only 610 mm (24 in); and Tarascon, at 476 m (1560 ft) in the valley of the Ariège in the Pyrenean foothills, receives 790 mm (31 in), while Saurat, 16 km (10 miles) away but at twice its altitude, has 1730 mm (68 in).

Snowfall

The occurrence of snow and the duration of a snow cover is also mainly a function of relief, for though it has been known to fall even along the Riviera, its mean frequency is only about three days along the French coasts and from ten to fifteen in the lowlands. The Vosges and Jura have a snow cover for about fifty days above about 450 m (1500 ft), and on the higher summits it may lie for five months; the mountain roads are closed intermittently. In the Alps most of the passes above about 1800 m (6000 ft) are closed from October to June (p. 379). The heaviest snowfall is received in the Pyrenees; the observatory on the summit of the Pic du Midi de Bigorre usually records a depth of at least 6 m (20 ft). The snow-line retreats with amazing rapidity in early summer; avalanches are widespread and swollen torrents foam down the valleys.

LAND USE AND AGRICULTURE

France is virtually self-sufficient in respect of many commodities, and has an export surplus of some; it is, for example, the sixth producer of wheat in the world, after the U.S.S.R., the U.S.A., China, Canada and Australia. Cultivation is widespread; only in the high mountains and bleak plateaus, and on the sandy stretches of the Landes and the Mediterranean coast, are there any appreciable empty areas. The range of products is probably greater than in any other European country, from meadow grass, potatoes, sugar beet, fodder crops and wheat to maize, olives, vines, peaches, citrus fruits and tobacco. The age-old utilization of the varied environment has resulted in some highly characteristic and specialized activities, in the production of, for example, wine and cheese, with their distinctive local character and reputation, both for sophisticated urban markets and for export; one has only to visit the colourful market in any country town to appreciate the variety of produce and the discrimination of the French housewife.

Soils

A generalized survey of the soils is difficult, partly because of the variety of types developed on geological outcrops ranging from Archaean rocks to alluvial flats, partly because they have been modified by centuries of intensive cultivation. Drainage, marling, the application of shell-sands and seaweed, even the transference in barges of soil from one locality to another, have made the present distribution almost artificial.

In the Central Massif soils derived from the granitic and schistose rocks are base-poor, coarse and infertile. The surfaces of the newer basalt flows are rocky and arid, though older volcanic rocks have

14*

decomposed to form dark base-rich soils. The soils of the limestone Causses vary from the terra rossa which floors the depressions to a thin indissoluble residue of coarse material lying on the solid rock. The granite plateaus of Armorica and the Vosges also bear thin gravelly soils, heavily leached and acid in quality. The Jura have moderately fertile calcareous soils, especially in the valleys and depressions where these are derived from marls and clays. Soils in the Alps and Pyrenees vary from those on boulder-clay and alluvium on the valley floors to thin scree soils on the higher slopes.

Even in the lowlands large areas carry only poor soils; in Aquitaine the sands of the Landes cover some 15 500 sq. km (6000 sq. miles), heavily leached and underlain by an impermeable hardpan, and in the Sologne, within the great bend of the Loire, sands underlain by clay have resulted in poor leached heath soils, with waterlogging caused by the impeded drainage. In the lower Rhône valley and the Mediterranean coastlands, the gravel fans and terraces are in summer a scene of bleached and dusty aridity.

The most fertile soils are found on the undulating chalk or limestone plains, especially where there is a veneer of limon (p. 290). Much of the Paris Basin has warm, well-drained, loamy soils, suited to wheat and sugar beet, though where the limon mantle is absent the calcareous soils are thin and dry. By contrast, the Gault Clay of Champagne humide and the Oxford Clay of Lorraine form heavy, rather cold soils, though when drained they support excellent pasture. The alluvial terraces are cultivated along the lower Seine and its tributaries, in the Plain of Alsace, in the 'garden of France' along the middle Loire, and in the Saône–Rhône valley, especially where there is a contribution of limon (as in Alsace) or of calcareous downwash from the higher slopes.

Intensive agriculture over long periods of time has enabled soils to be improved in many naturally unfavourable areas. Sunny south-facing slopes are terraced, with stone walls retaining the precious soil. In Brittany loads of shell-sand and seaweed are brought from the shore to sweeten and add humus to the acid soils. Drainage has reclaimed large areas of heavy clayland, the alluvium-covered floodplains, and the marshlands of the Rhône delta and the coasts of Normandy and Brittany. Conversely, irrigation has made usable much of the dry gravel soils of Languedoc. Since 1945 the area of improved land has been greatly increased, particularly through large government-sponsored schemes and where consolidation of holdings has made reclamation practicable.

Forests

Some 13·5 million ha (33 million acres), or about a quarter of the total area of France, is forested, an increase of 2·1 million ha (5·2 million acres) over 1938. The reason for this quite high proportion is the considerable area which is too high, too steep, too bleak or with too poor soils for cultivation, so that forests form the only practicable economic use.

The forests may be divided into three categories. The Mediterranean woodland has been ravaged through the centuries by cutting for fuel and timber, and by clearance for cultivation; natural regeneration has been precluded by close grazing, especially by goats. As a result, much has degenerated into maquis, a close evergreen shrub vegetation on siliceous rocks, or into garrigue, a thin, more stunted vegetation on limestone. Some Mediterranean species of trees survive in small stands, especially on hills behind the coast, notably the Aleppo and maritime pine, ilex and kerm oak, chestnut, plane, maple and groves of cypresses.

Temperate forests, consisting of oak, beech and many other deciduous trees are found over much of northern and western France, while farther south in Aquitaine the cork and pedunculate oaks appear. These woodlands are not extensive, as much of the land has been cleared for agriculture, though a few forests have been specially preserved, notably the Forêt d'Orléans and the Forêt de Fontainebleau to the south-west of Paris. A large proportion of this woodland occurs in small patches around farms and villages, and especially in northern France as avenues along the country roads. Deciduous forests are also found in the Pyrenees, where the more humid western uplands were once covered with magnificent forests of ash, which still clothe the steeper slopes. In the central Pyrenees beech is dominant on the lower slopes, succeeded by conifers at higher altitudes, and copses and lines of plane, poplar, maple, hazel, lime, birch and alder grow on the valley floors where they have not been cleared for agriculture. In the eastern Pyrenees, the various evergreen oaks, especially kerm and cork oak, gradually become dominant, with pines at higher elevations.

The third group, covering the higher and bleaker upland areas, are predominantly coniferous. Three altitudinal zones may generally be distinguished: a lower zone of pine, fir and beech, a middle zone of larch and Arolla pine, and an upper zone where the trees are dwarfed and isolated, gradually giving way to alpine meadows. In the damper northern parts of the French Alps the spruce is dominant, while farther south the thinner woodland consists of larch and Arolla pine.

Afforestation. Widespread afforestation has taken place as part of definite State policy, which has been accelerated since 1945. In 1968 about 15 per cent of the forest was state-owned, maintained under a strict code of forest law, about 22 per cent is owned by the communes, forming a valuable local asset, and the remainder is in the hands of private individuals. While much of the planting of blocks of trees on reclaimed land takes place in State forests, private planting has been encouraged with financial aid from the *Fonds Forestier National.* This policy has aimed at reducing the large imports of softwood and pulp, at making good the areas clear-felled during 1940–45, in fixing coastal sand-dunes, notably in the Landes, in making use of re-claimed land of otherwise little value, as in the Sologne, and in combating rainwash, torrent erosion and avalanches in the mountains. The success of this policy is shown by the fact that between 1947 and 1968 about 1 million ha (2·5 million acres) of forest were planted, replanted or improved.

Organization of Agriculture

The French farmer, though sometimes limited by his traditional outlook, is industrious, thrifty and conscious of his importance in the national economy. Ownership of land is esteemed, both from sentimental reasons and from the practical fact that a plot of land represents a safe investment. About 32 per cent of the total area is classified as arable land, 25 per cent as pasture, and 25 per cent under forest. But nearly 7 per cent is returned as 'non-cultivated agricultural land', about the same proportion consists of wholly uncultivated land, and even on some of the cultivated land yields are so low as to be almost uneconomic.

Until recently many aspects of agriculture seemed backward, and yields per ha were as a rule appreciably below those in Belgium, the Netherlands and Denmark. Mechanization has proceeded slowly; as late at 1957 about 70 per cent of the farmers did not own a tractor, and applications of fertilizer were at a comparatively low level. Various reasons account for these disabilities. In the first place, far too many workers sought to make a living from the land, producing too little per head and at too high a cost; consider-able government subsidies have been necessary. Before the War over 7 millions, about 36 per cent of the active population, were engaged in agriculture, but since 1945 the number has been appreciably reduced by the drift from the land, and by 1968 had fallen to a seventh of the total workers, almost 3 millions. The rural exodus has been an obvious feature of the Alps, the Central Massif and Brittany, where the struggle against poverty has been abandoned in favour of more attractive work and wages in the towns. It has also been noticeable, for different reasons, in the northern lowlands, where the creation of large farms and increasing mechanization have necessitated less labour. Paradoxically, this tendency has resulted in a shortage of agricultural labour, particularly of a seasonal character; as a result, large numbers of foreigners are employed, some permanently, some seasonally.

Another reason for the low productivity was the small size of many farms. In 1931 about 85 per cent of the holdings were less than 10 ha in extent, and nearly 40 per cent were less than 1 ha; many of the latter consisted of vineyards, orchards and market gardens, but the general effect on agriculture of too many non-viable units was adverse. This fragmentation of holdings is the result partly of a long process of *morcellement*, the equal division of property under Napoleon's Civil Code among the heirs on the death of a landowner (modified in 1961). It is also the result of *parcellement*, an equitable division to ensure that each heir obtained a share of the different types of land and soil in the holding. Another cause, affecting the northern part of France, was the three-field system of rotation, whereby a farmer required a share in each field. As a result, a single holding usually consisted of a series of scattered strips. In 1891 it is recorded that the farmland of France comprised 151 million separate 'parcels'.

After the War of 1914–18, the government took the first effective steps to combat this excessive division of land. Especially in communes in the war-devastated north, syndicates were encouraged and assisted to carry out a process of consolidation known as *remembrement*. In 1941, under the stress of wartime shortages, a new law was passed, which, slightly modified by subsequent legislation, is the basis of the modern *Service du Remembrement*. At the request of private landowners and tenants, or of a communal administration, a commission may be set up to examine a proposed collective consolidation project and if approved it is put into effect, a process similar in many ways to the enclosure movement in Britain during the Agrarian Revolution. The work is carried out by the *Service du Remembrement*, a department of the Ministry of Agriculture, the cost being met mostly by a government subsidy, a small proportion by a levy on the landholders involved. In addition, 29 regional organizations (*Sociétés d'Aménagement Foncier et d'Establissement Rural*) were established to acquire land, create viable farms, improve farmbuildings, and carry out programmes of drainage and irrigation. The beneficial results include more rational farming methods, the practicability of mechanization, an increase in productivity both per head and per unit of area, the possibility of an integrated arable–livestock economy, for livestock could not easily be kept on unenclosed land, and the release of a large amount of labour into industry. It has been estimated that between 1950 and 1968 the number of farms decreased by 20 per cent, and the numbers employed in agriculture by 25 per cent, thus releasing labour for industry.

A growing proportion of the land is farmed by large capitalized companies employing managers, about half by owner-occupiers, and a third by tenants. The system of share tenancy (*métayage*), under which the landlord provides the land, implements and livestock, and in return takes part of the produce, has long contributed to inefficient and wasteful cultivation; this is now of minor importance, involving less than 2 per cent of all farms.

Agriculture suffered as the result of the German occupation, though sheer necessity compelled an intensive cultivation of every scrap of land. But lack of fertilizers and vine sprays, shortage of implements and labour, the withdrawal of nearly 2 million prisoners and much conscription for forced labour, the destruction of farm buildings and communications in the areas of hostilities, all exercised an adverse effect. During and following the war years, acute shortage of food was evident in the towns, though less so in the country, and a flourishing 'Black Market' was rife for some time.

Since 1945 agriculture has played a considerable part in the government's economic planning. American aid was used to carry out the mechanization and re-equipment of farms, schemes of reclamation, rural housing and electrification, and the provision of fertilizers. The third national plan (p. 426) devoted considerable attention to agriculture by means of public works, subsidies and advisory services. Co-operatives have increased in number, especially in the dairy industry and among vine growers.

Both totals and average yields per unit of most cereals, and even more strikingly of fodder crops, have increased since 1950 (Fig. 81), and in 1968 the output of wheat reached a record of 14·9 million tons, though the poor harvests of 1966 and 1967 yielded under 12 million tons. The number of cattle increased from 16 millions in 1950 to

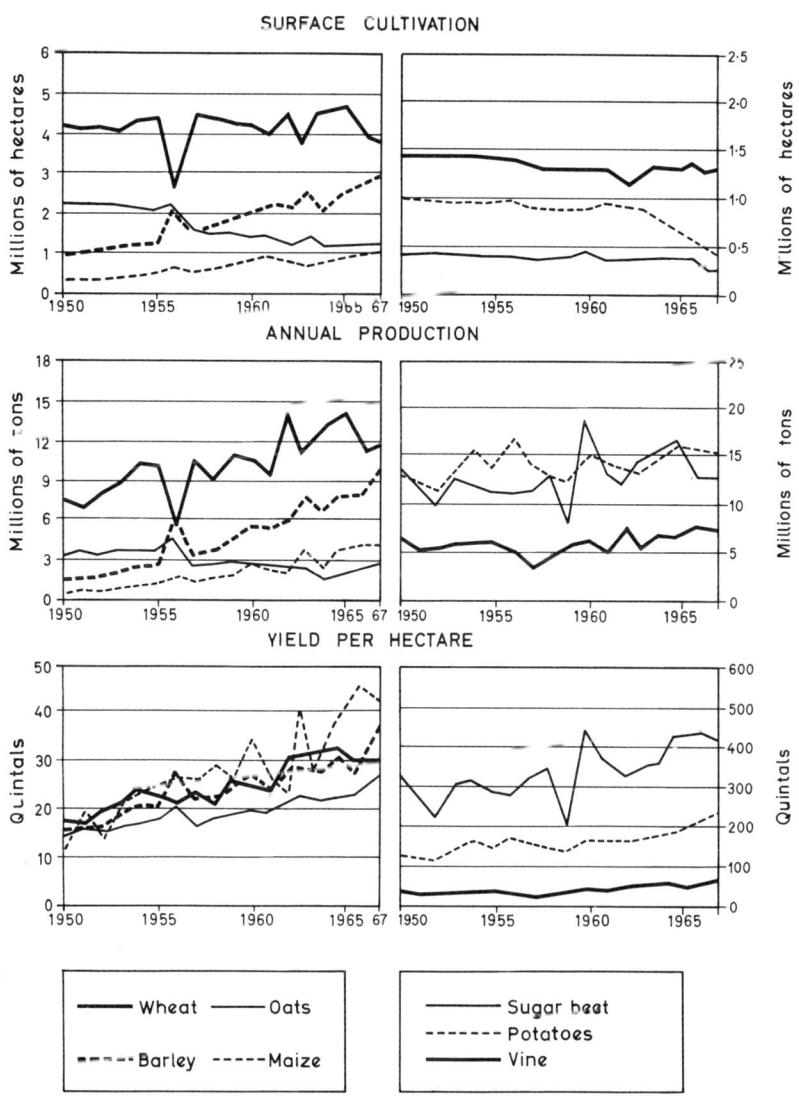

Fig. 81. Trends in French agricultural production, 1950–67
(After *Annuaire Statistique de la France*, 1968)

21·9 millions in 1968, and pigs from 7 millions to 11 millions. Agriculture, without revealing the striking developments shown by manufacturing industry, has thus made an appreciable contribution to France's economic growth since 1945.

Arable Farming

Cereals are widely grown, occupying half the arable area. Only in the extreme north-west do the cool damp conditions preclude the successful cultivation of wheat, and as a result it occupied about half the area under all cereals, and a quarter of the arable land. The area under wheat has declined since 1938 by about 600 000 ha, but the yield increased from under 10 million tons in that year to 14·9 million tons in 1968. This is a reflection partly of the conversion of low-yielding marginal lands to grassland, partly to increased applications of fertilizers, partly to the introduction of better hybrids. The most important wheat-growing areas are in the departments around and to the north and east of Paris, on the low limestone and chalk plateaus covered with fertile limon in Beauce and Brie, Picardy and Artois, where wheat is grown in rotation with sugar beet, sometimes also with fodder crops and barley; the countryside forms a vast chequerboard of unfenced fields, where cultivation is highly mechanized. Other areas of high yield are in northern Aquitaine, the Saône valley and the plain of Alsace. Actually, in recent years too much wheat has been produced, and the Government has been faced with embarrassing problems of surpluses.

The second most important cereal is now barley, grown mainly in northern France and in Alsace; most is consumed locally as fodder, but malting barley has increased in importance. Before 1957 oats was the second cereal in yield, concentrated in the damper northern and western parts of the country for use as fodder. Its decline in output, from 5·4 million tons in 1938 to only 2·5 million tons in 1968, is a result of the decrease in the number of horses. Rye, too, has dwindled to less than a third of its former yield, though some is still grown on the poor lands of the Central Massif, the granitic soils of southern Brittany, the drier parts of Aquitaine, and the Pyrenean valleys. The output of maize has quadrupled since 1938, largely because of the introduction of new hybrids and its value as fodder; it is grown mainly in the south-west, where conditions are moist, warm and virtually frost free, with some new hybrids in the Paris Basin, the Saône–Rhône valley and the Rhineland. About 140,000 tons of rice are produced annually on the reclaimed delta-lands of the Rhône, where the crop is harvested by modern combines; rice is milled at Arles.

The two most important root crops are potatoes and sugar beet, their output in 1968 being 10 and 18 million tons respectively. Potatoes are mainly grown for local consumption, though any surplus is fed to pigs or made into industrial alcohol. Two notable producing districts are Brittany (for new potatoes) and the Alsatian plain near Strasbourg. Sugar beet is grown in rotation with wheat on the loamy well drained soils of the northern plains, so that normally France can supply its own sugar requirements. The pulp from the refineries is fed to cattle.

Other crops include buckwheat in Brittany and the Morvan, flax in the Scarpe and Lys valleys of Flanders, tobacco in the Rhineland and Aquitaine under a State monopoly, a little hemp in the lower Loire valley, and hops in Alsace.

Horticulture and Fruit-growing

Market gardening is highly developed as the result of intensive labour, the markets provided by the large towns, and the keen interest taken in food by the people, affording a constant demand for fresh vegetables and fruit. This is exemplified especially in French Flanders, along the Seine valley floor below Paris, and on the reclaimed marshlands of the Somme valley. In certain districts, as around Bordeaux, Strasbourg and Metz, peas, beans, asparagus and other vegetables are grown specifically for canning and bottling.

Two areas are particularly important for the cultivation of *primeurs*, early and out of season vegetables, for despatch to the Parisian and other urban markets. In Brittany vegetables are grown in small sheltered 'pockets', virtually free from frost and with an early spring. Along the coast of the Mediterranean and in the lower Rhône valley the age-old pattern of the economy (wheat, olives and vines) was revolutionized by the development of the tourist industry, which necessitated more produce for local consumption, while better communications enabled perishable crops to be produced for distant markets. Tiny plots of land are exploited assiduously, protected by fences from the blast of the mistral. The succession of produce includes cauliflowers and lettuce during the winter, new potatoes as early as March, artichokes from March to June, early peas, spinach, onions, carrots and tomatoes. The cultivation of flowers for the cut-flower trade, perfume and seeds has achieved an outstanding success. In some districts specialization is practised, but more usually the smallholder grows a variety of items to spread his risks and provide some continuity of output. Competition to produce earlier crops has forced the use of cloches and greenhouses even in this favourable climate. Irrigation is widely used, taking water through a canal from the Rhône above Arles, and leading it through the coastal plain near Béziers and Narbonne; about 240 000 ha (600,000 acres) are irrigated.

The range of climate and the amount of sunshine make practicable the production of many fruits, cider apples in Normandy and Brittany, peaches, apricots, figs, olives, almonds, mulberries, citrus and even pomegranates on the Mediterranean coastlands. Cherries are grown in the Rhône valley on the limestone terraces, peaches in Roussillon and in a triangle to the east of Avignon, apples, plums and cherries in Alsace, walnuts in Périgord and Isère, sweet chestnuts on the Central Massif and in Corsica, black currants around Dijon, and olives on the limestone slopes of the Midi.

Viticulture

Though second to Italy in quantity of wine produced, France exports a far greater amount and is pre-eminent in the production of fine wines. The vine can withstand periods of frost, but it requires a moderate rainfall in spring and early summer, continuous sunshine during late summer and autumn, and it prefers a well-drained, calcareous, stony soil on a limestone slope with a southern aspect. The climate is too cloudy and humid beyond the vine's effective northern limit (Fig. 82). The marginal areas, where exceptional care is required, produce some of the finest qualities, though climatic fluctuations result in vintage and non-vintage years. The superb summer of 1959 produced an enormous yield, but, conversely, 1956 was climatically adverse, especially for the Bordeaux vineyards, where chilling mists and frost persisted in the valleys from January to April.

The area under vines grew steadily from Roman times, reaching a record of about 2·5 million ha (6 million acres) in 1874, but a serious blow was dealt in 1863 by the appearance in Languedoc of the phylloxera, an aphid of American origin. It multiplies prodigiously, living in galls on the leaves and the roots where it cannot be reached by spraying, and the affected vines become stunted and die; by 1884 every vine-growing part of France was affected. In 1891 it was discovered that stocks from the eastern U.S.A. were almost immune, and an immense programme of grafting European scions on to these stocks was begun; while not wholly resistant, these vines are affected much less seriously.

Though the phylloxera was defeated, the wine industry has never really recovered its former position. It has had to face increasing competition from Italy, Spain and North Africa and later from South Africa and Australia; Algeria, being for a long time within the French customs area, was able to ship huge quantities of very cheap *vin ordinaire*. Between the Wars, prohibition in the U.S.A. and rapidly increasing excise duties in England severely hit exports, as did the world economic crisis of 1930–34. Since 1950 there has been some government effort to discourage wine drinking in France, though this has not made much headway.

In an effort to reduce the dangerous dependence on a single crop, with its fluctuating yield and price, the government has encouraged, with the aid of subsidies, the conversion of vineyards to other crops.

Fig. 82. French wine-producing districts
(After the *Guide Michelin*)
The main districts are shown in large capital letters, and some of the more famous wines are named.

Nevertheless, their area still totals about 1·3 million ha, and the yield, about 66 million hl (15 million gallons) in 1968, is not much below the record of 18 million in 1875.

More than half comes from the Midi, especially from the departments of Hérault (where a third of the surface is covered with vines), Gard and Aude; here monoculture is carried to its extreme, though only a minute proportion of this yield consists of quality wine.

Aquitaine, particularly along the valleys of the Garonne, Dordogne and Charente, not only produces a quarter of the French total, but its output is three times that of the pre-phylloxera period. About 90 per cent consists of quality clarets, Sauternes and Graves, of remarkable variety, the result of soils including alluvium, gravel, calcareous clay and sandy marl, and the traditions and practices of individual producers; most famed are the château vineyards. Holdings are usually small, five-sixths of them being less than 2 ha (5 acres).

For 40 km (25 miles) along the Côte d'Or from Dijon to Chagny, overlooking the Saône valley, tiered on the limestone slopes are rows of vines, from which are produced the superlative Burgundy wines. To the south the vineyards continue along the eastern slopes of the Central Massif, the best-known district being Beaujolais.

In the sunny climate of the Rhône valley really poor years, so common farther north, are rare, and vineyards extend over much of the Côtes du Rhône alone each side of the river.

The most northerly wine-producing district lies along the eastern edge of the Tertiary limestone escarpment of the Ile de France; the sparkling wine is known after the regional name of Champagne. Except for its south-eastern aspect, this district possesses no real advantages for vine cultivation; the soils are rather poor, and the area is so near the northern limit of cultivation that bad or indifferent years are common. Both total yield and quality therefore vary considerably, and it is to traditional skill in processing that champagne owes its reputation, although the uniform temperatures within the labyrinth of caves in the limestone and chalk is a major factor in the maturing processes. The output of champagne wine is small, a mere 320 000 hl (70,000 gallons) or so, but in good vintage year its value is considerable, since it constitutes one of the best known 'export wines'.

The Loire valley has extensive vineyards on its slopes (Plate LVIII). Touraine has long been famous for both white and red wines, while the Val d'Anjou produces a range of sparkling and still wines.

On the south-facing slopes of the Vosges foothills, 10 000 ha (25,000 acres) vines are grown on the calcareous down-wash from the Jurassic outcrops.

One important aspect of viticulture is the production of high-quality spirits and liqueurs. The best-known brandy is produced around the town of Cognac in Charente, though Armagnac, produced in southern Aquitaine, is regarded as but little inferior. The varied liqueurs and apéritifs, many of age-old reputation and jealously guarded formulae, also contribute to exports.

Livestock

A striking feature in recent decades, and especially since 1950, has been the increase in the area under fodder crops and grassland; in addition, more than half the production of cereals is fed to stock. About a quarter of the total area of France is classified as grassland, including the lowland *bocage* (the permanent pasture in the damper areas of the north-west), the meadows along the floodplains of rivers and on the heavy claylands of Champagne and Lorraine, and the short-ley grassland, clover and alfalfa in the arable rotation. Upland pastures comprise the *alpages* in the Alps, Jura and Pyrenees, the rather poorer pastures of the plateaus, and the scanty herbage of the limestone country of the Causses and the Fore-Alps. Around the coast are salt-marsh grazings, especially in Brittany, Vendée, Normandy and the Rhône delta. Crops grown specifically for fodder, in addition to cereals, include fodder beet, sainfoin, turnips, kale and other green crops, and an increasing amount of alfalfa.

The number of cattle has risen from 15·6 millions in 1938 to 21·7 millions in 1968, and pigs from 7·1 millions to 10·7 millions. Sheep have remained at about 10 millions, though horses and goats reveal a substantial decline.

Cattle are kept widely for both milk and meat. Most farms, even the small ones, have a few animals, and even on the Mediterranean coast, where summer drought precludes pasture, some animals are reared on the Rhône delta and others are kept for draught purposes. Important districts include the Central Massif (especially Limousin and Charolais), the Savoy Alps, the Paris Basin (notably in Brie and Valois), Picardy and Artois, and the Pyrenean foothills; the three outstanding cattle-rearing districts are Armorica, Charente and the Jura. Few countries produce so many different cheeses as France; some of the well-known varieties, many of which are exported to Britain, are located on Fig. 83. The output of beef and veal (widely produced as a byproduct of the dairy industry) can normally meet home requirements. In the northern lowlands, store cattle from Normandy, Limousin and Charolais are fattened on oil-cake and sugar-beet pulp.

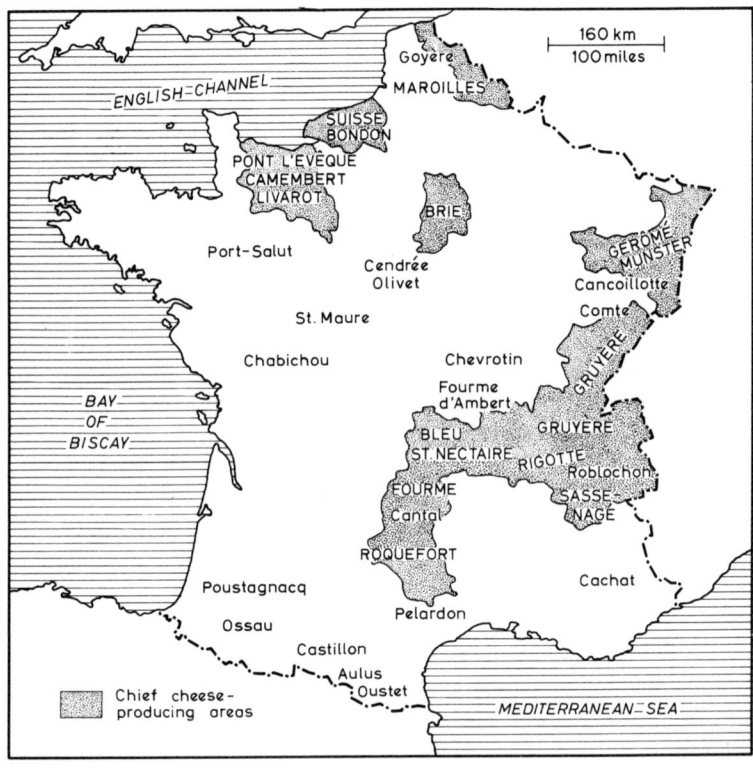

Fig. 83. *Varieties of French cheese*
(After the *Atlas de France*)

Sheep are reared in the Paris Basin, where they are folded on stubble and roots or grazed on the chalk and limestone pastures; in the Central Massif, particularly in the Grands Causses and the Cévennes; in the foothills of the Alps and the Pyrenees; on the drained marshes around the coasts, and on the Rhône delta. The Crau and Camargue districts provide winter grazing for flocks which spend summer on the Alpine pastures, moving slowly through

Provence along regular stock routes. The sheep arrive in the Crau towards the end of November and graze until mid-February, after which they spend a month on the cultivated meadows before returning to the foothills, the first stage of their summer journey to the alpine pasture. This transhumance is now carried out by rail. In the Grands Causses the limestone plateaus carry sweet though scanty grass, and for centuries sheep have been grazed; even today there are about 750,000 head, while other flocks come up from the Mediterranean coast during the summer. These sheep are kept principally for milk, from which is made Roquefort cheese, so called after the town which clings to the sides of the valley of the Soulzon. The caves, part natural, part artificially hollowed, maintain a constant temperature and humidity favourable for the maturing of the cheeses. The commercialization of cheese production has been helped by the development of co-operatives.

Pigs are kept on almost every farm and smallholding, since their products form an important part of the diet, the value exceeding that of beef and veal. A few districts specialize in pigs, notably Brittany, Limousin, Lorraine and Aquitaine, where they consume skimmed milk and whey.

Goats have declined considerably in number during the last half century, though they are still found in the Pyrenees, parts of the Central Massif and the Mediterranean lands, where they can survive on scanty pasture and scrubland which is useless for cattle. One special area of goat-breeding is the district of Berry, in the department of Cher on the northern margins of the Central Massif, where well-known goat-milk cheeses are produced. The widespread use of tractors on farms has resulted in the decline of horse-drawn vehicles; in 1938 there were about 2·7 million horses, in 1968 only 782,000. The chief horse-rearing areas are in Brittany and Normandy, where they are still used for ploughing.

Poultry are kept throughout the country, though with some special areas, as in the district of Bresse in the middle Saône valley, where poultry are reared both as a sideline on dairy and mixed farms, and on large poultry farms using intensive methods of production and fattening; Bresse capons are famous throughout France. Rabbits, geese and turkeys are bred on reclaimed land in the Sologne; the turkeys are sent to Paris and even to England for the Christmas market. Geese are reared for their livers in the Strasbourg district and in Périgord, where truffles grow on the roots of oaks below the surface of the ground, and are located with the aid of dogs or pigs; truffle-stuffed geese and capons are sent to the markets of Paris and elsewhere.

FISHERIES

France has an extensive coastline, and fishing directly employs about 31,000 people, while another 20,000 are engaged in ancillary occupations, such as handling and distributing the catch, canning and preserving, and boat-repairing.

The fishing industry, however, is not as important as might be expected, relative both to other activities and to other countries of north-western Europe. The annual catch, which usually varies between about 350,000 and 450,000 tons (though in 1957 it reached a peak of 537,000 tons), is appreciably less than that of Norway, Great Britain and West Germany. The disparity is less marked by value, especially if crustaceans and shellfish, notably lobsters and oysters, are included, while freshwater fisheries in rivers, lakes and artificial pools provide a valuable source of food. Sea fish do not play an important part in the diet, and the catch is more than adequate for home needs; much cod is marketed in dried or salted form in the Mediterranean countries and Latin America.

In pre-1939 days the industry suffered from poor organization, a multiplicity of small, badly equipped boats, and inadequate handling facilities at the ports. During 1939–45 nearly three-quarters of the craft were destroyed, and while replacement was at first slow, by 1968 there were about 13,800 registered boats, a third fewer than in 1938 but of much larger aggregate tonnage, mostly mechanized, and equipped with storage and refrigeration facilities. Commercial fishing is concentrated, and 60 per cent of the total catch is landed at only four ports: Boulogne (135,000 tons), Lorient (54,000), Concarneau (48,000) and La Rochelle (22,000). The only others of any importance were Douarnenez (19,000) and Dieppe (12,000).

Two-thirds of the catch by weight is made up of five species: cod, mackerel, sardine, herring and tunny, in that order, though in value tunny comes second to cod and the catch of herrings fluctuates so widely that in some years it takes first place. Large quantities of miscellaneous fish are sold unsorted in bulk, and unspecified amounts are consumed by the fishing population.

The most important centre for commercial fishing is Boulogne (Plate LXII), where activity is in the hands of large trawler firms.

Fast trains of refrigerator cars serve the Paris markets, and ancillary industries (curing, salting, packing, ice-making and the manufacture of fertilizers) are carried on. Dieppe handles the smaller vessels which return daily, and Fécamp is still one of the centres for fitting out trawlers which visit the Grand Banks of Newfoundland, based on St Pierre and Miquelon.

Along the coast of Brittany the sea may provide a farmer with a supplementary occupation or offer full-time employment. About 40 per cent of all personnel in the fishing industry live along this coast, and many of the 5,000 men employed in the trawler fleets of Boulogne are Bretons. Almost every bay and inlet has a few boats; Lorient, Concarneau and Douarnenez are the most important, though smaller harbours, such as Cancale, Paimpol, St Brieux, Tréguier, Lannion, Morlaix, Camaret, Brest and Audierne, each land a few hundred tons of fish. The chief catches are sardines and white tunny. Shrimps and shellfish are gathered mainly by women; oysters and mussels are cultivated in beds; and lobsters caught off the Portuguese and African coasts are stored alive in tanks at Roscoff, Concarneau and Audierne.

Farther south on the coast of Charente Maritime, La Rochelle is an important fishing centre. Arcachon, on the coast of the Landes, lands annually about 2,600 tons of fish, mostly sardines, with some sole and turbot, but oysters are its chief item; here and at La Tremblade and Marennes they are cultivated in beds.

The Basque coast was once one of the most active centres of the fishing industry; Bayonne, Biarritz, Bidart, Guéthary, Ciboure and St Jean-de-Luz have long been important. Fishing vessels went to Newfoundland and Arctic waters, and the Basque fishermen were second only to the Bretons in numbers and skill. Since the mid-nineteenth century this activity has declined, though St Jean is still an important centre for the sardine fisheries, and anchovy, tunny and mackerel are caught.

In spite of the long stretch of coast, the lagoons and the many villages, the Mediterranean littoral is not of any great importance; only 30,000 tons of fish are landed each year, though these figures refer only to fish sold commercially, and much is on a part-time and subsistence basis. About 1,900 men are engaged full-time, and many others fish occasionally, including Italians who come for the summer, living in camps among the dunes, before moving on to the Midi vine harvest. Red tunny, sardines, anchovies and mackerel are fished in the open sea; the Etang de Thau has oyster and mussel fisheries; and eels, lobsters and crayfish are caught in the lagoons. Farther east Marseilles and Toulon each has a small fishing fleet, but the annual catches amount to only a few thousand tons.

INDUSTRIAL PLANNING

France was faced in the post-1945 period with an enormous programme of economic development necessitated by four stringent years of occupation and the immense material destruction involved in the liberation of the country. Programmes were required to rebuild the shattered cities, ports and communications, to regain and improve upon past standards of living, to stimulate exports, to balance essential imports of food and raw materials, and to maintain a level of armaments in keeping with France's military commitments. The position was not helped by the unstable political situation until the constitution of the Fifth Republic came into force in 1958, and long periods of warfare in the overseas territories were a serious drain on resources. One regional problem involved the excessive concentration of economic activity in Paris, the result of the centralization there of political, administrative and financial power, and of the city's great growth of population. By contrast, large parts of southern and western France had stagnated or even declined for many decades, both demographically and economically.

Clearly some degree of overall planning was essential, involving both public and private sectors of the economy. Some direct nationalization was immediately effected; the *Banque de France* was nationalized in 1945, the coal-mining industry in 1946, and in the same year *Gaz de France* and *Electricité de France* were created. The largest aircraft manufacturing firm, *Sud-Aviation*, and the smaller *Nord-Aviation*, were also nationalized. In 1945 France's largest automobile producer was nationalized as the *Régie Nationale des Usines Renault*. In addition, the government is a major shareholder in such public corporations as the *Compagnie Nationale du Rhône*.

To carry out the modernization and re-equipment of the economy, it was necessary to formulate a series of overall plans, '*La Planification française*', under a permanent administrative body. The first plan, which was authorized in 1946, drawn up by M. Jean Monnet and published in 1947, ran until 1953 and was mainly concerned with basic heavy industry. The second plan (which produced severe inflation) ran from 1951–55; the third plan, from 1955–60, encouraged exports and sought to restore the balance of payments; the fourth

(1962–65) was largely concerned with regional development and the contraction of the agricultural labour force (p. 414). The Fifth Plan (1965–70) aimed at increasing national productivity generally, at stimulating research, and at working out wage structures.

In order to even out the radical contrasts in economic development in various parts of France, the government in 1955 set up machinery to produce regional plans to dovetail within and amplify the details of the national plans. Twenty-one regions were delimited, each with a plan within which the State, local authorities and private interests can co-operate, and through which investment can be directed. The first regional plan, which appeared in 1956, was for Brittany, and all have now been published. A major aim of regional planning has been to alter the pattern of industrial location, to discourage further concentration in Greater Paris and Lyons, to reduce rural unemployments by grants for the relocation of industry, and to concentrate new development in the west (Brittany), south-west and centre of the country.

The greater part of industrial activity was left in the private sector, though organized under a series of *Chambres Syndicales*; thus the *Chambre Syndicale de la Sidérurgie française* controls the iron and steel industry (Fig. 91).

There has been, it must be admitted, some disappointment at the slowness at which the regional plans have been implemented. Nevertheless, much has been done, including some slowing down of activity in the Paris region and a great stimulation of the Aquitaine and Midi-Pyrénées regions. The overall results are exemplified by five representative basic industries.

	1938	1946	1956	1963	1968
Steel (million tons)	6·2	4·4	13·4	17·6	20·4
Cement (million tons)	3·6	3·4	11·2	18·1	26·6
Fertilizers (million tons)	177·0	127·0	408·0	515·9	564·0(1967)
Electricity (milliard KWh)	20·0	23·0	53·8	88·5	117·7
Refined petroleum products (million tons)	5·0	2·2	25·0	43·0	70·3

FUEL AND POWER

Since the end of the War of 1939–45, the production, distribution and consumption of energy in France have increased markedly and changed in character. Statistics of the various categories of energy consumed (in terms of percentages of equivalent quantities of coal) afford some revealing contrasts between 1938 and 1967.

Percentages of total power consumed

	Coal, coke, lignite	Oil and petrol	Natural gas	Hydro-electricity
1938	80·4	11·0	0·0	8·6
1962	51·6	33·7	4·9	9·8
1967	34·7	49·3	5·2	10·8

Very nearly the same amount of coal was consumed in each of these years, 67·5, 72·9 and 63·9 million tons respectively, but other sources of energy increased markedly; expressed in absolute terms, the consumption rose from the equivalent of 84 million tons of coal in 1938 to 184 millions in 1967 (Fig. 84).

Coal

As late as 1850 France produced a mere 4 million tons of coal per annum, less than its small neighbour Belgium. No spectacular mid-nineteenth century development in industry occurred, as in Great Britain, while in 1871 the disaster of the Franco–Prussian War and the loss of Alsace–Lorraine profoundly affected progress.

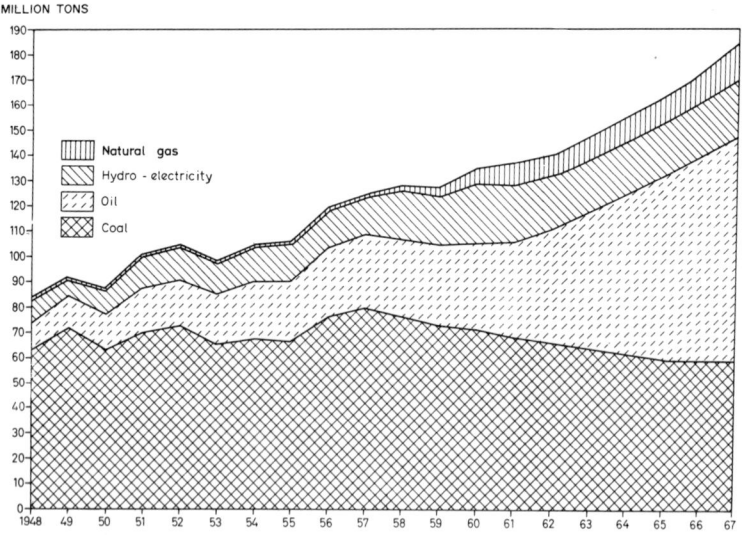

Fig. 84. Power production in France, 1948–1967
(After *Annuaire Statistique de la France*, 1968)
The energy value of each is given in terms of the equivalent quantity of bituminous coal.

Nevertheless, by 1914 the output of coal had attained 41 million tons per annum.

The vulnerability of the main coalfield on the north-eastern border was grievously demonstrated during the 1914–18 War, when surface installations and mining villages were devastated by the long drawn-out and concentrated warfare. The French exploited other fields, notably in the Central Massif, with the desperation of necessity, and managed to produce 19·5 million tons even in the trough year of 1915, and as much as 29 million in 1917. After the Armistice the process of restoration began, assisted by German reparations, the return of Alsace–Lorraine which included the Moselle field, and the use for fifteen years of the Saar. The northern coalfield was reconstructed on modern lines.

After the fall of France in 1940, output was maintained under German insistence at about 40 million tons, not including the Moselle field, which had been reincorporated as part of Alsace–Lorraine into the Reich. But at the end of hostilities stocks were non-existent, communications were disrupted, there was a grave shortage of labour, machinery, pit-props and trucks. Prewar foreign suppliers, especially Great Britain, were in no position to furnish much coal because of their own critical requirements.

In May 1946 the *Charbonnages de France* was created as the central controlling authority, within which operate nine regional organizations, the *Houillères de Bassin*. For some years the production of coal steadily increased; by 1952 the total exceeded the prewar figure and in 1958 it reached 60 million tons. Since then, as elsewhere in Western Europe, there has been a steady downward trend in coal production (about 42 million tons in 1968), largely because of the increasing use of oil and gas. Programmes of rationalization and modernization have been effected; between 1947 and 1968 the number of collieries was reduced to a third, as less efficient producers were closed down or several units were merged. The labour force has been reduced by half since 1950.

Consumption of coal, however, has remained steady at about 70–75 million tons, the balance being made up of imports from West Germany, the U.S.A., Poland and the U.S.S.R. (1·5 million tons in 1967). This large import results from the poor quality of much of the reserves, the high and increasing cost of mining, and the acute shortage of coking coal. Although new processes have been developed, particularly in Lorraine, where unsuitable coals through blending and processing can yield adequate metallurgical coke, considerable amounts of both coke and coking coal have to be imported, equivalent to about 40 per cent of the total consumed.

The output of coal in the nine regions in 1967 may be summarized:

Region	Chief producing areas	Output (million tons)
Nord and Pas-de-Calais	Douai–Anzin, Béthune–Lens	23·43
Lorraine	Petite Rosselle, Merlebach, Spittel, La Houve	15·03
Loire	St Etienne, Ste Foy	2·00
Cévennes	Alès	1·70
Blanzy	Blanzy, Montceau-les-Mines, Décize, Commentry	2·20
Aquitaine	Decazeville, Aubin, Carmaux, Albi, Graissesac	1·73
Auvergne	Brioude, St Eloi, Langeac, Brassac	0·80
Dauphiné	Maurienne, Tarentaise, Briançon, La Mure	0·75
Provence	Fuveau (lignite)	1·26
Total		48·90

The Northern Coalfield (Fig. 85). Underlying the sands and clays of Flanders in a synclinal depression lies the concealed coalfield of the Nord and the Pas-de-Calais; the Coal Measures, exposed on the surface farther to the east in Belgium, are found progressively deeper to the west. The field was affected not only by the Hercynian orogeny, but also by the fracturing associated with the uplift of the Ardennes during Tertiary times. In places overthrusting has forced older rocks over the Coal Measures, especially in the southwest of the field, and the coal is separated by faults into several productive areas; the two main basins are those of Douai–Valenciennes in the east and Béthune–Lens in the west. The mines average well over 400 m (1300 ft) and at times reach 900 m (3000 ft) below the surface. Many seams are thin and interrupted by faults, sometimes they dip at high angles, and the average thickness worked is only about a metre, making for difficult and expensive exploitation.

Despite these disadvantages, the field is still of vital importance to France, since it produces nearly half the output. About two-thirds comes from the Pas-de-Calais section, the most important areas being around Lens, Noeux, Béthune and Bruay. In the department of Nord, the main districts are near Douai in the west, Aniche, and as far east as Anzin and Condé. The quality of coal is extremely variable, not only in various parts of the field, but with depth; the upper seams consist of gas coal, the lower ones of semi-anthracite.

About half of the coal is consumed on the field itself at coke ovens, patent-fuel plant and thermal-electric stations. About a third of the

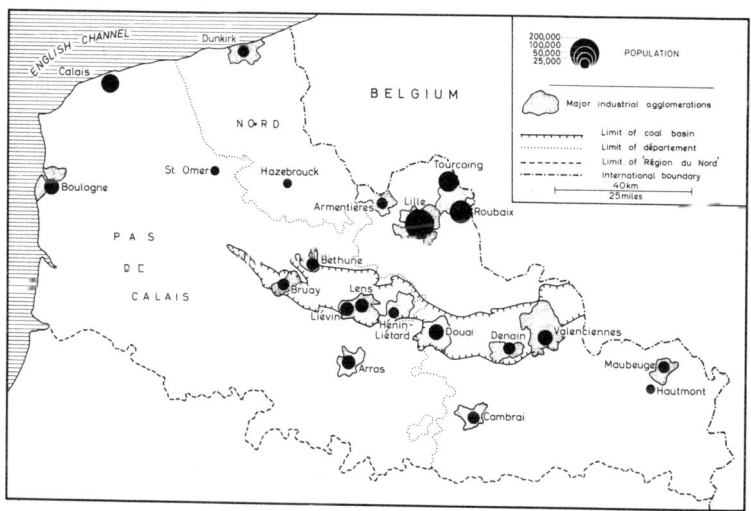

Fig. 85. The northern coalfield of France
(After I. B. Thompson)

coke output was made at pit-head cokeries, most of them large modern units. Considerably more than half of the gas manufactured is produced at these cokeries, and distributed over the north by a grid which links Béthune, Douai and Valenciennes with Lille district.

The Moselle Coalfield. The Coal Measures of the Saar Basin (p. 161) are continued across the border into Lorraine, though overlain by thick deposits of Triassic rocks. The field was actively worked by Germany between 1871 and 1918, then by France in the valley of the Rosselle, a left-bank tributary of the Saar. Between 1940 and 1944 it once more became German, but since then its output has rapidly increased, in 1967 reaching 15·0 million tons produced by eight collieries, twice as much as in pre-1939 years and nearly a third of France's total. A high yield per underground worker is an indication of the thick uninterrupted seams and the degree of mechanization, but the quality of the coal is not high.

Until recently Moselle coal was not suitable for making metallurgical coke unless mixed with Ruhr coal, but some modern cokeries use processes which make effective coke from the local coal alone.

The Central Massif Coalfields. The Coal Measures are preserved in down-faulted hollows or synclinal basins among the crystalline rocks. Although the fields are small and scattered, most are actively prosecuted as the centres of small industrial regions, notably the Loire field (St Etienne and Firminy) and the Blanzy field (Le Creusòt, Blanzy and Montceau-les-Mines).

Other Fields. About 1·6 million tons of lignite are mined annually in the Provence field, in the department of Bouches-du-Rhône. The bulk is consumed in thermal power stations; at Fuveau, to the north-east of Marseilles, it is used to generate power for reducing the bauxite mined locally. Non-nationalized mines produced about 1·5 million tons of lignite, mostly in the Landes, also supplying the thermal generators. About 700,000 tons of anthracite are mined in the Alpine valleys of Tarentaise and Maurienne, and in the valley of the Drac near La Mure.

Electricity

In 1946 a State agency known as *Electricité de France* (*E.D.F.*) was established to control the production, distribution and consumption of electricity throughout the country. Some producers were excluded from nationalization, notably those plants controlled by the national railway company, by the *Charbonnages de France* and by industry generally; most of these are thermal stations which sell excess power to *E.D.F.* As a result, while *E.D.F.* produces about 70 per cent of the total power, it distributes 95 per cent. Special relationships were established with the *Compagnie Nationale du Rhône* (p. 434), in which the Government is a major shareholder.

The contributions of hydro and thermal electricity to the total output is summarized by Fig. 86. In terms of installed capacity, thermal plants are ahead of hydro, the respective figures for 1968 being 16·9 and 13·7 million KW; in terms of output, hydro contributed 49 per cent of the total in 1963, but declined to 43 per cent in 1968. Some large thermal stations are used as supplementary sources of power at times of low water or hard frost when the hydro output is at a minimum, or as reserve plants standing by in a state of suspended animation to meet exceptional peak loads.

The creation of *E.D.F.* has made possible the development of an extensive grid system on a basis of 225 KV lines, of which by 1968

Plate LIV. *Les Haudères, an Alpine village at a height of about 1500 m (5000 ft) in the Val d'Hérens, Pennine Alps, Switzerland*

Plate LV. *The Vosges near Plainfaing, France*

Plate LVI. The Chamonix aiguilles in the French Alps. The high peak on the left is the Grandes Jorasses (4206 m, 13,800 feet); the Aiguille du Grépon is the dark castellated summit in the middleground; and the Nantillons Glacier is in the right foreground

Plate LVII. Chalk landscape near the eastern margins of the Paris Basin

Fig. 86. The output of electricity in France, 1910–1967
(After *Annuaire Statistique de la France*, 1968)

there were about 17 500 km (10,900 miles). During the last few years, some of the new stations have been linked by higher voltage lines (380 KV), totalling about 2800 km (1750 miles) by 1968.

Thermal Electricity. There are more very big thermal stations than hydro; of the 33 each producing over a milliard KWh in 1968, 24 were thermally operated. In the Paris region a group owned by E.D.F. includes the largest in France, at Montereau in Seine-et-Marne. Most are fuelled with coal brought by barge from the northern coalfield or from West Germany, or by oil, natural gas and nuclear power. The other concentrations of thermal stations are on the Nord

15

coalfield and in Lorraine, owned by the collieries and steel works. These units exist primarily to supply current to industry; coal slack, inferior grades of coal, coke-oven gas, blast-furnace gas and refinery gas, formerly waste products, are used to generate electricity, surplus current being sold to *E.D.F.* and put into the grid. Other large thermal plants are located in the neighbourhood of cities, ports and industrial districts. The Gardanne station north-east of Marseilles is fuelled with lignite from the nearby Fuveau field, and a station near Toulouse uses natural gas from Lacq.

Hydroelectricity. France is advantageously placed for the development of hydroelectricity, and almost half the total potential has been utilized. Several uplands provide catchments sufficiently lofty to afford considerable heads of water; the French Alps have extensive snowfields and glaciers; the Pyrenees contain many high-lying lakes; and exploitable rivers include the Rhine, the Rhône and the Dordogne.

The Rhône is the most important French river in terms of power potential. In 1934 the government sponsored the establishment of the *Compagnie Nationale du Rhône* to carry out a multi-purpose scheme for the production of hydroelectricity, the improvement of navigation, and the utilization of water for irrigation. The first station to be completed was Génissiat, 50 km (31 miles) downstream from Lake Geneva (Fig. 87), where the narrow valley, with cliffs rising nearly 300 m above the river, offered an obvious reservoir site. Work began in 1937 and though held up after the fall of France in 1940, the barrage, 80 m (260 ft) high, was completed in 1948; behind this a lake 22 km (14 miles) in length was created. The power plant at the base of the dam is the largest in France in installed capacity. Below Lyons twelve navigation loops are scheduled to by-pass sections of river, each with a power-station: the André Blondel station at Donzère-Mondragon above Orange was completed in 1952 (Fig. 88); Châteauneuf near Montélimar (1957); Baix-le-Logis Neuf above Montélimar (1960); Beauchastel below Valence (1963); Pierre Bénite just below Lyons (1966); Bourg-les-Valence (1968); and Vallabrègues between Avignon and Arles (1970). Five others are under construction or projected; the Rhône master plan, when completed, will generate some 13 milliard KWh annually.

The Rhine is the subject of a series of ambitious projects associated with the original plan for a left-bank Grand Canal d'Alsace with the dual function of overcoming the navigational difficulties of the river (p. 460) and of utilizing its hydroelectric potential. The first four stations were on the Canal itself: at Kembs (1932), Ottmarsheim

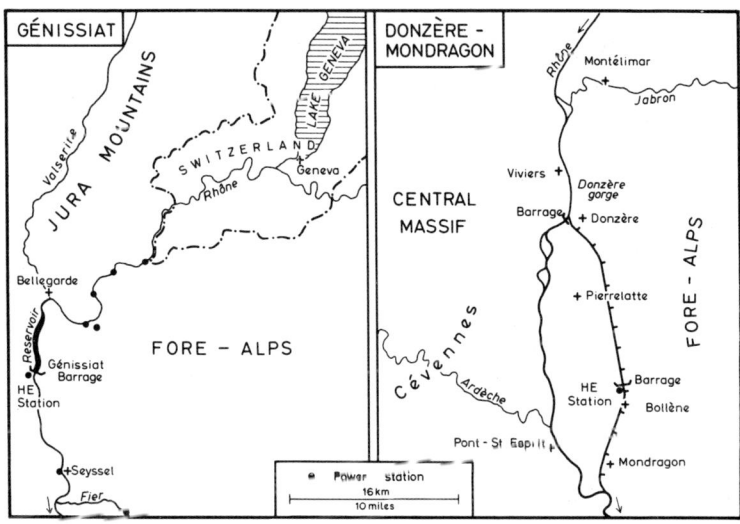

Figs. 87, 88. Hydroelectricity stations at Génissiat and Donzère-Mondragon

(1952), Fessenheim (1956) and Vogelgrun (1959). The second four stations were constructed on separate derivation loops along the left bank: Marckolsheim (1960), Rhinau (1964), Gerstheim (1970) and Strasbourg (1970), and will produce about 7 milliard KWh annually.

Some of the pioneering efforts in the production of hydro-electricity were pursued in the French Alps; the world's first power station was built near Grenoble in 1869. Up to 1939 the tendency was towards a large number of small stations, and the power was consumed locally in electrochemical and metallurgical factories along the valleys and by the electrified railways. Since 1945 the construction of numerous small projects has continued, though within an integrated plan. Chief developments concern the upper Isère basin, including the Tignes scheme completed in 1954, which involved the construction of a reservoir to flood the Isère valley. A huge earth barrage across the Durance at Serre-Ponçon was completed in 1959, the resulting lake filling the valley for 18 km (11 miles) upstream. The engineering feats in these Alpine valleys include taking water from the upper Isère valley (Tarentaise) through a tunnel under the mountains into the Arc valley (Maurienne), so affording a 150 m (500 ft) head of water for the underground Randens station.

While the industries of the Alpine valleys are the main beneficiaries, excess power is put into the grid; a 380 KV transmission line runs from Tarentaise to Génissiat and on to Paris.

Another area of hydroelectricity development is the Central Massif, which in 1968 produced one-quarter of the French total. Although the total potential is appreciably less than that of the Alps and the rivers experience a low-water régime in summer, their winter maximum is complementary to the minimum of the Alpine and Pyrenean streams which suffer from freezing. Most of the stations are strung out along the Dordogne, Cère and Truyère, with a few others on the Lot and the Tarn. The disadvantages are the rapid runoff over the crystalline rocks and the long periods of summer drought; at Bort-les-Orgues on the Dordogne the ratio between minimum and maximum rates of flow is 1 to 780. The solution has been the creation of a series of barrages to impound reservoirs; the total head of water between the highest and lowest of the Dordogne dams is 550 m (1800 ft). The largest dam, at Bort-les-Orgues, is 120 m (394 ft) high, the biggest station is Brommat, on the Truyère.

The Pyrenees possess a large potential, for they have a multitude of high-lying rock-basin lakes, which require only small barrages to increase appreciably their storage capacity. A few dams have been constructed, but there are no huge barrages as in the Rhône valley and the Central Massif, and the emphasis has been on the creation of numerous small enterprises. In all, about a hundred plants are in operation, producing a sixth of the French total, mainly supplying local industry and the French railways, though they contribute to the grid via the Lannemezan transformer station.

In the estuary of the Rance, near St Malo, a power station operated by the tides was completed in 1967. A dam was built across the estuary, containing a shipping lock, sluices, and 24 reversible turbines operated by the alternate ebb and flow of the tides. This station is now making 1 per cent of French electricity.

Nuclear Energy

The French government has adopted an ambitious nuclear power programme in order to ease the energy situation, since in 1960 only two-thirds of the country's production of energy was met from internal resources, and it was estimated that by 1970 the percentage would have fallen to 46 per cent. The first nuclear power-plant, at Marcoule near Avignon, was begun in 1953 and came into operation three years later. Since then, several other plants have been completed at Chinon in the Loire valley, in Brittany and on the Belgian border. It is stated that the new plants will produce power at about the same price as a conventional power station, and an official output target of 2 milliard KWh by 1970 was exceeded.

Petroleum

In 1968 nineteen refineries had a total capacity of about 97 million tons of crude oil. Only 2·8 million tons of oil were produced in France; eight companies work fields in various parts, but output has increased only slowly. The oldest field is in northern Alsace, where oil seepages were known and utilized as early as the fifteenth century near the village of Pechelbronn; the first oil was pumped in 1881, and a string of wells still operates, though output is small, only about 20,000 tons. A few recently drilled wells in the centre of the Paris Basin yield about 40,000 tons annually. The most productive district is in Aquitaine, where fields are worked in the Landes at Parentis–Born and near Lacq in the Pyrenean foothills; to the end of 1968 some 12 million tons had been extracted. The oil is piped to a refinery at Bordeaux.

France imported about 72 million tons of crude oil in 1967, including 34 million tons from the Middle East, 32 million tons from the Sahara, and 2·8 million tons from Venezuela. The Saharan deposits are increasing in importance, and are linked by pipelines to terminals on the Algerian coast at Bougie and La Skhirra, affording a short tanker haul across the Mediterranean to the Lavéra terminal near Marseilles. Libyan oil is similarly well placed with pipelines to coastal terminals at El Sider and Port Brega, and the growth of these two producing areas may have serious effects on the Middle Eastern fields.

The refineries (Fig. 89) are mostly owned by companies associated with the major world firms, though about 15 per cent of the industry is controlled by *l'Union Générale des Pétroles* in which the French State is a majority shareholder. The earliest refineries were built on the coast, but the attraction of inland markets has led to the construction of inland refineries, linked to the coastal terminals by pipelines (Fig. 89). These include two near Strasbourg at Herrlisheim and Reichstett, supplied with crude oil by the South European Pipeline, which runs for 770 km (480 miles) from its terminal at Lavéra to Strasbourg and on to Karlsruhe. Other inland refineries are at Feyzin near Lyons, Vern-sur-Seiche near Rennes, and two near Paris at Grandpuits and Porcheville.

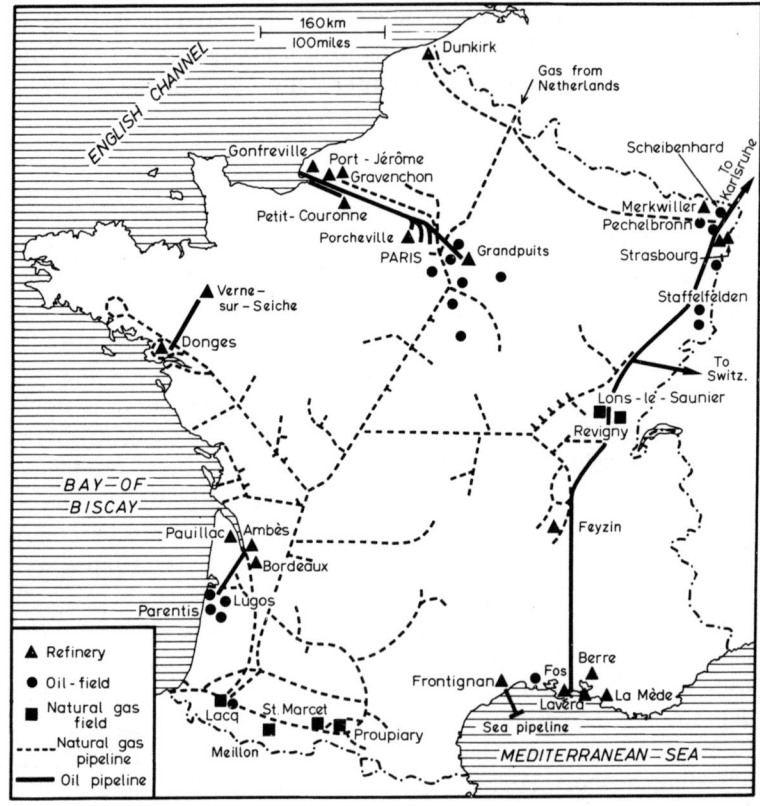

Fig. 89. Oil- and gas-fields, with pipelines and refineries, in France.

Natural Gas

Natural gas was first discovered in 1939 at St Marcet, 72 km (45 miles) south-west of Toulouse, and then after the War of 1939–45 in a larger field near Lacq, to the north-west of Pau. Both discoveries were byproducts of the search for oil, but it is now evident that the future of the fields lies rather in the gas. Starting with a short pipeline between St Marcet and Toulouse in 1942, the grid has been developed, and mains run to Bordeaux, Nantes, Lorient, Paris, Besançon and Lyons. In 1967 gas from the Dutch field at Slochteren (p. 262) began to flow through an international pipeline into France.

This natural gas is supplemented by increasing imports from North Africa. An 800 km (500 miles) pipeline brings gas from the Algerian field at Hassi Err'Mel to Algiers, where it is liquefied and transported by tanker to Lavéra.

The distribution of gas has been systematized and integrated under the nationalized authority, *Gaz de France*. Gas from coke ovens, blast-furnace gas, byproduct gas from the refineries and increasingly natural gas, both home-produced and imported, suitably standardized for calorific value, is put into the grid. Several underground gas-storage reservoirs have been established in 'geological traps', as at Beynes (40 km, 25 miles west of Paris) and at St. Illiers (near Mantes).

OTHER MINERALS

France is endowed with appreciable resources of four minerals: iron ore, bauxite, potash and common salt (Fig. 90). Limestone and chalk are widely quarried for cement-making; small amounts of tungsten, vanadium and uranium ores are mined in the Central Massif, Alps and Pyrenees; about 1·7 million tons annually of sulphur are obtained from the Pyrenean gas field and from pyrites deposits; and talc (hydrous magnesium silicate) is worked at Trimouns in the Pyrenean foothills, where the largest talc quarry in the world produced 205,000 tons in 1967.

Iron ore

With a production of 55·2 million tons of iron ore in 1968, France was fourth to the U.S.S.R., U.S.A. and Canada. Many minor deposits formed the basis of early metallurgical industries, but when smelting by coke developed and the scale of the industry increased, the scattered mines were rapidly exhausted or ceased to be economically workable. The dominance of the Lorraine ore-field is shown in the following figures of production:

	million tons				
	1929	*1937*	*1952*	*1962*	*1967*
Lorraine	48·0	35·4	37·8	62·4	46·0
Normandy	1·9	1·9	2·5	2·8	1·7
Anjou–Brittany	0·5	0·4	0·6	0·9	0·5
Others	0·3	0·1	0·4	0·2	1·0
Total	50·7	37·8	41·3	66·3	49·2

The Lorraine ore consists of limonite (hydrated oxide of iron) and siderite (a carbonate of iron) of oolitic structure and for the most part of a calcareous nature (and therefore self-fluxing), except in the Nancy basin where the matrix is siliceous. The iron content varies

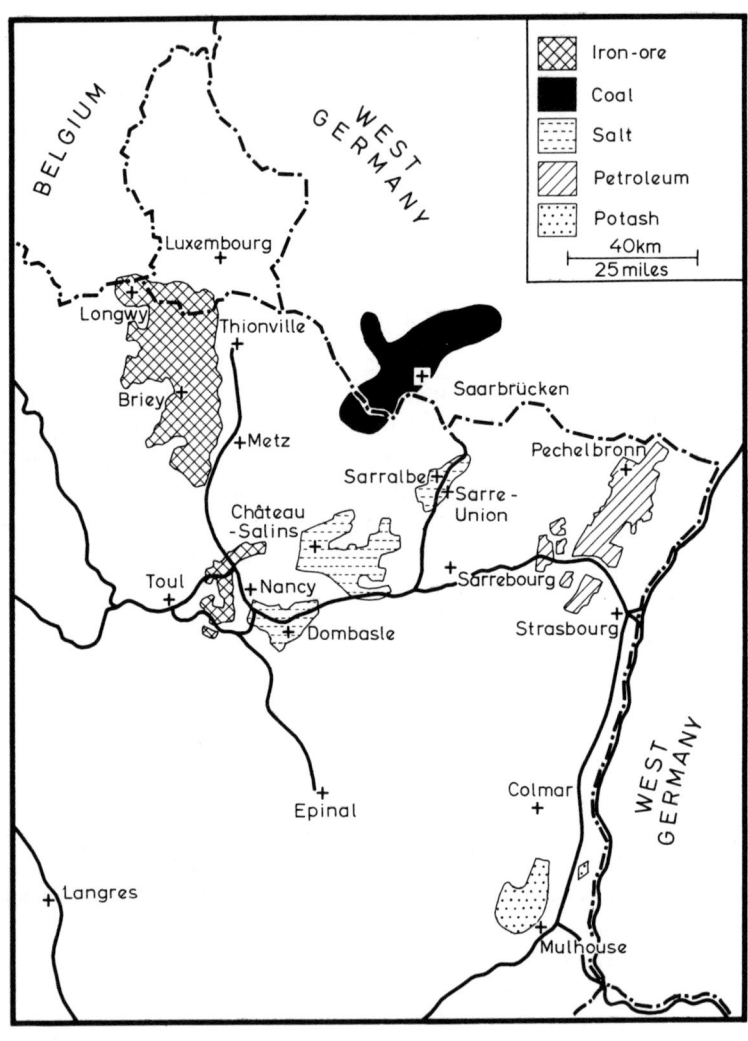

Fig. 90. Mineral resources of eastern France
(After *Carte industrielle de la Lorraine*)

from about 24 to 40 per cent, although the richer ores have been largely exhausted; the average content is now of the order of 33 per cent. The ore also contains phosphorus, and before the introduction of the Gilchrist–Thomas process, neither wrought iron nor steel could be successfully made from it; the term 'minette' was somewhat contemptuously applied in the early nineteenth century.

The minette field is located in the Jurassic limestone plateau between the valleys of the Meuse and the Moselle, with its apex near Nancy, its base lying 100 km (60 miles) to the north near the Luxembourg border. The strata dip gently south-westward; as a result, in the north and east the ore beds appear on the surface on the valley sides, but occur at progressively greater depths to the west. The main disadvantages of the deposits are the difficult terrain, with steep-sided valleys and escarpments, and the distance from supplies of adequate coking coal. On the other hand, the field has estimated reserves of 8,000 million tons, there is little structural disturbance so that the beds are continuous, and mining is highly mechanized. The deep valleys enable ore to be won by horizontal galleries (Plate LIX) and in some districts by open quarries. The geographical location which has brought travail to Lorraine three times in seventy years has meant that at the heart of the industrial complex of western Europe it has shared in its development. The ore-field is divided by intervening barren ground into four individual basins: those of Briey, Moselle, Longwy and Nancy, of which the first two are by far the most important.

The iron ores of Normandy occur near the eastern and southern margins of the Armorican massif, preserved in synclines within the Pre-Cambrian sandstones and quartzites. Where they were exposed on the surface by denudation, the carbonates were oxidized into haematites, though most have been worked out as a result of their accessibility, richness and freedom from phosphorus. Elsewhere the ore is a calcareous minette, of 30 to 40 per cent iron; five mines produced 1·7 million tons in 1967, of which two-thirds were smelted at Mondeville and Rouen, the rest was exported to Belgium, West Germany and Great Britain.

Anjou–Brittany. These ore-fields extend north-westward from Angers, a relic of the now vanished overlying Jurassic beds, occurring in ridges of sandstone among the Palaeozoic slates and shales. Five mines produced about 700,000 tons in 1967, most of which is consumed by the blast furnaces of the lower Loire steel works at Trignac.

The output of other mining areas in France is of relatively small importance. Some comes from the Pyrenees in the Tet valley near Prades, and in the upper Ariège basin near Ax-les-Therms and Saurat. Their chief advantage is that they are non-phosphoric haematites. Other small deposits occur in the Central Massif, for the most part now virtually worked out, but important in the past for the establishment of metallurgical industries.

France produces considerably more iron ore than its steel industry can consume; about two-thirds is smelted within the country, but 14 per cent of the total output goes to Luxembourg, 11 per cent to Belgium and 10 per cent to the Saar; none at all goes to the Ruhr. Despite this considerable export, France imported 4·8 million tons in 1967, some from Luxembourg, the result of firms owning properties and plants on either side of the border. The rest, obtained from such diverse sources as Labrador, South America, Liberia and Australia, is consumed by steel plants on the coast; from 1962, when the Dunkirk plant began operation, seaborne imports increased markedly.

Bauxite

The main commercial ore of aluminium, hydrated oxide of alumina, is known as bauxite from its occurrence near the town of Les Baux in Provence, where the ore has been preserved in 'pockets' among the limestone. Of about 2·7 million tons produced in 1968, 94 per cent came from this district in the department of Var, the rest from Hérault and Ariège. France is no longer the chief world producer, a position it held until the War of 1939–45, for consumption has risen so considerably that it now ranks behind Surinam and Guyana. The bulk of the bauxite is sent by rail to Gardanne near Marseilles, where it is reduced to alumina, and then to the Alpine valleys where it is smelted electrolytically.

Potash

In 1904, when Alsace was in German hands, deposits of potash in the form of sylvite were discovered in the Oligocene strata, deposited when the Rhine Rift Valley was a gulf of the sea in early Tertiary times. The deposits of the Forêt de Nonnenbruch contain between 12 and 22 per cent of potash, and the estimated reserves are 1,500 million tons. Before 1918 the owner of the field, the German *Kalisyndikat*, was mainly concerned with the exploitation of its own deposits between the rivers Weser and Elbe, the chief centre being Stassfurt (p. 218); this was the only major potash deposit worked in the world and the monopoly was jealously guarded, so that the annual output of the Nonnenbruch deposits was limited. With the reacquisition of Alsace by France the Stassfurt monopoly was broken, and within three years the Alsatian output had trebled. After 1945 the enormous demand for fertilizers resulted in a considerable increase of output; in 1968 France produced 1·8 million tons, nearly three times the highest prewar output, of which two-thirds was exported. Much of this potash, both crude and refined, is shipped down the Rhine to Antwerp, hence to the Benelux countries (the main customers), Great Britain and the U.S.A.

Salt

Common salt is an important raw material for the chemical industry, and France possesses considerable reserves; about 4·4 million tons were produced in 1968. Some is obtained by panning and solar evaporation in the lagoons along the coasts of the Mediterranean and the Bay of Biscay, but the main producing region for rock salt is Lorraine. The Triassic and older Jurassic rocks are notable for the immense deposits, formed by evaporation from former shallow gulfs of the sea. In the north the salt-field of Sarralbe in the Muschelkalk is exploited by brine-pumping at Sarralbe, Salzbronn and Haras. The salt beds of the Seille basin lie in the Keuper, from which brine is pumped at Château-Salins; those in the Sanon valley, occurring in the Lias marls, are worked at Varangéville and Dombasle. The salt provides the raw material for chemical works at Sarralbe and Dombasle (Plate LXI).

MANUFACTURING INDUSTRY

Iron and Steel

In 1968 France was the sixth world producer of crude steel, with an output of 20·4 million tons, about a fifth of the European Coal and Steel Community's total. The smelting of iron ore was active in Celtic and Gallo–Roman times in the wooded valleys of the Ardennes, Lorraine and Normandy. By 1780 there were more than a thousand widely scattered iron-making establishments, using charcoal and the small but rich deposits of iron ore. The English ironmaster William Wilkinson went to France in 1785 to build a cannon foundry near Nantes and then in conjunction with De Wendel, son of the founder of the present Lorraine firm, he erected at Le Creusot the first successful iron works with a coke-fired blast furnace on the continent of Europe. During the first three-quarters of the nineteenth century progress was slow, without the spectacular developments of England and Belgium. The minette ore of Lorraine was discovered during the early years of the century, but it was not then utilized because of its phosphoric nature. In 1871 Germany annexed the whole of the known minette field, except for the small Longwy and Nancy basins. The development of the Gilchrist–Thomas smelting process, by which a basic lining to the steel converter or open hearth is used to get rid of phosphoric impurities, revolutionized the position of Lorraine. Germany rapidly developed the steel industry in the annexed part of Lorraine, while France was stimulated to carry out geological research, which showed that the ore-field extended well to the west of the new boundary. But by 1913 the French output of crude steel was only 4·7 million tons, compared with the 18·9 million tons of Germany. The War of 1914–18 ravaged the industrial region in Nord and Pas-de-Calais, and stimulated heavy industry in Le Creusot and St Etienne in the Central Massif. At the end of the War Lorraine and Alsace were returned to France, which thereby inherited the flourishing German steel plants. The installations on the Nord coalfield were reconstructed with the aid of German reparations, and in 1929 French steel output reached an inter-war peak of 9·7 million tons.

When the world depression set in, steel production dropped abruptly to a trough of 5·6 million tons in 1933 and by 1938 it had only revived to 6·1 million; in the same interval Germany's production soared from about 6 million to 23 million, an eloquent commentary on the disparity of strength between the two countries. In 1940 Germany again annexed Alsace-Lorraine; though the remaining French industry was worked during most of the War at forced pressure, in the liberation year of 1945 only 1·7 million tons of steel were produced.

One of the major items in the postwar economic recovery was the rehabilitation of the steel industry under the guidance of the Monnet Plan (p. 426). This involved a vast capital investment to bring about modernization and re-equipment of plant. Several large consortia, such as *Wendel-Sidélor, Sacilor, Usinor* and *Sollac*, were incorporated, and a considerable measure of grouping and concentration took place; by 1968 80 per cent of the steel was produced by only six firms. Much modernization has been carried out with State financial aid. About half the steel made is 'basic Bessemer', 25 per cent 'open hearth', 15 per cent by the B.O.S. method (basic oxygen), which is increasing rapidly, and the rest in electric furnaces. Other recent developments include a cold-strip rolling mill at Montataire near Paris to provide sheet metal for the car industry, a wide-strip mill with an annual capacity of a million tons at Sérémange in Moselle, the integrated *Usinor* steel works at Dunkirk, opened in 1962, and the *Sacilor* integrated plant opened in 1970 at Gandrange in Lorraine.

The dominance of Lorraine is shown by the fact that 11·8 million out of the French total of 20·4 million tons of crude steel was produced in the regions Est I and Est II (Figs. 91–2). The former includes the steel works around Longwy and Nancy; in the latter the plants are situated along the foot of the limestone escarpment between Metz and Thionville, and along the valleys of the Orne and Fentsch (Plate LX).

The Nord steel-making region, which produced 2·1 million tons in 1968, comprises not only the northern coalfield, but also the adjoining departments of Oise, Seine and Seine-et-Oise; no iron ore is mined, but three-quarters of French coke is made on the coalfield. This steel industry depends partly on Lorraine ore and pig, partly on ore from Sweden, Liberia, Algeria and South America, and partly on local supplies of scrap. The biggest individual plant is on the coast at Dunkirk, the others mostly on the coalfield at Denain, Valenciennes, Anzin and Hénin-Liétard, and in the Sambre valley, notably near Maubeuge. Farther east, in Pas-de Calais, two outlying integrated plants are at Isbergues on the banks of the Aire Canal and at Outreau near Boulogne

Several centres of steel production are found in the Central Massif; these grew up on the small coalfields, using local ore deposits now exhausted or economically unworkable. No blast furnaces are in operation today; there are a few open-hearth converters, but most of the 250,000 tons of steel is made from Lorraine pig in electric furnaces. The main centres are St Etienne with the neighbouring towns of Firminy and Rive de Gier, Le Creusot with Blanzy and Guegnon, and Montluçon and Commentry in the basin of the upper Cher.

The most important centre in western France is the integrated plant at Mondeville, near Caen, which consumes Normandy iron ore and coking coal imported from West Germany by sea. Other steel plants are located on the lower Loire between St Nazaire and Nantes at Trignac, Basse-Indre and Couëron; the furnaces formerly obtained ore from the Anjou basin, but most now comes from Sweden and Spain. An integrated steel works is at Grand-Quévilly on the left bank of the Seine below Rouen.

The plants in the south-west and south-east are small specialized units, with the exception of the integrated works at Le Boucau on the banks of the Adour between Bayonne and the sea, established in 1882. It depends entirely on seaborne coal and iron ore, of which about a quarter of a million tons are imported through Bayonne.

Other works in the Alpine and Pyrenean valleys make special steels in electric furnaces. The Alpine centres are at Ugine in the valley of the Arly, an Isère tributary, at Moûtiers, Allevard-le-Cheylas and Venthon in the Isère valley, and at Montricher and St Michel-de-Maurienne in the valley of the Arc. The sole advantage is abundant power; pig-iron is brought in and the steels and alloys are sent away for the needs of specialized industries. In the Pyrenees the steel works, originally based on deposits of rich haematite but now using imported pig and scrap, are in the valleys of the Garonne and its tributaries at Pamiers and Tarascon.

Engineering

France both imports and exports steel, with a net annual excess of exports of about 1·2 million tons, leaving 19·2 million tons to be consumed by the 100,000 establishments which use steel as a major raw material; a map plotting these establishments would include almost every town in France (Fig. 91). The main concentrations are in the Nord and Pas-de-Calais, Lorraine, the central industrial region at St Etienne and Le Creusot, and Greater Paris. Many outlying centres are important: Montluçon, Commentry, Caen, Nantes–St Nazaire, Amiens, Châlons-sur-Saône, Rennes, Orléans, Tours, Toulouse and many more.

Heavy engineering is carried on for the most part near the steel-making centres, especially in Lorraine and the Nord. Locomotives and rolling-stock are made in the northern region at Lille, Denain, Jeumont, Valenciennes, Douai and Maubeuge; in the Centre at Le Creusot, St Chamond and Givors; in Alsace at Graffenstaden in the outskirts of Strasbourg, Mulhouse and Belfort; and in the northern and north-eastern suburbs of Paris at St Ouen and St Denis. Outlying centres are Nantes, Bagnères-de-Bigorre in the Pyrenees, and Clermont-Ferrand.

In shipbuilding capacity France ranks eighth in the world, and nearly half a million tons were launched in 1968 from yards on the Loire at St Nazaire and Nantes; on the Seine at Le Havre, Granville, Grand Quévilly and Le Trait; at Dunkirk; at La Ciotat, Port-de-Bouc and La Seyne on the Mediterranean; and at Bordeaux and La Pallice. The biggest yards are at St Nazaire, where the *Normandie* was built in 1935, the 55,000-ton *France*, the world's longest ship, in 1961 and several large tankers. Naval yards are at Brest and Toulon; in 1957 the carrier *Clemenceau* and in 1963 the carrier *Foch* were launched at Brest.

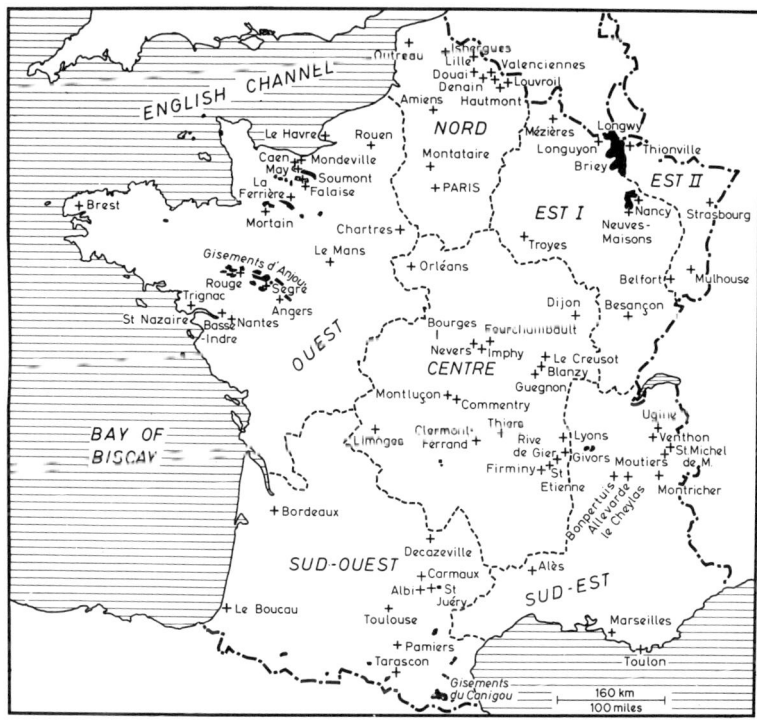

Fig. 91. Steel production in France
(After *Atlas de France*, with revisions)
The boundaries of the seven regions into which the industry is grouped under the
Chambre Syndicale de la Sidérurgie are shown. Ore-fields are in black. Towns
named are those in which major steel-making and steel-using industries are located.

One of the most rapidly expanding activities since the War of
1939–45 has been the production of automobiles, particularly of
the small cheap type. In 1968 about 1·8 million vehicles were produced; the most important makes were *Renault*, with its two major
plants in Greater Paris at Boulogne-Billancourt and Flin and others
at Le Havre and Cléon on the lower Seine, Le Mans, Hagondange
in Lorraine, Orléans, and Annecy in Savoy; *Citroën* at Grenelle
in Greater Paris, at Rennes in Brittany, at Strasbourg and at Reims;
Simca, now controlled by the American *Chrysler* company, with its
plants at Poissy on the banks of the Seine west of Paris, and at La
Rochelle and Sully near Orléans; and *Peugeot*, with its headquarters
at Montbéliard. Many of the auto-plants are in Greater Paris, where
materials can be conveniently brought together, there is a large labour

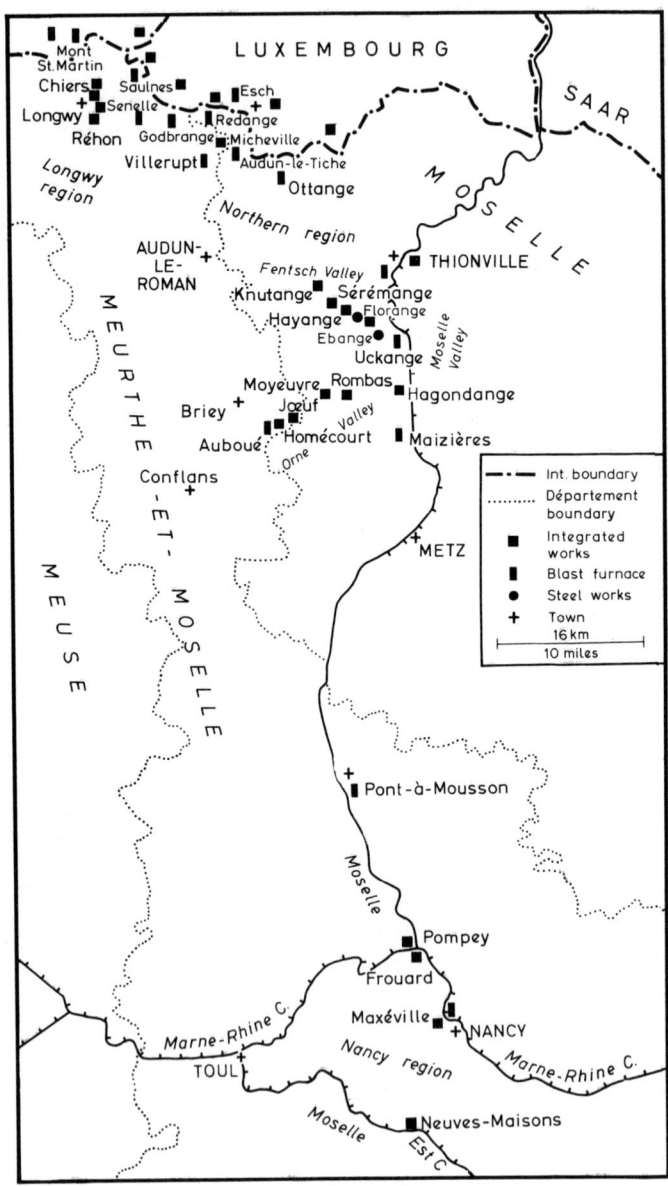

Fig. 92. Steel production in Lorraine
(After *Carte industrielle de la Lorraine* and *Atlas de France*)

supply and the vehicles are easily marketed, but nearly 30 other widely dispersed factories are involved in the industry. The industry employed over 300,000 workers in 1968, and in the same year over half a million vehicles were exported, a large number to the U.S.A.

The aircraft industry developed in the interwar years, at first mainly in the Paris district, though for strategic reasons many factories were transferred after 1931 to central, western and south-western France in Aquitaine and the Loire valley. Since 1945 both the civil and military sides have expanded enormously; it is fourth in the world after the U.S.A., U.S.S.R. and Great Britain. More than 200 separate firms are involved, but two nationalized concerns are pre-eminent, *Sud-Aviation* and *Nord-Aviation*. The former, the largest aircraft firm in Europe, with its headquarters near Toulouse and ten other plants, produces the successful *Caravelle* medium-range jet aircraft, and is collaborating with the *British Aircraft Corporation* in the development of the *Concorde*. *Nord-Aviation* is largely engaged on the production of guided missiles.

Chemicals

Several factors have influenced the development of a flourishing chemical industry. The first is the availability of coal, leading to the manufacture of chemicals associated with the byproducts of the coke ovens: coal-tar, benzine, naphthaline and such derivatives as ammonium sulphate, sulphuric acid and aniline compounds. The plants are located mainly on the Nord coalfield at Béthune, Douai, Lens, Liévin and other mining towns.

The second factor is the availability of salt, mainly in Lorraine (p. 443). As a result, the *Solvay* firm has factories at Sarralbe and Dombasle (Plate LXI), and at Dole in the Jura using brine pumped from Poligny. The potash near Mulhouse is another valuable raw material, used mainly for fertilizers (p. 442).

The third factor is the availability of hydroelectricity, for the production of calcium carbide and cyanamide requires the con-centrated and controlled heat of an electric furnace. The largest unit in the French Alps is at Argentière in the Durance valley below Briançon, while other factories are strung out along the Alpine valleys. The electrochemical industry is also active in the Pyrenean foothills; factories to the south of Lourdes on the Gave de Pau make nitrogenous and phosphoric fertilizers, and several other plants produce explosives.

The fourth factor is the development of the petrochemical industry, providing raw materials for the manufacture of detergents and synthetic textiles. These plants, usually owned jointly by the petroleum firms and chemical concerns, and linked by a web of products pipelines, include such large-scale groups as *Shell–St Gobain, Esso–Standard* with *Kuhlman*, and *B.P.* with *Péchiney*. A synthetic rubber plant is in operation at Port-Jérôme on the lower Seine. Gas from the St Marcet and Lacq fields contains much hydrogen sulphide, and the recovery of sulphur as a byproduct makes France the second producing country in the world. In 1919 the government established a company, the *Office Nationale Industriel de l'Azote*, whose plant has expanded enormously on the banks of the Garonne in the southern outskirts of Toulouse. It manufactures nitrogenous compounds from atmospheric nitrogen, using hydrogen obtained from blast-furnace gas, from oil refineries, and more recently from the St Marcet natural gas. Ammonia, nitric acid, nitrochalk, ammonium sulphate and ammonium nitrate are produced.

Apart from these specific examples, branches of the chemical industry are widely distributed in cities where large markets exist, in ports where such raw materials as phosphate rock can be imported, and on the waterways. The largest single centre is Paris, with pharmaceutical chemicals and cosmetics. Several large factories at Lyons produce pharmaceutical and photographic chemicals, explosives, and dyes for the textile industry. The influence of Lyons has resulted in large chemical plants in the Rhône valley to the south, notably at St Fons and the *Rhône-Poulenc* factory at Péage-de-Roussillon. The plastics industry is well developed, one of the largest units being at Quillan (between Perpignan and Carcassonne), owned by a subsidiary of *British Formica*. Other plants on the Nord coalfield use coke-oven gas as their main raw material.

Textiles

The textile industry is widely disseminated as a result of its long domestic traditions, and in 1967 about 5,000 enterprises employed 436,000 workers. Fig. 93 summarizes the relative importance in 1967 of the six main groups of textiles, according to production; cotton is now over five times as important as wool, and both synthetic (nylon) and artificial (rayon) textiles are now of considerable importance.

Notwithstanding this wide distribution, four distinct concentrations may be recognized. The first is in the north in Flanders, focused on Lille. The Plain of Flanders has been a leading textile manufacturing area since the Middle Ages, with a concentration in early times on woollens, using wool from the neighbouring chalk hills; later this was imported from the Cotswolds. Now consuming wool from Australia and South Africa, the industry is centred in the Roubaix–Tourcoing conurbation and near Cambrai. Linen manufacture has also flourished for centuries along the Lys valley, where flax was grown and the river water is soft for retting; home-grown flax now supplies only a fifth of the requirements, the rest being imported from the

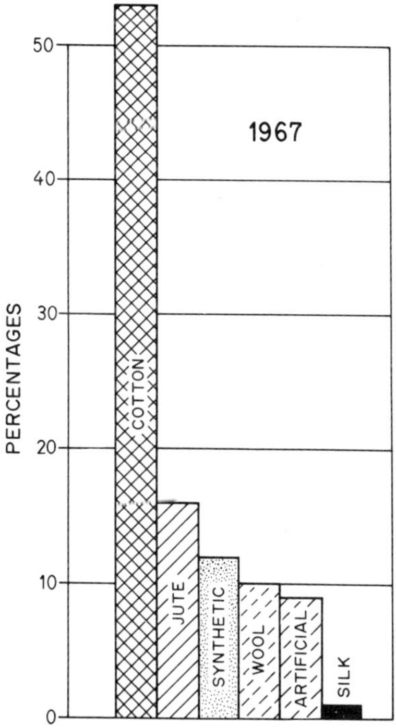

Fig. 93. French textile output, 1967 (After *Annuaire Statistique de la France,* 1968) The figures are expressed in percentages of the total amount of cloth produced.

Between 1962 and 1967, the percentage of cotton cloth has risen from 38 to 53, while the percentage of wool has fallen from 20 to 10.

U.S.S.R. and Poland. Fine linens still constitute an important product, mainly at Lille, with other factories in Amiens, Abbeville, Armentières, Hallines and Valenciennes. Cotton is important at Lille, Roubaix–Tourcoing, Armentières and La Bassée, and rayon, nylon and mixed fabrics are also produced. Associated industries are found in almost every town in Flanders, though especially in Lille and Roubaix–Tourcoing: carpets, hosiery, knitting wool, clothing, tapestries and furnishing fabrics.

The second textile centre is Rouen (Plate LXIII), where cotton has been pre-eminent since it was introduced into what had long been a textile district, making first woollens, then linen. Raw cotton, imported through Le Havre, is sent by rail to Rouen, and factories extend along both banks of the Seine and in the tributary valleys. A variety of other textile industries (rayon, nylon and clothing) has also developed there.

The textiles of Alsace originated in medieval times on a domestic scale with the advantages of local wool, pure soft water from the granitic uplands, fast-flowing streams for power, and long winters necessitating supplementary employment. Then in the eighteenth century small-scale calico and muslin manufacturing was established, and a little later the spinning of cotton was introduced as a cottage industry. As the nineteenth century brought the steam power of the Industrial Revolution, the Alsatian textile industry began to concentrate at Mulhouse and Colmar, though many small producers continued to function, supplying part-finished material or undertaking piece-work for the large centres. Most activity before 1871 was in Alsace, but after the new Franco–German boundary was drawn, many French workers migrated into the western valleys of the Vosges, with Epinal as the centre, and other factories were located down the Moselle–Meurthe valley as far as Nancy. Local specializations have survived in many places: Gérardmer produces fine linens, Soultz spins silk thread, and Barr is a hosiery centre. The chief cotton centres are still Epinal in the west, Mulhouse, Colmar and Belfort in the east. Although the emphasis is on cotton cloth, other products include sewing thread, printed calico, woollens, silk and rayon.

A fourth textile region is around Lyons, where silk making, which was introduced in the fifteenth century by Italian emigrés, developed as a domestic industry though organized by wealthy merchants, and the handloom weavers established themselves in workshops. Over a thousand silk-making enterprises are still active in Lyons and nearly 4,000 within the wider region, though large modern factories are responsible for an increasing proportion of the output. In 1968 France produced about 37,000 tons of silk cloth, 80 per cent in the Lyons area; half was exported, mostly to America, the rest going to the *haute-couture* firms of Lyons itself and especially of Paris. Rayon and nylon have developed rapidly, and of the twenty major factories in France ten are in the Lyons region, the largest at Decines to the east of the city.

These four regions are the main centres of textile production, but many smaller units are found in Normandy, Brittany, the Central Massif and the French Alps. Some retain their ancient specializations, such as the manufacture of lace at Calais, Le Puy and Alençon, velvet at Amiens, blankets at Orléans, flannel at Reims, hosiery and knitwear at Troyes, and ribbon at St Etienne. Finally, Paris is one of the world's largest centres of clothing manufacture, from ready-made to *haute-couture*.

Other Industries

It would be possible to give a lengthy catalogue of other industrial activities, many of which are small-scale but of quality and repute. Thus fine porcelain is made at Sèvres near Paris and at St Yrieix near Limoges; gloves at Grenoble and Millau; watches and clocks in the Jura, with the industry centred on Besançon. Some specializations are by contrast on an enormous scale, an example being rubber tyres at Clermont-Ferrand. Here little development took place until the invention of the pneumatic tyre and the growth of the cycle and automobile industry, but after 1890 progress was immense, associated with the name of *Michelin*, now the single largest company in France; the three factories, damaged by aerial bombardment in March 1944, have been rebuilt and re-equipped.

Many cities, especially the ports, are industrial centres. Marseilles has vegetable oil-refining, soap-making, the manufacture of fertilizers from North African phosphates, flour-milling, sugar-refining, ship-repairing and marine engineering, the manufacture of cement, furniture, glass, paper, cardboard, biscuits and foodstuffs generally, while around the Etang de Berre are three large oil refineries and several petrochemical works. An example of an inland industrial centre is Strasbourg, which has engineering works in its suburb of Graffenstaden, two recently built oil refineries, chemical works, rayon factories, and plants which manufacture a variety of electrical equipment. As a result of the city's position on the fertile Alsatian plain, it has developed food-processing activities: the canning of fruit and vegetables, the preserving of *pâté de foie gras*, tobacco-processing, chocolate-making, brewing and distilling. Tanning, paper making and printing have been carried on there for centuries.

COMMUNICATIONS

The relative importance of the different modes of transport, in respect of freight traffic, is shown by the tonnages conveyed in

1968; these totalled 1200 million tons by road (an estimated figure based on a traffic census), 229 million tons by rail, and 102 million tons by inland waterway.

Much damage was done to the transport systems during 1940–44, partly by the resistance movement, partly by strategic bombing, partly during military operations in the north, and partly through demolitions by the retreating German forces. Temporary repairs were effected rapidly, but it was several years before the bridges, locks and port installations were completely restored.

Route Patterns

The French networks of roads and railways are dense, and reflect the influence of two factors. The first is the centripetal effect of Paris; roads and railways focus on the capital with an unequalled emphasis. The second is the position of the lowlands relative to each other and the intervening uplands, with the river systems. The Paris and Aquitaine Basins are linked by the 'gate' of Poitou between Armorica and the Central Massif. Aquitaine communicates with the Midi by the Col de Naurouze at an altitude of 191 m (627 ft), forming the watershed between the Bay of Biscay and the Mediterranean; because it leads over from Aquitaine it is sometimes given the name of *la porte d'Aquitaine*, but as Carcassonne dominates the approach from the east it is also called the Gate of Carcassonne. The Saône–Rhône corridor, bounded by the edge of the Central Massif on the west and the Fore-Alps on the east, is the main avenue between northern France and the Mediterranean, and contains a remarkable concentration of routes; an *autoroute*, replacing *Route National 7*, carries an immense traffic to the east of the Rhône from Lyons to Avignon, and other roads and railways follow the river, though in places with considerable difficulty. The Rhône is an inadequate and little-used waterway. From the northern end of the corridor the Rhineland can be reached through the gap of Belfort between the Vosges and the Jura; Belfort, at a height of 350 m (1150 ft), has always possessed strategic significance, and has been a fortress town since the thirteenth century. Through this gap goes the Rhône–Rhine Canal, now being enlarged to take vessels of 1350 tons. Between the Saône–Rhône corridor and the Paris Basin lies the Plateau de Langres, the watershed of central France, which lies at an altitude of 450–600 m (1500–2000 ft), crossed by several roads and railways, including lines from Paris to Marseilles and to Basle. Even two canals cross this divide; the Burgundy Canal links the Yonne with the Seine via Dijon, though it requires 189 locks, and the Marne–Saône Canal passes to the east of Langres in a tunnel.

Frontier Routes

With the exception of Flanders, the land boundaries of France cross uplands which present problems for routeways. In the northeast is the Ardennes, though penetrated by the canalized Meuse. The crest-line of the Vosges, the German–French boundary between 1871 and 1918 and again between 1940 and 1944, is crossed by several road passes, notably the Col de la Schlucht (1139 m, 3737 ft), and by two railways. But the chief routes are via the Saverne Gap to the northwest of Strasbourg, which is followed by the Paris–Strasbourg railway line, the Marne–Rhine Canal which climbs up from Strasbourg by fifty-two locks, and the Strasbourg–Nancy main road.

The arc of the Jura between France and Switzerland does not attain any great altitude, yet its succession of parallel ridges and valleys make it a distinct obstacle. Several transcontinental lines which run south-eastward from Basle, Belfort and Dijon were difficult to build, but they carry a heavy international tourist traffic to Switzerland and Italy. The passes, which include the Col de la Faucille at 1320 m (4331 ft) between St Claude and Geneva, may be intermittently blocked by snow in the winter, usually on the eastern side, but rarely for any length of time.

The curve of the western Alps from Lake Geneva to the Mediterranean forms the Franco–Italian border zone, 290 km (180 miles) in length. Though the trend lines run broadly from north to south, transverse valleys on both the French and Italian sides have facilitated the construction of routes, and the region has been opened up both for tourists and industry. There are several international passes 1800–2100 m (6000–7000 ft) high: the Petit-St Bernard between Bourg-St Maurice and Aosta, the Mont Cenis between Lanslebourg and Susa, the Mont Genèvre between Briançon and Cesana Torinese, and the Col de Larche between Barcelonnette and Cuneo. The road tunnel under Mont Blanc between Chamonix and Courmayeur was completed in 1964; 12 km (7·5 miles) long, it is the longest road tunnel in the world, entering on the French side at 1204 m (3950 ft) and leaving on the Italian side at about 1370 m (4500 ft). Large numbers of cars and an extensive service of autocars penetrate far into the upper valleys. The famous Route des Alpes has been developed from Lake Geneva to Nice, crossing from valley to valley over the cols; the highest is the Col de l'Iséran at 2769 m (9085 ft), open only from early July to mid-October, which links the upper Isère valley with that of the Arc.

Only two trans-Alpine railways link France and Italy. The more northerly utilizes the Mont Cenis (or Fréjus) tunnel, 13·7 km (8·5 miles) long, constructed during 1857–70, the first of the trans-Alpine tunnels. The other runs north-eastward from Nice and crosses the Col de Tende into Italy before descending to Cuneo, hence to Turin.

The Pyrenees form a barrier more than 400 km (250 miles) in length between the Bay of Biscay and the Mediterranean. Though in altitude they do not compare with the Alps, they are more continuous, rising abruptly from the Basin of Aquitaine to a uniform crest line; for a distance of 160 km (100 miles) the lowest pass is over 1800 m (6000 ft). Many valleys penetrate the mountains, but almost all end in high-walled *culs-de-sac*. Roads lead up to the boundary ridge, and five cross into Spain; the highest, the Envalira (2407 m, 7897 ft), links Ax-les-Thermes with Lerida via the little state of Andorra, and is blocked until June. The easiest routes into Spain are by way of the narrow coastal plain on the west from Bayonne to San Sebastian or Pamplona, by the low Col de la Perche, and in the east from Perpignan over the Col du Perthus. The Pyrenean railway systems are limited, although the Hendaye and Cerbère lines around the western and eastern flanks were opened as early as 1864 and 1878 respectively. The Col de la Perche was traversed by a narrow-gauge line to the Spanish frontier in 1911, but a crossing of the boundary-ridge was not effected until 1928, when the line over the Col de Somport was opened. In the following year another line was completed from Ax-les-Thermes up the Ariège valley to the Col de Puymorens, under which the line passes in a tunnel nearly 6 km (3·5 miles) long. These two lines are little used, except for tourist traffic within France, for the change of gauge at the Spanish frontier precludes any through traffic.

Roads

The road network is one of the densest in the world, second only to Britain in relation to area, yet it is even less adequate than that of Britain to meet the needs of modern traffic.

The foundations of the road system were laid by the Romans; the modern network follows many of these lines. The pattern of the present system was established by Napoleon I, who created the *routes nationales* focusing on Paris and linking the main provincial cities, and the *routes départementales*, which were built by local authorities in response to local needs. The system of *routes nationales* now totals 80 000 km (50,000 miles), with a remarkably even density. The departmental and local roads total another 480 000 km (300,000 miles), though a large proportion is of dubious quality; this local network reflects closely the relief, the density of population and the degree of economic development.

The government has inaugurated a motorway (*autoroute*) programme, and is widening existing highways and improving surfaces, especially removing *pavé*. By the end of 1968 about 1100 km (680 miles) of motorway had been completed, notably the north-south route from Rouen to Marseilles via Paris and Dijon; the Lille–Paris motorway; some sections near Nancy, Strasbourg and Grenoble; and part of the coast road from Fréjus via Cannes and Nice to the Italian frontier. The largest individual road scheme so far has been the Mont Blanc tunnel (p. 455).

Railways

The centripetal effect of Paris on the pattern of French railways is even more striking than on that of the roads, mainly because during the great period of trunk-line construction between 1842 and 1859 nine main lines were authorized, seven of which radiated from Paris to Strasbourg, Marseilles, Toulouse, Bayonne, Nantes, Le Havre and Lille; the other two cross-country lines linked Bordeaux with Marseilles and Dijon with Mulhouse. The country was thus divided into sectors, each with an apex and terminal station in Paris, and each operated by a major company: *Nord, Est, Paris–Orléans* (*P.O.*), *Midi* (the last two were merged in 1933), *Ouest*, and *Paris–Lyons–Méditerranée* (*P.L.M.*). Later, a state-owned system (the *Etat* line) was created in the west and south-west, and in 1923 the *Alsace–Lorraine* line became state-operated. During the interwar years the financial position of these companies deteriorated so rapidly that in 1938 they were merged to form the *Société Nationale des Chemins de Fer français* (*S.N.C.F.*), in which the State holds 51 per cent of the capital. The system is operated in five regions, corresponding to sectors of the previous companies.

The *Nord* region serves the northern coalfield, the Lille district, and the Channel ports of Dunkirk, Calais and Boulogne. The *Est* region serves the eastern Paris Basin, Lorraine and Alsace. The

Ouest region covers Normandy, Brittany, and the west coast as far as Bordeaux. The *Sud-Ouest* serves Orléans, Limoges, Toulouse, Bayonne, and the Mediterranean coast as far east as Sète. The *P.L.M.* provides direct routes to the Midi, and to Switzerland and Italy, with Dijon as the junction from which routes fan out. The passenger from the Channel coast must pass through Paris, unless he uses one of the two important routes parallel to the north-eastern border: Calais–Lille–Metz–Strasbourg–Basle, or Calais–Lille–Reims–Dijon.

By 1938 the total route length was about 42 000 km (26,000 miles), but since the War some uneconomic lines have been closed, and the length in 1968 was about 37 400 km (23,000 miles). Apart from the initial work of postwar reconstruction, a progressive programme of modernization has been instigated. The *S.N.C.F.* receives considerable state subsidies and road competition is more restricted than in Britain, while the longer distances favour economic freight transport by rail. Long-distance passenger transport maintains high standards of comfort, speed and punctuality; the luxurious 'Mistral', now electrified, makes the journey from Paris to Nice (1088 km, 676 miles) at an average speed of 120 km (74 miles) per hour, while the 'Sud' express averages the same speed for the journey from Paris to Bordeaux. The *S.N.C.F.* operates several sections of international express routes, including 'Cisalpin' (Paris–Milan), 'L'Arbalète' (Paris–Zürich), 'Oiseau Bleu' (Paris–Brussels), the 'Simplon-Orient' (Paris–Milan), the 'Blue Train' (London–Paris–Nice–San Remo), and the two London–Paris through-trains, the 'Golden Arrow' and the 'Night Ferry'.

One of the main features of modernization has been electrification. Before 1938 about 3200 km (2000 miles) had been converted from steam, including the section of the Mont Cenis line from Culoz to Modane, and the Paris–Le Mans and the Paris–Bordeaux–Hendaye lines. Since the War this programme has been accelerated; the route length electrified by 1968 (Fig. 94) totalled 8813 km (5476 miles), and about 80 per cent of all traffic, passenger and freight, is handled by electrified lines. Great progress has also been made in the replacement of steam locomotives by diesels.

Inland Waterways

In 1968 there were 7550 km (4690 miles) of waterway in France, but these figures are misleading, for although minimum dimensions for waterways were laid down by the Freycinet Act in 1877, these are sufficient only to take the small Flemish barge (*péniche*) of 300 tons

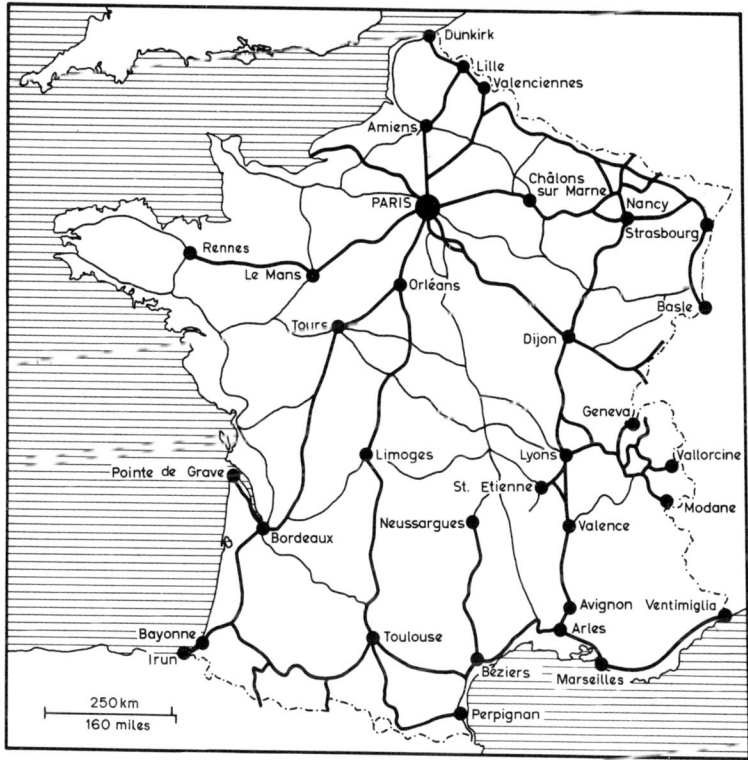

Fig. 94. The mainline railway system of France
(After *Annuaire Statistique de la France*, 1968)
The heavier lines indicate electrified tracks.

capacity. At least a third of the waterways do not attain even this and are commercially unimportant.

Several long rivers radiate from the heart of the country, but most are of relatively little use for navigation. The Loire and the Garonne suffer from irregular régimes, steep gradients and fluctuating channels. From Lyons to the sea the Rhône passes alternately through deeply trenched gorges and enclosed basins where deposition of gravel and alluvium blocks the channel, thus braiding the stream; its Alpine tributaries, Isère, Durance and Drôme, make the position worse by their contributions of flood-water and rock-waste. The creation of a navigable waterway between Lyons and Marseilles depends on the construction of a series of lateral loops, with barrages and ship-lifts, which is being carried out by the *Compagnie Nationale du Rhône* as part of a great multi-purpose scheme (p. 434). One important section of the future Marseilles–Lyons water route is the 31 km (19 miles) Marseilles–Rhône Canal, which penetrates the hills north of the port by means of the Rove Tunnel, completed in 1927.

The section of the Rhine in Alsace is also handicapped by a steep gradient and a swift current, variable depths, and the deposition of silt from its Alpine headstreams. Yet because of its situation the river has been used for centuries and much effort has been expended in regularization. The result is that a minimum depth of about 2·4 m (8 ft) can usually be maintained as far upstream as Strasbourg–Kehl. Between Kehl and Basle the river is negotiable by barges of 1,000 to 1,500 tons towed by powerful tugs.

Since Alsace returned to France after the War of 1914–18, that country has been concerned with a left-bank lateral canal, with the dual function of overcoming the navigational difficulties of the Rhine and of utilizing its hydroelectricity potential (pp. 434–5). The first stage was designed to overcome a serious obstacle on the river near Kembs below Basle, the Istein Bar of Jurassic limestone, by means of a barrage across the Rhine and a bypass loop of 6·4 km (4 miles), rejoining the Rhine below the Istein rapids. Since 1950 *Electricité de France* has completed three further loops, each with its power station. The whole position was, however, radically altered in June 1956, when a general agreement was reached between West Germany and France. The latter agreed not to proceed with this canal beyond the northern end of the fourth loop, beyond which the river itself is being improved by four stabilizing barrages. This improvement of the Rhône and the Rhine, together with the enlargement and modernization of the old Rhône–Rhine Canal through the Gap of Belfort, is part of the 'Grand Canal du Rhône au Rhin', to be completed in 1975, which will form a water-link between the Mediterranean and North Seas. The modern Port de Bourgogne, south-east of Belfort, is approaching completion.

The upper Moselle is of little value, though it is followed by the Canal de l'Est as far as Epinal, and from Metz to Thionville sections of its course are utilized by a lateral canal. Now that the river has been regularized from Thionville to Koblenz (p. 176), affording a direct link between Lorraine and the Ruhr, it has become a very important waterway; in 1968 it conveyed 2 million tons of coal and coke upstream and 1·5 million tons of steel downstream.

By far the most useful system of waterways is in the north-east, where a pattern focused on the lower Seine links Paris with the northern and eastern industrial districts and with southern Belgium. Much regularization has been necessary, and the depth of water is controlled by weirs. The Marne, Oise and Aisne are paralleled along their upper courses by lateral canals; this was easier and cheaper than extensive regularization of the rivers. The Seine has been much improved for navigation; between Marcilly and Paris many locks and barrages are required, and cuts have been made through tortuous sections. Below Paris the Seine provides a waterway in which a depth of 3 m (10 ft) is maintained by weirs, built during the interwar period both to check flooding and to assist navigation. The river carries the greatest volume of traffic of any French waterway, since not only is it joined by several major tributaries, but it forms an important line of communication between Paris and the ports of Rouen and Le Havre. The various sections carried between 8 and 12 million tons of freight in 1968, about a quarter consisting of coal. In 1968 the wharves within the municipality of Paris handled 3·7 million tons, and ranked third to Strasbourg and Rouen, though if all the ports within the Paris conurbation are included it was easily first with about 23 million tons.

Link canals connect the Oise and the Aisne, and the Aisne and the Marne; others join the Seine system to the Flanders waterways to the north (the St Quentin Canal), the Sambre–Meuse system in the east (the Sambre–Oise and Ardennes Canals), the Rhine to the south-east (the Marne–Rhine Canal), the Saône to the south (the Marne–Saône and Burgundy Canals), and the Loire to the south-west (the Nivernais, Loing and Orléans Canals). These links have not been easy to construct because of the concentric cuestas; the Sambre–Oise Canal, for example, needs thirty-eight locks in its 66 km (41 miles) across the chalk divide. In recent years several new canals have been constructed: the Canal du Nord (a direct link between the Somme and the Oise), a canal from Dunkirk to Valenciennes, and another from Dunkirk to Denain; all take 1350 ton barges.

The French waterways in 1968 handled 102 million tons of freight, of which minerals, cement and bricks accounted for 45 million, oil and petrol for 18 million, and coal and coke for nearly 10 million.

Air Transport

In 1933 *Air France* was created by merging four independent air transport companies, and has developed into the largest airline in continental Europe, flying worldwide services; in 1968 it conveyed 4·59 million passengers, compared with 2·5 million in 1958. Five other companies are concerned with freight transport and internal services. Paris has become one of the great air-terminals of the world; its two airports at Orly and Le Bourget accommodated 4·9 million passengers in 1967, and a third is under construction. Marseilles and Nice were also used by international airlines, handling just under a million passengers each.

Ports and Mercantile Marine

France is well endowed with natural harbours, adjacent to the busiest shipping routes in the world. Its length of coastline and outlook on several seas, however, have precluded concentration on a single port which might thereby attain world rank, as in the case of Rotterdam or Antwerp, and has resulted in the development of a number of ports of lesser status, each with its own hinterland and with its activities confined to 'national traffic'. Rotterdam handles a greater volume of freight than all the French ports combined, and Antwerp exports more French steel than any French port. In 1964 the government announced a plan for subsidizing the main ports (p. 464) by paying 80 per cent of the cost of new installations, instead of 50 per cent as previously.

Ports such as Rouen, Nantes and Bordeaux are situated up the estuaries of the major rivers at a distance from the sea. The difficulties of maintaining a channel have led to the development of outports in the case of the last two, and large vessels dock at Le Havre at the mouth of the Seine estuary. The port of Dunkirk, whose traffic has increased 60 per cent since the steel works opened in 1962, and the ferry ports of Calais, Boulogne and Dieppe lie on a gently shelving coastline, with offshore banks necessitating much dredging, the construction of long approach jetties, turning basins and docks.

Cherbourg stands on the northern shores of the Cotentin peninsula; for a natural harbour its site is poor, but its advantage lies in a mid-Channel position. It was a minor naval port for centuries, though its value was limited because of its exposed situation. In the period after 1920, the decision to make Cherbourg a transatlantic terminal and port of call was implemented by the construction of two inner moles, with liner berths providing depths of 12 m (40 ft). The port was seriously damaged in the later stages of the last War, but as it was needed as a supply port for the Allied forces, temporary facilities were rapidly installed. After its return to the French authorities, schemes of restoration and improvement were steadily pushed ahead, a new railway terminal was built, and the ocean basin was reconstructed. It is also the terminus of a car ferry with Southampton, opened in 1964.

The chief Mediterranean port, Marseilles, has a poor natural harbour, considerable physical obstacles separate it from the Rhône valley, and development inland has been cramped by the hills. The coast does, however, form a right-angle sheltered from the north and east, with deep water offshore, no tidal range, and an absence of silting unlike the Rhône delta and the Languedoc coast to the west. The modern port lies behind a breakwater parallel to the coast, along which basins and quays have been constructed. Much development has taken place at Lavéra and in the Etang de Berre to the north-west, particularly in the provision of tanker terminals. A terminal taking 200,000-ton tankers on the shores of the Golfe de Fos was opened in 1967.

The two best natural harbours are the naval ports of Brest and Toulon. The former is situated on the northern side of the Rade de Brest, a large sheet of water reached from the open sea through an easily defensible channel. In places least depths exceed 18 m (60 ft), and most of the port is accessible at the lowest tides to vessels drawing 10 m (32 ft); the only locks required are for entry to the dry dock. During the War of 1939–45 the port was used by the Germans as a submarine base, and the installations were heavily damaged from the air. At the liberation it was hardly usable, for nearly 2,000 vessels were sunk in and around the waters, but by 1949 the naval port was once again functioning and it has an important rôle as a N.A.T.O. port. Toulon has been a Mediterranean base for many centuries; both outer and inner roadsteads are protected from strong gales, while the hilly peninsulas provided sites for shore batteries. It has experienced critical phases of naval history, and has been blockaded on many occasions; its most tragic hour was when the French fleet was scuttled there in November 1942. Both port and town were damaged during the War, but much reconstruction has taken place.

The Channel ferry ports are by far the most important group for passenger traffic, handling annually about 3·7 million passengers each way. On the Mediterranean coast about 230,000 people pass to and from Corsica through Marseilles and Nice, while Marseilles and Port-Vendres handle traffic with North Africa.

Le Havre and Cherbourg are pre-eminent as North Atlantic terminals, though with rather different rôles. The latter is used only by foreign liners, while Le Havre is the port for French liners. Cherbourg has a car-ferry service with Southampton and Dunkirk has developed as an important container terminal.

It is difficult to evaluate the importance of ports by freight because of the contribution of petroleum, both crude oil arriving in ocean tankers and refined oil shipped away in coastal tankers. Five ports are pre-eminent in total freight tonnage:

		(*1967*)		
	Imports		*Exports*	
		million tons		
		of which		*of which*
	Total	*crude oil*	*Total*	*refined oil*
Marseilles	53·61	47·65	7·63	4·78
Le Havre	32·39	27·63	3·80	3·21
Nantes–St Nazaire	8·81	6·05	2·37	2·04
Dunkirk	12·93	5·16	3·59	0·81
Rouen	5·89	0·74	5·34	3·11
Bordeaux	4·93	2·62	2·40	1·31

Before 1939 the French mercantile marine totalled about 2·9 million gross tonnage and was eighth in the world, but during the War about two-thirds was destroyed. In the long view this has proved to be an advantage, for a steady policy of rebuilding has been pursued and by 1968 the tonnage had reached 5·5 million, of which two-thirds was less than fifteen years old. The mercantile marine is now tenth in the world in tonnage. French ships are largely employed in transporting freight to and from home ports, and play little part in the world carrying trade.

COMMERCE

The main categories of imports comprise such raw materials as non-ferrous ores and metals, raw textiles, timber and pulp, oilseeds, leather and rubber, and fuel (including oil, coal and coke). Unlike Britain, France's imports of food are not large, in fact in 1967 the value of cereal exports was greater than that of imports.

The chief exports are iron ore (nearly 17 million tons in 1968), phosphates, chemicals, raw steel, manufactured goods including automobiles, machinery and textiles, and foodstuffs such as wine, wheat, vegetables, fruit and cheese.

The importance of membership of the European Economic Community is shown by the fact that in 1968 two-fifths of France's foreign trade by value was with the other members, West Germany being by far the most important, followed by Belgo-Luxembourg and Italy. Other trading partners are the U.S.A. and, much lower down

Plate LVIII. Agricultural landscape near St Maure between Tours and Poitiers

Plate LIX. An iron ore adit mine, Lorraine

Plate LX. The Sidelor *steel works at Rombas, Lorraine*

Plate LXI. The Solvay *chemical plant at Dombasle, France, with the Marne-Rhine Canal in the foreground*

the list than in pre-1939 days, Great Britain. Trade with the 'franc zone' (p. 398) has grown steadily, now accounting for about an eighth of the total, and though exports to the zone are rather higher than imports, the unbalance in recent years is much less than formerly.

POPULATION AND SETTLEMENT

In 1801 France had a population of 27·3 million, with a density of about 51 per sq. km (132 per sq. mile); both figures were the highest in Europe; at that time, for example, Great Britain had only about 11 million. The population continued to grow steadily, reaching 36 million by 1850, though thereafter the rate of increase slowed down; between 1850 and 1938 the total grew by less than 6 million, while in the same time Germany's population increased by 30 million. The slow French growth was partly due to the 1914–18 War losses of about 1·8 million men, particularly among the young and lower middle-aged groups, directly reflected in an estimated 2·4 million fewer births. Between the Wars the birth rate remained one of the lowest in Europe, partly reflecting a desire to limit the fragmentation of land in rural areas (p. 413), partly because of a lowness of national morale and an unwillingness to produce children to face a dubious future; in five of the interwar years deaths exceeded births. But for the immigration of about 1·2 million foreigners, caused mainly by the shortage of labour in agriculture and in many branches of industry, the population would not have increased even by the little it did to about 42 million in 1938; during these years, in proportion to its population, France was the leading country in the world for immigration, with 515 immigrants for every 100,000 inhabitants, as compared with 492 in the U.S.A. During the years 1939–46 the population actually decreased by about 1·5 million, the results of 750,000 war dead and an inevitably low birth rate; the 1938 total was not regained until 1951.

After 1946, stimulated by state assistance under the new social security schemes and family allowances and by tax reliefs, the birth rate increased rapidly; between 1946 and 1950 it was 21 per 1,000, and since 1950 it has stabilized at about 18 per 1,000. The population total at the census of 1962 was 46·5 million, and this has risen to 50·1 millions in 1969. Thus the population has grown more rapidly, by over 10 millions in nineteen years, than at any time in the last hundred years.

But this growth has been exceedingly uneven in different parts of the country; about 45 per cent of the increase has been absorbed

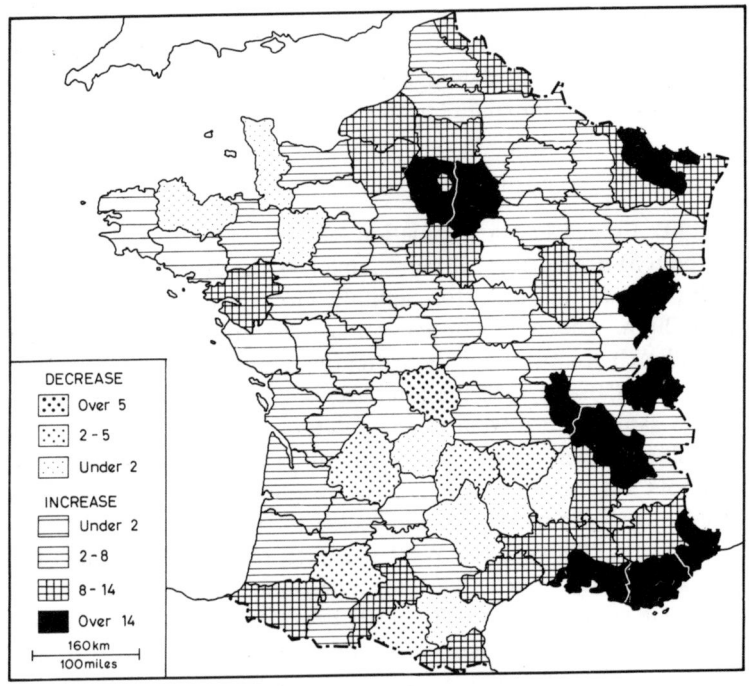

Fig. 95. Changes in the population of France, 1954–62, by departments
(After *Annuaire Statistique de la France*, 1964)
The figures represent percentage changes in individual departments.

by Greater Paris. Fig. 95 summarizes the changes between the cen-
suses of 1954 and 1962 by departments; fifteen showed a net loss,
mostly in the Central Massif and Brittany, a result of a movement
to a more attractive existence and better wages in Paris, the industrial
north and north-east, and other large towns. The total has been
increased by a considerable influx of repatriates from Algeria,
about 650,000 in 1962, and by foreign immigration, though the
overall number of foreigners permanently resident in France is
only about half the figure for the mid-twenties, partly because a
considerable number have become naturalized.

Distribution of Population

The density of population for the country as a whole was 91 per sq.
km (235 per sq. mile) in 1968, appreciably lower than in neighbouring
countries (except Spain), only a quarter that of the Netherlands,
and half that of West Germany. The density on the basis of de-

partments is shown for 1962 on Fig. 96. Several relatively thinly
populated areas stand out, with averages of less than 40 per sq. km
(100 per sq. mile). The Alpine departments of Hautes- and Basses-
Alpes have the lowest figures, though the higher density for the adjacent
Savoie and Haute-Savoie reflect the progress of industrialization in the
valleys. Much of the Central Massif, with its bleak uplands and poor
soils, has low and in places still declining figures, emphasized by
the steady exodus of young people to the towns, with a resultant
falling birth rate. The forested Landes and the high Pyrenees are
other obvious regions of low density, as are the limestone *côtes*
in Meuse and Haute-Marne, and the chalklands of Champagne.
Though the interior plateaus of Brittany are thinly inhabited, a
coastal belt of much denser population raises the average.

A few departments stand out with densities of over 190 per sq. km
(500 per sq. mile), and three, in addition to those wholly occupied
by Paris, have over 380 (1,000). These contain large industrial

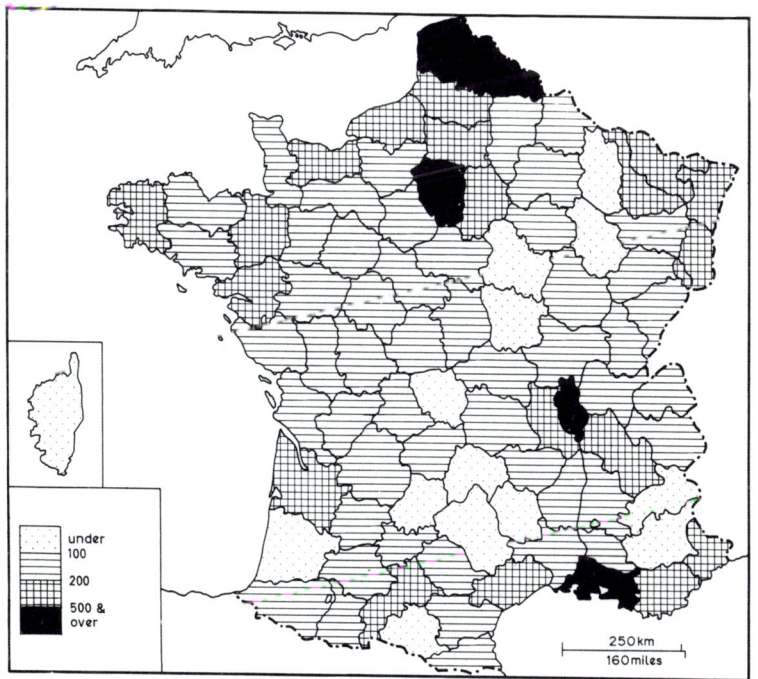

*Fig. 96. Density of population of France, 1962, by departments
(After* Annuaire Statistique de la France, *1964)*

agglomerations, notably Nord and Pas-de-Calais (the northern coal-field), Rhône (the Lyons industrial region), Bouches-du-Rhône (Marseilles and its hinterland), and the departments forming Greater Paris (p. 398). A more detailed map would show numerous smaller concentrations, as in Lorraine, Alsace, around most ports and regional centres such as Toulouse, Nantes and Bordeaux, and along the Riviera coast, where Nice is now the fifth city of France.

The rest of France has an average population of between 40 and 80 per sq. km (100 and 200 per sq. mile), much of it rural, with con-centrations around the regional centres. Only three regions have rural populations of any density: coastal Brittany, the wine-growing district of Hérault, and the plain of Alsace, though smaller, more discontinuous areas are found along the valleys of the Rhône, Garonne and Loire.

Rural Settlement

In the north and east most people live in small nucleated villages, partly because of the need for concentrating houses around a deep well in the chalk and limestone country, where surface water is limited, partly because of the legacy of open-field agriculture (p. 416). In many parts, especially in the Ardennes, the Vosges and Normandy, this nucleation resulted from the establishment of settlements in clearings within the woodland, akin to the *Waldhufendörfer* of Germany (p. 185). In modern times, especially in Flanders and Lorraine, small compact *cités-ouvrières* have been built to house the workers from a nearby colliery or large factory. In southern France compact villages were perched on defensible hills, while medieval settlements (*bastides*), commonly with a rectangular plan, were founded in Aquitaine.

By contrast, in the west and centre of France settlement is relatively dispersed or even thinly scattered, especially in Brittany, Normandy and the Central Massif; for example, in the Breton *bocage* a peasant has his farmhouse within his own fields. One reason for dispersal is the plentiful supply of water on the impermeable rocks, another is that the uplands offered less scope for agriculture and the farms were necessarily widely scattered among the extensive pasture lands.

Towns and Cities

A distinction is made in the French Census between the urban population, which in 1962 totalled 29·4 million, and the rural, with 17·1 million. On this basis the urban population comprises

64 per cent of the total, a distinct increase on the 52 per cent of pre-1939 years. It must be remembered, however, that a commune is classed as urban with a grouped population exceeding only 2,000, and many little market towns and even large villages are included. Two population figures are quoted for most French towns, the town proper (the *ville*) and what is termed the *agglomération*, including contiguous satellite towns. The Ville de Paris had 2·6 millions in 1968, but included within the official agglomeration are 23 satellite communes, making the total for Greater Paris about 8·2 millions, clearly a figure more indicative of the urban area.

On the basis of agglomeration totals (which are used in this Chapter as indicative of the urban position, fifteen towns in 1968 had populations exceeding 250,000, a further thirty-four exceeding 100,000. There is an enormous gap between Paris and the next largest cities, Lyons (1·07 million) and Marseilles (964,000); the growth of the capital at the expense of the rest of the country, especially since 1950, has compelled the government to attempt measures to check this tendency. The basis of the French plan is to create eight 'urban complexes' by expanding existing cities, or pairs of nearby towns; these are Lille–Roubaix, Nancy–Thionville, Strasbourg, Lyons–St Etienne, Marseilles–Aix, Toulouse, Bordeaux, and Nantes–St Nazaire. A new plan for Paris in 1965 proposed the creation of eight cities along the valley of the Seine, both above and below the capital.

Of the forty-nine agglomerations exceeding 100,000, all are manufacturing centres, eight are ports, two are resorts (Nice and Cannes), and two are naval bases (Brest and Toulon). Most are provincial cities, administrative, business, shipping and servicing centres for a considerable district, often the seat of a bishopric or a university, and well fitted to act as a regional capital. Such are Mulhouse, Limoges, Montpellier, Orléans, Angers, Rennes, Tours, Le Mans and Grenoble, while many more towns of between 50,000 and 100,000 fall into the same category. These towns are spread over France with remarkable evenness, except for the cluster in the Paris region.

REGIONS

The distinctive geographical regions (Fig. 78) comprise four upland massifs, together with the island of Corsica (two-thirds of which consists of a Hercynian crystalline block), three systems of fold mountains, and seven basins, valleys and coastal plains.

1. *The Paris Basin*

The greater part of northern France is underlain by a shallow syncline filled with Mesozoic and Tertiary limestone, chalk, sandstone and clay. These deposits were folded into a gentle basin by the Alpine earth movements, so that the rocks dip inwards from the margins (Fig. 80). These movements also caused flexures which have produced significant results in the landscape, and several distinct anticlines can be traced in Artois, forming a prominent line of hills bordering the Plain of Flanders, and in Boulonnais and Bray; the last two have been breached and 'unroofed', so that Jurassic clays and limestones are exposed, surrounded by infacing chalk escarpments. Over much of the area lies a thin patchy covering of clay-with-flints, gravels on the river terraces, alluvium on the floodplains, and limon.

The Basin is drained mainly by the Seine system, although in the north-east the Somme and in the south-west the middle Loire are included. Most of the Seine's upper tributaries, including the Aube and the Yonne, rise on limestone plateaus in the south, and the main river is joined in the neighbourhood of Paris by two right-bank tributaries, the Marne and the Oise.

In the centre a low plateau of Tertiary limestone, the Ile de France, is bounded by a prominent edge; it comprises numerous distinctive pays, including Beauce, which is thickly limon covered, to the south-west of Paris, and Brie to the south-east. Beyond this lies a surrounding area of chalk, broad in the north behind the English Channel, where it forms the undulating plateaus of Artois and Picardy, from 150 to 210 m (500 to 700 ft) above sea level. Farther south the chalklands are known as *Champagne pouilleuse*, a rather dry country because of the permeable nature of the chalk. Beyond that is an outcrop of Gault Clay, once an area of marsh, shallow lakes and damp soils, hence its name of *Champagne humide*. Though much reclamation has been effected, many small lakes remain, and the soils carry permanent pasture. In the east Jurassic limestones form the cuestas of Lorraine, in the south the plateau of Langres, and in the west the low plateaus of lower Normandy.

The rolling expanses of loamy soils grow wheat and sugar beet; here are France's largest farms and most productive food-growing areas. Where the chalk and limestone have no limon cover, the thin soils grow pasture grazed by sheep, which are also folded on fodder crops and stubble. Prosperous dairy farms on the well watered claylands supply milk to Paris and other towns, and for making such well-known cheese as Brie. Along the valley floors are carefully cultivated market gardens, orchards are widespread, and on the outer south-east facing slopes of the Ile de France escarpment are the champagne vineyards. The valley of the Loire below Orléans is so well cultivated that it is known as 'the garden of France'. Parts are still wooded, including oak and beech woods on the claylands, and conifers on the sandy ridges of the Argonne.

The Paris Basin has been closely settled for many centuries, though the population is unevenly distributed. Over the limestone and chalk country, people live in villages or large farms, and the towns are situated in gaps through the ridges or at points where roads cross the rivers. Most are market and servicing towns, with industries including the processing of agricultural products, such as milling and sugar-refining, and the manufacture of textiles originally based on wool from local sheep, paper, glass and pottery. Large towns include Amiens (137,000) on the Somme, the centre for Picardy and Artois; Reims (168,000) in the east, the centre of the champagne industry, Troyes (114,000) on the upper Seine; Orléans (168,000) on the bend of the Loire; and Caen (152,000) in the west, with nearby iron and steel industries based on local ores.

Along the coast are the ferry ports for the cross-Channel services: Boulogne to Dover and Dieppe to Newhaven. Boulogne is the main French fishing-port (Plate LXII), the liner port of Le Havre (247,000) is situated on the northern shore of the Seine estuary, and Rouen (370,000) is 130 km (80 miles) from the sea (Plate LXIII).

Paris (Fig. 97) has grown from a Gaulish settlement on the Ile de la Cité below the Seine–Marne confluence to be the leading city of continental Europe. The population of the ville is about 2·6 million, but if the surrounding communes in the agglomeration are included, the total is more than three times as great. Many factors account for its size and importance. It is the seat of the highly centralized government of France, and the centre of both the road system and the rail network. The quays along the Seine handle about 23 million tons of freight a year from the northern coalfield, the agricultural lands around, and Rouen. Paris has a variety of manufactures, not merely the world-renowned *haute couture* and *articles de luxe*, but everything from cars to musical instruments, paper and linoleum. Paris is a world city, a centre of commerce and finance, of life and thought (Plate LXIV).

2. *Flanders*

Between the chalk hills of Artois and the Belgian frontier lies French Flanders, an area of lowland crossed by the upper waters of the Lys, Dendre and Escaut (Scheldt). Its relief includes drained marshland near the coast, alluvium-covered valley floors, sheets of Eocene clay forming undulating plateaus, and some low hills capped by Pliocene sandstone. During the trench warfare of 1914–18, French Flanders was devastated, towns were terribly damaged, and many villages obliterated.

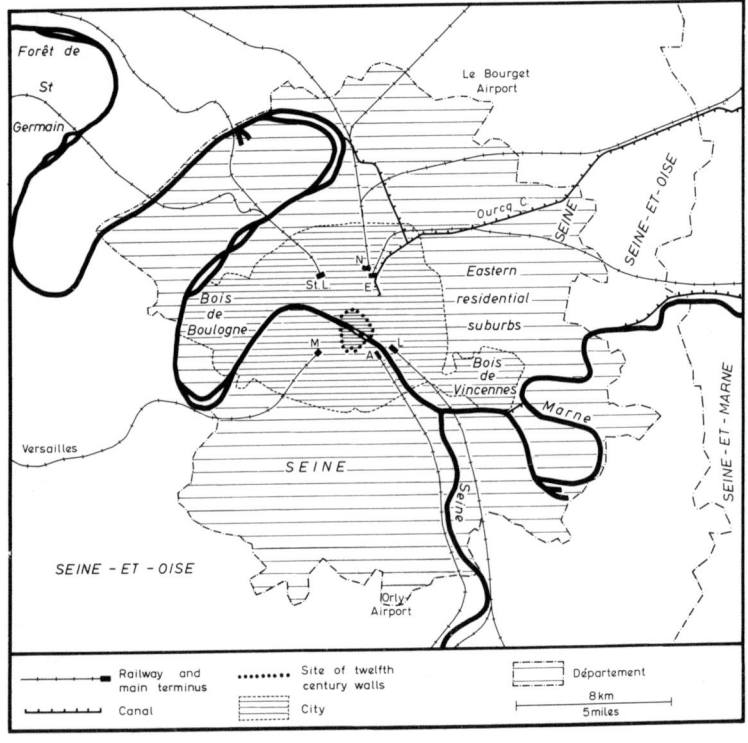

Fig. 97. Paris
(After *Environs de Paris, Carte Michelin au 100,000ᵉ*)
Note. New *départements* have been created around Greater Paris (p. 398).

Here agriculture and industry come into close contact. Large fields of wheat and sugar beet occupy most of the land, and flax, hops, potatoes, chicory and vegetables are grown. Agriculture is carried on intensively, much of it on a horticultural scale, for holdings are small and high yields are general. Dairy farming is intensively practised to supply the densely populated industrial districts, most holdings having a herd of two or three animals.

Underlying the newer rocks in the departments of Nord and Pas-de-Calais is the northern coalfield (Fig. 85), which produces half the country's output. In the west the main mining towns are Béthune and Lens, farther east are Douai and Valenciennes. Much coal is consumed on the coalfield at coke ovens and power stations, and is used for steam-raising in the factories, but some is sent, usually by waterway, to Paris and elsewhere. A large chemical industry produces coal-tar, ammonia, fertilizers, dyes and acids. The three main groups of industrial activity comprise the production of steel, engineering, and the manufacture of textiles. Ore and pig-iron come by rail from Lorraine and by sea through Dunkirk, and over 3 million tons of steel are made at Valenciennes, Denain, Dunkirk and elsewhere; this is indeed France's *pays noir*. The manufacture of textiles, at first based on local wool, has long been important; the main centre is Lille, with a population of nearly 190,000 and over 880,000 in its agglomeration (including the twin towns of Roubaix–Tourcoing), the largest textile centre in France.

On the coast Calais and Dunkirk are ferry ports of entry to France from Dover. Dunkirk also has a commercial port which in terms of freight is the third largest in France (handling annually 5 million tons of crude oil and 4·5 million tons of iron ore), and its industries include a large oil refinery and the new *Usinor* steel works.

3. *The Ardennes*

A small portion of the Ardennes uplands extends into France, trenched across by the Meuse valley and forming the plateau of Rocroi; the highest point attains about 410 m (1345 ft). Parts of the plateau are cultivated, yielding poor crops of potatoes and cereals, and much is under permanent pasture. The chief town is Rocroi, at a height of nearly 390 m (1300 ft). Slate is quarried at a number of places.

4. *Lorraine*

Lorraine lies between the outer ridges of the Paris Basin and the Vosges. In 1871 its eastern part was absorbed with Alsace into Germany, and though it was returned to France in 1918, the same thing happened in the 1940–44 period. It consists of a series of Jurassic limestone ridges, in turn the Portland, Corallian and Oolitic, alternating with valleys developed in the clays and marls. The more resistant limestones form cuestas, each with an eastward-facing escarpment dissected by deep valleys into spurs and outlying fragments, and a back-slope forming a plateau sinking gently to the west. The Meuse flows northward in a valley entrenched in the Corallian limestone, while farther east the Moselle receives many tributaries from the Vosges and from the clay-covered lowlands of eastern Lorraine.

Thin grey soils have developed on the limestone, damp alluvial soils on the floodplains, clay soils, fertile but heavy, rather cold and sometimes waterlogged, in the vales, and coarse hungry soils on the sands and gravels. Where the clays can be drained wheat, oats and potatoes are grown, malting barley and hops are cultivated for a large local brewing industry, and permanent grassland supports dairy cattle. On south-facing slopes vines and orchards of stone-fruits are grown.

Lorraine is much more important as an industrial than as an agri-cultural region, and has three main sources of wealth: coal, iron ore and salt (Fig. 90). In the north the Coal Measures of the Saar Basin in West Germany continue across the boundary into France to form the Moselle coalfield. From the Jurassic limestone over 46 million tons of iron ore were mined in 1967, and a major steel-making region based on these ore-fields has developed (p. 445); Lorraine produces four-fifths of French pig-iron, two-thirds of the crude steel and over half of the finished steel, with the chief centres Nancy, Longwy, Briey and Thionville (Fig. 92). Large deposits of common salt provide the raw material for several chemical works.

The chief town is Nancy (258,000), situated on the Meurthe above its junction with the Moselle, and with a variety of industries. Three other towns have long been important as route centres and as fortresses guarding the approaches to Paris: Metz (166,000) and Toul on the Moselle, and Verdun on the Meuse; the defence of the last in 1916–17 cost the lives of half a million men.

5. *The Vosges*

The Vosges rise gradually in Lorraine, then fall steeply along the western side of the Rhine valley. The High Vosges in the south have an average altitude of about 900 m (3000 ft), rising to rounded granite summits of which the highest is 1426 m (4679 ft), covered with moorland, bogs and rough pasture. Farther north the Bunter Sandstone of the Low Vosges forms flat tabular summits flanked by steep forested slopes. Short streams flow rapidly eastward to join the Ill and the Rhine, and have worn steep, gorge-like valleys.

The Vosges carry a snow-cover which on the high summits may lie for five months. The high pastures are used for summer grazing by dairy cattle, the milk being made into cheese at both farmhouses and small co-operative dairies. Farther down the slopes farming is more mixed in character; patches of cereals and vegetables are cultivated, with groves of chestnuts, walnuts, cherries and peaches, and the lower slopes are terraced for vineyards producing the white Alsatian wines.

The villages and towns in the valleys of the Vosges have an air of quiet prosperity, partly because they are busy markets, partly because of tourist activity (Gérardmer receives 100,000 visitors each year), and partly because of their industries, notably textiles. Forestry is important and numerous sawmills and pulp mills are active; pit-props and timber are sent away, and small factories make barrels, furniture, toys and sabots. Several paper mills use local pulp and the pure mountain water.

6. *The Plain of Alsace*

The valley of the Rhine from Basle to Mainz consists of a broad trench (p. 190), the south-western portion of which is in France. Beyond the damp floodplain, a series of terraces covered with alluvium, gravel and loess rise towards the foothills of the Vosges. The Rhine receives one tributary, the Ill, which flows northward for 130 km (80 miles) almost parallel to the main river, joining it north of Strasbourg. The floodplain, known as the *Ried*, is covered with sheets of alluvium and gravel, and was formerly very swampy, interspersed with 'islands' of gravel and clumps of trees. Much has been reclaimed, as indicated by the drainage channels and the water-meadows, though parts are still marshy and liable to flooding in winter.

The sands and gravels are mostly covered with woodland, the alluvium is under permanent pasture, and the loess soils grow wheat, maize, barley, sugar beet, tobacco and potatoes. Hops, produced on smallholdings, supply the numerous Rhineland breweries in both France and West Germany. In addition to apples, plums and cherries, such fruits as peaches, apricots and vines flourish on the slopes, and market gardens produce vegetables for the urban populations and for canning at Strasbourg. Large numbers of dairy cattle are grazed on the pastures in summer, stall-fed in winter.

Potash is mined in the south near Mulhouse, and oil is obtained near Pechelbronn and Staffelfelden. The most important industry is the manufacture of textiles, which began on a domestic scale in the foothills of the Vosges, and is now concentrated in Mulhouse, Colmar and Belfort. These towns have other industries, notably engineering and the manufacture of chemicals and fertilizers from the potash.

The capital of Alsace is Strasbourg (335,000), situated within the branches of the river Ill about 3 km (2 miles) from the Rhine, and with a large river port (Fig. 98). The city is a centre of communications, and has many industries, particularly engineering, food-processing, tanning, paper-making and printing. Two large oil refineries were opened in 1963 (p. 437) at Reichstett–Vendenheim and Herrlisheim to the north of the city.

The Rhineland has long been an area of contention between France and Germany; most people speak dialects of German and many are bilingual. In some parts of Alsace German speakers are in a majority, and many personal and place names are in the German form.

7. *The Saône–Rhône Valley*

The valley of the Saône, continued to the south of Lyons by that of the Rhône, forms a corridor between central France and the Mediterranean Sea. The Rhône is not a good waterway (p. 459), but the Saône is more useful since it flows placidly and is linked by canals to the Rhine and the Marne. Several projects have utilized the Rhône for navigation, irrigation and power production, and a multi-purpose plan is in progress under the *Compagnie Nationale du Rhône*. The valley of the Saône is broad and flat-floored, with terraces rising to the foothills of the Jura on the east and to the slopes of the Central Massif on the west. By contrast, to the south of Lyons the Rhône valley consists of a series of basins, each separated by a narrow gorge-section where the hills approach closely.

As the climate changes southward from a régime in the north with continental tendencies to one in the south with distinctive Mediterranean features, so does the landscape, from the meadows, arable fields and woodlands of central Europe, to a bright sunny Mediterranean scene of limestones and silvery shrubs, arid and dusty in summer. In the Saône valley fodder crops are grown to support dairy herds, and on the slopes of the Côte d'Or terraced

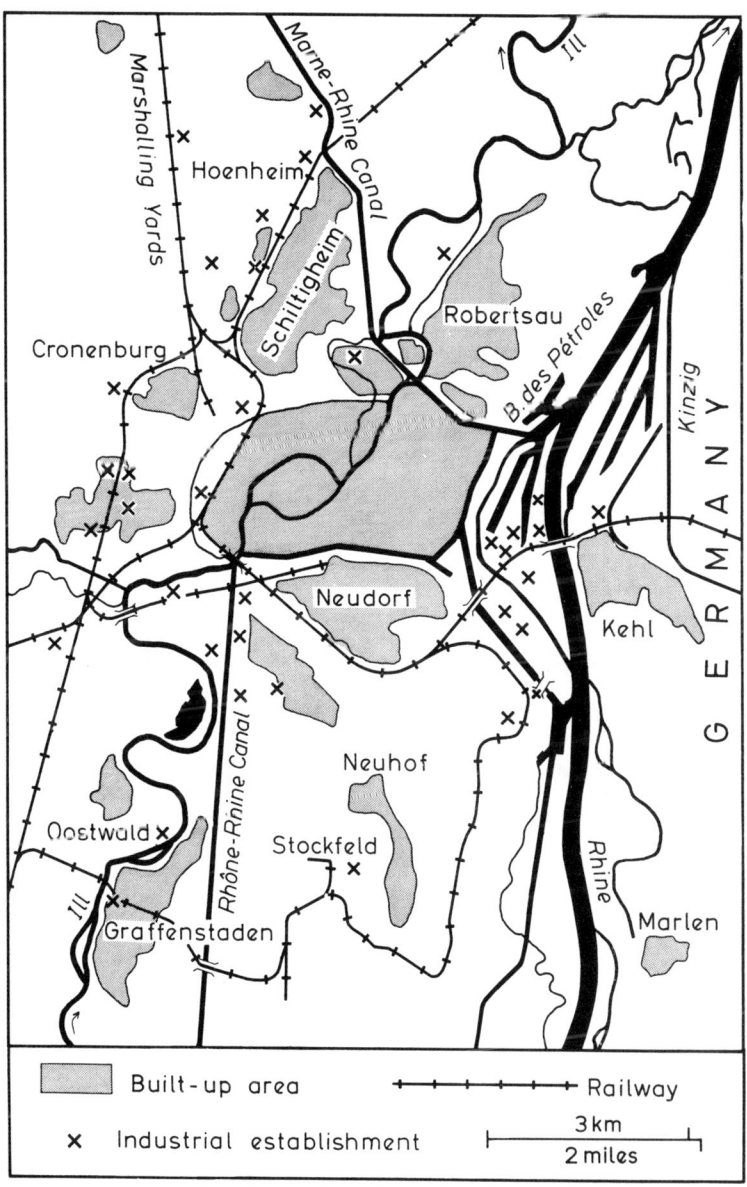

Fig. 98. Strasbourg
(After *Atlas de France*, with revisions)

vineyards produce Burgundy wines. Farther south in the Rhône valley, particularly near Avignon, cultivation is carried on with the help of irrigation; the market gardens are divided into tiny plots protected by windbreaks of cypress hedges and hurdle fences against the mistral.

The Saône–Rhône valley is quite densely, though rather unevenly, populated. In the north small towns are situated at crossing points of the Saône, and others concerned with the wine trade stand at the foot of the steep slopes. Dijon (184,000) is an important route centre, where almost every main railway-line from southern and south-eastern France converges on its way to Paris. It also has a variety of industries processing foodstuffs, notably mustard and tobacco, and making chemicals and metallurgical products.

Lyons, founded by the Romans as *Lugdunum* on a hillock over-looking the right bank of the Saône, has grown into a flourishing city (Fig. 99). It has a wide range of activities, administrative, com-mercial and industrial, for it is the regional centre for much of south-eastern France and is a focus of communications. Despite the

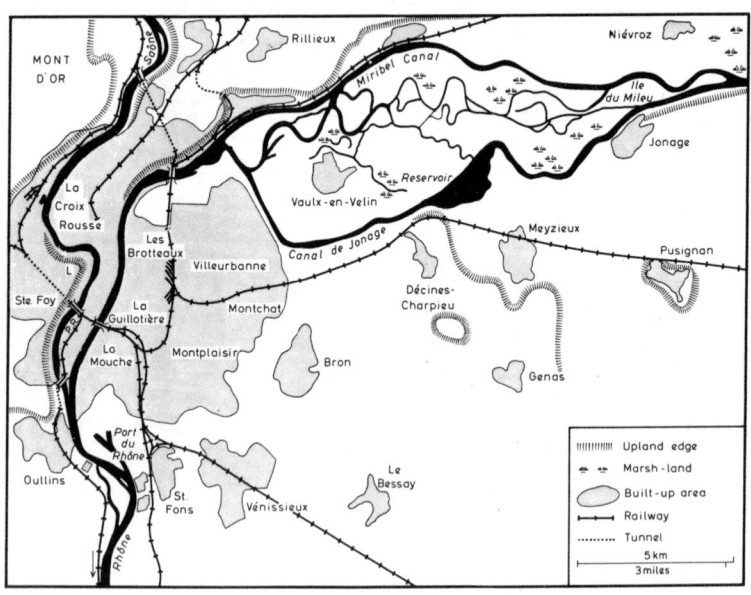

Fig. 99. Lyons
(After *Carte de France au 50,000ᵉ*)
The Pierre Bénite Canal, completed in 1965, forms a direct link south and east of Lyons around the city.

navigational disabilities of the Rhône, Lyons is the tenth river port in France in terms of tonnage handled, for the Saône is a quite busy river. Many workers are employed in the silk industry, originally based on raw silk from locally reared silkworms, though most now comes from Japan and the Middle East. The Lyons area is also responsible for over half the total French production of rayon and nylon. Other industries include metallurgical and electrical manufactures, pharmaceutical chemicals, and the processing of foodstuffs.

To the south of Lyons small towns are strung out along the river, usually where the valley opens out between the gorge sections. Many were Roman settlements and bridge towns, and preserve legacies of their past: Vienne, Valence, Montélimar, Orange and the largest, Avignon, with 73,000 people. They are now centres for agricultural districts, and have food-processing industries. With the availability of electric power, several factories have grown up, such as the *Rhône–Poulenc* chemical works south of Vienne, the plutonium refinery at Pierrelatte and the electro-metallurgical works of *L'Ardoise* near Avignon.

8. *The Jura*

The Jura form a crescent-shaped limestone upland, extending for 240 km (150 miles) from the southern end of the Rhine Rift Valley to the Rhône near Lyons. Although limestone is the dominant rock, water is plentiful, underground drainage systems have developed, and resurgences are common. Several large rivers, the Doubs, Ain and Rhône, flow westward in zigzag courses, for they usually follow for a time a longitudinal valley (*val*) between two ridges, then cut across a transverse ridge in a steep-sided gorge (*cluse*).

Marked contrasts are evident in the Jura between the northern end, where a distinct bleakness is apparent, and the southern part which possesses a certain brightness. The sides of the mountains are swathed with conifers, notably spruce, interrupted by limestone cliffs which rise, too steeply to support vegetation, from the meadows in the valleys. Along the river banks stretches of water-meadow, sometimes irrigated by a network of channels, produce several crops of hay for winter feed. Farther away from the rivers, strips of arable land grow wheat, oats, potatoes and turnips, and on the slopes are orchards.

There are about 350,000 head of dairy cattle, out of 600,000 cattle of all kinds. Before 1914 cattle-rearing was restricted to the high pastures, often owned in common by members of a commune, for little of the valley floor could be spared for grazing. These upland pastures are still used, and have been considerably improved by fertilizers, but in the valleys about half the arable was converted into pasture between the Wars; moreover, there has been greater concentration on fodder crops and on the improvement of meadows. Transhumance is still practised, families taking the animals up to the *alpages* from May to September, but most cattle are now kept permanently in the valleys. Some of the milk is sent to chocolate factories at Geneva and Pontarlier, and much consumed in liquid form in local towns or sent farther afield to Lyons and even to Paris. But the chief product is cheese, and the term *Gruyère* has been applied to Jura produce for centuries. These magnificent cheeses are made in small dairy chalets, in recent years also at factories in Pontarlier, Dole and Lons-le-Saunier. Some co-operative societies collect the milk, deliver it to the factories, and then sell cheese to the merchants. Other activities include the production of processed cheese, cream, butter and casein.

The Jura have long been a minor industrial area, using the tumbling streams to drive watermills. Now several large hydro-stations are in operation, including France's biggest at Génissiat on the Rhône near Bellegarde. Manufacturing, the legacy of 'châlet industries' which occupied winter leisure and which still afford an addition to family incomes, includes timber working, food-processing, watch- and clock-making, the cutting and polishing of precious stones, and the making of watch glasses and spectacles. A few larger towns on the margins, Besançon (116,000), Montbéliard (115,600), the home of the *Peugeot* company, and Lons-le-Saunier, have grown into industrial centres.

9. *The French Alps*

The mountainous region of south-eastern France is part of the fold-mountain system of the Alps, sweeping in a curve round the western margins of the North Italian Plain (Fig. 79). On the west are the limestone blocks of the Fore-Alps, divided by river valleys into units such as Grand Chartreuse, Vercors and Devoluy. In the east the sedimentary zone of the High Alps, with the constituent ranges of the Graian Alps, the Cottian Alps and the Maritime Alps, are composed mainly of metamorphosed sedimentary rocks; involved in these are several blocks of crystalline rock: the Mont Blanc massif, Belledonne, Pelvoux, Mercantour and several more. Two main Rhône tributaries, the Isère and the Durance, cross the ranges from east to west.

The Alps have been much affected by glaciation, and glaciers and snowfields still cover about 500 sq. km (200 sq. miles). Mont Blanc culminates in a snow hump reaching 4807 m (15,771 ft), with slopes falling away steeply on each side; from the snowfields filling the hollows between the granite ridges, glaciers move downwards, the largest the well-known Mer de Glace. While parts of the mountains carry a permanent mantle, the whole Alpine region is snow-covered during the winter, and the passes above 1800 m (6000 ft) are usually closed from October to May. After a severe winter, especially when a rapid spring rise of temperature occurs, damage from avalanches and flood melt-water may be considerable.

A gradual change in climate can be seen between the northern and southern ends of the French Alps, from Continental to Mediterranean types, resulting in marked differences in landscape and agriculture. In the north are snowfields and glaciers, pine woods and meadows, while in the south are dry limestone plateaus, with poor pasture and scrub in the higher parts and chestnut woods and olive groves on the lower slopes. Agriculture extends along the valleys far into the mountains; in the north the economy is dependent on cattle-rearing, though strips of wheat, potatoes and other vegetables are grown, and on the south-facing slopes apples, plums, cherries and vines flourish. In the south the summers are warmer and drier, and on the poor pastures cattle are replaced by sheep reared for wool, skins and milk; large flocks move down in winter to the valleys, even to the Rhône delta. On terraced slopes tiny patches of wheat, maize, tobacco, almonds, lavender and apricots are carefully cultivated.

Forestry and forest industries are a valuable contribution, especially in the north, where more than half of the area is wooded. Much is planted for fuel, for the timber industries, to check soil erosion, and as avalanche breaks. Every chalet has its huge pile of wood stacked for the winter, and large quantities of pit-props are sent away.

Industrial activity has expanded as a result of the development of water power, for about 150 stations generate a third of the hydroelectricity made in France. Part is transmitted elsewhere by high tension lines, the rest is consumed locally, and some of the valleys contain lines of factories; large-scale electrometallurgical and chemical industries include the refining of aluminium from

bauxite, the making of steel alloys in electric furnaces, and the production of calcium carbide and other chemicals. The focus of this
industrial region is Grenoble (332,000), which has large silk and
rayon factories, and makes electrical apparatus, paper, leather, gloves
and cement, and contains the National Nuclear Research Centre.

The whole region from the shores of Lake Geneva to the Mediterranean coast is popular with tourists; there are the pleasant spas
of Evian, Aix and Annecy, and the mountaineering and winter
sports centres of Chamonix and La Bérarde. The *Routes des Alpes*
comprises one of the finest series of mountain roads in Europe. The
high passes are crossed and the lonely valleys are penetrated by
roads, and hotels are found in remote centres.

10. *The Mediterranean Coastlands*

The coastline between the Italian and Spanish boundaries is
backed by a region often known as the Midi. In the centre an
expanse of sand and mud forms the ever-growing delta of the
Rhône, between whose main outlets are the lagoons and saltmarshes
of the Camargue, the northern part of which has been reclaimed as
pasture for the black cattle and the famous white stallions, for
growing rice, and for vegetables; the last supply a new American
cannery at Vauvert. To the east of the main river, in the Crau,
sheets of water-worn gravel were deposited by the Durance when in
Pleistocene times it entered the sea directly, though it now joins the
Rhône near Avignon. The coast of Languedoc to the west of the
delta is lined with dunes backed by lagoons and saltmarshes, into
which flow rivers such as the Hérault and the Aude. By contrast, to
the east of the delta in Provence the coast is bordered by cliffs
and rocky peninsulas alternating with deeply cut bays. The two
crystalline massifs of Maures and Esterel reach the coast east of
Toulon, forming headlands, rocky islands, occasional broad bays,
and deep narrow indentations.

Behind the coast outcrops of limestone are widespread, and in
eastern Provence the land rises steeply to the southern ranges of the
Maritime Alps. In Languedoc the land ascends in a series of gravel-
covered steps towards the south-eastern slopes of the Central Massif,
across which such swiftly flowing rivers as the Ardèche have worn
spectacular gorges. In the south the semicircular plain of Roussillon
is mostly covered with alluvium, sand and sheets of Pliocene gravels,
with a coastline bordered by dunes, lagoons and marshes glisten-
ing white with salt encrustations, or brown with reed beds.

Upon this very varied relief the Mediterranean climate has imposed its characteristics, reflected in both the landscape and the way of life. The summer drought, emphasized by the widespread occurrence of limestone and of highly permeable gravels, has resulted in a vegetation cover with xerophytic characters. Holm-oak and cork-oak forests once covered large areas, but their clearance exposed the slopes to the rains, and much soil erosion has resulted. In many places the vegetation has deteriorated into scrubby aromatic garrigue: cistus, rosemary, thyme, juniper, thorny bushes and dwarf evergreen oak. In response to autumn and winter rains, an intermittent covering of grass spreads over the gravels.

For centuries agriculture has consisted of the typical Mediterranean crops, wheat, vine and olive, using both the terraces of better soil and the alluvial plains where irrigation water is available. Much cultivation is small-scale, though varied; some farmers grow vegetables on irrigated land near a village, farther up the terraced slopes are patches of wheat and maize, then fruit trees such as peaches are succeeded by vines, and on the upper slopes are groves of olives and sweet chestnut. In some parts more specialization is practised; to the west of the Rhône the main activity is the cultivation of vines, and in Provence the mild winter and spring temperatures have encouraged the growth of early vegetables, flowers and fruit. In Roussillon apricots, olives, peaches and almonds flourish on the warm dry slopes of the gravel-covered plateaus and terraces, and vines are grown for the production of wines and liqueurs. A scheme is in progress to irrigate 240 000 ha (600,000 acres) with water brought by the Canal de Languedoc from the Rhône above Arles (240 km, 150 miles long), running westward parallel to the coast, and supplemented with water from the rivers Hérault, Aube and Aude.

In comparison with their past glories, most of the little ports of the Midi, such as the walled town of Aigues-Mortes, are decayed; only Sète, with its harbour and oil refinery, is now of any importance. Inland are such attractive towns as Montpellier (171,000), Nîmes (125,000), Béziers and Narbonne, with food-processing industries; at Nîmes is the third largest wholesale market in France, linked with local co-operatives and by 'telex' with the main European markets.

To the east of the Rhône delta, away from the silt and mud deposited near the mouth of the river, are Marseilles (Fig. 100) and the naval base of Toulon. With a population of 954,000, the Marseilles agglomeration is third in France, and it is the largest port in terms of freight, handling about a quarter of all French seaborne commerce, particularly from Algeria and the Middle East. It is an important industrial town, but the hills rising steeply behind the town limit expansion, and most developments now take place around the reclaimed shores of the Etang de Berre and Golfe de Fos (p. 463). There are four large oil refineries and several petrochemical plants; factories process imported foodstuffs and make soap, margarine and cement, and at the port are ship-repairing and marine engineering.

Formerly the western coastlands were bordered by marshes, lagoons and dunes, with only a few fishing villages, but in recent years modern tourist resorts, camp-sites and marinas are being developed. In the east are the long-established luxury resorts of the Côte d'Azur. The four main centres, Cannes, Nice, Monte Carlo and Menton, and the innumerable smaller ones, cater for a half-million visitors between Christmas and Easter and many more in summer. The Côte d'Azur has thus profited by its mild sunny climate, its south-facing aspect and protection from the mistral, and its sandy bays and rocky coves.

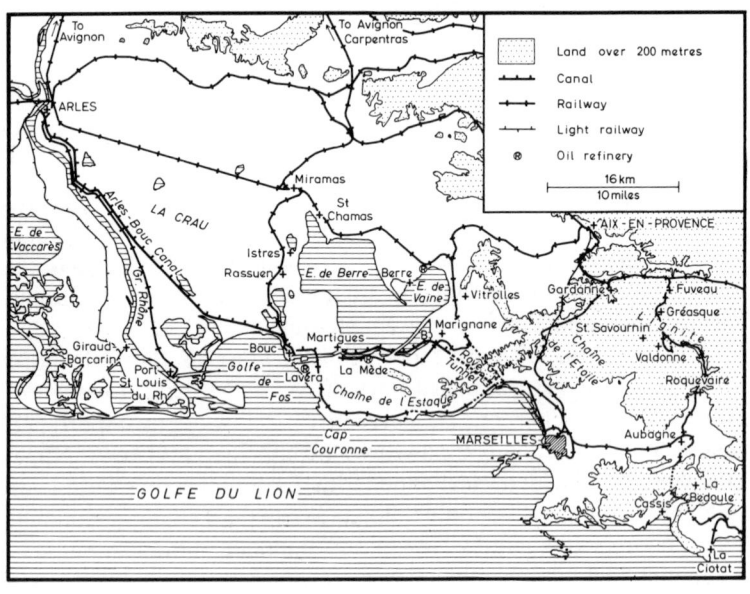

Fig. 100. The Marseilles region
(After *Carte de France au 200,000ᵉ*)

A new refinery has been opened on the shores of the Golfe de Fos.

11. *The Pyrenees*

The high serrated central line of the Pyrenees consists of numerous jagged peaks rising from a series of high plateaus; in altitude they do not compare with the Alps, for their highest summit, the Pic d'Aneto (Mont Néthou), which is in Spain, attains only 3404 m (11,168 ft). Though the mountains carry heavy winter snow, the permanent snowfields and glaciers are small in extent, and are confined to the central Pyrenees over 3000 m (10,000 ft). The Quaternary glaciation has left its stamp on the landscape with lofty arêtes, pyramid peaks, over-deepened valleys and innumerable cirque-basins, the best known being Gavarnie and Troumouse at the head of the Gave de Pau. For much of its length the crest-line divides the headwaters of streams flowing northward into France and those southward into Spain. The two main French systems are the Garonne (whose headstreams rise in Spain) with its tributary the Ariège, and the Adour, joined by many streams with the local name of *gave* (a foaming torrent). As limestone rocks are widespread, underground drainage is common, and there are huge cave systems; the most remarkable is the Gouffre de Pierre St Martin, which is entered by a vertical shaft 346 m (1135 ft) deep.

Mixed farming is practised, with the emphasis on livestock, cattle in the west and centre, and sheep and goats in the east; as the snows melt in summer, the animals are taken to the upland pastures, returning to the valley farms to be stall-fed in winter. Several factories process milk into butter and cheese. The western Pyrenean valleys are famous for horse-rearing; these animals are still used for draught purposes, and mules are bred mainly for export to Spain. In the west on the lower slopes a little wheat and maize are grown, with rye in the higher valleys, potatoes, beans, pumpkins and other vegetables, and orchards of apples and plums. In the east agriculture resembles that of the Mediterranean lands; terraces edged by stone walls grow vines, olives, almonds, peaches, apricots, and even oranges and pomegranates in favoured places, nurtured by streams from the melting snows.

In the valleys the old craft industries utilize wool, hides, timber and small deposits of iron ore. Wooden products include sabots, furniture, rosaries and religious statuary, and many small textile mills are active. By contrast, large-scale modern manufacturing largely depends on the availability of hydroelectric power from the Pyrenean stations. Aluminium is refined, high-grade alloys and special steels are made in electric furnaces, chemicals are produced, and there are several electrical engineering plants and aircraft works. The most important industrial towns in these lower Pyrenean valleys are Tarbes, Bagnères-de-Bigorre, Pamiers and Tarascon.

One further contribution to the economic life is tourism, attracted by the mountain scenery, the heavy winter snowfall which encourages winter sports, and the mineral springs; more than fifty places are spas, with Pau and Lourdes the main centres.

12. *The Basin of Aquitaine*

The triangular Basin of Aquitaine is an extensive, rather monotonous lowland of gently undulating hills, low plateaus and broad valleys, an area of Mesozoic and Tertiary limestone, sandstone and clay. Widespread superficial deposits include drift laid down over the foreland by the Pyrenean Quaternary glaciers, and the contributions of the main rivers. The Garonne flows diagonally across the basin to the Gironde estuary, receiving many tributaries, both from the Pyrenees and from the Central Massif, notably the Dordogne. Two other rivers drain the basin, the Charente in the north and the Adour in the south-western corner. The heavy winter rainfall, snow-melt and rapid runoff from the steep surrounding slopes cause flooding; loads of material are swept down, the coarsest gravels and sand over the floodplains, the finest materials reaching the estuary of the Gironde.

In the south-west sheets of fine sand, in places blown into dunes, cover the Landes, which lie behind a straight coast fringed with dunes. In their former state they were covered with lagoons and marshes, thickets of scrub and stunted evergreen oaks, but much has now been drained and planted with conifers, mostly maritime pine, which check the encroaching movement of the dunes. There has been some development of the tourist industry along the coast, with its fine sandy beaches and pleasant sunny climate.

The way of life over Aquitaine is mainly rural and agricultural, and more than half of the arable land is under cereals, notably wheat and maize; market gardens are intensively cultivated on the terraces, and orchards and vineyards are widespread; in the neighbourhood of Bordeaux quality clarets and other high-grade wines are produced. Cognac, in the valley of the Charente, and Armagnac in the south, are the centres of brandy-making districts.

In Charente about 300,000 of the 540,000 cattle are dairy animals. This development has been furthered by the inclusion of short ley grass within the arable rotation and an increase in fodder crops, while water-meadows along the valleys have been improved by fertilizing and irrigation. The dairy industry has been stimulated by the increase in co-operative methods, which are better developed than anywhere else in France; the first co-operative dairy was established in 1888, and the societies are now organized within a central association, the emphasis being on the production of butter, which has a widespread reputation. In addition, young beef stores are bought in Limousin and fattened in Charente.

Apart from the processing of agricultural products, some manu-facturing has developed, based on electricity and local natural gas (p. 438). A large steel works at Le Boucau near Bayonne uses imported coke and ore, and other activities, including the manu-facture of aircraft and chemicals, are located here, as far as possible from the eastern borders.

Numerous small towns each serve as a market centre for a particular district. Along the coast are several fishing ports, with factories canning tunny and sardine, the former naval port of La Rochelle whose main importance is now in fishing, and seaside re-sorts. In this mainly rural part are two of the country's largest cities, Bordeaux and Toulouse. The former, with a population of about 249,000 but with a total agglomeration of 555,000, the fifth in France, has long been a great port, though 100 km (60 miles) up the Gironde estuary (Fig. 101). It has many industries, including three oil refineries; it is the centre of the Bordelais vineyards, and the commercial capital of south-western France. At the other end of the Garonne valley, Toulouse is situated at the western approach to the Gap of Naurouze between the Montagne Noire and the foothills of the Pyrenees, and a focus of road, rail and inland waterways. It is a market and servicing centre for a large area, and its wide range of manufacturing includes the processing of local agricultural produce, chemicals and explosives, and textiles; the great aircraft factory of *Sud-Aviation* is nearby. It is, in fact, a striking example of a city with well developed regional functions.

13. *The Central Massif*

This upland, bounded by the 300 m (1000 ft) contour and composed of varied rocks among which ancient crystallines are dominant, occupies about a sixth of the area of France. Its maximum altitude is only 1886 m (6188 ft), the Puy de Sancy in Auvergne, but it maintains a high average of about 900 m (3000 ft). Much consists of gently

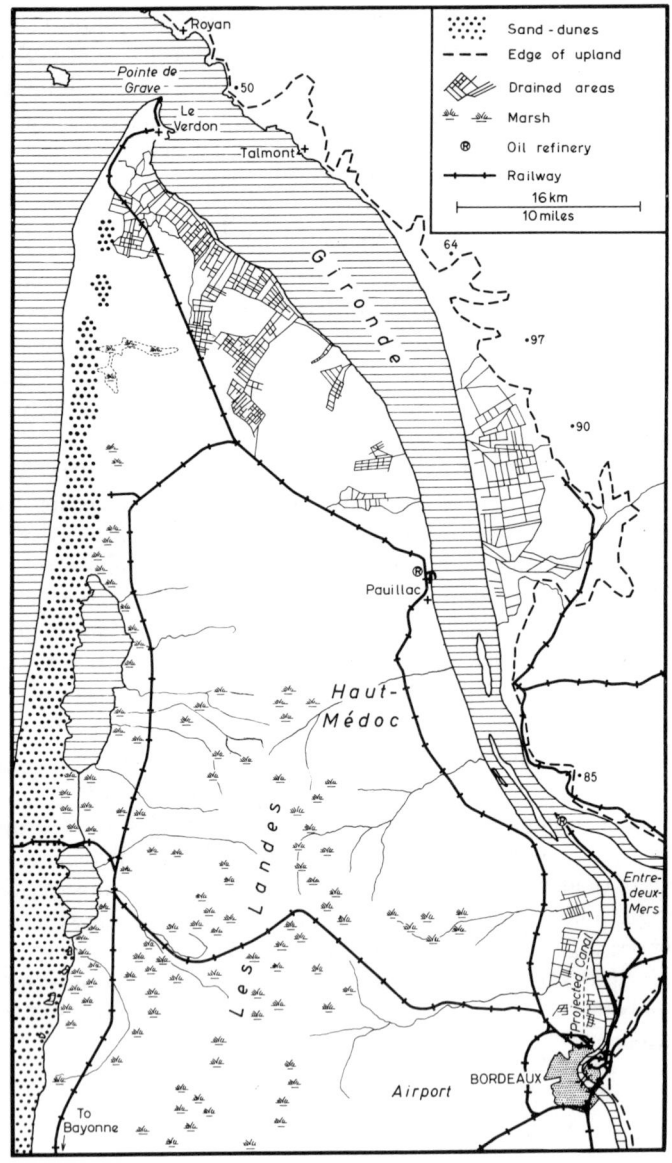

Fig. 101. Bordeaux
(After *Carte de France au 200,000ᵉ*)

undulating plateaus, including Limousin, the Montagne Noire, Vivarais and Margeridc, while the Morvan projects boldly from its north-eastern corner as a horst, defined on the east and west by clear-cut faults. Among the granitic and gneissic rocks lie several small down-faulted basins, where Coal Measures have been preserved. In the south a synclinal depression in Mesozoic times was the scene of

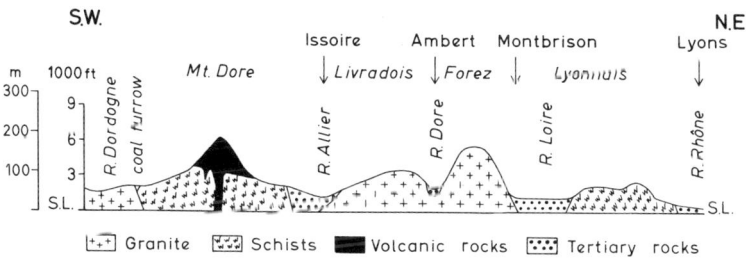

Fig. 102. *Generalized section across the Central Massif*
(After A. Cholley *et al.*)

extensive deposition of Jurassic limestone, which survives to form the plateaus, dissected by gorges, of the Grands Causses. In the central part of the Massif, known as Auvergne, groups of small volcanic peaks (*puys*) rise above the general level, with the large cones of Mont Dore (Fig. 102) and Cantal, and lava flows have solidified to form such basalt plateaus as those in Velay. During the earth movements which formed the Alps, the massif was tilted to-wards the west and north, leaving along the east and south-east a steep edge, its most striking part known as the Cévennes. As a result of this tilting, most rivers rise near the high south-eastern edge to flow northward (the Loire and Allier) or westward (the Lot, Tarn and Dordogne) to the Bay of Biscay.

Though some areas are too damp and bleak for anything but moorland, parts of the south are too dry and sun-scorched in summer for anything but poor scrub. These contrasts are reflected in the agriculture; in the high plateaus of the north-west rye, buckwheat and potatoes are grown; in the valleys of the Loire and Allier rich soils derived from the volcanic rocks support wheat; and vines, olives and mulberries flourish on the terraced slopes of the south. The main emphasis is on the rearing of cattle, sheep and goats, which can make use of the rather meagre upland pastures; in the centre and north cattle are reared both for beef, for the markets of Paris, Lyons and elsewhere, and for milk. Dairying is widely practised, using the milk of both cows and ewes; the latter is made into cheese at Roquefort.

The Central Massif is hardly an industrial region, yet it contains several important centres. Their few advantages include tiny scattered coal basins, some small-scale deposits of ores, and kaolin, timber, skins and hides. The rivers, used for centuries to work mill-wheels, have now been harnessed by modern schemes; barrages have been built along the Dordogne, Lot and Truyère valleys to hold up water for the summer months, when the river flow diminishes, and supply power stations linked into the grid. Craft manufactures long carried on in the small towns include the making of leather, textiles, lace, paper and wooden articles, and with the help of electric power many still flourish. St Etienne, Le Creusot and Alès, centres of steel production, were formerly based on the coalfields and on small ore deposits now mainly exhausted; pig-iron from Lorraine is now used, and specialized articles, often of high-grade steel, are produced. The proximity of the industrial areas of north-eastern France to a vulnerable border has encouraged the development of armaments in this more remote region. Other manufactured products include chemicals on the coalfields, tyres at the *Michelin* works in Clermont-Ferrand, and pottery at St Yrieix near Limoges.

Although most of the Central Massif is an area of scanty population, St Etienne (331,000), Clermont-Ferrand (205,000) and Limoges (148,000) are centres for a considerable area, and have varied manufactures. Other smaller industrial towns include Le Creusot and Montceau-les-Mines in the north-east, Alès in the south-east, Decazeville and Rodez in the south-west, and Montluçon on the northern margins. Several towns, such as the fashionable spa of Vichy and Le Puy in the upper Loire valley, cater for tourists.

14. *Armorica*

Armorica refers to the indented coastline and hinterland of a peninsula projecting into the Atlantic Ocean; its westerly portion is sometimes called Brittany, after the ancient province of Bretagne, while the eastern section was once part of Normandy. Armorica is an upland area mostly between 180 and 360 m (600 and 1200 ft), though dropping steeply to the coasts. Masses of granite form rounded plateaus, the line of the Montagnes d'Arrée in the north and of the Montagnes Noires in the south; the highest point attains only 384 m (1260 ft). Basins and depressions lie among the uplands, notably the valley of the Aulne, known as Châteaulin, opening into the Rade de Brest.

The rugged coast is the combined result of a slight submergence of the edge of the worn-down uplands in late Quaternary times, constant erosion by the sea of rocks of different degrees of resistance, and the accumulation of sand and mud in sheltered bays. This submergence flooded portions of the valleys, forming a ria coast with winding indentations, between which project long peninsulas with archipelagoes and submerged rocks extending seaward for over twenty miles. Castellated cliffs over 90 m (300 ft) high, caves, arches and stacks form a picturesque coastline. In the extreme west is the Ile d'Ouessant, known to English seamen for centuries as 'Ushant'. In the inlets accumulate beaches of gravel and sand, backed by dunes and marsh and fronted by tidal flats. An example is the Baie du Mont St Michel in the western angle of the Cotentin, from whose flats rises the granite mass of Mont St Michel, linked to the mainland by a causeway and crowned by an eleventh-century abbey. Parts of the flats have been reclaimed to form pasture, notably the Marais de Dol to the west of Mont St Michel and the St Michel polders.

The Breton peninsula, exposed to air masses from the Atlantic Ocean, is characterized by high humidity, cloudiness, fine drizzling rain, and mild temperatures along the coast. The plateaus in the interior are bleaker and wetter, in places covered with moorland, and with areas of bog in the depressions. But a surprisingly high proportion of Armorica, between 70 and 80 per cent, consists of either arable land or permanent grassland; Manche has two-thirds of its surface under grassland, the highest proportion of any department in France. Most of the farmland is in small fields enclosed by an earth bank with a thick hedge, forming the characteristic *bocage* country (Plate LXV). Some of these fields grow fodder crops, potatoes and cereals, usually oats and barley, and vegetables take advantage of the early springs and freedom from frost; they are sent by rail to Paris and by boat from St Malo, Morlaix and other small ports to Britain. Apple orchards are widespread, from which cider and the potent liqueur *Calvados* are made. The main activity is dairy farming, and nearly a fifth of the dairy cattle in France are found here. Much milk is made into cheese, including such well-known varieties as Camembert and Port-Salut; a fifth of the pigs in France are kept and fattened on skim-milk; and numbers of young bullocks are shipped away for fattening. Except during the worst weather on the uplands, cattle can be left out of doors through the year.

The surrounding seas both provide the farmers with a supplementary source of livelihood and offer full-time employment. Small fishing harbours are scattered about the coast, with the larger ones of Lorient, Concarneau and Douarnenez, and both inshore and deep-sea fishing in the Bay of Biscay and further afield are carried out.

While Armorica as a whole is thinly populated, numerous towns are strung out round the coast. Some of these are ports, notably Cherbourg, Nantes and its outport, St Nazaire. Nantes carries on much 'colonial trade', and has processing industries, while St Nazaire has shipbuilding yards and marine engineering works. A large oil refinery is at Donges, between St Nazaire and Nantes. Brest is France's leading naval port, with shipbuilding yards, mainly for warships. Cherbourg's dockyards completed the *Rédoutable*, France's first nuclear submarine, in 1967. Other small towns situated around the coast include fishing ports, the small port of St Malo, with connections to the Channel Islands, and resorts taking advantage of the general charm of the Breton landscape.

The only inland town of any size is Rennes, the capital of Brittany, a centre of communications, with commercial and servicing functions, and a famous university. Its industries include tanneries, shoe factories, chemical works, a large oil-refinery at the nearby Vern-sur-Seiche, and the *Citroën* plant opened in 1951 just outside the town.

15. Corsica

This mountainous island, about the size of Wales, is situated in the western Mediterranean basin 160 km (100 miles) from mainland France. The western two-thirds of the island consists of a horst-like mass of crystalline rocks, which has been deeply dissected, so that rugged ridges with many fine peaks rise steeply from the deep valleys; the highest, Monte Cinto, is 2710 m (8891 ft) (Figs. 103, 104). The north-eastern part, including the peninsula of Cap Corse, is lower, but still very rugged. While the east coast is bordered by dunes, lagoons and salt-marshes, the west coast has rocky ridges, with cliffs and offshore islets alternating with deeply cut gulfs.

Corsica has a climate of warm sunny summers (21 to 24° C. at sea-level) and mild winters (10° C.). Its island position slightly reduces summer temperatures, and diurnal land and sea breezes are experienced around the coast. Rainfall varies according to position; on the west coast the mean total is about 750 mm (30 in), while in the mountains it is as much as 1500 mm (60 in), mostly falling in winter in the form of snow, though none lies permanently.

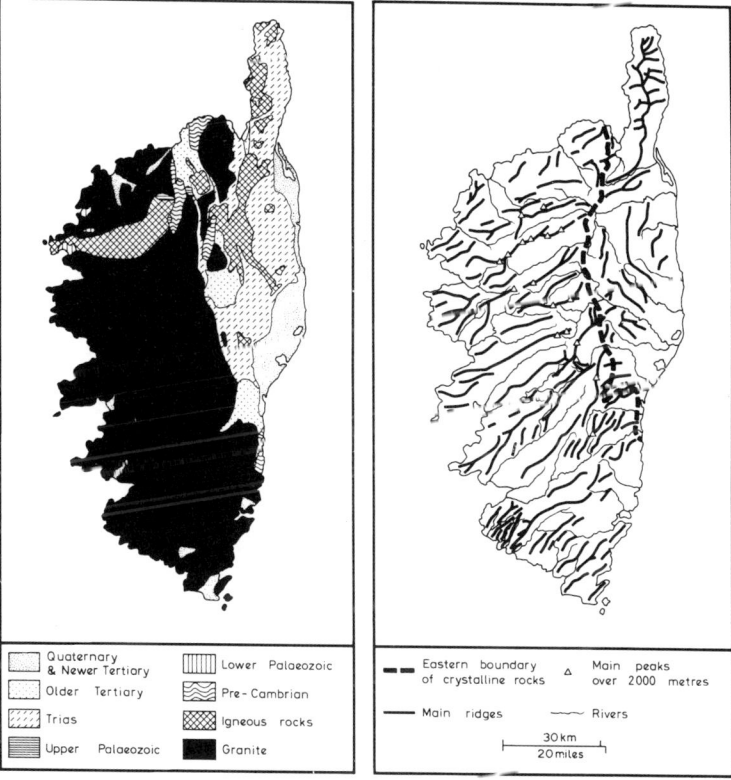

Quaternary
& Newer Tertiary   Lower Palaeozoic

Older Tertiary   Pre-Cambrian

Trias   Igneous rocks

Upper Palaeozoic   Granite

Eastern boundary   Main peaks
of crystalline rocks   over 2000 metres

Main ridges   Rivers

30 km
20 miles

Figs. 103, 104. Structure and relief of Corsica
(After *Atlas de France*)

The hot dry summer causes the predominant vegetation to be evergreen drought-resistant scrub (*maquis* or *macchia*); most of the shrubs are aromatic (lavender, rosemary, thyme, broom, cistus) and their fragrance may be detected out at sea, hence the term 'Scented Isle'. Corsica was once thickly forested, but cutting for timber and charcoal burning, still widely practised, have cleared great areas. Some forests of evergreen oak and chestnut remain, and large tracts of conifers, especially Corsican pine (which grows to a great size), have been planted.

A mere 3·5 per cent of the surface is classified as cultivated land, only half of what it was in 1860, much having reverted to maquis; over 40 per cent of the total area is now waste, and cultivation occupies only small tracts in the valleys, laboriously constructed

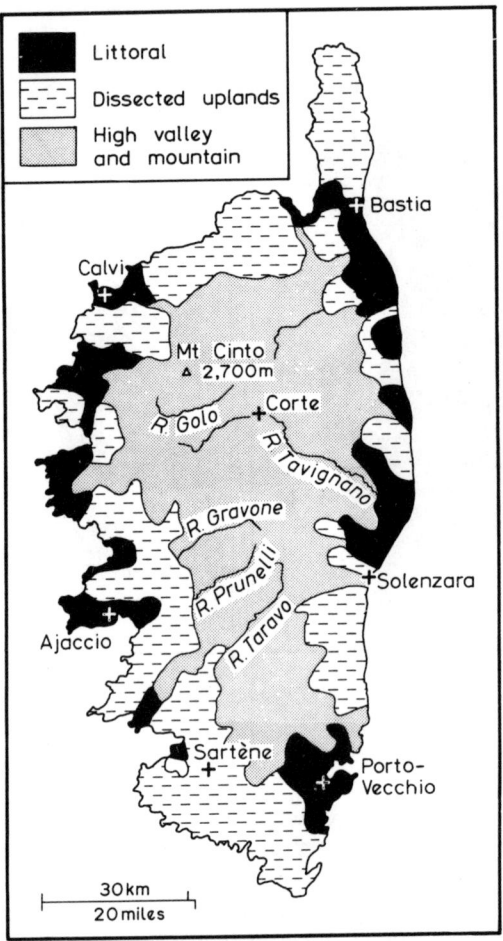

Fig. 105. *Categories of land in Corsica*
(After I. B. Thompson)

terraces on the hillsides, and in recent years parts of the east coast plain (Fig. 105). Groves of olives and chestnuts provide additional sources of food; the national dish is *polenta*, a kind of cake made of chestnut flour. Agricultural methods are backward and yields are low; although most people are employed in agriculture, more than half of the island's food supplies have to be imported. Large numbers of sheep and goats graze on the rough pastures and scrub; *broccio*, a kind of curdled cheese, is a staple item in the diet.

Industries are small-scale and dependent on agricultural and forest products. Macaroni is made from the hard wheat flour, olive oil is refined, lobster and tunny are canned, and pipes are carved from the roots of heath plants. Efforts have been made to develop a tourist industry, exploiting the climate and scenery of this romantic Mediterranean island, and several modern hotels have been built in recent years.

But Corsica is a poor place, with a large adverse balance of trade and requiring considerable help from mainland France. Its population is only about 270,000 with an average density of only about 31 per sq. km (80 per sq. mile); more than a quarter live in Ajaccio (the capital) and Bastia (the largest city and main port). These are linked by a narrow-gauge railway, but roads and railways have been constructed only with difficulty; in many parts mule-tracks are the only means of communication. The central problem of Corsica results from massive rural depopulation, land abandonment, and the exodus of young people from the island.

In 1955 the French government instituted a *Plan d'Action Régionale* for Corsica, with two main aims of developing tourism and stimulating agriculture, so that the island might be put on a commercial footing. Special attention has been paid to the east coast plain, where some 50,000 acres of uncultivated land are under development. Here the maquis was cleared and new farms created, whose owners or tenants are obliged to follow systems of cultivation prescribed by the development agency. Agricultural development is carried out under the control of *La Société pour la Mise en Valeur Agricole de la Corse*, on which both State and private interests are represented; there is much State financial assistance. Irrigation systems have been constructed, and large numbers of citrus trees, the most profitable form of farming, have been planted. Considerable progress has been made in this reclamation. At first the chief difficulty was to find sufficient suitable farmers, and a number of Algerian repatriates were encouraged to settle; recently there has been much more interest in the scheme, and indeed even a clamouring for new farms.

CHAPTER THIRTEEN

Trends towards European Unity

SINCE 1945 some of the countries of Europe have become closely grouped in various ways. Three main factors account for these groupings: a desire for military strength, a desire for economic benefit, and an idealist desire for a European parliament and system of government that ultimately might do away with national rivalries.

The military grouping has developed to meet possible aggression by the U.S.S.R. It started as Western Union, set up in 1948 when Britain, France, Belgium, the Netherlands and Luxembourg signed the Treaty of Brussels. This was widened in the following year into the North Atlantic Treaty Organization (N.A.T.O.), often known as the Atlantic Alliance, by the addition of the U.S.A., Canada, Denmark, Iceland, Italy, Norway and Portugal. In 1951 Greece and Turkey also became members. It has been described as a security league of free nations, and its military strength has been highly organized as a deterrent to aggression.

The nature and extent of the contribution of the Federal German Republic (West Germany) to the defence of western Europe presented certain problems, which led to a rejection by France in 1954 of a proposed European Defence Community. The *impasse* was ended by the creation of Western European Union, within which West Germany and Italy joined the five Brussels Treaty powers; under its terms the arms production of West Germany was to be controlled, but it was to share in the defence programme, and in 1954 West Germany joined the Atlantic Alliance. Western European Union remains as a useful link-body between the six Community countries and Great Britain.

Various economic groupings have taken place in order to help Europe, which was in a difficult position after the War. The Organization for European Economic Co-operation (O.E.E.C.) was established in 1948 by sixteen nations: the then twelve N.A.T.O. countries, together with the neutrals Austria, the Irish Republic, Sweden and Switzerland; West Germany joined in 1955 and Spain in 1959. The O.E.E.C. was set up to organize the economic development of these countries by means of American aid, originally offered by Mr Marshall, the Secretary of State (hence the popular

Plate LXII. The fishing harbour and new blocks of flats at Boulogne

Plate LXIII. The Seine at Rouen

Plate LXIV. Paris, viewed across the Seine towards Sacré Coeur de Montmarte

Plate LXV. The bocage *country of Brittany, near Rosporden*

name of 'the Marshall Plan'). It has established many committees to guide agriculture, industry and transport, and it has done much to promote the prosperity of the countries of western Europe. In 1960 it was decided that O.E.E.C. had outlived its purpose, and in the following year it was replaced by the Organization for Economic Co-operation and Development (O.E.C.D.). This includes the existing eighteen members, with the U.S.A. and Canada; in other words, it is an Atlantic economic community, though in addition Japan became a member in 1964. It has taken over most of the functions and administrative machinery of O.E.E.C.

Another most effective grouping is the European Coal and Steel Community, established in 1951, which was really the first major step towards the Economic Community. It originated from a desire by France to place under a common authority the heavy industry of France and Germany. This would mean that the Ruhr coalfield could develop for the benefit of western Europe, but without the risk of its becoming the arsenal of a revived Germany which might once again threaten the peace. The Benelux countries and Italy also joined and a 'High Authority' was established in the city of Luxembourg. All tariffs on the movement of coal, coke, iron ore, pig-iron and steel have been removed within the six countries, transport charges have been reduced, research programmes developed, and industry has received many benefits. The E.C.S.C. countries thus form a powerful industrial bloc. Great Britain, though not a member of E.C.S.C., has a link by way of the Council of Association, established in 1955, which performs a useful function in maintaining contacts at an official level, in discussing markets and price levels, technical research, and health and safety in industry.

In recent years the E.C.S.C. has experienced increasing difficulties, partly political, partly economic. The problems are partly due to the over-production of coal, which has led to stock-piling, and a number of collieries have been closed. This has been caused by the competition of oil and natural gas, and by the importation of cheap American coking coal and coke. Other problems have arisen in the steel industry, because of over-production and the growing competition of other countries.

Other groupings have been made for purposes of trade. The European Economic Community, established in 1959, includes the Benelux countries, France, West Germany and Italy. This group gradually removed tariff barriers until by 1968 there was complete free trade between them; when this Common Market is in full operation, it will be the largest trading bloc the world has ever known, larger than the U.S.A. or the British Commonwealth. For some time negotiations proceeded with a view to Great Britain joining the Community, but these broke down in January 1963, largely as a result of the intransigence of France. In 1960 Greece became an associate member. After the resignation of President de Gaulle in 1969, the French government indicated that its attitude to British entry was now favourable, and the application of the U.K. and other countries is under consideration (1970). The six E.E.C. countries also formed the European Atomic Energy Community (*Euratom*), to promote the use of atomic energy. In 1967 the three Communities merged their three executives into a single Commission.

Great Britain has taken the initiative in creating another trading association among other European countries, with Norway, Sweden, Denmark, Austria, Switzerland and Portugal, originally known as 'the Outer Seven', and now referred to as the European Free Trade Association. Finland has become an associate member.

The effective grouping of countries for idealistic motives is less easy to achieve, since this does not offer the obvious direct benefits of military and economic associations. The Council of Europe was set up in 1949 as a first step. Eighteen countries are members, and they send their Foreign Ministers to a Committee and other representatives to a Consultative Assembly at Strasbourg. This is really the first 'European parliament', but it has no powers, except to offer recommendations to its member countries. It discusses a wide range of social, political and legal matters, though it has nothing to do with any kind of military activity. A regional organization with somewhat similar outlook is the Nordic Council, established in 1953 by Denmark, Norway and Sweden, and joined in 1955 by Finland. This meets annually for discussion, but military policy is excluded.

The dominant alignments behind most of the various groupings are clearly those of the Atlantic Alliance and of the Communist *bloc*, acutely reflected in the division of Germany and indeed of Berlin. But there are also those countries who are neutral and unaligned in a military or strategic sense: Austria, Finland, the Irish Republic, Switzerland, Spain, Jugoslavia and Sweden. Yet all these countries realize that isolation is impossible and impracticable in the modern world; all but Jugoslavia are members of O.E.C.D., and that country has member status for agriculture; the Irish Republic and Austria are members of the Council of Europe; Austria and Switzerland are members of E.F.T.A.; all but Switzerland are members of the International Monetary Fund and of the United Nations Organization, and that country participates in the work of most of the U.N. agencies.

FURTHER READING

The geography of north-western Europe, as of many other parts of the world, is so dynamic and changeable that a book of this nature may in some respects be out of date as soon as it appears, notably in aspects of the economic geography, although the physical basis is more enduring. Students may find it profitable to follow the writer's example and keep a card-index or file in which all new information is systematically entered. This may be derived from articles in *The Times*, especially from its valuable supplements; *The Financial Times*; the *Listener*; *The Times Industrial Review*; and other publications of authority and repute. The house magazines of the great firms, such as *Progress* (beautifully produced by *Unilever*), or special bulletins and reports issued by the Petroleum Information Bureau and the British Iron and Steel Federation, may at times contain relevant material. A wealth of information is provided by the numerous reports and bulletins published by the European Economic Community and the Coal and Steel Community. *Kiesing's Contemporary Archives*, immaculately indexed, provide up-to-date information under the entries for the various countries.

Statistical material is a major problem, partly because of its embarrassing abundance, yet a keen student should strive to keep abreast of the changes indicated in the statistical publications. All the countries described in this book produce yearly statistical summaries, such as the *Annuaire Statistique de la France* and the *Jaarcijfers voor Nederland*. The United Nations' Organization issues both a *Statistical Year-book* and a *Monthly Bulletin of Statistics*, which can be consulted in many reference libraries. More conveniently, perhaps, material may be obtained from the most recent edition of *The Statesman's Year-book* or *Whitaker's Almanack*, should only summary figures be required. One of the most invaluable publications is the annual *Geographical Digest*, produced by George Philip & Son, Ltd., the first issue of which appeared in 1963, which provides an admirable summary of statistical and other material derived from a wide range of sources.

Various geographical periodicals can be consulted with profit, notably *Geography*, the *Geographical Journal*, the *Scottish Geographical Magazine* and the popular and well illustrated *Geographical Magazine*. The American periodicals *Geographical Review*, *Annals of the Association of American Geographers* and *Economic Geography* frequently contain articles relevant to north-western Europe. The more advanced student will require to consult the geographical periodicals published in the respective countries, if he is able to obtain access to them. Unfamiliarity with the language may be a difficulty, though it should not be with such as the *Annales de Géographie,* and in many foreign journals an English summary is commonly printed, as in the Dutch publication *Tijdschrift voor Economische en Sociale Geografie.* The writer's card-index contains many hundreds of references to such articles, which to list here would be space-consuming.

The following bibliography includes some of the more readily available books on the various countries, published for the most part in English. These have their own detailed bibliographies which can be consulted by a student with special interests. Care should be taken to consult the latest edition.

(1) *Chapters 2–5 The Scandinavian Countries*

    (a) P. Caraman, *Norway* (Longman, 1969).

    (b) W. R. Mead, *Farming in Finland* (Athlone Press, 1953).

    (c) W. R. Mead, *An Economic Geography of the Scandinavian States and Finland* (University of London Press, new edition, 1968).

    (d) R. Millward, *Scandinavian Lands* (Macmillan, 1964).

    (e) A. C. O'Dell, *The Scandinavian World* (Longman, new edition, 1962).

    (f) R. R. Platt (ed.), *Finland and its Geography* (Duell Sloan and Pearce, Inc., New York, 1965).

    (g) A. C. Sömme (ed.), *The Geography of Norden* (Heinemann, 1961).

(2) *Chapters 6, 7 West and East Germany*

    (a) R. E. Dickinson, *The Regions of Germany* (Routledge and Kegan Paul, 1945).

    (b) R. E. Dickinson, *Germany: A Regional and General Geography* (Methuen, 1953).

    (c) T. H. Elkins, *Germany* (Christopher, 1968).

    (d) The relevant chapters of A. F. A. Mutton, *Central Europe* (Longman, new edition, 1968).

    (e) N. J. G. Pounds, *The Ruhr* (Faber and Faber, 1952).

    (f) N. J. G. Pounds, *The Economic Pattern of Modern Germany* (John Murray, 1963).

    (g) K. A. Sinnhuber, *Germany: its Geography and Growth* (John Murray, 1960).

(3) *Chapters 8, 9, 10 The Benelux Countries*

    (a) A. Demangeon, *Belgique, Pays Bas, Luxembourg,* vol. II of the *Géographie Universelle* (Armand Colin, Paris, 1927).

(h) P. George and R. Sevrin, *Belgique, Pays-Bas, Luxembourg* (Presses Universitaires de France, 1967).

(c) The relevant chapters of F. J. Monkhouse, *A Regional Geography of Western Europe* (Longman, new edition, 1968).

(d) F. J. Monkhouse, *The Belgian Kempenland* (Liverpool University Press, 1949).

(e) J. van Veen, *Dredge, Drain and Reclaim: the Art of a Nation* (M. Nijhoff, The Hague, 1955).

(4) *Chapter 11 Switzerland*

There is no separate geographical account of Switzerland as yet in English, though there are many guide-books and general works. One of the best summaries in English is the Supplement on Switzerland issued by *The Times*, on 15 February 1964. The relevant chapters in A. F. A. Mutton, *Central Europe* (Longman, new edition, 1968) give much detail An excellent descriptive account of the Alpine regions is R. L. G. Irving, *The Alps* (Batsford, 1939). See also F. Imhof, *Atlas der Schweiz* (Bern, 1965) and H. Tschäni, *Profil der Schweiz* (Zürich, 1967).

(5) *Chapter 12 France*

(a) G. Chabot, *Géographie Régionale de la France* (Masson et Cie, Paris, 1966).

(b) E. Estyn Evans, *France: A Geographical Introduction* (Christopher, 1937).

(c) D. Faucher (ed.), *La France: Géographie—Tourisme* (Larousse, Paris, 1952).

(d) A. Demangeon, *Géographie économique et humaine de la France*, the second and third parts of vol. VI of the *Géographie Universelle* (Armand Colin, Paris, 1946, 1948).

(e) E. A. de Martonne, *The Geographical Regions of France* (Heinemann, London, 1933).

(f) E. A. de Martonne, *Géographie physique de la France*, the first part of vol. VI of the *Géographie Universelle* (Armand Colin, Paris, 1947).

(g) The relevant chapters of F. J. Monkhouse, *A Regional Geography of Western Europe* (Longman, new edition, 1968).

(h) H. Ormsby, *France: A Regional and Economic Geography* (Methuen, revised edition, 1950).

(i) P. Pinchemel, *La Géographie de la France* (2 volumes, 1964), in an English translation by C. Trollope and A. J. Hunt (Bell, 1969).

(j) D. I. Scargill, *Economic Geography of France* (Macmillan, 1968).

(6) *Chapter 13 Trends towards European Unity*

G. Parker, *The Logic of Unity. An Economic Geography of the Common Market* (Longman, 1968).

U. Kitzinger, *The European Common Market and Community* (Routledge and Kegan Paul, 1967).

Index